LEARNING AND
INSTRUCTION

LEARNING AND INSTRUCTION

Richard Hamilton
University of Houston

Elizabeth Ghatala

McGraw-Hill, Inc.
New York St. Louis San Francisco Auckland Bogotá
Caracas Lisbon London Madrid Mexico City Milan
Montreal New Delhi San Juan Singapore
Sydney Tokyo Toronto

This book was developed by Lane Akers, Inc.

LEARNING AND INSTRUCTION

4 5 6 7 8 9 10 FGRFGR 9 9 8 7

ISBN 0-07-023163-X

This book was set in Optima by Ruttle, Shaw & Wetherill, Inc.
The editors were Lane Akers and Bernadette Boylan;
the production supervisor was Elizabeth J. Strange.
The cover was designed by Joseph Gillians.

Library of Congress Cataloging-in-Publication Data

Hamilton, Richard J., (date).
    Learning and instruction / Richard Hamilton, Elizabeth Ghatala.
        p.   cm.
    Includes bibliographical references (p.   ) and index.
    ISBN 0-07-023163-X
    1. Learning, Psychology of.   2. Cognitive learning theory.
3. Teaching—Case studies.   I. Ghatala, Elizabeth Schwenn.
II. Title.
LB1060.H345   1994
370.15′23—dc20   93-21680

ABOUT THE AUTHORS

RICHARD HAMILTON received his Ph.D. in cognitive psychology at the University of Illinois at Chicago in 1983 and is an associate professor of Educational Psychology at the University of Houston, where he has taught since 1986. Dr. Hamilton has also held appointments at Wright State University and University of Wisconsin-Madison. He is the author of journal publications and proceedings on human learning, cognition, and instructional applications of cognitive theory, and he recently coedited the volume *Philosophy of Science, Cognitive Psychology and Educational Theory and Practice.* He also regularly reviews for the *Journal of Educational Psychology, Journal of Experimental Education,* and *Science Education.* Dr. Hamilton is a member of AERA, APA, and APS.

ELIZABETH GHATALA is a researcher in the area of learning strategies and metacognition. She received her Ph.D. in educational psychology from the University of Wisconsin-Madison. While serving as a research scientist at the Wisconsin Research and Development Center for Cognitive Learning, she coauthored a book entitled *Conceptual Learning and Development* with H. J. Klausmeier and D. A. Frayer (published by Academic Press, 1974). Dr. Ghatala is professor of Educational Psychology at the University of Houston, where she has taught since 1976.

To the Loves of My Life
Leslie, Marcus, and Megan Hamilton

R. H.

To Karen and Fred,
the Loves of My Life
and To Gurumayi, My Teacher

E. G.

CONTENTS IN BRIEF

CONTENTS

PREFACE

Learning and Instruction is designed for courses that introduce students to theories and principles of human learning and their application to instruction. Such courses typically carry titles such as Theories of Learning, Learning and Instruction, and Theories and Practice of Human Learning. We also feel that it could be used in educational psychology courses that focus primarily on theories of human learning. Whatever its label, the objective of such courses is to prepare reflective teachers who not only understand the theories and principles of human learning but are able to use this knowledge to solve real-life teaching problems. With this in mind, we built the following features into our text.

Two-Part Book Plan

In writing this text, we have gone a step beyond existing texts in this field. Rather than simply describing contemporary theories and giving a few examples of their application to teaching, we have developed an interrelated, two-part text. Part One presents, illustrates, and compares contemporary theories of learning. Part Two then provides an opportunity to apply these theories *in an integrated fashion* to a series of short cases that are organized around the following learning outcomes: cognitive and metacognitive strategies, positive attitudes and motivation to learn, retention of verbal information, and intellectual skills. Thus, in contrast to the usual approach, which presents theory X and then discusses how it can be applied, we provide an extra step: short cases organized around a common instructional problem (e.g., how to motivate students) and discuss how to apply all relevant theories to its solution.

Theoretical Coverage

Part One offers a comprehensive coverage of contemporary learning theory. In addition to presenting the usual theories, we have, to the delight of our reviewers, included a separate chapter on Vygotsky.

Method of Presentation

We believe that a text on learning theory should practice what it preaches. Therefore, to help students comprehend and apply the Part One theories, we have employed the following learning devices:

- *Common Chapter Format*—To facilitate comparing and contrasting theories, we have used a common format for all Part One chapters. Moreover, the presentation of each theory ends with a discussion of the following core questions: What is learned? What is the emphasis on environmental versus organismic factors? What is the source of motivation? What produces transfer? and, What are the important variables in instruction? Part One then ends with a lengthy review that compares and contrasts the position of each theory on these core questions.
- *Questions, Exercises, and Cases*—To ensure active processing of the theoretical material, we have inserted questions and exercises into all of the Part One chapters following the presentation of important concepts and principles. Answers are provided at the end of each chapter. Similarly, the Part Two cases provide a further opportunity for students to manipulate and thereby master the theoretical material.

Pedagogy

In addition to the common formats and the inserted questions and exercises, each Part One chapter contains the following pedagogical devices: lists of learning objectives, tables that summarize and compare important material, and itemized, end-of-chapter summaries that review the major principles and concepts.

Acknowledgments

With great appreciation, we would like to thank Lane Akers, our editor, for his support, effort, and insights, as well as the many reviewers who read all or portions of the manuscript during its long gestation period. Primary among these are Professors Loren Anderson, University of South Carolina; Ruth Garner, Washington State University at Vancouver; and Carol Ann Kardash, University of Missouri. Others who contributed valuable feedback at earlier periods include Myron Dembo, University of South Carolina; David Gleissman, Indiana University; William Goodwin, University of Colorado at Denver; Elizabeth McEntire, Baylor University; and Gary Stuck, University of North Carolina.

I, Richard Hamilton, would also like to especially thank Elizabeth Ghatala, my mentor and friend, for her guidance and support during the last six years. I wish her luck in her "new life." I will miss her.

I, Elizabeth Ghatala, express my gratitude to the University of Houston for granting me a sabbatical while writing this book, and to my colleagues and good friends in the educational psychology department for their support over the past 17 years.

Richard Hamilton
Elizabeth Ghatala

THE THEORIES

INTRODUCTION TO THEORY

OBJECTIVES

1. State the definition of theory and describe its three functions.
2. Identify six criteria for judging the adequacy of a learning theory.
3. Define "learning" and be able to identify instances and noninstances of learning using the definition.
4. Identify five core issues on which learning theories can be compared.
5. Compare and contrast the behavioral and cognitive perspectives on learning.

This is a book about how people learn. Although written primarily for teachers, the information contained here can also be very useful to parents, counselors, health-care workers, trainers in businesses and corporations, or anyone, for that matter, who seeks to guide or influence other people's behavior, attitudes, or knowledge.

Psychologists have been studying how organisms learn for decades. Before that the task was undertaken by philosophers. From all this intensive study a mountain of facts and observations has emerged about the learning process, enough to fill scores of books the size of this one. To save you the time it would take to read all these rather dry books, we have decided instead to write about theories of learning. That is because facts, to be useful to the human mind, have to be embedded within a comprehensible structure that organizes and relates them. The importance of context, or having an organizing structure for processing and understanding facts, in itself constitutes one of the most significant facts about human learning, which most of the theories in this book will address.

What Is a Theory?

Theory is a term about which volumes have been written by philosophers of science. However, we will simplify the picture and define a **theory** as *a set of* *related general statements used to explain particular facts.* The related general statements have variously been called axioms, theorems, assumptions, principles, or laws. Which of these terms is used has to do with whether the general statements are self-evident beliefs and logical deductions (assumptions, axioms, theorems) or whether they are generalizations derived from results of scientific studies (principles, laws). We will skirt this fine point and simply call them general statements.

The particular facts referred to by the general statements are either discrete observations or measurements (e.g., John, a 16-year-old, smokes marijuana; Mary, a 12-year-old girl, is 60 inches tall), or summaries of observations or measurements (e.g., the percentage of 16-year-olds who smoke marijuana; the average height of 12-year-old girls).

Let's illustrate with a simple theory consisting of only one general statement (keeping in mind that the typical theory consists of numerous general statements). Our simple theory states that:

Viewing violence leads to aggression.

A particular fact that the theory explains is the observation that children who view war movies more often choose to play with toy guns than children who do not view war movies. Note that the theory relates very broad categories of circumstances and behaviors. That is, there are many sets of circumstances in which viewing violence can occur (ranging from a Roadrunner cartoon to a hockey match) and many different behaviors indicative of aggression. The particular fact (playing with guns after seeing war movies) that the theory explains is thus a specific instance of the general statement.

Functions of Theory

We can use our simple theory to illustrate the functions that theory performs. Scientific research can proceed in several different ways. One way is to start with a theory and derive testable hypotheses from the theory. A **hypothesis** is a prediction about what will be observed in a scientific study if the theory is valid. Hypotheses are often stated in an if-then format. One hypothesis that follows from the theory that viewing violence leads to aggression is that if we watch children for a period after the Saturday matinee movie, then those who saw the latest Rambo escapade should exhibit more gunplay behavior than those who chose to see the latest Spielberg fantasy. *Here the main function of the theory is to lead to the discovery of new facts.* Each time a new fact is correctly predicted by the theory, we not only gain a new bit of information about the world, but, in addition, the theory gains validity or credibility.

But not all scientists do research to test a theory. Another way scientific research proceeds is to start with a problem that needs a solution or with an interesting question. For example, a school psychologist may notice an outbreak of pretend gunplay on the playground. She may wonder if it has anything to do with a series of war movies that has appeared in local theaters recently. She may interview children and find that those who report having seen the war movies exhibit more instances of gunplay behavior than those who report not having seen the war movies. If the researcher stops here, the study is of very limited usefulness because it has produced a single isolated fact. Suppose the researcher searches the research literature and finds somewhat similar facts discovered in other studies. For example, one researcher found that teens who report watching violent programs on television are more apt to be arrested for crimes involving assault than teens who report not watching violent television shows. Another finding is that fans at soccer matches are more likely to riot than fans at tennis matches. Now our researcher faced with this set of facts might propose a theory that would summarize all of them: Viewing violence leads to aggression. *Here the function of theory is to summarize and interrelate a set of disparate facts.* It is much easier to remember a few general principles than a whole list of facts.

The third function of theory is to explain facts or observations. Note that our simple theory states that viewing violence leads to or causes aggression. This is one way of explaining the facts that have been gathered. Another explanation is that people who are naturally prone to aggression (for whatever reasons) also prefer to view violence. This theory provides a quite different explanation of the same set of facts. One may ask, "Which theory is true?" But truth is not usually a criterion we can apply to theories. Statements of fact can be either true or false, but theories cannot be proven to be true or false. It is conceivable that even though a theory has correctly predicted ten-thousand-and-one facts, it may tomorrow lead to predictions not supported by the evidence. We will discuss criteria that we can use to judge the adequacy of a theory in a moment. First, let's consider the nature and importance of learning theories.

WHAT ARE LEARNING THEORIES AND WHY ARE THEY IMPORTANT?

In the preface we said that we would be inserting questions throughout the book to (1) see if you are awake, and (2) give you the opportunity to actively engage with the material. The questions are not difficult but do require you to reflect on the material you have just read. So your first question is given below. *You may write your answer in the space provided* before *you look at the answer given at the end of the chapter.*

Question 1.1: What is a learning theory? _____

_____

_____

A learning theory thus enables us to make sense out of facts about learning. When we theorize about learning, we are proposing which facts are most important for understanding how people learn and what kinds of relationships among the facts are most significant (Thomas, 1985). A learning theory is like a lens through which we can view situations, such as a teacher and students interacting in a classroom, a solitary individual reading a book, a counselor and a client interacting in a therapy session. The theory leads us to attend to certain elements of a situation while ignoring others and to see the selected elements in a particular pattern (Thomas, 1985). Thus, when a person adopts a particular theory, she takes on a set of beliefs concerning what questions about learning are valuable, what methods for studying these questions are legitimate, and what the nature of learning is (Miller, 1989).

Well, you might protest, if a person chooses not to look through a theory lens, can't she see "just the facts—the *real* facts." No, not really, because creating a system or structure for making sense out of data seems to be a characteristic of the human mind. So even though we may not be aware of it, we are always viewing every situation we encounter through a lens consisting of our beliefs (theories). It is literally true that if you change your beliefs your perceptions will automatically change in any given situation. So you can see that the theory you adopt makes quite a difference in terms of how you perceive classroom events and how you might respond to them and take action to optimize learning. An important reason for studying learning theories is that it leads us to examine our own private beliefs about learning. These beliefs, often based on observations of a limited number of individuals, may be an incomplete reflection of the learning process.

Criteria for Judging Theories

Since theorists may have dramatically different ideas about what is important, a large number of theories may emerge in the same area of investigation. This is true of the area of human learning. We must be able to tell a good theory from a bad theory. Thomas (1985) suggests six criteria for doing that:

1. *A good theory accurately reflects the facts of the real world.* There are several reasons why a theory might not accurately reflect the facts of the world. A theorist may study only a few individuals and then improperly apply conclusions to many individuals. It is customary in psychological and educational research to study a sample of individuals and then extend the resulting conclusions to a larger population. But the sample must accurately represent the population. That is why researchers like to draw random samples from a population. Random sampling insures that the sample is representative of the larger population. When samples are very small or not representative, the conclusions may well not reflect what is true for the entire population. For example, there was early criticism of Piaget's theory because his general statements about children's thinking were based on observations of only a few children (just his own children at the beginning). It wasn't until his observations were replicated on larger and more representative samples that other scientists gave credence to his theory.

Another reason why a theory may not accurately reflect the world is that a theorist may study only one facet or situation and then generalize to other situations. For example, a theorist may construct a theory of learning based on her observations of how children memorize lists of words under laboratory conditions and then use the theory to explain how children memorize historical names and dates in the classroom. The theory may not accurately reflect the facts in the latter situation.

Each of the theories that we will study all meet this criterion of accurately reflecting the facts within the situations studied by the particular theorist. However, we need to be aware that any given theorist has studied learning in some but not other circumstances. For this reason no single learning theory accurately reflects the facts of the total domain of human learning. As we study each theory we will note its boundaries. That is, we will determine for what kinds of people and for what kinds of situations the theory provides an accurate rendering of the facts. Later, in the second half of the book, we will use this information to selectively apply theories to achieve distinct learning outcomes.

2. *A good theory is stated in such a way that it is clear and understandable.* Anyone with reasonable competence should be able to understand (1) the situations in the world referred to by the theory; (2) the meanings of the terms used; (3) the key assumptions of the theory; and (4) how the explanations and predictions are derived from the assumptions. The theories we shall study have all fared well by this criterion in that they have survived the scrutiny of experts in the field. This does not mean, unfortunately, that the theories are equally transparent to the nonexpert. All of the theories will require you to learn new terms or new meanings for old terms, and most will require you to conceptualize the learning process in a new way. So it may not seem that a theory is clear until we acquire the competence to understand it.

3. *A good theory is useful for predicting events in the future.* Some theories are quite good at explaining why past events occurred but are not so good at predicting events in the future. For example, one of the criticisms leveled at Freud's view of the learning process is that while it can explain a person's current behavior in terms of the learning resulting from childhood events, it is very difficult to predict a person's future behavior based on the theory. In contrast, the theories we will study often yield accurate predictions of an individual's learning performance, based on an analysis of past events and current circumstances.

4. *A good theory is internally consistent.* Basically, this means that the parts of the theory fit together logically and that one doesn't have to set aside one part of the theory in order to understand another part.

5. *A good theory is based on as few unproven assumptions as possible.* This is also referred to as the law of parsimony, which states that if two theories fit the facts equally well, it is better to choose the simpler one. Basically, the more complex the theory the more difficult it is to understand and use.

6. *A good theory is testable.* Recall that one function of a theory is to lead to the discovery of new facts. The process is one in which hypotheses derived from the theory are tested by seeing if they accurately predict the outcomes of scientific studies. When a hypothesis derived from a theory is confirmed, the validity of the theory is enhanced. In order for this verification process to proceed, the theory must produce hypotheses that can be disproved.

Let's take as an example the two simple theories proposed earlier to account for various facts concerning aggressive behavior.

Theory 1: Viewing violence causes aggression.
Theory 2: People who are naturally aggressive prefer viewing violent events.

Both theories are in accord with the facts observed thus far—that children who see war movies exhibit more gunplay than children who do not see war movies, that there are more riots at soccer matches than at tennis matches, and that teens who view violent TV programs are more often arrested for assault than teens who report not viewing violent TV programs. In each case, the aggression could have been caused either by the viewing of violence or by naturally aggressive individuals who gravitate to the violent scenes.

Let's see if we can devise a situation for which the theories would make different predictions. Suppose through careful screening we are able to sample children with no history of aggressive behavior. We then randomly divide the children into two groups. One group will be exposed to violent war movies; the other group will view a nonviolent action film for an equal length of time. Both groups will then be observed in the same play environment under identical conditions.

The situation just described is called an **experiment,** which is the research methodology most widely used by scientists to investigate learning. The basic characteristic of an experiment is that the researcher manipulates one variable, in this case the type of film viewed by the children, and measures a second variable, here, aggressive play behavior of children. All other variables are controlled (the characteristics of the children, the play conditions, etc.). If there is a difference on the measured variable (e.g., more aggressive behavior in one group than the other), it can generally be concluded that the difference was caused by the manipulated variable.

Now our theories predict different outcomes for the experiment. Theory 1 would predict a higher incidence of aggressive behavior among children exposed to the war movie. Theory 2 would predict no difference between the groups since children in the groups were equal on aggressive predisposition before the introduction of the film. The outcome of the experiment will thus confirm one of the hypotheses and disconfirm the other. Both theories are testable because they lead to hypotheses that can be disconfirmed by the results of the experiment.

However, suppose we were to add to Theory 1 another element which we will call the Suppression Factor. The theory now states that viewing violence leads to aggression; however, when cues in the environment alert subjects that aggression will be punished, they suppress it. We have now rendered Theory 1 untestable because if the experiment shows that the children who saw the war movies did not play with guns more often than children who didn't see the war movies, we could simply invoke the Suppression Factor and say that there must have been cues present (even though we can't specify them exactly) that neutralized the effects of viewing violence. Hence the theory cannot be disconfirmed by this outcome.

It should make us uncomfortable when a theory can predict all possible outcomes of a learning experiment. When we examine the research evidence supporting each of our learning theories, we will usually find instances in which certain aspects of the theory have been disconfirmed. If not too numerous, such disconfirmations are a healthy sign that the theory is testable.

The Domain of Learning

Jennifer, a fourth grader, hears her teacher say that the formula for water is H_2O. Later, she writes on a test that the formula for water is H_2O. When presented this description, some students in our classes have argued that Jennifer has exhibited learning. Other students have argued that Jennifer could be just parroting back by rote what her teacher said, so she has not really learned anything.

Question 1.2: What do you think—has Jennifer learned? (Write your answer here before peeking at the answer at the end of the chapter.)_____

_____

_____

Most theorists accept the following definition of learning because it is useful for identifying the kinds of events that learning theories should explain, while excluding other kinds of events:

Learning is a relatively permanent change in an individual's knowledge or behavior that results from previous experience.

Each part of the definition mentions an attribute or characteristic that an event must have in order to be considered as an instance of learning. Let's consider each part of the definition.

1. *Learning is a change in knowledge or behavior.* This part of the definition reflects the fact that theorists differ in their view of what is learned from previous experience. Behavioral theorists claim that learning consists of changes in behavior, while cognitive theorists focus on changes in knowledge. Most theorists of both persuasions accept the notion that learning is not something that can be observed directly. We can only infer that learning has occurred from observing the overt responding or performance of an individual. Therefore, performance of some observable behavior is a necessary indication of learning but is not necessarily identical to the learning. For example, in school settings, we often conceive of learning as the acquisition of knowledge. But how do we know that knowledge has been acquired? We usually provide students with opportunities to demonstrate what they have learned through spoken or written responses. However, we don't usually equate the spoken or written responses with the knowledge that has been acquired; we treat them as mere reflections of the students' knowledge. Performance measures are important, unless students show a change in responding, we have no basis for inferring that learning has occurred.

The distinction between learning and performance is important, even for learning theorists who focus on changes in behavior. This is because it is quite possible for an individual to learn a new behavior yet not show it in his performance. For example, Robert (a fastidious sort) may have learned to change the oil in his car by watching the mechanic. However, he may not exhibit this behavior unless circumstances absolutely compel him to perform the task. Thus, absence of changes in performance is not an infallible indication that learning has not occurred. The incentives provided to the learner and his motivation to respond, as well as other factors, can influence performance.

2. *The changes brought about by learning are relatively permanent.* Changes in responding can be produced by other factors besides learning. The characteristic of relative permanence helps us to rule out changes brought about by such things as fatigue or warm-up which dissipate rapidly. Drugs can produce changes in responding, but these also disappear when the drug wears off. Learning results in change that is more enduring yet still only relatively permanent. We are all aware of the sometimes ephemeral nature of learning.

3. *Learning results from previous experience.* Many changes that we see, particularly in young children, are the result of growth or maturation of the skeletal, muscle, and nervous systems. They are excluded from the domain of learning since such changes cannot be tied to specific experiences of the child. Also, some behaviors, such as jumping after a loud noise, are instinctive or reflexive (wired into the nervous system), not learned.

Let's return to Jennifer, who has written the formula for water after hearing her teacher state it, and use the definition to classify her behavior. We simply go through the attributes given in the definition and determine if they are all present. Was there a change in her knowledge or behavior? Yes, assuming she did not know and therefore would not have been able to state the formula prior to her teacher's statement. Was the change relatively permanent? Yes; at least, it lasted long enough for her to answer the test questions. Whether she will retain the information much beyond the test is another matter. Did the change result from previous experience? Yes, specifically from hearing the teacher's statement. So, regardless of whether we would judge it to be desirable, meaningful, or worthwhile, according to our definition, Jennifer has learned.

To gain more practice identifying instances of learning and excluding situations that are not learning, do the following exercises. The answers can be found at the end of the chapter. You will benefit more by reasoning through your answers and *then* checking them against ours.

Exercise 1.1: Indicate for each of the following descriptions whether it is an example of learning or not, and if it is not learning, indicate what it is.

1. John blinks as a cold puff of air is blown in his eye.

---

2. Despite many attempts on the part of her parents to coax her, baby Alice (two months) does not roll over. At three months, Alice rolls over.

---

3. Scott reads in his science book that the planet is 48 billion years old. Later, he tells his mother that the planet is 48 billion years old.

---

4. Police recruits were presented with a different image for each eye—one neutral and the other depicting some form of violence. Third-year trainees reported seeing more violent pictures than did first-year trainees.

---

5. During the first hour of target practice, Jim scores 50 bull's-eyes. During the second hour he hits 35 bull's-eyes. At the next practice session, Jim again scores 50 hits.

---

6. Bobby's ability to focus on school tasks improved significantly after he began taking Ritalin under his doctor's supervision.

Core Issues on Which Learning Theories Differ

Although the learning theories we will study are all attempts to make sense out of the facts about learning as defined earlier, as we shall see, the theorists' views of the hows, whys, and wherefores of learning differ markedly. As we present each theory, we will describe its position on each of five core issues. These are not the only issues on which learning theories differ, but they are some of the most important issues to consider when deciding which theory to apply in any given situation.

Core Issue 1: What is learned according to the theory?   The issue of what is learned refers, in part, to the fact that each theory addresses quite different areas within the total domain of learning carved out by our definition. That is, each theory looks at only some types of learning outcomes that result from only certain kinds of previous experience. For example, classical and operant conditioning theories focus on changes in conditioned responses that result from environmental stimulus and response relationships. Information processing theory focuses on changes in perception, comprehension, and problem solving brought about by experiences that add to the individual's knowledge base and processing strategies. Cognitive-developmental theories focus on qualitative changes in thinking that come about as an individual interacts with her physical, logical, and social-cultural environments. Social learning theory focuses on changes in behavior, perception, and reasoning that result from observing the behavior of others. Thus, each of the theories we will study provides valuable insights into one or more important learning outcomes (see Table 1.1). However no one theory addresses all learning outcomes. Therefore, teachers really need to be conversant with a variety of theories in order to produce a wide variety of learning in students.

Another aspect of this core issue has to do with the nature of the inferences that theorists make concerning unobservable changes inside the organism that give rise to the observable changes in responding. Radical behaviorists such as Skinner do not make inferences about what happens inside the learner because they believe that such inferences are unnecessary and, even worse, misleading. Other behavioral theories and all cognitive theories do assume there is something

TABLE 1.1 TYPES OF LEARNING OUTCOMES AND PRIOR EXPERIENCE STUDIED BY DIFFERENT THEORISTS

Theory	Type of outcome studied	Prior experience studied
1. Classical and operant conditioning	Conditioned responses	Environmental stimulus and response contingencies
2. Information processing	Perception, comprehension, and problem solving	Experiences that change knowledge base and processing strategies
3. Cognitive-developmental	Thinking	Interaction with the physical, logical, and social-cultural environments
4. Social learning	Behavior, perception, reasoning	Observation of others

inside the learner that changes with experience and that underlies observable changes in responding. However, theories differ in the nature of the internal changes that are believed to constitute learning.

The background and training of theorists may be related to their preference for a particular type of explanatory mechanism. For example, Piaget's training in biology and epistemology perhaps predisposed him to view development and learning in terms of changes in individuals' logical knowledge structures brought about by their attempts to adapt to the environment. Pavlov's training in neurophysiology certainly influenced him to explain conditioning in terms of underlying neural changes in the brain. Information processing theorists' background in computers strongly predisposed them to explain learning in terms of the storage and retrieval of information in memory.

As we study each theory we will ask: (1) On what types of learning outcomes and learning conditions does the theory focus? and (2) What types of internal, unobservable mechanisms are claimed to underlie these outcomes?

Core Issue 2: What is the relative emphasis on environmental versus organismic factors in learning? Although all theories view learning as resulting from the interaction of the learner with the environment, they differ in how much importance is given to environmental factors as opposed to factors inside the organism. In some theories, the learner is a relatively passive subject of environmental forces, whereas in other theories the learner plays a more active role in learning. Which view is adopted has powerful implications for how one structures schools and classrooms.

Core Issue 3: What is the source of motivation for learning? Theories differ in their view of what motivates people to learn. Do we learn to obtain rewards? Do we learn to attain a sense of mastery? Do we learn because of natural curiosity? Some theorists give little attention to motivational forces. Some postulate a single source of motivation; some postulate several sources. The locus of motivational forces (internal needs or external stimuli) also differs across theories. We shall ask for each theory: What motivates learning and how does motivation fit into the overall picture of the learning process? Motivation is an important concern in the classroom, so, in addition to considering how each learning theory treats the issue of motivation, we shall in Chapter 9 present some theories that deal explicitly with motivation for learning.

Core Issue 4: How does transfer occur?   How is it that something learned in one situation carries over to another situation? Transfer, or often lack of transfer, is of central concern to teachers, so we shall see how each theory deals with this core issue.

Core Issue 5: What are important variables in instruction?   Learning theories are not theories of instruction, but each one implies factors that should be present in order for learning to occur optimally. As we discuss each theory we will determine the instructional variables the theory holds to be most important.

BRIEF HISTORICAL BACKGROUND

When attempting to understand a theoretical position, it is helpful to know something about the historical context in which the theory was developed. Virtually all of the ideas we will encounter as we study more contemporary theories have been around in one form or another for a long time. So let us embark on a brief tour (with the emphasis on brief) through the history of learning theory.

The field of learning is a subarea within psychology which itself grew out of philosophy in the late 1800s. The earliest theories of learning that retain more than historical interest were the stimulus-response (S-R) theories. They were attempts of early pioneers in twentieth-century psychology to objectify the study of learning. Stimuli (conditions in the environment) and responses (actual behavior) are observable and hence can be studied scientifically. This early perspective gave rise to behaviorism, a major branch within learning theory. Arising in tandem with S-R behavior theory was a second major division in learning theory: cognitivism. Cognitive theorists are typically more interested in the scientific study of perception, problem solving, and understanding than in the study of behavior per se. Because these two perspectives, behaviorism and cognitivism, have pervaded the field of learning from its beginnings, it is important to understand their underlying assumptions and to trace the theories developed within each perspective.

The Behavioral Perspective

Behaviorism arose in the early twentieth century in reaction against structuralism and functionalism, two approaches to psychology that focused on the study of conscious experience. The chief methodology of these approaches was introspection or self-report of one's own thoughts and images. Early behaviorists such as John Watson and Edward Thorndike regarded the study of conscious experience as a dead end and the method of introspection as nonscientific. According to behaviorism, the proper subject matter of psychology is activity rather than structures. While most behaviorists never denied the existence of private mental and emotional experience, they did deny that it could be studied scientifically by means of introspection. All behaviorists are concerned with analyses of observable stimulus and response events. Some behaviorists (Watson, Thorndike, Guthrie, and Skinner) confined themselves to observable phenomena while others (Pavlov, Hull) also included internal, unobservable variables in their explanations of learning. The methodology for behaviorist learning theorists is primarily the scientific experiment in which stimulus variables can be objectively manipulated and response variables can be reliably measured. Many of the learning experiments conducted by behaviorists used animals as subjects. This reflects another basic assumption of this approach. That is, behaviorists believe that learning follows the same laws regardless of species. While some species may be able to learn more complex behaviors than other species, the basic mechanisms by which learning occurs are the same in humans, rats, and flatworms.

Behaviorist Theorists

Ivan P. Pavlov (1849–1936) was a Russian physiologist credited with one of the major observations in the field of psychology. As with many great discoveries, Pavlov's was a result of serendipity. In the course of his work on the digestive system, Pavlov observed that some of the dogs in his laboratory began to salivate before they were fed. This behavior occurred only in dogs who had been in the laboratory for some time. Pavlov developed the model of classical conditioning to explain this phenomenon. Briefly, the model starts with an unlearned connection between a stimulus (e.g., meat) and a response (salivation). When the unlearned stimulus (meat) is presented repeatedly in conjunction with another, neutral, stimulus such as the laboratory assistant or the sound of a bell, the neutral stimulus begins to elicit the response (salivation). This model has formed the basis for many formulations of learning. We will discuss classical conditioning in Chapter 2 because it represents an extremely important form of learning that teachers need to be aware of.

John B. Watson (1878–1958), the founder of American behaviorism, extended Pavlov's classical conditioning model to explain human emotional learning. Basically, Watson believed that all humans are born with the same limited number of reflexes consisting of unlearned behaviors such as the knee jerk as well as the unlearned emotional reactions of fear, love, and rage which occur in response to specific stimuli. For example, loud noises and loss of support elicit fear, stroking and fondling elicit love, and confinement elicits rage. According to Watson's theory, all our emotional reactions in later life can be explained on the basis of classical conditioning involving these unlearned stimulus-response connections. While the particulars of Watson's theory of emotional development have not been supported by later, objective, studies of emotional responding in infants, it remains true that many human behaviors, particularly emotional reactions, are acquired through classical conditioning. (For an especially vivid illustration, of this conditioning, notice your reaction to the sound of the drill when you next visit your dentist's office.)

Edwin R. Guthrie's (1886–1959) approach to learning is best summed up by quoting his one major law: "A combination of stimuli which has accompanied a movement will on its reoccurrence tend to be followed by that movement" (Guthrie, 1952). Guthrie went on to say that the "bond" or connection between the stimulus and response is established all at once at full strength and is not strengthened by practice.

Basically, Guthrie's theory says that in a given situation we will do whatever it is that we did when last in that situation. But this can't be right! Certainly teachers observe that a student will cut up in class one minute, and the very next minute he will quietly do his seat work. Well, according to Guthrie, any given stimulus situation such as a classroom consists of many, many component stimuli. He would claim that the stimuli accompanying each response (cutting up or quietly working) are quite different and that a teacher could discover with careful analysis which particular elements of the total classroom situation are active in eliciting these different responses. But surely performance improves with practice; any teacher can see that! Well, according to Guthrie, any performance, even a simple one like throwing a ball, involves many, many component movements, each of which must become connected to a specific stimulus element in the situation in the proper sequence. Each of these molecular S-R connections is formed full strength in one trial. However, it may take many trials for all of the component habits involved in the smooth execution of ball throwing to be formed. In other words, Guthrie's principle of one-trial learning applies to the molecular level of behavior involving individual muscular movements and not to the molar level of behavior named in acts like ball throwing and walking.

Guthrie's theory of learning is quite similar to Pavlov's and Watson's in that the *primary mechanism involved in habit formation is contiguity of stimulus and response*. Rewards or reinforcement play no necessary role in learning. As in the case of practice, once again, Guthrie has a clever explanation of the apparent effects of rewards in terms of his basic principle. Suppose your dog approaches you and you give him food. The next time your dog sees you, he approaches. Didn't the dog learn to approach you because of the pleasurable consequence of receiving food? No; according to Guthrie, the dog approached on the second occasion because that is the last thing he did on the first occasion. The presentation of food simply changed the stimulus situation so that approaching you was the last response he made to the stimulus of seeing you from a distance.

One of Guthrie's great appeals lay in his ability to give anecdotal applications of his theory to everyday situations involving the making and breaking of habits. For example, he described the case of a young woman student who had noisy neighbors who insisted on playing the radio loudly. She was unable to study because of the noise until a friend suggested she read mystery novels in the noise. The novels held her attention enough that she was able to study in the presence of the noise after a week.

Guthrie described several methods for breaking undesirable habits. For example, in the *exhaustion method,* one repeats the bad habit until one is exhausted and stops responding. The last thing done in the situation is *not* making the undesired response. The *threshold method* involves presenting the stimulus that forms part of the undesirable S-R bond (habit) but presenting it so faintly that it does not elicit the undesirable response. The stimulus is then presented repeatedly over trials and its intensity is increased over time. The intensity increase is never enough to elicit the response. Thus, a new response (the response of not responding) gradually replaces the old response. By the time an intensity is reached that would initially have provoked the undesirable behavior, a different habit has been formed. The techniques described by Guthrie for making and breaking habits have become established procedures in behavior modification, which we will describe in Chapter 2.

Edward L. Thorndike (1874–1949), in agreement with Watson and Guthrie, saw learning as the formation of bonds between stimuli and responses. He thought of these bonds as neural connections—hence the term connectionism has been applied to his theory. However, in contrast to Pavlov, Watson, and Guthrie, who emphasized contiguity as the primary mechanism in habit formation, Thorndike's theory relied heavily on the principle of reinforcement. Thorndike stated a number of laws explaining how connections are "stamped in" and "stamped out" of the organism, the most important of which is the Law of Effect (Thorndike, 1913). Briefly, the law asserts that *responses that precede a satisfying state of affairs are more likely to be repeated, whereas responses just prior to an annoying state of affairs are more likely not to be repeated.* Thorndike objectively defined a satisfying state of affairs as one the organism does nothing to avoid or attempts to maintain and an annoying state of affairs as one the organism does nothing to maintain or seeks to end.

Another major law that Thorndike stated is the Law of Exercise, which maintains that *bonds between stimuli and responses are strengthened by being exercised frequently, recently, and vigorously* (Thorndike, 1913). These two laws, of exercise and effect, along with five subsidiary laws constituted Thorndike's system, which was to have a major influence on later theorists such as Hull and Skinner, who are also reinforcement theorists.

It is interesting that Thorndike, like other early behaviorists, placed great importance on the application of his theory particularly to the realm of education. In fact, he is regarded as the founder of Educational Psychology although most of his research used animals as subjects. For example, his analysis of problem solving as the gradual stamping in of the correct response through trial and error was based on observations of a hungry cat attempting to escape from a cage to get a piece of fish lying nearby. The cat could open the door of the cage by pulling a string hanging from the top of the cage. The cat's initial response would be to scratch at the door, paw up and down, scratch at the walls, etc., until by accident it would pull on the string and escape. Over numerous trials, the time it took the cat to escape grew shorter and shorter until finally it would immediately pull the string when put into the box. This view of learning and problem solving when applied to education had the predictable outcome of justifying repetitious drill approaches to instruction.

Clark L. Hull (1884–1952) produced a theory that for sheer complexity and grandness of scope has never been equaled in the annals of psychology. Even a brief summary of his theory, which encompasses all of behavior (animal and human), is impossible here. We will content ourselves with identifying some of Hull's most influential ideas.

First, while Hull, like previous behaviorists, characterized learning as the formation of stimulus-response connections, he was the first to hypothesize unobservable variables (called *intervening variables*) inside the organism which mediate or intercede between stimuli and responses. The intervening variables were states or characteristics of the organism that varied predictably with changes in stimulus variables and, in turn, were reflected by various changes in behavior. For example, one intervening variable in his system is drive (D) which increased in magnitude with the length of time the organism was deprived of a biological necessity such as food or water. Increasing drive is reflected in behavior in terms of increased activity, exploration of the environment, eating or drinking behavior, and so on. This single intervening variable can thus explain the relationship between a class of stimulus variables (those acting to increase D) and a class of responses (behaviors in reaction to increasing D). Hull postulated hundreds of such intervening variables and carefully specified how each was related to observable stimulus and response variables. This approach of postulating internal unobservable mechanisms in explaining behavior change was quite different from earlier S-R theorists and is symbolized as S-O-R theory (the O stands for states and processes inside the organism). This type of theory has become a model for most contemporary behavior theorists, with the exception of Skinner.

Hull also introduced an approach to theory building called the *hypothetical-deductive method.* In this method, a few basic assumptions are clearly stated, and from the assumptions are deduced theorems or hypotheses that can be tested by experiment. Hull's system included 17 basic assumptions from which were derived 133 theorems (Hull, 1952). While initially greeted with much enthusiasm, this approach to constructing theories of learning passed out of favor when it became apparent that the method is not workable in practice. It was not as easy as Hull believed to derive unambiguous tests of theorems (Malone, 1990).

Hull was a master at providing explanations of complex phenomena such as knowledge, insight, and purpose in terms of simple habit mechanisms. However, having read a number of these explanations, we can attest to the mind-numbing complexity of argument that is required to do so. Hull's reductionist tendency was carried forward by his numerous students and followers, who have explained such phenomena as relationship learning (McClelland, Clark, Roby, & Atkinson, 1949) and social learning and imitation (Miller & Dollard, 1941) in terms of simple habits.

Burrhus Frederic Skinner (1904–1990) is the most widely known and influential behaviorist. Largely because of his popular writings and autobiography (Skinner, 1983), his name has become almost synonymous with this perspective. While Skinner shows many similarities to other behaviorists, he is unique in several respects. First, he remained adamant in his opposition to explanations of behavior in terms of unobservable mechanisms. For Skinner, such explanations only translate what we wish to explain (behavior) into other terms, such as the language of neurons or electronic devices. Substituting this language does little to explain behavior, and its invocation may obscure the real explanations of behavior which lie in the past history of the individual. Another important distinction between Skinner and other reinforcement theorists such as Thorndike and Hull is his notion that learning consists of the association between the response and the reinforcement, not the connection between the stimulus and the response. Thus, stimulus variables that precede the response play far less of a role in Skinner's explanation of behavior than do the consequences that follow responses.

Skinner resembles other behaviorists such as Watson and Guthrie in his acceptance of thinking and other forms of private experience. Like them, he viewed thinking and feeling as activities that, like any other activities, are explainable in terms of environmental stimulus and response contingencies. He also shared the penchant of behaviorists to extend principles based on research with animals to humans and to attempt to explain complex human behavior such as language in terms of simple forms of conditioning. Skinner, like Thorndike, was very concerned with education and devoted much effort to applying his theory to instruction. We will discuss the most notable of these applications, programmed learning and behavior modification, in Chapter 2.

The Cognitive Perspective

As we have seen, behaviorism arose out of a negative reaction to mentalistic approaches that had previously characterized psychology. In turn, **cognitivism** arose out of negative reaction to behaviorism. Specifically, cognitive psychologists eschew the behaviorist approach of analyzing behavior into molecular or elemental units. They believe that such reductionism is too simplistic to provide adequate explanations of complex human behavior. In addition to viewing behavior in more molar or global terms, cognitivists also insist that human behavior is purposive and goal directed. In contrast, behaviorists do not include purpose or intention in their analysis, preferring instead to look only at relationships between stimulus and response variables. A third major difference between the two perspectives is that the cognitive approach focuses mainly on processes such as perception, thought, and consciousness and looks at behavior only to infer laws of mental activities. The behaviorist is primarily focused on formulating laws of behavior per se. A final way in which some cognitivists differ from behaviorists is their willingness to postulate complex explanatory concepts that are not always clearly and precisely linked to objective stimulus and response variables. However, many cognitive theorists are as rigorous, precise, and objective as any behaviorist. Table 1.2 summarizes the major differences between the cognitive and behavioral approaches to learning.

Cognitive Theories

While behaviorism was primarily a movement of American psychology, cognitivism has been more heavily influenced by European psychology—first by the German Gestalt movement of the early twentieth century and then by Swiss

TABLE 1.2   MAJOR DIFFERENCES BETWEEN BEHAVIORAL AND COGNITIVE APPROACHES

Behavioral theory	Cognitive theory
Analyzes behavior into *molecular* or elemental units	Deals with *molar* or global units of behavior
Does not ascribe purpose or intention to behavior; includes only stimulus-response relationships in its explanations	*Attributes goals and purpose* to human behavior
Focuses on formulating *laws of behavior*	Focuses on *describing mental processes* inferred from behavior

psychologist Jean Piaget and Russian psychologist Lev Vygotsky. American cognitive theorists, such as Tolman and Bruner, and information processing theory have incorporated European influences yet maintained their own distinct brand of cognitive theory.

Gestalt theory was the product of three psychologists—Kurt Koffka (1886–1941), Wolfgang Kohler (1887–1967), and Max Wertheimer (1880–1943). All three studied at the University of Berlin, all had training in philosophy and psychology, and all eventually immigrated to the United States. The term "gestalt" means whole, which clues us that Gestalt psychologists were vehemently opposed to procedures that analyze behavior. According to Gestaltists, behavior cannot be understood in terms of its molecular parts because *"the whole is greater than the sum of its parts."* What this statement, which has become a cliché, means is that the whole exhibits properties that cannot be understood by analyzing it into its constituent parts. For example, water has properties such as wetness and liquidity which are not even present in its oxygen and hydrogen constituents. A psychological example of the emergent properties of the whole is the phi phenomenon, discovered by Wertheimer. In this phenomenon, two or more lights flashing alternately are not perceived simply as flashing lights but rather as moving lights. This movement is a property of perceiving the whole and underlies our ability to perceive neon signs and movies. Music is another example of perceiving wholes rather than their constituent parts. We ordinarily hear not the isolated parts (notes) but the tune or melody (whole).

The major concern of the Gestaltists was to discover the laws governing the perceptions of wholes. Because they made no distinction between perception and thinking, the laws governing perception were also seen as laws of thinking and problem-solving. In contrast to the behaviorist view of problem solving, which emphasized trial and error processes, the Gestaltists characterized problem solving in both humans and apes as involving insight, which is the sudden perception of relationships among elements of a problem situation.

The Gestaltists also viewed learning and memory in terms of the laws governing the perception of wholes. One of their most important contributions to psych l gy was to point out that what one remembers in any situation is determined more by how one interprets or perceives the total situation than by the objective elements present. For instance, your memory of the last sentence may include the word psychology and not the stimulus psych l gy which was actually present. We tend to perceive such incomplete patterns as complete forms (Law of Closure) and our memories reflect this tendency to "fill in" or infer perceptual information. In later chapters, we shall elaborate on Gestalt conceptions of perception, memory, and problem solving and relate them to other cognitive theories.

Edward C. Tolman (1886–1959), a member of the psychology faculty at Berkeley, was a contemporary of Guthrie, Hull, and Skinner and thought of himself as a behaviorist. However, his brand of behaviorism differed in fundamental ways from the traditional variety. First of all, *Tolman assumed that all behavior is purposive*—that is, behavior is directed toward some goal. *Moreover, behavior is directed by cognitions related to goals rather than by S-R connections.* Tolman avoided reducing behavior to its smallest elements and instead focused on large units of behavior that are governed by a single purpose (e.g., food-seeking behavior).

Tolman argued that learning involves the development of *cognitive maps* or internal representations of relationships between goals and behavior as well as the environment in which the goals are to be found. For example, what a rat learns as a result of exposure to a maze, according to Tolman, is not a series of left- and right-turning responses connected to appropriate stimuli, but rather the structure of the maze and an expectancy that food will be found in the goal box. Like traditional behaviorists, Tolman used animals as subjects, and he and his students were masters at devising experiments that produced results contrary to traditional S-R expectations.

Tolman did not believe that reinforcement was necessary for learning as some behaviorists avowed. This notion was tested in an experiment in which rats were allowed to spend several nights in large mazes without being fed (Buxton, 1940). A strict reinforcement theorist such as Hull would predict that the rats would learn very little as a result of this exposure. However, when the rats were subsequently fed briefly in the goal box and then placed immediately in the start box, half of them ran to the goal box without a single error. This result was interpreted by Tolman to mean that rats are capable of learning (i.e., developing cognitive maps) in the absence of reinforcement. This was called *latent learning* because it was not exhibited in the rats' performance until a reward was provided. Thus, Tolman argued that rewards influence performance, not actual learning.

Cognitive-developmental theory was being developed at about the same time that Tolman was conducting experiments to test his theory of purposive behaviorism. However, **Jean Piaget** (1896–1980), a Swiss psychologist, was using a radically different methodology in the development of his cognitive theory. Piaget's basic approach was to observe children in various problem situations. However, he was not so much interested in children's solutions to the problems as in the reasoning they used to justify their solutions. This methodology of observation plus interview probes smacked heavily of earlier introspective approaches. This was probably one of the reasons why Piaget's work was virtually ignored by American psychologists until the 1960s, when the strict behaviorist position began to lose some of its power and influence in the psychological community.

Consistent with his early training in biology and his interest in genetic epistemology (study of the origins of knowledge), Piaget's theory deals with the development of human intelligence. His basic position is that as children attempt to adapt to their environment, they develop increasingly effective reasoning processes that in turn allow them to construct more adequate representations of the world. The emphasis is on understanding how individuals at different ages build or construct their view of reality.

One part of Piaget's theory deals with the processes by which adaptation occurs and the factors such as maturation and social interaction that influence it. Another part of his theory provides a description of the stages through which children's reasoning progresses as they grow from infancy through adolescence. According to Piaget, each qualitatively different stage is marked by the emergence of new cognitive abilities and the construction of new representations of the world that allow more effective interaction with the environment. Both of these aspects of Piaget's theory will be discussed in Chapter 6. We will also discuss **Robbie Case's** theory which combines many of Piaget's assumptions concerning cognitive development with processing mechanisms suggested by information processing theory. Case's approach has been called neo-Piagetian theory. Piaget's theory, along with Case's neo-Piagetian offshoots, has had a significant impact on school curricula, instructional procedures, and evaluation practices which we will also discuss in Chapter 6.

In Chapter 7, we will consider the Russian psychologist **Lev Vygotsky's** (1896–1934) sociohistorical view of cognitive development. Vygotsky's theory differed from Piaget's in its emphasis on the importance of language to cognition and the crucial role that social, historical, and cultural factors play in the child's acquisition of reasoning and knowledge.

Information processing theory, unlike the others covered in the book, is not associated with a single or even a small group of theorists. Rather, many cognitive psychologists have conducted research and developed theories within this general framework. This approach to explaining human cognition had its beginning in the late 1950s and early 1960s when psychologists such as Herbert Simon (Newell, Shaw, & Simon, 1958) and George Miller (Miller, Galanter, & Pribram, 1960) proposed theories of thinking and problem solving that incorporated the computer as the basic metaphor for the human mind, replacing the telephone switchboard metaphor implicit in S-R theory.

A computer takes input usually from keys pushed on a keyboard and transforms it into a qualitatively different internal representation (a pattern of electrical charges). It performs operations on this representation and finally converts it into some output, usually a pattern on a monitor. The output is qualitatively different from either the input or the representation. It might appear that information processing theory is simply substituting new labels for the behavioral terms of stimulus (input), intervening variable (central processing), and response (output). The difference is that behaviorists assume that internal events are very similar to external observable events. For example, they explained a change in strength of an overt response to a given overt stimulus in terms of the strengthening of a bond or link between the neural event representing the stimulus and the neural event representing the response. Thus, internal processes were considered to be a series of covert stimulus-response bonds. In contrast, the internal events in the information processing approach are considered to be "programs" or transformations that do not at all resemble covert stimulus-response bonds. Just as a computer's internal processes are quite different from the input and output, so a human's processes bear no resemblance to connections between stimuli and responses (Martindale, 1991).

In Chapters 3 and 4, we shall discuss information processing approaches to learning which emphasize the central phenomena of attention, perception, and memory. In Chapter 5, we shall discuss information processing approaches to the more complex mental activities of thinking and problem solving.

The next two theorists that we will consider have attempted to integrate the behavioral and cognitive approaches. On the one hand, their theories are quite cognitive in that they explain learning in terms of purely mental activities and structures that bear no resemblance to overt behavior. On the other hand, they are behaviorist because they are interested in explaining behavior and behavior change, whereas strictly cognitive theorists are not interested in behavior except as a means of inferring mental activity.

Social learning theory, like information processing theory, covers a number of theorists who take a similar perspective. However, in Chapter 8 we shall focus on the theory of **Albert Bandura.** As the name implies, social learning theory asserts that much of human learning takes place through social interactions. Humans can and do acquire much of their knowledge and behavior by observing others. This emphasis on *vicarious learning* contrasts with the behaviorist's insistence on direct experience of stimuli, responses, and reinforcements. Bandura argues that we don't have to experience directly the painful effects of certain actions; we can learn from observing the negative consequences that befall others who perform those actions. Similarly, we don't have to learn new behaviors through a process of trial and error, which is very time consuming, but can watch successful models. As we observe a model's performance, we create a cognitive representation that enables us to subsequently perform the new behavior. Whether or not we actually perform the behavior depends on our motivation and available incentives. So, like many behaviorists, social learning theorists view reinforcement as an important factor governing behavior or performance but not as crucial to learning.

Robert Gagné's approach to learning is unique because instead of starting with a particular formulation of the learning process (e.g., associations between stimuli and responses; execution of programs; insight) and then attempting to fit that formulation to human learning, he started with an analysis of the types of performance and skills that humans are capable of and then provided an explanation for this variety. This approach reflects Gagné's work in the military where it became apparent to him that no one theoretical formulation of learning provided an adequate basis for instruction across all the situations and tasks encountered in real-world training settings. In fact, according to Gagné, there are at least five different types of learning outcomes involving different internal cognitive processes that are enhanced by distinctly different environmental conditions. For example, learning verbal information (e.g., the definition of patriarchy) is a type of learning governed by processes different from those governing learning a motor skill (e.g., tying square knots), which in turn is different from learning an intellectual skill (e.g., phonetically decoding words). Gagné's explanation for acquisition of learning outcomes draws heavily on information processing constructs. However, he draws on behavioral concepts such as reinforcement and practice when explaining actual performance and transfer of learning. Gagné's theory forms a basis for the design of instruction related to the learning outcomes which we will cover in the second part of this book.

REVIEW OF MAJOR POINTS

1 A theory was defined as a set of related general statements used to explain particular facts.

2 Theories enable us to (1) discover new facts about the world; (2) summarize sets of disparate facts; and (3) explain facts or observations.

3 A learning theory is a set of related general statements that explain facts about learning.

4 Six criteria are useful for judging the adequacy of learning theories. Good theories (1) adequately reflect the facts; (2) are clear and understandable; (3) are useful for predicting as well as explaining; (4) are internally consistent; (5) are based on as few unproven assumptions as possible; and (6) are testable.

5 Most theorists accept the definition of learning that states that learning is a relatively permanent change in an individual's knowledge or behavior that results from previous experience. This definition is useful for excluding phenomena such as maturation, fatigue, and drug states, which produce behavioral change, and for including internal changes that have not, as yet, been manifested in behavior.

6 Five core issues on which we will compare theories are: (1) What is learned? (2) What is the relative emphasis on environmental versus organismic factors in learning? (3) What is the source of motivation for learning? (4) How does transfer occur? and (5) What are important variables in instruction?

7 The behaviorist perspective explains learning in terms of observable (or inferred) stimulus and response events. Behaviorists view mental activities such as thinking like any other activity. They attempt to analyze behavior into its molecular elements, and their preferred methodology is the experiment. Some early behavioral theorists include Pavlov, Watson, Guthrie, Thorndike, Hull, and Skinner.

8 Cognitive views of learning arose as a negative reaction against behaviorist views. Cognitive theorists assert that behavior cannot be understood by analyzing it into molecular units. The whole has properties that are not apparent in its components. Cognitivists emphasize central processes rather than stimulus and response events and are interested in behavior only as means of inferring mental activity. Brief descriptions were given of Gestalt theory, Tolman's purposive behaviorism, cognitive-developmental theory, and information processing theory.

9 Several theories such as social learning theory and Robert Gagné's theory integrate the cognitive and behaviorist perspectives on learning.

ANSWERS TO QUESTIONS AND EXERCISES

Question 1.1: It follows from what we said about theory that a learning theory is a set of general statements that explains particular facts about learning. (We told you the questions would be easy.)

Question 1.2: Yes, Jennifer meets all the attributes included in the definition of learning. Answering this question before reading about how scientists define learning may have revealed your own private beliefs about how learning occurs.

Exercise 1.1: 1. Not learning—John's blink is a reflex. 2. Not learning—Alice's feat is because of maturation. 3. Learning. 4. Learning—the perception of third-year recruits has changed because of their training experience, although it is difficult to specify exactly the nature of the response change or the exact experiences that have brought it about. (We borrowed this example from Lefrançois, 1982.) 5. Not learning—Jim is exhibiting effects of fatigue. 6. Not learning—Bobby's ability to focus would disappear if the drug were discontinued.

REFERENCES

Buxton, C. E. (1940). Latent learning and the goal gradient hypothesis. *Contributions to Psychological Theory, 2,* 6.

Guthrie, E. R. (1952). *The psychology of learning* (rev. ed.). New York: Harper & Row.

Hull, C. C. (1952). *A behavior system.* New Haven, CT: Yale University Press.

Lefrançois, G. R. (1982). *Psychological theories and human learning* (2nd ed.). Monterey, CA: Brooks/Cole.

Malone, J. C. (1990). *Theories of learning: A historical approach.* Belmont, CA: Wadsworth.

Martindale, C. (1991). *Cognitive psychology: A neural-network approach.* Pacific Grove, CA: Brooks/Cole.

McClelland, D. C., Clark, R. A., Roby, T. B., & Atkinson, J. W. (1949). The projective expression of needs: IV. The effect of the need for achievement on thematic apperception. *Journal of Experimental Psychology, 39,* 242–255.

Miller, G. A., Galanter, E., & Pribram, K. H. (1960). *Plans and the structure of behavior.* New York: Holt.

Miller, N. E., & Dollard, J. (1941). *Social learning and imitation.* New Haven, CT: Yale University Press.

Miller, P. H. (1989). *Theories of developmental psychology.* New York: W. H. Freeman.

Newell, A., Shaw, J. C., & Simon, H. A. (1958). Elements of a theory of human problem-solving. *Psychological Review, 65,* 151–166.

Skinner, B. F. (1983). *A matter of consequences.* New York: Knopf.

Thomas, R. M. (1985). *Comparing theories of child development* (2nd ed.). Belmont, CA: Wadsworth.

Thorndike, E. L. (1913). *Educational psychology* (Vols. 1–3). New York: Teachers College.

2

CLASSICAL AND OPERANT CONDITIONING

OBJECTIVES

1. Given examples of classical conditioning, label the components of conditioning and identify the type and order of conditioning.
2. Explain the importance of emotional conditioning in the classroom.
3. Describe the factors that determine classical conditioning.
4. Describe three ways in which classically conditioned responses can be eliminated. Identify any problems in using each method.
5. Describe the position of classical conditioning on the core issues.
6. Given examples of operant conditioning, classify them as involving positive or negative reinforcement or positive or negative punishment. Identify the examples as primary or secondary conditioning.
7. Describe the factors that determine operant conditioning.
8. Describe three methods for eliminating operant responses and identify any problems in using each method.
9. Describe two technological applications of operant conditioning in education.
10. Describe the relationship between classical and operant conditioning.
11. Identify the position of operant conditioning on the core issues.

In this chapter, we will discuss conditioning, a form of behavioral change or learning primarily studied by behaviorists. We will examine two types of conditioning: classical and operant. Almost everyone in our culture has some familiarity with conditioning from the popular press. So it is important for you to examine any preconceptions that might bias your interaction with the material before you begin reading. For example, you may view conditioning as applying only to lower animals or as trivial and irrelevant to the kinds of learning that go on in the classroom. Some of you may view conditioning techniques as dangerous methods involving "brain washing" and coercion, not appropriate for use with students.

It is true that many conditioning studies are conducted with animals. However, many studies are also done with humans, and they show not only that conditioning takes place in a wide variety of species ranging from flatworms to humans, but that the process of conditioning is very similar across species. The notion that conditioning is trivial (or not applicable to humans) may come from associating this form of learning with dogs salivating to bells and rats pressing bars for food pellets. While such animal studies have indeed played a major role in conditioning research, conditioning principles have also been demonstrated to play a powerful role in students' acquisition of emotional reactions, attitudes, skills, and prosocial behaviors. Similarly, the view of conditioning as a means of controlling and coercing people probably stems from attributing too much power to conditioning. Many people underestimate the complexity of this form of learning and the myriad factors that influence it. In fact, although people are constantly being conditioned naturally just by interacting with their physical and social environments, it is often difficult to condition people at will.

CLASSICAL CONDITIONING

In the movie *Jaws,* director Steven Spielberg demonstrated his entertainment genius by using classical conditioning principles to scare people out of their wits. The movie is about a great white killer shark that terrorizes a small town on the east coast. The shark is not actually seen until late in the movie, by which time Spielberg has thoroughly conditioned us. In a vivid scene from the movie, a young woman is swimming alone in the ocean on a beautiful moonlit night. All is peaceful, but then (softly at first) comes an intense, nervous sort of music that builds in volume until, at its climax, the young woman is attacked and dragged screaming under the water by something unseen and horrible. Another scene shows a large holiday crowd at the beach. Children are playing and swimming in the water. All is peaceful and happy until, suddenly, that music comes again. The audience immediately becomes restless, the music builds, and then at its peak, a little boy is attacked and dismembered by something unseen (but we know from preceding dialogue that it's the shark). Now, for the rest of the movie all Spielberg has to do is to play that musical theme and audience members respond with fearful anticipation and dread because he has skillfully led them to associate the music with the shark's attack. One can get a very direct experience of emotional conditioning involving fear by watching *Jaws.* Indeed, most movie and TV directors worth their salt use the principles of classical conditioning to condition both positive and negative emotions in their audience. See if you can detect attempts at emotional conditioning in the next movie or TV commercial you view.

Components of Classical Conditioning

We will examine the components of classical conditioning using the original laboratory situation in which the phenomenon was first discovered by Ivan Pavlov. Pavlov was a physiologist who won the Nobel prize for his work on the role of the glands in digestion. In his investigation of the salivary glands, he devised a way of observing the amount of salivation by diverting the flow of saliva through a tube surgically implanted in the wall of a dog's mouth. Thus, when food was placed in the dog's mouth, the resulting saliva could be collected in a beaker and measured (see Figure 2.1).

In the course of these experiments, Pavlov noticed that dogs began salivating before the food (meat powder) was placed in their mouths. They would salivate at the sight of the food or, even more interesting, at the sight of the lab attendant who usually brought the food. Any other observer might have dismissed these events—most people believe it is "natural" for organisms to salivate at the sight of food. However, Pavlov noted that these "psychic secretions" as he later called them occurred only in dogs who had been in the laboratory for some time, and were absent in dogs naive to the laboratory situation. This could mean only that these salivating responses were learned. Pavlov spent the rest of his life investigating the conditions under which such learning occurred.

The first component of classical conditioning is the **unconditioned stimulus.** This is a stimulus that naturally elicits a response. The food in the dog's mouth is the unconditioned stimulus in Pavlov's situation. Food placed in the mouth elicits the response of salivation. Salivation to the food in the mouth is called the **unconditioned response.** The connection between the unconditioned stimulus and unconditioned response is reflexive or unlearned. *Any stimulus that reflexively elicits a response can be used as an unconditioned stimulus.* Other examples of reflexes include blinking when a puff of air hits the eyeball, flexing a limb following an electric shock, and jerking the knee after a tap to the patellar tendon.

The next component of classical conditioning is a neutral one called the **conditioned stimulus** that does not originally elicit the unconditioned response. In Pavlov's situation the neutral stimulus often used was the sound of a bell. Prior to conditioning, when the bell was sounded the dog might prick up its ears and look

FIGURE 2.1 Pavlov's conditioning stand. (From Chance, 1979.)

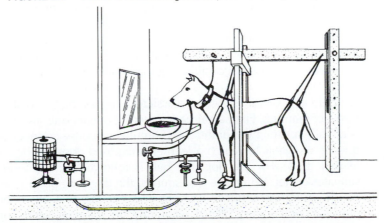

toward the sound, but it certainly would not salivate. The critical happening in conditioning, as Pavlov discovered, is that when the conditioned stimulus (bell) is repeatedly presented just before the unconditioned stimulus (food), the bell comes to elicit the salivation response that originally occurred only to the food. When the salivation occurs to the conditioned stimulus, it is called the **conditioned response.** The conditioned response is a learned response that resembles the unconditioned response except that it is elicited by the previously neutral stimulus. The components of classical conditioning are diagrammed as follows:

$$
\begin{array}{ccc}
\text{unconditioned stimulus} & \rightarrow & \text{unconditioned response} \\
\text{food} & & \text{salivation} \\
\text{conditioned stimulus} & \rightarrow & \text{conditioned response} \\
\text{bell} & & \text{salivation}
\end{array}
$$

Through the repeated pairing of the two stimuli, the dog learns that the bell signals the presentation of food, and it reacts to the bell in the same reflexive way in which it reacts to the actual food.

Type of Conditioning and Emotional Reactions

Pavlov distinguished between two basic types of conditioning. **Appetitive conditioning** involves an unconditioned stimulus that is positive or something that the organism would ordinarily seek out, such as food, water, or sexual stimulation. In **defense conditioning,** the unconditioned stimulus is something negative that the organism tries to avoid, such as electric shock or pin pricks. The most important fact concerning both types of conditioning is that, in addition to whatever other responses they elicit, *all unconditioned stimuli elicit emotional responses.* In appetitive conditioning, positive emotional reactions (e.g., feelings of satisfaction, liking, attraction, interest, pleasure, or delight) occur as part of the unconditioned response. In defense conditioning, one or more negative emotional reactions (e.g., feelings of fear, anxiety, aversion, dislike, hatred) are automatically elicited by the unconditioned stimulus. So, for example, at the same time that the dog is learning to salivate when the bell sounds, it is also learning to like the bell. In the same way, when a flash of light is paired with a painful shock to the paw, the dog not only learns a foot flexion response to the light but learns to fear the light. This is the aspect of classical conditioning that makes it relevant to the classroom situation.

There are several aspects of classical conditioning that distinguish it from other forms of learning. First, as already noted, it occurs only in situations where there is already a strong unconditioned stimulus-response connection. Second, the sequence of events to which a learner is exposed does not depend upon what the learner does. (For the dog, the bell is followed by the food whether the dog salivates or not. When the bell sounds, the dog may open its mouth and thereby get the food faster, but this response is not one that has been learned through classical conditioning.) Third, what indicates learning is a change in the effectiveness of the conditioned stimulus in eliciting the response that previously occurred only to the unconditioned stimulus. As noted above, the individual may learn other responses in the situation (e.g., to approach or to run away when the conditioned stimulus is presented). However, only the automatic response (e.g., the salivation and the emotional reaction) to the conditioned stimulus is a result of classical conditioning. The other responses are a result of operant conditioning, which we will study later in this chapter. Before we explore further the intricacies of this form of learning, let's try an exercise.

Exercise 2.1: Identify whether each description is or is not an example of classical conditioning. If it is, then label the components of conditioning and identify each example as either appetitive or defense. Include the emotional reactions likely to be evoked by the unconditioned and conditioned stimuli.

1. John has eaten curry for dinner. Later that evening with the curry aftertaste still remaining, he contracts stomach flu. From then on he avoids curry because it makes him queasy.
   Classical conditioning? Yes No
   Type? Appetitive Defense

   Unconditioned Stimulus:_____

   Unconditioned Response:_____

   Conditioned Stimulus:_____

   Conditioned Response:_____

2. Mary, a lifelong coffee drinker, gets a boost in arousal even when she drinks Sanka.
   Classical Conditioning? Yes No
   Type? Appetitive Defense

   Unconditioned Stimulus:_____

   Unconditioned Response:_____

   Conditioned Stimulus:_____

   Conditioned Response:_____

3. Joe has not been doing his homework. Mr. Brown, his teacher, promises him extra free time each day he hands in his homework. Joe begins to hand in his homework regularly.
   Classical Conditioning? Yes No
   Type? Appetitive Defense

   Unconditioned Stimulus:_____

   Unconditioned Response:_____

   Conditioned Stimulus:_____

   Conditioned Response:_____

4. At the beginning of the school year, Ms. Jones would say, "Boys and girls"

and then loudly clap her hands. The kindergarten children would stop whatever they were doing and pay attention to her. Later in the year, she could get their attention by softly saying "Boys and girls."

Classical Conditioning? Yes No

Type? Appetitive Defense

Unconditioned Stimulus:_____

Unconditioned Response:_____

Conditioned Stimulus:_____

Conditioned Response:_____

Order of Conditioning

The examples of classical conditioning we have encountered thus far have involved **primary** or first order conditioning. In primary conditioning, the unconditioned stimulus naturally elicits an unconditioned response with no prior learning. As we have seen, we can convert a neutral stimulus into a conditioned one by pairing it with the natural, unconditioned stimulus. Afterward, we can pair a new neutral stimulus with the conditioned stimulus we have just created and thereby produce another conditioned stimulus. This process is called **secondary conditioning** and is illustrated in the following diagram:

$$\text{primary} \quad \text{food} \rightarrow \text{salivation}$$
$$\text{bell} \rightarrow \text{salivation}$$

$$\text{secondary} \quad \text{bell} \rightarrow \text{salivation}$$
$$\text{light} \rightarrow \text{salivation}$$

Like primary conditioning, secondary conditioning can be either appetitive or defensive. Come to think of it, we have already encountered an example of secondary conditioning. Remember *Jaws*? The audience already has fear responses to the sight of a shark, to the word "shark," and to the sight of blood. These are conditioned responses—we are not born with any built-in responses to any of these stimuli, not even the sight of blood. We feel fear or anxiety at the sight of blood (conditioned stimulus 1) because it has been paired in the past with feeling pain from a wound (unconditioned stimulus). We feel anxious when we see a shark (conditioned stimulus 2) because we have seen sharks accompanied by the sight of blood. We feel anxious at the sound of the word shark (conditioned stimulus 3) because it has been paired with the sight of the shark. In the movie, the music becomes a conditioned stimulus when it is paired with one or more of these conditioned stimuli. Many of our emotional reactions, our likes and dislikes, our fears and our joys, are a result of such higher-order conditioning.

Carolyn and Arthur Staats have done research on secondary conditioning in which the neutral stimuli were nonsense syllables and the conditioned stimuli were words that presumably elicited emotional reactions. For example, college students watched while nonsense syllables such as YOF, LAJ, and QUG were flashed on a screen. At the same time the students repeated words spoken by the experimenters. For some students the syllable YOF was always paired with a positive word such as "beauty," "gift," and "win," while the syllable XEH was always paired with a negative word such as "thief," "sad," and "enemy." For other students the procedure was reversed—YOF was paired with unpleasant words and XEH was paired with pleasant words. Students then rated the syllables on a seven-point scale ranging from unpleasant to pleasant. The nonsense syllables took on the emotional tone of the words with which they had been paired. That is, YOF was rated as pleasant when it was paired with pleasant words and as unpleasant when it had been paired with unpleasant words (Staats & Staats, 1957).

In another experiment, Staats and Staats (1958) used this same procedure except that they paired names of nationalities (e.g., Swedish, Dutch) with either pleasant or unpleasant words. Again, the names took on the emotional tone of the words with which they were paired. It does not seem too farfetched to suppose that many of our attitudes toward people, including our prejudices, are acquired through such secondary conditioning involving verbal stimuli. Such words as "Negro," "communist," "catholic," "Jew," and "honky" are all originally neutral stimuli like YOF and XEH that acquire their emotional meaning through secondary conditioning. While the words are not the same as the objects they represent, there is evidence that if the word "Jew" is paired with such adjectives as "stingy" and "conniving," it will affect how we will respond to a person as well as to the word (Williams, 1966).

Some Implications of Classical Conditioning

Let's spell out the implications of what we have learned about classical conditioning so far. Many people dismiss classical conditioning because, after all, what is so interesting about a dog learning to salivate to a bell? The bell predicts food and makes the dog anticipate it; he salivates because he expects food. This is not such a big deal. But what is a big deal is that the dog salivates whether it wants to or not, whether it expects food or not. In fact, in many cases of classical conditioning, awareness on the part of the learner plays no role (Malone, 1990). Furthermore, as we have seen, classical conditioning results in many more interesting outcomes than salivating to bells.

A good deal of behavior, especially emotional behavior, can be accounted for in terms of either primary or secondary classical conditioning. The adaptability that conditioning brings has tremendous survival value. We must respond not only to stimuli which in themselves bring immediate benefit or harm but also to other stimuli which only signal the approach of these stimuli. Thus, we can be grateful that we feel fear at the sight of a snake and not only when it bites us. What's more, the adaptability of humans is enhanced greatly by higher-order conditioning involving language. We can shout "snake" while on a hike and our companions will respond as if they had seen the snake. And many of the things we enjoy in life produce pleasure because they have become conditioned stimuli. The sight of a loved one's face, a sunny day, or a flower can cheer us, thanks largely to conditioning. Many of the characteristics that make us unique individuals are due to our own particular histories of classical conditioning. For example, do you blush when someone compliments you? Do you enjoy meeting new people? Do you feel a shiver when you gaze at the stars? These and countless other emotional reactions that make up our sense of personal identity are due to classical conditioning.

However, conditioning like everything else has its dark side. We can acquire maladaptive as well as adaptive emotional responses through conditioning. For example, we can learn to fear harmless animals. Also, many conditioned stimuli elicit negative emotional reactions. For example, the sight of an overcast sky or a withered plant may sadden us, thanks to conditioning. Are you afraid to speak before a group? Are you uncomfortable with certain ethnic or racial groups? None of us is completely free of such reactions and, like our positively conditioned emotional responses, they make us who we are.

Many behaviors associated with mental illness are largely due to classical conditioning. Fetishes (sexual arousal at the sight of certain objects) and phobias are examples. Certain physical complaints such as asthma, headaches, and ulcers may partly be due to classical conditioning. We say that such diseases are caused by stress, but what is actually happening is that certain stimuli (such as criticism from one's teacher or hostile looks from one's students) are conditioned stimuli for certain physiological reactions, and these physiological reactions, in turn, produce organic disorders. For example, criticism from one's teacher elicits muscle tension which produces a headache.

Of course, classical conditioning occurs constantly in the classroom. Students (and teachers) acquire emotional responses to many stimuli in the school setting because these stimuli have systematically come just before stimuli that already elicit strong emotional responses. For example, many students feel anxious at the sight of math problems, probably because in the past they have experienced failure in working out math problems. Failure at tasks is itself a conditioned stimulus for anxiety because it has often been followed by criticism, disapproval, or punishment by adults. Students who fail frequently at school tasks will almost certainly acquire negative emotional reactions, not only to the tasks themselves but also to stimuli (such as the teacher) that are consistently paired with the failure. These conditioned negative emotional reactions then serve to interfere with the student's subsequent attempts to perform. Thus, a vicious cycle is set in motion.

Some students appear to be at higher risk of this type of negative conditioning. Clearly, students from homes where failure is punished and who lack prerequisite skills for successfully learning school tasks can easily acquire school anxiety. The role of the teacher is both preventive and corrective. The teacher can prevent school anxiety from developing in the first place by carefully monitoring each student's failures and intervening before emotional responses can be strongly conditioned to aspects of the school environment. Prevention is not possible when teachers encounter the student after the conditioning has occurred. However, once negative emotional conditioning has occurred, there is much that the teacher can do to help the student eliminate it. We will discuss elimination of classically conditioned responses in a later section. First, we need to discuss the factors that determine classical conditioning. This is information that you can use because teachers do wish to take an active role in conditioning positive emotional reactions and attitudes toward school and learning tasks.

Factors That Determine Classical Conditioning

Chance (1979) discusses a number of factors that need to be considered when attempting to bring about classical conditioning.

Pairing of Neutral and Significant Stimuli   One factor that determines how easily conditioning occurs is how the neutral stimulus and the significant or unconditioned stimuli are paired. *Normally, for good conditioning, the neutral stimulus should precede the unconditioned stimulus.* The ideal situation is when the conditioned stimulus appears and then after a brief interval the unconditioned stimulus comes on while the conditioned stimulus is still present (see Figure 2.2). For example, the teacher says, "Boys and girls" and, before finishing the phrase, claps her hands loudly. If the interval from the beginning of the neutral stimulus to the beginning of the significant stimulus is long, the arrangement is called **delayed conditioning.** This situation is less effective for conditioning than the first arrangement. If the neutral stimulus comes on and goes off before the significant stimulus comes on, it is called **trace conditioning** (see Figure 2.2). For example,

FIGURE 2.2   Various temporal arrangements of the conditioned and unconditioned stimuli in classical conditioning. The period when the conditioned stimulus and the unconditioned stimulus are on is shown for five types of pairings.

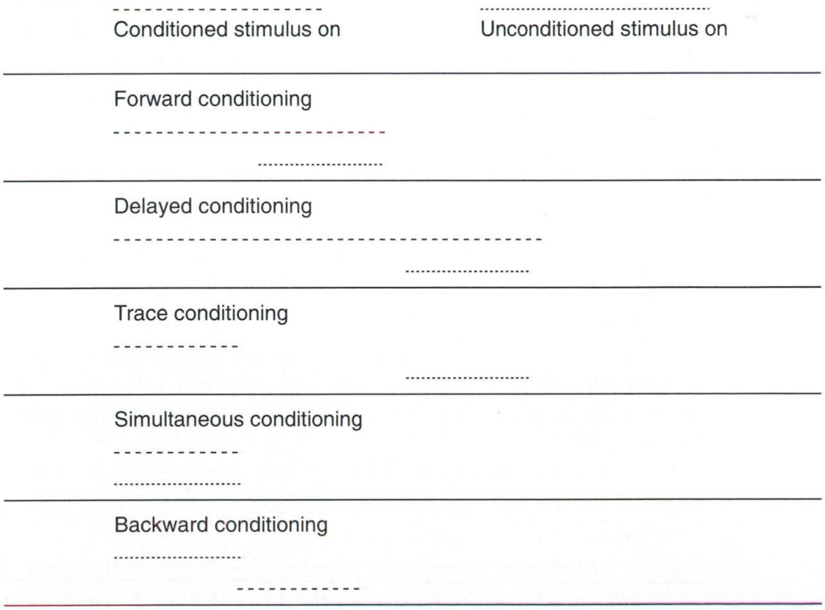

Conditioned stimulus on	Unconditioned stimulus on
Forward conditioning	
Delayed conditioning	
Trace conditioning	
Simultaneous conditioning	
Backward conditioning	

the teacher says, ''Boys and girls'' and then pauses before loudly clapping her hands. Trace conditioning is usually less effective than conditioning in which the conditioned stimulus is maintained until the unconditioned stimulus begins. However, all of the above arrangements result in conditioning because in all instances the neutral stimulus signals the onset of the unconditioned stimulus. If the neutral stimulus comes on simultaneously with the significant stimulus (**simultaneous conditioning**) or follows it (**backward conditioning**), very weak or no conditioning results because in both cases the neutral stimulus has no value as a signal that the significant stimulus is coming.

Interstimulus Interval   Another factor that determines conditioning is the time interval between the beginning of the neutral and the beginning of the unconditioned stimuli. The length of the time interval that produces good conditioning may vary, depending upon the response being conditioned. However, for the types of responses usually conditioned in the classroom setting, research indicates that from about half a second to a second between the onset of the neutral stimulus and the onset of the significant stimulus results in optimal conditioning.

Number of Stimulus Pairings   The more frequently students experience the pairing of the neutral and the unconditioned stimulus, the more likely that a conditioned response will be established. However, the conditioning curve is negatively accelerated. That is, the first few pairings will increase greatly the strength of the conditioned response while subsequent pairings will add less and less to the strength of the response.

Number of Times the Neutral Stimulus Occurs Alone   The effect of the number of pairings of the stimuli also depends upon how often the neutral stimulus occurs alone without being followed by the unconditioned stimulus. In general, the more times the neutral stimulus occurs without the unconditioned stimulus, the less effective is conditioning. For example, a teacher may obtain good conditioning by following the phrase ''Boys and girls'' with a loud hand clap five times during the initial school day. However, conditioning would be much slower if the teacher were also sometimes to speak the phrase without following it with the clap. Conditioning in the real world (outside the laboratory) is often erratic because the neutral stimulus sometimes occurs without the unconditioned stimulus. *Consistency is the key, then, when teachers are seeking to condition attentional or other types of responses in the classroom.*

Question 2.1: Often when the phone rings we receive important news. Why don't most of us experience a strong emotional reaction when we hear the phone

ring?_____

_____

_____

Characteristics of the Learner   Classical conditioning does not proceed at the same rate for all species or for all individuals within a species. For example, sheep, rabbits, and people condition more easily than rats, cats, and pigs (Chance, 1979). Some individuals within a species condition more easily than other individuals. Although there is not much research on the specific temperamental or biological characteristics that are related to conditioning, we need to be aware that there are internal (probably genetically determined) factors that influence the ease of conditioning. We do know that moderate levels of arousal are associated with better conditioning than low or high levels (Taylor, 1951).

Prior Experience with Neutral Stimuli   Another way individuals differ in their rate of conditioning depends upon their previous exposure to the stimulus that will serve as the conditioned one. For example, consider once more the teacher trying to condition the students to quiet down and pay attention when she says "Boys and girls." If a student has been exposed to this phrase often in the past and it has never been followed by an unconditioned stimulus, it will take longer to establish the conditioned response than if a student has little prior exposure to the phrase. Being exposed to a stimulus that is not paired with a significant stimulus interferes with the ability of that stimulus to become a conditioned one. This phenomenon is called **latent inhibition.** The kindergarten teacher trying to condition attention might do well to choose a neutral stimulus that children are unlikely to have encountered much in the past.

Another way prior experience with a neutral stimulus can affect later conditioning is called **sensory preconditioning.** In this case, two neutral stimuli such as a bell and a light are repeatedly presented together but not paired with an unconditioned stimulus. Then one of these stimuli, say the bell, is paired with food so that it becomes a conditioned stimulus for salivation. Now, the second neutral stimulus, the light, when presented will elicit the conditioned response even though it had never been paired with the unconditioned stimulus. In general, a stimulus will become a conditioned stimulus more rapidly if it has been paired with another stimulus that has subsequently become a conditioned stimulus.

Sensory preconditioning is very similar to higher-order conditioning except that the steps occur in a different order. Both procedures represent ways that an individual can develop a conditioned response to a stimulus that has never been directly paired with an unconditioned stimulus. Sensory preconditioning might account for some cases of test anxiety. First, school (neutral stimulus 1) is associated with tests (neutral stimulus 2). If school is then later associated with some traumatic event (unconditioned stimulus), then not only will school become a conditioned stimulus eliciting anxiety, but tests may become a conditioned stimulus for anxiety as well (Klein, 1987).

Generalization

After he had conditioned a dog to salivate to a previously neutral stimulus, Pavlov noticed a peculiar thing—not only did the dog salivate to the particular stimulus that had been paired with the unconditioned stimulus, but it would also salivate to other, similar, stimuli. This phenomenon, called **stimulus generalization,** refers to the fact that when a stimulus becomes a conditioned stimulus, other stimuli similar to it can also elicit the conditioned response.

An excellent example of generalization in the context of emotional conditioning is provided by the case of little Albert. Albert was an 11-month-old child whom John B. Watson and his associate Rosalie Rayner (1920) conditioned to fear a white rat. Albert at first showed no fear of the rat and would reach for it when it was presented. However, Albert did show an unconditioned fear response to loud noises. The conditioning trials consisted of (you guessed it!) presenting the rat, and as Albert reached for it, sounding a loud noise behind Albert's head. After only a few such pairings, Albert showed the fear response—originally elicited only by the loud noise—whenever the rat was presented. Watson and Rayner then tested to see if other, previously neutral, stimuli would also elicit the fear reaction. They presented Albert with a dog, a rabbit, cotton wool, a Santa Claus mask, and building blocks. None of these stimuli had been present when the rat was paired with the loud noise; however, several of them did elicit the fear response. The more similar the item to the rat, the stronger the reaction. Therefore, the rabbit produced the greatest generalization while the building blocks produced no reaction.

In the above descriptions, physical similarity to the conditioned stimulus is the basis for generalization (called **primary stimulus generalization).** Conditioned reactions can also spread to stimuli that are similar in meaning to the conditioned stimulus (called **secondary stimulus generalization).** For example, Razran (1939) established conditioned responses to words such as "style," and "urn," and then presented subjects with words that were either synonyms ("fashion," "vase") or homonyms ("stile," "earn"). While conditioned responses occurred to both types of words, generalization was much greater in the case of the words similar in meaning. Such semantic generalization occurs readily in the classroom. For example, if racial labels such as black and Chicano are associated with positive adjectives (e.g., "industrious," "competent," "honest"), positive emotional responses should be conditioned to these racial labels and should, in turn, generalize to other terms such as Negroes and Mexicans.

Discrimination

The opposite of the generalization process is **discrimination,** whereby an individual learns to inhibit the conditioned response to stimuli similar to the conditioned stimulus. Discrimination occurs when stimuli that are similar to the conditioned stimulus are not followed by the unconditioned stimulus. For example, our kindergarten teacher, who is attempting to condition her children to stop all activity and attend when she says "Boys and girls," may find that initially the children generalize the attentional response to other phrases as well. For example, they may all stop what they are doing and direct their attention to her when she calls one student by name—"John, please come here." However, if she continues to administer the unconditioned stimulus only after the target verbal phrase, the students will gradually learn to limit their attentional response to that phrase.

Eliminating Conditioned Responses

So far we have been concerned with the acquisition of conditioned responses. But it is very important for teachers to know how to help students get rid of conditioned responses that are maladaptive. One common approach is to hope that the child will simply forget the conditioned response. It is true that a conditioned response will weaken with the passage of time; however, in order for forgetting to occur, the individual must not come in contact with the conditioned stimulus. This is often difficult to arrange in the real world. Research has shown that just keeping children away from feared objects so that they will forget their fear is very ineffective (Jones, 1924a). Fortunately, there are two, more effective, ways to eliminate conditioned responses.

Extinction of a conditioned response is a procedure in which the conditioned stimulus is presented and not followed by the unconditioned stimulus (note that this is different from forgetting, which involves withholding the conditioned stimulus). After a number of trials in which the conditioned stimulus is presented without the unconditioned stimulus, the conditioned response disappears. However, it is not gone for good: After a short rest period, the conditioned response will once again be elicited by the conditioned stimulus. This reappearance of the conditioned response after extinction trials is known as **spontaneous recovery.** Usually when the conditioned response spontaneously recovers, it is weaker than before extinction and will become even weaker as more extinction trials are given. Finally, it will disappear completely.

The teacher who is attempting to extinguish a conditioned response in a student (say, a conditioned fear of answering questions in class) would first have to ensure that the conditioned stimulus (being called on to answer a question) occurs repeatedly without being followed by the unconditioned stimulus (ridicule, criticism). This process would have to be conducted over many sessions until the child no longer feels fear or anxiety when she is called on in class. Extinction, then, can be a time-consuming process.

Another drawback is that in the real world of the classroom, it is often difficult to ensure that the unconditioned stimulus never follows the conditioned stimulus. In the above example, the teacher can control her own responses, that is, make sure never to show anything but positive reactions to the child's attempts to answer questions. However, other children may laugh at or ridicule the student's responses. If this occurs, the result will be to strengthen, not eliminate, the conditioned fear response.

Another reason why one cannot count on extinction is that people tend to avoid a stimulus they have learned to fear, thus reducing the chances of encountering the conditioned stimulus in the absence of the unconditioned stimulus. For example, a person who has learned to fear answering questions because of a history of ridicule following responses typically avoids situations requiring answering questions. This minimizes any chance of disassociating question answering from ridicule. Because of these difficulties in implementing extinction, a third method of eliminating conditioned responses is often used.

In the method of **counterconditioning,** the conditioned stimulus is paired with a stimulus that elicits a response that is incompatible with the unwanted conditioned response. For example, funeral homes make use of counterconditioning when they place flower arrangements around the casket. The sight of the casket elicits sadness; the sight of flowers elicits positive emotional reactions. When you send flowers or candy to someone in the hospital you are using counterconditioning. But beware, counterconditioning can backfire! This is probably what happened to one friend who, after a long stay in the hospital, became depressed at the sight of flowers. To prevent this backfiring when using counterconditioning, the conditioned stimulus for the unwanted conditioned response is kept at a weak level at first and then only gradually strengthened. For example, if a child fears dogs, getting him a puppy might work. At first the puppy doesn't resemble a full-grown dog much. As it grows it becomes more and more similar to the feared conditioned stimulus, but only gradually. In the meantime, positive emotional responses are being conditioned as the child plays with the puppy.

John Watson and Mary Clover Jones (Jones 1924b) used counterconditioning with a 3-year-old child named Peter who had acquired many fears. In contrast to little Albert, however, Peter's fears were acquired naturally—not in the laboratory. Peter was a bundle of neuroses, fearing rabbits, fur coats, feathers, cotton wool, frogs, and other things. The researchers began to eliminate these fears by bringing a rabbit into view but keeping it far enough away so that it did not disturb Peter, who was enjoying a snack. On each successive trial, they would bring the rabbit closer but never close enough to frighten Peter. Finally, Peter was able to hold the rabbit on his lap without anxiety. The effects of counterconditioning as well as those of extinction generalize to similar stimuli. When Peter was no longer afraid of the rabbit, he had also lost his conditioned fear response to fur coats, feathers, and cotton wool. His fear of frogs would be less diminished because of the greater dissimilarity to the rabbit.

In the case of the child who becomes anxious when called on in class, counterconditioning might work something like this. At first the child is asked questions only when she is working in a small, informal group setting in which she feels relaxed. Moreover, the teacher ensures that the questions are ones that the child can easily answer. Gradually, the child's feeling of anxiety when called on is replaced with relaxation. When the child seems comfortable answering questions in this setting, then the teacher begins to ask questions of her in the large class setting but still poses only easy questions. Gradually, the teacher can increase the difficulty level of the questions, although she should always be ready to drop back to easier questions if the child exhibits anxiety.

The example of counterconditioning just described is similar to the technique of **systematic desensitization** developed by Joseph Wolpe (1961). In Wolpe's version the individual is taught progressive relaxation, a method for inducing total body relaxation. Then while relaxed, the person imagines situations related to a feared object or event. The imagined situations have been carefully arranged in a sequence so that ones used early do not arouse very much fear while ones coming later are more frightening. While in a state of relaxation, the person visualizes each scene in the fear hierarchy. If at any point the individual begins to feel anxious, he drops back to a less feared stimulus in the hierarchy. This therapeutic technique has been used quite successfully to help people overcome fears. One of the authors, who suffered from an intense fear of flying, can attest to the effectiveness of systematic desensitization.

Exercise 2.2: Make up an example of classical conditioning in which a student acquires a negative emotional response to some aspect of the classroom situation. Identify the following:

Unconditioned stimulus:_____

Unconditioned response:_____

Conditioned stimulus:_____

Conditioned response:_____
Describe how you would use counterconditioning to eliminate the undesirable conditioned emotional reaction.

_____

_____

_____

_____

_____

The Core Issues

It's time to examine the position of classical conditioning on the core issues identified in Chapter 1.

1. *What is learned?* In classical conditioning, a reflexive response is acquired to a stimulus that previously did not elicit that response. More generally stated, the learning outcomes dealt with in the domain of classical conditioning included the acquisition of emotional reactions and attitudes. Some theorists such as Watson have argued that the conditioned response is the basic building block of all learned behavior. While this is certainly overstating the importance of classical conditioning, it should be clear that this is indeed a powerful form of learning that teachers need to be able to control.

Another aspect of what is learned has to do with the mechanism that underlies classical conditioning. Pavlov explained the acquisition of conditioned responses in terms of the formation of neural connections between the neurons representing the unconditioned stimulus and the neurons representing the conditioned stimulus. He explained the phenomena associated with conditioning, such as generalization, discrimination, and extinction, in terms of the spread of excitation or inhibition in the cerebral cortex. Most behavioral theorists understand classical conditioning as involving the formation of a connection between the conditioned stimulus and the unconditioned response.

In contrast, cognitive theorists have proposed that in classical conditioning the individual processes and stores information about the relationship between stimuli in the environment (Bolles, 1972). Thus, in this view, rather than learning a connection between a stimulus and a response, the learner acquires an expectancy that the conditioned stimulus will be followed by the unconditioned stimulus. Neither the stimulus-response nor the expectancy explanation has earned recognition as *the* explanation of classical conditioning. Fortunately, we do not have to wait for a resolution of this theoretical dispute before using the principles and facts of classical conditioning to establish positive emotional reactions and attitudes in the classroom, while using extinction and counterconditioning to eliminate negative reactions and attitudes.

2. *Emphasis on environmental versus organismic factors.* Classical conditioning tends to emphasize the role of the environment in bringing about learning. The individual is rather passively acted on by stimuli in the environment. Moreover, the conditioned response is one that the individual can do little to control.

3. *Source of motivation.* Basically, there is little attention given to the role of motivation in classical conditioning. If the organism is awake and somewhat alert, learning occurs whether the individual wants it to or not. However, once having been unwittingly conditioned, it may take considerable motivation for people to willingly undergo extinction or counterconditioning in order to become free of their conditioned fears. Emotional pain is probably the factor that motivates most people to seek treatment.

4. *Transfer.* Stimulus generalization or the tendency for stimuli that are physically or semantically similar to the conditioned stimulus to elicit the conditioned response accounts for transfer.

5. *Important variables in instruction.* When attempting to condition positive emotional reactions and attitudes toward learning tasks and other elements of the school environment, it is crucial that the teacher control the occurrence of conditioned and unconditioned stimuli. The timing of their occurrence is another critical variable—the conditioned stimulus should precede the unconditioned stimulus by half a second or so. Repeatedly pairing the conditioned and the unconditioned stimulus is another critical variable in this type of instruction. When attempting to eliminate negative emotional reactions or attitudes, it is important to ensure that the unconditioned stimulus does not follow the conditioned stimulus. Additionally, the teacher needs to pair with the conditioned stimulus other stimuli that evoke responses that are antagonistic to the conditioned response. And, once again, repetition of the extinction-counterconditioning trials is important.

OPERANT CONDITIONING

At about the same time that Pavlov was working on classical conditioning, E. L. Thorndike was studying animal intelligence. During his studies of cats in puzzle boxes (see Chapter 1), he came to the conclusion that animals (including man) did not solve problems by reasoning them out, but rather by randomly trying out a variety of responses. Some responses produce positive consequences, some produce aversive consequences. Behavior is modified by the effects it has on the environment, a principle Thorndike called the **Law of Effect.** The law of effect states that when a response in a given situation is followed by a satisfying state of affairs, it tends to be repeated. When a response is followed by an annoying state of affairs, it tends not to be repeated. The procedure by which a response becomes more or less likely to be repeated depending upon its consequences is called instrumental learning.

Today, largely as a result of the work of B. F. Skinner, we refer to instrumental learning as operant conditioning and to consequences as reinforcers and punishers. Skinner adapted Thorndike's law of effect by leaving out any reference to subjective states of the organism. That is, for Skinner a reinforcer is anything which increases the probability of the behavior it follows, and a punisher is anything which decreases the behavior it follows. There need be no reference to what is satisfying or annoying to the organism. Skinner is quite content to treat reinforcement as an empirical fact rather than a theoretical construct. According to him, if you want to know if some consequence is a reinforcement for a particular individual, the only way to find out is to see if that consequence increases the probability of responses that it follows. If it does, then by definition it is a reinforcer.

This approach of defining reinforcement by its effects on behavior is circular, as critics of Skinner have pointed out. Other behaviorists have attempted to avoid such circularity by positing unobservable mechanisms that explain why reinforcements work. For example, Hull proposed that reinforcers work because they reduce drives (e.g., food is reinforcing because it reduces hunger). But Skinner regarded all such attempts to explain empirical laws of behavior in terms of unobservable abstractions as unnecessary. He believed that it is enough to say that there is a correlation between certain kinds of behavior and certain kinds of consequences. According to Skinner, this kind of behavioral law is useful in and of itself; nothing is gained (in fact, clarity is lost) by explaining behavioral laws in other terms.

Components of Operant Conditioning

The first component of this form of conditioning is an emitted response called an **operant response.** An operant is any response produced by the organism which, in turn, produces consequences in the environment. *An operant is freely emitted by the organism and not elicited by a stimulus as is the case in classical conditioning.* Skinner recognized that some forms of behavior are reflexively elicited by stimuli. He called this **respondent** behavior and described its acquisition in terms very similar to Pavlov's. However, he maintained that most behavior is operant rather than respondent. There is no specific stimulus that can be identified which will consistently and automatically elicit an operant response. Since most behavior is operant (e.g., walking, talking, working, and playing all involve operant responses), Skinner devoted most of his energy to discovering the laws governing the learning of this type of behavior.

The second component of operant conditioning is the **stimulus consequence** in the environment brought about by the emitted response. There are various kinds of consequences, as we will discuss in a moment. In general, a consequence is either a reinforcement which increases the probability of the operant's being repeated or a punishment which decreases the probability of the operant.

In addition to the above components which are always present in operant conditioning, there is also usually a **discriminative stimulus,** which is one that indicates whether a given response will be reinforced or punished. For example, the enter sign over a door tells you that you will be reinforced if you attempt to go into the store through that door. A stop sign tells you that you will be punished (by an accident or a ticket) if you proceed without stopping. Through learning, our operant responses are brought under the control of such discriminative stimuli. However, such control is only partial. For example, the operant response of reaching for food will take place only when food is present, but it is not elicited by the sight of the food in the way that salivation is. Rather, it also depends on hunger, social circumstances, and a variety of other stimulus conditions. Although much of Skinner's analysis of behavior was concerned with ways in which operants are brought under the control of discriminative stimuli, he did not consider it useful to think of operant behavior as made up of specific stimulus-response connections.

Types of Conditioning Procedures

Reinforcement In this procedure, the strength or probability of a response is increased. There are two kinds of reinforcement procedures: positive and negative. When an operant is strengthened by the appearance of a stimulus consequence or by an increase in the intensity of a stimulus consequence, we have **positive reinforcement.** For example, if you are teaching a dog to shake hands, you might give it a bit of food when it lifts its paw. The dog's response of lifting its paw will be strengthened. Praising students when they raise their hands to answer increases the probability that they will raise their hands the next time you ask the class a question. Another kind of reinforcement procedure involves the removal of, or decrease in, the intensity of a stimulus and is called **negative reinforcement.** For example, taking aspirin is reinforced by (i.e., strengthened by) the reduction of pain. Misbehaving is reinforced by removal from a boring class. Any procedure using negative reinforcement is called **escape** or **avoidance** conditioning because the individual learns to make a response that will enable him to escape from or entirely avoid an aversive stimulus.

Punishment In this procedure, the strength or probability of a response is decreased. As with reinforcement, there are two kinds of punishment. **Positive**

punishment involves the appearance or increase in intensity of a stimulus following the operant. For example, a dog's response of jumping up on people is punished (decreased in strength or probability) by rapping it on the forepaw when it does so. Similarly, a student's response of talking in class is decreased or punished by ridicule. **Negative punishment** involves removal of or decrease in intensity of a stimulus. For example, a 6-year-old who throws his spoon while at the dinner table might be punished by having her food removed. A student who talks in class might be punished by having to miss recess.

A System for Categorizing Consequences

We have found that students in our classes sometimes have difficulty distinguishing between these various types of conditioning procedures. In particular, they tend to confuse negative reinforcement and punishment. We have found that it helps to use the following system, although it involves using subjective terms such as "pleasant" and "unpleasant" of which Skinner would not approve. Nonetheless we provide it as a rule of thumb (often called a heuristic) for categorizing stimulus consequences.

To categorize a stimulus consequence, we need to consider two properties or attributes that it can have. First is the hedonic nature of the consequence—its pleasantness or aversiveness. A pleasant consequence is something an individual seeks out under normal circumstances. An aversive stimulus is something most individuals would avoid if possible. We can rely on our own subjective judgment to determine whether a consequence is pleasant or aversive. The second attribute of the consequence is its arithmetic sign, positive or negative. A positive stimulus is one that is added to a situation or one that is increased in intensity. A negative stimulus is one that has been taken away from a situation or one that has been decreased in intensity. Table 2.1 shows that these attributes can be combined to create a classification matrix consisting of four cells.

The top-left cell contains stimuli that are pleasant and positive (added or increased). Adding something pleasant following a response is positive reinforcement. The bottom-right cell contains negative aversive stimuli—subtracting something aversive from the situation following a response is negative reinforcement. Both of these cells then contain stimuli that will strengthen the responses they follow. The top-right cell contains positive aversive stimuli—adding something aversive following a response is positive punishment. The bottom-left cell contains

TABLE 2.1   REINFORCEMENT AND PUNISHMENT

	Pleasant stimulus	Aversive stimulus
Positive (added to the situation after a response)	Positive reinforcement	Positive punishment
Negative (taken from the situation after a response)	Negative punishment	Negative reinforcement

negative pleasant stimuli—subtracting something pleasant from the situation following a response is negative punishment. Both of these cells contain stimuli that
will decrease the strength of a response.

You can use this classification matrix to make decisions about the nature of
particular stimulus consequences. Tentatively, you decide if a stimulus is pleasant
or aversive by your own subjective judgment based upon your own experience.
However, what is actually pleasant or aversive depends upon the prior history of
each individual. *So the only way to be absolutely sure that a stimulus has been
correctly classified for a particular individual is to do what Skinner suggests—
observe behavior.* If the behavior that the consequence follows increases in frequency or probability, then you are sure the consequence is reinforcement (either
positive or negative). If the behavior decreases in frequency, then you can be sure
that the consequence is punishment (either positive or negative). The table allows
you to make a tentative guess about the nature of a stimulus consequence prior
to trying it out with students. Now let's put these principles to work in the following
exercise.

Exercise 2.3: Tentatively identify each of the following as either positive reinforcement, negative reinforcement, positive punishment, or negative punishment.

Response	Consequence
1. John says, "Look at me."	Classmates turn and look.
2. Sue has not done her homework.	Father turns off the TV.
3. Tom is wrestling with his friend and says, "Stop; you're hurting me."	His friend stops twisting his arm.
4. A kid grabs his friend's toy.	His friend punches him.
5. A student falls asleep in class.	His classmates ridicule him.
6. Student raises his hand.	The teacher calls on him.
7. Student promises to behave.	Teacher says he can stop writing lines.
8. Student talks during class.	Teacher does not let him go out for recess.

Order of Conditioning

When the consequences following responses are inherently reinforcing or punishing, then we are dealing with **primary operant conditioning.** For example, food, water, and sex are primary reinforcers. Examples of primary aversive stimuli are shock and pin pricks. In a sense we come into this world genetically disposed to be reinforced or punished by primary reinforcers and punishers—our survival depends upon it. However, when we consider operant conditioning in everyday life, especially in the classroom, it is clear that most reinforcers and punishers do not fit the above category. Most things that reinforce behavior in people are not inherently reinforcing but have acquired their capability to reinforce through learning. Some examples of **secondary reinforcers** are praise, smiles, attention, and money. Some examples of **secondary punishers** are criticism, frowns, and the word ''no.'' Some of these stimuli, particularly the **social reinforcers** (e.g., smiles, praise, a pat on the back) and **social punishers** (e.g., frowns, angry looks, contemptuous tone of voice), are used so often that they seem to be intrinsically positive or aversive. Yet the reinforcing power of such stimuli does depend upon experience.

Question 2.2: How do you suppose that stimuli become secondary reinforcers or punishers? You should be able to answer this by making use of what you have already learned in this chapter._____

_____

Virtually any stimulus can become a secondary reinforcer or punisher (Zimmerman, 1957). However, depending upon the exact nature of their prior experience, a stimulus that is a secondary reinforcer for one individual may be a neutral stimulus or even a secondary punisher for another person. For example, when as an infant Jennifer experienced adult attention, it was usually accompanied by feeding and gentle stroking. Thus, adult attention is now a conditioned stimulus for pleasant emotional reactions. In contrast, Mike experienced adult attention most often in the context of rough and abusive treatment. Adult attention for Mike is a trigger for negative emotional responses. Consequently, any behavior of Jennifer's that receives the teacher's attention is reinforced or strengthened; any behavior of Mike's that draws adult attention is likely to decrease in frequency. Fortunately, Mike's teacher knows something about classical conditioning and is able to extinguish his anxiety to adult attention and replace it with positive emotional responses through counterconditioning.

Because of individual differences in prior conditioning, it is difficult to know before the fact whether a stimulus will be a reinforcer or punisher for a particular individual. Often in educational settings, we apply secondary reinforcers and punishers based upon our intuition (as we did in the exercise). This is useful as a starting point. However, we must be careful to observe what actually happens to a particular student's behavior when we use these reinforcers or punishers in the classroom.

Teachers can make use of classical conditioning procedures to create secondary reinforcers to be used in the classroom. For example, tokens can reinforce behavior if they can be exchanged for things that are already reinforcers, such as snacks, movies, or play time (Kelleher, 1957; O'Leary & Drabman, 1971). In creating secondary reinforcers you must consider all the factors discussed earlier that influence classical conditioning. Most notably you must regularly re-pair the secondary reinforcer with primary reinforcers or else extinction will occur.

We usually think of a reinforcer as something that happens to the organism after it acts upon the environment. But sometimes a response is reinforced if it leads to another response. This principle is sometimes referred to as Grandma's Rule: Eat your spinach and then you can go out and play. More formally, it is known as the **Premack Principle** (Premack, 1965; Timberlake & Allison, 1974) which states that high probability behavior will reinforce low probability behavior. This principle works well in the classroom, where children can be reinforced for engaging in less preferred behavior, such as studying, by following it with preferred activities, such as drawing or reading stories. Since most high-frequency or preferred activities are learned, they are a type of secondary reinforcer.

Question 2.3: What do you think would happen if you followed a high-probability behavior with a low-probability behavior?_____

_____

_____

Factors Determining Operant Conditioning

Response-consequence Interval   The gap between an act and its reinforcing or punishing consequence affects the rate of operant conditioning. In general, the shorter the interval, the better the conditioning (Johnson, 1972; Logan, 1960). This is most easily seen when considering learning tasks which involve **intrinsic reinforcers** and punishers that are naturally embedded in the task (Chance, 1979). For example, in learning to play a tune on the piano by ear, the consequences that produce learning are the sounds of the correct notes (reinforcers) and the sounds of incorrect notes (punishers). Now suppose you have a hearing impairment that makes it difficult to discriminate notes. It is theoretically possible for you to learn to play by ear if someone yells "good" whenever you hit correct notes and "bad" whenever you produce wrong notes. The main difference is that in the latter case, the artificial or **extrinsic reinforcers** will be slightly delayed whereas the natural consequences would follow the appropriate responses immediately. This is why learning is usually more efficient when students are directed to attend to naturally occurring consequences or feedback.

One reason that immediate consequences usually produce better results is that a delay allows time for other responses to occur. In this situation, the intervening behavior and not the desired act is reinforced (Chance, 1979). Usually we think of behavior as *causing* a reinforcer or punisher. But as Skinner (1948) demonstrated, sometimes this logical or causal connection between a response and its reinforcer does not exist. That is, the reinforcer follows a response merely by coincidence—yet the response increases in probability nonetheless. Skinner called this **superstitious behavior.**

In one experiment, Skinner placed pigeons in a **Skinner box** (a device created by him for studying operant conditioning). The box usually contained a lever hooked up to a food magazine which delivered food pellets when it was depressed, but a variation containing a disk which could be pecked to activate the food magazine was used with the pigeons (see Figure 2.3). In this particular study, the food magazine had been modified so that it delivered food at fixed intervals, say every 15 seconds, regardless of what the pigeon was doing. Skinner found that most animals tested developed some clear-cut response—turning in counterclockwise circles, head bobbing, floor pecking, and so on. Skinner's explanation of this strange ritualistic behavior is quite simple. When the reinforcer was delivered, the pigeon had been doing something, for example, bobbing its head. Thus, the head bobbing response was reinforced. Since a reinforced response is likely to be repeated, the pigeon was probably bobbing its head when the reinforcer came again, thus making it an even more probable response.

Superstitious behavior is not limited to pigeons. A good deal of our everyday behavior seems to be superstitious—brought about by accidental reinforcement. The student who crosses her fingers while taking a test, the student who ducks his head slightly when the teacher asks a question, and the teacher who wears a certain outfit on evaluation day are all exhibiting behaviors which were followed coincidentally by reinforcing outcomes. The point of all this is that when attempt-

FIGURE 2.3 A pigeon in a Skinner box. (Drawing by Freddie Ghatala, age 12.)

ing to increase or decrease the probability of certain target behaviors, we must be sure that the reinforcer or punisher follows the desired response immediately; if not we could end up influencing some irrelevant response.

Consequence Characteristics   The amount or intensity of the consequence that follows a response can affect operant conditioning. In general, consequences that are very small or weak will be ineffectual in reinforcing behavior. On the other hand, consequences that are very strong can have powerful emotional side effects that may interfere with conditioning (Mowrer, 1960). This is most likely to occur with strong punishers that produce fear and anxiety which can interfere with learning. However, even positive reinforcers, if too strong, can interfere with learning. The teacher who rewards good behavior during study period by announcing an extra 10 minutes of recess may find the students too excited to attend to the next lesson. In short, moderate consequences, neither too strong nor too weak, are best.

Schedule of Reinforcement   The pattern of response consequences is called a **schedule of reinforcement.** When a response is reinforced each time it occurs, it is called **continuous reinforcement.** Continuous reinforcement leads to rapid acquisition of a new response. Normally, after a response has been acquired and is occurring with high probability, it is a good idea to stretch out the reinforcement by sometimes reinforcing the response and sometimes not. This is called partial or intermittent reinforcement. There are four basic types of intermittent reinforcement.

In a **fixed interval schedule,** a given response is reinforced but then is not reinforced again until a fixed interval of time has elapsed. A pigeon who has learned to peck the disk in a Skinner box may then be put on a fixed interval schedule so that after a peck is reinforced, all subsequent pecks are ignored until an interval of, say, five seconds has elapsed. The first peck after the five-second interval is then reinforced. An organism on a fixed-interval schedule will typically respond rapidly just prior to the end of an interval and then slow its rate immediately after reinforcement. If one were charting its rate of responding, a scalloped curve would result (see Figure 2.4).

In a **variable interval schedule,** the period during which responses are not reinforced varies around some average. In a five-second variable interval schedule, a pigeon may be reinforced for pecking after two seconds, eight seconds, six seconds, and four seconds. The average interval of nonreinforcement is five seconds, but the actual length of the intervals will vary.

In a **fixed ratio schedule,** each nth response is reinforced. For example, a pigeon may be reinforced on every fifth peck. In a **variable ratio schedule,** reinforcement occurs after an average of n responses. In a five-response variable ratio schedule, for example, the pigeon may be reinforced after two responses, then after eight responses, six responses, and four responses. So on the average, the organism is reinforced after five responses but the actual number of responses reinforced varies randomly.

These schedules of reinforcement have their counterparts in everyday life. Most

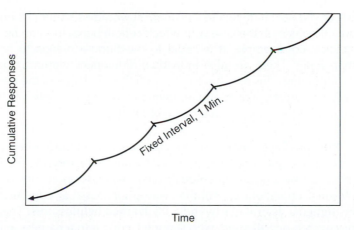

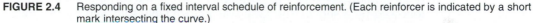

FIGURE 2.4   Responding on a fixed interval schedule of reinforcement. (Each reinforcer is indicated by a short mark intersecting the curve.)

games of chance, for instance, involve reinforcements delivered on a variable ratio schedule. This kind of schedule produces high rates of responding and great resistance to extinction, as anyone who has been to a gambling casino can testify. Jobs that involve receiving a weekly or monthly paycheck resemble the fixed interval schedule except that in the Skinner box, the organism is reinforced for the first appropriate response after the interval elapses. The paycheck is not contingent upon a specific response at the end of the week, but upon working continuously during the week. This difference probably diminishes the scalloping effect in this case. A closer example of an interval schedule is looking for a bus that is normally on schedule (fixed interval) or not on schedule (variable interval). Working on commission or at piece rate is like the fixed ratio schedule.

The common effect of partial reinforcement, regardless of the exact nature of the schedule, is that it produces higher rates of responding and greater resistance to extinction than does continuous reinforcement. On the other hand, continuous reinforcement produces faster acquisition of a response than does partial reinforcement. Thus, in the classroom, the teacher might at first reinforce some desired behavior each time it occurs. Then, when the behavior is occurring with high probability, she may begin to gradually stretch out the reinforcers. For example, Freddie may be given a sticker each time he completes a worksheet. When he consistently works quietly at his desk on assignments, the teacher may begin to reinforce every two completed assignments, then every five, and then every ten or so. This procedure results in rapid acquisition of a behavior which will remain strong even when it is only occasionally reinforced. Putting students on partial reinforcement for desired behavior ensures that they will continue the behavior when you are not around to reinforce it.

Characteristics of the Learner   The principles of operant conditioning apparently hold for all species and all individuals in a species. Obviously any species which did not abide by the law of effect would be extinct by now. However, there are differences in the ease with which certain behaviors can be conditioned across species. For example, it is easier to condition a pigeon to peck a disk for food than a pig. There are also individual differences within a species as to ease of conditioning. This may have to do with the efficiency of the perceptual-motor and nervous systems. For example, mentally retarded people are harder to condition than subjects in the normal range of intelligence.

Previous Experience   Another factor related to the learner which will influence ease of operant conditioning is prior learning history. As we have already seen, what will be a positive reinforcer often depends upon someone's prior history of classical conditioning. Another way prior classical conditioning can influence instrumental learning is by inducing **learned helplessness.** This phenomenon was discovered by Seligman, who strapped a dog into a harness and presented a tone, followed by a shock. The tone was unavoidably followed by the shock, for in classical conditioning procedures nothing the dog does can influence the occurrence of the unconditioned stimulus. Next, the dog was put into a box divided by a barrier. When a shock was delivered through the floor of the box, the dog could escape by jumping over the barrier. Typically, a dog learns to escape the shock very quickly, but the dogs exposed to the unavoidable shock did not learn to escape. Instead, after initially reacting to the pain by struggling and running around, these dogs just lay down and passively accepted the shock (Maier & Seligman, 1976). It seemed as if the dogs had learned from the inescapable shock experience that nothing they did made any difference. Hence they were unable to learn new behavior that would enable them to escape when it became possible. Since the original demonstration with dogs, learned helplessness has been found in many other species, including humans.

Question 2.4: Can you describe a set of circumstances that might produce learned helplessness in a school setting?_____

_____

_____

Prior operant conditioning can also influence later operant learning. That is, some individuals may be ready to learn some particular behavior because they have learned a prerequisite behavior while others who have not learned the prerequisite behavior may not be able to.

ACQUIRING NOVEL BEHAVIOR THROUGH OPERANT CONDITIONING

It may have occurred to you by now that in order for operant conditioning to occur a response must be emitted and then either reinforced or punished. If this is so, how can conditioning result in *new* behavior? Well, one way is to simply wait until the desired new behavior occurs spontaneously and then reinforce it. But this could be a long wait, especially if the desired behavior is complex. Skinner hit upon a technique called **shaping** for training novel behavior. This technique involves initially reinforcing any behavior that approximates the desired act and then progressively reinforcing each response that is closer and closer to the desired act. Skinner used shaping to teach a pigeon to bowl, certainly a novel behavior for a pigeon! First, he designed pigeon-sized pins, an alley, and a ball that would move down the alley if pecked in just the right spot. Now, the challenge was to get the pigeon to peck the right spot on the ball with consistency. Skinner began by reinforcing the pigeon whenever it approached the ball. Before long the pigeon was spending a large part of its time close to the ball. Then Skinner began reinforcing the pigeon only if it pecked in the direction of the ball. Once the pigeon was consistently pecking at the ball, Skinner changed the rules again and the pigeon was reinforced only for pecks that moved the ball in the general direction of the pins. Once this was learned, it was possible to fine tune the response to one that would move the ball rapidly against the pins. The pigeon was now a bowler!

In another instance, Skinner trained a rat to pull a string that would release a marble from a rack, to pick up the marble with its forepaws, to carry it to a two-inch high tube, to lift the marble to the top of the tube, and to drop it in. The rat's behavior is a complex chain of responses, and each response in the chain was shaped through differential reinforcement of successive approximations (Skinner, 1938). Shaping combined with **chaining,** the linking together of responses to form a complex behavioral act, is a technique that has been used successfully by animal trainers (think about this the next time you see an animal act in the circus or at an aquarium). These techniques can also be used with preverbal or nonverbal humans (Fisher & Gochros, 1975). However, they are probably not the most efficient way to teach complex behaviors in school. We would most likely resort to verbal instruction or demonstration if we wanted a student to perform some new skill. However, reinforcement would still play an important role in maintaining the behavior once acquired.

Generalization and Discrimination

Reinforcement or punishment of an individual's behavior always occurs in a particular situation in the presence of certain stimuli. These stimuli become signals that a particular behavior will be reinforced or punished (i.e., they become discriminative stimuli, as discussed earlier). In addition, when a response is reinforced in the presence of certain stimuli, it is likely to occur in the presence of other, similar, stimuli. For example, a pigeon that is reinforced for pecking a disk of a given color will also peck at other disks that are similar in color. They are less likely to peck at disks that are very different in color from the original training disk (Guttman & Kalish, 1956). Likewise, if a response is punished in the presence of certain stimuli, it is less likely to occur in similar situations. This is called **stimulus generalization,** a phenomenon we have encountered in classical conditioning.

As in classical conditioning, the degree of generalization depends upon the degree of similarity between stimuli, whether that similarity be physical or semantic in nature (Guttman & Kalish, 1956; Spence, 1937). Generalization is thus responsible for the carryover of behavior learned in one situation to other, similar, situations, and it occurs with great frequency in both the natural and social environment. For example, the responses learned in order to ride a bicycle are helpful when learning to ride a motorcycle; arithmetic operations are useful in both geometry and algebra; social skills learned on the playground can be useful in the classroom.

In some cases, responses appropriate to one situation are not appropriate to a similar situation, and the individual must learn to respond differently in each. In other words, when reinforced for a particular response in one situation and not in another the individual learns to **discriminate** between the two stimulus situations and emit the response only in the first situation. Likewise, if a response is punished in one situation and not in a similar situation, it will decrease in frequency in the first situation but persist in the second. We make such discriminations all the time. For example, students soon learn that wisecracks and jokes will get a laugh from Ms. Casey in history class but will be reprimanded by Mr. Johnson in English, or that certain behaviors approved of in the peer gang will not be reinforced in the classroom or at home.

As indicated earlier, a stimulus that indicates whether a given response will be reinforced or punished is a discriminative stimulus. Effective use of operant conditioning in the classroom is critically dependent upon establishing discriminative stimuli that will cue desired generalization or discrimination. When teaching a response that you want students to generalize to other situations, you must be sure that stimuli present during acquisition resemble stimuli present in those other situations. One way to ensure this is to simulate those situations you wish behavior to generalize to in the classroom. For example, if you desire students to use critical reading skills in their everyday (i.e., outside school) lives, then it would be useful to teach those skills in the context of reading magazines (even *Mad* magazine), newspapers, story books, and other texts that students encounter outside of school. In general, using a variety of tasks and situations when teaching skills will help to establish a wide variety of stimulus cues that will promote generalization. On the other hand, when you desire students to apply particular behaviors or skills in some situations and not in others, you must point out or highlight the stimuli that differentiate between the situations.

Eliminating Operantly Conditioned Responses

Some behaviors learned through operant conditioning are maladaptive to the individual. Stated another way, learned responses that once enabled individuals to cope effectively with their environment may no longer be effective if the environment changes. For example, a child who gets attention by crying or acting out at home is likely to have problems with this type of attention-getting behavior at school. Likewise, a child who was coaxed by overzealous parents or teachers into overly difficult tasks may have learned to cope with failure by avoiding new tasks. Initially this behavior was adaptive in that it protected the child's self-esteem; however, it becomes maladaptive if it leads to avoidance of tasks within the child's capability.

Viewing "undesirable" behavior as "maladaptive" is useful because it helps us to understand *that* all *behavior is acquired initially because it is reinforced by the environment and thus enables the individual to adapt to that environment.* Unfortunately, not all families and schools in our society provide healthy environments that encourage healthy adaptations. Operant views also help us to focus on the consequences in the environment that may be reinforcing the undesirable behavior. This allows us to alter the environment rather than blame or shame the child, who is merely responding to those consequences. So the question becomes, when behavior is brought about by a maladaptive environment, how can that behavior be modified? As with classical conditioning, behavior learned through operant conditioning may be forgotten. But, as you no doubt remember, forgetting is not an efficient way to modify learned behavior. There are three better methods.

Extinction   In operant conditioning, extinction refers to the process of withholding the consequences of a response. Most of the research on extinction involves withholding positive reinforcement and indicates that when reinforcement no longer follows a response, that response gradually declines in frequency (e.g., Skinner, 1938). Moreover, extinction of a response in one situation generalizes to similar situations (Skinner, 1938). Of course, extinction will generalize to similar situations only if reinforcement is also withheld in those situations. For example, if one parent avoids reinforcing temper tantrums but the other parent reinforces them, the child will soon discriminate and have tantrums in the presence of one parent but not the other.

Question 2.5: The accommodating parent is a D_ _ _ _ _ _ _ _ _ _ _ _ _ _

S_ _ _ _ _ _ _ for the child's tantrum behavior.

Several factors play a role in determining the rate or ease with which a response extinguishes. First, there is the matter of how thoroughly the response has been learned in the first place. The behavior of a child who has gotten attention by throwing tantrums for 10 years will be harder to extinguish than that of one who has been throwing fits for 10 weeks. In general, the more a response has been reinforced, the more slowly extinction will proceed (Williams, 1938).

Another factor is how much effort a response requires. A response that requires little effort is usually harder to extinguish than one requiring great effort (Capehart, Viney, & Hulicka, 1958). So, other things being equal, a child's performance worthy of Dennis the Menace will actually be easier to extinguish than the behavior of a child who merely whimpers and whines.

Undoubtedly, the most powerful factor in extinction is the schedule of reinforcement governing a response prior to extinction. As we have already discussed, intermittent reinforcement results in slower extinction than does continuous re-inforcement. This phenomenon is known as the **partial reinforcement effect.** One reason that attention-seeking responses (desirable ones as well as the temper-tantrum variety) are usually slow to extinguish is that we adults are inconsistent reinforcers. Depending upon our mood and other factors, we sometimes reinforce such responses and at other times ignore them. Remember, when a response is intermittently reinforced, the individual learns to continue responding in the absence of reinforcement because sooner or later the response will pay off. For extinction to occur, the individual must realize that the situation has changed so that now the response will never pay off. In general, the more nonreinforced responses during acquisition, the greater the resistance to extinction (Weinstock, 1958).

Although extinction is a relatively effective and trouble-free way of eliminating unwanted behavior, there are potential problems that you need to be aware of. One potential problem has already been suggested.

Question 2.6: Suppose that Janie's parents have decided to ignore her inappropriate behavior, but after awhile they give in. What is likely to happen to the

behavior and why?_____

_____

_____

Another problem with extinction is that one is not always able to withhold all reinforcing consequences. If you have a student who disrupts the class by clowning around, you may have figured out that the attention you give the student for misconduct is actually reinforcing the behavior. So you may decide to put the clown's behavior on extinction by ignoring it. Unfortunately, this is unlikely to work because you are not the only source of reinforcement in the classroom. The laughter of other students may be enough reinforcement to keep the clown in business. To use extinction effectively you must be able to remove *all* of the reinforcers that follow the unwanted behavior.

Another difficulty is that often a behavior that has apparently been extinguished will reoccur for no reason. Such spontaneous recovery is no problem as long as it is not followed by reinforcement. A related problem is that in the first stages of extinction, there is apt to be a sudden increase in the behavior (perhaps due to frustration). The danger here is that the person doing the extinguishing, seeing a sudden increase in the behavior, will conclude that it is not working and discontinue the procedure. Persistence! Another reaction to watch for in the early stages of extinction is an outburst of emotional behavior which also is probably a result of the frustration experienced when a favorite response no longer pays off. If such emotional outbursts are not reinforced by the adult's attention, they will soon subside.

Differential Reinforcement   This is a technique that combines extinction of an undesired response with reinforcement of desirable behavior. A particularly effective form of differential reinforcement involves reinforcing a response that is incompatible with the undesired response. For example, a child who is always getting into fights will change her behavior quickly if fighting is no longer reinforced but being friendly is. Often there is no particular response that is incompatible with the undesired behavior; in this case, any behavior *but* the undesired behavior should be reinforced. For example, the child who sucks his thumb could be reinforced for doing anything but sucking his thumb. A child who is constantly watching TV could be reinforced for doing anything but watching TV—talking to others, reading, walking around, etc.

Sometimes we wish not to completely eliminate a response, but to reduce its frequency. In those cases, we can **differentially reinforce a low rate** of the behavior. For instance, a student who is constantly asking for the teacher's assistance when he is supposed to be working independently could be ignored for a short interval and then attended to only if he has not emitted attention-seeking behavior in the interval. The duration of the interval could then be gradually lengthened until a low rate of attention-seeking behavior is achieved. In general, differential reinforcement is a faster way to eliminate behavior and avoids some of the problems of extinction. Table 2.2 summarizes and compares these two methods of eliminating operant responses.

Punishment   There is little doubt that the use of punishment results in quick suppression of the undesired behavior. However, there are some very serious

TABLE 2.2   COMPARISON OF EXTINCTION AND DIFFERENTIAL REINFORCEMENT

	Extinction	Differential reinforcement
Definition	Withholding the consequences of a response	Withholding consequences of an undesired response while reinforcing a desired behavior
Characteristics	Results in decrease in the frequency of the response; generalizes to similar situations; ease of extinction depends upon degree of initial learning, amount of effort required to make the response, and reinforcement schedule during learning	Results in decrease in the frequency of the response; generalizes to similar situations; depends upon the same factors as extinction; in general, works faster than extinction
Applications	When using extinction, be sure to persevere in the face of initial increases in response frequency and emotional outbursts; try to eliminate *all* sources of reinforcement for the behavior	If possible, reinforce behavior that is incompatible with the undesirable response; if there is none, then reinforce *any* response *but* the undesired one

problems entailed in its use. One problem with punishment is that it makes clear to the individual being punished what behavior is *not* acceptable but, unlike differential reinforcement, does not indicate what behavior *is* appropriate.

A second problem with punishment is that it may itself become a conditioned behavior. For example, a harried mother slaps her child who is whining and pulling at her in the grocery store. The child momentarily stops this annoying behavior. The mother has been negatively reinforced, and her tendency to slap the child under similar circumstances in the future is increased. Thus, the *punisher is being operantly conditioned by the consequences of her behavior*—something to remember the next time we feel the urge to punish someone "for his own good." This aspect of punishment perhaps accounts for its wide use in our society. Additionally, punishing a child provides an opportunity for the child to learn (through social modeling, a theory to be discussed later in this book) that punishing others is acceptable behavior. It is not surprising that the vast majority of parents who abuse their children were themselves abused as children.

Another side effect of punishment is that it invariably produces a negative emotional response in the individual being punished. This emotional response then becomes associated with the stimuli present in the situation, including the punisher. This association is formed through classical conditioning. Thus, the parent administers punishment (this could be positive punishment such as a slap or spanking, or negative punishment such as grounding the child). The experience of the aversive situation is an unconditioned stimulus that elicits pain, fear, resentment, etc. Through repeated pairing, the sight of the parent comes to elicit these negative emotions. Since the parent is usually angry or upset and usually precedes the punishment with threats or warnings, the child's negative emotional response is likely to be elicited by the sight of the angry parent and the presence of the warning or threat. This emotional conditioning sets the stage for a type of operant conditioning called **escape learning.** The child learns behaviors (through negative reinforcement) that allow him to escape from the negative emotions elicited by the sight of the parent and the threats. Thus, a child may run away physically or "tune out" the situation. *The important thing for a parent or teacher to remember is that the repeated use of punishment invariably conditions fear and resentment toward the punisher.*

Question 2.7: Moderate punishment in the form of spankings, detention after school, or traffic tickets may suppress the unacceptable behavior yet fail to produce a permanent change. Reflect on your own behavior with respect to exceeding the speed limit to tell why this is so._____

_____

_____

_____

_____

One form that punishment often takes in the classroom is the verbal reprimand. Several studies have shown that reprimands, intended as a mild form of punishment to reduce the frequency of certain behaviors, actually increase the frequency of those behaviors (Thomas, Becker, & Armstrong, 1968). This seems to be especially true in classrooms of adolescents where upsetting the teacher is a favorite activity reinforced by peers. Reprimands and other forms of mild punishment signal to the student, albeit in a negative way, the behaviors that are important to the teacher. A general rule of the classroom can be stated thus: *Those behaviors that receive the teacher's most concerned and genuine interest are those that occur with the highest frequency.* This applies to behaviors that are both desired and undesired by the teacher (Gentile, Frazier, & Morris, 1973).

Alternatives to Punishment   From everything we have said about punishment, you may have gathered that, in general, there is not much to recommend it as a procedure for eliminating undesirable behavior. You are absolutely correct. There is only one situation in which punishment might be warranted, and even then it should not be used in isolation. That situation is one in which individuals will suffer life-threatening injuries unless their behavior is immediately stopped. For example, if a child darts out into the street, punishment can be used to suppress the behavior and save the child's life. However, because of discrimination learning, as discussed above, punishment alone will reduce the frequency of running into the street only when the parent is present. What the parent must do in addition is differentially reinforce alternative behavior. For older children this could involve teaching them the correct way to cross the street and then reinforcing them for doing so. For a younger child, the parent might reinforce any behaviors that keep the child away from the street. *In general, reinforcing alternative behavior is a far better method than punishment.*

A method that has been found effective in dealing with unacceptable behavior is called **time out from reinforcement** (Brown & Tyler, 1967). In this method, a child who is engaging in inappropriate behavior is removed from the situation (to another room) without any show of emotion for a specified period of time. The time-out room is one in which the individual is socially isolated and which does not afford any other type of reinforcements. Usually the individual is allowed to return early to the situation from which he was removed as a reward for good behavior in the time-out room. This procedure can work well with adolescents who derive social reinforcement from peers for "getting a rise out of the teacher." Strictly speaking, time out involves a form of negative punishment because it requires the removal of a pleasant or desired stimulus. However, if used appropriately, time out from reinforcement emphasizes the positive side of behavior rather than just punishing undesirable behavior. That is, it tells the child that certain behavior will be reinforced. Also, as pointed out earlier, it lets teachers (or parents) remove themselves from a situation in which arguments or reprimands might have the effect of increasing the undesired behavior. This time out for teachers or parents gives them an opportunity to avoid excessive anger and to shift their focus to rewarding appropriate behavior.

Technologies Based on Operant Conditioning

Skinner and others who have done laboratory research to discover the principles of operant conditioning have spent almost as much time and energy in applying these principles to complex practical situations. We shall discuss two technologies—behavior modification and programmed learning—that have been developed from basic operant conditioning research. Both of these applications have had great impact on education.

Behavior Modification   While most parents and teachers (indeed, most people) attempt to influence the behavior of others and thus could claim to be in the business of behavior modification, the term is technically reserved for a distinct approach to learning based upon operant conditioning. The distinctive characteristics of behavior modification which set it apart from other approaches to influencing others are (1) its focus upon behavior (as opposed to focusing on feelings, attitudes, or beliefs); (2) the specificity of its goal (to either increase or decrease a particular behavior or set of behaviors); and (3) its exclusive reliance upon techniques of operant conditioning to achieve behavioral change (Hill, 1981). Given the negative side effects of punishment, behavior modification relies exclusively upon reinforcement and extinction to achieve its goals. Probably the best way to convey how behavior modification works is to give some examples.

Behavior modification was used by Hart, Allen, Buell, Harris & Wolf (1964) with two nursery-school children who cried excessively. The crying was usually not of the respondent variety (an unconditioned response to a painful stimulus) but seemed to be operant in nature (designed to produce consequences for the children). The behavior modifiers first had to decide what change in behavior was desirable. Since the children appeared to be otherwise well adjusted, it seemed appropriate to focus on the crying behavior itself instead of attempting to train the children to deal more effectively with their environments. The second step was to determine what was reinforcing all this crying. After observing the children in the nursery-school situation, the researchers found that (surprise!) the attention the children were getting from the teachers when they cried was reinforcing the crying behavior. The third step was to train the teachers to ignore the children when they cried and to reinforce them when they reacted to frustration in more constructive ways. The result was a rapid decrease in crying behavior. That the change resulted from the procedures was indicated by the fact that the crying rapidly increased in frequency when the teachers were told to begin once more to pay attention to the children when they cried.

Gentile, Frazier, & Morris (1973) describe how a behavior modifier would approach a common problem of teachers, especially teachers of special education classes: the child with a short attention span. Usually are such children are labeled as hyperactive or as having an Attention Deficit Disorder (the latter is apparently the more ''in'' label these days). The behavior modifier would ignore such diagnoses and labels as irrelevant to the problem, which is that the child, in someone's opinion, does not attend long enough to the presented task. When the typical classroom consequences of a child's short attention span are analyzed, it is usually found that when the child is attending to some task, the teacher is happy because she can use that time to work with other children. Thus, the child is ignored when attending to the task. When the child stops working and does something else, the teacher reminds her that she should be working and often takes her by the hand and leads her back to her work space. Thus, the consequence of not attending to the task is to receive the teacher's attention. The solution once again is obvious. The teacher must reinforce the child when she is attending and not when she is behaving inappropriately. At first the child must be praised (or given some other effective reinforcer) whenever she is on task. As the child begins to work for longer periods, the teacher can lengthen the intervals between reinforcement, gradually shaping a longer and longer attention span.

These examples seem so obvious that we may be in danger of missing their essential points, one of which is that for most of us it feels unnatural to ignore problem behavior. Most of us feel that if we do not deal with problems they will get more and more out of hand. So we attend to the problems while applying "benign neglect" to desirable behaviors. *It is well worth the time and effort for teachers, parents, or therapists to do a behavioral analysis of any given problem to determine how they may be reinforcing undesired behaviors while ignoring desired behavior.* The problem will usually go away if this pattern is reversed. Another critical feature of behavior modification that we must attend to is timing. The reinforcement must follow immediately upon the desired response. Also important is the schedule of reinforcement. Continuous reinforcement of desired behavior is used until the behavior is occurring with some regularity, at which time an intermittent reinforcement schedule can be adopted.

For some children attention or praise from the teacher for appropriate behavior may not be an effective reinforcer. An alternative is to look for reinforcers that the children find attractive. Since what is reinforcing can vary widely across children, behavior modifiers have relied on the use of tokens or points that the children can earn for engaging in desired behavior. They then can exchange these tokens for desired prizes. This system of reinforcement has been called the **token economy** and has been demonstrated to work well in the classroom (Karraker, 1971; O'Leary & Drabman, 1971).

Behavior modification has also been used with some success in the treatment of more severe behavior problems exhibited by autistic children and schizophrenics. Moreover, in addition to the situation in which one person tries to modify the behavior of another, behavior modification can be used as a technique of **self-control** (Hill, 1981). For example, an individual could successfully modify his own overeating behavior by reinforcing alternative noneating behaviors and by eliminating or reducing the discriminative stimuli in the environment that prompt overeating (e.g., attendance at parties).

Objections to Behavior Modification   Some ill-informed objections to behavior modification assume that aversive control is involved. As pointed out, behavior modifiers are all too aware of the dangers and ineffectiveness of punishment and avoid its use except in extreme cases, such as to prevent self-injury in autistic patients. Other objections to behavior modification are more serious and need to be considered.

One objection is that by reinforcing students with prizes or praise, they will become materialistic and never enjoy learning for its own sake. In other words, they will become hooked on extrinsic reinforcement and not discover the intrinsic reinforcement of learning. We shall deal with the well-intentioned critic here and not the hypocritical one who, on the one hand, decries the use of incentives yet sees no problem in using grades, punishment, and even legal means to coerce students into going to school and doing work they despise. Such critics ignore the fact that they themselves would not find their own jobs intrinsically rewarding enough to engage in without a paycheck.

To answer the well-intentioned critic, it needs to be pointed out that some skills or conceptual abilities are not intrinsically motivating to someone in the beginning stages of learning. In fact, just the opposite is true: The beginning stages of learning many skills are fraught with frustration and error (and sometimes pain, as in learning to ride a bicycle). In the early stages of learning, children need the encouragement and praise and even concrete rewards provided by adults. It is only after the learner gains sufficient skill at a task, be it riding a bike or reading, that engaging in the task becomes rewarding in itself. *A good reinforcement program,* as we have indicated, *starts out with continuous reinforcement at the beginning stage of learning, followed by intermittent reinforcement in the later stages of learning when the individual starts receiving intrinsic reinforcement.* In addition, as progress in the skill or behavior develops, less emphasis should be placed on tangible reinforcers, such as food or tokens, while more emphasis should be given to social reinforcers, such as praise and attention.

The introduction of extrinsic reinforcers does seem to be counterproductive in situations where students are already deriving intrinsic reinforcement from some behavior. A number of studies indicate that participation in enjoyable activities can be increased by introducing extrinsic reinforcers, but it will *decrease* below its original frequency once the external reinforcers are removed (see Lepper & Green, 1978). In one study, preschool children who had previously been reinforced for drawing activities were less likely to choose to draw in a free-play situation than children whose drawing activity had not been externally reinforced (Lepper, Greene, & Nisbett, 1973). Thus, it appears that *extrinsic reinforcement is not advisable for behaviors that are already occurring through intrinsic motivation. However, it is valuable for beginning stages of learning skills when there is little or no intrinsic reinforcement.*

Another objection to behavior modification is that the changes it produces are only temporary: If reinforcement is stopped the changes in behavior disappear. Behavior modifiers are not too distressed by this criticism because behavior in their view is always a function of the contingencies of reinforcement. A change in behavior will last only as long as the change in environmental reinforcement contingencies. Thus, whether children who have acquired good study habits as a result of a token economy continue that behavior after the token economy is gone depends upon other reinforcers' taking over, such as the fun of learning or the satisfaction of pleasing the teacher. If none of these "natural" reinforcers is strong enough to maintain the studying behavior, then of course it will extinguish. The problem is not the token economy but the absence of alternative reinforcement contingencies in the classroom environment.

A final objection to behavior modification is that the person who is being systematically reinforced loses freedom and comes under the control of the person controlling the reinforcers. Skinner has replied to this particular criticism by noting that we are all controlled by many contingencies, some deliberate, some accidental. Moreover, many of the deliberate contingencies are aversive. That is, in our society one is usually ignored if behaving appropriately and punished if some law or social convention is broken. Skinner (1956) asks: If the contingencies of positive reinforcement are more effective than others, and at the same time more pleasant to the learner and more beneficial in their effect, what is the criticism? Yet responsible professionals persist in the criticism that behavior modification is mechanistic and dehumanizing, representing simply the power of one person over another (Gordon, 1970) rather than the mutual sharing of ideas by which behavioral change ought to come about.

Realistically, as Hill (1981) points out, this difference between behavior modification and other techniques of influence is greatly exaggerated. It is true that behavior modification is most frequently used in situations where there is a power imbalance (e.g., schools, prisons, families). What behavior modification probably replaces in these situations is only rarely a true process of mutual negotiation and rational discussion. More often it replaces some mixture of punishment, shaming, fear of authority, and tricky arguments. In short, the benefits of behavior modification seem to us to outweigh the risks. However, this is an issue on which teachers and parents need to reflect and come to their own conclusions. What is clear is that using behavior modification often forces adults to recognize *that it is their own behavior that provides the reinforcement contingencies that support "undesirable" behavior in children. Thus, what needs to be changed is not solely the child's behaviors but the adult's behavior as well.*

Programmed Instruction   Skinner advocated an approach to instruction in classrooms that incorporated many of the principles found useful when training animals. He treated classroom learning like any other situation in which certain behavior, in this case verbal behavior, is to be shaped. The student must progress gradually from the familiar to the unfamiliar, must learn the required discriminations, and must be reinforced. To accomplish this Skinner invented the learning program. While Skinner was greatly attached to the notion of presenting learning programs by means of teaching machines, it is the program, not the machine, that is of the essence. A **program** is a series of items or frames that both present information and test students on the information. Each frame requires the student to respond to the information in some way (e.g., fill in a blank, answer a multiple-choice question). The learner is given immediate feedback. If he has answered correctly, this constitutes the reinforcement. If his answer is incorrect, the learner can study the correct answer so that he can be reinforced next time.

Skinner preferred to make the learning requirements so gradual and initial cues so obvious that errors were minimized. For example, a frame from a program teaching students the principles of operant conditioning might be this: "Rewarding a dog with food for doing a trick *reinforces* his tendency to do the trick, so the food is called a r _____ r." Even with no prior knowledge of the topic, the reader has no difficulty filling in the blank because of the presence of hints or prompts. Usually, the first time a concept is presented, the **prompts** are very strong. Once the correct answer has been given, the question can be asked again with weaker and weaker prompts until none are needed anymore. This process of gradually weakening the prompts until the response can occur in their absence is known as **fading.**

Skinner favored the kind of program described above. Known as a **linear program,** it requires all learners to go through the same frames in the same order, with each frame calling for a written response. As indicated, the program has a small step-size, making the transitions easy and ensuring a low error rate. Although good and poor learners are allowed to vary in the rate at which they go through the frames, one criticism of this kind of program is that it does not make sufficient allowances for individual differences.

Another kind of program was developed so that instruction could be more individualized. In this program, called a **branching program,** learners answer multiple-choice questions, and each answer leads to a different next step. The right answer might lead to reinforcement ("That's right!") followed by a frame presenting new information to be learned. Each wrong alternative would lead to a different set of frames depending upon the source of the learner's error as diagnosed by his selection of that particular alternative. So, for example, a learner might be sent to a frame that reviews information presented in previous frames. Or a learner might be directed to a frame that presented new information to clarify a misunderstanding or fill in the gaps that led to that particular wrong answer. Eventually, after branching through these remedial frames, learners would be returned to the same track as those who got the right answer. This kind of program does not require steps as small as a linear program since remedial materials are available. The larger step-size allows good learners to proceed more rapidly.

The advent of the computer has made possible the creation of very sophisticated branching programs which in essence provide students with a programmed tutorial. In fact, **computer assisted instruction (CAI)** has nearly replaced the older notion of programmed instruction. However, the basics of the learning program are the same whether delivered by computer, programmed text, or programmed workbook. The computer is just a better technology for presenting information in diverse ways (maps, graphics, etc.). Moreover, most students today have been raised on home computer games and find the computer to be highly motivating, especially when gamelike features are incorporated into learning programs.

A final point concerning programmed instruction is that while originally designed to incorporate principles of operant conditioning into education in a systematic way, the critical ingredient of a successful program is appropriate structuring of the material (Hill, 1981). What concepts have to be introduced before others? What ideas are best presented as subtopics or applications of other ideas?

In short, how is the particular area of knowledge structured and how can this structure best be presented to beginners? These are questions, as we shall see, that are the basis of cognitive approaches to instruction, and, indeed, most contemporary learning programs are being written by cognitive psychologists rather than by behavioral psychologists. It is the latter group, however, that deserves the credit (or blame, according to some who believe that programs and especially the machines that deliver them are dehumanizing education) for the existence of programmed instruction.

RELATIONSHIPS BETWEEN CLASSICAL AND OPERANT CONDITIONING

We have discussed two types of conditioning in this chapter, and because we have discussed them separately and in different contexts, we might have led you to believe that the events leading to one or the other type of conditioning also occur at different times and in different contexts. *In fact, this is not the case. Usually, these two types of conditioning occur together.* For example, when the rat presses a lever for food reinforcement, the sight and feel of the lever are also being learned as conditioned stimuli for salivation. When Pavlov's dogs learned to salivate to the sound of a bell that was paired with food, they also, if given the chance, would have learned an operant response in order to get the food faster. Little Albert, who was classically conditioned to fear a white rat that was paired with a loud noise, also learned flight responses that were reinforced by escaping from the rat.

In short, the two forms of conditioning often influence each other. Instrumental conditioning influences classical conditioning mainly by determining what classical conditioning situations the individual gets exposed to (Hill, 1981). For example, if you learn instrumentally how to find food, that food then has a chance to act as an unconditioned stimulus for salivation. If, through operant conditioning, you learn to avoid an aversive stimulus, you minimize the chances for that aversive stimulus to be the unconditioned stimulus for classical conditioning.

Conversely, a classically conditioned emotional response can interfere with the performance of an operant response. For example, if a rat is busy lever-pressing to get food and then hears a tone that had been previously paired with a strong shock, the rat will act as if it is too upset to work for food. In other words, the appearance of a conditioned stimulus involving a strong emotional response will interfere with instrumental conditioning (Rescorla & Solomon, 1967).

Often, in real life, the emotional response that interferes with instrumental learning is acquired during the process of instrumental learning. Take the case of a first-grader who is finding it more difficult to grasp the essentials of reading than are her classmates. If her teacher or peers ridicule her, or treat her as inferior by placing her in a "special" (read "dumb") reading group, she is being conditioned to have negative feelings toward reading. These classically conditioned gut reactions to the reading instruction situation will most likely interfere further with learning to read. That classical conditioning usually occurs simultaneously with operant conditioning means *"that you can never teach knowledge, skill, or cog-*

nitive process without at the same time connecting some emotion or feeling to the content, materials, or teacher'' (Gentile et al., 1973, p. 29). The question is not whether to teach affect but, rather, whether the affect is positive or negative. This is a strong argument, as we pointed out earlier, for the use of positive reinforcement and the elimination of aversive control in the classroom.

Even though classical and operant conditioning typically occur simultaneously and influence each other, there are differences between the two that can help us to distinguish between them and use them appropriately. One difference that should be apparent by now is the kind of behavior that lends itself to each conditioning procedure. *As a rule of thumb, classical conditioning works best with behaviors that are controlled by the autonomic nervous system.* Such behaviors are salivation, heart rate, emotional reactions, and other automatic bodily responses. *Operant conditioning procedures work best with voluntary behaviors produced by the striated muscles.* This rule is generally useful for keeping the two conditioning procedures straight in your mind, as long as you realize that it is not entirely precise. In fact, some of the most exciting work in conditioning today involves **biofeedback,** which is a method for bringing automatic bodily processes into our awareness so that operant conditioning procedures can be applied to change them. For example, people can learn to control heart rate, blood pressure, and other functions previously thought to be outside the realm of instrumental conditioning.

To sum up the relationship between these two types of behavior, Hill (1981) suggests that we think of operant conditioning as the process by which we learn the behaviors and skills needed to get what we want in life. Thus, operant or instrumental conditioning permits us to learn the *means* toward our goals. Classical conditioning, in contrast, is the *source* of many of our goals. The reinforcers (or goals) of instrumental learning are generally stimuli that elicit emotional reactions: joy, lust, curiosity, and so on. Or, in the case of escape learning, the reinforcers involve removal of stimuli that elicit responses of fear, shame, sorrow, or other unpleasant emotions. Some of these reinforcers elicit these reactions naturally, but most acquire the power to cause emotional reactions because they have been conditioned to do so by being paired with unconditioned stimuli. It is because of these emotional reactions, largely learned, that stimuli serve as positive goals to be achieved or negative ones to be escaped and avoided. Thus, classical and operant conditioning work together to provide the goals and the means for human activities.

The Core Issues

We can now examine the position of operant conditioning on the core issues. In Table 2.3 we compare classical and operant conditioning on these core issues.

1. *What is learned?* In operant conditioning an individual learns to make a particular response in a particular situation. For Skinner the response or behavioral change *is what is learned.* In other words, Skinner would not accept the notion

TABLE 2.3   COMPARISON OF CLASSICAL AND OPERANT CONDITIONING ON CORE ISSUES

Core issue	Classical conditioning	Operant conditioning
What is learned?	A reflexive response is acquired to a stimulus that did not previously elicit that response	The individual learns to make a particular response in a particular situation
Emphasis on environmental versus organismic factors	Emphasis on environment—the learner is passively acted upon by stimuli and has no control over the conditioned response	Emphasis on shaping of the learner by reinforcement contingencies in the environment; the learner has some control over conditioned responses
Source of motivation	Motivation plays little role—conditioning occurs whether the individual is motivated or not	Biological drives such as hunger must be present in primary conditioning; reinforcers can become incentives which motivate behavior
Transfer	Stimulus generalization	Stimulus generalization
Variables in instruction	Timing and repetition of the pairing of unconditioned and conditioned stimuli	Nature and timing of reinforcement. Instructional elements: behavioral objectives, task analysis, entering behavior, instruction, assessment, supportive environment

presented in Chapter 1 in which learning is something that is inferred from by changes in behavior. To Skinner, learning is not inferred from a change in behavior—it *is* the change in behavior. For Skinner, the principles of operant conditioning are sufficient because they work, and we do not gain anything—and perhaps create confusion—by speculating about internal unobservable mechanisms that explain why they work. Other psychologists, however, are not satisfied with the fact that the procedures of operant conditioning work; they want to know why they work.

One explanation of operant conditioning, associated with behaviorists, is S-R theory. We reviewed S-R theories in Chapter 1. Briefly, you may remember that theorists such as Thorndike believed that operant conditioning involved the formation of a connection or bond between a stimulus (such as the bar in a Skinner box) and a response (such as pressing). Reinforcement was thought to be a necessary condition for formation of the connection. Hull essentially adopted this view of conditioning and added an explanation of why reinforcement increased the strength of connections or habits. Hull believed that reinforcement works because it reduces some drive within the organism.

Question 2.8: What is the name of the S-R theorist who believed that contiguity, not reinforcement, is the important factor in the formation of S-R bonds? a. Edward Tolman b. Edward Guthrie   c. Kenneth Spence   d. David Premack.

Another approach to explaining operant conditioning is called expectancy theory. In this view the procedures of operant conditioning result in the acquisition of certain expectations. In classical conditioning, expectancy theory posits that the organism learns that certain events are followed by certain other events. In operant conditioning, the organism learns that certain responses are followed by certain events. In other words, classical conditioning involves the formation of stimulus-stimulus (S-S) expectancies, while operant conditioning involves the formation of response-stimulus (R-S) expectancies. Edward Tolman was the earliest expectancy theorist. Contemporary cognitive learning theorists would tend to view operant conditioning in these terms also (Bolles, 1972). Just as with classical conditioning, neither theory gives a completely adequate explanation of all the phenomena of operant conditioning. But, fortunately, we do not have to wait for a theoretical resolution. We can, as Skinner urges, apply the procedures of operant conditioning to achieve valuable learning outcomes in the classroom even if we do not know exactly why they work.

2. *Emphasis on environmental versus organismic factors.* Operant conditioning tends to emphasize the role of the environment in bringing about learning. Certainly species differ in ease of conditioning, with humans being by far the most easily conditioned (but dolphins are pretty close, and they will work for fish). Individual differences in conditionability have to do with genetic endowment. Basically, however, the laws of operant conditioning are the same for all species and all individuals within a species. In operant conditioning there is, of course, an interaction between the individual and the environment. The person responds and the response produces a consequence. So the organism is viewed as an active participant in learning. However, the most potent factor in learning is the nature of the environmental stimuli which follow and shape a response.

3. *Source of motivation.* When a primary reinforcer such as food is used as reinforcement, the organism must be hungry in order for responding to occur. Such deprivation-determined drives are not as important when secondary reinforcers such as praise are used.

Reinforcement comes after the response that it reinforces and hence can "confirm" a response once it has occurred. Normally, however, people appear to be striving to achieve something that they desire. This "something" is referred to as an incentive. According to Hill (1981), we can think of an incentive as an anticipated reinforcer. When one has repeatedly experienced a reinforcer, one learns to expect it, want it, and work to achieve it. It can then serve not only to reinforce behavior that has already occurred but also to inspire behavior that has not yet occurred. Teachers use incentives such as grades, tokens, and prizes all the time to get students to perform. Learning and motivation are closely related. On the one hand, it is through learning that most reinforcers and incentives come into existence. On the other hand, reinforcers and incentives influence both what we learn and what we do with what we have learned.

Skinner's position is that motivation, as we usually think of it, is a result of operant conditioning. That is, motivation, as indicated by willingness to engage in an activity over a prolonged period of time, is a behavior shaped by reinforcement.

4. *Transfer.* As with classical conditioning, generalization is synonymous with transfer. When a response is reinforced in a particular situation, other situations that are similar to the first either physically or semantically will serve to cue that response.

5. *Important variables in instruction.* Earlier we reviewed several factors that influence operant conditioning, such as response-reinforcement interval and schedule of reinforcement. These factors must be considered when applying operant conditioning in the classroom to bring about desired behavior. Behavioral psychologists, including Skinner, who have attempted to apply operant conditioning to academic instruction stress certain additional principles. First, the goals or objectives of instruction must be stated in behavioral terms. **Behavioral objectives** state what the student should be capable of doing after instruction. Once behavioral objectives have been set, the task or material is analyzed and structured so as to support learning. When we discussed programming, it was pointed out that the learner is presented with information in a gradual way and is required to respond to that information so that he or she can be immediately reinforced or given corrective feedback. This sort of programming requires a careful **task analysis** of the material to be learned, so that it can be broken down into small steps and so that component concepts or skills are mastered before attempts are made to learn superordinate skills.

Once the task or material has been structured, it is important to start each learner at the appropriate point in that structure. To do this the teacher must assess the students' **entering behavior.** That is, what concepts or skills related to the material have the students already mastered? During instruction itself, it is important to allow individuals to proceed at their own pace and to continually monitor individuals so as to diagnose and remediate learning difficulties. Finally, the teacher assesses students to determine if each has met the instructional objectives. The **behavioral assessment** should be based on the particular behaviors specified in the behavioral objectives.

Approaches to instruction based upon operant conditioning emphasize a positive, supporting environment. The underlying principle of this approach is that desirable responses can be shaped and maintained through reinforcement. Undesirable responses are maintained by the same reinforcing consequences. Thus, it is vital that teachers become aware of the reinforcement contingencies that are operating in the classroom and gain control of them in order to promote desired behavior. In many cases, the teacher's natural tendency to ignore students until they do something wrong must be reversed. Attention should be focused on good, desirable, normal behavior rather than problem behavior.

REVIEW OF MAJOR POINTS

1 Classical and operant conditioning are two forms of learning that occur with high frequency in the classroom. It is important that teachers understand and apply the principles governing these two types of conditioning.

2 Classical or Pavlovian conditioning involves attaching a reflexive response, originally elicited by an unconditioned stimulus, to a neutral stimulus, which is then labeled conditioned. Because all unconditioned stimuli elicit emotional responses in addition to other responses, classical conditioning can be viewed as emotional conditioning. In appetitive conditioning, positive emotions are conditioned. Defense conditioning involves negative emotions. In primary conditioning, the unconditioned stimulus naturally elicits an emotional response. In secondary conditioning, the unconditioned stimulus is a previously neutral stimulus that has acquired the capability of eliciting an emotional response through prior conditioning.

3 Factors that determine classical conditioning include: (a) How the neutral stimulus and unconditioned stimulus are paired. For optimal conditioning, the neutral stimulus should precede the unconditioned stimulus. (b) The interstimulus interval should be short—about half a second to a second. (c) The pairing of the neutral with the unconditioned stimulus should be repeated often for optimal conditioning. (d) The neutral stimulus should not occur without being paired with the unconditioned stimulus for optimal conditioning. (e) Conditioning also depends upon certain biological characteristics of individuals as well as their prior experience with the neutral stimulus.

4 Once a response has been conditioned to a neutral stimulus, other stimuli that are physically or semantically similar to that stimulus will also elicit the response. This is called stimulus generalization. Discrimination is the opposite of generalization and involves learning to inhibit the conditioned response to all stimuli except the conditioned stimulus.

5 Classically conditioned responses can be eliminated in several ways. Forgetting involves a weakening of the conditioned response over a lengthy time interval during which the individual is not exposed to the conditioned stimulus. Forgetting is not an effective way to eliminate conditioned responses. Extinction involves presenting the conditioned stimulus without the unconditioned stimulus, which sometimes can be difficult to accomplish in the real world. Counterconditioning is the most effective method and involves pairing the conditioned stimulus with one that elicits an incompatible response. Systematic desensitization is an example of counterconditioning.

6 Operant conditioning (also called instrumental learning) is a type of learning in which responses emitted by an individual produce consequences that either strengthen or weaken the response.

7 Reinforcement always strengthens the response it follows and can be either positive or negative. Punishment always weakens a response and is either positive or negative.

8 Consequences can be either inherently reinforcing or punishing (primary conditioning) or can acquire their capability to reinforce or punish through learning (secondary conditioning). Secondary reinforcers or punishers are learned through classical conditioning.

9 Factors that determine operant conditioning are: (a) The interval between the response and the consequence—the shorter the interval, the better the conditioning. (b) Moderate consequences, neither too strong nor too weak, are optimal. (c) The schedule of reinforcement can be either continuous or intermittent. Initial acquisition of a response is best accomplished with continuous reinforcement, while maintenance of the response is achieved by switching to intermittent reinforcement.

10 When a response is reinforced in the presence of certain stimuli, those stimuli become signals that the behavior will be reinforced. They are called discriminative stimuli. Other stimuli that are physically or semantically similar to the discriminative stimuli will also come to signal reinforcement through a process of stimulus generalization. Discrimination involves learning to emit the response only in the presence of the discriminative stimuli and not in the presence of similar stimuli.

11 Operant responses can be eliminated through extinction (withholding consequences following the response), differential reinforcement (reinforcing a response that is incompatible with the undesirable response), and punishment. Some combination of the first two is usually effective. Punishment has negative side effects and should normally be avoided.

12 Behavior modification and programmed instruction are two technologies based on operant conditioning.

13 Classical and operant conditioning almost always occur together. It is good to keep in mind that one can never teach knowledge or skill without connecting some emotion to the content, material, or teacher.

14 The position of classical and operant conditioning on the five core issues was summarized in Table 2.3.

ANSWERS TO QUESTIONS AND EXERCISES

Exercise 2.1: 1. Yes, Defense. Unconditioned Stimulus: illness. Unconditioned Response: nausea (disgust, dislike). Conditioned Stimulus: taste, smell, sight of curry. Conditioned Response: queasy feeling, disgust, dislike. 2. Yes, Appetitive. Unconditioned Stimulus: ingestion of caffeine. Unconditioned Response: arousal of nervous system, pleasant high. Conditioned Stimulus: taste of coffee. Conditioned Response: arousal, pleasure. 3. This is not classical conditioning—there is no response that is reflexively elicited by a stimulus. This is an example of operant conditioning which we will discuss later in this chapter. 4. Yes, Appetitive. Unconditioned Stimulus: moderately loud clapping. Unconditioned Response: orienting toward the noise (paying attention to it). Conditioned Stimulus: "Boys and girls." Conditioned Response: attending to the teacher.

Question 2.1: If every time we received a phone call it presented important news (good or bad), we would jump out of our skins when we heard the phone ring. However, many times phone calls are routine and uneventful. Thus, most of us do not have a strong emotional reaction to the sound of the telephone. On the other hand, many of us do have a strong emotional response when the phone rings in the middle of the night because most of these kinds of calls do herald dramatic events.

Exercise 2.2: Unconditioned Stimulus: anything in the classroom or school environment that elicits fear, anxiety, disgust, etc., either naturally or as a result of learning. Unconditioned Response: fear, anxiety, disgust, or any other negative emotion elicited by your unconditioned stimulus. Conditioned Stimulus: any neutral stimulus that is repeatedly paired with the unconditioned stimulus. Conditioned Response: fear, anxiety, disgust, etc., that is now elicited by the previously neutral stimulus; any procedure that pairs the conditioned stimulus with a stimulus that elicits relaxation, pleasure, or other positive emotional response. This has to be done so that the conditioned negative response is weaker than the positive response. This procedure must be gradual and repeated over time to extinguish the negative response and replace it with the positive conditioned response.

Exercise 2.3: 1. Positive reinforcement. 2. Negative punishment. 3. Negative reinforcement. 4. Positive punishment. 5. Positive punishment. 6. Positive reinforcement. 7. Negative reinforcement. 8. Negative punishment. Please note that these classifications are tentative, based upon subjective judgments of whether a particular stimulus is pleasant or unpleasant. The only way to be absolutely sure that the classifications are correct is to observe what happens to behavior. (For example, if the frequency of John's saying ''Look at me'' is increased after his classmates look at him, then we know for sure that gaining classmates' attention is positively reinforcing for John.) However, this classification scheme is useful because it allows us to tentatively predict the likely effects of stimuli on behavior.

Question 2.2: Yes, our old friend classical conditioning! Neutral stimuli such as smiles or praise become reinforcing because they have been paired with primary reinforcers such as food and physical stroking. Other neutral stimuli such as frowns and the word ''no'' have been paired with naturally aversive stimuli such as slaps or physical restraint. School grades become reinforcers by being paired with social approval, an instance of higher-order classical conditioning.

Question 2.3: This would be punishment. For example, a student who misbehaves in class has to write lines. In fact, responses or activities can be used as positive and negative reinforcers and as positive and negative punishers, and can be so classified by using the system presented earlier.

Question 2.4: One circumstance that can induce learned helplessness in school children would be to require them to perform tasks that are too difficult for them because they are not developmentally mature enough. Failure is guaranteed no matter what the child does or how hard he tries. Later when he is mature enough to learn the task, he may not do so because of his prior learning.

Question 2.5: Discriminative stimulus. Just testing to see if you are awake. Also, this question provides a preview of programmed instruction—one important application of operant conditioning to education.

Question 2.6: The behavior will be strengthened because the parents have essentially put Janie on a partial reinforcement schedule. So extinction inconsistently applied will make matters worse because it results in the partial reinforcement effect. Once you institute extinction, you had better be prepared to stick with it!

Question 2.7: We simply have formed a discrimination. We do not perform the unacceptable response of speeding when the police are around. However, when they are not around most of us exceed the speed limit. The ease with which such discrimination learning takes place severely limits the effectiveness of punishment.

Question 2.8: If you selected b. Edwin Guthrie and it was not a lucky guess, you have a great memory! You may continue on with the core issues. If you selected a response other than b., your memory stinks, but you are probably better at answering higher-level questions. You might review the section on Guthrie's theory in Chapter 1. This is an example of an item in a b_____ program.

REFERENCES

Bolles, R. C. (1972). Reinforcement, expectancy and learning. *Psychological Review, 79*, 394–409.

Brown, G. D., & Tyler, V. O., Jr. (1967). The use of swift, brief isolation as a group control device for institutionalized delinquents. *Behavior Research and Therapy, 5,* 1–9.

Chance, P. (1979). *Learning and behavior.* Belmont, CA: Wadsworth.

Fisher, J., & Gochros, H. L. (1975). *Planned behavior change: Behavior modification in social work.* New York: Free Press.

Gentile, J. R., Frazier, T. W., & Morris, M. C. (1973). *Instructional applications of behavior principles.* Monterey, CA: Brooks/Cole.

Gordon, T. (1970). *P. E. T. Parent effectiveness training.* New York: Wyden.

Guttman, N., & Kalish, H. I. (1956). Discriminability and stimulus generalization. *Journal of Experimental Psychology, 51,* 79–88.

Hart, B. M., Allen, K. E., Buell, J. S., Harris, F. R., & Wolf, M. M. (1964). Effects of social reinforcement on operant crying. *Journal of Experimental Child Psychology, 1,* 145–153.

Hill, W. F. (1981). *Principles of learning: A handbook of applications.* Sherman Oaks, CA: Alfred Publishing.

Johnson, J. M. (1972). Punishment of human behavior. *American Psychologist, 27,* 1033–1054.

Jones, M. C. (1924a). The elimination of children's fears. *Journal of Experimental Psychology, 7,* 382–390.

Jones, M. C. (1924b). A laboratory study of fear: The case of Peter. *Pedagogical Seminary, 31,* 308–315.

Karraker, R. J. (1971). Token reinforcement systems in regular public school classrooms. In C. E. Pitts (Ed.), *Operant conditioning in the classroom.* New York: Thomas Y. Crowell.

Kelleher, R. T. (1957). Conditioned reinforcement in chimpanzees. *Journal of Comparative and Physiological Psychology, 49,* 571–575.

Klein, S. B. (1987). *Learning: Principles and applications.* New York: McGraw-Hill.

Lepper, M. R., & Greene, D. (1978). *The hidden costs of rewards.* Hillsdale, NJ: Erlbaum.

Lepper, M. R., Greene, D., & Nisbett, R. E. (1973). Undermining children's intrinsic interest with extrinsic rewards: A test of the "overjustification" hypothesis. *Journal of Personality and Social Psychology, 28,* 129–137.

Logan, F. A. (1960). *Incentive.* New Haven, CT: Yale University Press.

Maier, S. M., & Seligman, M. E. P. (1976). Learned helplessness: Theory and evidence. *Journal of Experimental Psychology: General, 105,* 3–46.

Malone, J. C. (1990). *Theories of learning: A historical approach.* Belmont, CA: Wadsworth.

Mowrer, O. H. (1960). *Learning theory and behavior.* New York: John Wiley & Sons.

O'Leary, K. D., & Drabman, R. (1971). Token economy programs in the classroom. *Psychological Bulletin, 75,* 379–398.

Premack, D. (1965). Reinforcement theory. In D. Levine (Ed.), *Nebraska symposium on motivation* (Vol. 13). Lincoln: University of Nebraska Press.

Rescorla, R. A., & Solomon, R. L. (1967). Two-process learning theory: Relationships between Pavlovian conditioning and instrumental learning. *Psychological Review, 74,* 151–182.

Skinner, B. F. (1938). *The behavior of organisms: An experimental analysis.* New York: Appleton-Century-Crofts.

Skinner, B. F. (1948). Superstition in the pigeon. *Journal of Experimental Psychology, 38,* 168–172.

Skinner, B. F. (1956). Freedom and the control of men. *American Scholar, 25,* 47–65.

Spence, K. W. (1937). The differential response in animals to stimuli varying within a single dimension. *Psychological Review, 44,* 430–444.

Staats, A. W., & Staats, C. K. (1958). Attitudes established by classical conditioning. *Journal of Abnormal and Social Psychology, 57,* 37–40.

Staats, C. K., & Staats, A. W. (1957). Meaning established by classical conditioning. *Journal of Experimental Psychology, 54,* 74–80.

Taylor, J. A. (1951). The relationship of anxiety to the conditioned eyelid response. *Journal of Experimental Psychology, 41,* 81–92.

Thomas, D. R., Becker, W. C., & Armstrong, M. (1968). Production and elimination of disruptive classroom behavior by systematically varying teacher's behavior. *Journal of Applied Behavior Analysis, 1,* 35–45.

Timberlake, W., & Allison, J. (1974). Response deprivation: An empirical approach to instrumental performance. *Psychological Review, 81,* 146–164.

Weinstock, S. (1958). Acquisition and extinction of a partially reinforced running response at a 24-hour intertrial interval. *Journal of Experimental Psychology, 46,* 151–158.

Williams, J. E. (1966). Connotations of racial concepts and color names. *Journal of Personality and Social Psychology, 3,* 531–540.

Williams, S. B. (1938). Resistance to extinction as a function of the number of rein-forcements. *Journal of Experimental Psychology, 23,* 506–522.

Wolpe, J. (1961). The systematic desensitization treatment of neuroses. *Journal of Mental and Nervous Disease, 132,* 189–203.

Zimmerman, D. W. (1957). Durable secondary reinforcement: Method and theory. *Psychological Review, 64,* 373–383.

3

INFORMATION PROCESSING THEORY I: KNOWLEDGE, PERCEPTION, AND COMPREHENSION

OBJECTIVES

1. State two key ideas that Gestalt psychology contributed to contemporary cognitive psychology.
2. Distinguish between declarative and procedural knowledge and give an example of each.
3. Describe the characteristics of schemas; then analyze a schema from your own long-term memory in terms of these characteristics.
4. Describe the function of sensory memory in input processing.
5. Describe the role of schemas in perception. State two ways teachers can enhance students' perception.
6. Describe the role of schemas in language comprehension. State two ways teachers can enhance comprehension.
7. Explain the relationship between the concepts of attention, mental effort, and working memory.
8. Identify three ways a teacher can help students make the best use of limited working-memory capacity.

With this chapter, we begin discussing cognitive theories that have relevance for understanding learning. We will not call them theories of learning because, in fact, the cognitive theories that we will cover are much broader than that. Information processing theory, for example, attempts to account for perception, comprehension, remembering, thinking, decision making, and a host of other processes. Thus, in contrast to behavioral theory, learning is not the major focus of information processing theory. In fact, as opposed to the other theories that we consider in this book, it is not really a single coherent theory. It is, rather, a framework or world view that has been adopted by many cognitive psychologists to guide their research into mental processes. In Chapter 1, we mentioned some of the assumptions of this approach.

Question 3.1: Can you remember at least two assumptions of the information processing approach to the study of human cognition? Please make the attempt

to remember and then check the answer at the end of the chapter._____

Since the early sixties, psychologists working within the information processing framework have produced numerous explanations of various cognitive processes such as attention, perception, comprehension, retention, and problem solving. One approach to their research is to review these various subareas and present the theories related to them. Although this approach allows for an encyclopedic coverage of a wealth of material, we have not chosen it. For one thing, we do not wish to bog you down with theoretical distinctions that are extremely interesting to the cognitive researcher but of little use to those wishing to apply information processing theory to enhance learning. We have opted instead to present a consensus view of how humans process information because we believe that despite differences in emphasis or detail among theorists (which we will certainly point out in passing), there is agreement on certain basic principles. In this and the next chapter, we will present an integrated view of the information processing system based upon contemporary theories. In this chapter, we will examine the structures and processes that underlie perception and comprehension. Then in Chapter 4, we will look at how we remember information. We will then be ready in Chapter 5 to consider how we use information that we have in memory to solve problems. Since chapters 3, 4, and 5 all deal with one theory (or theoretical framework), we need to discuss the core issues only once at the end of Chapter 4, after our discussion of the information processing system which is the heart of the theory.

In the present chapter we will first take a look at the contributions of Gestalt psychology to the development of information processing theory. Then we will present an overview of the information processing system so that you can gain some initial familiarity with its structures, processes, and contents. Then we will examine what happens to information that comes into the system through the senses. In this chapter we will trace information as it is perceived and comprehended. Then in Chapter 4 we will continue the story with an examination of how this information is added to our permanent knowledge.

GESTALT ANTECEDENTS OF INFORMATION PROCESSING

You will recall from Chapter 1 that Gestalt psychology was an important school of thought which contributed several key ideas on which much of contemporary cognitive theory is based. One of these ideas is that our perceptions are mental constructions that tend to impose order on our incoming sensations. That is, rather than attending to bits and pieces of stimuli, we organize them into wholes according to a set of laws or principles that govern how people assign meanings to visual or aural stimuli. These principles of perceptual organization which were proposed early in this century (see Koffka, 1933) are still accepted today as useful in understanding why people respond to information as they do.

Principles of Perceptual Organization

Law of Continuity The law of continuity states that we tend to perceive smooth continuities rather than abrupt changes. For example, the zigzag line at the top of Figure 3.1 is usually seen as a continuous line and not as separate lines making up the bottoms of triangles. Similarly, the bottom part of Figure 3.1 is typically perceived as two lines crossing at A rather than as a pair of V-like shapes touching at A.

Law of Closure This law holds that incomplete figures tend to be seen as complete. In Figure 3.2, the two drawings, though incomplete, tend to be seen by most people as a rectangle and a triangle. Our perception tends to fill in the missing parts of the figures.

Law of Proximity The law of proximity states that things that are close together are grouped together in perception. The dots in the top part of Figure 3.3 are seen as columns because they are closer together vertically than horizontally. However, the dots in the bottom of the figure are seen as rows because of their greater horizontal proximity.

FIGURE 3.1 The law of continuity. Perceptual organization tends to preserve smooth continuities rather than abrupt changes.

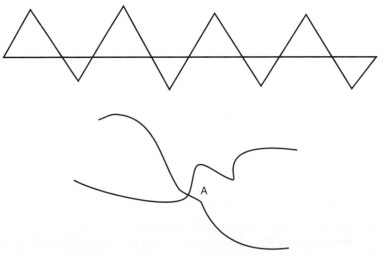

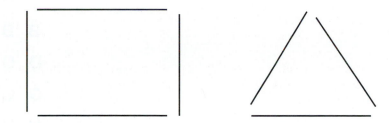

FIGURE 3.2   The law of closure. Incomplete figures tend to be seen as complete.

Law of Similarity   The law of similarity refers to the observation that similar objects tend to be perceived as related. So in Figure 3.4, even though the horizontal and vertical distances between letters are the same, most people see rows in the top figure and columns in the bottom figure because the same letter is repeated.

Law of Pragnanz   This law was proposed later than the other laws in an attempt to provide an overarching principle from which the other laws could be derived. The law of Pragnanz holds that of all possible organizations that could be perceived in a stimulus array, the one that actually will occur is the one that possesses the best, simplest, and most stable form. Thus, the rows of letters in

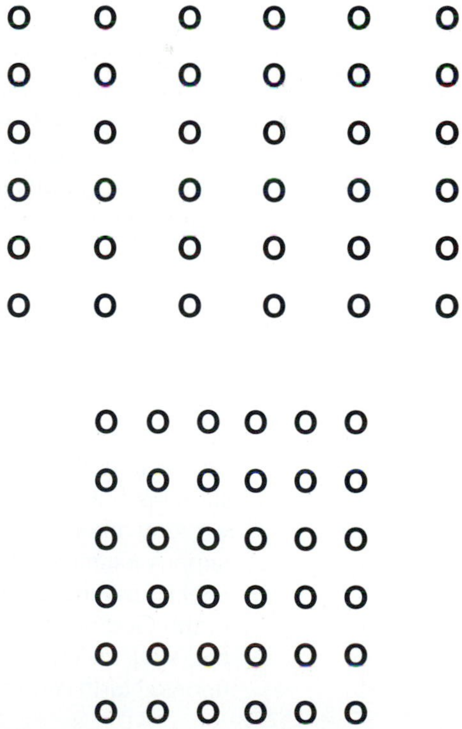

O   O   O   O   O   O

O   O   O   O   O   O

O   O   O   O   O   O

O   O   O   O   O   O

O   O   O   O   O   O

O   O   O   O   O   O

O O O O O O

O O O O O O

O O O O O O

O O O O O O

O O O O O O

FIGURE 3.3   The law of proximity. Things close together are grouped together.

O O O O O O

```
B  B  B  B  B

D  D  D  D  D

G  G  G  G  G

H  H  H  H  H

Y  Y  Y  Y  Y


B  D  G  H  Y

B  D  G  H  Y

B  D  G  H  Y

B  D  G  H  Y

B  D  G  H  Y
```

FIGURE 3.4   The law of similarity. Similar objects tend to be perceived as related.

Figure 3.4, the rows of dots in Figure 3.3, and so on are perceived rather than their alternatives because they are the "best" forms.

Gestalt theorists believed that during the process of perception, memory traces for the perceived stimuli were formed and that the same laws of organization governed memory as well as perception. Thus, what we remember is determined by our perceptions rather than by the actual stimulus. The validity of these laws of perception and memory remain unchallenged today. However, as we shall see, recent advances in information processing theory allow us to give a more adequate explanation than Gestalt theory of why these laws are valid.

Role of Prior Knowledge in Perception and Memory

Another key idea contributed by researchers in the Gestalt tradition is that our prior knowledge greatly influences our current perception and subsequent memory for stimuli. That is, perception and memory are not reproductions of the actual stimulus but rather are constructions based upon prior knowledge. Thus, when we remember something, we are reconstructing our perceptions of the event. A famous example of the role of prior knowledge in memory was provided by an English psychologist named Bartlett (1932). Although Bartlett was not a member of the Gestalt school, his view of memory was similar to Gestalt notions. Bartlett had subjects read a brief story called "The War of the Ghosts" which was based upon a North American Indian legend and thoroughly grounded in Indian culture.

Thus, the British subjects had no cultural background knowledge for the story. Bartlett assessed subjects' recall of the story at different time intervals.

Exercise 3.1: Read Bartlett's story, "The War of the Ghosts," and then without looking back write down as much of the story as you can remember.

One night two young men from Egulac went down to the river to hunt seals, and while they were there it became foggy and calm. Then they heard war cries, and they thought: "Maybe this is a war party." They escaped to the shore, and hid behind a log. Now canoes came up, and they heard the noise of paddles, and saw one canoe coming up to them. There were five men in the canoe, and they said:

"What do you think? We wish to take you along. We are going up the river to make war on the people."

One of the young men said: "I have no arrows."

"Arrows are in the canoe," they said.

"I will not go along. I might be killed. My relatives do not know where I have gone. But you," he said, turning to the other, "may go with them."

So one of the young men went, but the other returned home.

And the warriors went on up the river to a town on the other side of Kalama. The people came down to the water, and they began to fight, and many were killed. But presently the young man heard one of the warriors say: "Quick, let us go home: that Indian has been hit." Now he thought, "Oh, they are ghosts." He did not feel sick, but they said he had been shot.

So the canoes went back to Egulac, and the young man went ashore to his house, and made a fire. And he called everybody and said: "Behold, I accompanied the ghosts, and we went to fight. Many of our fellows were killed, and many of those who attacked us were killed. They said I was hit, and I did not feel sick."

He told it all, and then he became quiet. When the sun rose he fell down. Something black came out of his mouth. His face became contorted. The people jumped up and cried. He was dead. (From Bartlett, 1932, pp. 23–26.)

Cover the story and then write down as much of it as you can remember. Turn to the end of the chapter to compare your recall with one of Bartlett's subjects.

_____

_____

_____

_____

_____

_____

_____

_____

_____

OVERVIEW OF THE INFORMATION PROCESSING SYSTEM

Information processing theorists often use flow charts to depict schematically the flow of information through the system. Figure 3.5 identifies the structures and processes that researchers most commonly include in information processing models. A brief consideration of the model in Figure 3.5 will give you an overview of the system's components, each of which will be elaborated later.

Information from the external world is initially represented in its original sensory form in *sensory registers.* There are separate sensory registers for each sense modality, and presumably they can hold large quantities of information but only for a matter of milliseconds. The information in the sensory register is lost at the end of that time unless it can be described during the *pattern recognition* process. Most of the patterns we encounter are familiar, and recognition consists in classifying a pattern as a cat, the letter ''b,'' the word ''cup,'' and so on. When we recognize a familiar pattern we are using information that we already have in memory. Following pattern recognition, information is entered into *short-term memory,* where the capacity is smaller but the representations are more durable, lasting for seconds. Short-term memory is also referred to as *working memory*—a mechanism for holding information while we evaluate it and think about it. It is in working memory that we apply strategies for remembering or solving problems. Its capacity is limited, however, and if something is not done to the information once it is in short-term memory, it will be lost. If a person performs some cognitive operations on the information in short-term memory, it will be stored in *long-term memory,* where presumably it is stored indefinitely. With this brief introduction we begin our detailed examination of the system, beginning with long-term memory.

LONG-TERM MEMORY

As depicted in Figure 3.5, a major component of the information processing system is **long-term memory,** which we can think of as a vast repository for our knowledge about the world and our experiences in it. *From an information processing perspective, learning consists of storing new information in long-term memory and subsequently retrieving it.*

Kinds of Knowledge Contained in Long-term Memory

Information processing theory deals with knowledge and the processes used to act upon that knowledge. Cognitive psychologists have classified different types of knowledge contained in long-term memory.

Episodic Knowledge   There are two classes of information stored in long-term memory. Episodic knowledge is our memory for the personally experienced events which make up our lives. These episodic memories not only reflect what happened but when and where it happened. The major feature of this kind of autobiographical memory is the existence of a ''personal tag,'' and the basis of retrieval is an

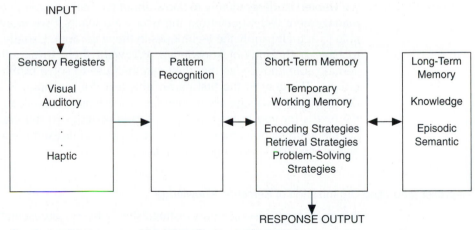

INPUT

Sensory Registers	Pattern Recognition	Short-Term Memory	Long-Term Memory
Visual Auditory . . . Haptic		Temporary Working Memory — Encoding Strategies Retrieval Strategies Problem-Solving Strategies	Knowledge Episodic Semantic

RESPONSE OUTPUT

FIGURE 3.5   Structures and processes of the information processing system.

association with a particular time or place (Tulving, 1983). For example, remembering that you had eggs and bacon for breakfast this morning is an episodic memory, as are memories of childhood experiences and memories of specific conversations with friends.

Semantic Knowledge   In contrast, semantic knowledge consists of memories that are not tied to an individual's personal history but rather transcend a particular context. Semantic knowledge refers to knowledge of general concepts and principles and their associations. For example, that people in this culture often eat eggs and bacon for breakfast is semantic knowledge, as is the information that a robin is a kind of bird and that lemons are yellow. Our organized knowledge of words and concepts and how they are associated is part of our semantic knowledge. It is obvious that much of what we need to remember in our daily lives in order to orient ourselves in time and space and conduct our affairs is episodic in nature. On the other hand, much of what we learn in school is semantic in nature.

Types of Semantic Knowledge   We can classify semantic knowledge into several types (J. R. Anderson, 1983a, 1987). **Declarative knowledge** is verbalizable knowledge about the world. Declarative knowledge is *knowing that* something is the case. For example, *we know that* the earth revolves around the sun. *We know that* lemons are yellow. Whenever we can fit a bit of knowledge into the *knowing that* frame, we are dealing with declarative knowledge. **Procedural knowledge** is *knowing how* to perform activities. For example, we *know how* to drive a car, tie our shoelaces, add whole numbers, identify the topic sentence of a paragraph.

The distinction between declarative and procedural knowledge, or between knowing that and knowing how, is important because, as we shall see later, each calls for different types of instruction. That is, we would teach quite differently if we wanted students merely to know about (verbally describe) effective classroom management techniques from the way we'd teach if we wanted students to be able to actually apply the techniques in the classroom. Usually, we want students to have both kinds of knowledge. We want them to acquire large bodies of verbalizable knowledge that they can then use to solve problems and make decisions. The goal of the first part of this text, for example, is for you to acquire declarative knowledge about theories of learning; the goal of the second part of the text is for you to learn to apply this knowledge in the classroom to achieve certain learning outcomes with your students. As this example implies, declarative and procedural knowledge often interact.

Representation and Organization of Semantic Knowledge

Information processing theory distinguishes between representations of knowledge (knowledge units) that are contained in long-term memory and the processes that operate on these knowledge representations. Let's first consider the various ways that our knowledge about the world is represented in long-term memory.

Concepts   A concept is a mental representation of a category of some kind (things, actions, situations, etc.). Concepts allow people to sort stimuli with similar characteristics into categories. Suppose you are a member of an expedition to a completely alien planet. You will find that at first the stimuli in the new environment are unique. You have no idea of what is safe and what is dangerous except for some rough analogies from your experience on earth (i.e., large creatures with teeth may be more dangerous than small creatures without teeth). Thus, the band of explorers may not behave adaptively at first, and there may be a reduction in their number. Survival depends upon finding some way to make sense of the alien world and to deal with environmental diversity. Extraterrestrial explorers, then, as well as newcomers here on earth, solve this problem by forming and using concepts.

Lumping stimuli together through concepts allows new stimuli to be responded to as class members rather than as unique entities. As residents of earth, we have all formed certain concepts that reflect the categories of our common environment. For example, concepts such as "up," "down," "water," "sky," "sun," "moon" are likely to be similar across all people on earth. Other natural concepts such as "tree" and "bird" may differ for people who experience quite different environments. That is, the trees and birds encountered in the Amazon rain forest are quite different from those encountered in the desert. The point is that concepts are abstractions from experience, so variations in concepts reflect variations in the physical and cultural environments to which people are exposed. Many, many concepts are taught in school. In fact, schooling is one of the chief means of inculcating and standardizing the concepts held by members of a culture.

Propositions   A proposition is a statement composed of two connected concepts that asserts something about the world and can be judged to be true or false. Some examples of propositions are: *Some people are teachers. Cars have wheels.*

All men are mortal. Each involves two concepts linked by a verb. Much of our declarative knowledge appears to be stored in memory and communicated to others as propositions (J. R. Anderson, 1976). Sentences and paragraphs in texts (like this one) can be viewed as ordered lists of propositions (Kintsch, 1988). For example, the complex sentence, *The mother of the spelling bee winner, Marsha, is Mrs. Smart who is a terrible speller,* can be analyzed into three propositions or idea units: (1) Mrs. Smart is the mother of Marsha; (2) Marsha won the spelling bee; and (3) Mrs. Smart is a terrible speller. The three propositions which underlie the meaning of the complex sentence are expressed here as sentences, but it is important to realize that the propositions are not the sentences themselves; rather they are the meanings of the sentences. Our memory contains the meaning of information, not its exact form.

Productions   Propositions can be viewed as units of declarative knowledge, whereas productions are a way of representing procedural knowledge. Productions are condition-action rules. That is, they produce certain actions when specified conditions are present. Here are two examples of productions:

Production A

IF   Figure is two dimensional And figure
is three-sided And figure is closed
THEN   Classify figure as triangle
And say "triangle" (Gagné, 1985)

Production B

IF   Encounter word I do not know
THEN   Look the word up in the dictionary

As you can see, productions have two clauses. The IF clause specifies the condition or set of conditions that must be present for a given action or set of actions to take place. The THEN clause lists the actions that are to take place. Production A above is a procedure for classifying figures as triangles. It specifies three conditions in its IF clause that must exist before the action of classification can take place. The second production specifies what to do when one encounters an unfamiliar word.

Generally, productions that have been well practiced run off automatically. That is, if the conditions specified in the IF clause exist, then the action specified in the THEN clause occurs without our having to think about it. This means that productions are dynamic and reactive to the environment. In contrast, propositions are less reactive to the environment and are more static in nature.

Question 3.2: How would you test to find out if a student has learned the *production* for triangles? How would you test to find out if the student has learned the *proposition* for triangle?

The outcome of a production can often supply the conditions to "fire" other productions in a sequence of cognitive processes and actions. Consider the following set of productions:

IF car is locked, **THEN** insert key in lock.
IF key is inserted in lock, **THEN** turn key.
IF door unlocks, **THEN** return key to vertical.
IF key is vertical, **THEN** withdraw key.

These productions are said to be organized into a production system in which the flow of control passes from one production to another. That is, each production provides the conditions needed for the next production to take place (J. R. Anderson, 1985). Such action sequences, if well practiced, can run off automatically. Thus, production systems are useful for modeling many complex cognitive activities, such as reading, that occur unconsciously in the expert reader (Just & Carpenter, 1987).

Networks of Propositions or Productions   One thing is clear: The average adult and even the average child holds an enormous amount of semantic information in long-term memory. Just guesstimate how many concepts you know. Thousands? Hundreds of thousands? How many propositions can you generate from these concepts? Millions? How many productions do you have? In order to be useful to us, this vast amount of information has to be well organized. If it were not organized, we simply would not be able to use information when we needed it.

A number of models have been developed to show how semantic information is organized in memory. Most of these models use the concept of a **network** to portray the organization of memory (J. R. Anderson, 1983a, 1983b; Collins & Loftus, 1975; Collins & Quillian, 1969). In such models, the networks consist of **nodes,** which are cognitive units (usually concepts but sometimes propositions), and **links,** which represent relations between the cognitive units (see Figure 3.6). In addition, each unit has connections with features that characterize that item. For example, in Figure 3.6 the concept "bird" is characterized by *breathes air* and *has feathers.* A complete network would include all of a person's knowledge about birds. In the network, the shorter the link between two nodes the stronger the association between the concepts. So *bird* and *feathers,* which are strongly associated, have a short link, while *animal* and *skis,* which are weakly associated, have a longer link between them.

One key feature of network models is called **spreading activation,** which means that when one node in the network is activated, closely associated nodes (those with short links) also tend to be activated. The closer an item is to one that is currently activated, the more likely it is to also become activated. Research based on such network models of long-term memory (using both human subjects and computer simulations) indicates that the models can account for our ability to comprehend sentences (such as "A robin is a bird"), answer questions (such as "Is a robin a bird?"), and draw inferences (such as "A robin has feathers").

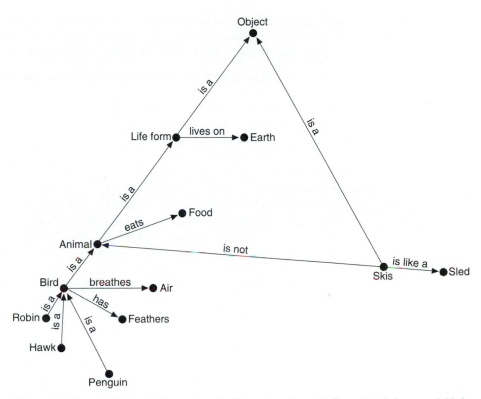

FIGURE 3.6   A fragment of semantic knowledge represented in a network model. The network is expandable in all directions. The closer two nodes are, the more similar those items are perceived to be. (From R. W. Howard, *Concepts and Schemata*, 1987.)

The networks described above represent the organization of declarative (statable) knowledge. Procedural knowledge can also be viewed as organized into networks of productions called **production systems** (J. R. Anderson, 1985), which we described earlier.

Images   Imagery is a form of knowledge representation built around the physical dimensions of objects and events. That is, just as a picture of a table contains information about the relative size and arrangement of the table parts, so does the mental image of a table. Thus, an image is physically similar to the object it represents (called an analog representation), while a proposition is physically distinct from the object it describes (called a discrete representation). There is a good deal of evidence that we use images in thinking and problem solving.

Exercise 3.2: Mentally solve the following problems:

1. John is smarter than Joe. Harry is smarter than Pete. Harry is less smart than

Joe. Who is the smartest boy? Who is the least smart?_____

2. How many window panes does your living room have?_____
3. Form a mental image of your car (or of a car you know well). View the car from the side and focus your attention on the trunk area at the rear. The question is, what kind of hood ornament does the car have?_____

In addition to their use in problem solving, images can also help people remember information better. There are many memory tricks that involve forming visual images. For example, one memory technique developed by the ancient Greeks, who often had to give long orations without the aid of notes, is called the **method of loci.** In this method, the memorizer uses a well-known route in which certain distinctive landmarks are encountered in a certain order. For example, you could use the route between your home and office or between home and school, or you could use a route through your home. Then as you mentally trace this well-learned route you place one major point from your speech at each of the landmarks. To be more effective you must form vivid visual images linking the points with the landmarks. Then, as you are giving the talk or speech, you simply retrace the route and retrieve each point from its landmark. This will also work for remembering your shopping list or for remembering a list of tasks you want to accomplish during the day.

While images are very useful in solving problems and in enhancing memory, there is considerable debate among cognitive theorists as to whether images are actually stored in long-term memory. Some theorists believe that information in long-term memory can be stored in two ways—as verbal strings (essentially propositions) and as visual images (Paivio, 1979). Other theorists believe that information in long-term memory is only stored in one format, such as propositions (Anderson & Bower, 1973; Kosslyn, 1978). These latter theorists assert that people build images in their short-term memory based upon more abstract representations (e.g., propositions) stored in their long-term memory. Once an image is constructed, its spatial and other physical attributes can be used. That is, we can then ''look'' at the internal image display of certain abstract information held in long-term memory. For example, when asked which is higher off the ground, a horse's knees or the tip of its tail, people often claim that this information became available only after they generated an image.

The theoretical debate about whether images are actually stored in long-term memory or whether they are generated only from underlying propositional knowledge is far from being resolved. However, this controversy does not prevent us from instructing students in the use of imagery in learning and problem-solving tasks.

Schema Theory of Knowledge Representation   Schema theory, developed in the 1970s and 1980s, is another way of representing declarative and procedural knowledge. Schemas (the basic units of knowledge in this view) have both static and active qualities. At times they appear to operate automatically but at other times seem to be used consciously. Schemas not only represent verbalizable knowledge about things and situations, they also guide behavior. Thus, schemas consist of both declarative and procedural knowledge. Because it attempts to describe the use of schemas in perception, comprehension, memory, and learning, we believe that schema theory is quite useful in education.

Schemas are knowledge structures that represent the general features of classes of objects, events, or situations (Rumelhart, 1980; Rumelhart & Ortony, 1977). Examples of object schemas are *human face, car, cup, pencil, book.* In fact, we have in long-term memory many, many schemas that represent the general features of objects. Examples of schemas that represent events and situations are the *buy* schema and the *going to a restaurant* schema.

A schema is a *wholistic structure* which represents the interrelations between the components of an object or event. We can think of a schema as having a *slot* or *variable* for each component. For example, the schema of a *human face* includes slots for the components of lips, chin, nose, eyes, etc. The face schema prescribes that the parts be organized in a certain way: The eyes are above the nose, the lips are below the nose and above the chin. A schema places constraints on what can fill its slots. For example, an object will be recognized as a face only if it has features which qualify as eyes, lips, nose, etc. But the slots will accept a range of values, so there is some flexibility in what can fill the slots. This flexibility accounts for our ability to recognize in Figure 3.7 a normal face (A), a very sketchy cartoon drawing (B), and a deviant, cyclopean face (C). The latter face does not fit the schema exactly, because it has only one eye rather than the prescribed two, but still it is an acceptable face because most of the elements are present in the correct arrangement. There are limits beyond which something will not be recognized as a face, as illustrated by (D) in Figure 3.7, in which all the elements are present but not in the prescribed arrangement.

Another example is the schema *buy*. It consists of several slots: a buyer, a seller, money (or some medium of exchange), and the item bought. The slots are arranged in a certain way to represent the temporal sequence of actions making up the event. First, the buyer gives money to the seller, who then gives the item to the buyer. If the actions are not arranged in this way, then the event is not an instance of the *buy* schema. For example, if a person gives money to another person and gets nothing in return, then the situation is an instance of a different schema, perhaps the *gift* or the *rob* schema.

FIGURE 3.7   Examples of instantiations of the human face schema. A, B, and C are reasonable instantiations because they match the schema reasonably well. However, D is too discrepant to be an instantiation. (From R. W. Howard *Concepts and Schemata*, 1987.)

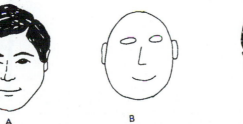

A   B   C   D

Schemas have a number of important characteristics (Rumelhart, 1980; Howard, 1987). One characteristic is that while schemas themselves are abstract representations, they have specific **instantiations.** A schema is instantiated when its slots are filled in with stimuli. The facts depicted in Figure 3.7 are instantiations of the *face* schema. If you recently bought a car, that transaction was an instantiation of the *buy* schema. You filled in the buyer slot, the car filled in the slot for the item bought, and the car dealer filled in the seller slot. The next person you see, whether known to you or a stranger, will instantiate your *face* schema. The person's specific eyes will fill in the eyes slot, the person's nose will fill in the nose slot, etc. Thus, the schema, as we shall elaborate on later, acts as a pattern-recognition device.

Another characteristic of schemas, as mentioned earlier, is that their slots can usually be filled with a fairly wide range of values. The slot for an item sold in the *buy* schema can be filled with an almost infinite variety of things or services ranging from insurance to apples to the services of a plumber. The nose slot of the *face* schema will accept noses of widely different sizes, shapes, and distances from other parts of the face.

Some slots can be filled in by **default.** Look at the stimulus in Figure 3.8 and identify it. Most people have no trouble identifying the figure as a cube, although they can see only three sides of it. The visible parts of the figure filled in enough slots of the *cube* schema to activate or instantiate it. The remainder of the *cube* schema's slots had expected or default values assigned to them based upon what we know about cubes. If you see someone leaving a grocery store with a bag of groceries, you can fill in many details of what probably just happened from your *buy* schema. For one thing, you know that the person probably handed over money for the groceries. Thus, schemas allow us to fill in or infer lots of information that is never specifically presented.

Schemas are **embedded** within each other. Each of the components of the *face* schema, for example, is itself a schema which, in turn, is composed of subschemas. Thus, the *eye* is a schema having slots (subschemas) for *pupil, iris, lens,* etc. Going in the other direction, the *face* schema is embedded in the *human body* schema,

FIGURE 3.8 The figure pictured instantiates most people's *cube* schema even though only three sides are visible and can be fitted to the schema's slots. The other slots are filled by default or inference. (Drawing by Freddie Ghatala, age 12.)

which is embedded in the more general schema for *humanity*. Thus, schemas are organized into part-whole structures with more general, inclusive, and abstract schemas subsuming more specific subschemas, which in turn subsume still more specific schemas.

Exercise 3.3: Choose a schema from your long-term memory. It can be an object schema (e.g., *car, tree*), a schema for a place (e.g., *classroom, university*), or one for an event or action (e.g., *driving a car, earning a degree*). Analyze the schema as to its slots, values that can fill those slots, subschemas embedded in the schema, and a more general schema that it is embedded in._____

_____

_____

_____

_____

Schemas can be activated in **bottom-up** or **top-down** fashion. The top refers to the mind and the bottom to environmental stimuli. Thus, if you are sitting quietly in your office and suddenly smell smoke, most likely this will activate your *fire* schema and impel you to appropriate action. In this case, the schema was activated through the senses, that is, from the bottom up. In other cases, a mental schema can lead us to make certain interpretations of environmental stimuli. For example, consider the following sentence contained in the CIA's manual for espionage agents: "Bugs are often concealed in unlikely places." In this sentence the word "bugs" likely elicited the schema associated with small, covert listening devices rather than the schema associated with small insects. This interpretation stems from the top-down influence of the espionage schema which had just been activated in the preceding sentence. In top-down processing, the context or instructions given to individuals, rather than the item being perceived, activates a schema. While these examples show one process operating to the exclusion of the other, top-down and bottom-up processing usually occur simultaneously. That is, our perceptions result from a combination of information coming in through the senses and conceptual information.

Table 3.1 summarizes the various knowledge units proposed by information processing theorists. While each form of knowledge representation provides a useful way of conceptualizing long-term memory, schema theory has been tremendously appealing to cognitive psychologists and to educators because it emphasizes the critical role of existing knowledge in the processing of new information. Although schema theory has been criticized for vagueness and generality (Alba & Hasher, 1983), current cognitive research has been heavily influenced by it. Our description of the remainder of the information processing system and the processes of perception, comprehension, and remembering reflect the influence of schema theory.

TABLE 3.1 SUMMARY OF KNOWLEDGE UNITS IN LONG-TERM MEMORY

Knowledge unit	Description	Uses
Concepts	Mental representations of categories	Used to sort similar stimuli into categories so that environmental diversity can be reduced; organized into networks
Propositions	Statements composed of two concepts that make true or false assertions about the world	Used to represent declarative knowledge and to make assertions, answer questions, and derive inferences; organized into networks
Productions	Condition-action rules consisting of if-then clauses which often run off automatically	Used to represent procedural knowledge such as skills; organized into action sequences called production systems
Images	Analog or picturelike representations of objects and events	Used to represent spatial and other physical dimensions of stimuli; useful in memory and problem-solving tasks; probably not stored directly in long-term memory, but generated when needed
Schemas	Wholistic structures consisting of variables or slots that represent the interrelations between the features of objects, events, or situations	Used in perception, comprehension, remembering, and problem solving; organized into part-whole hierarchies

INPUT PROCESSING

There are two basic avenues or routes of processing in the memory system (see Figure 3.5). One is input processing, which starts with an external stimulus and proceeds through the sense organs to activate a schema in long-term memory. *Input processing involves perception, comprehension, and remembering of information.* The second route of processing, called output processing, starts with the excitation of schemas in long-term memory and ends with some type of response. This is the avenue of processing involved when we use knowledge stored in long-term memory to perform motor skills, think, or solve problems. We shall discuss input processing in this and the next chapter and reserve discussion of output processing until Chapter 5. Now let's trace the route of input processing and see what is involved.

Sensory Memory

First, an external stimulus impinges upon a sensory receptor and becomes represented in **sensory memory.** Sensory memory is a mechanism for holding for a fraction of a second all of the information from the environment that excites our sensory receptors. Sensory memory is presumed to be a literal copy of the input, and there are thought to be as many types of sensory memories as there are sense receptors. So there is a visual sensory memory containing copies of retinal images, an auditory sensory memory containing auditory images or echoes, and memories associated with the receptors for smell, taste, touch, etc. We shall review the characteristics of the visual and auditory sensory memories because research has focused almost entirely on these receptors.

Suppose you were shown an array of letters such as those in Figure 3.9 for a brief time, say, 500 milliseconds. If you then tried to report the letters, chances are that you would be able to remember about four of them. This is the performance level of subjects in experiments by George Sperling (1960), who was the first psychologist to do research on visual sensory memory. Sperling wondered whether only four letters were reported because that was all the subjects registered or whether more letters had been registered but had been lost before they could be reported. Sperling developed a clever technique to answer this question. Instead of asking subjects to report all they saw, he asked them to report only one of the rows of letters by cuing them with tones of different pitches. A high-pitched tone meant subjects were to report the top row, if the tone were of middle pitch, they were to report the middle row, and a low tone indicated the bottom row. Because subjects did not know which row they were to recall until after the array had disappeared, this method provided a means of sampling the information available from the total array. That is, the number of letters recalled in this partial report method could serve as an estimate of the total number of letters they actually had available when they began their recalls. By varying the delay between the disappearance of the array and the tone, Sperling could estimate how long the information was retained.

Sperling found that if the tone occurred immediately after the array disappeared, subjects could report about three of the four letters from the cued row. This means that they had nine total letters (three rows times three letters) available in sensory memory. A delay in the tone, however, decreased the number of letters available and this decrease was very rapid. After only half a second, subjects recalled only one of the letters from a row, indicating that only three total letters were available from the array. These results indicate that people register a great deal of information that they see in brief presentations. However, after the information is removed from sight, it is available only very briefly—about a half second.

Another question that Sperling addressed was whether meaning is assigned to information in the visual sensory memory. Sperling presented arrays which con-

D H K L

F Q N C

FIGURE 3.9   Example of a stimulus array used in Sperling's research on visual sensory memory.

S M Y P

tained both numbers and letters. Subjects were then given cues indicating that they were to recall either numbers or letters. Such cues would work only if meaning (number or letter) had been assigned to the stimuli. Unlike the location cues described earlier, the number/letter cues were found to be ineffective, suggesting that the information held in sensory memory is not processed for meaning.

The research on the visual sensory memory has been replicated using aurally presented information (see Darwin, Turvey, & Crowder, 1972). The results closely resemble those of Sperling. That is, immediately after presentation, a large amount of information is available in the auditory sensory memory, but after about three seconds most of the information is no longer available. Moreover, the ineffectiveness of meaningful (number/letter) cues once again indicates that sensory memory contains relatively unprocessed information.

Sensory memory is crucial to perception in that it provides a mechanism for momentarily holding information coming in over our sense receptors so that it can be further processed. The research on sensory memory has some implications for teaching (Glover, Ronning, & Bruning, 1990). First, the short duration of information in sensory memory points up the need to carefully pace the delivery of information to students so as not to overwhelm sensory memory capacity. Second, there may be some benefits to presenting information both aurally and visually since entering the same information into both memories should increase the chances for further processing. In fact, multisensory presentations involving all the senses should enhance learning by making more information available from sensory memory.

Perception

When an input enters sensory memory, the system immediately begins to process it by analyzing its features and attempting to match these features with knowledge in long-term memory. This is the first stage of perception and is called **pattern recognition.** It is the essential element of perception which is the process by which meaning is assigned to a stimulus input. While there have been various theories of pattern recognition proposed over the years, the view presented here is based upon schema theory, which seems to incorporate the basic ideas of previous views.

According to a schema-theoretic view, a schema in long-term memory is activated when one or more features of a stimulus in sensory memory fit the slots of the schema. The activated schema will then drive the system to search for more information or features to fill the rest of its slots. In this early stage of perception, feature analysis and initial schema activation is conducted automatically, that is, without attention, and can go on simultaneously for many inputs coming in via different receptors. However, individuals cannot fully process everything they are seeing, hearing, tasting, smelling, touching all at the same time. So the person is said to "select" certain receptors (or input channels) for focal attention. Information in the sensory memory corresponding to the selected channel will undergo further processing. That is, with the addition of attention, the schema can become more fully activated (in the sense of filling in more of its slots with stimulus features). When a schema is sufficiently activated, we experience recognition of the stimulus as a particular kind of thing, for example, a face, the letter "a," the word "cat."

Question 3.3: What do you suppose happens to information coming in over unattended channels?_____

_____

_____

The Constructive Nature of Perception   As you recall from our demonstration of the cube (see Figure 3.8), during perception some slots of a schema may be filled in by inference rather than by features actually present in the stimulus. As a general rule, the process of perception involves going beyond the information given. Perception is not simply seeing what is "out there." Rather, *perception involves constructing an interpretation of environmental stimuli by using knowledge contained in our schemas.* The constructive nature of perception can explain how in some circumstances people can witness the same event and literally perceive different things. This most often happens under circumstances in which the stimulus input is degraded, as when there is poor light or when events unfold very rapidly. Under such circumstances (e.g., witnessing an automobile accident or a robbery), there is a greater tendency for people to fill in missing information. Such fill-in information may vary from one person to another depending upon differences in their schemas.

The Role of Context in Perception   As we saw earlier, an appropriate schema is activated by an incoming stimulus as a result of the pattern-recognition process (bottom-up processing) and/or by the context surrounding a stimulus (top-down processing). The profound role of context in perception is illustrated in Figure 3.10. The middle shape on the left side of the figure is seen by most people as the letter "B." However, the same shape on the right side of the figure is not seen as a B but rather as the number 13. The surrounding context thus led to quite different perceptions of the same shape. Activation of the *letter* schema facilitated closure in the A-B-C row. Activation of the *number* schema prevented the operation of closure in the 12-13-14 row. This demonstration also indicates that the Gestalt laws (e.g., closure, similarity, proximity) described earlier may be derived from the effects of context on schema activation (Roth & Frisby, 1986).

Schemas and Perception: Implications for Teaching   Schemas provide a means of recognizing patterns and assigning meaning to incoming stimuli. Once

FIGURE 3.10   Context effects in perception.

activated, whether by stimulus, context, or instruction, a schema then affects the information we take in. Schemas even tell us where to look. For example, if we wish to determine what someone is feeling, our *person* schema tells us to look at his face. However, if we wish to determine a person's wealth or status, our *person* schema tells us to look at his clothes and possessions. Similarly, a student whose schema for *average speed problems* has been activated will begin looking for information relevant to the following problem: *Mr. Ross flies 900 miles to El Paso and then 300 miles to Cottonville. If his flying time was 5 hours and 20 minutes, and his stopover time was 1 hour and 15 minutes, what was his average speed?* The student will perceive certain information as relevant (total flying distance, total flying time) and will ignore other information such as stopover time. His schema will then direct him to perform certain operations on the selected information (convert time to minutes, divide total distance by total time, etc.). Thus, schemas direct attention to relevant information and filter out irrelevant information. Since we can absorb only a limited amount of information, schemas provide a way to extract what is most important for our purposes.

It is important for teachers to be aware of how schemas influence and sometimes enhance students' perception. First, teachers should ensure that students acquire the schemas necessary to construct desired perceptions. For instance, for a young student to "see" the difference between "b" and "d" or for an older one to recognize different word-problem types requires background knowledge in the form of specific schemas. Additionally, teachers can aid perception by providing contexts and instructions that activate appropriate schemas (more on this later). Finally, teachers need to be aware that beginning or less knowledgeable students must be carefully guided. Teachers can help such students to perceive critical information by directing their attention to relevant aspects of the situation.

Language Comprehension

Role of Schemas in Comprehension   When the processes of pattern recognition and perception are applied to verbal messages contained in text or speech, we refer to the outcome as comprehension. Comprehension involves discovering a schema or schemas that provide a plausible account of the message and allow us to assimilate it to something we know (R. C. Anderson, 1977; Rumelhart, 1984).

Exercise 3.4: Please read the following short passage and then go to the explanation at the end of the chapter.

The procedure is actually quite simple. First you arrange things into different groups. Of course, one pile may be sufficient, depending on how much there is to do. If you have to go somewhere else due to lack of facilities, that is the next step; otherwise you are pretty well set. It is important not to overdo things. That is, it is better to do too few things at once than too many. In the short run, this may not seem important, but complications can easily arise. A mistake can be expensive as well. At first the whole procedure will seem complicated. Soon, however, it will become just another facet of life. It is difficult to foresee any end to the necessity for this task in the immediate future, but then one can never tell. After the procedure is completed one arranges the materials into different groups again. Then they can be put in their appropriate places. Eventually they will be used once more and the whole cycle will then have to be repeated. However, that is part of life. (Bransford & Johnson, 1973.)

As in perception, we use our schema to make inferences, to fill in information not explicitly stated in the message, and to interpret any ambiguous elements of the message.

Exercise 3.5: Read the following passage drawn from a study by Anderson, Reynolds, Schallert, and Goetz (1977). As you read, try to figure out who Rocky is.

Rocky got up slowly from the mat, planning his escape. He hesitated a moment and thought. Things were not going well. What bothered him most was being held, especially since the charge against him had been weak. He considered his present situation. The lock that held him was strong, but he thought he could break it. He knew, however, that his timing would have to be perfect. Rocky was aware that it was because of his early roughness that he had been penalized so severely—much too severely from his point of view. The situation was becoming frustrating; the pressure had been grinding on him for too long. He was being ridden unmercifully. Rocky was getting angry now. He felt he was ready to make his move. He knew that his success or failure would depend on what he did in the next few seconds.

Describe who or what Rocky is and then see explanation at end of the chapter.

The passages used in the two preceding exercises are intentionally ambiguous or vague in order to illustrate the role of schemas in the comprehension process. However, it should be understood that comprehension of all verbal messages, even those written to be as explicit and unambiguous as possible, involves the use of schemas stored in long-term memory to construct an interpretation of the message. Thus, the meaning of messages is not "in the text" but rather in our heads.

Schemas and Comprehension: Implications for Teaching   The role of schemas in comprehension makes them particularly important in education, in which a basic goal is to get students to understand material. To do so, teachers must either align new material with students' existing schemas or give them a new schema that they can then use to understand the material. Teachers need to be aware that comprehension failure results either when students lack the necessary background schemas for assimilating new material or when students possess requisite schemas but fail to activate them. It is also possible that students may fail to comprehend a message in the manner intended by the teacher because they have assimilated it to a schema different from the one the teacher had in mind.

One way that teachers can help students activate relevant schemas is to provide them with an **advance organizer** before presenting new material. According to Ausubel (1968), who originated the concept, advance organizers provide a "scaffold" which can subsume more detailed material. More recently, the concept has been revised by schema theorists to mean any kind of overview material presented before a lesson which serves to activate relevant schemas so that the new material can be assimilated to them (Derry, 1984; Mayer, 1984b). Recent research indicates that organizers containing concrete examples of things that students will encounter in the lesson are better than abstract organizers. In addition, the organizer should contain material familiar to students (Glover, Ronning, & Bruning, 1990). Aside from being concrete and familiar, advance organizers can take a variety of forms, including discussions, outlines, drawings, diagrams, and short passages from texts.

Exercise 3.6: Figure 3.11 contains an advance organizer for the following lesson on radar. Please study the material in Figure 3.11 for 60 seconds and then read the radar passage.

The Radar Lesson

Radar means the detection and location of remote objects by reflection of radio waves. The phenomenon of acoustic echoes is familiar: sound waves reflected from a building or cliff are received back at the observer after a lapse of a short interval. The effect is similar to your shouting in a canyon and seconds later hearing a nearly exact replication of your voice. Radar uses exactly the same principle except that the waves are radio waves, not sound waves. These travel very much faster than sound waves, 186,000 miles per second, and can cover much longer distances. Thus, radar involves simply measuring the time between transmission of the waves and their subsequent return or echo and then converting that to a distance measure.

To send out the radio waves a radio transmitter is connected to a directional antenna which sends out a stream of short pulses of radio waves. This radio pulse that is first transmitted looks very much like the effect of tossing a pebble into a quiet lake. It creates concentric circles of small waves that continue to grow outward. Usually both a transmitter and a receiver are employed separately but it is possible to use only one antenna in which pulse transmission is momentarily suppressed in order to receive echo pulses. One thing to remember, though, is that radar waves travel in fundamentally straight lines and that the curvature of the earth eventually interferes with long-range transmission. When you think about the reception of the returning pulses or echoes you should remember that any object in the path of the transmitted beam reflects some of the energy back to the radio receiver. The problem then becomes transmitting the pulses picked up by the receiver to a display mechanism for visual readout. One mechanism in large use is the cathode-ray tube, a familiar item in airport control towers, which looks somewhat like a television screen.

It is easiest to understand how radar is displayed if you begin with one of the earliest models used around the 1930s. These types of displays were able to focus

There are five steps in radar.

1. Transmission: A pulse travels from an antenna.

2. Reflection: The pulse bounces off a remote object.

3. Reception: The pulse returns to the receiver.

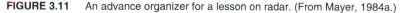

4. Measurement: The difference between the time out and the time back
   tells the total time traveled.

Out   Back

5. Conversion: The time can be converted to a measure of distance, since
   the pulse travels at a constant speed.

_____ seconds =_____ miles

FIGURE 3.11   An advance organizer for a lesson on radar. (From Mayer, 1984a.)

the broad radar pulse into a single beam of light which proceeded from the left of screen to the right. When no object impedes the traveling radar pulse it continues its travel until lost from the screen on the right. When there is an object present the pulse would strike it and begin to travel back to the receiver. When the object is struck by the radar pulse, it creates a bright spot on the face of the screen and the distance of the object can be measured by the length of the trace coming from the object back to the receiver. With this model, however, you are able to measure only the distance of an object and not its absolute location, since the beam of light on the screen actually presents the entire width of the broader radar pulse.

Models employed today use two simple techniques which make location of objects much easier. First, the transmitter now operates much like the searchlight used in airports. It emits a single beam of radar pulses that make continuous circular sweeps around the area under surveillance. Secondly, the display screen is adjusted so that its center corresponds to the point where the radar pulses begin. The radar pulse seen on the screen operates like the second hand of a clock, which continually moves. When an object is present, it leaves a bright spot on the face of the screen. An additional feature is that the face of the screen actually shows a maplike picture of the area around the radar giving distance and, of course, location. Thus, it is very easy now to determine the location of objects by noting their location on the screen's map. (From Mayer, 1983.)

Did the advance organizer help you to understand the radar lesson? Why do you think it helped? Please answer and then see comments at end of chapter.____

_____

_____

A final implication of schema theory is that teachers need to realize that many students possess schemas that actually interfere with the acquisition of new information. For example, Nussbaum (1979) interviewed children of various ages to determine their schema of the *earth as a cosmic body.* Children held quite different conceptions of *earth,* which appeared to develop with age. The particular conception of the earth that a child possessed determined her understanding of new information. For example, some children viewed the earth as flat. They accommodated the notion that the earth is round by conceiving of a flat, round disk. In later conceptions, the earth was seen as a ball that had been cut in half, the flat cross section forming the ground where people live with the sky as a dome above.

In the above example, the children's existing schemas are actually misconceptions which need to be either modified or replaced by a new, more adaptable schema. Much geology and geography instruction would be incomprehensible to children who held such misconceptions because the material could not be easily assimilated. Material that cannot be understood with existing schemas is either ignored, compartmentalized, distorted, or learned by rote. The schemas that students bring to school are ones that they have constructed from information gained through their interactions with the world. These schemas may often be highly resistant to change because, although they may be incorrect in the eyes of modern science, they have previously helped students to make sense of the world. Helping students correct misconceptions by constructing more adequate schemas is a prime task of good teaching.

Short-term Memory

We are at the point of input processing where a schema in long-term memory has been activated, thus allowing us to recognize and comprehend incoming information. At this stage it is said that the information has entered short-term memory (refer to Figure 3.5). In some early information processing models of memory, such as that of Atkinson and Shiffrin (1968), short-term memory was conceived of as a "place" for temporarily holding information until it was used. This short-term store was postulated to hold a limited amount of information for a limited duration, roughly 30 seconds. However, the individual could extend the life of information in the short-term store by rehearsing it. For example, if you look up a telephone number you can "keep the number in mind" by repeating it over and over to yourself until you can get to the phone and dial it. At that point, you stop rehearsing it and within 30 seconds it is lost from short-term memory. In order to retain information for longer periods of time, it would have to be transferred to long-term memory. In this model, rehearsal was seen as the mechanism by which information was transferred from short-term to long-term memory.

More recent models of memory do not view short-term memory as a "place" where information is held for brief periods. Rather, short-term memory is viewed more as a working memory, that part of the memory system where mental work is performed. However, before discussing this view, we need to examine the concept of attention more closely. As we have seen, attention is a critical ingredient in both perception and comprehension. It is also the key to understanding contemporary views of short-term or working memory.

Attention   In contemporary information processing theory, attention is viewed as a person's allocation of cognitive resources to the tasks at hand. Kahneman (1973) likens attention to mental effort and then draws the analogy between mental effort and electrical power. When we devote attention to a task, we put mental effort into it in the same way that we would put electrical power into a machine that we wanted to use. Just as there are limits to how many electrical appliances we can run in our home without blowing a fuse, there are limits on how much mental effort we have available to perform tasks simultaneously. Although there are individual differences—some people can do more things at the same time than others—most people can perform only a limited number of tasks at the same time.

The number of tasks a person can do simultaneously depends not only upon her mental capacity (ability) but also upon the nature of the tasks being attempted. Tasks vary in the amount of cognitive resources or mental effort they require for successful completion, just as machines vary in the amount of power they require. It takes more power to run an air conditioner than a window fan, for instance. Some tasks are **automatic,** that is, they can be performed without attention or conscious awareness. One example of an automatic task that we have already encountered is the initial perceptual analysis of stimuli contained in sensory memory.

One clue that a task involves automatic processing is that it can be carried out simultaneously with other tasks. For example, for a skilled driver in light traffic driving requires little, if any, attention. Such a driver can listen to the radio and carry on a conversation with a passenger while driving. A novice driver, on the other hand, may have to devote more mental effort or attention to the driving task and hence may not be able to converse normally while driving. Indeed, even a veteran may find that he loses the thread of the conversation when traffic becomes heavy and driving more complicated. This example indicates that the amount of attentional capacity required by a task depends both upon its complexity and how practiced one is at the task. Many tasks can become virtually automatic with lots of practice.

The example also illustrates that when we reach the limits of our attentional capacity, we have to decide how to allocate attention. Usually there is a primary task such as driving that is selected for attention, thus diverting resources from other, more secondary, tasks such as conversing with a passenger. The relative importance of tasks determines which one(s) of them will be selected for attention when attentional resources are exceeded. Of course, relative importance of tasks can differ among individuals, which explains why some students opt to attend to a conversation with a peer rather than the teacher's instructions. Helping students select appropriate tasks for attention is a critical function of teaching because what is not attended to will not be perceived or comprehended.

Another way that teachers can help students manage their limited attentional resources is to provide practice on basic processes until they become automatic. Automatic processes allow students to use fewer cognitive resources in completing the same task, thus freeing up attention for other tasks. For example, if decoding skills are automatic, students can devote more attention to the task of comprehending a reading passage. To gain true automaticity in most skills requires extensive practice, usually hundreds of hours. Thus, the real job of the teacher is to motivate students so that they will stay on task long enough to acquire the practice needed for automaticity.

We can now relate attention to the memory system. One way to view short-term memory is to equate it with attentional capacity. Giving focal attention to incoming information corresponds to entering the information in short-term memory. Any mental activity that uses attentional capacity takes place in short-term memory. Because attention is identified as mental effort or "work," we can think of short-term memory as working memory.

Working Memory   Working memory is the "place" where attention-demanding tasks such as adding sums in the head, holding a list of digits for a brief time, and solving problems or thinking about something are performed. By "place" we do not mean that working memory occupies a particular location in the brain; rather it refers to a distinct *function* of the information processing system. To say that something is "in" working memory is to say that it is being consciously processed. Thus, *subjectively, working memory corresponds to our conscious awareness.* How much can we be aware of at any one time? This is a question about the storage capacity of working memory, and to answer it we must elaborate on that concept.

Most conceptions of working memory (e.g., Baddeley, 1986; Case, 1985) suppose that in order to perform tasks such as the ones mentioned above a person needs to operate on information and briefly store the products of those operations. Both operating on information and storing it require mental effort or attention, and hence, are conducted in working memory. For example, if you are solving the problem 26×32 mentally, you would operate (multiply) to get the intermediate products 52 and 78 and then hold these in working memory while adding them together there.

The operating and storing components of any task can be conducted simultaneously as long as the total effort (attention) required does not exceed the limited supply available. If the total effort needed by any task does exceed the supply, then effort or attention has to be allocated among the components of the task. This often means that there is a trade-off between operating and storing in working memory. That is, the more effort spent operating on information, the less the storage capacity of working memory. This means that a person who is skilled in conducting the operations called for by a particular task will have to expend less of his limited attentional capacity on the operations and will thus have more capacity left over for storing information.

In general, the more complex the task, the more storage that is required, because complex tasks involve more steps or operations than do simple problems. Thus, it follows that people who are able to store the most in working memory (while simultaneously operating on the information) are those who are able to solve more complex problems. As we shall see in Chapter 6, developmentally based increases in the storage capacity of working memory have been postulated by some developmental theorists to be the major reason why adults and older children are capable of solving more complex problems than are younger children.

In general, then, the storage capacity of working memory is a critical factor in determining students' performance on tasks of all kinds. Because the capacity of working memory depends upon an individual's facility with the task, the best way to measure the capacity of working memory is to use tasks that require people to both process and store information. For example, Daneman and Carpenter (1980) have measured the capacity of working memory during reading by having subjects read a set of two to six sequentially presented sentences and then recall the last words of the sentences. While reading each sentence, subjects judged its truth value. Thus this task required processing the sentences in order to comprehend them and storing their last words.

Daneman and Carpenter found that the reading span (the number of last words recalled) ranged from two to five among college students, and that students with longer spans scored higher on reading comprehension tests such as the verbal SAT than did students with shorter spans. This correlation means that poor readers have less storage capacity in working memory than do good readers. The lower storage capacity of poor readers is, in turn, probably due to their inefficient reading processes, such as word recognition, which leave less attentional capacity for storing the products of reading. The less the storage capacity at any one time, the more difficult it is to grasp the interrelationships between words and phrases; hence, comprehension suffers.

It should be noted, however, that working memory does not have a single storage capacity. For example, a poor reader in Daneman and Carpenter's study might have a larger storage capacity and hence better performance on a task (say, mathematics) involving more familiar operations than a good reader having less mathematical facility. Researchers have measured working memory capacity on a variety of tasks (e.g., reasoning and logical skill tasks) and have found very strong positive correlations between students' storage capacity and their task performance (Kyllonen & Christal, 1990; Kyllonen & Stephens, 1990). Table 3.2 provides a summary of the major features of short-term (working) memory and long-term memory.

Dealing with Limitations in Working Memory   It may be helpful to use the analogy of a workbench when thinking about how to deal with limitations in working memory. Working memory is like a workbench that students use to construct things like solutions to problems, or interpretations of texts, or new sets

TABLE 3.2 CHARACTERISTICS OF SHORT-TERM (WORKING) MEMORY AND LONG-TERM MEMORY

	Working memory	Long-term memory
Function	Locus for operating on and storing information in the course of performing mental tasks	Locus for storage of information until needed for tasks being performed in working memory
Capacity	Can hold very limited amounts of information; capacity varies with the complexity and familiarity of the task being performed	Can hold vast amounts of information in highly organized fashion
Duration	Information in working memory is lost within 30 seconds if it is not attended to	Information resides in long-term memory virtually permanently

of propositions representing facts to be added to long-term memory (see Figure 3.12). The materials used in construction are retrieved from long-term memory as the student perceives environmental stimuli and activates relevant knowledge about the task at hand. Most construction jobs involve a number of steps, so the workbench has to hold the materials until they are needed as well as provide a space for actual construction. As shown in the picture, when storage space becomes crowded, items can be pushed off the bench and become unavailable when needed. The worker shown in Figure 3.12 is an adult who has a relatively large workbench. Child labor laws notwithstanding, children also work at building mental constructions, but their workbenches are smaller than those of adults. For example, a kindergarten child's workbench is about half the size of the adult's.

There are three things teachers can do to help students make the best use of their limited workbench space. First, be aware of the size of your students' workbenches and try to avoid tasks that require more storage space than they have available. For example, if you tell a kindergarten child to put the white blocks in the box, she will happily comply. If, however, you tell her to put the white blocks in the box, put the green blocks in the bag, and leave the red blocks on the table, she will most likely become hopelessly confused, and repeating the instructions will not help. A second grader will handle this task with ease.

Second, the workbench storage space can be increased by judicious use of **chunking.** Notice in Figure 3.12 how well organized the workbench is: Materials are carefully stacked, and similar materials are grouped together so that they take less room on the bench. This is what chunking does for working memory.

Exercise 3.7: Read the following string of letters once quickly; then close your eyes and repeat back, in order, as many of the letters as you can remember.

FB ITW AI BMC IA

How many did you remember?_____

Turn to the back of the chapter for your working memory score.

FIGURE 3.12   Working memory serves as a "workbench" in the human information processing system. (From Klatzky, 1975.)

Chunking involves integrating stimuli (e.g., letters, numbers, words, phrases) into meaningful higher-order units. A **chunk,** then, is a stimulus pattern that has a unitary representation in long-term memory. For example, the letter "A," the number 5, the word "clown," the phrase "Too many cooks spoil the broth," and the picture of a face are all chunks for individuals with the requisite schemas in long-term memory. For many members of this culture CIA, IBM, etc., are meaningful chunks. However, for a young child or someone from a different culture these groups of letters would not have a unitary representation. Thus, chunks are a result of learning and experience. Helping children to chunk will allow them to store more in working memory. With young children (and older ones as well), who may lack the knowledge base to chunk semantically, rhyme and rhythm can be used to chunk items. For example, the alphabet can be changed from a string of 26 letters to: *abcd efg hijk lmnop qrs tuv wx yz.*

Presenting materials so that the chunking capability of the student is used is a good idea. But remember that the chunks that children can form depend upon prior learning and experience within a particular stimulus domain. For example, a kindergarten child will see 111 as three numbers while an older child will see it as one number. Similarly, extended practice in reading will enable a child to develop techniques for chunking letters together into words and thereby free memory capacity to focus on the meaning of the sentence. It is well to remember that chunking is specific to a stimulus domain. That is, experience with numbers will not lead to improvements in memory capacity for processing letters and words, and vice versa. In sum, providing lots of domain-specific experience is one way of increasing students' working memory capacity.

The third way of helping students overcome limitations on working memory is to help them become faster, more efficient workers. Someone who works quickly and efficiently does not need as much construction space for as long a time as a slow, inefficient worker. In terms of working memory, a more efficient worker is one who can execute processes with little or no conscious effort or attention. This means, as we pointed out earlier, helping students practice the skills required by important academic tasks until they become automatic.

We will pause now in our coverage of input processing and review what we have learned about information processing theory thus far. In the next chapter, we will see how, according to the theory, we remember information that we have perceived and comprehended.

REVIEW OF MAJOR POINTS

1 Information processing theory is a framework that has been adopted by many cognitive psychologists to guide their research into mental processes. Gestalt psychology contributed many ideas, including the laws of perceptual organization (laws of continuity, closure, proximity, similarity, and Pragnanz) that anticipated information processing constructs.

2 Long-term memory is a vast storehouse for our knowledge about the world. It contains episodic (personal experiences) and semantic knowledge. Semantic knowledge is generalized knowledge that transcends a particular context and includes declarative and procedural forms.

3 Semantic knowledge is represented in a variety of ways in long-term memory, including concepts, propositions, productions, images, and schemas. Different theorists emphasize one type of representation more than others. The knowledge in long-term memory is highly organized, with most theorists characterizing it in terms of networks of nodes (cognitive units) and the links (relations) between them. When one node in the network is activated, this activation spreads to neighboring nodes in the network. The closer the node, the quicker and more strongly it is activated.

4 Schemas are knowledge structures in long-term memory for representing the general features of objects, events, and situations. Schemas have slots for the components of objects and events and include information about the interrelations among components. A schema is instantiated (activated) by having a stimulus fill one or more of its slots. Missing information can be filled in by referring to the default values of the schema's slots. Schemas are embedded one within another and are at various levels of abstraction.

5 Input processing starts when a stimulus is represented in sensory memory. Sensory memory is a mechanism for holding, very briefly, a copy of information coming in over our sense receptors so that it can be further processed. Perception involves analyzing the features of the stimulus in sensory memory and fitting them to the slots of a schema in long-term memory. This activated schema will then allow us to recognize the stimulus. The important point that schema theory makes is that perception is not a process in which we ''record'' external stimulation like a video camera. Rather, *perception is a process by which we construct interpretations of external stimuli using the schemas in long-term memory.*

6 Schemas also play an important role in comprehending verbal messages. Comprehension is finding a schema or schemas that allow us to make sense of a message. As in perception, we use our schemas to fill in information not explicitly stated in the message. Thus, the meaning of the message is not in the text but rather in our heads.

7 Once perception or comprehension processes have resulted in an activated schema, the information is said to be ''in'' short-term memory. Short-term memory is viewed as the part of the memory system where mental work is performed, hence the name working memory. It roughly corresponds to our consciousness.

8 Mental work requires mental energy, which corresponds to contemporary views of attention. Humans are conceived to have a limited supply of mental energy or attention with which to perform various tasks. Tasks vary in terms of the amount of attention required to perform them. Some tasks are automatic, which means that they can be performed without attention. Other tasks require varying amounts of attention. We can perform several tasks simultaneously as long as the total attention required does not exceed our capacity. If capacity is exceeded, we must decide how to allocate attention among the tasks. Tasks can become automatic with much practice.

9 To perform most tasks in working memory requires operating on information and storing the products of operations. Both operating and storing require attention, which means that there is often a trade-off between these two functions. In general, the more efficiently (automatically) an individual can conduct basic cognitive operations, the more she will be able to use her limited attention to store information in working memory. This, in turn, will enable her to perform more complex cognitive tasks. This is one reason why information processing theorists put great emphasis upon automatizing basic cognitive skills and finding other ways (e.g., chunking) of enabling students to cope with the storage limitations of working memory.

ANSWERS TO QUESTIONS AND EXERCISES

Question 3.1: Since information processing theory is primarily concerned with how the memory system operates, we thought a straight memory question would help prime you for this chapter. We are not so much interested in your actual answer as in getting you to reflect on what mental processes might be involved in answering such a question. First, you might not have even attempted an answer because you knew that you did not have the information in your memory, either because you did not read Chapter 1 (shame!) or you read it so cursorily that you are confident you cannot recall any of its details. This sense of what is or is not retrievable from memory is one aspect of metamemory (our knowledge about our memory) and is important in guiding our memory attempts.

Second, if you had a feeling that you might have some relevant information stored in memory, then you probably attempted to search for it, perhaps by using cues like "Let's see, information processing is a cognitive theory; what did they say about cognitive theories in Chapter 1?" Getting something out of memory is very dependent upon having a useful cue that will help us find a particular bit of knowledge in the vast amount of information that we have stored in memory. That you realized that you might find knowledge about information processing theory under *cognitive theory* and not under *cities of the world* is sensible and reflects the fact that our memories are meaningfully organized. Oh, by the way, two assumptions of the information processing framework are that computers provide a useful metaphor for human cognition and that mental processes are "programs" or transformations that do not resemble overt behavior.

Exercise 3.1: Here is a recall protocol from one of Bartlett's subjects.

Two youths were standing by a river about to start seal-catching when a boat appeared with five men in it. They were all armed for war.

The youths were at first frightened, but they were asked by the men to come and help them fight some enemies on the other bank. One youth said he could not come as his relations would be anxious about him; the other said he would go, and entered the boat.

In the evening he returned to his hut, and told his friends that he had been in a battle. A great many had been slain, and he had been wounded by an arrow; he had not felt any pain, he said. They told him that he must have been fighting in a battle of ghosts. Then he remembered that it had been queer and he became very excited.

In the morning, however, he became ill, and his friends gathered round; he fell down and his face became very pale. Then he writhed and shrieked and his friends were filled with terror. At last he became calm. Something hard and black came out of his mouth, and he lay contorted and dead.

In addition to rather poor recall even at short retention intervals, Bartlett found that subjects recalled only the gist or theme of the story. From that gist they constructed a reasonable story that made sense out of the material recalled. The story constructions, however, often had errors and distortions that made the story fit their own cultural background. Does your recall protocol fit this description?

Question 3.2: Someone who has the *triangle* production in long-term memory should be able to correctly classify new examples of triangles. Someone who has information about *triangle* stored in propositional form should be able to state that a triangle is a closed figure with three sides. In other words, these forms of representation underlie different kinds of performance. Someone with only de-clarative knowledge represented by mental propositions can state the definition of *triangle* but may not be able to classify figures as triangles. Someone with procedural knowledge represented in the form of a production can classify trian-gles but may not be able to state the definition of *triangle*.

Exercise 3.2: 1. John is the smartest, followed by Joe, Harry, and finally Pete. Huttenlocher (1968) found that people often solve logical deduction problems like this one by constructing mental images. For example, they might imagine a line and place dots (one representing each person) along it. The smarter a person was, the farther to the right the dot would be placed. As long as they remembered whom each dot stood for, it was easy to read off who was smarter than whom. Note that in this case, people are using a spatial image to provide an analog representation of the abstract dimension of intelligence. Of course, not all subjects used images; some used linguistic strategies. Did you use some type of imagery strategy?

2. People often form a mental image and then count the window panes in order to answer this question. Meudell (1971) found that people who reported more window panes took longer to respond to this question, which means it took them longer to count than people reporting fewer panes. This is what we would expect because images are analog (picturelike) representations. If people were simply retrieving a proposition from long-term memory (such as, *"My living room windows contain 10 panes."*), then there should be no relationship between number of panes and response time. How did you go about answering this ques-tion?

3. In answering the question about the hood ornament, people report the sensation of scanning from the rear of the car to the front. This appears to indicate that we scan mental images in much the same way that we scan pictures, and that images have picturelike attributes such as size and distance. (Kosslyn, 1985.)

Exercise 3.3: We chose the event schema *eating out in a restaurant* to illustrate schema analysis. The general slots in this schema are: being seated, having one's order taken, consuming the food, paying the bill, leaving. The schema specifies that these components occur in a certain order. First one arrives, then is seated, and so on. Each slot can be filled with a wide range of stimuli. The order-taking slot will accept many different kinds of people as waiters (including singing ones and topless ones or even machines). The food slot can be filled with almost an infinite variety of items. Each slot is a subschema with slots of its own. For example, the order-taking slot is a schema with slots for the waiter, the menu, the customer. The schema is quite general so that it includes similar events in all kinds of restaurants. Particular restaurants subsumed under this general schema would include such things as cafeterias and drive-ins, each requiring a somewhat different sequence of events. The *restaurant* schema is, in turn, embedded in a more general schema called *eating out,* which also subsumes the *picnic* and *going to a dinner party* schemas.

Question 3.3: You guessed it—it is lost after a few seconds. This is why, even though we may be aware that someone is talking to us, and can even respond with a nod or a mumbled "uh huh," if we are intent on reading or watching TV, we will not fully perceive the message, much to the speaker's annoyance. However, as we now know, the input from other channels is held briefly in sensory memory, so if we can switch our attention to an unattended channel quickly enough, we might be able to "get to" the information held there before it disappears. As a general rule, we are always receiving and initially processing many more stimuli than we ever actually perceive or even become aware of. For example, if you direct your attention to the soles of your feet you will discover a whole host of sensations that activate perception of this part of your anatomy.

Exercise 3.4: The material makes little sense, but this is not because you cannot perceive and assign meaning to the individual words and sentences. On the contrary, the vocabulary is simple and no grammatical rules are violated, yet the sentences don't seem to hang together or lead to any meaning. However, the passage does make sense if a schema is suggested that can provide a plausible account of it. Give it the title "Washing Clothes" and reread it. Now it should make perfect sense because you can assimilate it to your schema for washing clothes. This schema provides an account of the passage because it has the necessary slots for assimilating the objects, qualities, and actions mentioned in the passage. The information in the passage fits the schema, producing the subjective sense that it has been comprehended. We experience a "click" of comprehension whenever we can fit a message to a schema.

Exercise 3.5: Like many readers you may have decided that Rocky is a prisoner in jail. There are enough segments in the passage that match people's *prisoner* schema for it to provide a reasonable interpretation. On the other hand, you may have decided, as do many readers, that Rocky is a wrestler. There are many elements of the passage which seem to fit people's *wrestler* schema. The meaning you constructed for the passage, and how you interpreted certain elements such as "escape," "being held," and "severely penalized," depends upon the specific schema you adopted. The meaning you construct determines a great deal about what you will remember. If we could test people's memory for the passage, as did R. C. Anderson et al. (1977), we would find large differences in the particular elements of the passage people remembered. This is presumably because the schema being used to interpret a message guides attention. People reading from the prisoner perspective would attend most closely to aspects congruent with that schema, while those reading from a wrestler perspective would focus more on elements relevant to wrestling. Memory for the passage might also reflect inferences drawn while reading and, since these inferences involve drawing upon information contained in the activated schema, these would be different for readers employing different schema. For example, use of the *wrestler* schema would lead to the inference that Rocky is clothed in wrestling trunks, while prison garb would be inferred by those using the *prisoner* schema.

Exercise 3.6: The advance organizer should help you to understand the radar passage because it presents a concrete model of the principles to be learned. The organizer does not add any information that is not in the lesson, but it does provide a familiar way to organize the passage. Mayer (1983) found that students who were given the advance organizer before listening to the passage recalled more conceptual information from the passage and were better able to solve problems based on the lesson than were students who did not receive the organizer. However, advance organizer subjects performed worse than no organizer subjects on tests of verbatim recognition and factual recall. The advance organizer apparently helped learners to put the information into their own words and to organize the lesson around the major points of the passage.

Exercise 3.7: If you followed instructions, you should have been able to remember somewhere in the range of five to nine letters. Now let's try it again. Read the following letters quickly; then close your eyes and repeat them back in order:

FBI   TWA   IBM   CIA

How many did you remember this time? Usually people remember all twelve of the letters this time. This is an example of chunking.

REFERENCES

Alba, J. W., & Hasher, L. (1983). Is memory schematic? *Psychological Bulletin, 93,* 203–231.

Anderson, J. R. (1976). *Language, memory, and thought.* Hillsdale, NJ: Erlbaum.

Anderson, J. R. (1983a). *The architecture of cognition.* Cambridge, MA: Harvard University Press.

Anderson, J. R. (1983b). A spreading activation theory of memory. *Journal of Verbal Learning and Verbal Behavior, 22,* 261–195.

Anderson, J. R. (1985). *Cognitive psychology and its implications* (2nd ed.). New York: Freeman.

Anderson, J. R. (1987). Skill acquisition: Compilation of weak-method problem solutions. *Psychological Review, 94,* 192–210.

Anderson, J. R., & Bower, G. H. (1973). *Human associative memory.* Washington, DC: Winston.

Anderson, R. C. (1977). The notion of schemata and the educational enterprise. In R. C. Anderson, R. J. Spiro, & W. E. Montague (Eds.), *Schooling and the acquisition of knowledge.* Hillsdale, NJ: Erlbaum.

Anderson, R. C., Reynolds, R. E., Schallert, D. L., & Goetz, E. T. (1977). Framewords for comprehending discourse. *American Educational Research Journal, 14,* 376–382.

Atkinson, R. C., & Shiffrin, R. M. (1968). Human memory: A proposed system and its control processes. In K. W. Spence & J. T. Spence (Eds.), *The Psychology of learning and motivation: Advances in research and theory* (Vol. 2). New York: Academic Press.

Ausubel, D. P. (1968). *Educational psychology: A cognitive view.* New York: Holt, Rinehart & Winston.

Baddeley, A. D. (1986). *Working memory.* Oxford: Clarendon Press.

Bartlett, F. C. (1932). *Remembering: A study in experimental and social psychology.* Cambridge: Cambridge University Press.

Bransford, J. D., & Johnson, M. K. (1973). Consideration of some problems in comprehension. In W. G. Chase (Ed.), *Visual information processing.* New York: Academic Press.

Case, R. (1985). *Intellectual development: Birth to adulthood.* New York: Academic Press.

Collins, A. M., & Loftus, E. F. (1975). A spreading-activation theory of semantic processing. *Psychological Review, 82,* 407–428.

Collins, A. M., & Quillian, M. R. (1969). Retrieval time from semantic memory. *Journal of Verbal Learning and Verbal Behavior, 8,* 240–248.

Daneman, M., & Carpenter, P. A. (1980). Individual differences in working memory and reading. *Journal of Verbal Learning and Verbal Behavior, 19,* 450–466.

Darwin, G. J., Turvey, M. T., & Crowder, R. G. (1972). An auditory analogue of the Sperling partial report procedure: Evidence for brief auditory storage. *Cognitive Psychology, 3,* 255–267.

Derry, S. J. (1984). Effects of an organizer on memory for prose. *Journal of Educational Psychology, 76,* 98–107.

Gagné, E. D. (1985). *The cognitive psychology of school learning.* Boston: Little, Brown.

Glover, J. A., Ronning, R. R., & Bruning, R. H. (1990). *Cognitive psychology for teachers.* New York: Macmillan.

Howard, R. W. (1987). *Concepts and schemata.* London: Cassell.

Huttenlocher, J. (1968). Constructing spatial images: A strategy in reasoning. *Psychological Review, 75,* 550–560.

Just, M. A., & Carpenter, P. A. (1987). *The psychology of reading and language comprehension.* Boston: Allyn & Bacon.

Kahneman, D. (1973). *Attention and effort.* New York: Prentice-Hall.

Kintsch, W. (1988). The role of knowledge in discourse comprehension: A construction integration model. *Psychological Review, 95,* 163–182.

Klatzky, R. L. (1980). *Human memory* (2nd ed.). New York: Freeman.

Klatzky, R. L. (1984). *Memory and awareness.* New York: Freeman.

Koffka, K. (1933). *Principles of Gestalt psychology.* New York: Harcourt Brace Jovanovich.

Kosslyn, S. (1978). Imagery and cognitive development. In R. S. Siegler (Ed.), *Children's thinking: What develops?* Hillsdale, NJ: Erlbaum.

Kosslyn, S. (1985). Mental imagery ability. In R. J. Sternberg (Ed.), *Human abilities: An information processing approach* (pp. 151–172). New York: Freeman.

Kyllonen, P. C., & Christal, R. E. (1990). Reasoning ability is (little more than) working memory capacity. *Intelligence, 14,* 389–433.

Kyllonen, P. C., & Stephens, D. L. (1990). Cognitive abilities as determinants of success in acquiring logic skill. *Learning and Individual Differences, 2,* 129–160.

Mayer, R. E. (1983). Can you repeat that? Qualitative and quantitative effects of repetition and advance organizers on learning from science prose. *Journal of Educational Psychology, 75,* 40–49.

Mayer, R. E. (1984a). Aids to prose comprehension. *Educational Psychologist, 19,* 30–42.

Mayer, R. E. (1984b). Twenty-five years of research on advance organizers. *Instructional Science, 8,* 133–169.

Meudell, P. R. (1971). Retrieval and representation in long-term memory. *Psychonomic Science, 23,* 295–296.

Nussbaum, J. (1979). Children's conceptions of the earth as a cosmic body: A cross-age study. *Science Education, 63,* 83–93.

Paivio, A. (1979). *Imagery and verbal processes.* Hillsdale, NJ: Erlbaum.

Roth, I., & Frisby, J. P. (1986). *Perception and representation.* Philadelphia: Open Press.

Rumelhart, D. E. (1980). Schemata: The building blocks of cognition. In R. J. Spiro, B. C. Bruce, & W. F. Brewer (Eds.), *Theoretical issues in reading comprehension.* Hillsdale, NJ: Erlbaum.

Rumelhart, D. E. (1984). Understanding understanding. In J. Flood (Ed.), *Comprehension.* Newark, DE: International Reading Association.

Rumelhart, D. E., & Ortony, A. (1977). The representation of knowledge in memory. In R. C. Anderson, R. J. Spiro, & W. E. Montague (Eds.), *Schooling and the acquisition of knowledge.* Hillsdale, NJ: Erlbaum.

Sperling, G. (1960). The information available in brief visual presentations. *Psychological Monographs, 74* (Whole No. 498).

Tulving, E. (1983). *Elements of episodic memory.* Oxford: Oxford University Press.

4

INFORMATION PROCESSING THEORY II: REMEMBERING

OBJECTIVES

1. Identify encoding activities that are instances of deep processing. Identify instances of shallow processing.
2. Distinguish between maintenance and elaborative rehearsal.
3. Identify one instance each of an elaboration strategy, an organizational strategy, and a mnemonic strategy.
4. Describe the principle of encoding specificity and its implications for teaching and test construction.
5. Describe three metacognitive skills involved in remembering.
6. Describe five out of eight essential ingredients of effective strategy instruction.
7. Identify the position of information processing theory on the core issues.

In our discussion of input processing in Chapter 3, we saw that representations in long-term memory are activated and processed to produce perceptions and comprehensions that are temporarily stored in working memory. Now we are ready to address the issue of how new information is added to long-term memory. In fact, remembering what we perceive and comprehend is what most people consider to be the primary function of the information processing system. There are three kinds of processes involved in remembering: encoding, retrieving, and metamemory. This last process helps us decide which encoding and retrieval processes to use on particular tasks. Let's consider encoding processes first.

ENCODING PROCESSES

Encoding means placing new information into long-term memory. We are already familiar with the first stage of encoding, which is perceiving and comprehending a stimulus input. Remember how this involved analyzing stimulus features and activating schema(s) in long-term memory? Now, when a schema is so activated and is "in" working memory, a memory for the perceived input is formed in long-term memory. The long-term memory consists of a copy of the activated schema plus environmental information that was fitted into the schema's slots (Rumelhart, 1980). For example, you are introduced to a stranger at a party. Your *face* schema is activated, enabling you to perceive the incoming visual sensations. Later you can recognize your new acquaintance when you meet him on the street because during perception, a copy of the *face* schema containing the unique components of his face was stored in your long-term memory.

Thus, memories are formed as a by-product of perception. It is well to remember that such memories are not simply copies of the environmental stimulus. Rather, memories for experienced events are our interpretations of those events and contain embellishments and inferences. (Remember the inferences that went into your perception of even a simple stimulus like the cube!) Memories are also formed as a by-product of the comprehension process. As we read text or listen to conversations we use our activated schemas to make inferences and elaborations. (Remember Rocky!) As we know now, the initial processes of perception and comprehension (up to the point of pattern recognition) are pretty much automatic, requiring very little mental effort or attention. However, there are many information processing theorists who believe that unless further, more effortful, encoding activities are carried out in working memory, the long-term memory for the material will not be very strong. In addition to being effortful, encoding activities that result in strong memories must deal with the meaning or semantic features of the material.

Question 4.1: We will describe a memory experiment and see if you can predict the outcome. This experiment uses an incidental memory task—subjects are not told that their memory for the material will be tested. One group of subjects listens to a list of words and is instructed to think of a rhyming word for each word in the list. Another group listens to the same words, but instead of rhymes, its members are asked to think of an appropriate adjective if the word is a noun, or an appropriate noun if the word is an adjective. After both groups finish their task, they are given a surprise test in which they are asked to recall as many words on the list as possible.

Which group will have better recall? Why do you think so? (Please answer and then turn to the end of the chapter.)_____

_____

_____

Depth of Processing

Craik and Lockhart (1972) developed a framework for thinking about how different kinds of encoding activities affect memory. In their perspective, memory critically depends upon what learners do as they interact with new information. If students are engaged in activities that require them to focus on the meaning or semantic base of the new information (*deep processing* in Craik and Lockhart's terms), then memory for the material will be better than if students engage in activities that focus on the superficial, surface aspects of the material (shallow processing). Examples of classroom tasks that require deep processing include telling students to read an essay so that they can tell about it in their own words; having students demonstrate addition and subtraction facts using manipulatives; having students predict the outcome of a science demonstration.

Question 4.2: What activities might result in shallow processing when reading an essay, learning addition and subtraction facts, and learning a science principle?

Effortful Processing

In general, effective encoding activities require students to make more difficult or effortful decisions while learning. Effortful decisions are presumed to result in more distinctive memories (Jacoby & Craik, 1979). For example, Glover and his associates (Glover, Bruning, & Plake, 1982; Glover, Plake, & Zimmer, 1982) have conducted research designed to determine how student decision-making during reading affected recall. First, these studies show that requiring students to make decisions about what they read results in better recall than not requiring decisions. The difficulty level of the decisions was varied by using the taxonomy of learning outcomes created by Bloom and his associates (Bloom, Englehart, Furst, Hill, & Krathwohl, 1956). This taxonomy distinguishes between lower levels of learning (i.e., knowledge, comprehension) in which facts, concepts, and rules are learned and understood, and higher-level learning outcomes (i.e., application, analysis, synthesis, and evaluation) in which knowledge is used and transformed. Students' recall improved as they moved from simpler, less difficult, decisions at the lower level of the taxonomy to more complex and more difficult decisions at the upper end. Thus, if we want students to retain more of the instructional material that they need, one approach is to require them to make decisions (or answer questions) while interacting with the material (note the questions and exercises in this book). In general, more difficult and complex decisions and questions result in better retention.

Elaboration of Processing

In general, the more effortful a semantic encoding activity is, the more it requires the learner to elaborate upon the meaning of the material; the more semantic elaboration, the better the retention (Anderson & Reder, 1979; Craik & Tulving,

1975). One way to increase semantic elaboration is to provide learners with a richer, more elaborate, context. This approach is illustrated by one of the experiments in Craik and Tulving's (1975) study. College students were given a semantic judgment task in which they determined whether a word would fit into a sentence frame. There were three levels of sentence complexity: simple (e.g., She cooked the _____.), medium (e.g., The ripe _____ tasted delicious.), and complex (e.g., The small lady angrily picked up the red _____.). For half of the judgments, the words fitted the sentence frames and for half they did not. After completing 60 judgments, subjects were asked to recall as many words as they could. They were then shown the original sentence frames and asked to recall the word associated with each sentence. This latter test is called cued recall because students could use the sentences as retrieval cues. The results showed that students' recall of the words increased with the complexity of the original sentence frames. This was true for both cued and noncued recall tests. However, the more elaborate code was not effective if the word did not fit the sentence. This finding suggests that the elaboration must be consistent with the meaning of the word in order to be effective.

Elaboration appears to be especially effective when it helps to tie new information together.

Question 4.3: Suppose we asked you to read a series of sentences involving a particular kind of man and a particular kind of activity. For example:

The fat man read the sign.
The hungry man got into the car.

Suppose also that we elaborated the sentences by adding phrases to them. Sometimes the phrases were like the following:

The fat man read the sign warning him about the thin ice.
The hungry man got into the car to go to the restaurant.

Other times the phrases were like the following:

The fat man read the sign that was two feet high.
The hungry man got into the car and drove away.

Then, we tested your memory by giving you the sentences with blanks in place of the adjectives "fat" and "hungry." Which type of elaboration (first set or second set) do you think would help you to recall more? Why?_____

_____

_____

Elaborate processing requires encoding the same material in different but related ways. As you semantically elaborate upon the material, you are linking the to-be-learned material with more and more of the knowledge that is already in your long-term memory. This facilitates memory for the material in a couple of ways. First, it makes the material more accessible by providing more ways or routes for retrieving the material. Second, elaboration may help learners to infer what the information was likely to have been when the information itself cannot be recalled (Anderson, 1985).

Effortful encoding activities are usually what teachers have in mind when they use the term "learning strategies." The above discussion of encoding processes provides criteria for evaluating the potential effectiveness of a learning strategy. In general, the most effective strategies require students to deal with the meaning of the material. Additionally, as the semantic decisions that are required by a strategy increase in difficulty, memory improves. Finally, strategies that require elaborate encodings lead to much better memory than strategies that result in sparse or redundant encodings. Let's examine some learning or encoding strategies with these criteria in mind.

Encoding Strategies

A **cognitive strategy** is any conscious mental activity that can be deliberately undertaken to achieve a cognitive goal. Everyday school examples of cognitive goals include reading and understanding a passage, solving for the unknown variable in an equation, remembering a list of vocabulary words. There are as many types of cognitive strategies as there are cognitive goals. However, some major categories of cognitive strategies include text-comprehension strategies, problem-solving strategies, and strategies for remembering information. We shall deal with this last category here. Problem-solving strategies will be discussed in Chapter 5, while comprehension and other cognitive and metacognitive strategies will be covered later in this chapter and in Chapter 7.

Rehearsal　The strategy of rehearsal always involves the notion of recycling through the material and usually involves subvocalizing (i.e., repeating the material over and over to oneself). One type of rehearsal, **maintenance rehearsal** (Craik, 1979), utilizes only these two components. The cognitive goal of this type of rehearsal is to keep material active in working memory. This is the type of rehearsal used when we look up a telephone number and want to remember it just long enough to dial it (for example, repeating 749-7343 over and over to oneself until the number is dialed). Research indicates that this is a highly efficient way to hold information in consciousness for a short time without producing very good long-term retention (Bjork, 1975; Klatzky, 1984). Sometimes our cognitive goal is simply to hold onto certain information until we no longer need it. We don't want to clutter up our long-term memory with telephone numbers that we seldom use, for example. Maintenance rehearsal is also useful in problem-solving tasks in which we need to keep certain information available in working memory only long enough to solve the problem. Mathematical word problems provide a common school example.

However, if our cognitive goal is to retain the rehearsed information in long-term memory, we need to employ another type of rehearsal called elaborative rehearsal. **Elaborative rehearsal** is recycling of the to-be-remembered material in such a way that it is related to other information (Craik, 1979). For example, one could subvocalize the telephone number 749-7343 while noticing that 49 is the square of 7 and 343 is the cube of 7. Or one could personalize the number by relating parts of it to other, well-known, numbers such as one's social security number or birthdate. For example, one could notice while rehearsing that 749 corresponds to the month, July, and year, 1949, that one was born. With young children rhyme and rhythm can be used in elaborative rehearsal (as in the alphabet example in Chapter 3). However, as we now know, forms of elaborative rehearsal that entail semantic relations with other material will be more effective than forms based upon more surface characteristics.

Elaboration   Elaboration does not occur only as part of rehearsal. More generally, **elaboration** is the process of *adding to* the information being learned. The addition could be an inference, an example, a detail, an image, or any other mental construction. It may seem paradoxical that adding more information makes something easier to remember, but that is the case. As we saw earlier, effective elaborations tie together the to-be-learned material and relate it to knowledge already in long-term memory. Elaboration was first studied in the context of paired-associate learning tasks. To find out what a paired-associate task is, do Exercise 4.1. By the way, is it possible that you are *not doing the exercises and questions?* Are you skipping them altogether or just reading them and not attempting to answer them? If so, you are cheating yourself of valuable learning experiences, not to mention lots of fun. Enough said (for now).

Exercise 4.1: Study the following pairs of items for two minutes, and then *with the list covered* take the test which requires you to recall the second item in each pair when given the first item. Following recall, turn to the end of the chapter for an explanation.

Study List

Pencil—Soldier	Cow—Ball	Hammer—Cup
Window—Desk	Giraffe—Watch	Tree—Picture
Duck—Leaf	Chimney—Rock	Fence—Rug
Bucket—Pillow	Lamp—Apple	Monkey—Cowboy

Recall Test

Write in the word that was paired with each word.

Fence _____	Lamp _____	Chimney _____
Giraffe _____	Hammer _____	Tree _____
Duck _____	Monkey _____	Cow _____
Pencil _____	Window _____	Bucket _____

Paired-associate learning is an important variety of learning that occurs in school and, thus, has been extensively studied in educational research. Examples of school-learning tasks involving paired associates include learning the names of the letters of the alphabet, learning the names of new objects, learning the definitions of new vocabulary words, and learning the capitals of the states. Research indicates that some (but certainly not all) high-school and college-age students spontaneously use visual and verbal elaborations to learn paired associates (Pressley, Levin, & Bryant, 1983; Rohwer, 1973). Older elementary students do not use elaboration spontaneously, but can create both verbal and visual elaborations (at least with concrete materials) when so instructed and thereby improve their recall. Kindergarten and first-grade students can use elaborations that are provided by the teacher but should not be expected to generate them on their own (Levin & Kaplan, 1972; Reese, 1977; Rohwer, 1973). Incidentally, if you do not know precisely what the term "visual and verbal elaborations" means as used in this paragraph, you *did* skip the exercise. Why don't you go back and do it now—we'll wait for you.

Elaboration has also been studied in the more complex context of learning facts and concepts from text and lessons. Many studies have indicated that getting students to elaborate while reading and studying text aids retention (E. Gagné, 1985; Reder, 1982). Encouraging students to explain an idea in their own words or to relate new information to a familiar, concrete situation increases the chances of elaboration and benefits retention. For example, Mayer (1980) asked college students to read a manual on computer programming in which one programming command was described on each page. After reading each page, some students were asked to explain the command in their own words and relate it to a concrete, familiar situation (elaboration group). Other students read each page without elaborating. Students in the elaboration group recalled more conceptual information from the booklet and performed better on problem-solving tasks that involved applying commands to new tasks as compared with the nonelaborating students.

Implications for Teaching   Teachers can enhance elaboration by asking students to draw pictures of the material they are learning, summarize part of a text or lesson in their own words, and produce their own examples of new concepts. Using metaphors and analogies when teaching new concepts can be beneficial, especially if students are helped to elaborate on the relationship between the familiar concept and the new concept (Hayes & Tierney, 1982). For example, in a lesson on the American revolution it could be explicitly pointed out how a *revolution* is like a *volcano.* However, in order for analogies and metaphors to be useful, students must be familiar with the analogous material. One way to select familiar analogies is to ask your students to produce their own metaphors and analogies. This approach has been found to help Hispanic fifth-grade children's recall and comprehension of stories (Linden & Wittrock, 1981). Finally, students can be asked to make inferences to extend the concepts being learned. For example, if learning about revolutions, students could be asked which nations are likely candidates for future revolutions and why (Howard, 1987).

To summarize, elaboration is a powerful encoding strategy for enhancing long-term memory for material. As you may have surmised from the above examples, elaboration is a broad category of strategies encompassing many specific and diverse techniques.

Question 4.4: Many study strategies familiar to teachers, such as summarizing, note taking, generating inferences, asking and answering questions, and generating images are potentially but not necessarily elaborative strategies. In order to qualify as true elaborative strategies such activities must have what two attributes?

_____

_____

_____

Organization   In addition to elaborating upon the material to be learned by thinking of related ideas, examples, images, or details, students can optimize their learning and retention by **organizing** the material. Organization is a process in which material is divided into subsets, and the relations within and between subsets are noted.

Exercise 4.2: Study the list of words given below for one half-minute and then, _with the words covered,_ write down as many of them as you can recall. Turn to the end of the chapter for your memory rating.

Study List

Schema, Contiguity, Schedule, Encoding, Salivation,
Neutral Stimulus, Reward, Chunk, Generalization,
Proposition, Operant, Punishment

Recall

_____

_____

_____

Organization has been studied in situations like that illustrated in Exercise 4.2, where subjects are given lists of items to learn which have some apparent organization. Subjects' recall is then examined to determine whether they used the categories to organize their recall. This materials-induced organization assumes of course that subjects are familiar with the categories in the list. The results from such studies consistently show that organization enhances recall (e.g., Bousfield, 1953; Jenkins & Russell, 1952; Reitman & Rueter, 1980).

Materials-induced organization has also been studied with narrative prose (Thorndyke, 1977) and expository text (Meyer, 1977). These studies indicate that when reading material is well organized, students recall more of the information than when organization is poor. Moreover, Glynn and DiVesta (1977) found that providing college students with a topical outline to study before they read a passage about various kinds of minerals enhanced their recall of details from the passage when they were compared with a group not receiving the outline.

Implications for Teaching   In addition to presenting material that is well organized or providing students with outlines, teachers can teach students to organize the material. In fact, *getting students to organize and elaborate on their own should be a conscious instructional goal,* because in real life they will often encounter materials that are not well organized or elaborated. Instructing students to outline the material while studying will improve retention, especially if students are required to generate an organization that is *different from* the organization in the text (Shimmerlick & Nolan, 1976). Apparently, reorganizing the material requires more mental effort than simply using the organizational structure given in the material.

Outlining is a good organizational strategy which many teachers attempt to teach students. **Outlining** techniques require students to identify the main ideas in the material and then decide how they are related. In traditional outlines the only kind of relation is subordination of one topic to another. Recently, researchers have developed techniques for organizing expository prose that go beyond the traditional outline. For example, Dansereau and associates (Dansereau, 1978; Holley, Dansereau, McDonald, Garland, & Collins, 1979) have developed a technique called **concept mapping,** which utilizes spatial organization of ideas based upon a variety of links between them. For example, one idea may be a *part of* another idea, or one idea may *lead to* another idea, and so on. Figure 4.1 shows a concept map derived from a chapter on wounds in a nursing textbook.

Holly et al. (1979) provided college students with 5½ hours of training on a hierarchical mapping technique. Following training, the students used the technique to study a 3,000-word passage taken from a geology text. A control group simply read the passage. Five days later, all subjects took four tests: essay, concept cloze, multiple-choice, and short-answer. The experimental group outperformed the control group on the combined concept cloze and essay scores, both of which were designed to tap main ideas. There was no difference between the groups on the combined multiple-choice and short-answer scores, both of which were designed to tap details. Further analysis indicated that the technique was most beneficial for low-ability college students. This approach probably would benefit high-school and junior-college students as well (see Lambiotte, Dansereau, Cross, & Reynolds, 1989, for a review of research on concept mapping).

Other researchers have taken the approach of identifying the organizational structures most frequently found in expository textbooks and then teaching students to recognize these structures (Cook, 1982; Meyer, Brandt, & Bluth, 1980). For example, Cook (1982) trained college students to recognize prose structures that are found in science textbooks (i.e., *generalization, enumeration, sequence, classification, and compare/contrast*). When compared with a control (no training) group, students who received the training recalled more high-level information from science passages. Apparently, knowing about text structures makes it easier for students to form a coherent mental organization for new material.

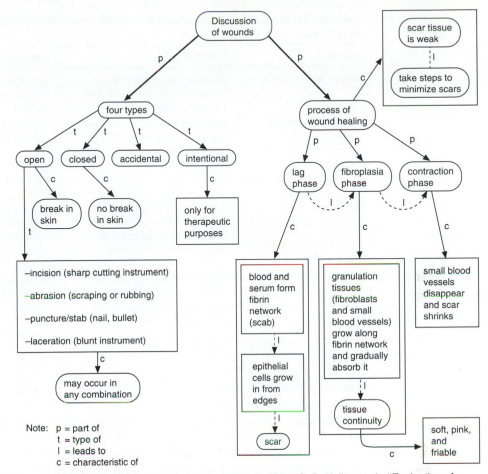

FIGURE 4.1   A concept map of a chapter from a nursing textbook. (From C. D. Holley et al., "Evaluation of a Hierarchical Mapping Technique as an Aid to Prose Processing," in *Contemporary Educational Psychology*, vol. 4, pp. 227-237, © 1979. Used by permission of Academic Press and the author,1979.)

To summarize, organization, like elaboration, is a broad category that includes many specific strategies, ranging from grouping words into categories to generating complex networks of ideas. All specific organizational techniques have in common the goal of improving long-term retention by grouping and relating the subparts of the to-be-learned material. Teachers can stimulate organization by being sure the material they present is coherently organized and by teaching students to organize materials on their own. Table 4.1 summarizes the encoding strategies we have discussed thus far.

Mnemonics   Mnemonics are very precise strategies for helping people remember information (Bellezza, 1981). In general, mnemonics work by relating unknown information to well-learned information. In other words, *we can view mnemonics as specific instances of elaboration.* We treat them as a separate

TABLE 4.1   SUMMARY OF REHEARSAL, ELABORATION, AND ORGANIZATION ENCODING STRATEGIES

Strategy	Function	Examples
Maintenance rehearsal	Recycling/subvocalization information in order to keep it in consciousness	Verbatim repetition of spelling words; repeating a telephone number
Elaborative rehearsal	Recycling information while relating it to other information in order to add the material to long-term memory	Repeating the spelling of a word while relating it to other words you already know; repeating a telephone number while relating it to your birthdate
Elaboration	Adding to the information being learned in order to tie it to familiar material and thus make it more memorable	Forming an image relating a state and its capital; drawing a picture of material in a text; using analogies and metaphors
Organization	Dividing the material into subsets and noting the relations between them in order to enhance memorability of the material	Grouping vocabulary words into superordinate categories; outlining; creating spatial networks showing relations between concepts in a text

category of encoding strategies because of their specific nature and because the study of mnemonics is an honored tradition dating back at least to the ancient Greeks. In this section, we will describe some mnemonic techniques that may be helpful in the classroom.

Many of the most familiar mnemonics utilize **rhymes** (*i before e except after c*) or **poems** (*thirty days hath September, April, June, and November . . .*). **Physical tags** are another common mnemonic. For example, to remember the number of days in each month, make a fist and then label the knuckle above the little finger on the left hand "January." The space between this and the next knuckle is labeled "February," the next knuckle is labeled "March," the next space, "April," and so forth in sequence—see Figure 4.2. The months that occupy knuckles all have 31 days; the months assigned to spaces have 30 days (except, of course, for February).

Many memory tricks used in the classroom are variations on **first-letter mnemonics** in which the first letters of items to be remembered are used to form a phrase (e.g., **E**very **g**ood **b**oy **d**oes **f**ine can be used to remember the lines of the treble clef) or a word (e.g., **FACE** stands for the spaces of the treble clef). Other examples are **Roy G. Biv,** which stands for the colors of the spectrum, and **HOMES,** which stands for the great lakes—Huron, Ontario, Michigan, Erie, and Superior. You can create first-letter mnemonics to remember lists of items such as a grocery list. For example, you could formulate the word "camera" in order to remember the list consisting of *cheese, apples, milk, eggs, raisins,* and *artichokes.* Although many students report making use of first-letter mnemonics (Boltwood & Blick,

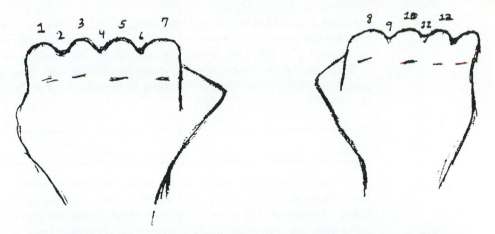

FIGURE 4.2   Physical mnemonic for remembering number of days in each month: 1 = January, 2 = February, etc. Months on knuckles have 31 days. Months between knuckles have 30 days. (Drawing by Freddie Ghatala, age 12.)

1978), there has been very little research on their effectiveness. Our best advice is that if a particular first-letter mnemonic can be easily formulated for the to-be-remembered material, it can be pointed out to students as a potential aid to their memory.

A very well-researched and effective mnemonic strategy for remembering lists of items is called the **peg method.**

Exercise 4.3: To use the peg method you first need to memorize the following simple rhymes. Please study and commit them to memory.

One is a bun
Two is a shoe
Three is a tree
Four is a door
Five is a hive
Six is a stick
Seven is heaven
Eight is a gate
Nine is a line
Ten is a hen

Now that you know the pegs you can use them to "hang" things on. Let's take a grocery list consisting of:

apples, bread, celery, milk, cereal, detergent,
ice cream, and butter.

For each item on the list create a visual image of it interacting with one of the pegs. For example, visualize an apple between the two halves of a large hamburger bun. See a loaf of bread stuffed into a shoe. Mentally hang bunches of celery from the limbs of a tree. Continue until you have each item visually connected to one of the pegs. It should take only a few seconds to form each image.

To recall the list, mentally run through the rhymes and "see" each item on its peg. Write the grocery list here without looking back at it and then check your score at the end of the chapter.

_____

_____

The peg method has been shown to be effective in learning lists of various kinds (Bugelski, Kidd, & Segmen, 1968). Glover and his colleagues have done extensive research that shows that the method is effective for remembering things other than lists. Examples include written and oral directions (Glover, Harvey, & Corkill, 1986; Glover, Timme, Deyloff, Rogers, & Dinnel, 1987) and steps in complex procedures (Glover, Timme, Deyloff, & Rogers, 1987). These latter applications take advantage of the fact that the peg system can be used to preserve the temporal order or sequence of items on a list if that information is important. In sum, the peg system is very effective and it can be taught to students easily. In our experience, students enjoy learning and using this mnemonic system although they will have to be reminded to use it initially.

In Chapter 3 we described the **method of loci,** which is a mnemonic strategy dating back to the ancient Greeks (Yates, 1966). This method compares well to the peg method for memorizing lists of items and their sequence. Both the peg and loci methods require that the "hooks" (the rhymes in the peg system and the locations in the method of loci) be perfectly memorized and that imagery links be formed between the items and the hooks. This requires some expenditure of time and effort, and sometimes students resist the methods on these grounds. However, in our experience, if they can be motivated to learn them, most students report that they are worth the effort.

One of the most powerful and well-researched mnemonic techniques is the **key-word method.** Originally devised as a method for foreign language vocabulary learning (Atkinson & Raugh, 1975), the technique has been extended by Levin, Pressley, and their associates to many other situations. The method involves two steps, which we will illustrate for learning that the Spanish word "carta" means "letter" in English. The first step is forming the *acoustic link* between the foreign word and a familiar (and concrete) English word. That is, the unknown word is associated with an English "key word" that sounds like part of it. For example, the Spanish word "carta" can be linked to the English word "cart." This link is easy to learn because of the acoustic similarity between the key word and the foreign word. The next step is forming an *imagery link* that combines the key word with the translation of the foreign word. For example, the learner could imagine a postal letter in a shopping cart (see Figure 4.3). After learning these linkages, whenever the learner sees or hears the word "carta" he will think of "cart" which will activate the image from which he can retrieve the translation, "letter."

In an experiment in which college students were given 15 minutes to learn 60

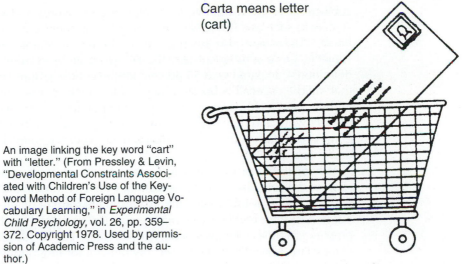

Carta means letter
(cart)

FIGURE 4.3   An image linking the key word "cart" with "letter." (From Pressley & Levin, "Developmental Constraints Associated with Children's Use of the Key-word Method of Foreign Language Vocabulary Learning," in *Experimental Child Psychology*, vol. 26, pp. 359–372. Copyright 1978. Used by permission of Academic Press and the author.)

Spanish to English vocabulary pairs, one group was given pretraining in using the key-word method and was provided with key words. Sample pairs with key words in parentheses included "charo" (charcoal) "puddle"; "gusano" (goose) "worm"; "nabo" (knob) "turnip". The control group was given the same amount of time to learn the same pairs and was also provided with the key words. These subjects were instructed to rehearse the pairs. On the test, which required subjects to write the English word when given the Spanish word, the key-word group scored 88 percent, compared with 28 percent for the control group. These results have been replicated with college students learning Russian vocabulary (Atkinson & Raugh, 1975; Raugh & Atkinson, 1975).

Such experiments suggest that the key-word method is much more effective for college students than is the frequently used rehearsal or recitation method. It is likely that these benefits would also hold for high-school-age foreign-language learners. The method seems to work best for this age group when the instructor provides the key word and the learner provides the image. However, Pressley and Levin (1978) and Pressley (1977) have found that elementary-school-age children have difficulty in generating appropriate images even when they have been trained to do so. These authors suggest that with children, the teacher needs to provide the key words *and* images.

One way to adapt the key-word technique for younger children is illustrated by Levin, McCormick, Miller, Berry, and Pressley (1982), who used the method to teach fourth-grade students English vocabulary words such as "celebrate," "gesture," "hesitate," and "persuade." The key-word group learned a key word for each of the vocabulary words. The key word sounded like part of the unknown word, e.g., "purse" for the word "persuade." Then the experimental subjects were given pictures showing the key word interacting with the definition of the vocabulary word, such as a woman being *persuaded* to buy a purse. At the bottom of the picture, the word's formal definition was given (see Figure 4.4). The control subjects were given training in recognizing the words and were provided with sentences such as "The lady's friend was trying to persuade her to buy a pocketbook." They were also given the same formal definitions as the experimental subjects. On a subsequent test, the key-word group recalled 83 percent of the definitions compared with 55 percent for the control group. These results indicate that children's recall is boosted by providing pictures that connect the key word and definition. However, it seems to be important that the pictures include both the key word and the vocabulary word since it was found that conditions which eliminated either of these elements from the picture resulted in diminished recall (Levin et al., 1982).

While studies of the key-word method with elementary-school-age children support the conclusion that it substantially increases vocabulary learning, the fact that the teacher must provide the images in the form of pictures is a drawback in our minds, since regular usage may require too much of a teacher's already scarce preparation time. Perhaps teachers could create key words and pictures only for vocabulary words that seem especially difficult for most children to remember.

FIGURE 4.4   Key-word picture for learning the definition of "persuade." (From Levin, McCormick, Miller, Berry, & Pressley, "Mnemonic versus Nonmnemonic Vocabulary Learning Strategies for Children" in *American Educational Research Journal,* vol. 19, pp. 121–136, Figure 1. Copyright 1982 by the American Educational Research Association. Reprinted by permission.)

On the other hand, teachers might try the following modified version of the method, which does not require students to generate interacting images. In a study by Pressley, Levin, and McCormick (1980), elementary-school children learned key words for Spanish words, and then experimental subjects were instructed:

The Spanish word _____ sounds like _____ (key word) and means _____. Make up a sentence in your head about a _____ (key word) and a _____ (translation) doing something together in order to remember the meaning of _____ (Spanish word).

The control children were told:

The Spanish word _____ means _____. Try hard to remember that the Spanish word _____ means _____.

Both groups spent the same amount of time learning; however, on a subsequent test the experimental subjects remembered 72 percent of the words while the control subjects remembered only 27 percent. Thus, this version of the key-word method, which appears easier for teachers to implement (they provide only key words), does seem to facilitate vocabulary learning in younger (second grade) and older (fifth grade) elementary students. We would bet that this particular version could be adapted to learning English vocabulary words as well as foreign vocabulary.

There is evidence that the key-word method can be successfully adapted to a variety of school tasks. For example, the method works well for memorizing medical terminology, functions of various biochemicals, cities and their products, famous people and their accomplishments, states and capitals, and the U.S. presidents in order of their terms (Levin, 1981).

Since vocabulary acquisition is a major task in school, especially during the elementary grades, teachers should be ready to try encoding strategies such as the key-word method that have been shown to work in numerous controlled studies. Moreover, because the key-word strategy can be adapted to various school tasks, its mastery seems well worth the time and effort. Table 4.2 summarizes the various mnemonic strategies we have discussed.

Implications for Teaching   Mnemonics are specific procedures for making material more memorable. They are instances of elaboration because they add information (often rhymes and visual images) that ties the to-be-learned material together and relates it to what we already know. Mnemonics are specifically tailored for memorizing certain kinds of information. For example, the peg method and the method of loci are primarily useful for remembering lists of items in a particular order. The key-word method is useful for remembering associations between items, and although it has typically been used in learning foreign and English vocabulary, it will work wherever one can derive acoustic and imagery links between two stimuli. We recommend that teachers use mnemonics as an adjunct to instruction and that they teach students to use them where appropriate.

TABLE 4.2   SUMMARY OF MNEMONIC TECHNIQUES

Technique	Description	Uses
First-letter mnemonics	The first letters of items to be remembered are used to form a phrase or word	Remembering sequence of items or list of items
Peg method	Numbers 1–10 are associated with rhyming words (one is a bun, two is a shoe . . .); each item to be remembered is then imaged interacting with one of the pegs (a bottle of milk dancing with a bun)	Remembering lists such as grocery items or errands; also useful for remembering temporal or spatial sequences, as in directions or steps in a complex procedure
Method of loci	Items to be remembered are linked with distinct landmarks along a familiar route	Remembering the key points in a speech, lists of items
Key-word method	The first item to be learned is linked with a familiar word to which it is acoustically similar; this key word is then linked to the second item to be learned by means of an image or sentence	Remembering the English translations of foreign words; definitions of English words; technical vocabulary; states and capitals; presidents and their terms

Students who know how to execute specific mnemonics and who also know how to use other elaboration and organization strategies have the potential to become independent learners. To realize this potential, they need other kinds of knowledge which we will discuss a little later in this chapter under the topic of metacognition.

RETRIEVAL PROCESSES

Remembering depends upon more than encoding. In order to remember something that we have stored in long-term memory, we have to be able to retrieve it. **Retrieval** is the process of accessing information in long-term memory and placing it in short-term memory. Remember that in information processing theory, to ''place'' information in short-term memory simply means to bring it into consciousness. Actually we have really already discussed some aspects of retrieval, since pattern recognition (perception) is a form of retrieval. The retrieval involved in perception (e.g., recognizing a stimulus as a cat or recognizing the word ''cat'') is extremely rapid and largely automatic. Here we will elaborate on more effortful forms of retrieval that are involved in remembering previously encoded information.

Retrieval Cues

The act of retrieval begins with some sort of cue. A **retrieval cue** is a stimulus that initiates a search for some representation in long-term memory. The more effective the retrieval cue, the better will be retrieval. *In general, to be effective a cue must be present both at encoding and at retrieval.* This characteristic of memory is called **encoding specificity.**

Question 4.5: We will describe an experiment by Tulving and Osler (1968). See if you can predict the results based upon encoding specificity.

One group of subjects learned a list of 24 words. A second group learned the same list, but each of the 24 to-be-learned words was paired with a weak associate (e.g., "boy"-"child"). Then at the time of testing, each group was divided into two groups, one that received the weak associates as retrieval cues and one that did not get retrieval cues. Thus, there were four groups:

Group 1: Learned with associates, tested with associates.
Group 2: Learned with associates, tested without associates.
Group 3: Learned without associates, tested with associates.
Group 4: Learned without associates, tested without associates.

Rank-order the groups from best to worst in terms of recall performance on the

test, and then check your answer._____

_____

The phenomenon of encoding specificity has been demonstrated so often and with so many different types of materials that it is recognized as a basic principle of memory performance. The principle of encoding specificity means that encouraging students to generate elaborations (as in Group 2 in Question 4.5) will not enhance memory for the material unless the elaborations are somehow reinstated on the test. On the other hand, activating related knowledge at the time of the test (as in Group 3) will not enhance performance if that knowledge was not also activated during encoding.

Types of Memory Tests

Suppose your instructor announces a quiz on the material in this chapter. Would it make a difference in how you studied if you knew that the quiz would consist of multiple-choice questions rather than essay questions? It would for most students. Students who expect a **recall test** such as an essay exam prepare by focusing on the organization of the material, by relating important ideas, and by practicing recall of the material. Students expecting a **recognition test** such as a multiple-choice exam prepare by becoming familiar with the material and discriminating items from each other so that they can pick out relevant information from distractors on the test (Kintsch, 1986). Students report studying harder for essay tests than for recognition tests. This makes good sense because laboratory studies indicate that recognition is easier than recall (Kintsch, 1970).

Given these differences in preparation, it is not surprising that students who receive the type of test they expect perform better than students who receive a type of test they do not expect (Carey & Lockhart, 1973; Glover & Corkill, 1987). Apparently, this is another instance of the operation of encoding specificity. The cues generated when studying for a recall test do not match the cues present on a recognition test and vice versa. This is simply more evidence for the importance of context in memory and the fact that memory is enhanced when the contexts of encoding and retrieval are similar.

Reconstructive Processes

The discussion of retrieval thus far may have given you the impression that given the proper retrieval cues, remembering is just a matter of locating the appropriate memory in long-term storage and then reading it off. This view of retrieval is not correct. For one thing it assumes that during encoding a verbatim copy of the stimulus event is stored. We know from our discussion of schemas that this is not the case. Rather, in perception and comprehension we *construct* and store an *interpretation* of a stimulus event, using sense data plus inferences and elaborations drawn from our schemas. Thus, at the time of retrieval, we utilize our schemas to *re*construct our interpretation of the event from fragments in memory. Rumelhart (1980) has drawn the analogy between perception and remembering. *If perception is using a schema to make sense of incoming sense data, then remembering is using a schema to make sense of data from memory.* Much research supports this reconstructive view of remembering and the role of schemas in retrieval (e.g., Carmichael, Hogan, & Walter, 1932; Kardash, Royer, & Greene, 1988; Spiro, 1977).

In one study, subjects were shown a variety of figures (Carmichael, Hogan, & Walter, 1932). One, for example, was a pair of circles connected by a line (see Figure 4.5). One group was told that it was a pair of eyeglasses; another group was told it was a dumbbell; a third group was not given a label for the figure. Later when asked to draw the figures from memory, the group given no labels tended to draw the figure accurately; however the group who were given the eyeglass label tended to draw eyeglasses while those given the dumbbell label drew dumbbells. Thus, the schema activated at the time of learning (and reactivated at the time of retrieval) determined what the groups recalled.

FIGURE 4.5   Sample figure used in Carmichael et al. study.

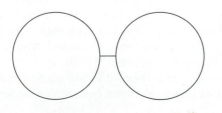

Labels

Eyeglasses   **Dumbbell**

Spiro (1977) asked subjects to read a story and then gave them a new fact that was either consistent or inconsistent with the implications of the story. Later when recalling the story, subjects' memory seemed to be distorted to accommodate the new fact, particularly when that fact contradicted the schema activated to make sense of the story.

Distortions can also be induced into subjects' memories of eyewitnessed events. For example, Loftus and Palmer (1974) showed subjects a film of a car crash. Some were later asked how fast the cars were going when they *smashed* into each other, and others how fast when they *hit* each other. Those given the "smash" wording gave higher estimates of the cars' speed, and even though there was none in the film, "smash" wording subjects were more likely to report having seen broken glass when asked about its presence. Once again, what is recalled is affected by the schema activated at the time of retrieval.

In summary, none of the above research findings supports the notion that retrieval consists of passively "reading out" memories that are copies of stimulus events. The reconstructive view of remembering emphasizes that students construct interpretations of new information based upon existing schemas. Students remember the gist of the encoded material and then use their schemas to reconstruct the information at the time of a test. The exception to this characterization of remembering is verbatim recitation of material that has been rotely memorized (poetry verses, the Pledge of Allegiance, etc.). This type of memory performance is usually more difficult to achieve and often requires effort *not* to assimilate the material to existing schemas that can cause distortions in recall. In contrast, remembering meaningfully learned material is a reconstructive process.

Implications for Teaching

To enhance memory retrieval, teachers need to consider the context of remembering. In general, memory performance will be better if there is a match between cues present at encoding and at retrieval and if there is a rich context for retrieval. Practically, this means that teachers need to encourage students to meaningfully elaborate and organize the material during encoding, using strategies we discussed earlier. This will ensure that many cues are encoded with the material. Then, teachers need to construct tests that provide students with the cues encoded during learning.

Another point is that the context of remembering also consists of the activities that students engaged in to prepare for the test. We have noted that students prepare differently for recognition and recall tests. It is important to give students information about the nature of the test and *deliver the type of test promised.* Finally, teachers who intend that the information acquired by students carry beyond the test must realize that to use information in new contexts (e.g., in "real life" situations and in later educational endeavors), students must retrieve that information given the cues in those contexts. "Teaching for transfer," in the view of information processing theory, means to ensure that information is encoded in many ways and with the widest possible range of cues.

METACOGNITIVE PROCESSES

We have considered processes responsible for getting information into long-term memory (called E _ _ _ _ _ _ _ processes) and the processes responsible for getting information out of long-term memory (called R _ _ _ _ _ _ _ _ processes). Now we can discuss the third set of processes in remembering called metacognitive processes. **Metacognition** refers to one's knowledge about one's thought processes, whereas cognition refers to the thought processes per se. (Flavell (1979, p. 906) defines metacognition as ''that segment of your stored world knowledge that has to do with people as cognitive creatures and with their diverse cognitive tasks, goals, actions, and experiences.'' An example would be Delores's believing that she learns better if she puts the information in her own words than if she repeats it verbatim from the text. Another example would be Ms. Smith's belief that her first graders will learn more easily if she groups similar vocabulary words together for them.

Baker and Brown (1984) distinguish two types of metacognition: (1) knowledge about cognition and (2) regulation of cognition. Knowledge about cognition includes a person's knowledge about his or her own cognitive resources and the compatibility between the person's characteristics as a learner and the learning situation. Baker and Brown believe that knowledge about cognition is stable over time. For example, if Delores believes today that she learns better by putting information into her own words, she is likely to continue to believe that tomorrow and next week. Knowledge about cognition is a form of declarative knowledge in that it can be stated by the learner. Like other forms of declarative knowledge stored in memory, knowledge about cognition may not be accurate. Baker and Brown also believe that knowledge about cognition is late developing and therefore is more complete in the older learner. The second type of metacognition, regulation of cognition, consists of the ''self-regulatory mechanisms used by an active learner during an ongoing attempt to solve problems. These indexes of metacognition include *checking* the outcome of any attempt to solve the problem, *planning* one's next move, *monitoring* the effectiveness of any attempted action, and *testing, revising,* and *evaluating* one's strategies for learning.'' (Baker & Brown, 1984, p. 354). These activities are thought to be unstable because the learner may use them on some occasions and not others. They are forms of procedural knowledge and are rarely statable. Although they are more often used by older children and adults, even young children can regulate their own activities on a simple problem. Table 4.3 summarizes these two types of metacognition.

Metacognition includes knowledge about and regulation of various cognitive processes. For example, knowledge about and regulation of understanding communications is called metacomprehension. In this chapter we will be concerned with knowledge about and regulation of memory, which is called **metamemory** (Flavell & Wellman, 1977). Actually, you exhibited metamemory earlier when you realized that you would study differently for an essay test from the way you would for a multiple-choice test.

Adults have extensive knowledge about their own memory. That is, most adults know that some tasks call for deliberate attempts to remember while other tasks

TABLE 4.3   SUMMARY OF TWO TYPES OF METACOGNITION

Type	Definition	Characteristics
Knowledge about cognition	Knowledge about one's own cognitive resources and their compatibility with the learning situation	Stable over time; can be stated by the learner; may not be accurate; more developed in older learners
Regulation of cognition	Self-regulatory processes used by learners during an ongoing attempt to solve problems; includes planning, checking, monitoring, evaluating	Unstable over time; not statable by learners; relatively independent of learner's age

do not. They also know that some memory tasks are easier for them than others, and they can verbally describe many techniques or strategies for learning and remembering information. All of this knowledge about memory is acquired through experience with various kinds of memory tasks over many years. We would expect, then, that children would know considerably less about memory than do adults, and that is the case (Kail, 1990).

In addition to knowledge about memory, adults have acquired memory regulation skills which enable them to *diagnose* learning tasks, *select* appropriate learning strategies, and *monitor* the effectiveness of those strategies. Once again, children with less experience in the domain of learning have less developed metamemory skills than do adults (Kail, 1990). Let us examine each of these metamemory skills in turn.

Diagnosis

When confronted with a memory task, we adults might begin by forming a rough estimate of the difficulty of the task which, in turn, would help us select an appropriate strategy for achieving our mnemonic goal. In forming this assessment of task difficulty, we would weigh the effects of two classes of variables, those having to do with the characteristics of the to-be-remembered material and those having to do with the nature of the retrieval situation. The characteristics of the material that we would consider are such things as sheer amount of material to be learned (the more information to be learned, the more difficult the task), the familiarity of the material (the more our related knowledge, the easier it will be to learn), and its semantic organization (the better the material is organized, the easier it will be to remember). Developmental research indicates that young children in kindergarten, first, and even second grade are less able than adults and older children to assess accurately the difficulty of memory tasks because they have less knowledge of the factors influencing task difficulty (Kail, 1990; Kreutzer, Leonard, & Flavell, 1975).

One important instance of young children's naiveté about memory tasks is illustrated in experiments concerning their awareness of the limits of their working memory (Flavell, Friedrichs, & Hoyt, 1970; Yussen & Levy, 1975). In both studies, researchers asked subjects to predict the number of pictures they would be able to recall. The researcher first briefly showed the subject a card with a single picture on it. Then, the card was covered, and the subject predicted whether she could remember the picture. On subsequent trials, the procedure was repeated, except that the number of pictures on the cards increased up to a maximum of 10. After the prediction task, the subject was tested to see how many pictures she could actually hold in working memory. The results are shown in Figure 4.6, which combines data from both studies. It is clear from the figure that nursery-school and kindergarten children consistently overestimate the capacity of working memory. The predictions of older children become increasingly realistic, until by grade four, children estimate nearly as accurately as adults. That young children are totally oblivious of the limitations of working memory is not due to a general inability to predict their own abilities and behavior, however, since young children can accurately predict their performance in other domains. For example, they can predict how far they are able to jump (Markman, 1973).

One implication of children's unrealistic view of their working memory capacity is that they may not see the need to engage in learning strategies to make material memorable. In the laboratory, practice on short-term memory tasks does seem to make children more realistic in their predictions of working memory storage capacity (Markman, 1973; Yussen & Levy, 1975). Teachers can help younger children form more realistic beliefs about their working memory capacity by simply giving them practice (with feedback) on tasks that require remembering

FIGURE 4.6   Predicted and actual working memory span capacity as a function of grade. N = nursery school, K = kindergarten. (From Kail, *The Development of Memory in Children.* Copyright 1990 by W. H. Freeman and Company. Reprinted by permission.)

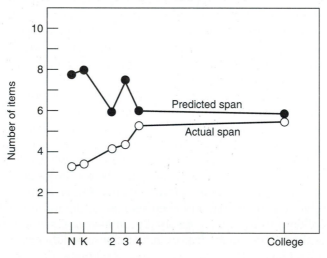

items. For example, short-term memory games might be arranged using the names of characters in a story, telephone numbers, and instructions for a task involving several steps.

Young children's assessment of memory task difficulty also depends upon their knowledge of retrieval demands. Studies have shown that many kindergarten children have a sense that recognition is easier than recall; however, it is not until first grade that they understand *why* recall is harder (Speer & Flavell, 1979). A slight majority of kindergarten children interviewed by Kreutzer, Leonard, and Flavell (1975) knew that the required format of recall (i.e., verbatim versus paraphrase) makes a difference in the ease of the test. The percentage of children understanding the difference increased with each grade until, by fifth grade, all children indicated that paraphrase recall of a story would be easier than verbatim recall. Finally, children's understanding that increasing the time interval between learning and retention makes retrieval more difficult develops with age. Approximately 60 percent of kindergarten and first-grade children and over 90 percent of third- and fifth-grade children understand the effect of time interval on retention (Kreutzer et al., 1975).

Selecting Appropriate Strategies

After a student assesses the difficulty of a learning task by evaluating the factors influencing it, she must select a learning strategy that will enable her to accomplish the task successfully. In order to select an appropriate strategy, a child must first know the strategy. However, the research literature clearly shows that simply knowing a strategy does not mean that a child will automatically select it when needed. That is, if children are taught to use learning strategies such as rehearsal, organization, and elaboration, their performance on learning tasks improves immensely as a result. This is especially the case with young children in kindergarten through third grade. However, unless they are provided explicit information about the value or utility of the strategy for improving their performance, they will not maintain the strategy in the absence of prompts from adults (e.g., Cavanaugh & Borkowski, 1979; Kennedy & Miller, 1976; Kramer & Engle, 1981; Paris, Newman, & McVey, 1982; Ringel & Springer, 1980).

These findings point up the importance of the teacher's providing metacognitive information about the usefulness of strategies while teaching them to children. Beyond this, however, these results suggest that such feedback may be effective with children because they do not monitor their own performance and, consequently, have no way of evaluating strategy effectiveness.

Monitoring Strategy Effectiveness

A skilled learner is one who keeps track of how well he is doing on a task (Am I learning the material? Am I remembering the material? Am I comprehending the material?) so that he can direct his learning activities. On the basis of information gained through monitoring, the student may decide to shift strategies or continue with the present strategy. He may decide that no further study is needed or that he needs to continue studying. Moreover, information gained through monitoring progress on a task can become a permanent part of the student's knowledge of strategies. For example, he may decide, as a result of self-monitoring, that strategy X is better for this kind of task than strategy Y. In summary, monitoring results in two important outcomes. First, use of a particular strategy can be continued, discontinued, or modified in light of its consequences. Second, monitoring can add knowledge to long-term memory concerning how to use a strategy and the benefits gained from it. This metacognitive knowledge gained through monitoring can then influence one's strategy selections in future learning situations. There is evidence that the ability to monitor the effectiveness of strategies develops with age.

Pressley, Levin, and Ghatala (1984) described and demonstrated for subjects two strategies for learning vocabulary definitions and then allowed them to practice using each strategy. One strategy was the key-word method described earlier in this chapter, and the other was a much less effective simple rehearsal strategy. Subjects were then given a new set of definitions to learn and told that they could use either strategy. The major question of this study (and several others using essentially the same procedures) was whether subjects could ascertain which strategy was more effective and whether they would then select the more effective strategy. The answer turned out to depend upon two factors—age of the subjects and whether they were tested on the material learned by the strategies before making their strategy selection. Adult subjects who merely practiced with the strategies but were not tested on the material did not realize that the key-word method was the more effective strategy. When practice was followed by a test (without performance feedback), adults overwhelmingly chose the key-word strategy for the new task. The researchers concluded that adults do monitor and that they use information gained through monitoring to select good strategies. However, tests are apparently necessary for monitoring to occur.

Older grade-school children can also monitor test performance although less accurately than do adults. However, they do not spontaneously think about which strategy has been more effective for them when choosing a strategy for a new task. If they are reminded to "think back" to their experience with the strategies just before making a strategy decision, they can then choose the more effective strategy (Pressley, Ross, Levin, & Ghatala, 1984). Young children do not seem to realize that one strategy is more effective, even when asked to monitor their performance (McGivern, Levin, Pressley, & Ghatala, 1990). In light of this evidence, Ghatala and her associates have attempted to ascertain whether young children who do not monitor can be trained to do so.

In a series of studies with first- and second-grade children, Ghatala et al. used game-like situations (e.g., drawing games) to teach children the skills of "keeping track of how well you are playing," "seeing which method of playing the game works best," and "choosing the best method." (Lodico, Ghatala, Levin, Pressley, & Bell, 1983; Ghatala, Levin, Pressley, & Lodico, 1985; Ghatala, Levin, Pressley, & Goodwin, 1986). Later, the children practiced two methods (strategies) for playing a memory game, with one of the methods (an elaboration strategy) producing objectively higher performance than the other (a simple rehearsal strategy). Finally, they were asked to choose one of the strategies to use on a new but similar memory game. Children who received the strategy-monitoring training more often chose the better strategy than children who did not receive the monitoring training. When asked why they chose a particular strategy, trained subjects typically would say things like "It helps me to learn better," while control subjects tended to give reasons that were unrelated to performance (e.g., "It's fun," or "It's easy.").

These studies indicate that young children who do not spontaneously monitor their own learning performance can be trained to do so. However, the training must explicitly focus children's attention on the linkage between using a strategy and improved performance. They also need to be shown that choosing the best strategy will enhance their learning (Ghatala, 1986). Young students who received the monitoring training tended to forget to use it in later situations unless prompted by the instructor (Ghatala, Levin, Pressley, & Goodwin, 1986).

Implications for Teaching

Earlier we stated that students who know how to use a variety of elaboration, organization, and mnemonic strategies have the potential for becoming independent learners. However, in addition to knowledge of specific strategies, students need metacognitive knowledge and skills in order to use those strategies on their own. We believe that one of the most helpful things teachers can do for students today is to provide them with the tools of independent learning. In today's world, knowledge becomes obsolete within 10 years or so, but learning skills can be used for a lifetime. Teaching students to use effective encoding strategies is time well spent. However, strategy teaching is effective only if it empowers students to take charge of their own learning.

TEACHING STRATEGIES FOR LEARNING

Based upon interviews with teachers (Clift, Ghatala, Naus, & Poole, 1990) and research on strategy instruction (see Pressley, Snyder, & Cariglia-Bull, 1987; Pressley, Harris, & Marks, 1992), we recommend that learning strategies be explicitly taught to students from the early elementary grades throughout high school. A teacher at any given grade level would do best by focusing on a few strategies that are appropriate for that age level rather than overwhelming students with many strategies. One successful approach to strategy instruction is called the **direct explanation approach** (Duffy, Roehler, Meloth, & Vavrus, 1986; Pressley et al., 1987) and consists of the following components:

Direct Explanation Approach to Strategy Instruction

1 Alert students that you are teaching them a strategy or method for learning. This directs their attention to the strategy as the goal of learning.

2 Explicitly point out the positive connection between using good study strategies and performance. Also point out that good strategies require mental work but that this effort pays off in higher performance.

3 Teach the strategy using verbal description and demonstration wherein you model your mental processes while using the strategy.

4 Provide metacognitive scaffolding by telling students why the strategy works and when (for what kinds of tasks) it works.

5 Reward students for using strategies and induce them to attribute good performance to hard work and use of strategies. If students attribute success to effort and strategy use, they will be motivated to attempt further learning tasks. If they attribute failure to lack of effort or use of a poor strategy rather than lack of ability, they will not give up but rather try harder or look for a better strategy (Clifford, 1984).

6 Provide varied practice in using the strategy. Initially describe and model the strategy and then provide help as the students execute the strategy. This help may be gradually faded as students are cued to use the strategy on different lessons and tasks for which it is appropriate. Extensive and varied practice with strategies will lead to their being automatized and generalized to a variety of learning tasks.

7 When testing over content learned via the strategy, give feedback on the strategy-performance link. In addition, teach students specific ways to monitor their performance—for example, to assess by self-testing whether they have mastered the material (Leal, Crays, & Moely, 1985).

8 Evaluate for independent use of the strategy and prompt students if they are not spontaneously using the strategy.

In summary, students can be taught to select and monitor strategies on their own, and we suggest that this become a high priority objective for teachers. The direct explanation approach makes as explicit as possible the invisible reasoning employed when experts use the strategies being taught (Roehler, Duffy, & Johnson, 1988). We will discuss an alternative method to the direct explanation approach for teaching strategies in Chapter 7.

THE CORE ISSUES

We will conclude this chapter on information processing theory by summarizing the position of the theory on the core issues.

1. *What is learned?* Stated most generally, *learning from the information processing perspective is adding new knowledge to long-term memory.* Depending upon their view of how knowledge is represented in long-term memory, different theorists have described the learning process in slightly different terms. For example, learning is the process of linking new propositions to old propositions in the propositional network (Gagné, 1985). Learning is the acquisition of new pattern-recognition and action procedures (Anderson, 1987).

Schema theorists use the terms **accretion** and **tuning** to describe the learning process (Rumelhart & Norman, 1978). Accretion is adding details to existing schemas. For example, a teacher has a schema for *reinforcement* as giving kids treats when they behave well. She hears another teacher talk about reinforcing her students with free time. The first teacher may then add the detail that activities can be used as reinforcers. Most learning, especially that of adults who have many schemas already in long-term memory, involves this kind of accretion of detail.

Tuning is more complex than accretion because it involves minor modification of the schema. For example, a teacher's schema for *reinforcement* does not usually include negative reinforcement, that is, terminating an aversive stimulus following a student's desired response. Most teachers think of this as punishment. If the teacher's *reinforcement* schema can be modified to include aversive stimuli, then tuning will have occurred.

There is a point in the modification of schemas in which prior schemas become so reorganized that they are quite different from the old ones. This is referred to as **restructuring** of schemas. This is a difficult and significant kind of learning that can involve a change in a person's "world view" (much as when a child passes from one cognitive stage to another in Piaget's theory—see Chapter 6). For example, a teacher, as a consequence of taking a course on learning theories, shifts from a primarily behavioral view of *reinforcement* to a cognitive view. These major shifts or restructurings of schemas occur over long periods of time and can be accompanied by much resistance. After all, humans often have attached to their schemas strong attitudes and values that make it difficult for them to embrace new ones. Think of how difficult it must be for someone from a fundamentalist religious background to shift his or her religious views as a result of majoring in science while in college. In any case, learning new schemas typically proceeds as follows: First, an attempt is made to use old schemas by adding details and tuning and, if this fails, restructuring occurs as a last resort. This view of learning, once again, points to the crucial role of prior knowledge.

2. *Emphasis on environmental versus organismic factors.* In comparison with behavioral conditioning theories, the environment plays much less of a role in information processing theory. The major factors that influence learning are inside the organism. These include relatively permanent characteristics of individuals, such as working-memory capacity, as well as factors that are more malleable, such as the individual's knowledge base and learning strategies. From the perspective of information processing theory, individuals are active learners who seek out strategies for controlling their own processing. The environment plays a role by providing the encoding and retrieval contexts that can activate knowledge structures and strategies within the learner. However, in contrast to conditioning theories, the environment is not viewed as having a reality independent of the individual. As we have seen, for example, a person's perception of an environmental stimulus depends as much upon his schemas as upon the nature of the stimulus per se.

3. *Source of motivation.* Information processing theory has little to say about motivation. Most theorists of this persuasion would consider the source of motivation for learning to be a need to make sense of the world. Humans are meaning-seeking creatures who derive satisfaction from constructing representations that allow them to understand the universe and their role in it.

4. *Transfer.* Knowledge learned in one setting will transfer to a new setting to the extent that cues in the new setting activate appropriate representations in long-term memory. Thus, transfer is viewed as a special case of retrieval and will be enhanced by factors that enhance retrieval.

Question 4.6: Speaking of retrieval. . . . We pointed out two things a teacher could do to enhance transfer. What are they?

(1)_____

(2)_____

Could you use more retrieval cues? Try these questions instead:
(1) What can teachers encourage students to do at the time of encoding to enhance

later transfer?_____

_____

(2) What can teachers provide students with in a new educational setting that will

increase the chances that transfer will occur? _____

---

5. *Important variables in instruction.* The important variables in instruction are those that influence perception, comprehension, and remembering. To review briefly, perception and comprehension both depend upon attention and activation of appropriate schemas. In the classroom, teachers can guide students' attention to relevant aspects of the learning task and present the material so that the students' limited working memory capacity is not overwhelmed. Teachers can also activate students' relevant schemas prior to introducing new material. If students do not possess schemas appropriate for comprehending the new information, the teacher must back up and teach that material first.

A major factor that influences remembering is the encoding activities that students use when interacting with the material. *In general, the more the students elaborate on the meaning of the material, the better will be their memory for it.* Teachers can devise activities for students that will ensure that they elaborate on the material (posing questions that require drawing inferences from the material, requiring students to rephrase the material in their own words, instructing children to draw pictures of the material, etc.). Even more important for students' long-term success as independent learners, teachers need to explicitly teach them a variety of elaboration, organization, and mnemonic strategies along with metacognitive knowledge concerning why, when, and where to use the strategies.

Remembering is also influenced by the nature of the retrieval context. Teachers need to provide a rich context for retrieval that includes cues that match those present during encoding. To enhance transfer, a teacher needs to help students build in a variety of cues during learning that will match cues in the transfer situation.

REVIEW OF MAJOR POINTS

1 Remembering involves encoding, retrieval, and metamemory processes. Encoding (forming new long-term memories) is optimal when learners perform effortful activities that require them to deal with the meaning of the material. Various classes of encoding strategies, such as elaboration, organization, and mnemonic strategies were described. In virtually every instance, an effective encoding strategy is one that adds information to (elaborates on) the to-be-learned material. This adding-on process makes the material more cohesive and relates it to knowledge already in long-term memory.

2 Retrieval begins with a retrieval cue that initiates a search for the encoded information. Effective retrieval cues are those present at both encoding and retrieval. Retrieval is best viewed as a reconstructive process in which we use schemas to interpret memory data.

3 Metacognition is knowledge about one's thought processes, including knowledge about how memory works. Metacognitive skills involved in remembering include the ability to diagnose learning tasks, select appropriate learning strategies, and monitor the effectiveness of those strategies. Young children typically need assistance or training in these skills.

4 We recommend that teachers provide explicit instruction in learning strategies. We described one approach (direct explanation approach) to teaching strategies and promised to describe other ways of teaching strategies in later chapters.

5 Regarding the core issue of what is learned, information processing theory is quite clear that learning is adding new knowledge to long-term memory in the form of new concepts, propositions, procedures, or more elaborated and finely tuned schemas. Factors inside the organism that govern perception, comprehension, and remembering play a larger role in the learning process than do environmental factors. Humans are motivated to learn because they have a need to make sense of the world. Transfer is retrieval of information from long-term memory in settings different from those in which the material was initially encoded. The most important variables in instruction are those influencing attention, activation of prior knowledge, and retrieval context.

ANSWERS TO QUESTIONS AND EXERCISES

Question 4.1: The group thinking of appropriate adjectives and nouns will recall more words than the group thinking up rhymes. The reason for this difference in performance is that thinking of appropriate modifiers and modificands requires subjects to deal with the meanings of the words, while thinking of rhymes requires more superficial analysis of the acoustical/physical features of the words.

This finding of greater retention associated with more meaningful encoding activities has been replicated many times (see Craik & Tulving, 1975; Hyde & Jenkins, 1969).

Question 4.2: One shallow processing activity frequently found in school textbooks is to require students to find the definitions of key vocabulary words. The student can simply repeat verbatim the definitions given in the text. This activity, in contrast to telling about the text in one's own words, does not require students to deal with the meanings of larger chunks of text and perhaps not even with the meanings of the words. Using flash cards and other kinds of drill on math facts is a shallow processing activity which does not deal with the meaning of the operations. It should be noted that we are not ruling out the use of these kinds of drill. In fact, acquiring automaticity in mathematical operations will demand some kind of speeded drill. However, the *initial learning* of math facts should emphasize conceptual understanding rather than rote memory. Finally, simply having students observe the science demonstration followed by a statement of the principle by the teacher would probably result in shallow processing.

Question 4.3: When experiments like this have been done by Stein, Bransford, and their colleagues (Stein & Bransford, 1979; Stein, Bransford, Franks, Owings, Vye, & McGraw, 1982), fifth graders and college students recalled the sentences elaborated as in the first set of sentences much better than the second set. They called the elaborative phrases in the first set *precise elaborations* because they explained the connection between the man's characteristic and his activity. The second set of *imprecise elaborations* did not help to tie the information in the sentence together. In order to be effective, the elaboration must clarify a concept (such as *fat man*) relative to the context (*thin ice*).

Exercise 4.1: So now you know that in a paired-associate learning task the learner is given pairs of items, such as two words or two pictures. The job is to associate the two words so that the second member of a pair can be recited when the first member is presented. We are interested in how you went about learning the pairs of items. If you tried to make up meaningful contexts that would connect the items in each pair, you were using elaboration. For example, to learn the pair *Cow—Ball* you could form a visual image of a cow kicking a ball. For the pair *Giraffe—Watch* you could visualize a giraffe wearing a large watch around its neck. Generating visual images to connect the items is called **visual elaboration.** Instead of visual elaboration you might have used verbal contexts such as short sentences to meaningfully connect the items. For example, *"The window shattered on the desk"* is a **verbal elaboration.**

Question 4.4: To qualify as elaboration an activity must make the material more meaningful by adding information that relates the material to the learner's existing knowledge. So, for example, summarizing in one's own words would most likely lead the learner to add information from existing knowledge. However, summarizing by reciting verbatim sentences from the text or lesson would not be elaborative. Additionally, to qualify as an elaboration strategy, an activity must require cognitive effort. For example, some inferences occur almost automatically during perception and comprehension as a consequence of our schemas' filling in missing information based upon their default values. (Perception of the cube was one example.)

Automatic inferencing also occurs during reading. For example, when subjects read a sentence like "The postman pushed the doorbell," they often recall it as "The postman *rang* the doorbell"; or if they read "The paratrooper leaped out the door," they very likely recall it as "The paratrooper *jumped out of the plane.*" Subjects are usually unaware that they have added information to the input sentences based upon schematic knowledge (Brewer, 1977). These kinds of automatic processes do not qualify as encoding strategies. Remember that, by our definition, a strategy is a conscious mental activity that is deliberately undertaken to achieve some cognitive goal.

While some strategies can become virtually automatic after much practice, they are initially conscious and deliberate. Even after they become automatic, we still have control over them in the sense that we can "turn them off" at will. In contrast, the automatic inference process demonstrated above is outside the learner's control. That is, Brewer (1977) found that subjects still made the inferences compelled by the above sentences even when instructed to memorize the sentences in verbatim form, "as if you were a tape recorder."

Exercise 4.2: We are not interested so much in how many words you recalled from the list but whether or not you made use of the categories in the list. The items could be grouped into terms related to operant theory—punishment, reward, operant, schedule; classical conditioning theory—contiguity, neutral stimulus, generalization, salivation; and information processing theory—schema, encoding, chunk, proposition. If you noticed and utilized the organization inherent in the list, then you probably clustered items from the same category together in recall. You may have noticed that having the categories available during recall helped you to think of the items in each category. Those who used the category organization scheme probably recalled more of the words than those who did not.

Exercise 4.3: Your recall should have been virtually perfect. Now that you have the rhyme memorized, you can use it to remember lots of things—the chief exports of a country, the steps in a procedure, the errands you need to do that day, and so on. Incidentally, the peg method can be used over and over without producing interference. We use it almost daily to remember groceries and various tasks to be accomplished (e.g., pick up the dry cleaning, get oil checked in the car, change the filter on the air conditioner) without getting confused by lists from last week or yesterday.

Question 4.5: As you probably predicted, the subjects in Group 1, who learned with the associates and were tested with them, performed the best on the test. You might have expected groups 2 and 3 to do better than Group 4. After all, Group 2 elaborated on the material and Group 3 should benefit from activation of knowledge related to the to-be-recalled material. However, the subjects who received the associates *either* at encoding *or* at recall but *not at both* did not perform any better than the subjects who did not receive the associates at all. *The conclusion is that having cues is important for retrieval, but cues are only effective if they were stored with the material at the time of encoding.*

Question 4.6: (1) The teacher can encourage students to elaborate upon the material in a variety of ways, since this builds in more retrieval cues and increases the probability of including cues that will be present in new educational and noneducational settings. (2) In a later educational transfer situation, the teacher can provide retrieval cues that match those encoded by students during acquisition, as we hope we did in the second version of this question.

REFERENCES

Anderson, J. R. (1985). *Cognitive psychology and its implications* (2nd ed.). New York: Freeman.

Anderson, J. R. (1987). Skill acquisition: Compilation of weak-method problem solutions. *Psychological Review, 94,* 192–210.

Anderson, J. R., & Reder, L. M. (1979). An elaborative processing explanation of depth of processing. In L. S. Cermak & F.I.M. Craik (Eds.), *Levels of processing in human memory.* Hillsdale, NJ: Erlbaum.

Atkinson, R. C., & Raugh, M. R. (1975). An application of the mnemonic keyword method to the acquisition of a Russian vocabulary. *Journal of Experimental Psychology: Human Learning and Memory, 104,* 126–133.

Baker, L., & Brown, A. L. (1984). Metacognitive skills and reading. In P. D. Pearson (Ed.), *Handbook of Reading Research.* New York: Longman.

Bellezza, F. S. (1981). Mnemonic devices: Classification, characteristics, and criteria. *Review of Educational Research, 51,* 247–275.

Bjork, R. A. (1975). Short-term storage: The ordered input of a central processor. In F. Restle, R. M. Shiffrin, N. J. Castellan, H. R. Lindman, & D. B. Pisoni (Eds.), *Cognitive theory.* Hillsdale, NJ: Erlbaum.

Bloom, B. S., Englehart, M. D., Furst, E. J., Hill, W. H., & Krathwohl, D. R. (1956). *Taxonomy of educational objectives: The classification of educational goals. Handbook I: Cognitive domain.* New York: McKay.

Boltwood, C. R., & Blick, K. A. (1978). The delineation and application of three mnemonic techniques. *Psychonomic Science, 20,* 339–341.

Bousfield, W. A. (1953). The occurrence of clustering in randomly arranged associates. *Journal of General Psychology, 49,* 229–240.

Brewer, W. F. (1977). Memory for the pragmatic implications of sentences. *Memory & Cognition, 5,* 673–678.

Bugelski, B. R., Kidd, E., & Segmen, J. (1968). Image as a mediator in one-trial paired-associate learning. *Journal of Experimental Psychology, 76,* 69–73.

Carey, S. T., & Lockhart, R. S. (1973). Encoding differences in recognition and recall. *Memory & Cognition, 1,* 297–300.

Carmichael, L., Hogan, H. P., & Walter, A. A. (1932). An experimental study of the effect of language on the reproduction of visually perceived forms. *Journal of Experimental Psychology, 15,* 73–86.

Cavanaugh, J. C., & Borkowski, J. G. (1979). The metamemory-memory "connection":

Effects of strategy training and maintenance. *Journal of General Psychology, 101,* 161–174.

Clifford, M. M. (1984). Thoughts on a theory of constructive failure. *Educational Psychologist, 19,* 108–120.

Clift, R. T., Ghatala, E. S., Naus, M., & Poole, J. (1990). Exploring teachers' knowledge of strategic study activities. *Journal of Experimental Education, 58,* 253–263.

Cook, L. K. (1982). *The effects of text structure on the comprehension of scientific prose.* Unpublished doctoral dissertation, University of California, Santa Barbara.

Craik, F. I. M. (1979). Human memory. *Annual Review of Psychology, 30,* 63–102.

Craik, F. I. M., & Lockhart, R. S. (1972). Levels of processing: A framework for memory research. *Journal of Verbal Learning and Verbal Behavior, 11,* 671–684.

Craik, F. I. M., & Tulving, E. (1975). Depth of processing and retention of words in episodic memory. *Journal of Experimental Psychology: General, 104,* 268–294.

Dansereau, D. F. (1978). The development of a learning strategies curriculum. In H. F. O'Neill, Jr. (Ed.), *Learning strategies.* New York: Academic Press.

Duffy, G., Roehler, L., Meloth, M., & Vavrus, L. (1986). Conceptualizing instructional explanation. *Teaching and Teacher Education, 2,* 197–214.

Flavell, J. H. (1979). Metacognition and cognitive monitoring: A new area of cognitive-developmental inquiry. *American Psychologist, 34,* 906–911.

Flavell, J. H., Friedrichs, A. G., & Hoyt, J. D. (1970). Developmental changes in memorization processes. *Cognitive Psychology, 1,* 324–340.

Flavell, J. H., & Wellman, H. M. (1977). Metamemory. In R. V. Kail & J. W. Hagen (Eds.), *Perspectives on the development of memory and cognition.* Hillsdale, NJ: Erlbaum.

Gagné, E. D. (1985). *The cognitive psychology of school learning.* Boston: Little, Brown.

Ghatala, E. S. (1986). Strategy-monitoring training enables young learners to select effective strategies. *Educational Psychologist, 21,* 43–54.

Ghatala, E. S., Levin, J. R., Pressley, M., & Goodwin, D. (1986). A componential analysis of the effects of derived and supplied strategy-utility information on children's strategy selection. *Journal of Experimental Child Psychology, 41,* 76–92.

Ghatala, E. S., Levin, J. R., Pressley, M., & Lodico, M. G. (1985). Training cognitive strategy monitoring in children. *American Educational Research Association, 22,* 199–216.

Glover, J. A., Bruning, R. H., & Plake, B. S. (1982). Distinctiveness of encoding and recall of text materials. *Journal of Educational Psychology, 74,* 522–534.

Glover, J. A., & Corkill, A. (1987). The spacing effect in memory for prose. *Journal of Educational Psychology, 79,* 198–200.

Glover, J. A., Harvey, A. L., & Corkill, A. J. (1988). Remembering written instructions: Tab A goes into slot C, or does it? *British Journal of Educational Psychology, 58,* 191–200.

Glover, J. A., Plake, B. S., & Zimmer, J. W. (1982). Distinctiveness of encoding and memory for learning tasks. *Journal of Educational Psychology, 74,* 189–198.

Glover, J. A., Timme, V., Deyloff, D., & Rogers, M. (1987). Memory for student performed tasks. *Journal of Educational Psychology, 79,* 445–452.

Glover, J. A., Timme, V., Deyloff, D., Rogers, M., & Dinnel, D. (1987). Oral directions: Remembering what to do when. *Journal of Educational Research, 81,* 33–53.

Glynn, S. M., & DiVesta, F. J. (1977). Outline and hierarchical organization as aids for study and retrieval. *Journal of Educational Psychology, 69,* 89–95.

Hayes, D. A., & Tierney, R. J. (1982). Developing readers' knowledge through analogy. *Reading Research Quarterly, 17,* 256–280.

Holley, C. D., Dansereau, D. F., McDonald, B. A., Garland, J. C., & Collins, K. W. (1979). Evaluation of a hierarchical mapping technique as an aid to prose processing. *Contemporary Educational Psychology, 4,* 227–237.

Howard, R. W. (1987). *Concepts and schemata.* London: Cassell.

Hyde, T. S., & Jenkins, J. J. (1969). Recall for words as a function of semantic, graphic, and syntactic orienting tasks. *Journal of Verbal Learning and Verbal Behavior, 12,* 471–480.

Jacoby, L. L., & Craik, F. I. M. (1979). Effects of elaboration of processing at encoding and retrieval: Trace distinctiveness and recovery of initial context. In L. S. Cermak & F. I. M. Craik (Eds.), *Levels of processing in human memory.* Hillsdale, NJ: Erlbaum.

Jenkins, J. J., & Russell, W. A. (1952). Associative clustering during recall. *Journal of Abnormal and Social Psychology, 47,* 818–821.

Kail, R. V., Jr. (1990). *The development of memory in children* (3rd ed.). New York: Freeman.

Kardash, C. M., Royer, J. M., & Greene, B. A. (1988). Effects of schemata on both encoding and retrieval of information from prose. *Journal of Educational Psychology, 80,* 324–329.

Kennedy, B. A., & Miller, D. J. (1976). Persistent use of verbal rehearsal as a function of information about its value. *Child Development, 47,* 566–569.

Kintsch, W. (1970). Models for free recall and recognition. In D. A. Norman (Ed.), *Models of human memory.* New York: Academic Press.

Kintsch, W. (1986). Learning from text. *Cognition and Instruction, 3,* 87–108.

Klatzky, R. L. (1984). *Memory and awareness.* New York: Freeman.

Kramer, J. J., & Engle, R. W. (1981). Teaching awareness of strategic behavior in combination with strategy training: Effects on children's memory performance. *Journal of Experimental Child Psychology, 32,* 513–530.

Kreutzer, M. A., Leonard, C., & Flavell, J. H. (1975). An interview study of children's knowledge about memory. *Monographs of the Society for Research in Child Development, 10* (1, Serial No. 59).

Lambiotte, J. G., Dansereau, D. F., Cross, D. R., & Reynolds, S. B. (1989). Multirelational semantic maps. *Educational Psychology Review, 1,* 331–367.

Leal, L., Crays, N., & Moely, B. E. (1985). Training children to use a self-monitoring study strategy in preparation for recall: Maintenance and generalization effects. *Child Development, 56,* 643–653.

Levin, J. R. (1981). The mnemonic '80s: Key words in the classroom. *Educational Psychologist, 16,* 65–82.

Levin, J. R., & Kaplan, S. A. (1972). Imaginal facilitation of paired-associate learning: A limited generalization. *Journal of Educational Psychology, 63,* 429–432.

Levin, J. R., McCormick, C. B., Miller, G. E., Berry, J. K., & Pressley, M. (1982). Mnemonic versus nonmnemonic vocabulary learning strategies for children. *American Educational Research Journal, 19,* 121–136.

Linden, M., & Wittrock, M. C. (1981). The teaching of reading comprehension according to the model of generative learning. *Reading Research Quarterly, 17,* 44–57.

Lodico, M. G., Ghatala, E. S., Levin, J. R., Pressley, M., & Bell, J. A. (1983). Effects of meta-memory training on children's use of effective learning strategies. *Journal of Experimental Child Psychology, 35,* 263–277.

Loftus, E. F., & Palmer, J. C. (1974). Reconstruction of automobile destruction: An example of the interaction between language and memory. *Journal of Verbal Learning and Verbal Behavior, 13,* 585–589.

Markman, E. (1973). *Factors affecting the young child's ability to monitor his memory.* Unpublished doctoral dissertation, University of Pennsylvania.

Mayer, R. E. (1980). Elaboration techniques that increase the meaningfulness of technical text: An experimental test of the learning strategy hypothesis. *Journal of Educational Psychology, 72,* 770–784.

McGivern, J. E., Levin, J. R., Pressley, M., & Ghatala, E. S. (1990). A developmental study of memory monitoring and strategy selection. *Contemporary Educational Psychology, 15,* 103–115.

Meyer, B. J. F. (1977). The structure of prose: Effects on learning and memory and implications for educational practice. In R. C. Anderson, R. J. Spiro, & W. E. Montague (Eds.), *Schooling and the acquisition of knowledge.* Hillsdale, NJ: Erlbaum.

Meyer, B. J. F., Brandt, D. H., & Bluth, G. J. (1980). Use of top-level structure in text: Key for reading comprehension of ninth-grade students. *Reading Research Quarterly, 16,* 72–103.

Paris, S. G., Neuman, R. S., & McVey, K. A. (1982). Learning the functional significance of mnemonic actions: A microgenetic study of strategy acquisition. *Journal of Experimental Child Psychology, 34,* 490–509.

Pressley, M. (1977). Children's use of the keyword method to learn simple Spanish vocabulary words. *Journal of Educational Psychology, 69,* 465–472.

Pressley, M., Harris, K. R., & Marks, M. B. (1992). But good strategy instructors are constructivists! *Educational Psychology Review, 4,* 3–31.

Pressley, M., & Levin, J. R. (1978). Developmental constraints associated with children's use of the keyword method of foreign language vocabulary learning. *Journal of Experimental Child Psychology, 26,* 359–372.

Pressley, M., Levin, J. R., & Bryant, S. L. (1983). Memory strategy instruction during adolescence: When is explicit instruction needed? In M. Pressley & J. R. Levin (Eds.), *Cognitive strategy research: Psychological Foundations.* New York: Springer-Verlag.

Pressley, M., Levin, J. R., & Ghatala, E. S. (1984). Memory strategy monitoring in adults and children. *Journal of Verbal Learning and Verbal Behavior, 23,* 270–288.

Pressley, M., Levin, J. R., & McCormick, C. B. (1980). Young children's learning of foreign language vocabulary: A sentence variation of the keyword method. *Contemporary Educational Psychology, 5,* 22–29.

Pressley, M., Ross, K. A., Levin, J. R., & Ghatala, E. S. (1984). The role of strategy utility knowledge in children's strategy decision making. *Journal of Experimental Child Psychology, 30,* 491–504.

Pressley, M., Snyder, B., & Cariglia-Bull, T. (1987). How can good strategy use be taught to children? Evaluation of six alternative strategies. In S. Cormier & J. Hagman (Eds.), *Transfer of Learning: Contemporary research and applications.* New York: Academic Press.

Raugh, M. R., & Atkinson, R. C. (1975). A mnemonic method for learning a second-language vocabulary. *Journal of Educational Psychology, 67,* 1–16.

Reder, L. M. (1982). Elaborations: When do they help and when do they hurt? *Text, 2,* 211–224.

Reese, H. J. (1977). Imagery and associative memory. In R. V. Kail & J. W. Hagen (Eds.), *Perspectives on the development of memory and cognition.* Hillsdale, NJ: Erlbaum.

Reitman, J. S., & Reuter, H. H. (1980). Organization revealed by recall orders and confirmed by pauses. *Cognitive Psychology, 12,* 554–581.

Ringel, B. A., & Springer, C. J. (1980). On knowing how well one is remembering: The persistence of strategy use during transfer. *Journal of Experimental Child Psychology, 29,* 322–333.

Roehler, L. R., Duffy, G. G., & Johnson, J. (1988, April). *A creative tension between content and process: The instructional challenge in developing self-regulated readers.* American Educational Research Association, New Orleans, LA.

Rohwer, W. D., Jr. (1973). Elaboration and learning in childhood and adolescence. In H. W. Reese (Ed.), *Advances in child development and behavior* (Vol. 8). New York: Academic Press.

Rumelhart, D. E. (1980). Schemata: The building blocks of cognition. In R. J. Spiro, B. C. Bruce, & W. F. Brewer (Eds.), *Theoretical issues in reading comprehension.* Hillsdale, NJ: Erlbaum.

Rumelhart, D. E., & Norman, D. A. (1978). Accretion, tuning and restructuring: Three modes of learning. In J. Cotton & R. L. Klatzky (Eds.), *Semantic factors in cognition.* New York: Wiley.

Shimmerlick, S. M., & Nolan, J. D. (1976). Organization and recall of prose. *Journal of Educational Psychology, 68,* 779–786.

Speer, J. R., & Flavell, J. H. (1979). Young children's knowledge of the relative difficulty of recognition and recall memory tasks. *Developmental Psychology, 15,* 214–217.

Spiro, R. J. (1977). Remembering information from text: The 'state of schema' approach. In R. C. Anderson, R. J. Spiro, & W. E. Montague (Eds.), *Schooling and the acquisition of knowledge.* Hillsdale, NJ: Erlbaum.

Stein, B. S., & Bransford, J. D. (1979). Constraints on effective elaboration: Effects of precision and subject generation. *Journal of Verbal Learning and Verbal Behavior, 18,* 769–777.

Stein, B. S., Bransford, J. D., Franks, J. J., Owings, R. A., Vye, N. J., & McGraw, W. (1982). Differences in the precision of self-generated elaborations. *Journal of Experimental Psychology: General, 111,* 399–405.

Thorndyke, P. W. (1977). Cognitive structures in comprehension and memory of narrative discourse. *Cognitive Psychology, 9,* 77–110.

Tulving, E., & Osler, S. (1968). Effectiveness of retrieval cues in memory for words. *Journal of Experimental Psychology, 77,* 593–601.

Yates, F. A. (1966). *The art of memory.* Chicago: University of Chicago Press.

Yussen, S. R., & Levy, V. M., Jr. (1975). Developmental changes in predicting one's own span of short-term memory. *Journal of Experimental Child Psychology, 19,* 502–508.

5

INFORMATION PROCESSING THEORY III: CONCEPTS AND PROBLEM SOLVING

OBJECTIVES

1. Distinguish between the classical, prototypical, and exemplar views of concept representation.
2. Distinguish between the classical, prototypical, and exemplar views of concept classification.
3. Summarize the instructional implications of the classical, prototypical, and exemplar views of concept learning.
4. Describe how conceptual domains may influence concept learning and instruction.
5. Classify novel examples of well- and ill-defined problems.
6. Define "problem space" and how it influences problem solving.
7. Describe how a broad base of declarative knowledge influences problem solving.
8. Identify and describe analogical and difference reduction heuristics and methods for helping students acquire these heuristics.
9. Describe how schematic knowledge influences problem solving and identify three methods for enhancing or modifying that influence.
10. Describe three components of metacognitive problem-solving knowledge, the role of these components in problem solving, and methods for developing these components.

In chapters 3 and 4, we discussed the basic memory processes that are responsible for learning and remembering. This chapter will discuss two areas of complex learning that are dependent on these basic processes: concept learning and problem solving. Throughout this chapter, we will continually refer to ideas presented in the previous chapters.

Concept learning and problem solving have been selected for further discussion because they are important components of most classroom instruction. For example, courses in biology and chemistry require that students acquire concepts such as "cells," "molecules," "species," and "elements." This chapter will examine how students acquire these concepts, encode them in memory, and then use them to solve problems.

Our ability to learn concepts and solve problems is dependent on knowledge stored in long-term memory (LTM). As described in Chapter 3, long-term memory consists of episodic and semantic knowledge.

Question 5.1: Semantic knowledge, you may recall, includes two types of knowledge. Can you identify and describe each type? (If not, please go back to Chapter 3 and reread the section on LTM.)

In addition to the two types of semantic knowledge stored in LTM, concept learning and problem solving are also influenced by attention and short-term memory (STM). For example, given normal storage limitations of STM ($7 \pm$ units), complex problems with multiple subparts may overwhelm individuals during the problem-solving process. As an illustration, try to solve the following problem in your head:

Exercise 5.1: Judy, Celia, and Betty are a math teacher, a truck driver, and housewife, but not necessarily in that order. Judy can't drive and is married to the brother of the math teacher. Celia is the best friend of the truck driver. Betty had a bad experience with math in grade school and has avoided all contact with math since then. What is each woman's occupation? (Taken from Whimbey & Lochhead, 1986.)

Unless you are experienced with this type of problem, you probably had difficulty solving it in your head. That is because the amount of information that you need to juggle at one time exceeds your information processing capacity. (See end of chapter for the answer to Exercise 5.1.)

Processing limitations may also interfere with the acquisition and use of complex concepts that require retrieving other related concepts. For example, in order to understand the concept "inflation," an individual also needs to understand "economy," "buying power," "interest rates," "wages," etc. Accessing these concepts while attempting to understand inflation will severely tax an individual's attentional energy and require efficient retrieval processes.

In the following sections, we will describe an information processing approach to concept learning and problem solving. The first half of the chapter will focus on concepts, and their acquisition and use; the second half will focus on problem solving. Our discussion will include the different types of knowledge required for learning concepts and solving problems and will also show how the different components of an information processing system (e.g., working memory) influence each process. Finally, when appropriate, theory and research from traditional views of concept learning and problem solving will be integrated into the discussion.

CONCEPTS: ACQUISITION AND USE

A **concept** is an internal representation of a category of related stimuli (objects, events, and processes) which allows a person to sort those stimuli into that category. For example, substances that are edible and tasty and that satisfy our energy needs are labeled "food." Likewise, objects that allow us to sit, lie, or store things more efficiently are labeled "furniture." The labels are arbitrary and might easily be swapped. They are abstractions—creations of the mind by which we organize our experiences. The types of stimuli experienced in a given culture (snow vs. desert heat, industrialized vs. agrarian economies) often determine the types of concepts invented in that society.

It is important to emphasize that forming an abstraction is a constructive process, so that even within the agreed upon categories, there is still a high degree of variability from individual to individual (Barsalou, 1989). For example, if you were raised in New York, the concept "pizza" is described in terms of thin crusts, lots of cheese, oil, and garlic, and a small amount of tomato sauce. Alternatively, if you were raised in Chicago, the concept "pizza" is described in terms of thick, deep crusts, lots of cheese, and lots of tomato sauce.

The value of creating concept categories is that they allow us to organize the vast amounts of information that we encounter into meaningful units that can be stored in memory. Concepts have adaptive value in that they allow us to filter incoming stimuli and thereby make sense of our world. They allow us to identify regularities in our experiences. For example, although a New Yorker and a Chicagoan might disagree as to which pizza is best, each would agree that both fit the category of "pizza" and, consequently, each individual could easily adapt to minor differences in this concept. Without the creation of concepts, we would be forced to deal with every new experience without the benefit of prior experiences. That is, every time we encountered another example of pizza, we would be forced to recreate that concept and, consequently, there would be no continuity to our experiences.

Types of Concepts

There are many ways to categorize the different types of concepts. For example, we could differentiate between object and event concepts, artificial and natural concepts, or well- and ill-defined concepts (see Howard, 1987). However, within most instructional contexts, the most important distinction occurs between **concrete and abstract concepts.** Abstract concepts such as "democracy," "art," and "affect" tend to be more difficult to define, illustrate, and learn, whereas concrete concepts such as "chair," "rectangle," and "bird" are relatively easy to comprehend and use (Reed & Dick, 1968).

Abstract and concrete concepts differ along three dimensions: membership criteria, tangibility, and complexity (Newby & Stepich, 1987). **Membership criteria** refers to the clarity of the concept definition, that is, whether or not it is easy to differentiate between examples and nonexamples. Examples and nonexamples of concrete concepts are typically easier to differentiate than examples and nonexamples of abstract concepts. The definition of an abstract concept often depends upon the context in which it occurs. A comic strip appearing in a newspaper may not be considered "art," while the same comic strip, if framed and hung in a museum, might qualify as "art."

Tangibility refers to whether the criteria used to define a concept can be easily perceived. The definitions of most abstract concepts are not easily perceived criteria and, consequently, are intangible. While it may be easy to see, touch, and feel an example of a "chair," what does "culture" or "democracy" look and feel like?

Finally, **complexity** refers to how many related concepts are needed in order to understand a more abstract one. For example, understanding the concept of "democracy" requires understanding the notion "equity," which involves an understanding of "impartial," and so on. Learning an abstract concept, then, often requires learning an extensive system of related concepts.

Exercise 5.2: Categorize the following concepts as either concrete or abstract, and justify your answers:

a. car _____

b. love _____

c. bird _____

d. creativity _____

Information Processing Model of Concept Learning

An information processing model of concept learning involves (1) forming declarative and procedural knowledge of the concept and (2) integrating this knowledge into a set of related concepts (Tennyson & Cocchiarella, 1986). For example, an individual's knowledge of the concept "prose passage" includes a definition of the concept (declarative knowledge), procedures for applying the concept to novel instances (procedural knowledge), and connections with related concepts such as "poetry," "literary work," "fiction," and "nonfiction." This packet of knowledge is referred to as **conceptual knowledge.**

Declarative Knowledge and Concept Learning

Currently, there are three approaches to describing the declarative knowledge embedded in conceptual knowledge: a classical approach, a prototype approach, and an exemplar approach.

Classical Approach   The classical approach has a long history dating back to Locke (1689/1975). This view of concepts states that each consists of a set of critical attributes. **Critical attributes** are simply those features which define a concept and differentiate examples from nonexamples. Consequently, these attributes are important for making distinctions between related concepts.

Let's take the concept of "chair," which has three critical attributes. All chairs possess a back, have room for one person, and are high enough off the floor to produce an appropriate sitting position. In order to be classified as a chair, an object has to possess *all three* critical attributes. For example, a piano stool is for one person and produces an appropriate sitting position, but it does not have a back. Consequently, it is not considered a chair. Alternatively, a sofa has a back and produces an appropriate sitting position, but seats more than one person. Again, it is not considered a chair. As indicated earlier, critical attributes allow us to differentiate examples from related nonexamples.

Exercise 5.3: The following exercise consists of two parts.

Part 1: Please put a check next to each of the following words that describes an object that fits into the category of "weapon."

_____ bomb	_____ sword	_____ scissors	_____ shirt
_____ words	_____ sofa	_____ gun	_____ knife
_____ whip	_____ spinach	_____ foot	_____ spear
_____ screwdriver	_____ tea	_____ shoes	_____ peach

Part 2: Please rate the words that you checked in terms of whether they are good or bad examples of weapons. Use the following scale and write the number next to those words you selected:

5 = very good example; 4 = good example; 3 = OK example; 2 = bad example; 1 = very bad example.

We will come back to your answers to this exercise in the following sections.

Problems with the Classical Approach   The classical view assumes that critical attributes can be identified for all concepts, that all examples of a concept containing the critical attributes are equally good, and that one can easily decide concept membership by noting the presence or absence of the critical attributes

(Smith & Medin, 1981). Medin (1989), however, suggests that all three assumptions may be faulty. That is, evidence indicates that even experts cannot come up with the critical attributes for many concepts in their areas of expertise (Smith & Medin, 1981). For example, within the area of economics, when was the last time you saw two economists agree about whether or not we were in a recession? Even experts can't seem to agree on what critical attributes can be used to define the concept of "recession."

Research also indicates that some examples of concepts are considered better than others, or more prototypical of their category (Mervis & Rosch, 1981; Oden, 1987). In Exercise 5.3, you probably did not have much difficulty identifying good and bad examples of the concept "weapons." This suggests that not all examples are equal. If the classical approach were an accurate description of how we represent concepts, we would expect all examples possessing the critical attributes to be equally acceptable. Your responses to Exercise 5.3 (and related research) suggests otherwise.

Finally, research has found that people not only disagree with each other about the acceptability of various examples, but they are also inconsistent over time regarding their own views (Barsalou, 1989). Take a look at Table 5.1. It is more likely that you would classify "fist" as an example of a "weapon" in list A than in list B. The existence of certain words in list B predispose you to think of "fist" as a body part rather than as a weapon. Context, then, can play an important role in placing instances into particular categories. Again, this suggests that some concepts cannot be represented by critical attributes alone and that categorizing examples is often a subjective process. If all concepts are not best represented by critical attributes, then what alternatives are available? The following two approaches attempt to address the criticisms of the classical approach.

Prototype Approach Rosch (1978) suggests that many individuals appear not to categorize examples of concepts in all-or-none terms. She suggests that for many concepts (typically concrete ones), individuals appear to compare novel examples to what they consider to be the most typical example of that particular concept.

TABLE 5.1 WORD LISTS

List A	List B
gun	gun
fist	toe
club	fist
sword	foot
spear	sword
knife	spear

Exercise 5.4: Think about the concept "bird." Take a few minutes to write down a definition of this concept. In your definition, try to identify those attributes that are critical for membership. _____

_____

Please go to the answer section at the end of the chapter and compare your definition with the technical definition of "bird."

How did you do? How much overlap was there between your definition and the technical one? The one listed in the answer section is the zoological definition of "bird," so don't feel bad if yours did not include all that information. Most importantly, how did you go about deriving your definition? Did you first try to picture a typical bird and then identify the features of that bird? Most people do it this way. In this case, a robin is often what people think of when asked to describe the important features of a bird. Our experiences have led us to identify a robin or the features of a robin (e.g., wings, beak, flight, feathers) as those which most birds possess. However, if you were an Eskimo, you might have pictured a penguin. In short, a prototypical view of concepts is based on past experience with examples of a category. Individuals, then, abstract a typical set of features (a prototype) that becomes the mental representation for that concept.

Exemplar Approach   The exemplar view also suggests that we store a specific example of a concept in memory rather than a list of critical attributes (Smith & Medin, 1981). However, it differs from the prototypical view by suggesting that individuals often represent a concept by a distinctive and memorable example which may not be a typical example. As an illustration, some individuals may compare all examples of birds to a previously experienced eagle. Eagles are certainly not typical birds, but for some individuals, they may be the most memorable. In contrast to both the classical and prototypical views, the exemplar view of concepts does not assume that learners *abstract* attributes from previous examples. Rather, individuals are seen to store *specific* examples along with detailed descriptions without any abstraction and to use these to categorize future novel examples (Medin & Ross, 1989). A summary of the classical, prototypical, and exemplar views of concepts is presented in Table 5.2.

Question 5.2: Distinguish between the classical, prototypical, and exemplar views of concept representation. _____

_____

TABLE 5.2 THREE APPROACHES TO CONCEPT REPRESENTATION

	Nature of representation	Process for creating representation
Classical approach	Each concept is represented by a verbal description of its critical attributes; these attributes are necessary and sufficient to define the concept	The attributes are abstracted from everyday examples
Prototypical approach	Each concept is represented by either an image of an idealized example or by a verbal description of idealized attributes; the example and attributes represent typical examples of the concept	The attributes and examples are abstracted from everyday examples
Exemplar approach	Each concept is represented with an image or a verbal description of a distinctive and memorable example	No abstraction occurs; the verbal description or image of one distinctive example is encoded in memory

Exercise 5.5: Please generate a prototypical example and an everyday, memorable example for each of the following concepts. Your examples can be either verbal descriptions or pictures.

a. pizza

b. politician

c. catastrophe

d. tree

It is important to note that none of these approaches taken individually can capture the variety of ways in which our knowledge of concepts is represented in long-term memory (Anderson, 1990). An individual's concepts may be represented by critical attributes, prototypical attributes, best examples, and everyday, memorable examples. As an illustration, the concept "triangle" may be represented by the critical attributes ("a closed figure that has three straight sides"), by an idealized image of a "triangle" (e.g., △, an equilateral triangle), and by memorable examples of triangles (ones presented during instruction, yield signs, etc.).

The suggestion that concepts consist of both a verbal label or description and an image of an example is consistent with current research and theory which attempts to explain differences in the recall of concrete and abstract words (Pavio, 1991). Pavio proposes a dual-coding theory which states that concrete words are encoded with two independent memory codes (verbal label and image), whereas abstract words are encoded via a verbal label only. Having two memory codes provides a better chance of remembering the target item. Assuming that concrete concepts are more likely to be encoded with both a verbal description and a visual example would explain the ease with which concrete concepts are acquired in comparison with abstract concepts (Reed & Dick, 1968).

Declarative Knowledge and Concept Instruction

As indicated in the previous chapter, as we increase the number of ways to retrieve our knowledge from LTM, we also increase the probability that we will be able to access that knowledge when needed. Consequently, when teaching concepts we should use both verbal descriptions and images because this increases the number of cues available to retrieve the concepts. Creating images may be easy for concrete concepts like "chair" and "apple" but what about for abstract ones like "democracy" and "justice"?

Newby and Stepich (1987) suggest that abstract concepts can be made more concrete by using analogies. An **analogy** is an explicit comparison between two objects or events in which the similarities and differences between them are described. For example, one could say that justice is like a scale, since both are concerned with the process of balancing. Justice entails balancing arguments whereas scales entail balancing weights. Notice that the analogy compares the concept to be learned to another, familiar, concept that the student already knows. Consequently, the first step in this process is to identify an analogous concept that already exists in the student's repertoire.

Exercise 5.6: Identify concrete analogues for the following abstract concepts:

a. A turbine is like a _____. (Hint: Both are turned to produce electricity.)
b. A zero can be compared to a _____. (Hint: It has no value except as a placeholder.)
c. Red blood cells work like _____. (Hint: They transport materials through a system of passageways.)
d. Repentance is like _____. (Hint: Both are cleansing in their own way.)
(Adapted from Newby & Stepich, 1987.)

As indicated in Chapter 3, there are distinct limitations on our ability to attend to and store relevant information (limitations on STM). Consequently, when teaching concepts it is critical to focus students on the important aspects of the chosen examples and definitions. When reinforcing a verbal definition with a visual image or an actual object, be sure to (1) cue students to the important attributes of the image or object and (2) support their attentional and memory system with aids such as definitions written on the blackboard or on a handout.

For example, if you are trying to teach the concepts "vegetable" and "fruit," either you can use pictures of different vegetables and fruits or you can bring the real thing to class. In either case, you need to emphasize both the critical attributes (e.g., fruits have seeds) and prototypical attributes (e.g., fruits are typically sweet). In addition, you could have a written handout listing critical and prototypical attributes of fruits and vegetables. Also, you might bring to class highly distinctive and memorable examples of vegetables and fruits such as a very large pumpkin. Presenting examples in multiple formats (pictures, verbal description, real and distinctive objects) will help students create an elaborated code for the concept; that will add to the probability that the concept can be easily accessed and used.

Procedural Knowledge and Concept Learning

Concepts are used primarily to classify or categorize new experiences. For example, before deciding to eat a new entrée at a restaurant, we usually attempt to categorize it and access related knowledge and concepts. This section focuses on how procedural knowledge works, that is, how it allows us to classify novel instances of concepts.

As described in Chapter 3, one way to present procedural knowledge is with productions that consist of if-then statements. The "if" portion of productions lists a set of conditions that will trigger a specific activity described in the "then" portion of the production. For example, a production for "chair" (Production #1) is presented in Table 5.3.

The classical and the prototype/exemplar approaches make fundamentally different assumptions about the nature and use of procedural knowledge and, consequently, the process of classifying concept examples and nonexamples.

Classical Approach According to this approach, we categorize concepts by matching the critical attributes of a particular example against those of the general concept. If the match is successful, then it is classified as an example of that concept. This is an all-or-none view of the classification process. That is, an example has to have *all* critical features in order to be classified as an instance of a particular concept. Production #1 in Table 5.3 is an example of the classical approach to representing procedural knowledge. That is, the "if" condition statement consists of a list of attributes, all of which must be met in order for the piece of furniture to be classified as a "chair."

Prototype and Exemplar Approach According to the prototype approach, either an idealized (prototype) example or set of features is used to classify potential examples. If the example is similar enough to the prototype, then it will be classified as a member of the concept. This implies that some examples are more similar than others and, consequently, are better (more acceptable) than others. Classifying concepts then becomes *a matter of degree,* and the boundaries for what is or is not an example are often fuzzy. That is, it becomes difficult to separate bad examples from nonexamples. Take the case of penguins. Are they good, bad, or nonexamples of birds? If you view them as birds, it is likely that you will see them as not very good examples of birds. Sparrows, on the other hand, are likely to be classified as good examples. This is because the degree of similarity between sparrows and your prototype for the concept "bird" is probably very high, whereas for penguins it is likely to be low.

TABLE 5.3   EXAMPLES OF PRODUCTIONS

Classical view

Production #1
IF a piece of furniture has the following characteristics:
a back support;
a seating surface for one person; and
an appropriate sitting position off the floor
THEN the piece of furniture is a "chair."

Prototypical view

Production #2
IF a piece of furniture possesses a *similar set* of characteristics such as:
a back support;
a seating surface for one person;
an appropriate sitting position off the floor;
four legs; and
wood construction
THEN the piece of furniture is a "chair."

OR

Production #3
IF a piece of furniture is *similar* to:

THEN the piece of furniture is a "chair."

Exemplar view

Production #4
IF a piece of furniture is *similar* to:

THEN the piece of furniture is a "chair."

Likewise, the exemplar view involves categorizing novel examples according to the degree of overlap between them and the stored exemplar. Consequently, category membership is seen as a matter of degree, and concept boundaries are not clearly defined.

Due to the subjective nature of prototypical or exemplar-based productions, their application is not as clear-cut as those involving critical attributes. The basis for triggering a production lies in the perceived *degree of similarity* between the potential example and the criteria listed in the condition component of the production. (See Table 5.3 for examples.) The degree of perceived overlap needed to trigger the production will differ from individual to individual. For example, a chair which can seat one and a half people and which is only 3 inches off the floor may be classified as a chair by some individuals but not by others. The critical word in Productions 2 through 4 is "similar." Even when given identical sets of concept attributes or images, individuals may differ in terms of the degree to which a new instance has to be similar in order to be classified as an example. Again, this underscores the subjective nature of concept categories within the prototypical and exemplar views.

Question 5.3: Distinguish between the classical, prototypical, and exemplar views of concept classification._____

_____

_____

Procedural Knowledge and Concept Instruction

A student may be able to state the definition of a concept but not be able to categorize novel examples of it. In this case, the student would have appropriate declarative knowledge but not appropriate procedural knowledge. For example, a student might give an appropriate definition of "noun" but not be able to correctly differentiate between nouns and other parts of speech such as pronouns, adverbs, and gerunds. Consequently, it is important not to assume that students who can state the definition of a concept are capable of categorizing novel examples of that concept, that is, that they possess appropriate procedural knowledge.

The development of procedural knowledge requires practice classifying novel examples and nonexamples of the target concepts (Tiemann & Markle, 1978; Tennyson & Park, 1980; Tennyson & Cocchiarella, 1986). In the classical approach to teaching concepts, examples and nonexamples should be selected that will highlight the critical attributes of the target concepts. For instance, a teacher might pair together an example and nonexample of a target concept such as "chair." Both the example (a four-legged, wooden chair) and the nonexample (a four-legged wooden milk stool) might share certain irrelevant attributes, in this case, four legs and wood. They might also share certain critical attributes such as room for one person and a comfortable sitting height. However, the milk stool would be a nonexample because it lacked one critical attribute, a back. An example-nonexample pair which differs only by one critical attribute is referred to as a "matched" pair.

In addition, the classical approach to concept teaching suggests presenting a wide variety of examples in order that students might see how the critical attributes remain constant while the irrelevant attributes vary widely. For instance, when you are teaching the concept "chair," a wide variety of examples would include those that possess various numbers of legs or are made of various materials, those that have arm rests and those that do not, and those that swivel and rock.

Both the prototype and exemplar views suggest that teaching concepts should rely less on comparisons of critical attributes and more on comparisons to prototypical or distinctive examples. Research has found that presenting students with prototypes of mathematical and social science concepts produced high levels of concept acquisition (Dunn, 1983; Park, 1984; Tennyson, Youngers, & Suebsonthi, 1983).

Park (1984) compared a classical approach with a prototypical approach to teaching concepts. The to-be-learned concepts were drawn from operant conditioning: negative and positive reinforcement, and negative and positive punishment (sound familiar?). Subjects in the classical treatment were given an analytic list of the critical attributes and a two-by-two table which isolated each dimension of the critical attributes (similar to Table 2.1 presented in Chapter 2). In contrast, subjects in the prototypical treatment were given a set of best or prototypical examples (in addition to the teaching examples). Subjects in the classical treatment were asked to identify the critical attributes of a teaching example and then categorize each teaching example. In contrast, subjects in the prototypical treatment were asked to (1) compare the teaching example to the best examples; (2) select which best example was most similar to the teaching example; and (3) categorize the teaching example. The same set of teaching examples was used in each treatment. Subjects were given an immediate and a delayed (1 week) posttest which asked them to classify a novel set of examples of the target concepts. There was no difference between treatments on the immediate posttest; however, on the delayed posttest, subjects in the prototypical treatment group were able to correctly classify significantly more novel examples than subjects in the classical treatment group.

As the above results suggest, students will benefit if given a best example or a prototype and practice comparing novel examples and nonexamples with it. This will develop the students' ability to compare novel examples with a target example rather than to abstract and compare two sets of critical attributes.

For instance, if you wanted to teach the concept of "democracy," a prototype approach would present a prototypical example (e.g., United States government) and follow it with the presentation of novel examples (e.g., Canada) and nonexamples (e.g., Russia, Kuwait). Students should be instructed to compare the United States government with the novel examples and nonexamples and to identify differences. They might also be asked to determine *how well* the novel examples match the prototype (are they good examples or bad examples?). This would develop students' ability to make judgments of similarity rather than judgments based on one-to-one correspondence.

Exercise 5.7: Given the following definition of "game ball," create three pairs of teaching examples and nonexamples. Each pair needs to highlight a different critical attribute.

Definition of game ball: an object which is *roundish in shape*[1], *sufficiently rigid to maintain shape in repeated use*[2], and *manipulated in a game*[3]. (The three critical attributes are identified with superscripts.)_____

_____

_____

Conceptual Domains

Concepts are organized in long-term memory in clusters or **conceptual domains** (Anderson, 1990). As indicated in Chapter 4, the ease with which we can retrieve a concept from LTM will be significantly influenced by the number and nature of connections between that concept and others related to it. As we increase the number of connections between a concept and related ones, we increase the number of ways to gain access to that concept (Anderson, 1990). For example, a naturalist who has lots of experience with plants and gardens possesses an organized set of plant and garden concepts (e.g., bushes, flowers, grasses, fertilizers) with multiple connections to other biological and botanical concepts in LTM. In terms of information processing, the naturalist has a *well-elaborated* knowledge base of plant and garden concepts (see Chapter 4 if you don't remember the meaning of "elaboration" and "elaborative processing"). Consequently, the naturalist will more accurately and efficiently classify new instances of flowers or bushes than someone who does not have such experience and the resultant well-elaborated knowledge base.

Conceptual domains are most often represented in terms of a hierarchy or taxonomy. This is a specific type of network in which the graphic display of concepts captures their interrelationships. Figure 5.1 depicts a taxonomy for the category of "vehicles." As you can see, there is a horizontal and a vertical dimension to the taxonomy. As one moves up the taxonomy (vertical dimension), the degree of abstraction increases. For instance, as one goes from "four-door sedan" to "car" to "vehicle," each successive concept is considered less specific and more general. Also, each concept is considered an example of the next highest concept to which it is connected. In contrast, coordinate concepts (horizontal dimension) are mutually exclusive and share the same level of abstraction. For example, "four-door sedan," "pick-up trucks," and "city bus" are equally specific but mutually exclusive categories.

Rosch and her associates (1978), found that people normally access one level of a taxonomy more frequently than the others. She termed this most frequently accessed level of a taxonomy the "basic level." In Figure 5.1 the coordinate concepts of "car," "bus," and "truck" are identified as occurring at the basic level. When individuals refer to particular vehicles, it is more likely that they will refer to them as cars, buses, or trucks rather than as vehicles or as four-door sedans. "Vehicle" seems too abstract and "four-door sedan" seems too specific. The basic-level concepts capture the most important aspects of that class of object without being abstract or very detailed. Therefore, they offer a way of organizing the world by providing the most information for the least cognitive effort. Given the importance of conserving our mental energy, using basic-level categories is an adaptive way to organize our world.

Concepts tend also to be *learned* initially at the basic level of a conceptual domain (Rosch, 1978). For example, children tend to learn the concept "car," "bus," or "truck" sooner than "vehicle" or "four-door sedan." Examples at this level are usually more similar than at other levels. To illustrate, examples of

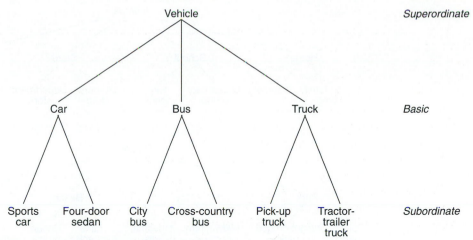

FIGURE 5.1   Taxonomy for the category of "vehicles."

different cars seem quite similar in comparison with examples of different vehicles (planes, cars, skateboards, etc.). Also, our patterns of interacting with examples of cars, buses, or trucks are very similar compared with our patterns of interacting with those of different vehicles. Finally, examples of basic-level categories tend to be more recognizable and familiar than concepts at other levels of the taxonomy (Cantor, Smith, French, & Mezzich, 1980; Murphy & Smith, 1982; Tversky & Hemenway, 1983). That is, one can make judgments as to whether an object is a car or a truck faster than judgments as to whether an object is a vehicle.

Exercise 5.8: For each of the three taxonomies presented in Figure 5.2, please identify the most likely basic-level categories and why.

Taxonomy A: _____

_____

Taxonomy B: _____

_____

Taxonomy C: _____

_____

Conceptual Domains and Concept Instruction

The nature of conceptual domains has important implications for sequencing and organizing instruction. The first step to sequencing concept instruction is the construction of a taxonomy, followed by identifying the basic-level categories.

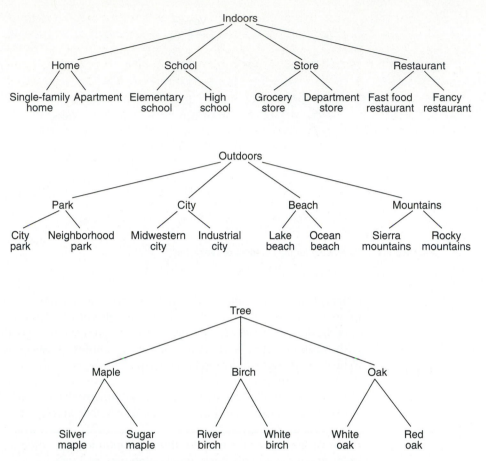

FIGURE 5.2   Taxonomies for the categories of "indoor environmental scenes," "outdoor environmental scenes," and "tree." (The "tree" taxonomy is taken from Howard, 1987, and the two "environmental scene" taxonomies are taken from Tversky & Hemenway, 1983.)

The basic-level categories should be taught first, since they are normally the easiest to acquire. As indicated earlier, superordinate concepts tend to be more abstract, and the subordinate concepts tend to be more detailed than basic-level categories. Increases in abstractness will make the concepts less meaningful because students will not have a concrete referent, while increases in detail may overload students' processing capabilities. This suggests that when teaching superordinate and subordinate concepts, there is a need to offer extra support to offset the students' potential difficulty in dealing with abstract and detailed information. For example, when teaching about vehicles (superordinate concept), use multiple examples of vehicles to give students concrete referents. Also, when teaching about specific types of trucks (subordinate concept), use a lot of external support (e.g., list of features, pictures highlighting details).

In terms of organizing instruction, the taxonomy should be used to identify related coordinate, superordinate, and subordinate concepts that may facilitate learning the target concept. Recall our discussion about teaching concepts using related examples? As Figure 5.3 shows, in order to better understand and use the concept "triangle," both superordinate concepts (e.g., closed figures) and coordinate concepts (e.g., trapezoids, parallelograms, circles) should be explicitly built into the instruction. The teacher should present students with the relevant taxonomy and emphasize the superordinate concept (closed figure) as part of the definition of "triangle" (a closed figure consisting of three straight lines). Also, the teacher can use examples of the coordinate concepts (trapezoids, parallelograms, etc.) as nonexamples. By explicitly identifying similar concepts and how they are related, the teacher is building an organized conceptual domain that can be used to transfer concepts to novel situations.

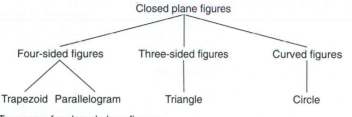

FIGURE 5.3   Taxonomy for closed plane figures.

Summary   A student's ability to acquire and use concepts depends on her ability to store, organize, and access relevant declarative and procedural knowledge in LTM. We have focused primarily on the ways in which we can represent conceptual knowledge and how this influences concept acquisition and use. In addition, we have indicated how attentional and short-term processes may facilitate or interfere with concept acquisition and use. Finally, based on this discussion, we have made suggestions for teaching concepts. In Table 5.4, we briefly summarize the instructional implications.

As indicated in the opening paragraphs of this chapter, the acquisition of a broad base of concepts is an important prerequisite to successful problem solving. The following sections will focus our attention on other types of information and knowledge that also contribute to successful problem solving. For example, we will discuss how a student's schemas can influence how he categorizes a problem and, consequently, how he tries to solve that problem. Also, we will describe how metacognitive knowledge facilitates successful problem solving. It is important to keep in mind, however, that schematic and metacognitive knowledge will not be helpful for solving problems unless a student has a broad base of conceptual knowledge.

TABLE 5.4   INSTRUCTIONAL GUIDELINES FOR TEACHING CONCEPTS

Teaching declarative knowledge

a) Focus students on critical defining attributes and prototypical attributes of examples and nonexamples.
b) Present prototypical and distinctive memorable examples.
c) Present examples and nonexamples in multiple formats.

Teaching procedural knowledge

a) Practice classifying a wide variety of novel examples.
b) Practice classifying very similar example/nonexample pairs (differ by only one critical attribute).
c) Practice comparing novel examples to prototypical and distinctive teaching examples.

Teaching a conceptual domain

a) Create a taxonomy of related concepts.
b) Identify basic-level categories.
c) Use the taxonomy to sequence and organize instruction.

PROBLEM-SOLVING ABILITY: ACQUISITION AND USE

Nearly everyone is faced with a multitude of daily problems. For example, how am I going to finish writing a new book, given other demands such as family and teaching? Alternatively, how can I avoid getting caught in morning traffic when there is road construction on all available routes? Finally, given a college professor's salary, how can I save enough money for my children's college education? These three situations have at least one thing in common: I am trying to reach some goal and having difficulty doing it. In all three cases, some type of obstacle is interfering with the attainment of that goal. We can define a **problem** as any situation in which there is an obstacle to obtaining a particular goal. In the above three situations, we can identify three distinct components to each problem (Mayer, 1992):

1 *Initial state or givens.* This consists of a description of existing conditions that need to be changed in order to attain the goal. In the above problems, the givens include current teaching and family schedules, available routes to work, and current financial situation and potential earning power.

2 *Goal state or solution.* This consists of the conditions that indicate the problem has been solved. In the previously presented problems, these include completion of the textbook, arriving at work on time, and paying for children's college education.

3 *Obstacles or barriers.* These refer to the conditions which obstruct the individual's ability to go from the initial state to the goal state. Obstacles can include such factors as lack of skill, lack of knowledge, lack of resources, failure to remember, and external conditions. The primary obstacles in the above problems range from lack of time and energy to road construction to limited earning power.

Well- and Ill-defined Problems

Problems differ in terms of the clarity of the givens, goals and obstacles. For example, look at Exercise 5.9 which is presented in Figure 5.4. The givens, goal, and obstacle are pretty clear: a piece of paper and pencil, writing the number 100 within a circle, and keeping pencil on the paper at all times, respectively. What is unclear, however, is a way to overcome this obstacle (see end of chapter for solution). This is an example of a well-defined problem. **Well-defined problems** include a clearly specified initial state, goal state, and obstacles. The "problem" of well-defined problems is how to overcome the obstacle.

In contrast to Exercise 5.9, we face many problems in our lives in which the goal is not clear. For example, faced with the problem of "leading a satisfying and happy life," we can see the initial state clearly; however, there are many uncertainties about the goal state. How are satisfaction and happiness defined? What level of satisfaction and happiness is required? Without a clear goal, it is impossible to identify methods for solving this problem. Alternatively, there are many problems in which *both* the initial state and the goal state are not clearly specified. For example, faced with the problem, "How can we reduce society's need for sex and violence?" we would have to ask: Reduce it *from what?* How do we define society, need, sex, violence? Even if we could answer these questions about the initial state, there are also ones about the goal state such as: Reduce it *to what?* I've just given two examples of **ill-defined problems,** where one or more components are not clearly specified and defined. The first step in dealing with any ill-defined problem is to try to make it well-defined. The first step in attempting to solve the above problem would be to find answers to the questions about both the initial and goal states. Given answers to these questions, the problem of how to reduce society's need for sex and violence would then be easier to solve.

FIGURE 5.4   Instructions for Exercise 5.9. Please draw the above (the number 100 in a circle) without lifting your pencil off the piece of paper.

Question 5.4: Please describe the three components of a problem and define well-defined and ill-defined problems._____

_____

_____

Exercise 5.10: Please classify the following problems as being either well-defined or ill-defined and explain why.

1. Prove the existence of God.
2. One-fourth is to 8 as 2 is to _____.
3. Create a method for safely discarding nuclear waste.
4. How may the crime rate in Houston be reduced?
5. The fire department wants to send booklets on fire hazards to all teachers and homeowners in town. How many booklets does it need? (Use the following statistics: Homeowners = 53,000; Teachers = 7,000; Teachers who own their homes = 6,000.)

Algorithms and Heuristics

Once we have identified the obstacles that need to be overcome, there are two types of methods we can use for overcoming them: algorithms and heuristics. **Algorithms** are guaranteed to lead to a correct solution if they are applied properly. In contrast, methods that are based on our best guess, rule of thumb, or general experience in solving problems and that do not guarantee a solution are referred to as **heuristics.** For example, please look at Exercise 5.11.

Exercise 5.11: A train travels 50 miles during the same time that a car travels 40 miles. How many miles will the train travel while the car travels 60 miles?

The initial state and goal state are clearly specified in this problem. That is, we know the rate of travel of the car in comparison with the train (40/50), and we are asked to calculate the distance traveled by the train when the car has traveled 60 miles. Clearly, in order to identify the initial and goal states we need to draw from our conceptual knowledge in LTM regarding cars, trains, miles, and proportions. Once we have identified the initial state and goal state, the next step is to identify a method for solving this problem. The way to solve it is to set up an algebraic equation with one unknown (40/50 = 60/x) and to solve for "x." This would involve: (1) reducing the fraction on the left to its lowest common numerator and denominator (4/5); (2) cross multiplying the two fractions in order to get rid of the fractions (4x = 300); and finally (3) dividing both sides of the equation by 4 in order to isolate the unknown variable (x = 75).

The methods employed to solve this problem are examples of algorithms. As indicated earlier, algorithms are guaranteed to lead to a correct solution if they are applied properly. Most mathematical problems have algorithms that can be used to solve them. For many other problems, however, there are no algorithmic solutions. For example, even if we could clearly specify the initial and goal states of the problem, ''How can we reduce society's need for sex and violence?'' it would be difficult to identify an algorithm that would guarantee a solution. Also, even when an algorithm is available, it may be very impractical and time consuming. For instance, suppose we forgot the combination to our locker at the health club. An algorithm for solving this problem would be to try all possible number combinations until we find the correct one. Clearly, even though this would guarantee a solution, it would be very time consuming. An alternative approach would be to first try meaningful sequences of numbers: birthdays, anniversaries, etc. In this case, we are using best guesses based on our past experiences. These ''best guess'' methods are referred to as heuristics. Although heuristics may turn out to be more efficient, there is no guarantee that they will solve the problem.

As suggested by the above discussion, problem solving involves the ordering of specific operations to obtain a solution. Early attempts to understand problem solving usually involved descriptions of the steps involved in solving problems.

Steps to Problem Solving

Wallas (1926) described problem solving as a four-step process: preparation, incubation, illumination, and verification. Preparation consists of defining and studying the problem, incubation involves a period of not working on the problem, illumination consists of identifying a possible solution, and verification involves testing the solution. Illumination was seen as an experience of insight, which was defined as a sudden discovery of the correct solution following a period of incorrect attempts based primarily on trial and error.

Polya (1957) introduced a four-step problem-solving method based upon his observations while employed as a teacher of mathematics: understanding the problem, devising a plan, carrying out the plan, and looking back. These steps overlap considerably with those of Wallas (1926). Understanding the problem required coming up with a correct representation of it. Polya suggested that the problem solver could better understand a problem by asking the following questions: What information is left out? What are the stated conditions? Are there any inconsistencies or redundancies? etc. For example, look at Exercise 5.12.

Exercise 5.12: How can we stop a 35-year-old teacher's need for sweets?

The initial and goal states of this problem are pretty vague. Missing information related to the initial state includes: How much does this individual weigh? Why does he need to curb his appetite? What is his health and physical condition? Also, the following question about the goal comes to mind: What does curbing one's need for sweets entail—no sweets, dropping from 10 candy bars a day to 5?

In devising a plan for solving the problem, Polya suggests a variety of approaches: Compare it with similar problems that you have previously solved, try to create and solve a similar problem, and break the problem down into smaller ones. We will discuss some of these approaches in more detail later in the chapter. Finally, carrying out the plan and examining the solution obtained are straightforward and involve verifying the information derived from the first two steps, that is, understanding the problem and devising a plan.

Both Wallas (1926) and Polya (1957) emphasize the importance of the first step in solving problems. Unless the problem solver clearly identifies the problem at hand, the problem-solving steps that follow will not lead to a solution. Although descriptive approaches to problem solving did not try to explain the cognitive mechanisms responsible for successful problem solving, their emphasis on the first step (clearly defining the problem) had an important influence on later approaches to problem solving.

In summary, we can divide up the components of a problem into an initial state, a goal state, and obstacles to solving the problem. The detail with which these components are described classifies them as either well-defined or ill-defined. Finally, there are two general methods that are used to solve problems: algorithms, which guarantee a solution or attainment of the goal state, and heuristics, which do not guarantee a solution but may generate one more efficiently.

Question 5.5: What is the most important step in trying to solve a problem and why?_____

_____

_____

INFORMATION PROCESSING APPROACH TO PROBLEM SOLVING

Newell and Simon were the first theorists to develop an information processing theory of problem solving. In a series of papers, they describe their attempts to program a digital computer to solve problems (Newell, Shaw, & Simon, 1958; Simon & Newell, 1971; Newell & Simon, 1972). They used a **computer simulation,** three-step method in order to program a computer to mimic human problem-solving behavior. The first step involved using all available evidence about human problem solving to develop computer programs that would solve problems. At the time, research on human problem solving indicated that many individuals would break a problem into subproblems and solve each subproblem until they attained an overall solution.

The second and third steps involved (1) comparing the computer's performance in solving problems with that of humans attempting the same problems and (2) modifying the computer program in order to reduce the differences between the performance of the computer and that of humans. These last two steps occurred repeatedly until there were minimal differences between the computer's and humans' problem-solving performance.

Once they had developed a program that closely approximated human problem solving on a specific task, they then evaluated the generalizability of the computer program by giving it other, more general, problems. Through the use of computer simulation, Newell and Simon hoped to identify the cognitive processes humans employ in solving problems.

One class of problems that Newell and Simon used extensively in their computer simulations was transformation. **Transformation problems** include clear initial and goal states, as well as methods for transforming the initial state to the goal state. The problem was to identify the most efficient set of moves to get from one to the other. Look at the following transformation problem:

Exercise 5.13: Missionaries-and-cannibals problem: The purpose of this problem is to transport missionaries and cannibals across a river under the constraint that cannibals can never outnumber missionaries, whether in the boat or on either side of the river. The initial state consists of five missionaries, five cannibals, and a boat that can hold three persons. All missionaries and cannibals start out on the left bank of the river, and the goal is to get all ten persons to the right bank.

Take a few minutes to try to solve this problem. Although it can be solved in 11 moves, most people end up taking 20 to 30. How did you do? Figure 5.5 depicts the most efficient way to solve this problem: Move from Oval A straight down to Oval Z (11 moves). As you can see from this diagram, problem solving was viewed as a series of transformations which were intended to move you from the initial state to the goal state.

In describing how this problem is solved, Newell and Simon created the term **"problem space"** to refer to the initial state, goal state, potential operations, and choices that an individual evaluates while solving a problem (see Figure 5.5). In its current usage, the idea of a problem space has been expanded to refer to the knowledge in LTM that is relevant to interpreting and solving a problem. A problem space delimits the area of LTM that is relevant to finding a solution to the current problem. For example, in the problem of how to finance my children's college education, the problem space would consist of all information and past experience related to the process of generating and saving large sums of money.

In addition to identifying the importance of an individual's problem space, Newell and Simon integrated the basic characteristics of information processing into their theory of problem solving. They were the first theorists to suggest that the capacity of working memory can dramatically influence how effectively we can solve problems. Take a minute to read through the following problem and try to solve it in your head.

Exercise 5.14: Messrs. Downs, Heath, Field, Forest, and Marsh—five elderly pigeon fanciers—were worried by the depredations of marauding cats owned by five not less elderly ladies, and, hoping to control the cats, they married the cat owners. The scheme worked well for each of them so far as his own cat and pigeons were concerned, but it was not long before each cat had claimed a victim and each fancier had lost his favorite pigeon.

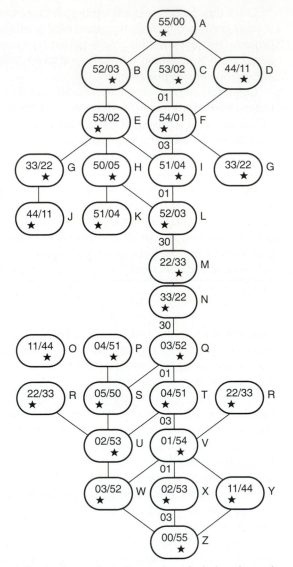

Within each oval, the numbers refer to the number of missionaries and cannibals on the left and right side of the river. The star indicates which side of the river the boat is on. For example, Oval L represents five missionaries and two cannibals on the left side of the river, no missionaries and three cannibals on the right side of the river, and that the boat is on the left side of the river.

FIGURE 5.5 Alternative ways to solve the missionaries-and-cannibals problem, Exercise 5.13. (Adapted from Simon & Reed, "Modeling Strategy Shifts in a Problem-solving Task," in *Cognitive Psychology*, vol. 8, pp. 867, 1976. Used by permission of Academic Press and the author.)

Mrs. Down's cat killed the pigeon owned by the man who married the owner of the cat which killed Mr. Marsh's pigeon. Mr. Down's pigeon was killed by Mrs. Heath's cat. Mr. Forest's pigeon was killed by the cat owned by the lady who married the man whose pigeon was killed by Mrs. Field's cat.

Who was the owner of the pigeon killed by Mrs. Forest's cat? (Taken from Hayes, 1987.)

Clearly, this problem exceeds the capacity of working memory, due to both the complexity of the operations necessary and the storage requirements. As indicated in Chapter 3, there is a trade-off between storing and using information in working memory. The more skilled a person becomes at conducting the operations called for by a particular task, the less attentional energy she will need to expend on those operations and consequently, the more capacity she will have left over for storing information. In general, the more complex the task, the more storage is required because complex tasks involve more steps or operations than do simple problems. Thus, it follows that people who are able to store more in working memory (while simultaneously operating on the information) are able to solve more complex problems than people who cannot store as much information in working memory.

Question 5.6: In Chapter 3, we described two ways in which we could expand our attentional capacity to deal with complex information. Please describe those two ways and how they might help in solving complex problems._____

_____

_____

Current Information Processing View of Human Problem Solving

Consistent with the lead of Newell and Simon, current information processing theories emphasize the effective use of mental processes and operations for successful problem solving (Andre, 1986; Voss, 1989). However, in contrast to Newell and Simon, who were primarily assessing general problem-solving behavior, current research has focused on **expert and novice problem solving** within specific content areas: physics, mathematics, chess, and so on (Chi, Glaser, & Rees, 1982).

The research on experts and novices has found that experts' superior problem-solving ability within their domain of expertise is due primarily to four factors: (1) domain-specific, verbalizable knowledge (i.e., declarative knowledge); (2) more effective strategies for solving problems (i.e., procedural knowledge); (3) larger chunks of related thematic knowledge within the content area (i.e., schematic knowledge); and (4) better ability to plan and monitor their problem-solving attempts (i.e., metacognitive knowledge) (Chi, Glaser, & Rees, 1982; Mayer, 1992; Rohwer & Thomas, 1989; Voss, 1989).

In order to understand how each of these four types of knowledge might contribute to the process of solving problems, let's look at the following math problem.

Exercise 5.15: Countertop tiles are sold in squares 25 cm on each side. How much would it cost to tile a rectangular countertop 5.5 m long and 4.4 m wide if the tiles cost $.65? (Adapted from Mayer, 1992.)

As indicated earlier, the first step in solving any problem is to come up with an accurate problem representation. In order to do this, you need to translate the problem statement with the aid of appropriate declarative knowledge. That is, you need to generate definitions of the concepts included in the problem statement ("squares" have four equal sides, "rectangles" have pairs of unequal sides, etc.). Given these definitions, you now know that each tile is 25 cm $\times$ 25 cm and the space to be covered is 5.5 m $\times$ 4.4 m. An additional important piece of declarative knowledge related to this problem is that one meter equals 100 centimeters.

Given this initial information, you then need to diagnose the problem (metacognitive knowledge) and categorize it. The stated goal of this problem is to find the cost of tiling the countertop. In order to do this, you need to calculate the area of the countertop. This problem would then be categorized as an "area" calculation problem and this would cue the appropriate schema related to the calculation area. Embedded in this schema would be both declarative and procedural knowledge related to the calculation, that is, the procedure for calculating area (area = length $\times$ width). Also, within the present problem, we need to make all relevant dimensions equivalent; consequently, some of the measurements need to be converted from centimeters to meters. This requires identifying procedures for converting 25 centimeters to meters (a division procedure).

Once you have come up with a problem representation (area calculation problem) and cued the appropriate schema, the next step is to develop a plan for solving the problem, and to execute this plan and monitor its effectiveness. To do that, you would again engage your metacognitive knowledge for solving problems. For this math problem, an effective plan would be:

1 convert 25 centimeters into meters;

2 find the area of the countertop by multiplying 5.5 $\times$ 4.4;

3 find the area of each tile by multiplying 0.25 $\times$ 0.25;

4 find the number of tiles by dividing the area of the countertop by the area of each tile; and then

5 find the total cost by multiplying the number needed by $.65.(Adapted from Mayer, 1992.)

Finally, you would access appropriate procedural knowledge (procedures for multiplication and division) and execute this plan, monitoring the output of each step.

As you can see, solving a problem requires the identification, access, and use of a variety of types of knowledge. The following sections will focus on the importance of each of the above types of knowledge to problem solving. Given the documented differences between experts and novice problem solvers, we will be referring to the expert-novice literature throughout these sections.

Declarative Knowledge and Problem Solving

Experts tend to have more factual or declarative knowledge within their area of expertise than do novices (cf. Chi, Feltovich, & Glaser, 1981; Larkin, McDermott, Simon, & Simon, 1980; Larkin, 1980a, 1980b; Mayer, 1992; Rohwer & Thomas, 1989; Voss, 1989). As indicated in the discussion of Exercise 5.15 (countertop tile problem), having relevant declarative knowledge was helpful in defining (representing) the problem. A large base of declarative knowledge relevant to content areas (mathematics, science, social sciences, etc.) will facilitate the process of creating an appropriate problem representation. As an illustration, please complete Exercise 5.16.

Exercise 5.16: Please read through the following two problem statements and come up with a problem representation. For example, is the problem asking you to calculate area?

Problem A: A car traveling 35 meters per second is brought to rest at a constant rate in 30 seconds by applying the brake. How far did it move after the brake was applied?

Problem B: Which is the best buy for peanut butter? Bottle A, which costs $1.75 for 12 ounces, or Bottle B, which costs $2.50 for 16 ounces? Once you have come up with a problem representation for the two problems, continue reading.

Unless you have just taken a standardized mathematics test or had a few courses in physics, coming up with a problem representation for Problem A was probably more difficult than for Problem B. Problem A is a distance problem and can be easily solved only if the following equation is available in declarative knowledge: distance = [(initial speed + final speed)/2] × time. In contrast, Problem B describes a situation that most of us have faced many times. Consequently, we have lots of relevant declarative knowledge that will help us create an appropriate problem representation (i.e., ratio problem: compare the product of 1.75/12 with 2.50/16).

A large base of relevant declarative knowledge increases the number of cues for accessing relevant knowledge (both declarative and procedural) in LTM. This, in turn, increases the probability of coming up with an accurate problem representation, the key first step in solving the problem. Without this large base of cues, a problem solver will be forced to search through many parts of LTM that are irrelevant to solving target problems.

Remember, however, from Chapter 4, that the nature of cues that are embedded with our knowledge during encoding will critically influence retrieval of that knowledge. As indicated in Chapter 4, the greater the overlap between the cues present during encoding of materials (e.g., studying for a test) and the cues present during retrieval of that information (e.g., taking a test), the greater the probability that retrieval will be successful.

Bransford and his colleagues have found that individuals often do not access available and appropriate knowledge when faced with novel problem-solving tasks (Bransford, Franks, Vye, & Sherwood, 1989; Bransford, Sherwood, Vye, & Reiser, 1986; McNamara, Miller, & Bransford, 1993; Sherwood, Kinzer, Bransford, & Franks, 1987). As an illustration, Perfetto, Bransford, and Franks (1983) conducted a series of studies in which they gave students cues that were associated with problems that they would be asked to solve later. An example of the kind of problems they were given is:

> A man living in a small town in the U.S. married 20 different women in the same town. All are still living and he has never divorced one of them. Yet, he has broken no laws. Can you explain?

Prior to being given these problems, some subjects were given clue information that was relevant to solving each problem. The clue which was relevant to solving the above problem is: "A minister marries several people each week." It is important to note that many cues were given to the subjects prior to the presentation of the problems. One group of subjects was given the problems and explicitly prompted to use the clue information to solve them. They solved most problems. In contrast, a second group of subjects was given problems and was not prompted to use the clue information. They were unable to solve most problems.

Even though all subjects were given the appropriate knowledge to solve the novel problems, when faced with these problems, they did not access that knowledge unless explicitly prompted (see also Gick & Holyoak, 1983). According to Bransford and his colleagues, the inability to see how current knowledge is relevant to present tasks and situations (unless prompted) is due to minimal overlap between the encoding context and the retrieval context. Thus, if subjects had acquired the clues while solving problems and then were asked to solve a similar problem, it is more likely that they would have accessed that clue to solve the second problem. As you will see in a later section, gaining access to relevant procedural knowledge can also be hampered by an individual's inability to see its relevance to the problem at hand.

Declarative Knowledge and Problem-solving Instruction

In order to ensure access to relevant declarative knowledge during problem solving, Bransford and his colleagues emphasize the importance of teaching with problem-oriented activities rather than fact-oriented activities (Cognition and Technology Group at Vanderbilt, 1992). **Fact-oriented activities** are aimed at the storage of information (e.g., increasing retention of information) and presenting to-be-learned information without any reference to mode of future use or context of future use. An example is teaching vocabulary words in list format. All this prepares the individual to do is to associate a definition with the word. Typically, however, we expect students to be able to use words to communicate their ideas and needs to others. If you want students to learn how and when to *use their vocabulary* in order to communicate with others, then the vocabulary words should be taught in activities that emphasize the communicative value of the word (asking someone for directions, negotiating with someone, etc.). In these examples, the context of instructional activities is matched with the context within which students are expected to use the to-be-learned information.

Problem-oriented activities involve the presentation of to-be-learned information within the context of future use and activities which require the student to use that information as it will be used in the future. For example, within science education, the specific contexts and activities built into instruction aimed at developing students who are knowledgeable consumers of science will differ tremendously from the contexts and activities built into instruction aimed at producing future scientists. In the former situation, activities and contexts which focus on evaluating and information seeking are emphasized, whereas in the latter situation, activities and contexts which focus on information and knowledge generation are emphasized (hypothesis generation, gathering data, data analysis, etc.). Both types of students may acquire the same set of declarative knowledge; however, the contextual cues which are associated with their declarative knowledge are different and, consequently, one group will perform best under one set of conditions while the other will perform best under a different set of conditions.

Research on the nature of expert and novice knowledge suggests that how knowledge is organized in LTM can also influence its accessibility (Chi, Feltovich, & Glaser, 1981; Lesgold, Rubinson, Feltovich, Glaser, Klopfer, & Wang, 1988; Rohwer & Thomas, 1989; Voss, 1989). Experts organize their knowledge around important higher order principles and solution plans (i.e., procedural knowledge). They also organize this higher order procedural knowledge and related declarative knowledge into large accessible units (schematic knowledge). For example, a medical expert will organize her declarative and procedural knowledge of cancer around important principles of the immune system and disease etiology. The declarative knowledge would include information related to cancer and its usual symptoms and related effects, while the procedural knowledge would consist of procedures for diagnosing and treating cancer. Given our previous discussion of the importance of embedding cues in LTM related to how and when to use our knowledge, organizing it in this way (around the immune system and disease etiology) should facilitate accessing this knowledge. That is, the medical expert will need to use her knowledge of the immune system and disease etiology when faced with specific symptoms and related effects. Detailed discussion of the importance of procedural and schematic knowledge to problem solving will occur in the following two sections.

Procedural Knowledge and Problem Solving

In most cases, when we have an algorithm to solve a problem, we can easily overcome any obstacles that might exist. For example, when faced with the tile countertop problem described earlier, if we know and can use the algorithm for calculating area, the problem is easily solved. As with the procedural knowledge which supports concept classification, algorithms *can be* represented with productions. Recall from the section on concept learning that a production consists of a set of conditions ("if" statement) which, if met, trigger some internal or external activity ("then" statement). Some examples of productions which represent problem-solving algorithms used in Exercise 5.15 are presented in Table 5.5. Productions which represent algorithms are similar in their detail to those which represent a classical view of concept classification. Consequently, as will be described later, teaching algorithms focuses on the acquisition of specific criteria or attributes related to their conditions of use.

If an algorithm is not available, we will be required to generate alternative strategies or methods for solving a problem. If you recall, these alternative best guess strategies are referred to as heuristics. In the following sections, we will discuss two types of heuristics: **analogical approach and difference-reduction approach.**

Analogical Approach   Many times we are faced with problems in which we may have a clear idea of both the initial state and goal state but have no ways to overcome the obstacle. In these situations, it is useful to compare the current problem with other, similar, problems and their solutions. This is referred to as solving a problem by **analogy.** Remember our earlier discussion of the importance of analogies in teaching concepts? There we defined an analogy as an explicit comparison between two objects or events in which the similarities and differences between them are described. Please take a moment to read through the following problem:

Exercise 5.17: Suppose you are a doctor faced with a patient who has a malignant tumor in his stomach. It is impossible to operate on the patient, but unless

---

TABLE 5.5   EXAMPLES OF PRODUCTION FOR ALGORITHMS AND HEURISTICS

Algorithms

IF goal is to convert centimeters to meters,
THEN divide the number of centimeters by 100.

IF goal is to find the area of a square,
THEN square the length of one side.

IF goal is to find the area of a rectangle,
THEN multiply the length of the longest side by the length of the shortest side.

Heuristics

Subgoaling:

IF goal is to transform the current state into a goal state,
THEN identify an intermediate state which successively approximates the goal state
        and attain this state.

Means-end analysis:

IF goal is to transform the current state into a goal state
THEN find the most important difference between the two states and eliminate this difference.

the tumor is destroyed the patient will die. Furthermore, there is a kind of ray that will destroy the tumor if it reaches the tumor at sufficiently high levels of intensity. Unfortunately, at this intensity the healthy tissue that the rays pass through on the way to the tumor will also be destroyed. At lower intensities the rays are harmless both to the healthy tissue and the diseased tissue. What type of procedure might be used to destroy the tumor with the rays and, at the same time, avoid destroying the healthy tissue? (Adapted from Duncker, 1945.)

Are you having difficulty solving this problem? If you are, please read the following scenario and look at Figure 5.6:

A general wants to capture a fortress located in the center of a country. There are many roads radiating outward from the fortress. All have been mined so that, while small groups of men can pass over the roads safely, any large force will detonate the mines. A full-scale attack is therefore impossible. The general's solution is to divide his army into small groups, send each group to the head of a different road, and have the groups converge simultaneously on the fortress. (Taken from Gick & Holyoak, 1980.)

Now go back and reread Exercise 5.17 and identify an analogous solution to that problem. It should now be much easier to see that a viable solution is to have low level X-rays converge on the tumor from various directions. In this way, no healthy tissue will be destroyed, yet the sum of the converging X-rays will destroy the tumor. Using the analogous fortress problem helped to identify the solution to the tumor problem. In order for analogies to be helpful, the problem solver needs to both recognize the similarity between two problems and recall the solution of the analogous problem.

Research has found that when subjects are prompted they will make use of analogous problems and solutions. However, without a prompt, most subjects do not make use of analogies (Gick & Holyoak, 1980). For example, subjects were given the fortress problem and solution described above prior to being given the

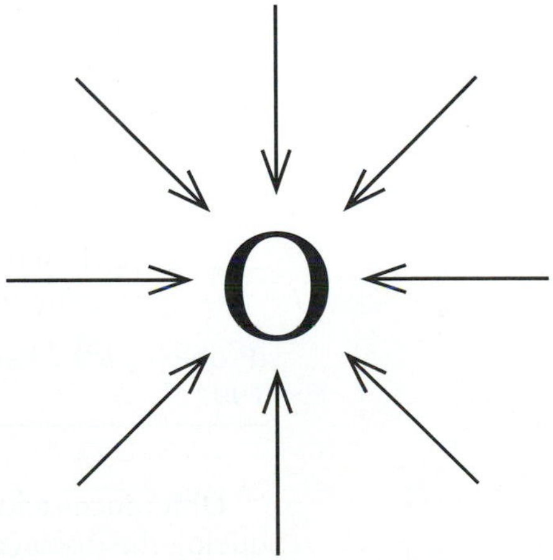

FIGURE 5.6   Graphic representation of solution to fortress problem.

tumor problem to solve. Those subjects whose instructions suggested that the two problems were related were much more likely to solve the tumor problem than subjects who were not given this suggestion. These results indicate that individuals have difficulty spontaneously recognizing the similarity between analogous problems.

How might we increase the spontaneous use of analogies? Gick and Holyoak (1983) and Catrambone and Holyoak (1989) found that inducing individuals to compare analogous stories and identify their similarity proved useful when attempting to solve a third analogous problem. Experience with prior analogous stories helped them spontaneously apply these stories to the later problem. This suggests that getting students to compare and contrast problems and their solutions may help them develop generalized knowledge that may be useful for later problem-solving situations.

Exercise 5.18: Read the following set of problems and identify those that are similar and could be solved using analogous methods. Also describe how the analogous problems can be solved. Identify similar problems by labeling them with the same letter: A, B, C, etc.

———— a) Apples were selling four for $1. How many could Jim buy for $4?

———— b) Cathy knows French and German; Sandra knows Swedish and Russian; Cindy knows Spanish and French; Paula knows German and Swedish. If French is easier than German, Russian is harder than Swedish, German is easier than Swedish, and Spanish is easier than French, which girl knows the most difficult languages?

———— c) You are facing west. You make an about-face and then turn left. Which direction is now on your right side?

———— d) Richard owes Dick $23.00. Dick owes Ricardo $8.00 and Rick $11.31. If, with Dick's permission, Richard pays off Dick's debt to Rick, how much does he still owe Dick?

———— e) A train travels 30 miles per hour for 3 hours. How far will it travel?

———— f) Paul, Sam, and Tom differ in height. Their last names are Smith, Jones, and Calvin, but not necessarily in that order. Paul is taller than Tom but shorter than Sam. Smith is the tallest of the three and Calvin is the shortest. What are Paul's and Tom's last names?

———— g) If mints cost 8 cents each and lemon drops cost 6 cents each, how much do two mints and five lemon drops cost?

(Problems are taken and adapted from Whimbey & Lochhead, 1986, and Mayer, 1992.)

Difference-reduction Approach   Difference-reduction heuristics involves reducing the distance between the initial and the goal state by successive approximations (Anderson, 1990). Two similar but slightly different types of difference-reduction heuristics will be discussed: subgoaling and means-ends analysis.

Subgoaling   Using a subgoaling approach to solve a problem involves breaking up the problem into a series of intermediate states between the initial state and the goal state. As an illustration, one approach to solving the missionaries-and-cannibals problem (Exercise 5.13) is to set up appropriate subgoals. For example, an initial subgoal would be to reach a situation in which there were three cannibals across the river by themselves without a boat. In fact, Simon and Reed (1976) compared the performance of subjects given this subgoal with a control group not given any subgoal and found that the control group required, on the average, 10 more moves to solve the problem than did the subgoal group.

One advantage of using subgoaling is that it can reduce the number of solution paths that need to be searched because the problem is broken down into mini-problems which may be more manageable. This clearly is helpful, given the limitations of our attentional energy and working memory capacity. There are however, some potential disadvantages: This is not a useful approach when the intermediate subgoals are not obvious. For example, faced with the problem of obtaining a new job, it is not clear what an appropriate subgoal would be: a new appearance? relocation? more schooling? In addition, Reed (1992) indicates that the use of subgoals may actually increase the time required to solve a problem because it involves repeated identification, that is, once a subgoal has been attained, the individual is then required to identify a new one (Hayes, 1966).

Exercise 5.19: Break the following problem into a series of subgoals which, if attained, should lead to a solution.

Problem: A student shows a great deal of anxiety about contributing to group discussions. His teacher would like him to be less anxious in this situation. How might you solve this problem?

Means-ends Analysis   Another difference-reduction heuristic which has received much attention is the means-ends analysis. This particular heuristic was studied extensively by Newell and Simon in their computer simulation program discussed earlier (Newell & Simon, 1972). This heuristic also involves creating subgoals. However, the process of identifying subgoals revolves around finding the most *important* difference between the initial state and the goal state and then creating a subgoal aimed at eliminating this difference. When using a **means-end analysis,** one continually identifies the most important difference between where one wants to be and where one is now. Once this difference has been identified, the next step is to find the *means* to attain this *end.* Thus, means-ends analysis involves a continuous identification process (1) identifying the most important difference and (2) identifying how to eliminate this difference. The subgoals refer either to eliminating the important differences or to obtaining the methods for eliminating these differences.

A means-end analysis differs from the subgoaling approach discussed earlier in that attaining each subgoal in the subgoaling approach immediately moves you one step closer to the final goal. In the means-end analysis, however, eliminating the most important difference often moves you away from the goal before moving you closer to it.

For example, in attempting to clean up my office (initial state = office is a disaster area; goal state = spotless office), the most important difference between the initial state and the goal state is one of cleanliness. How can I increase the cleanliness of my office? By storing and organizing the papers, books, etc., that are cluttering it up. At this point, I do not have any room left on my shelves or in my file cabinets. How do I make more room? To make room, I need to go through my books and clean out my files. This will require that I pile the stuff I want to save on the floor and also get a larger waste basket. How can I get a larger waste basket? I could talk to the secretary . . . and so on.

In this example, each question posed represents a subgoal that, I hope, is moving me toward my goal. Notice, however, that initially I had to make my office messier by piling material on the floor, in boxes, or in the garbage can. Consequently, I was not immediately moving closer to the goal state. However, once I had made more room in my files for materials, I could take paper which had been stacking up on my desks and file them away, thus moving toward the goal of a clean office. Also, notice that the first question—"How do I make more room?" is aimed at reducing the difference between the current state and the goal state, while the second question—"How can I get a larger waste basket?" deals with obtaining the methods for reducing the difference between the current state and the goal state.

Research on expert-novice differences in problem solving indicates that experts most often approach problems using a difference-reduction strategy (Mayer, 1992). For example, expert computer programmers, when faced with a programming problem, will proceed to break it into successively smaller parts (subgoals) based on differences between present conditions and the desired goal state (Jeffries, Turner, Polson, & Atwood, 1981). In contrast, although novice programmers do break problems into smaller parts, they soon abandon this organized approach and switch to random problem-solving activity.

Heuristics can also be represented with productions. However, as you can imagine, given the general nature of heuristics, the condition statements will not be as precise as you would find in the productions which represent algorithms (see Table 5.5 for examples).

Question 5.7: Please distinguish between a subgoaling and a means-ends analysis approach for solving problems._____

_____

_____

Procedural Knowledge and Problem-solving Instruction

As indicated earlier, algorithms are specific procedures or strategies that guarantee a solution to a problem. For example, in Exercise 5.15, if the appropriate information is inserted into the formula for calculating area, then a solution is guaranteed. Research indicates that problem-solving algorithms are most effectively taught within specific contexts to which they can be applied (Schoenfeld, 1985). That is, the conditions for using algorithms need to be explicitly taught and the algorithms need to be repeatedly practiced under these conditions. It is also important to practice these algorithms until they can be applied somewhat automatically. Given limited attentional resources, an individual's attentional energy is best directed toward higher level problem-solving processes, that is, planning and monitoring.

Whereas algorithms are tied to specific contexts, heuristics are intended to be "context-free" strategies. Unfortunately, research indicates that, although it is possible to teach students general problem-solving heuristics, students are not very likely to transfer these heuristics to novel problems (Larkin, 1980; Reif, 1980; Voss, 1989). That is, students tend to use general heuristics only in situations similar to those in which they were taught. For example, if students are taught a subgoaling approach to solving mathematics problems, they tend to restrict this subgoaling method to the specific type of mathematics problem that was used during training.

Schoenfeld (1979, 1982, 1985) evaluated the usefulness of training students to use general heuristics for solving mathematics problems (find an analogous simpler problem and adapt the solution of that problem to the current problem, break the problem into subgoals and try to attain each one, etc.). He found that the training was not successful unless the students were taught *when* to use the strategy.

Recall our Chapter 4 discussion on the teaching of learning strategies, where we indicated that research supported the use of a direct explanation approach to teaching strategies. An important component of this approach is a focus on *when* to use strategies. The results of Schoenfeld's experiments suggest that a direct explanation approach may also be useful for teaching general problem-solving strategies.

Question 5.8: Briefly summarize the important components of a direct explanation approach to strategy instruction and how it can be used to teach problem-solving heuristics._____

_____

_____

Given the importance of goal setting in difference-reduction heuristics, students should be given training in how and what type of goals to set. Research on goal setting suggests that specific, moderately difficult, and immediately attainable goals are best since they help maintain interest and motivation in solving a goal

(Locke, Shaw, Saari, & Latham, 1981). In addition, goals will direct an individual's attention to specific aspects of a problem situation and, consequently, will reduce the load on mental energy. Specific, moderately difficult, and immediately attainable goals will also produce more persistence in searching through LTM for related information because they will give the individual a clear end point at which to aim.

For example, in dealing with the problem of paying for my children's college education, Subgoal A would be more likely to induce a persistent search for related information than Subgoal B:

Subgoal A: Identify exactly how much money I will need to save in order to support 4 years of college education for each child.

Subgoal B: Obtain information concerning finance by taking a course at the community college next semester.

Subgoal A is specific, of moderate difficulty, and almost immediately attainable (by talking to a broker), whereas Subgoal B is general, may be difficult (in terms of time and expense), and is not immediately attainable. Although both subgoals may eventually lead to a solution to this problem, Subgoal A is more likely to keep me working toward a solution.

Finally, students should be given a wide range of problems to solve and should be asked to identify the similarities and differences between the types of problems and the related problem-solving methods (see Exercise 5.18 as an illustration). This will, it is hoped, facilitate a student's search for analogous problems and potential solutions when faced with a difficult problem.

Schematic Knowledge and Problem Solving

As described in Chapter 3, schemas are knowledge structures for representing classes of objects, events, or situations such as a human face, a buying event, or a restaurant visit. Schemas are said to consist of both declarative and procedural knowledge and are organized around a theme. Problem-solving schemas would include themes related to the different types of problems that one might encounter. For example, physics problems can be categorized as including fulcrum problems, velocity problems, and gravity problems. Once a schema is activated, it turns an individual's attention to a specific category of information. In problem-solving situations, activating the appropriate schema brings useful information to bear on the problem, but activating the wrong schema can interfere with problem solving, as Exercise 5.20 demonstrates.

Exercise 5.20: Carefully read the passage below once; then turn to the answer section at the end of this chapter and answer the question dealing with this problem.

You are the driver of a bus that can hold a total of 72 passengers (there are 36 seats that can each hold 2 passengers). At the first stop 7 people get on the bus.

At the next stop 3 people get off and 5 get on. At the next stop 4 people get off and 2 get on. When the bus arrives at the next to the last stop, 2 people get on and 5 get off.

Most individuals who read this information assume immediately that it is a calculation problem and activate their *calculation problem* schema. If you did this, then you activated the wrong information and probably had difficulty answering the question posed at the end of the chapter. Your immediate categorization of this problem interfered with your ability to solve it. Thus we see once again how important the initial problem identification step is. Until the appropriate schema is activated, there is little hope of solving the problem at hand.

As suggested above, individuals are often predisposed to approach problems in ways that reflect their prior knowledge and past problem-solving experiences. Early problem-solving research (1930–1950) focused a considerable amount of attention on obstacles to successful problem solving. In particular, this research showed that prior knowledge and experience can interfere with an individual's ability to see alternative approaches to solving problems and, consequently can interfere with finding a solution. One line of research which looked at prior knowledge effects focused primarily on the function and uses of objects (Duncker, 1945). Let's look at the following problem used in early Gestalt research (see Chapter 3 for a discussion of Gestalt theory) on problem solving (Maier, 1931, 1933).

Exercise 5.21: An individual is put into a room with two cords hanging from the ceiling to the floor that are just out of reach of one another. The following objects are also present: five nails, one hammer, three paper clips, and four candles. The goal of the problem is to tie the two cords together even though they are not long enough for you to grasp both at the same time.

Take a minute and try to solve this problem. When you think you have a solution or want to go on, please turn to the end of the chapter for the answer.

In order to solve this problem, you need to think of using the available materials in novel ways. As indicated at the end of the chapter, using the hammer as a weight would solve this problem. What makes this problem difficult to solve is the tendency to see only the customary usage of the hammer, that is, as a tool to be used with nails. You are **functionally fixed** to see a hammer only as a tool for pounding nails.

Research using variants on the above two-cord problem found that if subjects had previous experience using the given objects in their normal function (e.g., pliers, relays, switches), they were less likely to solve the problem by using that object in a novel way (i.e., as a weight) (Adamson & Taylor, 1954; Birch, 1945; Birch & Rabinowitz, 1951). Hence, this research is consistent with the view that schematic knowledge (in this case, uses and function of tools) can have an interfering effect on problem solving.

As indicated earlier, research on expert and novice problem solving found that

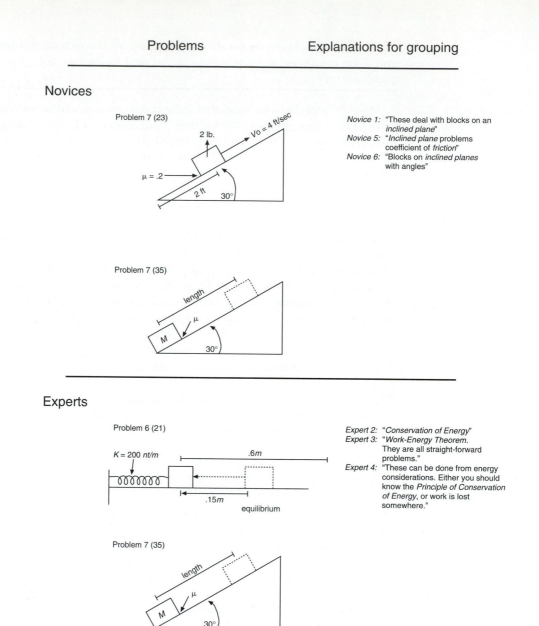

Problems   Explanations for grouping

Novices

Problem 7 (23)

2 lb.
$V_0 = 4$ ft/sec
$\mu = .2$
2 ft
30°

Novice 1: "These deal with blocks on an
          inclined plane"
Novice 5: "*Inclined plane* problems
          coefficient of *friction*"
Novice 6: "Blocks on *inclined planes*
          with angles"

Problem 7 (35)

length
μ
M
30°

Experts

Problem 6 (21)

$K = 200$ *nt/m*
.6*m*
.15*m*
equilibrium

Expert 2: "*Conservation of Energy*"
Expert 3: "*Work-Energy Theorem.*
          They are all straight-forward
          problems."
Expert 4: "These can be done from energy
          considerations. Either you should
          know the *Principle of Conservation
          of Energy*, or work is lost
          somewhere."

Problem 7 (35)

length
μ
M
30°

FIGURE 5.7   Novices' and experts' categorization of physics problems and their explanation for the grouping.
(Adapted from Chi, Feltovich, and Glaser, "Categorization and Representation of Physics Problems by Experts and Novices," in *Cognitive Science*, vol. 5, pp. 121–152, 1981. Used by permission of Ablex Publishing Corporation.)

novices tend to categorize problems based on superficial features while experts
tend to categorize problems based on deep fundamental features (Chi, Feltovich,
& Glaser, 1981; Silver, 1987). For example, novices in physics tend to categorize
problems which involve the movement of objects (see Figure 5.7) in concrete
terms such as the behavior of entities on inclined planes. In contrast, experts

would categorize these as problems related to Conservation of Energy (Chi, Feltovich, & Glaser, 1981).

As you can see, an individual's schematic knowledge is critical to successfully understanding and solving problems. Problem understanding must be considered in a broad context that includes both comprehending the problem statement and developing and encoding a reasonable representation of the problem. This is important because once a problem representation has been encoded, it activates a schema in LTM which then directs the search for a potential solution. If the wrong schema is activated, the search proceeds in an inappropriate direction.

Schematic Knowledge and Problem-solving Instruction

Given the purposive nature of schematic knowledge, it is important to induce students to perform a detailed analysis of the problem prior to seeking the solution. A student must be sure that her problem representation accurately reflects the nature of the problem. This process should involve a detailed analysis of not only the explicitly stated information, but also of any implicit information that can be assumed within the problem statement. For example, read through the following problem:

Exercise 5.22: Take six wooden matches and make four equilateral triangles without breaking any of the matches.

People tend to approach this problem by organizing and reorganizing the matches in an attempt to solve the problem (see Figure 5.8). If you have not already solved the problem, try to identify an implicit assumption that constrains your problem solving and the attempts depicted in Figure 5.8. Here's a hint: thr_ _ dimensional. These approaches (including yours, in all likelihood) all suffer from focusing on two-dimensional solutions when the problem requires a three-dimensional solution. Once you view this problem as three dimensional, it becomes easier to solve (see answer at end of chapter). This exercise underscores the importance of a detailed analysis of a problem *before* you embark upon trying to find a solution.

Two additional approaches for dealing with obstacles caused by inappropriate prior knowledge or inappropriate use of prior knowledge are fractionation and incubation. As indicated previously, most people have trouble finding a solution to the problem in Exercise 5.21 because they do not identify alternative uses for the objects involved in that problem. **Fractionation** would involve identifying the characteristics and functions of each object (e.g., light vs. heavy, round vs. square) or person (e.g., rich vs. poor, tall vs. short). Once you have done this, then you should look at the set of characteristics and see if any are relevant to finding a solution. Often, this process will allow you to identify unusual uses for the objects or people, which may help solve a problem. Basically, this approach is aimed at making the problem more concrete by identifying all explicit and implicit information embedded in that problem.

An alternative approach for dealing with interference caused by prior knowl-

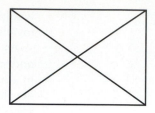

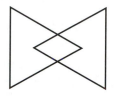

FIGURE 5.8   Incorrect attempts at solving Exercise 5.22.

edge or use of an inappropriate problem schema is to **incubate,** that is, to step away from the problem and do something completely different. For example, when I ask my students to try to solve the problem in Exercise 5.22, they initially have some difficulty. I usually stop them and show them a short (10–15 minutes) videotape on something that has nothing to do with the problem or with potential ways of solving the problem. Very often, when the students get back to the problem they will be able to break away from a two-dimensional perspective and solve it. Basically, viewing the short videotape gives them a period of incubation after which they can return to the problem and look at it with a fresh new perspective.

As indicated earlier, Wallas (1926) suggested that incubation is a necessary and important step in the problem-solving process. However, it is more useful to think of incubation as a method for interrupting and, it is hoped, overcoming the effects of an incorrect problem schema.

Metacognitive Knowledge and Problem Solving

In Chapter 4, we described **metacognition** as one's knowledge about and ability to control one's thought processes. Our metacognitive knowledge of problem solving consists of declarative, procedural, and motivational components. The declarative knowledge component involves our understanding of problem-solving tasks; the procedural component involves our ability to solve problems; and the motivational component involves our beliefs and attitudes about our problem-solving ability. Examples of the type of information included in the declarative component are the importance of clearly representing the problem prior to embarking on a search for the solution; differential difficulty and ease of problem types (e.g., word problems vs. formula problems); descriptions of algorithms and heuristics for solving problems; and an individual's preferences and style of problem solving. The declarative component is acquired through experience with a variety of problems involving a wide range of settings.

The procedural component of metacognition consists of the skills which we use to diagnose problem situations, select appropriate algorithms or heuristics, and monitor their effectiveness. As with an individual's declarative knowledge about problem solving, this procedural component develops with experience. Consequently, children would be expected to have less developed metacognitive processes related to problem solving than would adults.

Expert problem solvers have been shown to have more developed metacognitive ability within their domain of expertise than novices (Schoenfeld, 1985b; Voss, 1989). The most important procedural difference involves planning: the coordination of algorithms and heuristics and the monitoring of progress toward solving the problem. Experts guide their planning and monitoring process by posing and answering the following three kinds of questions: (1) what are you doing (i.e., what goal are you trying to attain), (2) what is the reason for doing it, and (3) how will the result be used later in the solution (Rohwer & Thomas, 1989; Schoenfeld, 1982, 1985a).

Finally, the motivational component concerns a student's beliefs and attitudes about her problem-solving ability. A good problem solver believes that she is capable of solving problems if she devotes lots of effort to the process. (Much more will be said about the importance of effort to success in Chapter 9.) Also, when a good problem solver fails, she will attribute it either to a lack of effort or to the use of an inappropriate algorithm or heuristic. Consequently, she will continue to approach problem-solving situations with the expectations that she will succeed (Rohwer & Thomas, 1989).

Metacognitive Knowledge and Problem-solving Instruction

The first step to improving a student's metacognitive knowledge of problem solving is to make him aware of the important components to successful problem solving. This involves explicitly discussing the importance of content knowledge, strategies, and schemas for solving problems. Just as I explicitly identified the different components of successful problem solving when discussing Exercise 5.15, teachers should explicitly describe how to solve representative problems within their specific domain (Schoenfeld, 1987).

The instructional techniques described in the previous sections for developing appropriate declarative, procedural, and schematic knowledge should also contribute to a student's metacognitive knowledge of problem solving. In addition, the teacher should underscore the *benefits* of developing each of these knowledge components. That is, *why* is it important to automatize basic algorithms; *why* is it important to create large, organized units of knowledge around high order principles; *why* is it important to be careful when creating a problem representation.

Finally, problem-solving instruction should emphasize the important relationship between effort and successful problem solving. One way to do this would be to present a problem, to devote very little effort toward solving the problem, and to fail. Then, with the same problem, devote lots of effort to finding the solution, and succeed. This will explicitly make the connection between high effort = success and low effort = failure. Also, do this with a variety of relevant problems.

As you may have already guessed (I hope!), a direct explanation approach would again be well-suited for increasing a student's metacognitive knowledge of what is required for successful problem solving.

Question 5.9: Why would a direct explanation approach be well-suited to increase students' metacognitive knowledge of problem solving?_____

_____

_____

As you can see from this discussion, problem solving is a complex and multi-faceted activity. Table 5.6 summarizes the important instructional issues related to each of the four types of problem-solving knowledge: declarative, procedural, schematic, and metacognitive.

In the second half of this chapter, we focused on a variety of problems (both academic and "real life" problems). The identified techniques for helping students develop their problem-solving capability are also relevant to your own problem solving. As a teacher, you will be faced with many classroom problems. If you prepare yourself to approach these problems as an "expert" problem solver, then you will be more likely to solve them. In the second half of this book, we will present ways to successfully identify classroom problems (i.e., create a problem representation) which will help you organize and solve them.

REVIEW OF MAJOR POINTS

1 A concept is an internal representation of a certain type or category of stimuli which allows a person to place similar stimuli in that category. They are abstractions—creations of the mind that help organize our experiences.

2 Within most instructional contexts, the most important categories of concepts are *concrete* and *abstract.* Examples of concrete concepts are typically easier to differentiate than examples and nonexamples of abstract concepts. Concrete concepts (e.g., table) are tangible and can be perceived, whereas abstract concepts (e.g., democracy) typically are not. Finally, due to the contextual nature of abstract concepts, one often needs to understand related concepts in order to fully understand the abstract one.

TABLE 5.6   SUMMARY OF IMPORTANT POINTS FOR TEACHING PROBLEM SOLVING

Declarative knowledge

a) Develop a broad base of domain-specific knowledge.

Procedural knowledge

a) Provide practice using algorithms and heuristics until automatic.
b) Teach the algorithms in the specific context in which they will be used, e.g., mathematics, social science.
c) When teaching algorithms and heuristics, identify how, when, and why to use each technique.
d) Teach students how to set specific, moderately difficult, and attainable goals.
e) Induce students to compare problems and their solutions in order to identify analogous problems *and* methods for identifying analogous problems.

Schematic knowledge

a) Teach students to perform detailed analysis of a problem prior to seeking a solution.
  i) Identify implicit and explicit assumptions.
  ii) Identify all characteristics and functions of problem entities.
b) Suggest to students that they take a break from a problem when having difficulty solving it (incubate).

Metacognitive knowledge

a) Explicitly teach (through verbal description, demonstration, and modeling) the important components of successful problem solving.
b) Explicitly identify the benefit of acquiring the important components of successful problem solving.
c) Identify and demonstrate the important link between high effort and successful problem solving.

3 An information processing approach to concept learning involves developing declarative knowledge (definition of concept) and procedural knowledge (procedures for using the concept) and integrating this knowledge within an appropriate conceptual domain, which is an organized set of related concepts (e.g., economics, eating).

4 There are three approaches to describing the declarative knowledge embedded in conceptual knowledge: the classical approach, the prototype approach, and the exemplar approach. The classical view states that each concept is defined by a set of critical attributes that each example must possess. A prototypical view suggests that, based on experience with many examples of a category, individuals abstract either a typical set of features or a prototype example that becomes the mental representation for that concept. The exemplar view also suggests that we store a specific example of a concept in memory rather than a list of critical attributes; however, it differs from the prototypical view by suggesting that the stored example is distinctive and memorable.

5 In teaching concepts, it is critical to (1) focus students on either the critical defining attributes or the prototypical attributes of teaching examples and nonexamples, (2) present prototypical and distinctive, memorable teaching examples, and (3) present the teaching examples and nonexamples in multiple formats (e.g., actual objects, visual images, written description).

6 Our ability to classify or categorize new instances and experiences as concept examples and nonexamples depends on procedural knowledge stored in LTM. There are three approaches to describing this procedural knowledge: the classical approach, the prototypical approach, and the exemplar approach. According to the classical approach, we categorize concepts by noting the critical attributes of a particular example and, if it possesses *all* the critical attributes, it is then classified as an example of that concept. According to the prototype approach, either an idealized (prototype) example or a set of abstracted features are used in classifying potential examples. If a potential example is similar enough to the prototype, it will then be classified as a member of the concept. As with the prototype view, exemplar concept classification involves evaluating the degree of overlap between novel examples and the stored exemplar. For both the prototype and exemplar views, classifying concepts then becomes *a matter of degree.*

7 The development of procedural knowledge requires practice classifying novel examples and nonexamples of the target concepts. The classical approach suggests teaching examples and nonexamples should be selected that will highlight the critical attributes of the target concepts. In addition, the classical approach suggests presenting a wide variety of examples in order to repeatedly focus the student on core critical attributes. Both the prototype and exemplar views suggest that teaching concepts should focus on developing students' ability to compare potential examples with a target example. In contrast, the classical view involves abstracting critical attributes of novel examples and comparing these with a set of remembered critical attributes associated with the target concept.

8 Within LTM, concepts are organized into conceptual domains and are most often represented in terms of a hierarchy or taxonomy. Particular levels of the relevant taxonomy are identified as "basic-level categories." Basic-level categories are coordinate (same level) concepts that are normally more familiar, are learned first, and are referenced more frequently than other levels of that domain. Examples within basic-level categories also tend to be more similar to each other than are examples at higher levels of the domain and tend to elicit more similar modes of interaction. Basic-level categories should be taught first, as they are usually the easiest to acquire. Taxonomies should be used as guides to identifying related concepts that may facilitate the learning of a target concept.

9 Problems can be divided into an initial state, a goal state, and obstacles to solving the problem. In addition, depending upon the detail with which these components are described, a problem is either well-defined or ill-defined. Also, there are two types of methods that are used to solve problems: algorithms, which guarantee a solution or attainment of a goal state, and heuristics, which do not guarantee a solution but may generate one more efficiently.

10 A problem space refers to the knowledge in LTM that is relevant to interpreting and solving a problem. A problem space limits the area of LTM that is relevant to finding a solution to the current problem.

11 Problems often exceed the capacity of working memory, due to both the complexity of the operations required and the storage requirements. People who are able to store more in working memory (while simultaneously operating on the information) are able to solve more complex problems than people who cannot store as much information in working memory.

12 Research on experts and novices has found that experts' superior problem-solving ability within their domain of expertise is due to their possessing (1) more verbalizable, domain-specific knowledge (i.e., declarative knowledge), (2) more effective strategies for solving problems (i.e., procedural knowledge), (3) more large chunks of knowledge organized around fundamental themes within the content area (i.e., schematic knowledge), and (4) more ability to plan and monitor their problem-solving attempts (i.e., metacognitive knowledge).

13 In order to become a more effective problem solver, an individual needs to acquire a large store of declarative knowledge related to the problem-solving domain. Consequently, in order to prepare students to be good problem solvers, a considerable amount of time and attention to building up content area knowledge is required. In order to ensure access to relevant declarative knowledge during problem solving, instruction should consist of problem-oriented activities. Problem-oriented activities involve the presentation of information within the context of future use and activities which require the student to use that information as it will be used in the future.

14 Algorithms and heuristics are methods or procedures for overcoming obstacles to problem solving. Algorithms are typically domain-specific methods whereas heuristics tend to be domain-general. Two types of heuristics are the analogical approach and the difference-reduction approach. Solving a problem by analogy involves (1) comparing the current problem with other, similar, problems that have been solved and (2) applying to the current problem the same method which solved the analogous one. A difference-reduction approach aims to reduce the difference between the current state and the goal state. One way to do this is by creating subgoals that will move one to the final goal by successive approximations. An alternative method is the means-end analysis in which an individual creates subgoals whose purpose is to eliminate the most important difference between the current state and goal state. In this way, although you eventually arrive at the final goal, each step may not move you closer to the goal state. Some steps may move away from the final goal in order that later steps may move forward. Both algorithms and heuristics are best taught through instruction which emphasizes the how, why, and when of using each approach, that is, a direct explanation approach.

15 Schemas consist of both declarative and procedural knowledge and are organized around a theme (baseball, clothes, art, etc.). Problem-solving schemas include themes related to the different types of problems that one may be expected to solve. Identifying the appropriate problem-solving schema is crucial since the activated schema contains the knowledge that is used to solve the problem. If the wrong schema is activated, there is little chance that its knowledge will be related to the problem. Hence, there is little chance of solving the problem.

16 Given the purposive nature of schematic knowledge, it is important to emphasize that students need to perform a detailed analysis of the problem prior to trying to find the solution. A student must be sure that her problem representation accurately reflects the nature of the problem. Part of this process should involve a detailed analysis of both the explicitly stated information and implicit information that can be assumed within the problem statement.

17 Our metacognitive knowledge of problem solving includes a declarative, a procedural, and a motivational component. The declarative component provides an understanding of problem-solving tasks and our problem-solving abilities. The procedural component provides skills for diagnosing and monitoring problem-solving efforts. The first step in improving students' metacognitive knowledge of problem solving is to make them aware of these important components. This involves explicitly discussing the importance of content knowledge, strategies, and schemas for solving a *variety* of problems. There should be explicit discussion of the similarities and differences between these problems. In addition to the specific methods discussed earlier for developing declarative, procedural, and schematic knowledge, the teacher should underscore the *benefits* of developing each of these knowledge components. A direct explanation approach would again be well-suited to this task.

ANSWERS TO QUESTIONS AND EXERCISES

Question 5.1: The two types of knowledge in semantic memory are declarative and procedural. Declarative knowledge refers to *what* we know, that is, to knowledge that we can verbalize. For example, when we state the definition of a concept, that definition is said to be stored as declarative knowledge. Also, stating the steps that are involved in solving problems reflects our declarative knowledge of problem solving. Procedural knowledge refers to *how* we guide our mental and physical activities. Classifying novel examples of concepts and solving novel math problems by using our specific mathematical procedures are both instances of procedural knowledge in this domain.

Exercise 5.1: Judy is the housewife, Celia is the math teacher, and Betty is the truck driver.

Exercise 5.2: Categorize the following concepts as either concrete or abstract and justify your answers:

a. car *concrete*—it is usually very easy to identify examples and nonexamples. Cars are very tangible, and understanding the concept does not depend on related concepts or the context within which the example is placed.

b. love *abstract*—it is often hard to differentiate between love and related concepts (lust, infatuation, duty, etc.). Love is not very tangible, and context often plays an important part in identifying whether something is an example of love.

c. bird *concrete*—it is usually not difficult to identify examples of birds. Birds are very tangible, easily perceived objects, and understanding the concept does not depend on related concepts or the context within which the example is placed.

d. creativity *abstract*—it is difficult to identify criteria for creative behaviors and to differentiate them from related concepts (intelligence, common sense, intuition, etc.). Creativity is not tangible, and context plays an important part in understanding the concept and identifying examples of the concept.

Exercise 5.4: The technical definition for bird is a warm-blooded vertebrate with wings and feathers; hind limbs variously adapted for perching, swimming, walking, scratching, etc.; shanks and toes usually without feathers, covered with cornified scales; beak or bill without teeth and covered with a horny sheath; neck flexible and often long; sternum large, usually with a prominent median keel; heart four-chambered, right aortic arch persistent; red blood corpuscles with nuclei; lungs with associated thin-walled sacs ramifying between visceral organs; syrinx at base of trachea; bladder absent, excretions semisolid; female with only one ovary and oviduct; fertilization internal; eggs incubated externally, with large yolk and limy shell; embryonic membranes present; upon hatching, young variously developed and dependent upon parents. (Taken from Pennak, 1988.)

Question 5.2: A classical view of concepts states that each concept consists of a set of critical, defining attributes. These attributes are necessary for category membership and serve to differentiate examples from nonexamples. This view assumes that critical attributes can be identified for all concepts, that all examples of a concept are equally good if they possess all the required critical attributes, and that one can easily decide concept membership by noting the presence or absence of these attributes. A prototype view also assumes some level of abstraction. However, the attributes that are abstracted are prototypical; that is, they typically but not always occur and are not necessarily critical or defining. In contrast, the exemplar view assumes that we do not perform any abstraction from everyday experience and that we store a distinctive and memorable example to represent a particular concept.

Exercise 5.5: We have listed only verbal descriptions below; however, as indicated in the directions, you could have represented examples with pictures.

	prototypical example	memorable example
a. pizza	a round very thick crust (2 inches deep) with lots of cheese and tomato sauce	a spinach pizza cooked in a bowl with a crust
b. politician	Warren Rudman	Huey Long (flamboyant former governor of Louisiana)
c. catastrophe	California landslide	earthquake in San Francisco
d. tree	an oak tree	a hollowed-out sequoia that you have driven through

Exercise 5.6:
a. A turbine is like a water wheel.
b. A zero can be compared to a bookmark.

c. Red blood cells work like trucks or trains.

d. Repentance is like soap.

Question 5.3: According to the classical approach, we categorize concepts by noting whether or not a particular example possesses *all* the critical attributes of a given concept. This is an *all or none* view of how we classify examples of concepts. According to the prototype and exemplar approaches, either an idealized (prototype) example or set of features or a distinctive example is used to classify potential examples. If a potential example is perceived as similar enough to the prototype or memorable example, then it will be classified as a member of that concept. Classifying concepts then becomes *a matter of degree,* and the boundaries for what is perceived as an example or not-an-example become quite fuzzy.

Exercise 5.7:
Pair 1: A baseball (example) and a baseball bat (nonexample). A baseball bat is sufficiently rigid to maintain shape in repeated use and is manipulated in a game but is not round in shape.

Pair 2: A basketball (example) and a medicine ball (nonexample). A medicine ball is round in shape and is sufficiently rigid to maintain shape in repeated use but is not manipulated in a game.

Pair 3: A billiard ball (example) and a water balloon (nonexample). A water balloon is round in shape and is manipulated in a game (childhood games—cops and robbers, etc.) but is not sufficiently rigid to maintain shape with repeated use. (Concept definition was taken from Tiemann & Markle, 1978.)

Exercise 5.8: The middle levels of all three taxonomies are most likely to be the basic-level categories since they are usually chosen as instances of these superordinate categories. For example, a maintained play area in a community is more likely to be referred to as a "park" than as a "city park" or "neighborhood park." These basic category examples also tend to be more similar and to elicit more similar modes of interaction than examples of concepts at the next higher and highest levels in the taxonomy. For instance, how one behaves in different homes is more similar than how one behaves across homes, schools, stores, and restaurants.

Exercise 5.9: The way to solve this problem is:
Step 1: Fold the bottom third of the paper up and over the middle third.

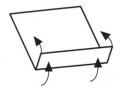

Step 2: Draw half the circle and the number 100 as depicted in the diagram.

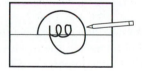

Step 3: While keeping your pencil on the upper third of the paper, unfold the bottom third and complete the circle around the number 100.

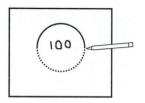

Question 5.4: The three components of a problem are the initial state, goal state, and obstacles. The initial state is the set of givens in a problem situation—the problem statement; the goal state is the solution to the problem; obstacles are the barriers which make it difficult to get from the initial state to the goal state. A well-defined problem is one in which all three components are clearly described, and the major task is to try to find a way to overcome the obstacle. In contrast, an ill-defined problem is a problem in which one, two, or all major components are not clearly described.

Exercise 5.10: Please classify the following problems as being either well-defined or ill-defined and explain why.
1. Prove the existence of God.
This is an ill-defined problem because there are many questions about the goal state. For example: Which God? What does it mean to "prove the existence of"? Also, what are the givens in this situation?
2. One-fourth is to 8 as 2 is to _____.
This is a well-defined problem because the givens are clear ($1/4 \times 8 = 2 \times$ unknown), the goal is to equate the two sides, and the primary obstacle is to appropriately use multiplication and division skills.
3. Create a method for safely discarding nuclear waste.
There are many questions related to this problem, but the most important ones are: How do we define "safely discarding"? And what kinds of nuclear waste, that is, from what process? Consequently, this is an ill-defined problem.
4. How may the crime rate in Houston be reduced?

Some of the questions that need to be answered before attempting to solve this problem are: Are we talking about the rate of all crime? How much of a reduction are we looking for? This is an ill-defined problem.

5. The fire department wants to send booklets on fire hazards to all teachers and homeowners in town. How many booklets does it need? (Use the following statistics: Homeowners = 53,000; Teachers = 7,000; Teachers who own their homes = 6,000.)

This is a well-defined problem. The givens are the statistics presented above while the goal is to calculate how many booklets on fire hazards are needed. The obstacle to solving this problem is identifying a method for calculating the number of booklets. One potential approach is to use venn diagrams.

Exercises 5.11, 5.12, and 5.13: The answers to these exercises are contained within the text.

Question 5.5: The most important step to solving problems is to come up with a clear representation of the problem. This means having a good idea of what the problem entails. Without this it is unlikely that you will come up with the solution to the problem.

Exercise 5.14: The answer is Mr. Heath.

Question 5.6: First, developing methods for *chunking information* would allow an individual to minimize the amount of attention devoted to storing information in working memory and maximize the attention that could be devoted to problem-solving operations. For example, an individual may have developed mnemonics for combining some of the steps described in a complex problem that is contained in Exercise 5.13. A related method is to *automatize the basic processes* that are employed during problem solving. For example, if an individual has extensive experience with problems within a particular domain (e.g., chess), she may quickly and automatically sort the important problem information from the unimportant and use the important information to create an appropriate problem representation. A seasoned or expert chess player can look at a board position, automatically classify the position, and then immediately access a variety of possible moves based on previous experience with this particular position. Once the problem has been appropriately categorized, the chess expert has reduced the load on working memory and can spend her time and mental energy on identifying a useful next move.

Exercises 5.15, 5.16, and 5.17: The answers to these exercises are presented in the text.

Exercise 5.18: Read the following set of problems and identify those that are similar and could be solved using analogous methods. Identify similar problems by labeling them all with the same letter: A, B, C, etc. Answers: a) A; b) B; c) C; d) D; e) A; f) B; g) A.

Problems a, e, and g are multiplication problems and can be solved with analogous multiplication operations:

Problem a: $4 \times 4 = 16$ apples; problem e: $3 \times 30 = 90$ miles; problem g: $8 \times 2 = \$.16$, $5 \times 6 = \$.30$, so it will cost $.46.

Problems b and f are verbal reasoning problems that can be solved by using a diagram of a continuum (see below) to keep track of the different comparative heights of the men and the difficulty of languages.

Problem b:

Step 1: German is harder than French

```
            G      F
   Harder |-------|-------| Easier
```

Step 2: Russian is harder than Swedish

```
            R      SW
   Harder |-------|-------| Easier
```

Step 3: German is easier than Swedish

```
            G     SW     G      F
   Harder |-------|-------|-------|-------| Easier
```

Step 4: Spanish is easier than French

```
            R     SW     G      F      SP
   Harder |-------|-------|-------|-------|-------| Easier
```

Step 5: Given this diagram, it is easy to identify that Sandra speaks the most difficult languages—Russian and Swedish. (Taken from Whimbey and Lochhead, 1986.)

Problem f:

Step 1: Paul is taller than Tom

```
             P      T
   Tallest |-------|-------| Shortest
```

Step 2: . . . but shorter than Sam

```
             S      P      T
   Tallest |-------|-------|-------| Shortest
```

Step 3: Smith is the tallest of the three and Calvin is the shortest

```
             S             C
   Tallest |-------|-------|-------| Shortest
```

Step 4: A look at the problem statement reveals that Jones is the third last name.

```
             S      J      C
   Tallest |-------|-------|-------| Shortest
```

Step 5: Comparing this diagram with the one generated in Step 3 indicates that Paul's last name is Jones and Tom's last name is Calvin. (Taken from Whimbey & Lochhead, 1986.)

Problems c and d are not similar to any other problem presented. Problem c can be solved by standing up and actually going through the directed movements, by visualizing the movements, or by drawing them out. (Answer is east.) Problem d is a basic math problem requiring subtraction: $23.00 − $11.31 = $11.69.

Exercise 5.19: An obvious series of subgoals for solving this problem would be to start with the least anxiety-provoking situation and slowly work your way to the most anxiety-provoking situation. For example, a potential subgoal would be to make the individual less anxious in low-pressure group situations, such as those involving a discussion with one friend about some familiar topic. Once this subgoal is attained, then other subgoals can be identified which would move him closer to the goal state, for instance, discussing something unfamiliar with the same friend, discussing something familiar with two people (one friend and one stranger).

Question 5.7: Subgoaling consists of identifying intermediate states which will eventually lead to the desired goal state. It is helpful because it can reduce the number of solution paths that need to be searched. This, in turn, reduces the load on memory and frees up attentional energy for dealing with other aspects of the problem. This approach works best when the subgoals are obvious. When they are not obvious, the individual may spend considerable amounts of time creating subgoals and, of course, this increases the overall time required to solve a problem.

The means-ends analysis has the same disadvantage as the above method, that is, the time required to continually create subgoals. The advantage of the means-ends analysis is that the goals are specifically aimed at reducing the most important difference between where you are now and the goal state. These subgoals will often take the form of eliminating obstacles to attaining the most important differences.

Question 5.8: A direct explanation approach to strategy instruction focuses on the *how, when,* and *why* of using strategies. With respect to the *how* of using a problem-solving strategy, the teacher explicitly teaches the strategy, using verbal description and demonstration, and involves students in extensive and varied practice. In terms of *when* to use a problem-solving strategy, the teacher needs to point out for what tasks the specific strategy works best (e.g., when doing ill-defined vs. well-defined problems). The teacher also stresses *why* to use the problem-solving strategy and why it works. This involves pointing out the positive connection between the strategy and successful problem solving. In addition, the teacher should indicate specific reasons why the problem-solving strategy improves performance (e.g., helps in the development of a problem representation; frees up attentional energy). A final and important aspect of direct strategy instruction is a focus on motivation. The teacher needs to emphasize that successful problem solving is a function of hard work and good problem-solving strategies. Students should then attribute success to this intense effort and to good problem-solving strategies; they should attribute failure to lack of effort or use of a poor strategy. This will make students more persistent in problem-solving situations.

Exercise 5.20: How many stops did the bus make?

Exercise 5.21: You could use the hammer as a *weight:* Tie it to the end of one rope; set that rope swinging toward the other rope; walk to the other rope; grab it; walk as far as you can back to the swinging rope; and when it swings toward you, grab it.

Exercise 5.22: The solution to this problem is to build a pyramid. Each side (including the base) is an equilateral triangle, and you can build it with six matches (see illustration below).

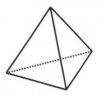

Question 5.9: Metacognition is responsible for the following: diagnosing problems, selecting appropriate problem-solving strategies, and monitoring their use. A direct explanation approach to teaching strategies would focus on the how, when, and why of strategies and their use. Focusing students on when to use strategies and why they work will help in the development of both diagnostic and selection abilities. That is, knowing the situations in which a strategy is appropriate and why that strategy is appropriate will cue important aspects of problem solving that will help in diagnosing a problem. Also, identifying the situations in which a strategy is most appropriate will help develop the selection abilities of students. Finally, understanding how to use a strategy and why it works will help students better monitor the use of the strategies and will help them to identify alternative strategies when they run into difficulty.

REFERENCES

Adamson, R., & Taylor, D. (1954). Functional fixedness as related to elapsed time and set. *Journal of Experimental Psychology, 44,* 288–291.
Anderson, J. (1990). *Cognitive psychology and its implications.* New York: W. H. Freeman.

André, T. (1986). Problem solving and education. In G. Phye & T. André (Eds.), *Cognitive classroom learning: Understanding, thinking, and problem solving.* New York: Academic Press.

Barsalou, L. (1989). Intraconcept similarity and its implications for interconcept similarity. In S. Vasniadou & A. Ontony (Eds.), *Similarity and analogical reasoning.* Cambridge: Cambridge University Press.

Birch, H. (1945). The relation of previous experience to insightful problem solving. *Journal of Comparative Psychology, 38,* 367–383.

Birch, H., & Rabinowitz, H. (1951). The negative effect of previous experience on productive thinking. *Journal of Experimental Psychology, 41,* 121–125.

Bransford, J., Franks, J., Vye, N., & Sherwood, R. (1989). New approaches to instruction: Because wisdom can't be told. In S. Vosnaidou and A. Ontony (Eds.), *Similarity and analogical reasoning.* New York: Cambridge University Press.

Bransford, J., Sherwood, R., Vye, N., & Reiser, J. (1986). Teaching thinking and problem solving. *American Psychologist, 41,* 1078–1089.

Cantor, N., Smith, E., French, R., & Mezzich, J. (1980). Psychiatric diagnosis as prototype categorization. *Journal of Abnormal Psychology, 89,* 181–193.

Catrambone, R., & Holyoak, K. (1989). Overcoming contextual limitations on problem-solving transfer. *Journal of Experimental Psychology: Learning, Memory, and Cognition, 15,* 1147–1156.

Chi, M., Feltovich, P., & Glaser, R. (1981). Categorization and representation of physics problems by experts and novices. *Cognitive Science, 5,* 121–152.

Chi, M., Glaser, R., & Rees, R. (1982). Expertise in problem solving. In R. Sternberg (Ed.), *Advances in the psychology of human intelligence.* Hillsdale, NJ: Lawrence Erlbaum.

Cognition and Technology Group at Vanderbilt. (1992). Anchored instruction in science and mathematics: Theoretical basis, developmental projects and initial findings. In R. Duschl & R. Hamilton (Eds.), *Philosophy of science, cognitive psychology and educational theory and practice.* Albany, NY: SUNY Press.

Duncker, K. (1945). On problem solving. *Psychological Monographs, 58* (*5,* Whole No. 270).

Dunn, C. (1983). The influence of instructional methods on concept learning. *Science Education, 67,* 647–656.

Gick, M., & Holyoak, K. (1980). Analogical problem solving. *Cognitive Psychology, 12,* 306–355.

Gick, M., & Holyoak, K. (1983). Schema induction and analogical transfer. *Cognitive Psychology, 15,* 1–38.

Hayes, J. (1966). Memory, goals, and problem solving. In B. Kleinmuntz (Ed.), *Problem solving: Research, methods, and theory.* New York: Wiley.

Hayes, J. (1987). *The complete problem solver.* Hillsdale, NJ: Lawrence Erlbaum.

Howard, R. (1987). *Concepts and schemata.* London: Casell Education.

Jeffries, R., Turner, A., Polson, P., & Atwood, M. (1981). The processes involved in designing software. In J. Anderson (Ed.), *Cognitive skills and their acquisition.* Hillsdale, NJ: Lawrence Erlbaum.

Larkin, J. (1980a). Information processing models and science instruction. In J. Lochhead & J. Clement (Eds.), *Cognitive process instruction.* Philadelphia: Franklin Institute Press.

Larkin, J. (1980b). Teaching problem solving in physics: The psychological laboratory and the practical classroom. In D. Tuna & F. Reif (Eds.), *Problem solving and education: Issues in teaching and research* (pp. 111–125). Hillsdale, NJ: Lawrence Erlbaum.

Larkin, J., McDermott, J., Simon, D., & Simon, H. (1980). Expert and novice performance in solving physics problems. *Science, 208,* 1335–1342.

Lesgold, A., Rubinson, H., Feltovich, P., Glaser, R., Klopfer, D., & Wang, Y. (1988). Expertise in a complex skill: Diagnosing X-ray pictures. In M. Chi, R. Glaser, & M. Farr (Eds.), *The nature of expertise.* Hillsdale, NJ: Lawrence Erlbaum.

Locke, E., Shaw, K., Saari, L., & Latham, G. (1981). Goal setting and task performance: 1969–1980. *Psychological Bulletin, 90,* 125–152.

Locke, J. (1689/1975). *An essay concerning human understanding* (crit. ed. by Peter H. Nidditch). Oxford: Oxford University Press.

Maier, N. (1931). Reasoning in humans II: The solution of a problem and its appearance in consciousness. *Journal of Comparative Psychology, 12,* 181–194.

Maier, N. (1933). An aspect of human reasoning. *British Journal of Psychology, 14,* 144–155.

Mayer, R. (1992). *Thinking, problem solving and cognition.* San Francisco: W. H. Freeman.

McNamara, T., Miller, D., & Bransford, J. (1993). Mental models and reading comprehension. In T. Pearson, R. Bair, M. Kamill, & P. Mosenthal (Eds.), *Handbook of reading research* (Vol. 1). New York: Longman.

Medin, M. (1989). Concepts and conceptual structure. *American Psychologist, 44,* 1469–1481.

Medin, M., & Ross, B. (1989). The specific character of abstract thought: Categorization, problem solving and induction. In R. J. Sternberg (Ed.), *Advances in the psychology of human intelligence* (Vol. 5). Hillsdale, NJ: Lawrence Erlbaum.

Medin, M., & Smith, E. (1984). Concept and concept formation. *Annual Review of Psychology, 35,* 113–138.

Mervis, C., & Rosch, E. (1981). Categorization of natural objects. *Annual Review of Psychology, 32,* 289–316.

Murphy, G., & Smith, E. (1982). Basic-level superiority in picture categorization. *Journal of Verbal Learning and Verbal Behavior, 21,* 1–20.

Newby, T., & Stepich, D. (1987). Learning abstract concepts: The use of analogies as a mediational strategy. *Journal of Instructional Development, 10*(2), 20–26.

Newell, A., Shaw, J., and Simon, H. (1958). Elements of a theory of problem solving. *Psychological Review, 65,* 151–166.

Newell, A., & Simon, H. (1972). *Human problem solving.* Englewood Cliffs, NJ: Prentice-Hall.

Oden, G. (1987). Concept, knowledge and thought. *Annual Review of Psychology, 38,* 203–227.

Park, O. (1984). Example comparison strategy versus attribute identification strategy in concept learning. *American Educational Research Journal, 21,* 145–162.

Pavio, A. (1991). Dual coding theory: Retrospect and current status. *Canadian Journal of Psychology, 45*(3), 255–287.

Pennak, R. (1988). *Collegiate dictionary of zoology.* Malbar, FL: Robert E. Krieger.

Perfetto, B., Bransford, J., & Franks, J. (1983). Constraints on access in a problem solving context. *Memory and Cognition, 11,* 24–31.

Polya, G. (1957). *How to solve it.* Garden City, NY: Doubleday/Anchor. (Originally published by Princeton University Press, 1945.)

Reed, H. & Dick, R. (1968). The learning and generalization of abstract and concrete concepts. *Journal of Verbal Learning and Verbal Behavior, 7,* 486–490.

Reed, S. (1992). *Cognition: Theory and application.* Pacific Grove, CA: Brooks, Cole.

Reif, F. (1980). Theoretical and educational concerns with problem solving: Bridging the gaps with human cognitive engineering. In D. Tuna & F. Reif (Eds.), *Problem solving and education: Issues in teaching and research* (pp. 39–50). Hillsdale, NJ: Lawrence Erlbaum.

Rohwer, W., & Thomas, J. (1989). Domain-specific knowledge, metacognition, and the promise of instructional reform. In C. McCormick, G. Miller, & M. Pressley (Eds.), *Cognitive strategy research: From basic research to educational application.* New York: Springer-Verlag.

Rosch, E. (1978). Principles of categorization. In E. Rosch & B. Lloyd (Eds.), *Cognition and categorization.* Hillsdale, NJ: Lawrence Erlbaum.

Schoenfeld, A.H. (1979). Can heuristics be taught? In J. Lochhead & J. Clement (Eds.), *Cognitive process instruction* (pp. 315–338). Philadelphia: Franklin Institute Press.

Schoenfeld, A. H. (1983). Measures of problem solving performance and of problem solving instruction. *Journal for Research in Mathematics Education, 13,* 31–49.

Schoenfeld, A. H. (1985a). *Mathematical problem solving.* Orlando, FL: Academic Press.

Schoenfeld, A. H. (1985b). Metacognitive and epistemological issues in mathematical understanding. In E. Silver (Ed.), *Teaching and learning mathematical problem solving: Multiple research perspectives* (pp. 361–379). Hillsdale, NJ: Lawrence Erlbaum.

Schoenfeld, A. H. (1987). What's all the fuss about metacognition? In A. Schoenfeld (Ed.), *Cognitive science and mathematics education.* Hillsdale, NJ: Lawrence Erlbaum.

Sherwood, R., Kinzer, C., Bransford, J., & Franks, J. (1987). Some benefits of creating macro-context for science instruction: Initial findings. *Journal of Research in Science Teaching, 24*(5), 417–435.

Silver, E. (1987). Foundations of cognitive theory and research for mathematics problem-solving. In A. Schoenfeld (Ed.), *Cognitive science and mathematics education.* Hillsdale, NJ: Lawrence Erlbaum.

Simon, H., & Newell, A. (1971). Human problem solving: The state of the theory in 1970. *American Psychologists, 26,* 145–149.

Simon, H., & Reed, S. (1976). Modeling strategy shifts in a problem-solving task. *Cognitive Psychology, 8,* 79–86.

Smith, E., & Medin, D. (1981). *Categories and concepts.* Cambridge, MA: Harvard University Press.

Tennyson, R., Chao, J., & Youngers, J. (1981). Concept learning effectiveness using prototype and skill development presentation forms. *Journal of Educational Psychology, 73,* 326–334.

Tennyson, R., & Cocchiarella, M. (1986). An empirically based instructional design theory for teaching concepts. *Review of Educational Research, 56,* 40–71.

Tennyson, R., & Park, O. (1980). The teaching of concepts: A review of instructional design literature. *Review of Education Research, 50,* 55–70.

Tennyson, R. D., Yonngers, J., & Suebsonthi, P. (1983). Acquisition of mathematics concepts by children using prototype and skill development presentation forms. *Journal of Educational Psychology, 75,* 280–291.

Tiemann, P., & Markle, S. (1978). *Analyzing instructional content: A guide to instruction and evaluation.* Champaign, IL: Stipes.

Tversky, B., & Hemenway, K. (1983). Categories of environmental scenes. *Cognitive Psychology, 15,* 121–149.

Voss, J. (1989). Problem solving and the educational process. In A. Lesgold & R. Glaser (Eds.), *Foundations for a psychology of education.* Hillsdale, NJ: Lawrence Erlbaum.

Wallas, G. (1926). *The art of thought.* New York: Harcourt Brace Jovanovich.

Whimbey, A., & Lochhead, J. (1986). *Problem solving and comprehension.* Hillsdale, NJ: Lawrence Erlbaum.

6

PIAGETIAN AND NEO-PIAGETIAN THEORIES OF COGNITIVE DEVELOPMENT

OBJECTIVES

1. Define "development" and describe how it differs from "learning."
2. Compare and contrast figurative and operative schemes and describe their role in cognitive development.
3. State the definitions of "assimilation," "accommodation," and "equilibration"; describe how these processes are related and how they influence the course of cognitive development.
4. Given descriptions of specific behaviors, classify them as involving primarily assimilation or accommodation.
5. Identify two important characteristics of each of Piaget's stages of cognitive development.
6. Describe two ways in which Case's neo-Piagetian theory is different from and similar to Piaget's theory of cognitive development.
7. State the definitions of "operational efficiency" and "executive control structures" and how these influence the process of cognitive development.
8. Briefly describe each of Case's neo-Piagetian stages of cognitive development.
9. Compare and contrast the position of Piaget's and Case's theory of cognitive development on the core issues.

In chapter one, we defined **"learning"** as a relatively permanent change in knowledge or behavior due to experience. In contrast, **"development"** is broader and more encompassing and can be defined as an orderly and relatively permanent change in knowledge or behavior due to learning and/or maturation. **"Maturation"** is the biological unfolding of an individual according to an inherited genetic plan. *Development, then, involves both experiential and biological changes in* *knowledge and behavior.* As an illustration, the high school student preparing for a test may have learned to take good notes during class, to anticipate teacher questions, and to pace her studying activities. She has also acquired the experience of taking a variety of tests in a variety of formats and conditions. In addition, she has cognitively matured such that she is able to concentrate longer and mentally manipulate multiple facets of information. All these combine to improve and develop her test-taking skills.

Due to the role of maturation in development, development always involves orderly change. The rate at which individuals change may differ but the sequence of changes that occur is typically the same across all individuals. For example, before a child is able to think logically about abstract events, he first needs to have developed the ability to think logically about concrete events. In contrast, the changes that occur during learning may or may not be orderly, depending on the nature of instruction and experience.

We include developmental theories in a textbook on learning because an individual's ability to learn from particular situations is critically influenced by her own level of maturity and development. For example, you would not be able to begin teaching a child how to speculate and hypothesize about future events until he has developed the ability to think and reason about abstract events. No matter how well you design learning activities, if a child has not attained a particular development level, he will not benefit from the instruction. Consequently, we need to identify the student's level of development and then design learning activities with this in mind.

The two cognitive developmental theories discussed in this chapter are Jean Piaget's theory of cognitive development and Robbie Case's neo-Piagetian theory of cognitive development. Jean Piaget (1886–1980), a Swiss-born psychologist, spent approximately 60 years studying how children think and reason. As you will see, his training in biology and philosophy contributed heavily to the creation of his theory of cognitive development. Robbie Case's neo-Piagetian theory offers a more modern view of development and learning that combines aspects of Piaget's theory with aspects of information processing theory. It is important to note, however, that Case's neo-Piagetian theory is one of many which integrate aspects of Piagetian theory with aspects of information processing theory (see Fischer, 1980; Fischer & Pipp, 1984; Siegler & Hodkin, 1982).

Both of these theories adopt a cognitive constructivist perspective on the process of development. As you recall from previous chapters, **cognitive constructivist theories** assume that individuals are actively involved in the process of acquiring and modifying their knowledge. That is, what we know about ourselves and the world around us is constantly evolving as new experiences cause us to modify our existing knowledge. For example, a young child will experiment with her food to see what the different types taste and feel like, what kind of noise they make when they hit the floor, and so on. The child is attempting to learn about both the nature of different foods and how she can modify her environment. In summary, both theories explain development in terms of everchanging knowledge and assume that individuals are actively involved in creating their knowledge and, consequently, in determining their development. Now let us turn to the first of these two theories.

PIAGET'S THEORY OF COGNITIVE DEVELOPMENT

According to Piaget, changes in behavior that occur during development are a result of changes in our **ability to reason** about the world around us (Piaget, 1964). We reason in order to adapt to our environment, and how well we reason determines how well we interact with that environment. For example, because an infant is capable of reasoning only about events that involve physical movement, she will interact with the world at a very concrete level. Her reasoning is limited to manipulating and grasping objects to see how they relate to other objects in the world. In contrast, an adolescent is capable of abstract reasoning and consequently is able to interact with the world on a logical and symbolic level. He is capable of systematically testing verbal hypotheses about hypothetical problems. Although both internal (reasoning ability) and external (modes of interacting with the environment) changes occur during development, *Piaget identifies the internal changes as primary and responsible for the external changes.*

Drawing from his training as a biologist, Piaget suggested that the development of reasoning and intelligence parallels the development of other biological systems of the body. Just as the digestive system allows us to derive life-sustaining nutrients from the foods we eat, so the cognitive system helps us extract information from the environment in order to understand and adapt to that environment. Also, since our biological systems are critically influenced by preset, innate mechanisms, one important influence on the development of reasoning and intelligence is maturation, that is, innate biological changes.

A variety of environmental factors also influences most biological systems. For example, the types of foods available will dramatically influence the development of the digestive system, as well as other biological systems that depend on its nutrients. Similarly, if a child is not allowed to explore and investigate the environment or is exposed to one that is impoverished, she is not likely to attain more complex levels of reasoning. According to Piaget, our attempts to adapt to the world stimulate higher and higher levels of reasoning which, in turn, increase our ability to adapt to the world.

Finally, Piaget used two methods of observation to verify the basic tenets of his theory. Out of the biological tradition, he used a **naturalistic observational method** which consisted of carefully observing children's behavior in natural environments (e.g., schools and homes) without any experimenter intervention. From the psychological and philosophical tradition, he developed a two-part method of **clinical observation.** First, the child is presented with a task and is asked to make a verbal or nonverbal response. Upon receiving the response, the experimenter then asks the child a question, poses a variation of the problem, or sets up a new situation. Thus a probe-response/new probe-and-response cycle is set in motion until the experimenter can clearly classify the child's developmental level. The following experimental description and protocol exemplifies the clinical observation method used by Piaget in his study of cognitive development. In this experiment, the investigator placed six tokens on the table in a straight line with equal spaces between them. The child's (Jon—4 years, 5 months) task was to pick out of the container the same number of counters. (Investigator's comments are in italics.)

"Take the same number as there are there (6 counters)."—Jon put 7 tokens close together, and then made the correct correspondence.—*"Are they the same?"*— "Yes."—Investigator then spread out Jon's row of tokens and asked: *"Are they the same?"*—"No."—*"Has one of us got more?"*—"Me."—*"Make it so you have the same number as I have."*—Jon closes his tokens up.—*"Are they the same?"*— "Yes."—*"Why?"*—"Because I pushed mine together." (Piaget, 1952, p. 151.)

As can be seen in this protocol, for Piaget, the correctness of a child's answer is secondary to the thought processes used to justify the answer. Piaget was most concerned with the logic that children employed to justify their answers.

The Process of Development

According to Piaget, all normal individuals follow the same pattern of development whether they are 10 months old or 70 years old. That is because, according to Piaget, all biological systems share specific characteristics and functions which operate throughout the life span. Piaget identified these as "functional invariants." According to him, the two **functional invariants** which constrain and encourage all types of development are organization and adaptation.

Organization   As indicated earlier, cognition is viewed as one of many biological systems that help us adapt to our environment. Each of these systems is highly **organized;** that is, each one follows a pattern of coordinated activities that allows it to fulfill a specific purpose or goal. For example, the respiratory system has a coordinated set of activities which enables us to draw oxygen from the air and pass it on to the circulatory system. The cognitive system is no different. We are born with organized ways of extracting information from the environment. According to Piaget (1967), our cognitive system pushes us to actively seek out information about the environment and then to organize it into an accurate picture of this world. The knowledge structure that is primarily responsible for our ability to reason and adapt to the environment is the **scheme.** *Schemes are specific patterns of mental or physical activity for acquiring information about the environment.* For example, infants will invariably grab novel objects. This *grabbing* scheme allows them to learn about the characteristics of these new objects. Alternatively, when a child mistakenly applies the label "cat" (i.e., cat scheme) to a dog, he learns both about the nature of cats as well as the nature of dogs. These structures both facilitate and constrain our interactions with objects, events, and people.

In Chapter 3, we discussed different types of knowledge and how they affected our ability to learn and remember. One particular type was schema. If you recall, "schema" was defined as a unit which represents verbalizable knowledge about things and situations and which guides behavior. For example, a *restaurant* schema would not only consist of the verbalizable knowledge about what occurs in restaurants and appropriate restaurant behaviors, but would also be responsible for guiding your ordering, eating, and paying behaviors. Schemas have both a static quality (verbalizable knowledge) and a dynamic quality (guiding behavior).

The Piagetian notion of "scheme" and this earlier notion of "schema" are very similar. Both are units of knowledge which are responsible for a wide variety of activities. Schemes and schemas are seen to be responsible for activities as simple as naming and labeling and also those as complicated as hypothesis testing and creating experiments. For Piaget, however, all schemes have primarily a dynamic quality; that is, they guide behavior. Schemes are labeled by the behavior sequences which they control. As described earlier, infants use a *grabbing* scheme to learn about the world around them. This scheme is described by the behavior sequence that it controls, that is, the activity of grabbing.

Initially, the child is born with a very specific set of reflex schemes. For example, in the newborn, the sucking reflex is one of the main avenues for accumulating information about the world. The infant learns about the world through oral sensations. If you have ever watched an infant come upon a new object, invariably she will try to put it in her mouth. She is attempting to gain information about the object by applying a scheme to it. The number and types of schemes that we have available to use will determine the way in which we interact with the world around us. They can be thought of as the principal tools of cognitive development. The richer our repertoire of schemes, the richer our mental life is apt to be.

As the child develops, these initial reflex schemes are modified and expanded in order to better deal with a wider variety of information. These initial schemes are primarily physical in that they require some observable motor behavior. As the child develops, these schemes become more and more internally directed and mental (see Figure 6.1). For example, once the child has acquired language, she is able to internally represent objects and events. Also, as the child engages in school activities, she will acquire increasingly sophisticated concepts (e.g., addition rules, grammatical rules) which allow her to better label and understand the world around her.

FIGURE 6.1   Change in types of schemes which occur during development.

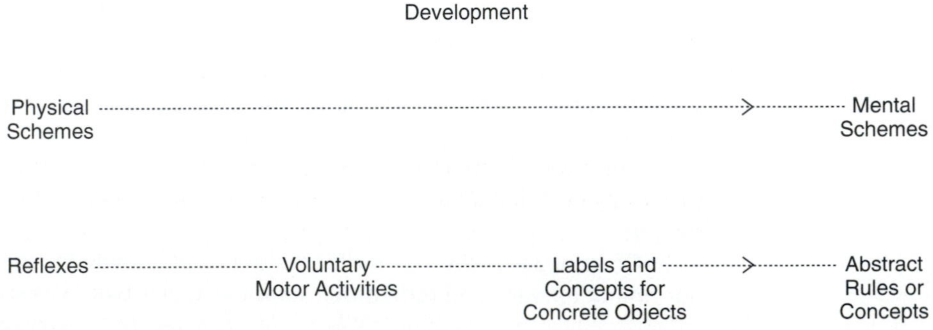

Question 6.1: What are schemes and what part do they play in cognitive development? _____

_____

_____

According to Piaget (1970b), there are two different types of schemes: figurative and operative. Each requires a different instructional approach and follows a different pattern of development. **Figurative schemes** attempt to represent reality as it appears (i.e., its physical properties) and, consequently, have a clear referent in the environment. Schemes for labeling different colors, shapes, and textures are figurative. Also, figurative schemes are responsible for our ability to draw and imitate external events, people, and objects. Finally, figurative schemes can be primarily internal, such as those responsible for our ability to create mental images. Reinforcement, imitation, and association are very important for the acquisition of these types of schemes. For example, the growth of a student's vocabulary depends upon the child's being reinforced for correctly repeating and imitating new words and correctly associating the words with their appropriate referents. Worksheets which match words and pictures are a commonly used strategy for developing figurative schemes.

In contrast to figurative schemes, **operative schemes** do not have a clear referent in the environment. These schemes allow us to separate the perceived character-istics of objects and events from their implied characteristics. Perceived charac-teristics are those referred to earlier, such as color and shape. Implied character-istics are those that cannot be directly perceived (e.g., number, mass, volume). For example, with experience a child will come to realize that the concept of "number" is not related to the physical configuration of the objects to be counted. To illustrate this, Piaget (1964) cites a friend's childhood experience. At the age of about 5 years,

> . . . he was seated on the ground in his garden and he was counting pebbles. Now to count these pebbles he put them in a row and he counted them, one, two, three up to ten. Then he finished counting them and started to count them in the other direction. He began by the end and once again found he had ten. He found this marvelous. . . . So he put them in a circle and counted them that way and found ten once again. (p. 12)

The concept of "number" is an implied characteristic in that it is not influenced by changes in the physical configuration of the objects involved. It is clear that operative schemes are required for the development of abstract reason-ing.

Operative schemes exist in an organized symbol system of words and numbers that can be manipulated in a logical manner. They are responsible for the internal (mental) manipulation and modification of knowledge. For example, with expe-rience a child will come to realize that no matter how she arranges objects to be counted or what their physical properties are, it will not influence the number of objects that exists or influence the process of counting. The child has internalized the activity of counting and has come up with a way of symbolically representing the products of counting, that is, "number."

Finally, the use of operations is governed by rules of symbolic logic. One of the basic rules of symbolic logic which governs the use of operations is that they are **reversible.** One way to reverse an operation is through **negation.** For example, in the domain of arithmetic, we can reverse the process of addition by employing the process of subtraction. That is, once we have added together two numbers and gotten their product, we know that each of these numbers is equal to the product subtracted by the other number. The numerical operation $2 + 3 = 5$ can be reversed as follows: $5 - 3 = 2$ or $5 - 2 = 3$. Another way to reverse an operation is through **compensation.** This process can be illustrated by the following classic Piagetian example (see Figure 6.2). A young child has acquired an appropriate set of operations related to volume when he realizes that changes in height of water containers can be compensated for by changes in the width of water containers. Consequently, even if a tall, slim container appears to have more water than a short, wide container, an "operative" child will be able to see that changes in one dimension can compensate for changes in a separate but related dimension of objects.

As the child acquires more and more operative schemes, he attains qualitatively higher and higher levels of cognitive development and becomes capable of employing logical reasoning in a variety of domains. According to Piaget (1970a), our ability to learn is primarily influenced by changes in our ability to reason which are keyed to the development of operative schemes.

FIGURE 6.2   Conservation of liquids.

Two equal glasses of liquid.

Pour one into a squat glass.

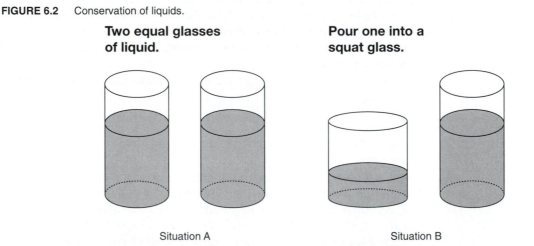

Situation A   Situation B

After the child has agreed that there is an equal amount of liquid in the two containers in Situation A, the liquid from one of the containers is poured into a shorter, fatter container as illustrated in Situation B. The child is then asked if the two containers in Situation B have the same amount of liquid. A preoperative child will indicate that the taller container holds more liquid.

With the development of operative schemes, a critical change in an individual's own development occurs. Piaget indicates that the individual is now capable of **reflective abstraction.** This refers to the ability to separate out the invariant characteristics of objects and events (e.g., number, mass, volume) from those characteristics which are tied to physical and perceptual experience (e.g., shape, size, color). As illustrated in Figure 6.2, if you pour the same amount of water from one size cup (short and fat) to another (tall and thin) you have clearly changed the physical and perceptual experience; however, you have not changed the volume of water in the different cups. A child who is capable of reflective abstraction can reason logically about concepts such as volume, mass, and number without being confused about physical appearance. (Examples of responses from children who have *not* acquired the ability of reflective abstraction can be found in Table 6.3.)

Question 6.2: Define "operative schemes" and describe why they are important to cognitive development. _____

_____

_____

Irrespective of the *type* of scheme (e.g., figurative or operative, mental or physical), each one is modified, expanded, or transformed in similar ways. Each also shares the same purpose, which is to allow the individual to *adapt* to her surroundings.

Adaptation   Adaptation is the second functional invariant that, in Piaget's view, controls all human development, including learning. Adaptation refers to our attempt to create an accurate view of the world around us so that we can successfully develop physically, emotionally, and intellectually. Adaptation occurs through the following two basic processes: **assimilation** and **accommodation.**

Assimilation is the process of fitting new information into existing schemes. When faced with a new situation, we normally try to relate the information in this new situation to what we already know about the world. In this way, we can deal with a wide variety of new situations in a meaningful and potentially useful way. In order to better understand the process of assimilation, let us look at the following illustration. Suppose a child has a scheme of *dog* that includes the following critical characteristics: "four legs, fur, and a tail." What would happen if she encountered a dog with no tail? The child would basically have three choices: (1) ignore the fact that the dog does not have a tail or assume it is there but not visible (in other words, distort her perceptions to match the current scheme for dog), and classify this instance as a dog; (2) either temporarily or permanently modify her scheme for dog, so that a tail is no longer a defining characteristic; or (3) ignore the dog. Assimilation is involved in choices 1 and 2. In both alternatives, the child classifies the new instance as a dog by relating it to existing or reworked schemes. Notice that in order to assimilate new experience we may sometimes distort our perceptions (e.g., ignore the presence or absence of critical attributes) in order to make them fit with our existing knowledge (schemes) of the world.

To Piaget, the assimilation process is how we integrate our experiences into schemes. Through assimilation we attempt to apply our existing knowledge of the world to new experiences and objects, and thereby integrate the new aspects of those experiences or objects into our existing scheme. Irrespective of whether we distort what we perceive, there is much about the experience that we record in an accurate fashion. In the tailless dog example presented earlier, the child may ignore the presence or absence of a tail but may accurately record color of fur, length of fur, sizes and shapes of snouts, and so on. In this way, she will be continually accumulating new and accurate information about the world around her. If a succession of tailless dogs is encountered, the child will eventually realize that rather than distorting her perceptions, she needs to change her existing schemes so that a tail is no longer part of her *dog* schema. This process of changing her schema to fit reality rather than changing her perceptions to fit her schema is called accommodation.

Accommodation is the temporary or permanent modification of schemes in order to more easily interact with the world around us. In the above example of a child meeting a tailless dog, accommodation occurred primarily in alternative 2. The child modified her scheme in order to assimilate her current experience with a tailless dog. Given the endless variety of situations to which our schemes are constantly being applied, changes (accommodation) in them are constantly occurring. For example, we are forever having to slightly modify our *sitting* scheme in order to comfortably sit in the variety of chairs, sofas, benches, and stools that we encounter. Additionally, given the week-to-week changes (e.g., new software and new equipment) that are occurring in the computer industry, our schemes for interacting with computers need to be continually modified in order for us to keep up.

Almost every instance of assimilation involves some form of temporary accommodation. It works like this: As we encounter some new situation (e.g., eating with chopsticks), we apply our existing scheme of eating utensils (knives, forks, and spoons) to the use of the chopsticks. We try to use them as we have previously used forks (assimilation) and find that that doesn't work. So we ask the waiter for instructions and, after a brief demonstration, learn how to correctly manipulate the chopsticks. Thereafter, whenever we think about eating utensils, our new, expanded scheme for them includes chopsticks, knives, forks, and spoons. Our old scheme has changed to accommodate chopsticks. Assimilation and accommodation must be considered twin processes that occur together.

Flavell (1962) presents the following as an example of how the processes of assimilation and accommodation interact during development:

An infant comes into contact for the first time with a ring suspended from a string. He makes a series of exploratory accommodations: he looks at it, touches it, causes it to swing back and forth. . . . Through past interactions with various other objects the child already possesses assimilatory structures (schemes) which set in motion and direct those accommodations. . . . The ring is assimilated to concepts of touching, moving, seeing, etc. . . . . The child's actions with respect to the ring are at once accommodations of these concepts to the . . . contours of the ring. (p. 51)

Question 6.3: Assimilation and accommodation are similar in that they both help _____. They are different in that assimilation is concerned primarily with _____, while accommodation is concerned primarily with _____.

Exercise 6.1: Given the following descriptions of behaviors, please classify the underlined behavior as an example either of assimilation or accommodation and explain why.

a. A student *attempts to relate Piaget's theory to knowledge* gained in a previous class. _____

_____

b. A student *changes her view of development* based on her readings in class.

_____

_____

c. A student *ignores new information* and maintains her old view of development.

_____

_____

d. The businessman *applies his negotiation skills to deal with a quarrel* between his son and daughter. _____

_____

e. The scientist *restructures his theory* after reviewing the results of his experiment. _____

_____

The process of assimilation and accommodation influences development and learning in a variety of ways. Assimilation results in constant activity because we are spontaneously applying old and new schemes in an attempt to understand and control our current experiences. Once a child has acquired a new scheme, she will spontaneously use the scheme over and over again in a variety of new settings. For example, once the child learns to pound with a hammer, she will try to gain more information about the world by using the hammer in different settings, many of which may be inappropriate. Also, as the child acquires language labels, she will be constantly applying them to her concrete experiences. Later, the child will acquire or create grammatical rules in order to establish relationships among her growing repertoire of language labels. Action labels like "jump" or "bark" will be connected to the *dog* scheme. Later still, small numerical rules of addition will be learned and applied to a variety of objects.

Children need opportunities in which to use and exercise their schemes freely and in various settings. Children are best able to do this during exploration and play. For Piaget (1962), exploration and play are central to cognitive development. During play, there is no attempt by the child to adapt to the "reality" of the outside world. The child applies her schemes for no other reason than the pleasure of manipulating them. Piaget (1962) presents the following observation as a good example of playing for the sake of playing:

> T. (0 years, 7 months), after learning to remove an obstacle to gain his objective, began to enjoy this kind of exercise. When several times in succession I put my hand or a piece of cardboard between him and the toy he desired, he reached the stage of momentarily forgetting the toy and pushed aside the obstacle, bursting into laughter. What had been intelligent adaptation had thus become play, through transfer of interest to the action itself, regardless of the aim. (p. 92)

Another good example is a child who creates imaginary playmates that she engages in novel situations (e.g., formal dining, mother-daughter conversations) which allow her to apply a variety of socialization schemes. The child benefits by exercising her schemes. These applications to imaginary situations provide practice in assimilating new experiences into her schemes. However, constantly engaging in such play activity, and the resulting assimilatory processes, will foster a distorted view of reality unless there is some attempt to change existing schemes in order to accommodate new aspects of the imaginary situation.

Permanent changes due to accommodations occur as a result of feedback from the outside world. Other peoples' reactions and actions, as well as perceptions of the physical environment, may be used as feedback or a cue to accommodate a specific scheme. For example, a child has just learned the scheme for bouncing objects and decides to apply the *bouncing* scheme to the crystal candy dish in the parlor. She is attempting to gain information about the world by applying (assimilating) this new object to her *bouncing* scheme. The bowl, unfortunately, does not bounce back. The child has received feedback from the environment. If she attempts to pick up the broken pieces, she will receive even more new feedback. In addition, the child is likely to receive verbal feedback from the adults in the surrounding environment. The consequences of using the *bouncing* scheme in this situation allows the child to modify (accommodate) her original scheme. That is, the *bouncing* scheme may now exclude such things as crystal, glass, and fragile objects.

According to Piaget (1967), we are all born with the ability to assimilate and accommodate. *While assimilation allows us to be constantly active and gain information about the world, accommodation allows us to benefit from this activity. That is, accommodation ensures that these activities result in useful learning.* It improves the "fit" between schemes or knowledge, and the real work to which we must adapt.

When our knowledge of the world is inaccurate, it produces conflicts. We all have a built-in tendency to reduce this conflict and attempt to regain some stability. **Equilibration** can be defined as this tendency to reduce cognitive conflict through the complementary processes of assimilation and accommodation (Piaget, 1985). During equilibration, some form of cognitive reorganization occurs as we attempt to establish a balanced cognitive state in which assimilation and accommodation processes are equally influential.

Equilibration occurs on three different levels: within a particular scheme, within a particular domain, and across all domains. Domains are specific areas of knowledge which share a particular focus and which are distinct from each other, for example, moral concepts (ideas about right and wrong), socialization concepts, number concepts, physics concepts, and drawing and illustration concepts. At the schematic level, when applications of a scheme fail to fit incoming perceptions, then equilibration leads to change or accommodation within that scheme. In the case of the tailless dog, the restructuring (accommodation) of the *dog* scheme to eliminate tails as a defining feature would occur because we tend to reduce conflicts. Whereas the above form of equilibration relates to a specific scheme, the following two types concern the reorganization of whole systems of schemes.

Within a particular domain, equilibration produces changes in the organization and structure of domain-related knowledge so that the child can reason similarly in all situations which relate to that domain. For example, during play and socialization activities, a child might gradually learn to empathize with the needs and interests of other children, thereby reducing his cognitive conflict in that situation. Having used empathy to reduce conflict in one play situation, the child might then learn to apply it to other play situations and eventually to a variety of social situations.

Finally, since empathic reasoning is essentially the ability to see a situation from more than one point of view, the child should learn to apply two-sided reasoning to all domains. Once an individual learns to focus on more than one aspect of social situations, this same form of reasoning should begin appearing in other domains, such as being able to coordinate two dimensions of a physics problem. Such qualitative changes in the ability to reason reflect a reorganization of the whole cognitive structure and are what Piaget refers to as movement from one stage to another.

Question 6.4: Define "equilibration" and explain why it is critical to the process of cognitive development. (Hint: What would happen if we did not have a

tendency to reduce conflict?)_____

_____

_____

Stages of Cognitive Development

Piaget proposed four **stages of cognitive development.** Within each stage, individuals exhibit a particular type of thinking and behavior which reflects a specific cognitive organization and structure. These unique structures each produce different types of interactions between the person and the environment and lead him to fundamentally different views of the world.

Because each stage is a transformation of the previous one, once individuals attain a higher stage, they cannot revert to a previous level of reasoning; it no longer exists for them. For example, once children learn that a ball still exists even though it may have rolled out of view, they can never return to the cognitive state of "unseen equals nonexisting." This process is referred to as the hierarchical nature of the stages. Piaget (1970a) states that these stages occur in sequence, that all learners proceed through them in the same order, and that no stage can be skipped. Furthermore, he assigns an age range to each stage. Keep in mind that these are only approximate ages and that some individuals will move through the stages at different rates. As can be seen in Table 6.1, each stage is qualitatively different from the previous one.

Sensorimotor Stage (Birth to 2 Years)   During this stage, the child learns about his environment through sensory impressions and motor actions (Piaget, 1962). The child's efforts to solve problems involve motor movements rather than the manipulation of ideas. As a result, we see children in this stage using tasting, touching, rolling, seeing, hearing, and pushing to learn about the world around them.

Major advances in cognitive development occur in this stage. The child begins the stage equipped with basic and reflexive schemes such as sucking, crying, and grasping. These unrefined schemes provide the basis for later, more sophisticated,

TABLE 6.1   SUMMARY OF PIAGET'S COGNITIVE DEVELOPMENT STAGES

Stages	Age range (approximate)	Characteristics
1. Sensorimotor	birth to 2 years	Behavior is basically reflexive; the child is totally egocentric; object recognition and object permanence develop; mental representation begins
2. Preoperational	2 to 7 years	Thinking involves more use of symbols; language skills develop; behavior is guided more by intuition than by logic; thinking remains egocentric
3. Concrete operational	7 to 11 years	The child relies on real, concrete things to solve problems; thinking becomes less egocentric; thought process can be reversed; conservation and classification tasks can be resolved
4. Formal operational	11 years and older	Logical and abstract thought develops; all variables are considered before decisions are made; not all adults reach this highest level; scientific thinking develops; learners can evaluate their own thinking

thought processes. *According to Piaget (1962), the child develops fundamental knowledge about four properties of the external world during this period: knowledge of objects, causation, space, and time.* Knowledge of objects can be seen in the infant's understanding that they are permanent; that is, an infant will search for objects which he has previously seen but which are not currently in view. As an example of an infant's understanding of causation, Piaget (1954) offers the following observations of Laurent (1 year, 1 month):

> Laurent is seated in his carriage and I am on a chair beside him. While reading and without seeming to pay any attention to him, I put my foot under the carriage and move it slowly. Without hesitation Laurent leans over the edge and looks for the cause in the direction of the wheels. As soon as he perceives the position of my foot he is satisfied and smiles. (p. 296)

Knowledge of space is evident as the infant probes the inside of containers, is able to negotiate detours by going around and over large objects, and is able to locate objects by sound. Finally, knowledge of time is evident in many of the behaviors described above. For example, the search for objects that he has previously seen but that are not currently in view indicates a rudimentary grasp of the temporal order of events in a specific sequence.

Although Piaget (1962) identified six substages that occur during the sensorimotor period of development, research has found that not all substages occur reliably (Fischer, 1980; Uzgiris & Hunt, 1975). Accordingly, our discussion will focus on those levels or substages that have the greatest conceptual and research consensus (Fischer & Silvern, 1985; see Table 6.2). At the *sensorimotor level,* the child voluntarily adjusts his actions to the characteristics of objects and people (e.g., tilting his head to look at a face, or closing his hand in order to grasp an object). Eventually, the child is able to coordinate his actions and differentiate means from ends. At this point, he has entered the second level, that is, *sensorimotor coordination of a few actions.* This is illustrated by an infant's using some object as a guide when crawling across the floor: The child's objective (toy, parent) becomes the end she seeks, and crawling is her means to that end. At this point, the child has acquired the ends-means concept.

TABLE 6.2   SENSORIMOTOR LEVELS OF DEVELOPMENT SUPPORTED BY RESEARCH

Level	Documented characteristics
1. Sensorimotor actions	Single actions and perceptions; first social responsiveness
2. Sensorimotor coordination of a few actions	Differentiation and coordination of means and end; attachment relation to caretaker
3. Sensorimotor system of several actions	Location of characteristics in objects and people—single words
4. Representation	Symbolization of people and objects, vocabulary spurt, multiword utterances

Source: Adapted from Fischer and Silvern, 1985.

A third level is the development of a *sensorimotor system of several actions.* Here, the child becomes capable of understanding that an object or person has some constant properties. For example, the family dog has hair, four legs, and a wagging tail, and it makes a barking sound. The child understands that these characteristics always accompany the family dog. This implies a conceptual understanding of the thing called "dog" and reflects the beginning of symbols, that is, thinking.

The last level, *representational thinking,* serves as the transition to the next stage. Within this level, children demonstrate an increased ability to use and manipulate symbols. Symbols are objects, events, or actions that represent something else by association, resemblance, or convention. For example, a stop sign is a symbol which becomes associated with the act of stopping your vehicle. Alternatively, because of its physical resemblance, a long, thin stick may be used as a gun during a neighborhood "war." Finally, our language consists of symbols (words) which are culturally agreed upon but arbitrarily associated with specific objects, events, and actions.

Within this last level of the sensorimotor stage, children often engage in pretend play, during which they talk to imaginary friends, allow one object (box) to represent a variety of other objects (house, train, plane), and take on a variety of imagined characteristics and roles. It is not until the next stage, however, that children begin to make full use of their ability to interact symbolically with the world.

Question 6.5: What is the primary way in which children who are in the sensorimotor stage of development learn about themselves and the world around

them? _____

_____

_____

Preoperational Stage (2 to 7 Years)   During this stage, the child significantly expands her use of symbols and language becomes increasingly important as a tool for dealing with the environment. Through language, the child is able to store a representation of previous environmental events and symbolically recall these events at a later time.

This ability to symbolically recall objects and events stems from the development of the **semiotic function,** which is the ability to use symbols or signifiers (Piaget, 1970a). During the preoperational stage, we can find several examples of this function: deferred imitation, symbolic play, mental imagery, and language. Deferred imitation occurs when the child is able to reproduce an action or sound long after the original action or sound was produced. The following observation by Piaget (1962) is a good example of deferred imitation:

Jacqueline (1 year, 4 months) has a visit from a 1½-year-old boy whom she used to see from time to time, and who, in the course of the afternoon got into a terrible temper. He screamed as he tried to get out of a playpen and pushed it backward, stamping his feet. Jacqueline stood watching him in amazement, never having witnessed such a scene before. The next day, she herself screamed in her playpen and tried to move it, stamping her foot lightly several times in succession. (p. 63)

In order for Jacqueline to have imitated the temper tantrum of the previous day, she needed to internally represent the activity by means of some symbolic mechanism.

An example of symbolic play is when a child pushes a box along the floor, imagining that it is a car, and makes appropriate car noises. In order for the child to play symbolically, she needs to have a mental image or picture of the objects or events that are being represented in her play. That is, the child has an image of what a car looks like, what it does, and even what it sounds like. Finally, the child's use of language can be seen when she describes to her parents something she needs (box) in order to complete her imaginary play scene. The language that the child uses is a product of past experiences with the described objects and events. In all these behaviors, the child is separating her schemes from the actual events and applying them to different but similar situations. The schemes are becoming generalized, more internalized, and detached from the physical environment.

Even though the child has advanced dramatically from the early part of the sensorimotor stage, there are limitations to his thought which prevent him from developing an accurate picture of the surrounding world. One of these limitations is the child's inability to conserve. **Conservation** is the understanding that the amount of something or its quality can remain the same even though our perception of it may change (Piaget, 1967). In a classic Piagetian conservation task, the child is presented with two identical containers, each holding the same amount of liquid. After the child agrees that the containers are filled equally, the liquid from one is poured into a taller, thinner container. The child, who viewed the pouring, is then asked if the containers still hold identical amounts of liquid (see Figure 6.2). Preoperational children typically respond that the taller and thinner container has more liquid. The typical child equates height with volume. It is not until the next stage that children see and indicate that the two beakers still have the same amount of liquid. Meanwhile, the preoperational child is unable to conserve across a variety of domains, as Table 6.3 shows.

Why is the preoperational child unable to conserve? There are two primary limitations to the child's thinking during this stage: centration and irreversibility.

Centration refers to the tendency to center on only one aspect of a situation at a time. The preoperational child cannot perceive complex situations in their entirety. In the liquid conservation task, she focuses only on the height of the beakers and fails to take account of their width. Although she can use symbols and reproduce past experiences, she cannot coordinate multidimensional situations when solving problems.

In addition, the preoperational child exhibits **egocentric thinking.** This does not mean she has a selfish personality, but that she tends to believe that everyone sees and experiences events as she does. Consequently, such children often fail to understand how others can think differently about a situation. They are, in

TABLE 6.3   SAMPLE PIAGETIAN CONSERVATION TASKS

Conservation of number

Step 1 Place two rows of coins so that they are in one-to-one correspondence and have the child judge that the rows contain an equal number of coins.

Step 2 Spread out one rows of coins until it is longer than the other. Ask the same child if each row still has the same number of coins.

A preoperational child will typically indicate that the row of coins which is longer has a greater number of coins.

Conservation of length

Step 1 Place two equal pieces of string side by side and have the child judge them to be of equal length.

Step 2 Change the shape of one and ask the child if the pieces of string are still of equal length.

A preoperational child will typically indicate that the string which is stretched out is longer than the string which is curvy.

Conservation of mass

Step 1 Place two equal balls of clay side by side and have the child judge them to be equal.

Step 2 Reshape one into a cylinder and ask if they are still equal.

A preoperational child will typically indicate that the two are no longer equal and that there is more clay in the cylinder.

---

effect, unable to place themselves in the shoes of another. This is a function of their inability to decenter from their own perspective and take other perspectives into account.

In a classic series of experiments, Piaget and Inhelder (1956) demonstrated egocentric thinking within the spatial-perceptual realm. In these experiments, they used a scale model of three mountains, photographs of the model taken from various positions around it, and a doll "observer" who viewed the model from the various perspectives. Preoperational and concrete operational children were asked to identify which photograph represented what the doll was seeing when it was placed at different positions around the scale model. The majority of preoperational children consistently selected the photograph which represented their own view of the mountains, regardless of where the doll was placed. Basically, they could not adopt someone else's perspective. In contrast, the majority of concrete operational children consistently selected the correct photographs to represent the doll's view of the mountains.

The preoperational child looks primarily at static states and ignores any transformations that might occur between them. For example, in the conservation of liquid task, the child focuses on the beginning state (identical heights of liquid) and the final state (two different heights of liquid) and ignores the transformation (pouring from one beaker to another) that occurred between the two states. The child does not perceive the transformation of one state into another (Piaget, 1967). Without this connection the child is unable to return to the starting point of the transformation and see that the two states are equal. In contrast, the child in the next (concrete operational) stage realizes that she can pour the liquid back into the original beaker and that the liquid will remain constant.

Children begin the preoperational stage as intuitive thinkers. They tend to reason more by how things appear to be than by how they really are. In other words they can easily be fooled by appearances. However, by the end of this stage, the child's schemes are more internalized and less tied to perceptual experiences. In addition, she is less egocentric and has developed schemes which are more general and abstract and, consequently, she is better able to deal with complicated problem-solving situations (Piaget & Inhelder, 1969). At this point, many of the child's schemes have been transformed into operations.

Question 6.6: Describe two limitations of preoperational thought. _____

Concrete Operational Stage (7 to 11 Years)   The concrete operational stage roughly parallels the elementary school years. However, some school children show an earlier movement into this stage, while many secondary school students and adult learners never advance past this level (Schwebel, 1975). Children at this stage possess operative schemes which allow them to think logically, in contrast to preoperational children, who are considered to be prelogical. As described earlier, operative schemes allow children to separate the perceived characteristics of objects, such as color and shape, from the implied characteristics of objects and events, such as number, mass, volume, density. To illustrate, with experience, a child will come to realize that the concept of weight is not related to the shape of objects. If two balls of clay weigh the same and are then transformed into different shapes (e.g., hot dog and cone shape), they will continue to have the same weight. The concept of weight is an implied characteristic in that it is not influenced by changes in the physical appearance of the objects involved.

The acquisition and development of logical thinking is evidenced by the concrete operational child's ability to approach a problem-solving situation more systematically than can the preoperational child. Two major skills involved in systematic problem solving are **classification** and **seriation.**

Children in this stage develop the ability to group a set of objects and then to group around a common attribute (Inhelder & Piaget, 1969). For example, if a child is given a platter of cookies varying in color, size, and shape, she can focus on one variable (e.g., color) and group the cookies accordingly. However, since the child can reverse actions, she could go back to the starting point and regroup the cookies based on another variable, such as shape. In this stage the child also begins to learn that categories can form a hierarchy, with one fitting into another (e.g., the category "cookies" fits into the category "food").

The process of seriation means the child can *order* things based upon a selected variable. Children can order objects in terms of height, length, weight, and so on. The emergence of this process signals the child's ability to place order and structure upon environmental stimuli. The only limitation of this seriation ability is its restriction to previously experienced concrete stimuli. For example, if a child were asked to order a set of canisters in terms of height and her only experience with seriation was with sticks, she would be unable to seriate the set of canisters.

According to Levin (1983), many accomplishments occur during the concrete operational stage, as shown in Table 6.4. Many of these accomplishments reflect the increasing importance of the school environment in the child's cognitive development. The ability to do well in any academic subject and to be able to cope with the academic environment (e.g., rules and regulations) requires concrete operational thinking.

The primary limitation to the concrete operational stage is that the child's logical thinking is restricted to previous experience. He has not yet gained the ability to use abstract, hypothetical situations as content for thinking, and cannot, for example, speculate about hypothetical events or experiences.

Question 6.7: Describe how acquiring classification and seriation skills allows the concrete operational child to be systematic about solving problems. _____

TABLE 6.4 ACCOMPLISHMENTS OF THE CONCRETE OPERATIONAL STAGE

1. Play:
   mastery of table games with rules, such as checkers; mastery of outdoor games with rules, such as soccer; spontaneous play involving different roles and shared understandings about who does what

2. Problem solving:
   plans ahead on familiar tasks such as drawing and building; abandons hypotheses when they are not confirmed; can explain what words such as "bicycle" mean; is less susceptible to perceptual illusions

3. Mathematics:
   can learn to add, subtract, multiply, and divide; understands equations, equalities, and inequalities

4. Comprehension of the physical world:
   distinguishes magic and pretend from what is real; understands that pouring water into a container of a different shape does not change the amount

5. Comprehension of the social world:
   uses kinship terms such as "sister" and "uncle" accurately; understands social rules, such as those governing marriage; emphasizes factors such as fairness in explaining right and wrong; shows increased ability to understand others' motives and intentions

Source: From *Child Psychology*, by Gerald Levin, Copyright 1983 by Wadsworth, Inc. Reprinted by permission of Brooks/Cole Publishing Company, Pacific Grove, California.

Formal Operational Stage (11 Years and Older)   The development of abstract thinking is a hallmark of the formal operational stage of cognitive development. No longer is the adolescent child bound to thinking about concrete things. He is now able to hypothesize about relationships among abstract concepts. Such thinking also permits the child to imagine and reason about possibilities and not just about events as they are. The emphasis on possibility rather than on what currently exists is often considered a special characteristic of adolescent thinking. The change that occurs in the adolescent during this stage is an increased ability to perform reflexive and scientific thinking.

The ability to use one's own imagination as content for further thinking is a major development. This advancement, called **reflective thinking,** permits the adolescent to consider and evaluate her own thinking, that is, to systematically approach problems. For example, if a student attempts to solve a problem but arrives at an unworkable solution, he can go back and examine his thinking that led to this solution. This self-evaluation may result in the conclusion that an unwarranted assumption was made or that faulty logic was applied. For instance, in trying to calculate how much food will be needed for a Saturday night party, an adolescent may come up with an estimate that is way beyond his expenses. He may then go back and reevaluate his assumptions (e.g., how many people are coming; will all of them be hungry; how much will they eat) and realize that some of these assumptions may not be realistic. The adolescent would then try to recalculate, given the new set of assumptions.

Another notable development during this stage is the ability to solve problems by using systematic combinations of the variables involved—that is, **scientific thinking.** This results in a more logical and methodological solution of problems, rather than reliance upon a trial and error approach. For example, a child trying to determine the proper mixture of paints to produce a certain color can mentally construct a list of all possible combinations. She can then proceed to test the possibilities until she arrives at the correct one. In fact, in some problems, the formation and testing of hypotheses is all done cognitively, without reliance upon concrete manipulation of variables.

Not all adults reach the formal operational stage (Kuhn, Langer, Kohlberg, & Hann, 1977). Those who do not continue to function at the lower stages described earlier. Alternatively, Arlin (1965) states that recent investigations suggest that a qualitatively different stage may occur beyond formal operations (see also Kitchener & Kitchener, 1981). This so-called fifth stage consists of problem-finding abilities. These abilities concern creativity and the structuring of ill-defined problems (e.g., How can we feed all the starving people of the world?).

Question 6.8: Describe how formal operational thought differs from concrete operational thought. _____

_____

_____

The child has now developed from solving problems via purely physical schemes to a point where she can solve them using abstract coordinated internal schemes (operations). At each stage, she is capable of more and more complex behaviors and thought (refer to Table 6.1).

Questions about Piagetian Theory

Piaget's is the most widely discussed and cited theory of cognitive development. However, Piaget has his critics. Some contend that a stage theory is misleading—that development is more gradual and continuous and that clear-cut stages simply do not exist (Luria, 1976). Other critics indicate that movement through the stages is not always invariant and that children can be in more than one stage at a time. For example, a child may be concrete operational in relation to mathematics but preoperational in relation to social roles (Brainerd, 1978).

Research has indicated that children at early stages of development are far more capable than Piaget's theory suggests (Gelman & Gallistel, 1978). As described earlier, Piagetian research found that preoperational children are egocentric and are incapable of taking another individual's perspective. But more recent research indicates that many preoperational children are not completely egocentric (Ford, 1979; Gelman, 1979). In a series of experiments, Flavell and his associates evaluated the perspective-taking abilities of 3- and 4-year-olds (Masangkay, McCluskey, McIntyre, Sims-Knight, Vaughn, & Flavell, 1974; Flavell, Everett, Croft, & Flavell, 1981). In the experimental tasks, the child and the experimenter faced each other across a small table. In one version of the task, a card with a picture of a cat on one side and a dog on the other was held vertically between the two. If the experimenter was looking at the cat, the child would be looking at the dog, and vice versa. The child was asked to indicate which animal the experimenter saw. The 3- and 4-year-olds had no difficulty doing this accurately. In another version of the task, a picture of a turtle was placed horizontally so that the turtle appeared upside down from one side of the table and right side up from the other. The 3-year-olds had difficulty identifying which orientation the experimenter was viewing; however, 4-year-olds were capable of performing this task accurately. According to Piagetian theory, both 3- and 4-year-olds are within the early part of the preoperational stage and, accordingly, should not have been able to successfully complete either version of the above task.

Researchers have also found that when transformations are hidden from sight (hence minimizing the potential of being misled by appearances), preoperational children are capable of conservation (Siegler & Hodkin, 1982). Finally, concrete operational children have been shown to demonstrate characteristics of logical thinking which are associated with formal operational thinking; for example, they have solved hypothetical deductive reasoning problems (Roberge, 1970).

The appearance of abilities at an earlier age than was proposed in the four stages of cognitive development indicates that experience may have a more pronounced effect on development than Piaget suggested. In fact, research has found that, with practice and training, acquisition of cognitive abilities can be accelerated (Field, 1987). For example, Golomb and Cornelius (1977) found that pre-operational children (4-year-olds) can be trained to successfully conserve mass and liquid. The researchers used a pretense-play training method. This method engaged children in a play situation that forced them to make justifications supporting the conservation of either mass or liquid. For example, in order to train for the conservation of mass, the experimenters transformed clay into various shapes (food, chair, truck, etc.) and asked a child how it was possible for one clump of clay to take on these different shapes. While engaging the child with these questions, they would maneuver him or her to use an argument based on reversibility: That is, the clay is the same in all instances because we can just reshape it from one form to another. Fifteen children were given three days of training (training group) and fifteen others were allowed to play with the same materials for three days but were not given any training (control group). At the end of three days, both groups were given a test of their conservation abilities. In the training group, six children demonstrated the ability to conserve either mass or liquid, four children demonstrated the ability to conserve both mass and liquid, and five children were not able to conserve. According to the experimenters, the conservers' justifications were straightforward, assertive, clear, and confident. In contrast, within the control group, fourteen children were unable to conserve, while one child acquired the ability to conserve both mass and liquid. The results of this experiment clearly indicate that specific training can accelerate the development of conservation abilities in preoperational children.

In reaction to many of these criticisms, a set of **neo-Piagetian theories** has appeared. Most of these theories have attempted to maintain the basic assumptions of Piaget's theory (e.g., qualitative, stagelike cognitive changes), while adding greater specificity to their descriptions. For example, neo-Piagetian researchers have shown the importance of practice on the acquisition of cognitive skills and have provided in-depth descriptions of the development of procedures such as those which underlie proportional reasoning, perspective taking, communication with others, and basic motor movements. We now turn to a description of one of these theories.

ROBBIE CASE'S NEO-PIAGETIAN THEORY OF COGNITIVE DEVELOPMENT

Robbie Case's neo-Piagetian theory also adopts a "stage" view of development. However, his is more detailed than Piaget's in two respects. First, he focuses on the variety of strategies that is involved in performing simple tasks such as visual tracking of interesting objects. Second, he attempts to explain individual differences in development by looking at both qualitative and quantitative changes in cognitive strategies. Qualitative changes have to do with the complexity and focus of strategies, while quantitative changes deal with increases in number and automatization (Case, 1978; 1985). Memory development is also identified as being critical to the performance of cognitive tasks. If this sounds vaguely familiar to you it is because such changes in cognitive strategies and memory development are critical in explaining learning within information processing theory. Case's neo-Piagetian theory links important structural ideas (i.e., stages of cognitive development) from Piagetian theory with important process ideas from information processing theory (i.e., memory and strategic processes) in order to explain development and learning.

A stage view of development isn't the only assumption about cognitive development that Case has carried over from Piagetian theory. Both theories assume that knowledge is actively constructed via internal operations and that these operations are organized into systems. Also, both assume that important processes and patterns of development are constrained by maturation.

Case, then, blends two models of development. His structural model focuses on the stages of development and the mechanisms responsible for transition from stage to stage. His process model focuses on the specific procedures or operations used to manipulate information and the factors which constrain the manipulation of this information. We will first discuss important changes in processing that occur during development and how they influence the course of development.

Processing Mechanisms That Influence Development

In the chapter on information processing theory, we discussed the importance of **working memory** to learning and remembering. As you should recall, working memory includes two specific functions: storage and operation. The storage function maintains information in working memory for either immediate or later use. The operation function manipulates the information by condensing, expanding, relating, and so on. Unfortunately, working memory is limited in terms of the amount of energy one can devote to storing and operating on information. In Case's theory, working memory is referred to as **short-term storage space (STSS).** An important determinant of development, according to Case, is the efficiency with which an individual can operate on and maintain information in the STSS. **Operational efficiency** refers to the maximum number of independent schemes that can be brought to full activation (attended to) simultaneously.

As in Piagetian theory, Case (1985) identifies two types of schemes: figurative and operative. **Figurative schemes,** you remember, are static and relate to fixed characteristics (size, color, shape) of objects and events. **Operative schemes,** however, are dynamic and are responsible for our ability to transform and manipulate (classify, order, sequence) information. Case's notion of an operative scheme is also very similar to information processing theory's notion of a procedure. That is, for Case, operative schemes become more efficient and eventually become coordinated with other schemes through the process of practice.

Although the capacity of STSS is fixed at birth, through maturation and practice we become more efficient at using it. Maturational changes are produced by increases in the myelinization of brain tissue. This ongoing biological change, when combined with practice, leads to increases in operational efficiency of STSS. As an individual practices the skills necessary to complete the tasks at hand, she becomes more proficient and the skills more automatic. This proficiency allows her to perform with less effort and attentional energy. In addition, practice permits the consolidation of separate simple schemes into larger, more complex ones. This process of consolidation is analogous to "chunking" (referred to earlier). That is, it integrates many schemes into one meaningful unit and thus frees up space and energy within STSS which can be devoted to the completion of more complicated cognitive tasks.

Question 6.9: Define "operational efficiency" and describe the two factors which are responsible for increases in the operational efficiency of STSS. _____

Structural Mechanisms That Influence Development

As indicated earlier, this theory is also a stage theory. Case suggests that we develop through a series of four stages that begins with very primitive mental structures which are linked to physical experience and eventually proceeds to higher levels consisting of an abstract intellectual system of thought (see Case & Sandieson, 1992). Case, like Piaget, believes that cognition develops through a universal series of stages in an invariant sequence and that these stages are hierarchical, that is, higher stages are reached by coordinating structures (ideas) derived from lower ones. However, for Case, an individual's movement through the stages may vary according to cognitive domains (see page 217). That is, one's thinking in domain A may be more advanced than in domain B.

The course of development within each stage is constrained primarily by the efficiency of STSS which, in turn, is linked to maturation and practice. Consequently, these two factors are important determinants of an individual's movement through the stages of development. In particular, the consolidation of schemes, which results from practice, is critical to fostering cognitive development.

According to Case, this consolidation is basically a three-step problem-solving process that he terms the **executive control structures.** Case explains that we structure our thinking by (1) identifying problem situations, (2) setting specific goals and objectives related to the problem situation, and (3) activating procedures (schemes) in an attempt to achieve these goals. For example, for an infant, a block moving out of view may represent a problem situation described as "an interesting object moving out of view." The objective or goal would then be to "put the object back into view." A strategy for accomplishing this would be to "move the head and eyes in the direction of the block, using visual input from the block as a guide" (see Figure 6.3). A control structure or space would thus consist of (1) problem situation, (2) objective/goal, and (3) strategy to obtain the goal. That is, our thinking is continually oriented to solve particular problems (e.g., returning interesting object back into view). Within this context, the complexity of the problem, objective, and procedures that we can deal with will be constrained by

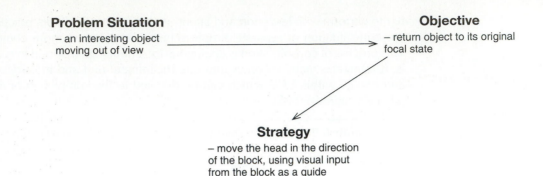

Problem Situation
– an interesting object
moving out of view

Objective
– return object to its original
focal state

Strategy
– move the head in the direction
of the block, using visual input
from the block as a guide

FIGURE 6.3   Example of sensorimotor control structure. (Adapted from Case, *Intellectual Development: Birth to Adulthood*, 1985. Used by permission of Academic Press and the author.)

the nature of the control structure or space that we are capable of developing. In essence, the control structures "control" or set limits on the types of problems that can be solved.

Whereas Piaget viewed the child as a developing scientist striving to create logical theories of the world and her interactions with the world, Case views the child as a problem solver striving to acquire better tools for solving more and more complex problems. As the child develops, the thought processes (control structures) she is capable of creating and employing become increasingly more complex, and they influence development by aiding the coordination of lower-order schemes into higher-order ones. When two lower-order schemes are repeatedly activated together, the child's executive control structures reorganize them into one higher-order scheme. This reorganization allows her to retrieve those schemes together in the future. This, in turn, requires less attentional energy and therefore increases the efficiency of STSS processing.

Question 6.10: Define "executive control structures" and describe how they influence the course of development. _____

_____

_____

As indicated earlier, according to Piaget, a critical change in an individual's development occurs when he becomes capable of **reflective abstraction.** That means being able to separate out the invariant characteristics of objects and events (e.g., number, weight, volume) from those characteristics which are tied to physical and perceptual experience (e.g., shape, size, color). According to Piaget, this ability depends on the development of operative schemes. In contrast, Case (1985) attributes the development of "reflective abstraction" to the executive control structures (innate problem-solving process). This innate process allows the child to step back and reflect on the nature of problems and to frame the current situation into a problem format. For Case, this ability to impose some voluntary control over one's own cognitive and affective experiences occurs very early in development.

Stages of Development

Case indicates that there are four stages of cognitive development: **sensory motor, relational, dimensional,** and **abstract dimensional** (see Table 6.5). These stages represent qualitatively different ways of interacting with the world. They differ by the level of the relationship that an individual is able to represent and manipulate and by the type of executive control structure they reflect. During the sensory motor stage, thought processes (control structures) are linked primarily to physical movements. A typical problem to be solved during this stage is how to get an interesting new object to or into one's mouth. The relational stage focuses on the development of thought processes which control the coordination of two distinct activities. At this point, a child is capable of pushing a toy car *and* vocalizing engine noises. This represents the coordination of physical movements with symbolic activities. In the dimensional stage, the child can focus on and coordinate

TABLE 6.5   SUMMARY OF CASE'S COGNITIVE DEVELOPMENT STAGES

Stages	Age range (approximate)	Characteristics
1. Sensory motor control structures	birth to 1½ years	Mental representations are linked to physical movements
2. Relational control structures	1½ to 5 years	Children can detect and coordinate relations along one dimension among objects, events, or people. For example, weight is viewed as bipolar—heavy and light.
3. Dimensional control structures	5 to 11 years	Children can extract the dimensions of significance in the physical and social world. They can compare two dimensions (e.g., height and width) in a quantitatiuve way.
4. Abstract control structures	11 to 18½ years	Children acquire abstract systems of thought that allow them to use proportional reasoning, solve verbal analogy problems, and infer psychological traits in other people.

Source: From *Theories of Developmental Psychology* by Patricia Miller. Copyright 1989 by W. H. Freeman and Company. Reprinted by permission.

multiple concrete aspects of objects and events. For example, he can now classify and reclassify a flower by its size, color, and shape, depending on the nature of tasks and problems at hand. Finally, during the abstract dimensional stage, the child is capable of coordinating multiple abstract aspects of objects and events. For example, when speculating about his future, an adolescent can juggle hypothetical career, family, and peer issues in order to find a suitable path to pursue.

Within each of these stages, the individual progresses through the same three substages: **unifocal, bifocal,** and **elaborated coordination.** As its name implies, each substage reflects a particular number of elements that can be represented and a particular way these elements are organized in the cognitive system. As an illustration of these substages, let's look at a sensorimotor child. At the unifocal substage, a child would be capable of using one physical/sensory scheme for obtaining one goal (e.g., a visual search for an object). At the bifocal substage, a child would be capable of both visually searching for the object and then reaching for it. Finally, at the elaborated substage, the child would be capable of visually searching for the object, reaching for it but realizing it is out of reach, and then using something separate (sheet, stick) to bring the object closer.

Each substage reflects increases in the operational efficiency of the STSS. As indicated earlier, these increases, which occur at each substage, are the result of maturation and practice. As the individual matures and practices critical skills, he becomes capable of performing them with less effort and attentional energy. Consequently, he is able to create more and more complex control structures. It is important to note that there is considerable overlap between stages. The elaborated coordination substage of the sensory motor stage, for example, overlaps with the initial substage of the relational stage. Consequently, even though there are qualitative differences between each stage, there is much continuity in the transition from one to another.

As indicated earlier, there are many similarities between the Piagetian view and Case's neo-Piagetian view of cognitive development and its stages. There are, however, three important differences (see Table 6.6) which relate to (1) the domain found within each stage, (2) the cognitive processes that lead from one stage to another, and (3) the role of instruction in facilitating movement from stage to stage. In Case's theory, an individual can be in different stages at one time. For example, in the social domain, an individual may be at the relational stage, whereas in the linguistic domain, she may be at the dimensional stage. For Piaget, once an individual moves to a higher stage, she should be capable of dealing with the world in all domains at that higher stage.

From Case's perspective, in order to identify an individual's level of cognitive development, one needs investigate each domain and identify the thought processes (control structures) that the individual is capable of employing within each of these domains. Piaget would indicate that the level of development demonstrated in one domain should exist within all others so there is no need to investigate them all. However, more recent research supports Case's view that children possess very different levels of skills in different domains (Brainerd, 1978). A good example of this is the child who is academically gifted in such abstract reasoning

TABLE 6.6   SUMMARY OF DIFFERENCES BETWEEN PIAGET'S AND CASE'S VIEWS OF STAGES AND DEVELOPMENT

	Piaget	Case
1. Domain specificity of stages	A child is within one stage across all domains. That is, if a child is preoperational in the social domain, she will be preoperational in all other domains (e.g., linguistic, moral).	A child can be in different stages at one time. That is, she can be in the dimensional stage in the social domain and relational in the mathematical domain.
2. Mechanism responsible for movement from one stage to another	Equilibration, which is a self-regulatory process that reduces the cognitive conflict between the child's view of the world and reality.	Self-regulatory process which consists of (1) an individual's tendency to structure his interactions in terms of problem situations and (2) the development of skills to solve these problems.
3. Role of instruction in development	Instruction is one of many environmental experiences that will influence development. It does not, however, play a critical part in development.	Instruction plays a critical part in development. It allows for practice of schemes and skills for solving problems, which directly influences cognitive development. Instruction also allows for the transmission of important cultural knowledge and skills.

domains as mathematics and science but seems unable to empathize with others in social situations.

Each theory identifies a different mechanism to explain movement between stages. As you recall from our earlier discussion, Piaget identified equilibration as the process that moves us from one stage to another. Equilibration is described as a self-regulatory tendency to reduce conflicts between our views of the world and reality. Movement from one stage to the next is a very slow process, requiring the transformation of all skills within all domains. Unfortunately, these processes were so globally defined by Piaget that they are very difficult to explain clearly. Case also indicates that we have a tendency toward self-regulation and that this tendency is partially responsible for moving us from one stage to another. However, Case is a bit more specific about this process. He identifies two important components: (1) an individual's tendency to structure his interactions in terms of problem situations and (2) the development of skills to solve those problems.

Individuals develop increasingly sophisticated procedures or schemes for solving problems through exploration, imitation, and instruction. Exploration is simply trying out new ways of doing things in a variety of settings. Imitation is attempting to repeat the performance of others. Finally, formal instruction plays an increasingly significant role in children's development at each successive stage. Each type of activity allows individuals to practice their new schema. As indicated earlier, this practice leads to the chunking or consolidation of multiple schemes into one unit and to increased operational efficiency of an individual's STSS.

Finally, a third important difference between the two views of cognitive development is the role of instruction. For Case, an individual's culture plays a critical role in cognitive development (Case, 1985). That is, each culture identifies the critical skills, knowledge, and values that should be imparted through the process of education and instruction. Interaction with adults in this culture, then, becomes an important mechanism by which children acquire higher and higher levels of cognitive development. As you will see in the next chapter, other theorists have also identified cultural influences as critically important to cognitive development (Bruner, 1964; Vygotsky, 1962).

Exercise 6.2: The statements listed below describe a variety of views related to the nature of cognitive development that are consistent with either Piaget's theory, Case's theory, or both. On the line next to each statement mark a "C" for those that are consistent with Case's theory, a "P" for those that are consistent with Piaget's theory, or a "B" for those that are consistent with both theories.

a. _____ Patterns of development are constrained by maturation.

b. _____ The child is viewed as a problem solver who acquires better problem-solving skills as he develops.

c. _____ Practice of specific skills plays a critical part during development because it increases the individual's ability to process information efficiently.

d. _____ A process critical to knowledge growth is the development and use of operations.

e. _____ Everyone goes through the same set of stages in the same order. However, not everyone may attain the higher-level stages.

f. _____ At any one time, children may be in different stages in different domains of knowledge.

After this introduction to Case's view of the stages of development, let us review each stage in order to give you a taste of the specificity by which he attempts to describe an individual's level of cognitive development (Case, 1985). As indicated earlier, each stage is defined in terms of the type of thinking (control structure) the individual is capable of employing within a particular problem domain.

Sensory Motor Control Structures (Birth to 1.5 Years) *In the first stage, cognition is linked primarily to physical movements.* As in all the stages which follow, advances within this one occur when the infant increases the number of schemes that she can employ to obtain specific goals. The three substages (unifocal, bifocal, and elaborated coordination) roughly correspond to the three levels presented under Piaget's sensorimotor stage. That is, each of these three substages subsumes or integrates previously discrete motor activities. For example, in an attempt to follow the movement of a block, a child may both employ a movement of the head to maintain visual contact *and* reach out to grab the block in order to get it back into view (see Figure 6.4).

This coordination of two distinct schemes into a new, more complicated one represents, according to Case, a movement from a unifocal to a bifocal substage. Notice also that as the child moves from lower to higher substages, there is an increase in the number of objectives that can be coordinated within a single problem situation. In the above example, the child had two objectives: (1) to locate the moving block and (2) to return it to its original position. A movement to the highest substage—elaborated coordination—would require the capability of adding even more objectives (e.g., using the block as a tool). The label "elaborated" implies adding and coordinating related schemes in order to obtain some new set of objectives (see Figure 6.5). *An important characteristic, then, for development from lower to higher substages is the integration of multiple schemes to obtain more and more complex sets of objectives.*

Relational Control Structures (1 to 5 Years)   In this stage, the young child is able to detect and coordinate bipolar relations among objects, people, and events. *That is, children are capable of thinking which focuses on not more than two clearly differentiated characteristics or attributes.* For example, during this stage, children can focus on both the "right" and "left" side of a structure when using building blocks.

Initially during this stage, the child is able to coordinate two different types of sensorimotor activities. For example, the child may coordinate physical movements and verbalization to perform a counting activity (see Figure 6.6). This

FIGURE 6.4   Bifocal sensorimotor control structure. (Adapted from Case, *Intellectual Development: Birth to Adulthood,* 1985. Used by permission of Academic Press and the author.)

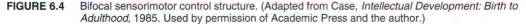
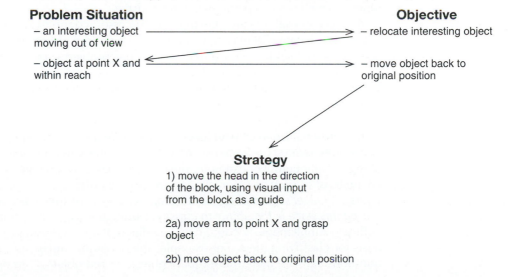

Problem Situation   **Objective**

– an interesting object ──────────────────────▶ – relocate interesting object
moving out of view

– object at point X and ◀────────────────────▶ – move object back to
within reach   original position

Strategy

1) move the head in the direction
of the block, using visual input
from the block as a guide

2a) move arm to point X and grasp
object

2b) move object back to original position

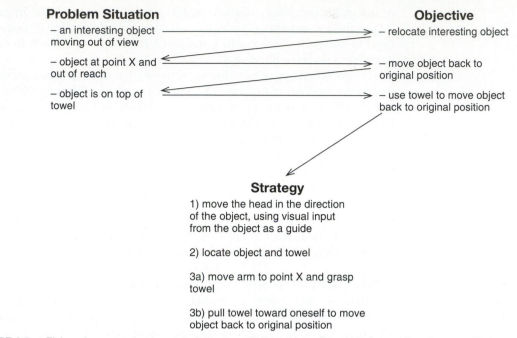

Problem Situation

– an interesting object
moving out of view

– object at point X and
out of reach

– object is on top of
towel

Objective

– relocate interesting object

– move object back to
original position

– use towel to move object
back to original position

Strategy

1) move the head in the direction
of the object, using visual input
from the object as a guide

2) locate object and towel

3a) move arm to point X and grasp
towel

3b) pull towel toward oneself to move
object back to original position

FIGURE 6.5   Elaboration sensorimotor control structure. (Adapted from Case, *Intellectual Development: Birth to Adulthood*, 1985. Used by permission of Academic Press and the author.)

represents a qualitative shift in cognitive functioning since each of these activities was originally developed within very different problem situations to obtain very different objectives. As the child progresses to the final substage, she is able to make finer and finer physical and perceptual distinctions. For example, with respect to counting, the child may gradually separate out and count only those objects which possess particular characteristics.

As you can well imagine, the thought processes (control structures) for the next two stages become increasingly complex. The child is able to deal with multiple objectives and strategies in order to solve her problems and eventually to deal successfully with abstract problems. Due to the integration and chunking of thought processes developed in the earlier stages, the child can now operate efficiently on more complicated problems.

Dimensional Control Structures (3.5 to 11 Years)   In this stage, the child can make more refined distinctions—objects and events can now differ quantitatively along a continuum. For example, she can organize and separate objects based on characteristics such as color, shape, size, and texture.

As in Piaget's third stage of development, one of the major skills acquired during this stage is the ability to classify. During this stage, the child develops the ability to simultaneously coordinate two different characteristics of an object as a basis for classifying them. For example, she becomes capable of answering such questions as, "Are there more square objects or red objects?" In order to answer

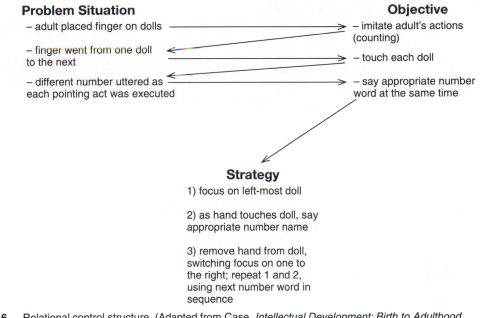

FIGURE 6.6   Relational control structure. (Adapted from Case, *Intellectual Development: Birth to Adulthood*, 1985. Used by permission of Academic Press and the author.)

this question, she needs to focus on both the shape and the color of objects presented to her (see Figure 6.7). As in Piaget's concrete operational stage, Case indicates that children's classification power is limited to previously experienced objects or persons.

Abstract Dimensional Control Structures (9 to 18 Years)   In this final stage, the child acquires abstract systems of thought that can be employed in a variety of reasoning contexts: proportional, spatial, causal, analogical, and social. Just as in Piaget's final stage, the child develops the ability to approach both abstract and concrete tasks in a systematic and scientific manner. However, Case's view of this stage allows for a detailed description of both the specific procedures and their coordination within the contexts of different reasoning tasks.

One example of thinking during this stage involves a proportional reasoning task. In this task, children are shown two sets of cups, each set containing a different combination of water and juice. One set may have three cups of water and two cups of juice, while another set may have five cups of water and three cups of juice (see Figure 6.8). The problem posed to individuals is this: "If we pour all the cups of one set into one container, which set of cups will produce the 'juiciest' drink?" According to case, in order to be able to successfully answer this question, the child must employ thought processes similar to that presented in Figure 6.9.

As you can see in Figure 6.9, the child is now capable of coordinating multiple objectives and procedures in order to deal with a complex reasoning task. The

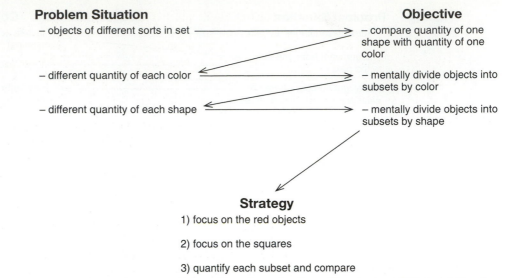

Problem Situation

– objects of different sorts in set

– different quantity of each color

– different quantity of each shape

Objective

– compare quantity of one shape with quantity of one color

– mentally divide objects into subsets by color

– mentally divide objects into subsets by shape

Strategy

1) focus on the red objects

2) focus on the squares

3) quantify each subset and compare

FIGURE 6.7   Dimensional control structure. (Adapted from Case, *Intellectual Development: Birth to Adulthood,* 1985. Used by permission of Academic Press and the author.)

child must demonstrate the ability to make multiple comparisons involving ratios not in unit form and employing them in a systematic manner. In order for it to be in unit form, the ratio of one liquid to the other must equal a whole number. For example, in Figure 6.8(b), the left- and right-hand sides have two cups of water for one cup of juice. In contrast, in Figure 6.8(e), the ratio of juice-to-water cups for the left-hand side is 2:33, and for the right-hand side it's 2:50. Being able to deal with ratios not in unit form indicates that the individual can engage in abstract thinking about objects and their relationships.

Exercise 6.3: Each statement listed below is a description of the capabilities acquired within one of the four stages of development proposed by Case's neo-Piagetian theory. Please identify to which stage each statement refers.

1. _____ The child is capable of coordinating two very distinct attributes (e.g., top and bottom) of objects, events, and people.

2. _____ The child acquires the ability to coordinate two different sets of characteristics (e.g., colors, shapes) of objects during classification.

3. _____ The child is capable of integrating diverse motor activities in order to deal with the world around him.

4. _____ The child is capable of reasoning in a variety of domains at an abstract level.

As you can see from the above description, there are many similarities between the cognitive developmental theories of Piaget and Case. As in Piagetian theory,

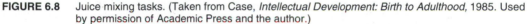

FIGURE 6.8   Juice mixing tasks. (Taken from Case, *Intellectual Development: Birth to Adulthood*, 1985. Used by permission of Academic Press and the author.)

the individual, according to Case, develops from being primarily physical and sensory in his interactions to a point where he is able to successfully deal with abstract situations. Also, the developmental stages in each theory center around similar changes. For example, the development of a symbol system is important in the second stage (preoperational, relational) in both theories. Classification is a critical skill acquired in the third stage (concrete operational, dimensional). Finally, the ability to reason at an abstract level and to deal with hypothetical situations is tied to the final stage of development (formal operational, abstract dimensional).

The Core Issues

In Chapter 1, we presented five core issues that capture important assumptions concerning the nature, process, triggers, and maintenance of learning. In the following discussion, we will compare and contrast the positions of Piagetian and neo-Piagetian theory on these core issues. Keep in mind that these are both theories of development and, consequently, the core issues here deal with developmental factors which are central to an individual's ability to learn (see Table 6.7).

1. *What develops according to the theory?* According to Piaget, changes in behavior during development are a function of changes in our ability to reason about the world around us. Changes in reasoning ability involve modifications in the nature of an individual's schemes, from those which are simple, one-dimensional, and based entirely on sensory input at birth to increasingly integrated and more abstract schemes in the concrete and formal operational stages. *For Case,*

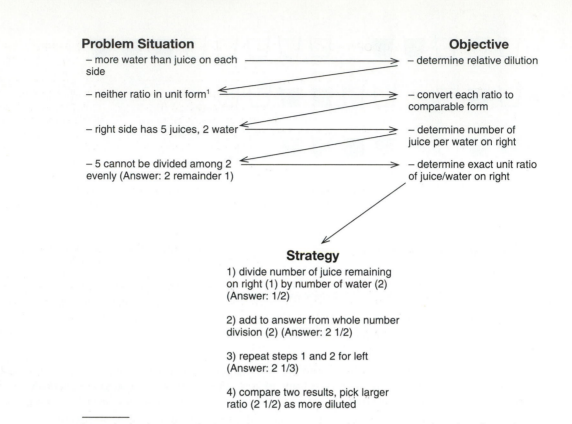

Problem Situation

– more water than juice on each side

– neither ratio in unit form[1]

– right side has 5 juices, 2 water

– 5 cannot be divided among 2 evenly (Answer: 2 remainder 1)

Objective

– determine relative dilution

– convert each ratio to comparable form

– determine number of juice per water on right

– determine exact unit ratio of juice/water on right

Strategy

1) divide number of juice remaining on right (1) by number of water (2) (Answer: 1/2)

2) add to answer from whole number division (2) (Answer: 2 1/2)

3) repeat steps 1 and 2 for left (Answer: 2 1/3)

4) compare two results, pick larger ratio (2 1/2) as more diluted

---

[1] In order for the ratio to be in unit form, one must know how many cups of one liquid exist for one cup of the other. For example, in Figure 6.8(b), the left-hand side has two cups of water for one cup of juice, whereas for (e), neither side is presented such that one can immediately translate the array of cups into a unit form.

FIGURE 6.9   Abstract dimensional control structure. (Adapted from Case, *Intellectual Development: Birth to Adulthood*, 1985. Used by permission of Academic Press and the author.)

however, changes in behavior and movement through the cognitive stages are due to increases in the operational efficiency of STSS. Modifications in the operational efficiency of STSS are due both to biological changes and to practice applying thinking skills. For both theories, the individual goes through a series of four distinct stages of development, with each stage building on previous ones.

2. *What is the relative emphasis of environmental versus organismic factors on development?* Both theories are interactionist in that they attribute approximately equal weight to the influence of environmental and organismic (biological) factors on development and learning. In Piaget's theory, the child has an innate tendency to interact with the environment in an attempt to understand and adapt to the world. If the child is not allowed to explore the environment or is exposed to an impoverished one, he will not develop to his full potential and will not attain more complex levels of reasoning. Both organismic factors (predisposition to engage the environment) and environmental factors (availability and quality of sensory input) interact to influence the cognitive development of the individual.

TABLE 6.7 SUMMARY OF PIAGET'S AND CASE'S POSITIONS ON THE FIVE CORE ISSUES

	Piaget	Case
1. How does cognition develop?	Cognitive development is due to changes in a child's ability to reason that occur because of biological changes and experiences.	Cognitive development is due to increases in the operational efficiency of STSS that are produced by biological changes and practice in applying thinking skills.
2. Relative emphasis of environmental versus organic factors on development?	Interactionist view which attributes equal weight to both factors on development.	Interactionist view which attributes equal weight to both factors on development.
3. Source of motivation for development?	Intrinsically motivated. When new experiences fail to fit into existing schemes, there occurs a need to resolve this conflict (i.e., equilibration).	Intrinsically motivated. An individual has an inherent need to organize her world into problem situations, identify objectives, and then devise appropriate problem-solving strategies.
4. How does transfer occur?	Transfer will occur when a child is presented with a wide variety of experiences at the appropriate developmental level.	Transfer will occur with practice within domains but not necessarily across domains. Practice, will, however, improve the operational efficiency of STSS which supports the development of more complicated skills across domains.
5. Important instructional variables?	Creation of challenging lessons aimed to stimulate cognitive development and which mirror the basic developmental order (i.e., physical to the abstract).	Facilitation of the child's problem-solving abilities through practice on a wide range of culturally valued problem domains.

Case's theory is also based on organismic interaction with the environment. However, for Case, these interactions are motivated by the desire to solve problems. As an individual develops, he perceives increasingly complex problems with multiple goals—problems whose solutions require increasingly complex thought patterns (schemes). In seeking to solve them, individuals simultaneously activate and integrate more than one scheme. By repeatedly combining previously isolated schemes, the individual produces more complex, multidimensional ones. Through practice, these new, complex schemes become just as automatic as the simpler ones and can be applied across a variety of situations.

The large part played by the environment within both theories suggests that educational experiences can fulfill an important role in influencing a child's cognitive development. For Piaget, an environment that encourages exploration would be the best means for fostering cognitive development. Allowing students to take the lead and direct their learning activities (i.e., guided-discovery activities) should best promote the development of their reasoning ability. For Case, an environment which encourages lots of practice with thinking skills would be best to foster cognitive development. Unlike Piaget, Case suggests that training in the use of thinking skills and strategies is an important determinant of the nature and speed of cognitive development.

3. *What is the source of motivation for development?* Piagetian theory believes that individuals have built-in tendencies that motivate them to interact with the environment and, consequently, to develop and learn. As indicated earlier, individuals are seen to be inherently active and are constantly attempting to accumulate information about the nature of the world through the process of assimilation. In essence, they are intrinsically motivated to gather information and become involved in experiences that will help in their development. When new experiences fail to fit into their existing schemes, there occurs a need to resolve this conflict (i.e., equilibration). This need motivates individuals to further interact with the environment and reorganize their world view as a means of resolving the conflict. *For Piaget, then, individuals are intrinsically motivated to develop.*

In Case's neo-Piagetian theory, individuals are considered natural problem solvers. Consequently, what motivates them is the inherent need to solve problems. Thus, a person is predisposed to organize her world into problem situations, identify objectives, and then devise appropriate problem-solving strategies. As the problems that she deals with become more and more complicated, the strategies required to solve them become more and more sophisticated. She is, then, motivated to develop more sophisticated ways to solve her problems. *As in Piagetian theory, the individual is intrinsically motivated to develop.*

4. *How does transfer occur?* As indicated earlier, according to Piagetian theory, changes in the structure and nature of knowledge (schemes) are responsible for the development of our reasoning ability. To Piaget, these changes are permanent in that once we have attained a certain level of reasoning ability we can never fall back to an earlier level. They are also universal; that is, they apply to all situations and domains. Consequently, once we have attained a certain level, we should be able to reason at that level within any content area or set of experiences. Our ability to transfer our skills to new situations will then be generalized and automatic, a function of global changes in our knowledge. To ensure transfer, a teacher should introduce a wide variety of experiences at the appropriate developmental level. The content of these experiences is not as important as the degree to which they force the child to rethink and change her current view of the world. Also, maturation is responsible for the specific timing of these "appropriate points" during development. Consequently, both biological and environmental factors will be responsible for the degree to which transfer of skills occurs within individuals.

In contrast to Piagetian theory, Case suggests that the content of experiences is critically important when promoting transfer of cognitive skills (see Case & Sandieson, 1992; Case, Sandieson, & Dennis, 1987). Developments in one domain do not necessarily transfer to others. However, practice of cognitive skills within a variety of domains will help with transfer by improving the operational efficiency of STSS and, consequently, pave the way for the development of more complicated cognitive skills in other domains. Transfer, however, is viewed as occurring primarily within a specific problem domain, not necessarily across problem domains.

5. *What are important variables in instruction?* According to Piaget, the child is inherently active and motivated to learn. Any discrepancies between new experiences and prior knowledge produces tension which, in turn, motivates the child to accommodate (change) her intellectual structure (existing schemes). The function of a teacher, therefore, is to construct classroom environments which challenge the child. In order to do this, the teacher must first evaluate the child's present level of cognitive functioning. As a teacher, you need to recognize that children view the world very differently (qualitatively differently) from adults' view. For example, a child operating at the preoperational level of thinking has centered and irreversible schemes. To challenge the child, some of the activities you create should require that she deal with her environment in a decentered and reversible manner. On the other hand, you would not present formal operational activities that require understanding abstract concepts such as "political responsibility" or "individual rights." In summary, to promote accommodation teachers must present tasks that cannot be totally explained by the child's existing system of schemes. We want something that doesn't quite fit. However, if the discrepancy is too great (requires too much accommodation), the child will be unable to cope, will become frustrated and quit. Finally, there is a particular order to acquiring information in particular domains (e.g., number, moral reasoning). The learning sequence must mirror the basic developmental order. This translates into developing a lesson plan which begins with repetition of purely physical schemes and gradually works its way to the mental manipulation of an internalized set of coordinated schemes (algorithms, ten commandments, etc.).

Case's neo-Piagetian theory views education as facilitating the development of the child's problem-solving abilities. Moreover, this problem solving should occur across as wide a range of culturally valued problem domains or subject areas as possible. The first step in this process is to specify the important abilities to be developed within the educational setting. This will differ depending on the culture in which the child resides. These abilities should be described in terms of control structures (problem-solving schemes): problem situations, objectives, and appropriate strategies. Within each problem domain, a very specific description of the schemes possessed by adults in that culture is required (see Figure 6.7). Once these schemes are identified, they need to be sequenced in terms of their levels, that is, their stages and substages. This sequencing of schemes provides a guide to curriculum development that teachers can use to organize developmentally appropriate learning experiences (see Figures 6.3–6.6 for examples of control structures—schemes—for early stages).

After organizing the curriculum according to schematic levels, teachers need to adapt the curriculum to the needs of each individual learner. That means considering (1) the child's existing developmental level, (2) the child's need for independent versus adult-regulated activity, and (3) the amount of task simplification, prompting, and carefully monitored practice that will lead to higher-level skills. The speed with which a child can progress will be a function of both environmental factors (instruction and practice) and organic factors (myelinization of nervous tissue) and their effects on the operational efficiency of STSS and the child's need for self-regulation.

As you can see, the implications for instruction within Case's theory overlap with those derived from the Piagetian perspective and the information processing perspective. It overlaps with the Piagetian perspective in its description of cognitive development as a series of qualitative changes in the nature of interactions between the individual and the world around him. Also, though education and instruction play a large part in the child's development, teachers still need to accommodate maturational changes (which will influence the capacity of the child's STSS). Case's instructional implications overlap with those derived from information processing theory in two ways. First, he identifies specific mental processes and strategies which underlie intellectual development and, second, he asserts that much practice is needed in order to acquire these operations and strategies.

REVIEW OF MAJOR POINTS

1 Development can be defined as a relatively permanent change in knowledge or behavior due to maturation and learning which occurs over an extended time span.

2 Both Piaget's and Case's theories of cognitive development are concerned with the changes that occur in the nature and structure of knowledge due to maturation and experience. Both theories assume that the individual is actively involved in this developmental process (i.e., they are both constructivist theories).

3 Piagetian theory indicates that changes in behavior that occur during development are a function of changes in our ability to reason about the world around us.

4 Piagetian theory indicates that there are two functional invariants which constrain and encourage all types of development: organization and adaptation. Our cognitive system is highly organized, its primary purpose and goal being to help us adapt to the world around us. The following structures and processes aid in the organization of experiences and in our adaptation to the world: schemes, assimilation, accommodation, and equilibration.

5 Schemes are units of knowledge which consist of specific patterns of mental or physical activity that enable us to understand and adapt to our environment. There are two types of schemes: figurative and operative. Figurative schemes consist of information about the environment which is essentially a copy of objects and events. In contrast, operative schemes allow the child to separate the invariant characteristics (number, volume, mass, etc.) of objects and events from those which are tied to physical and perceptual experience (size, color, shape, etc.).

6 Adaptation refers to our attempts to create an accurate view of the world around us, and it occurs through assimilation and accommodation. Assimilation is the process of fitting new information into existing schemes and has an integrative function. Accommodation is the temporary or permanent modification of existing schemes in order to more easily interact with new, incoming experiences from the world around us. It has a negotiation function.

7 Equilibration can be defined as the tendency to reduce cognitive conflict by attempting to maintain a level of balance through the complementary processes of assimilation and accommodation. During equilibration, some form of cognitive reorganization occurs which is intended to establish a state in which assimilation and accommodation are equally influential to cognitive development.

8 Piagetian theory proposes four stages of cognitive development: sensorimotor, preoperational, concrete operational, and formal operational. Within each stage, an individual exhibits a particular type of thinking and behavior which reflects a specific cognitive organization and structure. These unique structures allow for different types of interactions between the person and the environment and lead to fundamentally different views of the world.

9 Case's neo-Piagetian theory of cognitive development also adopts a stage view of development but focuses on the variety of cognitive strategies that is involved in tasks. It also attempts to explain differences between individuals' levels of development by looking at both qualitative and quantitative schematic changes. Moreover, cognitive development is critically tied to memory development. This theory blends two models of development, a structural or stage model and a process model.

10 A critical processing component within Case's theory is the operational efficiency of the individual's short-term storage space (STSS). Short-term storage space is similar to what information processing theorists refer to as working memory. They both have two functions: storage of information and operating on this information. The STSS is limited in terms of the amount of energy one can devote to these functions. Operational efficiency refers to the maximum number of independent schemes that can be brought to full activation (attended to) simultaneously within STSS. Although the capacity of STSS is fixed at birth, through maturation and practice our ability to use the existing capacity increases.

11 A critical structural component which influences cognitive development is the executive control structures. These structures are a product of our tendency to structure activities and interactions in terms of problems to be solved: problem situation, goals and objectives, and strategies to obtain those goals. As children develop, the control structures that they are capable of creating become more and more complex.

12 Each of the four stages (sensorimotor, relational, dimensional, and abstract dimensional) proposed by Case differ by the level of the relationship that an individual is able to represent and manipulate and the type of executive control structure they reflect. Within each of these stages, the individual progresses through the same three substages: unifocal, bifocal, and elaborated coordination. Movement through these substages reflects a particular number of elements that can be represented and a particular way these elements are organized in the cognitive system. Each substage reflects increases in the operational efficiency of the STSS.

13 The similarities between the Piagetian and neo-Piagetian view of stages are: (1) each divides cognitive development into four stages, (2) each stage represents a qualitatively different way of interacting with the world, (3) the child's cognitive development moves from being primarily sensory to being able to successfully deal with abstract situations, and (4) the stages are hierarchical, each one subsuming a previous one.

14 The differences between the Piagetian and neo-Piagetian view of stages include: (1) the fact that a child can be within different stages within different domains, (2) the mechanisms for movement from stage to stage, and (3) the role of formal instruction in facilitating movement from stage to stage.

15 In Piagetian theory the changes that occur during development are a function of changes in our ability to reason. In contrast, neo-Piagetian theory indicates that changes in behavior and movement through the stages are due to increases in the operational efficiency of STSS.

16 Both theories are interactionist theories in that they attribute approximately equal weight to the influence of environmental and biological factors on development and learning.

17 Both theories view the individual as being intrinsically motivated. Piagetian theory sees the need to possess an accurate view of the world as an innate motivator that drives us to explore the world and to compare newly acquired information with prior knowledge and experiences. Neo-Piagetian theory sees the individual as predisposed to organize the world into problem situations and to develop increasingly sophisticated ways of dealing with those problems.

18 In order to ensure that transfer occurs, Piagetian theory recommends introducing a wide variety of developmentally appropriate experiences during development. The content of these experiences is not as important as the degree to which they force the child to rethink and change (accommodate) her current view of the world. In contrast, neo-Piagetian theory suggests that the content of experiences is critically important in promoting the transfer of cognitive skills. Practicing cognitive skills within a variety of domains promotes transfer by improving the operational efficiency of STSS. This paves the way for development of more complicated cognitive skills in other domains.

19 Within a Piagetian framework, the function of a teacher is to construct classroom environments which challenge the child. In order to do that, the teacher must evaluate the child's present level of functioning. Within a neo-Piagetian framework, the function of a teacher is to facilitate the development of the child's problem-solving capabilities. The child should be given as wide a range of culturally valued problem domains or subject areas as possible.

ANSWERS TO QUESTIONS AND EXERCISES

Question 6.1: Schemes are units of knowledge which are responsible for a wide variety of specific and complex activities. They are the basic unit of knowledge involved in reasoning, and through their applications and use, they help us develop a more accurate picture of the world around us. In this way, they are instrumental in helping us to adapt.

Question 6.2: Operative schemes are a special type that is responsible for internalized activities (e.g., problem solving). They are employed in a logical manner and exist within organized systems of operations. That is, they are combined with other operations to make larger units of related knowledge. The acquisition and development of operations reflect qualitative changes in our reasoning ability. For example, operations allow us to "reflectively abstract." This ability is a critical component of higher-level thinking.

Question 6.3: Assimilation and accommodation are similar in that they both help *the individual adapt to his environment.* They are different in that assimilation is concerned primarily with *the integration of our experiences into our existing schemes,* while accommodation is primarily concerned with *the modification of our existing schemes because of our experiences.*

Exercise 6.1:

a. This is an example of assimilation because the student is attempting to integrate his current experience with his prior knowledge.
b. This is an example of accommodation because the student is modifying her current view of development (i.e., her current schemes related to development).
c. This is an example of neither assimilation nor accommodation. The student is neither attempting to integrate new information nor modifying her existing schemes in response to current and past experiences.
d. This is an example of assimilation because the businessman (by applying his negotiation skills) is relating this experience to his schemes on negotiation.
e. This is an example of accommodation because the scientist is changing his existing schemes (theory) because of his experiences (experiments).

Question 6.4: Equilibration is the tendency to reduce cognitive conflict by establishing a cognitive state of balance between the processes of assimilation and accommodation. Without this tendency it is unlikely that individuals would develop an accurate view of the world. Also, without this built-in tendency, individuals would not move to higher and higher qualitative levels of reasoning.

Question 6.5: Children who are in the sensorimotor stage of development interact with the world primarily through sensory impressions and motor actions. Children solve problems through motor movements rather than through the manipulation of ideas.

Question 6.6: The child's thinking during this stage is limited primarily in two ways. First, the child tends to center on one aspect of a situation at a time.

Consequently, situations which require the coordination of multiple elements will present a problem for him at this stage. Secondly, the child's thinking is irreversible. That is, he looks at static states and basically ignores how one situation got transformed into another. Consequently, he is unable to reverse transformation and reestablish original states.

Question 6.7: Classification skills allow the concrete operational child to organize stimuli in terms of selected characteristics such as color or shape. In this way, she is able to identify relations (red vs. green, round vs. square) between the selected characteristics. Seriation skills allow the child to *order* things based upon a selected variable. This will enable her to identify specific patterns such as "longer" or "bigger." Both the classification and seriation skills allow the child to impose some organized system on the objects she is manipulating and, consequently, systematically deal with concrete problems.

Question 6.8: Formal operational individuals are able to deal logically with a variety of hypothetical situations. They can reflect on the products of their actions and systematically manipulate their environment in order to test a variety of hypotheses. They can deal logically with the world of possibilities. In contrast, a concrete operational individual can deal logically only with the real world. That is, in order for him to be able to approach a problem systematically, that problem must deal with previously experienced situations.

Question 6.9: Operational efficiency can be defined as the maximum number of independent schemes that can be attended to simultaneously within STSS. We are limited in terms of how much mental energy we can devote to the manipulation of information in STSS. As we develop, we become more efficient at using our limited capacity. The two factors which influence the operational efficiency of the STSS are (1) myelinization of brain tissue (which results in greater nervous processing speed) and (2) practice employing schemes. With practice, simpler schemes become consolidated into more complex ones and, in the process, free up space and energy within STSS which can be devoted to the completion of more complicated tasks.

Question 6.10: Executive control structures consist of the following three components: problem situation, objective/goal, and strategy to obtain the goal. The strategic component consists of a set of procedures (operative schemes) for dealing with objects, events, and/or people. These structures help in the coordination of lower-order schemes with higher-order schemes. This coordination allows the individual to retrieve those schemes together in the future. This, in turn, requires less attentional energy, frees up the STSS by increasing its operational efficiency, and allows the child to deal with more complicated as well as qualitatively different problem situations.

Exercise 6.2:
a. ___B___ Patterns of development are constrained by maturation.
b. ___C___ The child is viewed as a problem solver who acquires better problem-solving skills as he develops.

Neo-Piagetian theory views the child as a problem solver whereas Piagetian theory views the child as a developing scientist.

c. ___C___ Practice of specific skills plays a critical part during development because it increases the individual's ability to process information efficiently.

Within Piagetian theory, practice of specific skills is not a critical part in development. Changes that occur are global in nature.

d. ___B___ A critical process to knowledge growth is the development and use of operations.

e. ___B___ Everyone goes through the same set of stages in the same order. However, not everyone may attain the higher level stages.

f. ___C___ At any one time, children may be in different stages in different domains of knowledge.

Within Piagetian theory, stage-appropriate thought processes and structures should be consistent across all domains.

Exercise 6.3:

1. ____relational stage____ The child is capable of coordinating two very distinct attributes (e.g., top and bottom) of objects, events, and people.

2. ____dimensional stage____ The child acquires the ability to coordinate two different sets of characteristics (e.g., colors, shapes) of objects during classification.

3. ____sensorimotor stage____ The child is capable of integrating diverse motor activities in order to deal with the world around him.

4. __abstract dimensional stage__ The child is capable of reasoning in a variety of domains at an abstract level.

REFERENCES

Arlin, P. (1975). Cognitive development in adulthood: A fifth stage? *Developmental Psychology, 11,* 602–606.

Brainerd, C. J. (1978). The stage question in cognitive-developmental theory. *The Behavioral and Brain Sciences, 2,* 173–213.

Bruner, J. S. (1964). The course of cognitive growth. *American Psychologist, 19,* 1–15.

Case, R. (1978). Intellectual development from birth to adulthood: A neo-Piagetian investigation. In R. Siegler (Ed.), *Children's thinking: What develops?* Hillsdale, NJ: Lawrence Erlbaum.

Case, R. (1985). *Intellectual development: Birth to adulthood.* New York: Academic Press.

Case, R., & Sandieson, R. (1992). New data on learning and its transfer: The role of central numerical structures in the development of children's scientific, social and temporal thought. In R. Case (Ed.), *The mind's staircase: Stages in the development of human intelligence.* Hillsdale, NJ: Lawrence Erlbaum.

Case, R., Sandieson, R., & Dennis, S. (1987). Two cognitive developmental approaches to the design of remedial instruction. *Cognitive Development, 1,* 293–333.

Field, D. (1987). A review of preschool conservation training: An analysis of analyses. *Developmental Review, 7,* 210–251.

Fischer, K. (1980). A theory of cognitive development: The control and construction of hierarchies of skills. *Psychological Review, 87,* 477–531.

Fischer, K., & Pipp, S. L. (1984). Process of cognitive development: Optimal level and skill acquisition. In R. J. Sternberg (Ed.), *Mechanisms of cognitive development.* New York: Freedman.

Fischer, K., & Silvern, L. (1985). Stages and individual differences in cognitive development. *Annual Review of Psychology, 36,* 613–648.

Flavell, J. (1962). *The developmental psychology of Jean Piaget.* New York: D. Van Nostrand.

Flavell, J., Everett, B., Croft, K., & Flavell, E. (1981). Young children's knowledge about visual perception: Further evidence for the level 1–level 2 distinction. *Developmental Psychology, 17,* 99–103.

Ford, M. (1979). The construct validity of egocentrism. *Psychological Bulletin, 86,* 1169–1188.

Gelman, R. (1979). Preschool thought. *American Psychologists 34,* 900–905.

Gelman, R., & Gallistel, C. R. (1978). *The child's understanding of number.* Cambridge, MA: Harvard University Press.

Golomb, C., & Cornelius, C. (1977). Symbolic play and its cognitive significance. *Developmental Psychology, 13,* 246–252.

Inhelder, B., & Piaget, J. (1969). *The early growth of logic in the child* (E. Lunzer & D. Papert, Trans.). New York: W. W. Norton.

Kitchener, K. S., & Kitchener, R. F. (1981). The development of natural rationality: Can formal operations account for it? In J. Meacham & M. R. E. Santilli (Eds.), *Social development in youth: Structure and content* (pp. 231–262). New York: S. Karger.

Kuhn, D., Langer, N., Kohlberg, L., & Hann, N. (1977). The development of formal operations in logical and formal judgements. *Genetic Psychology Monograph, 95,* 115.

Levin, G. (1983). *Child psychology.* Monterey, CA: Brooks/Cole.

Luria, A. R. (1976). *Cognitive development: Its cultural and social foundations.* Cambridge, MA: Harvard University Press.

Masangkay, Z., McCluskey, K., McIntyre, C., Sims-Knight, J., Vaughn, B., & Flavell, J. (1974). The early development of inferences about visual percepts of others. *Child Development, 45,* 357–366.

Miller, P. (1989). *Theories of developmental psychology.* San Francisco: W. H. Freedman.

Piaget, J. (1952). *The child's conception of number.* New York: Humanities.

Piaget, J. (1954). *The construction of reality in the child.* New York: Basic Books.

Piaget, J. (1962). *Play, dreams and imitation in childhood.* New York: W. W. Norton.

Piaget, J. (1964). Development and learning. In R. E. Ripple & V. N. Rockcastle (Eds.), *Piaget rediscovered.* Ithaca, NY: Cornell University.

Piaget, J. (1967). *Six psychological studies.* New York: Vintage Books.

Piaget, J. (1970a). Piaget's theory. In P. Mussen (Ed.), *Manual of child psychology* (3rd ed.). New York: Wiley.

Piaget, J. (1970b). *Science of education and the psychology of the child.* New York: Viking Press.

Piaget, J. (1985). *The equilibration of cognitive structures: The central problem of cognitive structures.* Chicago: University of Chicago Press.

Piaget, J., & Inhelder, B. (1956). *The child's conception of space.* London: Routledge & Kegan Paul.

Piaget, J., & Inhelder, B. (1969). *The psychology of the child.* New York: Viking Basic Books.

Roberge, J. (1970). A study of children's abilities to reason with basic principles of deductive reasoning. *American Educational Research Journal, 7,* 583–596.

Schwebel, M. (1975). Formal operations in the first year college student. *Journal of Psychology, 91,* 133–141.

Siegel, L., & Hodkin, B. (1982). The garden path to the understanding of cognitive development: Has Piaget led us into the poison ivy? In S. Modgil & C. Modgil (Eds.), *Jean Piaget: Consensus and controversy.* New York: Praeger.

Uzgiris, I., & Hunt, J. (1975). *Assessment in infancy: Ordinal scales of psychological development.* Urbana: University of Illinois Press.

Vygotsky, L. S. (1962). *Thought and language.* Cambridge, MA: MIT Press. (First published in Russian in 1934.)

7

VYGOTSKY'S THEORY OF COGNITIVE DEVELOPMENT

OBJECTIVES

1. Describe two similarities and two differences between the theories of Piaget and Vygotsky.
2. Describe Vygotsky's explanation of the difference between lower and higher mental functions.
3. State Vygotsky's general genetic law of cultural development and show how this law applies to speech development.
4. Describe how Vygotsky saw the process of internalization.
5. Describe Vygotsky's notion of how egocentric speech contributes to the child's cognitive development.
6. Explain the difference between Vygotsky's and Piaget's conception of the relationship between learning and development.
7. Define the zone of proximal development.
8. Define scaffolding and describe three (of six) scaffolding functions.
9. Explain how reciprocal teaching incorporates elements of Vygotsky's socioinstructional approach.
10. Describe Vygotsky's position on the core issues, and compare his position on each issue to that of Piaget.

GENERAL ORIENTATION

In this chapter, we examine yet another theory of cognitive development, that of Lev Vygotsky (1896–1934). Our reason for including Vygotsky in this book is that learning is at the core of his view of cognitive development. Although we are devoting considerable time to theories of development, as we pointed out in the previous chapter, learning and development are intimately related. Consequently, teachers who are primarily interested in promoting learning must be knowledgeable about developmental factors that impinge upon learning.

Vygotsky was a Russian psychologist whose intellectual roots were in literature and linguistics. His career as a theoretical and applied psychologist, which began following the Russian Revolution in 1917, was relatively brief due to his early death from tuberculosis. Vygotsky's contemporaries included the behaviorists Pavlov, Watson, and Thorndike, Gestalt psychologists Koffka and Wertheimer, and, of course, Piaget. Vygotsky was very aware of developments within these diverse theoretical frameworks and used them to sharpen his own theoretical views. In contrast, Vygotsky's work was, until recently, little known among American and European theorists. For example, Piaget knew of Vygotsky's work only 25 years after his death.

The late entry of Vygotsky's ideas into the mainstream of Western psychology was partially due to the suppression of his major works in the Soviet Union for a period of time because of a dispute in the Soviet psychological community. However, even after his work began to be disseminated in his own country, there was a delay in translating it into English. Consequently, his major book, *Thought and Language,* was not published in English until 1962, almost 30 years after his death. Vygotsky's influence on American psychology, which has grown steadily during the last two decades, is now at a peak largely because his views regarding the social contexts of learning and developing have been widely assimilated by cognitive and educational psychologists.

In this chapter, we shall first provide an advance organizer for Vygotsky's theory by comparing his views with those of Piaget and by pointing out some of the key influences on Vygotsky's thinking. We will then set forth Vygotsky's major ideas concerning development and show how he applied these theoretical notions to explain the development of speech (language) and its relationship to conceptual thought. Finally, we will examine his notion of the relationship between development and learning as well as his views on the role of instruction in development. These latter views have been very influential in contemporary cognitive approaches to instruction. Consequently, we will describe some of the recent work by Americans who have attempted to systematically apply Vygotskian notions to education.

Comparison of Piaget and Vygotsky

There are many similarities between Vygotsky's theory and that of Piaget and neo-Piagetians (see Tudge & Rogoff, 1989). Vygotsky and Piaget both argued that to really understand a psychological process, one has to study it genetically, meaning developmentally. They both believed that cognitive development involves qualitative transformations of thought patterns rather than gradual growth of existing patterns. Both theorists also have a dialectic view of the developmental process and of the relation between the individual and society. A **dialectic** view sees change emerging from conflict between opposing forces or ideas. The resolution of the conflict comes about by a transformation (often involving synthesis) of the opposing forces or premises into a qualitatively new entity. For example, as children go about their daily activities, their established ways of doing things don't always work because they fail to accommodate to (conflict with) the conditions of a new situation. Thus, children must develop new problem-solving methods that incorporate these conditions (Thomas, 1992). Both Piaget and Vygotsky regarded the roles of the individual and the environment as inseparable, and both believed that children are active in their own development, arriving at their knowledge of the world through active exploration of their environment.

Despite these similarities, there are some major differences between the two theorists. Although both acknowledged the role that the social world plays in cognitive development, they differed in their emphasis on social factors and their explanation of how social factors influence development. Social influences on development are not central to Piaget's theory, which focuses on the interaction of the child with his physical and mental environment. In Piaget's view, the child comes to understand the world by acting on it as an individual. He emphasized the role of equilibration in explaining developmental change, and he restricted the role of the social environment to accelerating or retarding the age at which children pass through the stages of development (Piaget, 1983).

In contrast, Vygotsky's theory asserts that individual development cannot be understood without reference to the social environment, both institutional and interpersonal, in which the child is embedded. Vygotsky emphasized how much social institutions, tools, and technologies (e.g., schooling, language and other symbol systems, mnemonic strategies, calculators, computers) influence the individual's thinking. These sociocultural devices for cognitive processing are made available to children through interaction with people who are more skilled than they.

The two theories also differ in their view of how social factors affect cognitive development. Piaget focused on the cognitive conflict (disequilibrium) that occurs as the individual acts on the physical environment. When an existing scheme is altered to accommodate new information, equilibrium is reestablished at a higher level (see Chapter 6). Piaget simply extended this notion by recognizing that disequilibrium can also be brought about by social interactions between children or between children and adults who hold different views. Attempts by individual children to reach a logical resolution of their internal cognitive conflict lead to cognitive development. Thus, according to Piaget, the social environment is just another source of experience or information that evokes conflict and adaptation in the child.

According to Vygotsky, the sociocultural environment does not just provide cognitive stimulation that triggers conflict and equilibration. Rather, it is literally the *source* of the child's higher cognitive processes. Higher mental processes such as voluntary attention or deliberate remembering are created and sustained by social interaction. The child internalizes processes that are first observed and practiced in social interactions. However, this internalization is not achieved through simple imitation of observed behaviors. Rather it involves the qualitative transformation of social activities to fit the child's level of comprehension. Explaining how social processes (external to the child) are transformed into internal mental processes is the main purpose of Vygotsky's theory, discussed below.

Another difference between Piaget and Vygotsky concerns the direction of development.

Question 7.1: According to Piaget, in what direction does development always proceed? This need not be a straight memory question. You can figure it out by thinking about the major tenets of Piaget's theory. Please answer and then turn to

the end of the chapter._____

_____

_____

Cognitive development in Vygotsky's theory is a result of social interaction which leads children toward the skills of their social partners.

Question 7.2: Given Vygotsky's emphasis on the role of social interaction in development, can you deduce his view of the direction of development? (Hint: How might children's development be affected by the characteristics of the people

they interact with?_____

_____

_____

Finally, most of the differences between Piaget and Vygotsky probably reflect an underlying difference in which aspects of development they were trying to explain. Piaget focused his attention on the development of logical thinking, especially on how children make qualitative shifts in their reasoning ability. He wanted to demonstrate that at each stage of development, the child possesses an internally consistent logic, a logic that differs qualitatively from that of an adult.

In contrast, Vygotsky was concerned with how culturally developed tools, thought, and language patterns are internalized and then used to understand the world. He thus focused on the ways in which more knowledgeable members of a culture pass on to less developed members culturally accepted practices and tools, of which language is the most important. Given this comparison with Piaget as background, let's now explore some of the major influences on Vygotsky's theory.

Influences on Vygotsky's Thought

Contemporary Psychological Theory   To understand Vygotsky's theory one needs to examine the climate within psychology in his time. In Chapter 1, we pointed out that in the early days psychology was dominated by two opposing views of human thought. First came espousers of structuralism and functionalism who studied conscious experience by means of introspection. Then came the behaviorists who ruled out the study of consciousness in order to make psychology a scientific discipline. Observable behavior was the only subject matter allowed in their approach.

Vygotsky saw the shortcomings of both of these schools. He saw the pitfalls in the introspective method, yet he also saw that behaviorists, by ruling out the study of mind and consciousness, blocked psychology from studying complicated problems of human behavior. In his own research, Vygotsky studied conscious thought processes, but he used newly developed objective measures which did not depend upon introspection. More importantly, he argued that to be scientific, explanations of consciousness must be sought in *material realms outside of consciousness.* Thus, he suggested that individual consciousness is built from the *outside* through relations with others. That is, we become aware of ourselves because we have become aware of others and thus can take the position of another toward ourselves.

Marxist Theory   Vygotsky's thinking was profoundly influenced by the Marxist philosophy on which the new Soviet state was founded. He viewed as his major task the development of suitable objective methods for giving scientific substance to the tenets of Marxist-Leninist doctrine. According to this doctrine, the intellectual skills or thinking patterns of an individual are not due to innate factors but, instead, are the result of activities practiced in the social institutions of the culture in which the individual grows up. Thomas (1992) points out three core assumptions of Marxist philosophy that Vygotsky incorporated into his approach to human development.

First, Marx asserted that people's consciousness (attitudes, conceptions of reality) is constructed from the production and distribution activities in which they engage. That is, consciousness does not precede or determine social existence but, rather, social existence determines consciousness. Vygotsky incorporated this position by picturing children engaging in activities and from these activities projecting the contents of their minds. Thinking does not create action; instead action creates thought. Mental development occurs as children internalize the products of their interactions with their environment.

Second, Marx asserted that societies develop through a process of resolving dialectic conflicts. As indicated earlier, the dialectical process of change is one in which an established idea or thesis is opposed by its opposite or antithesis. This intellectual conflict is then resolved by means of a revised conclusion or synthesis. Vygotsky applied this formula to child development by proposing that children's activities give rise to conflicts because their accustomed way of doing things (thesis) often cannot adequately encompass novel aspects of the current situation (antithesis). Children must develop new problem-solving methods that meet the challenge of the new situation (synthesis). Development is the result of internalizing new knowledge and skills that resolve each dialectical conflict. This new knowledge then becomes the child's new thesis which will, in turn, be challenged by new situations.

Third, Marx contended that societal development is a historical process within cultural contexts. A society's history is a chronology of purposeful change. By analyzing such change processes, we can understand how the society develops. The culture of a given society is a product of its past history and also provides the contextual foundation for future development. Vygotsky incorporated this cultural-historical approach into his theory of child development. On the one hand, he maintained that understanding children's development requires understanding the culture's historical background because it is the culture that forms the environmental context which spurs children's development. On the other hand, Vygotsky saw that each child's history (i.e., the succession of his dialectic conflicts and resolutions) determines the child's future development.

In summary, Vygotsky's theory represents a cultural-historical view of human development, in which the history of the society in which a child is raised and the child's own history of experiences within that society are both extremely important in determining the ways in which a child will be able to think. Let us now examine the major constructs in Vygotsky's theory.

Major Constructs in Vygotsky's Theory

According to Vygotsky, the higher mental functions of consciousness are products of **mediated** activity. The meaning of the term "mediated activity" should become clear as we proceed. The mediators of thought are psychological tools and means of interpersonal communication. Vygotsky made the analogy between psychological tools and material tools. Material tools mediate between the human hand and objects and thus are used to gain mastery over the external environment. **Psychological tools** are used to gain mastery over one's own behavior and cognition. Psychological tools have a *semiotic* nature. That is, they consist of signs and symbols or sign-symbol systems such as gestures, language, mathematical sign systems, and mnemonic techniques.

Vygotsky distinguished between **lower natural mental functions,** such as elementary perception, memory, and attention, which are biologically determined, and **higher cultural psychological functions.** These higher psychological functions appear gradually as the lower functions are transformed by incorporation of psychological tools. For example, elementary memorization by a young child involves a direct connection between stimulus events A and B. Pavlovian conditioning is one example of that. An older child might remember that B goes with A by using either an external or an internal mediator. An example of an external mediator might be a written note or a string around the finger, while internal mediators might be key words or images, or any of the mnemonic techniques we studied in Chapter 4.

A key point of Vygotsky's theory is that the psychological tools that enable the development of higher psychological processes come from outside the individual. They come from the surrounding culture, and they are transmitted through interactions with others who already possess them. This point was stated succinctly in Vygotsky's **general genetic law of cultural development,** which asserts:

Any function in the child's cultural development appears twice, or on two planes. First it appears on the social plane, and then on the psychological plane. First it appears between people as an interpsychological category, and then within the child as an intrapsychological category. This is equally true with regard to voluntary attention, logical memory, the formation of concepts, and the development of volition. (1981, p. 163)

Thus, Vygotsky was primarily interested in investigating how psychological tools and social relations are internalized. By **internalization** he meant the internal reconstruction of an external operation. Vygotsky saw a good example of the internalization process in the development of pointing. At first it is just an unsuccessful attempt to grasp something. The child attempts to grasp an object placed beyond his reach; his hands extend toward the object and his fingers make grasping movements. However, the situation changes fundamentally when the mother interprets the child's reaching movement as a communicative sign and gives him the object. The child then learns to direct this pointing behavior to other people rather than to an object, and eventually the action itself is transformed into true pointing. At this stage the child is using an external sign because it has meaning for others. Finally, the child himself comes to consciously understand the meaning of his own gesture, and it is at this point that it becomes a "gesture for oneself." That is, it becomes a psychological tool (Vygotsky, 1978).

From the above example of pointing, we can see that internalization consists of a series of transformations: (1) An operation that initially represents an external activity is reconstructed and begins to occur internally. (2) An interpersonal process (between people) is transformed into an intrapersonal one (within a person). (3) The transformation of an interpersonal process into an intrapersonal one is the result of a long series of developmental events. The process being transformed continues to exist as an external form of activity for a long time before definitely turning inward (Vygotsky, 1978).

Although Vygotsky attempted to explain the development of all higher mental functions in the above terms, the major focus of his theory was on the development of speech and its relation to thought. Speech has a special place in his theory because it plays a dual role. On the one hand, speech (language) is a psychological tool that helps one to form other mental functions. On the other hand, it is itself one of those mental functions. We turn now to Vygotsky's view of the development of speech and thought.

Thought and Language

Vygotsky's most popular and well-known book is entitled *Thought and Language* (Vygotsky, 1962, 1986). The title is somewhat misleading because it mistranslates the word that Vygotsky actually used, which was the Russian word for speech. Vygotsky used the word "speech" rather than the word "language" because, in keeping with the major thrust of his theory as outlined above, he was primarily interested in the social aspects of speech rather than the structure of the language system per se. Having said this, it is important to add that by the word "speech"

Vygotsky did not mean just verbal utterances. Rather, he had in mind the whole social milieu within which speech is embedded (Wertsch, 1979).

Vygotsky believed that thought and speech have different roots in development, with the two initially being independent. That is, in the development of the child there is a stage in which speech is preintellectual and thought is prelinguistic. At a certain point, however, these functions meet, whereupon thought becomes verbal and speech, rational. Thus, the intersection of speech and thought gives rise to verbal thought. In highly literate cultural settings, verbal thought eventually becomes the individual's primary form of thought. However, Vygotsky did not identify thought with speech, since he believed that even adults exhibit nonverbal thought (e.g., skilled tool use) and nonconceptual speech (e.g., rote recitation of material such as telephone numbers or memorized jingles). At the same time, he believed that the speech structures mastered by the child eventually become the basic structures of his thinking. Thus, Vygotsky was extremely interested in the development of speech and its internalization as a psychological tool for guiding thinking.

Speech Development   A critical notion of Vygotsky is that language arises initially as a means of communication between the child and the people in his environment. Only subsequently, upon conversion to internal speech, does it come to organize the child's thought. According to Vygotsky, speech development follows the same course and obeys the same laws as the development of all other mental operations involving the use of signs. Other examples include counting and mnemonic memorizing (Vygotsky, 1986). He found that these operations generally develop in four stages. Table 7.1 contains a description of each stage and the characteristic features of two illustrative sign-using operations, speech and memory, at each stage.

First is the **primitive or natural stage,** which lasts from birth until about age 2. At this stage, the child possesses only what Vygotsky (1978) termed *elementary* processes which are rooted in conditioned and unconditioned reflexes, that is, in the biological nature of the individual. They are totally and directly determined by stimulation from the environment. At this stage, speech (as well as other processes such as attention and memory) functions much as it does in lower animals. Early in this stage, speech consists of sounds representing emotional release—crying with pain, cooing with contentment. Next, as early as the second month, sounds appear that represent social reactions to other people's voices or appearance. The third type of natural (or thoughtless) speech consists of the child's first words which substitute for objects and desires. These words are conditioned by parents' and others' matching the words frequently to objects. The same type of conditioning can be observed in animal training.

The second stage of **naive psychology** begins at about age 2. In this stage, the child exhibits the beginnings of practical intelligence by recognizing characteristics of her surroundings and by starting to use tools. This phase in speech development is manifested by the correct use of grammatical forms and structures before the child understands the logical operations for which they stand. In this stage the

TABLE 7.1   STAGES IN THE DEVELOPMENT OF OPERATIONS USING SIGNS

Stage	Operation	
	Speech Characteristics	Memory Characteristics
1. Natural Child is not capable of using signs to regulate behavior	Babbling, emotional release, words learned through conditioning	Retention of mental images of actual experiences and objects
2. Naive psychological Beginnings of practical intelligence manifested in tool use	Child uses words to stand for things but does not understand symbolic function of language or the logic underlying the grammatical forms that he uses	Child uses external signs to cue recall only if the sign is a direct representation of the target memory
3. External sign use Child uses external signs as aids in solution of internal problems	Child uses egocentric speech first to accompany action and then to guide and plan behavior	Child uses external signs symbolically to aid in retrieval of target memories
4. Ingrowth External signs are transformed into self-generated internal signs	Egocentric speech goes underground as it develops into silent inner speech which becomes the basis for the child's thinking	Child generates internal mnemonics and logical connections that mediate recall

child feels the need for words and uses them to label things, but she does not clearly grasp the symbolic function of words. That is, to the child, the word has a fixed meaning. It is not a flexible symbol whose meaning can be changed by common agreement. For example, when asked whether one could call a cow "ink" and ink a "cow," children will answer, "no, because ink is used for writing, and the cow gives milk." At this stage, there is an inseparable connection between words and objects in the child's mind (Vygotsky, 1986, p. 223).

This same sort of nonsymbolic use of signs can be seen in the child's memory functioning. For example, in one study in which the task was to remember a list of words, auxiliary stimuli in the form of pictures were also provided. The pictures were unrelated to the words, however, and young children would only use a picture to aid retrieval if they could see in it the object to be remembered. For example, when asked to remember the word "sun" with the help of a picture showing an ax, one child pointed to a small yellow spot in the drawing and said "there it is, the sun." (Vygotsky, 1978, p. 48).

The accumulation of naive psychological experience enables the child to enter a third stage in which **external signs** and external operations are used *symbolically* to aid in the solution of internal problems. In this stage, the child counts on his fingers, uses external mnemonic aids (e.g., the string around the finger), and so on. In speech development this is the stage of **egocentric speech.**

Vygotsky saw egocentric speech as a key link leading from social to inner speech. Egocentric speech had been described by Piaget (1926) as "speech for

SPEECH
Stages of Development

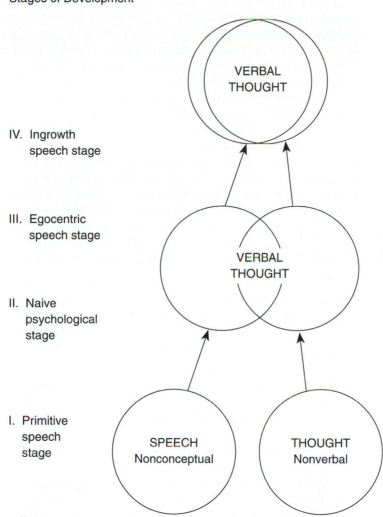

IV. Ingrowth
    speech stage

III. Egocentric
     speech stage

II. Naive
    psychological
    stage

I. Primitive
   speech
   stage

FIGURE 7.1   Vygotsky's view of the development of speech and its relationship to thought. (Adapted from Thomas, *Comparing Theories of Child Development*, 1992. Used by permission of Wadsworth Publishing Co.)

oneself, speech which is not intended for others." It is overt language that is carried out with apparent satisfaction even though it does not function to communicate. This type of speech can be observed both when children are alone and in social settings. Its function, Piaget believed, is "to chant" one's thoughts or actions, as in this exchange recorded by Bjorklund (1989) between two 5-year-old boys playing together in a sandbox: "I drive my truck over here, and then I drive beside your plane and I fill it up with stuff," says one child. Simultaneously, the other child is saying, "My plane's coming in for a landing. I drop bombs on your truck and crash into it. Boom!" According to Piaget, preschoolers' egocentric speech reflects their egocentric perspective of the world. As children become increasingly able to decenter and see the point of view of another, their egocentric speech disappears. Thus, for Piaget, egocentric speech plays no role in cognitive activity but is merely symptomatic of ongoing mental activity.

Vygotsky's research brought him to a quite different view of egocentric or private speech. In his studies, Vygotsky arranged for problems to arise during play-work activities of young children. For example, a pencil for the drawing task would be missing, or the paper would be too small. He observed that the amount of egocentric speech nearly doubled on these occasions as compared with the same activities without impediments. The child would try to grasp and remedy the situation in talking to himself. Vygotsky observed that in the beginning, egocentric speech may have the function of accompanying the child's activity and serving as a release of tension. However, it soon becomes an instrument of thought in the proper sense—in seeking and planning the solution to a problem. Vygotsky used the following example to show that egocentric speech is not just an accompaniment to activity but actually influences the child's activity:

> A child of five-and-a-half was drawing a streetcar when the point of his pencil broke. He tried, nevertheless, to finish the circle of a wheel, pressing down on the pencil very hard, but nothing showed on the paper except a deep colorless line. The child muttered to himself, "It's broken," put aside the pencil, took watercolors instead, and began drawing a *broken* streetcar after an accident, continuing to talk to himself from time to time about the change in his picture. (1986, p. 31)

In this example, the child's accidentally evoked egocentric utterance changed the course of his activity. Vygotsky's investigations also showed a gradual temporal shift in the interrelation of the child's activity and egocentric talk during this stage. Egocentric speech first came at the end of an activity, then was shifted toward the middle and finally to the beginning of an activity, taking on a directing, planning function.

Vygotsky also disagreed with Piaget's conclusion that egocentric or private speech simply dies out after age 7 or so. Instead Vygotsky concluded that egocentric speech "goes underground"; that is, it turns into inner speech which plays a fundamental role in mediating the child's thought. Egocentric speech thus splinters off from social communicative speech and becomes a separate linguistic form which serves as an intermediate stage leading to inner speech.

Fourth and final is the **ingrowth stage.** Here the external operation turns inward and undergoes a profound change in the process. For example, the child begins to count in his head and to use "logical memory." In speech development this is the final stage of inner, soundless speech in which the child manipulates language in her head. Now the child's thinking employs inner signs for solving problems. From here on, the individual will use inner speech (as well as outer speech) as tools in conceptual or verbal thought. According to Vygotsky, conceptual thought development is determined by language, i.e., by the linguistic tools of thought and by the socio-cultural experience of the child. Essentially, the development of inner speech depends on outside factors; the development of logic in the child, as Piaget's studies have shown, is a direct function of his socialized speech. The child's intellectual growth is contingent on his mastering the social means of thought, that is, language. (1986, p. 94)

In summary, speech, as well as all higher psychological functions such as mediated memory and voluntary attention, emerges in the process of cultural development and utilizes signs and tools. These functions develop through four stages between the time of birth and the years of primary school, age 7 or 8. The central feature of these higher psychological functions is "self generated stimulation, that is, the creation and use of artificial stimuli which become the immediate causes of behavior" (Vygotsky, 1978, p. 39).

Question 7.3: To help you tie Vygotsky's theory together, try explaining how the transition of egocentric speech into inner speech is an instance of Vygotsky's genetic law of cultural development presented earlier. This law, you may remember, states that each function in the child's cultural development appears twice: first, on the social level (interpsychologically or between people) and later, on the

individual level (intrapsychologically or inside the child)_____

_____

_____

_____

Relationship between Learning and Development

The educational relevance of any child development theory depends upon the relationship between learning and development postulated by the theory. Before examining Vygotsky's position, let's examine the positions of some theorists we have already studied. You guessed it—time for a question!

Question 7.4: Given your knowledge of Piaget's theory, how do you suppose he views the relationship between learning and development? (Hint: Would Piaget expect children at a lower developmental stage to be able to learn the same

material as children at a higher stage?)_____

_____

_____

_____

As you might expect, behavioral psychologists take quite a different position on the development-learning relationship from Piaget's. Basically, behaviorists such as Skinner and Thorndike argue that development *is* learning. That is, these theorists do not believe that there are *general* thinking abilities that develop as a result of processes such as maturation and equilibration. Rather, they believe that development is nothing but the gradual accumulation of many, many *specific* habits or skills. In this view, learning capability is not dependent upon developmental processes independent of learning. Rather, a child's readiness to learn any given subject depends only upon prior learning of prerequisite responses and skills. The implications of this view for teaching were set forth at length in Chapter 2 where we discussed task analysis and programmed instruction.

Vygotsky essentially rejected both of these views and took a new approach based upon the importance of social interaction in development. According to Vygotsky, "learning is not development; however, properly organized learning results in mental development and sets in motion a variety of developmental processes that would be impossible apart from learning. Thus, learning is a necessary and universal aspect of the process of developing culturally organized, specifically human, psychological functions" (Vygotsky, 1978, p. 90). This approach to learning and development was embodied in his concept of the zone of proximal development.

The Zone of Proximal Development

In the years just prior to his death, Vygotsky lectured and wrote extensively on problems of education, often using the term "educational psychology." It was in the course of applying his theoretical constructs to practical problems of educational psychology that he introduced the notion of the *zone of proximal development,* more accurately translated as "the zone of next or nearest development." This concept is clearly set forth in the following quote:

Suppose I investigate two children upon entrance into school, both of whom are ten years old chronologically and eight years old in terms of mental development. Can I say that they are the same age mentally? Of course. What does this mean? It means that they can independently deal with tasks up to the degree of difficulty that has been standardized for the eight-year-old level. If I stop at this point, people would imagine that the subsequent course of mental development and of school learning for these children will be the same, because it depends on their intellect. Of course, there may be other factors, for example, if one child was sick for half a year while the other was never absent from school; but generally speaking, the fate of these children should be the same. *Now imagine that I do not terminate my study at this point, but only begin it* [emphasis ours]. These children seem to be capable of handling problems up to an eight-year-old's level, but not beyond that. Suppose that I show them various ways of dealing with the problem. Different experimenters might employ different modes of demonstration and ask the children to repeat it, others might initiate the solution and ask the child to finish it, or offer leading questions. In short, in some way or another I propose that the children solve the problem with my assistance. Under these circumstances it turns out that the first child can deal with problems up to a twelve-year-old's level, the second up to a nine-year-old's. Now, are these children mentally the same?

When it was first shown that the capability of children with equal levels of mental development to learn under a teacher's guidance varied to a high degree, it became apparent that those children were not mentally the same age and that the subsequent course of their learning would obviously be different. This difference between twelve and eight, or between nine and eight, is what we call the *zone of proximal development. It is the distance between the actual developmental level as determined by independent problem solving and the level of potential development as determined through problem solving under adult guidance or in collaboration with more capable peers.* (Vygotsky, 1978, pp. 85–86, italics in original, emphasis is ours)

Thus, as shown in Figure 7.2, Vygotsky was concerned with the relationship between two levels of development: The level of *actual development,* which is the level at which the child can function independently, and the level of *potential development,* the area in which she can function with the help of others.

Vygotsky was very critical of psychological testing because it focused on "where a child has been" (i.e., his level of actual development) to the exclusion of the child's potential for growth. According to Vygotsky, a separate assessment of the level of potential development is necessary, because it can vary independently of the level of actual development. Assessing the level of potential development lets us take stock of budding processes that are ready to bloom. His concern with assessing the child's both actual and potential levels of development has grown into a philosophy of testing in the Soviet Union. There is increasing interest in this approach to assessment in the United States, which we will discuss in a later section.

Vygotsky was also critical of instruction whose learning goals are tied to developmental stages that have already been completed. In his words, such instruction "does not aim for a new stage of developmental process but rather lags behind this process. Thus, the notion of a zone of proximal development enables us to

Level of potential development
Determined by problem solving in
collaboration with more capable partner

ZPD

Level of actual development
Determined by independent problem
solving

FIGURE 7.2   The zone of proximal
development.

propound a new formula, namely that *the only 'good learning' is that which is in advance of development"* (1978, p. 89, emphasis ours). It follows from this that *"instruction is good only when it proceeds ahead of development.* It then *awakens and rouses to life those functions which are in a stage of maturing, which lie in the zone of proximal development"* (1956, p. 278).

Question 7.5: The notion that good instruction should lead or stimulate development follows directly from Vygotsky's General Genetic Law of Cultural Development. Explain this statement. (Sorry, this time you have to retrieve the law

yourself.)_____

_____

_____

_____

_____

_____

In summary, Vygotsky viewed learning as involving social interactions that push the child forward into his zone of proximal development where new developmental processes are triggered. There, these new processes are practiced until they are internalized and become part of the child's repertoire of independent abilities. Thus the zone of proximal development can be thought of as the developmental level that is just beyond the child's current level of functioning. There, the child encounters new cultural tools, which are practiced in social interactions with more experienced members of society until they become part of the child's independent functioning (Wertsch & Rogoff, 1984).

AMERICAN RESEARCH SPURRED BY VYGOTSKY'S THEORY

A major focus of cognitive and educational psychology in contemporary America is **cognitive self-regulation.** This topic is part of the larger one of metacognition which we discussed in Chapters 4 and 5. Metacognitive researchers, you may remember, are interested in how children become aware of their own cognitive processes and of their ability to take charge of their own learning and thinking. Vygotsky's theory is very useful in this regard because it posits both a mechanism for self-direction (private speech) and a process (internalization of social activities) by which self-regulation is acquired. Thus, it is not surprising that much current research attempts to elaborate upon constructs posited by Vygotsky. In the following section we shall review research related to (1) the self-directive role of private and inner speech of the child's cognition; (2) the concept of scaffolding; (3) reciprocal teaching; (4) peer interactions; and (5) assessment techniques based on the zone of proximal development.

Research on the Self-directive Role of Private Speech

Have you ever attempted one of those assemble-it-yourself-with-easy-to-follow-instructions-and-no-tools-required projects? If so, and if you are like us, you soon found yourself talking to yourself (e.g., "Let's see, do I insert tab A into slot B or does it go into slot C? Where's the #★@#&★@ screwdriver that I don't need?"). This example illustrates that private speech is not found only in young children, but commonly resurfaces in adulthood when we are faced with complex or novel problems.

Remember that Vygotsky believed that private (egocentric) speech plays a self-directive role in children's thinking and problem solving. That is, children talk to themselves in order to direct their own behavior. This *self-regulative* function of speech emerges from social interactions in which children's behavior is first guided by the speech of others. With age, Vygotsky believed, overt private speech goes underground to become inner speech. You may also recall that, in contrast to Vygotsky's position, Piaget believed that egocentric speech was merely an expression of the child's egocentric thinking and played no role in the child's cognition.

One of the earliest attempts to contrast the positions of Vygotsky and Piaget was conducted by Kohlberg, Yaeger, and Hjertholm (1968). These researchers assessed children's private speech while solving problems and categorized utterances according to their function. One category was speech that provided self-stimulation and word play; another category was speech that described the children's actions but did not direct it; finally, there was overt speech that served to direct problem solving. Kohlberg et al. charted the frequency of each type of speech for preschool and school-age children. It's always more fun to learn the results of a study after you have made some predictions, don't you think? So . . .

Question 7.6: Based upon Vygotsky's theory, what change in frequency pattern would you expect to see in each of these three speech categories as children get older? How would Vygotsky's prediction differ from Piaget's?_____

_____

_____

_____

Having made our bet, let's see what happened. Kohlberg et al. found that the frequency of word play and descriptive speech decreased and the incidence of private speech used to guide performance increased over the preschool years, peaking between the ages of 6 and 7. It declined thereafter. This trend was accompanied by an increase in inaudible mutterings with age, peaking between 8 and 10 years. This muttering was interpreted as evidence that overt private speech was being internalized into covert inner speech.

Researchers have also documented that the frequency of overt private speech increases when children are confronted with difficult tasks (Berk & Gavin, 1984; Goodman, 1981) and when adults are not present to exert control over children's activity (Kohlberg et al., 1968). However, several observations do not square with Vygotsky's theory. First, the relationship between the amount of children's private speech and their task performance has been found to be either nonsignificant (Fuson, 1979) or negative (Frauenglass & Diaz, 1985). Second, it was found that approximately half of the observed subjects engaged in no private speech at all. However, both of these observations could be influenced by the fact that the children in these studies were given nonverbal tasks involving mazes and block-design tasks in unfamiliar surroundings. Who in their right minds would talk aloud under such circumstances, let alone say what they were really thinking?

Recently, a naturalistic study by Berk (1986) compensated for these factors by comparing the private speech of first and third graders engaged in mathematics seatwork in their classrooms. It will come as no surprise to those who have taught that Berk found a very high incidence of private speech. Close to 98 percent of the children uttered comments related to the task at hand. Externalized speech decreased between grades 1 and 3, whereas internalized (subvocal) speech increased between these grades. IQ was positively related to the incidence of private speech for first graders and negatively related for third graders. This latter result is what you would expect since self-directive speech is normally internalized by the third grade so that only the slower third graders would still be talking aloud to themselves. Finally, the amount of task-relevant private speech was positively related to math achievement. Berk's findings offer clear support for Vygotsky's notion that private speech plays a significant role in children's cognitive development and self-regulation.

Instructing Children in Self-directive Speech

According to Vygotsky, inner speech often takes the form of an "inner dialogue" that reflects its social origins. That is, as a result of participating in problem-solving dialogues with adults who take the lead in verbalizing goals and strategies, the child learns to talk to himself in order to direct his own cognitive activity. It follows that a child will be deficient in self-directive inner speech if he does not have the opportunity to participate extensively in such social dialogues. Worse yet, he will be negatively influenced if he is exposed to adults who transmit maladaptive internal dialogues. Concern with this possibility led Meichenbaum and his associates to try to influence what individuals "say" to themselves while engaging in tasks.

Meichenbaum's program, called **cognitive behavior modification,** uses cognitive strategy training combined with principles of behavior modification to change not only the way students behave but how they talk to themselves when confronted with an academic task. Students are taught to make self statements that will guide them to their goal. These statements are usually a series of steps or reminders in the completion of a task but can also be statements that help students cope with frustration or distraction while maintaining their goal. The statements are initially modeled by the teacher, and students are trained to make the statements aloud while completing the task and then to fade the verbal statements to subvocalizations. The teacher directly reinforces and encourages self-reinforcement whenever the student's subsequent behavior is congruent with his internal dialogue.

Cognitive behavior modification has been used successfully to improve problem solving of impulsive children (Meichenbaum & Goodman, 1971), and to improve children's handwriting (Robin, Armel, & O'Leary, 1975), composition (Harris & Graham, 1985), and reading comprehension (Meichenbaum & Asarno, 1978). Meichenbaum's work can be interpreted as providing support for Vygotsky's theory as well as illustrating one educational application of self-regulatory inner speech.

Bruner's Concept of Scaffolding

Before Vygotsky's notion of the zone of proximal development was widely appreciated in the West, Bruner and Wood and their associates introduced the closely related concept of **scaffolding,** a process whereby an adult provides support to a child learning to master a problem (Bruner, 1978; Wood, Bruner, & Ross, 1976; Wood & Middleton, 1975). In scaffolding, an adult directs those elements of the task that are initially beyond the capacity of the child. This makes it possible for the child to participate in strategic activity without really understanding it completely. For example, the mother who is putting together a jigsaw puzzle of a ship with her 4-year-old child might give the child the subtask of finding all the pieces that have blue in them, pointing out that "these are all the ocean pieces." Then she might direct the child to find "all the pieces that have ship parts in them." Once all the pieces are classified, the mother can direct the child to "find me the piece of ocean that fits with this piece of ocean." In this example, the child may not fully understand how each activity contributes to the overall goal but can participate in each activity because the adult provides structure. Through repeated social dialogue of this nature the child comes to gradually understand the import of the more experienced individual's utterances and his or her own responses.

Wood, Bruner, and Ross (1976) discovered various aspects of the scaffolding process by observing 3-, 4-, and 5-year-old children being assisted by an adult in the task of constructing a pyramid from complex, interlocking blocks. The female tutor was given no special training or instruction but simply tried to gear her behavior to the needs of the individual child. She tried to maintain comparable procedures from child to child. Her aim was to allow each child to do as much as possible for himself, intervening verbally and then more directly if necessary to keep the child headed toward successful task completion. The child's success or failure at any point determined the adult's next level of response.

By observing the adult's interventions and the child's responses to them, the researchers discovered that the nature of the social dialogue changed greatly with the age of the child. With the 3-year-olds, the adult's role was primarily to induce the child into the task by stimulating her to perform actions that she was unable to recognize as solutions. With these very young children, who had their own ideas of what to do with the blocks, one of the main functions of the adult was to keep the goal of the task before the children's eyes by continually *showing* them what to do. With the 4-year-olds, who could keep the goal in mind, the adult's role was more to help them recognize, usually through verbalization, discrepancies between their attempted constructions and what was required by the task. Thus, the nature of the interventions shifted from showing to telling between the 3- and 4-year-old participants. Finally, the 5-year-olds needed assistance from the adult only when experiencing difficulty or checking out a solution.

Question 7.7: (Fill in the blanks.) According to Vygotsky, dialogue between adult and child will result in the child's internalizing new skills only if the joint task is one that is within the child's _____ _ _____ _____ (See answers at end of chapter.)

Wood, Bruner, and Ross list six scaffolding functions that may be carried out by adults who are assisting children on a task:

1 *Recruitment.* The adult must first engage the child's interest in and adherence to the requirements of the task. The younger the child, the more importance this function assumes.

2 *Reduction in degrees of freedom.* This involves simplifying the task by reducing it to subtasks. The child is allowed to concentrate upon subroutines that he can manage while the adult fills in the rest.

3 *Direction maintenance.* This involves keeping the goal of the task before the child who may tend to "wander" to other aims. This function also involves displaying enthusiasm and compassion to keep the child motivated as well as encouraging the child to move beyond those aspects of the task he has already mastered to risk the next step.

4 *Marking critical features.* The adult, by various means, accentuates certain features of the task that are relevant.

5 *Frustration control.* The adult helps the child overcome frustration by "face saving" for errors or by exploiting the child's "wish to please."

6 *Demonstration.* This involves considerably more than simply performing solutions in the presence of the child. It often involves "imitating" in idealized form a solution tried (or assumed to be tried) by the child. This gives the child the opportunity to "imitate" it back in a more appropriate form. Children apparently imitate only acts they can already do fairly well.

Other researchers investigating the way scaffolding occurs in more naturalistic settings have documented the importance of dialogue between parents and children in the acquisition of language and problem-solving skill. For example, Scollon (1976) uses the term "vertical constructions" to describe a pattern of conversation in which the child says something, the parents asks a question about the topic, and the child elaborates or comments on the topic. Over time, the child independently generates single utterances that include both the topic and the comment. Cazden (1983) identified another kind of scaffolding that occurs when adults and children play games (e.g., "peekaboo," "This little piggy went to market . . ."). In these language games, there are scripts that are initially produced entirely by the adult. Over time, as the child develops the ability to participate, the parents encourage the child to speak more of the script.

Rogoff, Ellis, and Gardner (1984) observed mothers preparing their children to engage in a classification task. They noted that the mothers assisted the children with novel problems by guiding transfer of knowledge and skills from more familiar contexts. The mothers did not demonstrate or explicitly instruct the children. Rather, learning occurred through a collaborative effort in which the parent scaffolded the participation of the child, gradually transferring more and more responsibility to the child over the course of the interaction.

In summary, scaffolding is the process by which an adult assists a child on tasks within the zone of proximal development. As Wertsch and Rogoff (1984) point out, there are three primary aspects to the scaffolding process to keep in mind. First, *working on a task in the zone of proximal development involves the joint consciousness of the participants.* That is, it involves a synchronized collaboration of two or more minds on solving a problem. At first, the participants do not have the same definition of the task or of the problem to be solved. However, through their continued interaction, the child's notion of the task comes to approximate that of the more expert adult. Second, *both participants help shape the interactions within the zone of proximal development.* The child's emerging skills and personal interests help to set the pace and direction of the interaction. The adult takes responsibility for providing scaffolding, as described above. Third, these adult-child interactions form a *dynamic goal-oriented system* that is organized around the tasks, encouraged activities, and tools of the culture.

Reciprocal Teaching

The above research concerning the role of social dialogue between adults and children in the acquisition of language and problem-solving skill applies to interactions outside of school settings. It might be expected that the same results would hold in classroom settings. However, studies examining student-teacher talk in the classroom indicate that dialogue of this type is not typical of classroom practice. Instead of being collaborative, most teacher-child interactions are dominated by the teacher. Teachers give directions, students nonverbally carry them out; teachers ask questions, students give brief (one word or phrase) answers (cf. Forman & Cazden, 1985).

The reason for this situation is understandable: Teachers feel (and rightfully so!) that it is quite difficult to manage meaningful dialogue with an individual student while sustaining the attention of a classroom group. It is in this context that Palincsar and her colleagues developed **reciprocal teaching,** an instructional procedure explicitly based upon Vygotsky's socioinstructional approach. Its aim is to help teachers use collaborative learning dialogues to teach self-regulated reading comprehension in the classroom (Palincsar, 1986; Palincsar & Brown, 1984; Palincsar, Brown, & Martin, 1987).

In reciprocal teaching, small groups of students and their teacher take part in discussions concerning small segments of shared text. The discussions are centered around the use of four strategies: predicting, questioning, summarizing, and clarifying. These strategies were chosen for several reasons: (1) They are activities that good readers routinely use but poor readers do not. (2) They both improve comprehension and provide the reader with the opportunity to monitor for understanding. For example, if one attempts to summarize a portion of text and fails, it signals that comprehension has not been achieved and some remedial effort such as rereading is necessary. (3) These particular strategies lend themselves well to scaffolding a collaborative dialogue.

Lessons revolve around an assigned text with either the teacher or a student leading the group discussion. After everyone reads a segment of text, the group leader summarizes the content. The leader then poses a question that might occur on a test. Discussion of the question then follows, with clarification provided as needed. Finally, the leader makes a prediction about future content. Over the course of a lesson all members of the group, including the adult teacher, take turns being the discussion leader. The following is an illustration of the process of reciprocal teaching adapted for first-grade students:

> The teacher reads the following text:
> "The pipefish change their color and movements to blend with their surroundings. For example, pipefish that live among green plants change their color to a shade of green to match the plants."
> Clare, the child leading the discussion, begins:
> One question that I had about this paragraph is: What is special about the way that the pipefish looks?
> Keith:
> Do you mean the way that it is green?
> Andy:
> It's not just that it's green: it's that it's the same color as the plants around it, all around it.
> Clare resumes:
> Yes. That's it. My summary is this part tells how the pipefish looks and that it looks like what is around it. My prediction is that this is about its enemies and how it protects itself and who the enemies are.
> Monty adds on to her summary:
> They also talked about how the pipefish moves . . .
> To which Keith rejoins:
> It sways back and forth.
> Andy adds:
> Along with the other plants.
> Ms. Mackey, the teacher, interjects:
> What do we call it when something looks like and acts like something else? The way that the walkingstick was yesterday? We clarified this word when we talked about the walkingstick.

Angel:

"Mimic."

Ms. Mackey:

That's right! We said/ we would say/ that the pipefish mimics the ————-

Students:

Plants.

Ms. Mackey:

OK! Let's see if Clare's predictions come true.

(From Palincsar, 1988.)

As you can see, the predicting, questioning, summarizing, and clarifying strategies serve to structure and support the discussion, while the teacher supports the children's participation in the dialogue. The amount of support given by the teacher varies across lessons and children. During the initial sessions, the teacher models the strategies by "thinking aloud" how she generates a summary, what cues she uses to make predictions, and so on. At first, many children have difficulty assuming the role of leader, and the teacher must support the students in a variety of ways. For example, she might prompt the student, provide the student additional information, or actually construct summaries and questions for the student to mimic. Day by day as students internalize the strategies, the teacher consciously turns over more and more responsibility for leading and sustaining the dialogue to them.

Question 7.8: From the description of reciprocal teaching given above, identify at least three specific aspects of the procedure that have been derived from Vygotsky's theory.————————————————————

————————————————————————————

————————————————————————————

Reciprocal teaching has been studied most extensively with children in their early teens who can decode text adequately but who have severe comprehension problems (Palincsar & Brown, 1984). In one study, the procedure was conducted by remedial reading teachers in small groups of five students for a period of 20 days. In comparison with control students, striking improvement was observed in trained students' ability to use the strategies and in their scores on comprehension measures. Even more importantly, the benefit of the training generalized to all classroom reading materials, with trained students showing better understanding of science and social-studies material that they encountered in class. This latter result supports the contention that *reciprocal teaching leads to the internalization of the strategies by the children.* This permits them to self-regulate their comprehension in settings quite different from those used in training.

Palincsar compared reciprocal teaching with a variety of other approaches to strategy instruction. For example, in one alternative approach, the teacher modeled the four strategies as she read the text, while the students observed and responded to her questions. Another approach involved isolated skill practice in which the students completed worksheet activities on each of the four strategies and received extensive feedback from the teacher. The reciprocal teaching procedure was superior to these other ways of imparting strategies (Palincsar, 1986). Recently, reciprocal teaching has also been successfully adapted for use with first-grade students who are academically "at risk": children from disadvantaged families or children referred from special education or remedial services (Palincsar, 1986).

In Chapter 4, we discussed the direct explanation approach for teaching strategies to students. That approach, you might recall, entails a combination of teacher modeling of strategies, independent strategy practice with feedback, generalization practice, and metacognitive information about why, when, and where to use the strategies (cf. Pressley, Snyder, & Cariglia-Bull, 1989). As far as we know, there has been no study directly comparing the relative benefits of the direct explanation and reciprocal teaching approaches to strategy instruction. Even in the absence of such research, we feel safe in saying that either of these approaches, if implemented properly, will result in children's acquiring self-regulated learning strategies. We need to point out, however, that it may be more expensive in terms of the teacher's time to implement reciprocal teaching with small groups of students than to use direct explanation with the whole class. On the other hand, reciprocal teaching seems particularly well-suited for slow and "at risk" students in special education settings.

Interactions between Peers

In all of Vygotsky's writings, social interactions that affect cognitive development are depicted as one-to-one relationships between one adult and one child. As we saw with reciprocal teaching, Western researchers have extended this notion to include one adult with a small group of children. Moreover, reciprocal teaching has also been successfully implemented with pairs of peers (Palincsar & Brown, 1984). Peer interaction has also been studied in schools in the context of peer tutoring and peer cooperation (e.g., Ehly & Larsen, 1980; Slavin, 1983). Although this research demonstrates that children can learn from other children, it has tended not to examine the processes by which peers may influence each other's learning or development.

Other research has examined peer interaction from a Piagetian perspective, focusing on the role of cognitive conflict induced by peer interaction (e.g., Ames & Murray, 1982). Recently, however, researchers examining peer interactions within a Vygotskian perspective have argued that peer interactions benefit children by requiring them to arrive at a shared perspective of the problem. For example, Forman and her associates (Forman, 1987; Forman & Cazden, 1985) studied 9- to 14-year-old children working in pairs on complex problems. They concluded that in the course of such joint problem-solving ventures, children learn to use speech to guide the actions of their partners and, in turn, to be guided by their partners' speech. Experience with this type of social regulation enables children to internalize the tools needed to master problems on their own.

Tudge and Rogoff (1989) have summarized the major conclusions of Vygotskian research related to the effects of peer interaction on learning and development as follows:

1 Young preschool children show limited benefits from peer interaction. They may be unable to provide each other with the type of scaffolded assistance that older children and adults can provide.

2 Peer interactions are most beneficial on tasks involving discussion of issues and sharing of perspectives. Adult-child interactions are more beneficial than peer interactions on tasks involving learning of skills and knowledge.

3 The condition that appears to most influence the effectiveness of social interactions between peers or between adult and child is that the partners achieve a joint understanding of a topic by working together and taking each other's perspective into account.

Assessing Zones of Proximal Development

One implication of Vygotsky's notion of a zone of proximal development concerns the design of diagnostic tests for children. Vygotsky was very critical of the use of IQ and achievement tests because they are static in nature. That is, scores on such tests reflect the end result of prior learning but do not provide a sensitive index of the potential for improvement over current performance. Moreover, there are strong reasons to believe that for many people, particularly those from disadvantaged backgrounds, such static test scores underestimate ability. In place of static IQ and ability tests, Vygotsky called for dynamic assessments of the child's learning ability, defined as the child's ability to benefit from adult aid.

Vygotsky had a strong impact on the development of testing in the Soviet Union, where the use of standardized intelligence tests has been widely criticized. In place of standard IQ tests, Soviet psychologists have concentrated on the development of clinical diagnostic tests that measure differences in learning potential. In this country, Brown and her colleagues have attempted to replicate and extend the Soviet findings with American children (Brown & Ferrara, 1985; Brown & French, 1979; Campione, Brown, Ferrara, & Bryant, 1984).

In Brown's research, a typical testing session consists of the initial presentation of a test item exactly as it would occur in an American IQ test. That is, the child is initially asked to solve a problem independently. If the child fails to reach the correct solution, an adult progressively adds clues that aid in solving the problem. By these means it is possible to assess how much additional information the child needs in order to solve the problem. The child's initial performance when asked to solve independently provides information comparable to that provided by standardized IQ tests. The degree of aid needed before the child reaches the solution is taken as an inverse indication of the width of her proximal zone. Once a solution on a particular test item is reached, another version of the original task is presented.

If the child needs fewer clues than before in order to reach a solution, transfer of the original solution (i.e., learning) is said to have occurred.

Using inductive reasoning tasks very similar to ones found on standardized IQ tests, Brown and her associates have examined the relationship between the dynamic measures yielded from the above procedures and traditional (static) IQ test scores. In one study of third- and fifth-grade children, they found that for two thirds of the children, IQ scores predicted learning speed (i.e., number of prompts the child needed to reach the solution). However, approximately one third of the children's learning speeds were not predictable from their IQ scores. The same was true for predicting transfer scores (i.e., number of prompts needed to solve transfer problems). That is, a third of the children's transfer scores were not predictable from their IQ scores. Overall, the IQ of almost 50 percent of the children did not predict learning speed and/or degree of transfer.

Within the wide range of normal ability children (IQ range 88–150) used in their study, the researchers found a number of distinct learning profiles, including (1) slow learners, narrow transferrers, low IQ (they called this pattern *slow*); (2) fast learners, wide transferrers, high IQ (*fast*); (3) fast learners, narrow transferers (*context bound*); (4) fast learners, wide transferrers, low IQ (*high scorers*). All of these profiles are hidden when one considers only the child's IQ score.

An additional finding by these researchers was that within the domain of inductive reasoning, estimates of children's zones of proximal development provided by two different tasks (i.e., letter series problems and matrix problems) were quite similar. This suggests that it is possible to take stable measures of children's learning potential *within* a domain. However, the authors point out that the concept of the zone of proximal development implies that a given child will have differing zones *across* a variety of domains. In fact, one of the disadvantages of the use of standardized tests to diagnose children's learning potential is that scores on such tests are often taken as a general estimate of a child's ability throughout the cognitive arena. For example, a child with IQ 80 or reading scores 3 years below grade level is labeled dull and is not expected to perform well in any academic domain. Such expectations, as we shall see in Chapter 9, tend to become self-fulfilling prophecies. Zone measures, being clearly specific to one cognitive domain, may curb the use of such broad characterizations of children's ability.

Another advantage of zone measures over static IQ or achievement measures is that not only do they diagnose a child's learning potential within a domain, but they can also provide the basis for prescribing the kind of instructional intervention the child needs to realize her potential. Clearly what is now needed is extension of Brown's work to academic tasks (reading, writing, math) so that the diagnostic and prescriptive information yielded by zone measures can be put to use by teachers in the classroom.

Implications of Vygotsky's Theory for Instruction

If all the development of a child's mental life takes place in the process of social intercourse, this implies that this intercourse and its most systematized form, the teaching process, forms the development of the child, creates new mental formations, and develops higher processes of mental life. Teaching, which sometimes seems to wait upon development, is in actual fact its decisive motive force. (Leont'ev & Luria, 1968, p. 365)

As the above quote from two of his closest collaborators indicates, Vygotsky clearly viewed instruction in school settings as an essential factor in children's cognitive development. In turn, his theory has clear implications for how that instruction should be conducted in order to optimize development. Let's spell out some of these instructional implications.

One implication stems from the central role of speech as a tool for thought and self-regulation. According to Vygotsky, children need to engage in overt, self-regulatory speech before they can engage in covert, inner speech. This means that during the early grades until the transition to inner speech is completed, teachers must not only tolerate but encourage *task-related* self talk. This will make for a somewhat noisy but effective environment for fostering self-regulation.

In the Vygotskian perspective, the ideal role of the teacher is that of providing scaffolding (collaborative dialogue) to assist students on tasks within their zones of proximal development. Until now this role has been operationalized only in school settings in the context of reciprocal teaching of self-regulated comprehension strategies. The teacher's role in reciprocal teaching is to *collaborate* with children in constructing the meaning of shared text. This collaborative dialogue is structured around basic comprehension strategies such as predicting, questioning, summarizing, and clarifying. This emphasis on collaboration and support instead of control and direction of instructional interactions is one of the major implications in Vygotsky's theory for teachers.

In line with the collaborative flavor of teacher-student interactions, a Vygotskian approach also encourages the use of cooperative peer interactions to promote learning and development. Situations in which children are required to discuss perspectives and arrive at a jointly constructed solution allow them to practice using speech to regulate others and subsequently themselves.

Finally, one of Vygotsky's most important contributions to education is his conception of "readiness" for instruction. Instead of waiting on development, Vygotsky emphasized the importance of locating skills or tasks that the child cannot do alone but can do if provided assistance from the teacher or a more capable peer. In other words, a child is ready to learn a task when he benefits from collaboration on the task. According to Vygotsky this is the only "good learning" because it stimulates development.

VYGOTSKY'S POSITION ON THE CORE ISSUES

Like Piaget, Vygotsky is a developmental theorist, so the core issues will deal with factors influencing the process of development. However, in his theory, learning and development are so closely interrelated that one is tempted to treat Vygotsky as a learning theorist.

1. *What develops according to the theory?* Vygotsky was concerned with the development of cultural knowledge and skills (e.g., language) that could then be used in cognition. The process of development is internalization of operations that first occur externally in social interactions with more mature members of the culture. In his general law of genetic development, Vygotsky makes a very strong claim about the social foundations of cognition. It is important to realize that he is not simply claiming that social interaction leads to the development of the child's abilities in problem solving. Rather, he is saying that the very means (especially speech) used in social interaction are taken over by the individual child and internalized (Wertsch, 1981).

2. *What is the relative emphasis on environmental versus organismic factors in development?* While Vygotsky places great emphasis on the child's sociocultural environment as the very source of higher psychological processes such as speech and verbal thought, it is clear that factors inside the child play an important role in development. For example, the child's first elementary structures for perception, memory, and so on are chiefly biologically determined. It is through the destruction, reconstruction, and transformation of these direct, reactive processes that higher, sign-mediated processes emerge. Another example is the child's zone of proximal development, which determines a child's readiness for acquiring particular skills. Development is optimal when an adult and a child engage in reciprocal interactions related to tasks within the child's zone of proximal development. Both partners contribute to such interactions: the child contributes readiness and interest; the adult contributes cultural tools, support, and direction.

Having said all this, it is apparent that Vygotsky placed more emphasis on sociocultural than organismic factors in development. The relationship he posited between learning and development makes this clear. Vygotsky regarded learning (the initial use of skill and knowledge) as the precursor and stimulator of development (the internalization of skills and knowledge). Thus, Vygotsky placed great weight on the role of adults, especially teachers, in producing the initial learning that stimulates cognitive development.

3. *What is the source of motivation for development?* The source of motivation for development resides both in the child and in the child's sociocultural environment. The child's inherent activity and curiosity impel exploration of physical stimuli and attention to other humans. Adults in the child's culture are motivated to engage in interactions with the child, during which they model and guide the child's use of cultural tools such as language. Although Vygotsky rarely discussed the concept of motivation, one senses that a primary goal of interactions between children and adults is to gradually free the child from dependence on the adult. Both partners work toward this end, the child by internalizing tools for self-regulation and the adult by transferring more and more responsibility for task completion to the child.

4. *How does transfer occur?* Transfer, or the use of knowledge and skills in new problem situations, is dependent upon the child's having first internalized skills and knowledge acquired from external sources. Thereafter, he is self-regulating. That is, he can search for similarities between new problems and old ones. The development of these processes, like any other mental function, occurs first as the child interacts with a more capable adult. The adult guides the transfer of knowledge and skills from more to less familiar contexts, thereby guiding the child in making connections. Both informal social interactions and formal instruction provide the child with models of an expert transferring prior knowledge and skills to a new problem (Rogoff & Gardner, 1984).

5. *What are important variables in instruction?* Given the crucial role that social intercourse plays in Vygotsky's theory, far and away the most important instructional variables are the nature and quality of interactions between the teacher and child, and between the child and peers. In successful teacher-child interactions, the teacher must determine the child's region of sensitivity to instruction (i.e., the child's zone of proximal development) and adjust her instruction to support the child's emerging capabilities. Within a Vygotskian perspective, the ideal teaching-learning process has been called "proleptic instruction" (Rogoff & Gardner, 1984). In this process, the student carries out simple aspects of the task as directed by the teacher. By actually performing the task with the teacher's guidance, the student acquires some of the teacher's understanding of the problem and its solution. This contrasts with explanation, where the teacher talks about the task, and with demonstration, where the teacher carries out the task rather than involving the student in the action. Proleptic instruction integrates explanation and demonstration while emphasizing the learner's guided participation. A critical feature of proleptic instruction is transfer of responsibility for the management of the interaction from the teacher to the child. At first, the teacher provides much structure and support, which she gradually reduces as she encourages the student's greater participation.

Successful peer interactions are those which involve cooperation and discussion of perspectives in order to arrive at a shared solution to some problem. In the course of peer interactions, it is important that each participant use speech to guide the actions of the other. Ideally, peer cooperative learning encourages sharing of perspectives, while adult-child instructional interactions result in the internalization of new knowledge and skills.

Question 7.9: How does Vygotsky's position on each of the core issues compare with Piaget's position?_____

_____

_____

_____

_____

_____

REVIEW OF MAJOR POINTS

1 Vygotsky and Piaget agreed that a dialectical approach best explains the development of psychological processes. They also agreed that development involves qualitative transformations of thought processes instead of gradual increments. Vygotsky and Piaget disagreed on the relative importance of the social versus the physical-logical environment in determining development, on the means by which social factors influenced development, and on the direction of development.

2 Three core assumptions from Marxist theory are incorporated into Vygotsky's theory. First, people's activities in social contexts determine their consciousness. Second, development of both societies and individuals occurs through a process of resolving dialectic conflicts. Third, understanding how society or individuals develop requires a cultural-historical approach.

3 According to Vygotsky, higher mental functions are mediated by psychological tools which come from an individual's culture. These tools are used to gain mastery over one's own behavior and cognition. Psychological tools are mainly semiotic; that is, they consist of signs or systems of signs such as language.

4 The child's first cognitions are nonmediated, natural mental functions such as direct perception, memory, and involuntary attention. Higher-level thinking gradually emerges as these lower functions are transformed through the use of psychological tools.

5 Vygotsky's general genetic law of cultural development describes how psychological tools are acquired by children. The law states that any function in the child's development appears first on the social plane, where it is used to regulate behavior between people, and second on the psychological plane, where it is used to regulate behavior within the individual.

6 Development is a process of internalizing social experiences. That is, interpersonal experiences are transformed into intrapersonal ones.

7 A major focus of Vygotsky was on the development of speech and its relation to thought. He believed that speech and thought are initially independent, but eventually merge to form verbal thought, which then becomes the individual's primary form of thought.

8 Because the child's speech structures become the basic structures of his thinking, Vygotsky considered it important to chart the development of speech. He found that speech (as well as all mental operations using signs) develops in four stages: the natural stage, the naive psychological stage, the stage of external sign use, and the ingrowth stage. Vygotsky believed that overt egocentric speech eventually splinters off from social communicative speech, becomes covert, and is used by the child to regulate his own behavior. That is, egocentric speech "goes underground" and becomes inner speech or verbal thought. This view of egocentric speech differs from that of Piaget, who believed that it eventually disappeared altogether.

9 In contrast to Piaget, Vygotsky believed that learning (initial skill or knowledge use) is a necessary aspect of development. Learning creates the zone of proximal development, which is the distance between the child's actual developmental level as determined by independent problem solving and the level of potential development as determined through problem solving under the guidance of a more capable partner. Vygotsky claimed that learning should precede and stimulate development.

10 Western research has validated Vygotsky's view of the role of egocentric or private speech in regulating the child's behavior. Cognitive behavior modification is a program of intervention aimed at improving cognitive performance by changing the way students talk to themselves when confronted with academic tasks.

11 The concept of scaffolding is closely related to the notion of the zone of proximal development. Bruner and Wood define "scaffolding" as the process whereby an adult provides support to a child learning to master a problem. In their studies, Bruner et al. discovered six scaffolding functions: recruitment, task simplification, direction maintenance, marking critical features, frustration control, and demonstration. These types of assistance from adults or more capable peers allow a child to participate in a task without really understanding it completely. Through scaffolded participation, the child gradually acquires the adult's understanding of the task.

12 Reciprocal teaching, developed by Palincsar, is an instructional procedure that is explicitly based on Vygotsky's theory. In this approach, children acquire self-regulated comprehension strategies by participating in dialogues with a small group of peers and an adult teacher. The teacher's role is to initially demonstrate the strategies and support the students' use of them in the context of a discussion in which teacher and students jointly construct the meaning of a shared text. Gradually, the teacher turns over more and more responsibility for the discussion to the students. Evidence indicates that reciprocal teaching results in children's internalizing strategies which they then transfer to other academic tasks. The method takes time but may be the best approach to use with "at risk" students.

13 Collaboration with peers on tasks which require the use of speech to regulate others' behavior benefits children's development. Peer interactions are most beneficial on tasks involving discussion of issues and sharing of perspectives rather than learning of knowledge and skills. Mutual understanding of a topic and sharing of perspectives must be present in order for interactions between peers or between a teacher and child to be successful.

14 Vygotsky was critical of the use of IQ and achievement tests because they only indicate a child's current level of development and not her potential for development. According to Vygotsky, the best indicator of a child's cognitive development is her response to instruction. Ann Brown and her associates have attempted to develop dynamic assessments of cognitive ability by measuring how quickly the child learns to perform on IQ-like tasks with adult assistance. Their research indicates that the learning speed of many children is not predictable from their IQ scores.

15 Some instructional implications of Vygotsky's theory include: (1) encouraging appropriate task-related self talk; (2) engaging in more dialogue with children wherein scaffolded support, collaboration, and transfer of responsibility to children are primary goals of the teacher; (3) using cooperative peer interactions to promote learning and development; and (4) focusing on skills or tasks that are slightly ahead of the child's current developmental level.

16 With regard to the core issues, Vygotsky was concerned with the development of knowledge and skills for using culturally developed tools for mediating cognition. He saw the importance of biological factors in development but placed more emphasis on social-cultural factors. The source of motivation for development is the child's natural curiosity and activity and the willingness of adults to model and guide the child's use of cultural tools. The child learns to apply knowledge and skills to new problems by interacting with more capable adults who at first guide this process of transfer. The child gradually internalizes the ability to make such connections on his own. The important variables in instruction are the nature and quality of interactions between teacher and child, and between the child and peers. The ideal teaching-learn process within the Vygotskian perspective involves "proleptic instruction" in which the child carries out challenging tasks under the guidance of the teacher or more capable peer.

ANSWERS TO QUESTIONS AND EXERCISES

Question 7.1: In Piaget's theory, development always proceeds in the direction of improvement. Children's notions of the world progress through stages which involve successively more adequate representations of the world.

Question 7.2: Vygotsky's theory allows for development to proceed in more than one direction. The tools and skills imparted to children by their social partners can differ both within and across cultures. The implication is that children learn skills from *more competent* partners, so there is a bias toward improvement in development. However, there is nothing in the theory that precludes the notion that children's interactions with others could lead to delays in development, abnormal development, or regression in development if social partners possess incorrect knowledge or if they do not believe that the child is capable of further development.

Question 7.3: Speech first appears on the social plane in that the first role of speech is communication—the child talks to others. Then the child transfers this collaborative form of behavior to the sphere of his individual psychological functioning—the child talks to himself—and this self talk begins to serve the function of self-regulation.

Question 7.4: Piaget would not expect children at, say, the preoperational stage of development to be able to tackle the same learning tasks as those at the operational or formal levels. Basically, Piaget's view is that learning depends upon and lags behind development. If a child's intellectual operations have not matured to the extent that he is capable of learning a particular subject, then no amount of instruction will prove useful. In fact, premature instruction in a subject before a child is developmentally ready for it is considered harmful. The teacher's main task in this view is to determine the child's developmental level because this forms the lower threshold of learning capability and indicates which subjects can be appropriately taught.

Question 7.5: In a nutshell, the general law of cultural development states that any function must occur between people before it occurs within the child as an individual psychological function. Thus, mental skills involved in performing tasks first emerge in social interaction with adults (teachers, parents, etc.) or more capable peers and then are internalized by the child. This social interactional view of development places the teaching-learning process at the heart of human development. However, for instruction to benefit development, it must be aimed at the child's zone of proximal development. That is, it must focus on those skills that are just emerging and it must provide the child with support and guidance until he is able to function independently.

Question 7.6.: Vygotsky would expect the frequency of the first two categories of private speech, word play and simple description, to decrease over the preschool and school years, and the frequency of speech serving a self-directive function to increase with age. Piaget would not expect the frequencies of these types of speech to change with age; he would simply expect all types of private speech to gradually disappear with age. Vygotsky would expect the incidence of *overt* private speech to disappear and the frequency of *covert* self-directing speech to increase.

Question 7.7: *Zone of proximal development.* That is, the task must be one that a particular child cannot do alone but can do when working with a more experienced partner. If the task is below the lower bound of the zone, it will not stimulate development because the child has already mastered the requisite skills. If the task is above the upper bound of the child's zone, it will not stimulate development because the child cannot understand the task well enough either to comprehend the meaning of the partner's task-related utterances and demonstrations or to recognize viable problem solutions when they are reached.

Question 7.8: First and foremost, reciprocal teaching involves a social situation where the new strategies are repeatedly used to regulate discourse between people. Through repeated modeling, students gradually learn to use these strategies internally to regulate their own comprehension. Second, the procedure capitalizes on the use of speech to regulate behavior and cognition. Third, the role of the teacher is to promote dialogue as a means of internalizing the strategies. You could also have mentioned that the goal of reciprocal teaching, to transmit tools (strategies) that mediate comprehension, is congruent with a Vygotskian perspective. Finally, the comprehension strategies being taught are skills that are in the child's zone of proximal development.

Question 7.9: Our answer to this question is contained in Table 7.2, which we hope confirms your answer. Incidentally, we have also included neo-Piagetian theory in the table for completeness.

TABLE 7.2   COMPARISON OF VYGOTSKY, PIAGET, AND NEO-PIAGETIAN THEORY ON CORE ISSUES

Core issues	Vygotsky	Piaget	Neo-Piagetian
What develops?	Ability to use culturally developed psychological tools	Ability to reason logically	Ability to reason logically
Emphasis on environmental or organismic factors	Greater emphasis on social-cultural than organismic factors	Equal weight to the physical-logical environment and organismic factors	Equal weight given to environmental and organismic factors
Source of motivation?	Curiosity and activity of child plus motivation of adults to pass on cultural tools	Child is intrinsically motivated to interact with the environment and to resolve cognitive conflict	Child is intrinsically motivated to solve problems and to develop ever more sophisticated strategies for solving problems
How does transfer occur?	Transfer occurs as the child learns to relate knowledge and skills to new problems; this occurs initially under adult guidance	Once a child has developed a given level of reasoning ability, he is able to apply it across a wide variety of settings	Transfer occurs as a child practices cognitive skills across a variety of domains and as the efficiency of STSS improves
Variables in instruction	The child's zone of proximal development; the nature and quality of interactions between teacher and child and between child and peers; proleptic instruction	Child's level of reasoning; environmental stimuli that induce cognitive conflict; sequence of instruction within a domain must mirror developmental progression	Capacity of child's STSS; identification of operations and strategies necessary for intellectual development; instruction must induce children to practice these operations and strategies

REFERENCES

Ames, G. J., & Murray, F. B. (1982). When two wrongs make a right: Promoting cognitive change by social conflict. *Developmental Psychology, 18,* 894–987.

Berk, L. E. (1986). Relationship of elementary school children's private speech to behavioral accompaniment to task, attention, and task performance. *Developmental Psychology, 22,* 671–680.

Berk, L. E., & Gavin, R. A. (1984). Development of private speech among low-income Appalachian children. *Developmental Psychology, 20,* 271–286.

Bjorklund, D. F. (1989). *Children's thinking: Developmental function and individual differences.* Pacific Grove, CA: Brooks/Cole.

Brown, A. L., & Ferrara, R. A. (1985). Diagnosing zones of proximal development. In J. V. Wertsch (Ed.), *Culture, communication, and cognition: Vygotskian perspectives.* Cambridge: Cambridge University Press.

Brown, A. L., & French, L. A. (1979). The zone of potential development: Implications for intelligence testing in the year 2000. *Intelligence, 3,* 255–277.

Bruner, J. S. (1978). The role of dialogue in language acquisition. In A. Sinclair, R. J. Jarvella, & W. J. M. Levelt (Eds.), *The child's conception of language.* New York: Springer-Verlag.

Campione, J. C., Brown, A. L., Ferrara, R. A., & Bryant, N. R. (1984). The zone of proximal development: Implications for individual differences and learning. In B. Rogoff & J. V. Wertsch (Eds.), *Children's learning in the zone of proximal development.* San Francisco: Jossey-Bass.

Cazden, C. B. (1983). Adult assistance to language development: Scaffolds, models, and direct instruction. In R. P. Parder & F. A. Davis (Eds.), *Developing literacy.* Newark, DE: International Reading Association.

Ehly, S. W., & Larsen, S. C. (1980). *Peer tutoring for individualized instruction.* Boston: Allyn & Bacon.

Forman, E. A. (1987). Learning through peer interaction: A Vygotskian perspective. *The Genetic Epistemologist, 15,* 6–15.

Forman, E. A., & Cazden, C. B. (1985). Exploring Vygotskian perspectives in education: The cognitive value of peer interaction. In J. V. Wertsch (Ed.), *Culture, communication, and cognition: Vygotskian perspectives.* Cambridge: Cambridge University Press.

Frauenglass, M. H., & Diaz, R. M. (1985). Self-regulatory functions of children's private speech: A critical analysis of recent challenges to Vygotsky's theory. *Developmental Psychology, 21,* 357–364.

Fuson, K. C. (1979). The development of self-regulating aspects of speech: A review. In G. Zivin (Ed.), *The development of self-regulation through private speech.* New York: Wiley.

Goodman, S. (1981). The integration of verbal and motor development in preschool. *Child Development, 52,* 280–289.

Harris, K. R., & Graham, S. (1985). Improving learning disabled students' composition skills: Self-control strategy training. *Learning Disability Quarterly, 8,* 27–36.

Kohlberg, L., Yaeger, J., & Hjertholm, E. (1968). Private speech: Four studies and a review of theories. *Child Development, 39,* 691–736.

Leont'ev, A. N., & Luria, A. R. (1968). The psychological ideas of L. S. Vygotsky. In B. B. Wolman (Ed.), *Historical roots of contemporary psychology.* New York: Harper & Row.

Meichenbaum, D., & Asarno, J. (1978). Cognitive behavioral modification and metacognitive development: Implications for the classroom. In P. Kendall & S. Hollon (Eds.), *Cognitive behavioral interventions: Theory, research, and procedure.* New York: Academic Press.

Meichenbaum, D., & Goodman, J. (1971). Training impulsive children to talk to themselves: A means of developing self control. *Journal of Abnormal Psychology, 77,* 115–126.

Palincsar, A. S. (1986). The role of dialogue in providing scaffolded instruction. *Educational Psychologist, 21,* 73–98.

Palincsar, A. S. (1988, April). *Dialogue, private speech, and the development of self-regulatory behavior.* Paper presented at the American Educational Research Association annual meeting. New Orleans, LA.

Palincsar, A. S., & Brown, A. L. (1984). Reciprocal teaching of comprehension-fostering and comprehension-monitoring activities. *Cognition and Instruction, 1,* 117–175.

Palincsar, A. S., Brown, A. L., & Martin, S. (1987). Peer interaction in reading comprehension instruction. *Educational Psychologist, 22,* 231–254.

Piaget, J. (1983). Piaget's theory. In W. Kessen (Ed.), *History, theory, and methods.* In
P. H. Mussen (Ed.), *Handbook of child psychology* (Vol. I). New York: Wiley.

Pressley, M., Snyder, B. L., & Cariglia-Bull, T. (1989). How can good strategy use be
taught to children: Evaluation of six alternative approaches. In S. Cormier & J.
Hagman (Eds.), *Transfer of learning: Contemporary research and applications.* New
York: Academic Press.

Robin, A. L., Armel, S., & O'Leary, D. (1975). The effects of self-instruction on writing
deficiencies. *Behavior Therapy, 6,* 178–187.

Rogoff, B., Ellis, S., & Gardner, W. (1984). Adjustment of adult-child instruction according to child's age and task. *Developmental Psychology, 20,* 193–199.

Rogoff, B., & Gardner, W. (1984). Adult guidance of cognitive development. In
B. Rogoff & J. Lave (Eds.), *Everyday cognition: Its development in social context.*
Cambridge, MA: Harvard University Press.

Scollon, R. (1976). *Conversations with a one-year-old: A case study of the developmental foundation of syntax.* Honolulu: University Press of Hawaii.

Slavin, R. E. (1983). *Cooperative learning.* New York: Longman.

Thomas, R. M. (1992). *Comparing theories of child development* (3rd ed.). Belmont,
CA: Wadsworth.

Tudge, J., & Rogoff, B. (1989). Peer influences on cognitive development: Piagetian
and Vygotskian perspectives. In M. G. Bornstein & J. S. Bruner (Eds.), *Interaction in
human development.* Hillsdale, NJ: Lawrence Erlbaum.

Vygotsky, L. S. (1956). *Selected psychological investigations.* Moscow: Izdstel'sto Aka-
demii Pedagogicheskikh Nauk SSSR.

Vygotsky, L. S. (1962). *Thought and language* (E. Hanfmann & G. Vakar, Trans.).
Cambridge, MA: MIT Press.

Vygotsky, L. S. (1978). In M. Cole, V. John-Steiner, S. Scribner, & E. Souberman (Eds.),
Mind in society. Cambridge, MA: Harvard University Press.

Vygotsky, L. S. (1981). The genesis of higher mental functions. In J. V. Wertsch (Ed.),
The concept of activity in Soviet psychology. Armonk, NY: Sharpe.

Vygotsky, L. S. (1986). *Thought and language* (A. Kozulin, Trans.). Cambridge, MA:
MIT Press.

Wertsch, J. V. (1979). From social interaction to higher psychological processes: A
clarification and application of Vygotsky's theory. *Human Development, 22,* 1–22.

Wertsch, J. V. (Ed.). (1981). *The concept of activity in Soviet Psychology.* Armonk, NY:
Sharpe.

Wertsch, J. V., & Rogoff, B. (1984). Editors' notes. In B. Rogoff & J. V. Wertsch (Eds.),
Children's learning in the "zone of proximal development." San Francisco: Jossey-
Bass.

Wood, D., Bruner, J. S., & Ross, G. (1976). The role of tutoring in problem solving.
Journal of Child Psychology and Psychiatry, 17, 89–100.

Wood, D., & Middleton, D. (1975). A study of assisted problem-solving. *British Journal
of Psychology, 66,* 181–191.

8

BANDURA'S SOCIAL LEARNING THEORY

OBJECTIVES

1. Identify one similarity and one difference between behavioral theory and social cognitive theory; identify one similarity and one difference between cognitive theory and social cognitive theory.
2. Describe Bandura's concept of triadic reciprocality and contrast it with environmental determinism and personal determinism.
3. Describe four effects of modeling on the observer and be able to identify instances of each.
4. Describe the attention, retention, and production processes involved in modeling and suggest ways that teachers can enhance them.
5. Describe the function of reinforcement according to Bandura and contrast this view with Skinner's view.
6. Define self-efficacy and differentiate it from outcome expectations.
7. Describe the three subprocesses involved in self-regulation of behavior and suggest specific ways in which teachers might enhance students' self-regulation.
8. Describe the position of social cognitive theory on the five core issues.

All of the theories that we have examined thus far have been either behavioral theories concerned with environmental factors that shape behavior or cognitive theories concerned with internal, mental processes. As teachers who have to be concerned with guiding both the behavior and mental processes of students, you may have found it difficult to reconcile the different approaches of these two theoretical camps. There is, however, a theoretical position that can help us integrate these apparently disparate approaches to learning. Social learning theory tempers behaviorism by emphasizing the role of cognitive processes in the acquisition and regulation of behavior. It moderates cognitive theory by incorporating reinforcement as an important factor that influences cognitive processes and controls behavior. Social learning theory expands upon both behavioral and cognitive theories by emphasizing the social nature of learning. That is, social learning theorists have traditionally studied how children acquire social behaviors such as aggression, sharing, and cooperation through observation and interaction with other people.

As with information processing theory, social learning theory is a framework or general theoretical approach that has encompassed the work of many theorists. The approach was originated in the 1930s and 1940s by Miller and Dollard and their associates, who proposed that imitation is the primary learning mechanism for most social behaviors (Miller & Dollard, 1941; Dollard, Doob, Miller, Mowrer, & Sears, 1939). Subsequently, social learning theory was spearheaded by Albert Bandura and his colleagues (Bandura & Walters, 1963) who initially attempted to explain the acquisition of aggression and other social behaviors through the mechanisms of observation and vicarious reinforcement. Over three decades, Bandura's theory has gradually become more cognitive until, in its latest version, he has renamed it **social cognitive theory** (Bandura, 1986). Bandura and his colleagues have also broadened the scope of the theory to encompass the learning of academic skills and concepts (see, for example, Rosenthal & Zimmerman, 1978; Schunk, 1981).

This chapter is based primarily upon Bandura's social learning theory. First, we will examine some similarities and differences between Bandura's theory and the other approaches to learning that we have already discussed. Then, we will examine the processes that govern observational learning. Finally, we will examine Bandura's theorizing with regard to self-regulation and motivation. Throughout our discussion, we will derive implications of Bandura's ideas for teaching academic and social skills and for classroom management.

COMPARISONS WITH OTHER THEORETICAL APPROACHES

Comparison with Behavioral Theory

Bandura's theory is similar to behavioral learning theory in that it is primarily concerned with behavioral change. A major difference between them lies in their conceptions of *how* people acquire complex, new behaviors.

Question 8.1: Do you remember how people acquire novel behaviors according to Skinner? Write your answer here before looking at the answer at the end of the chapter._____

_____

_____

Bandura finds it hard to believe that all or even most behavior is acquired in the way Skinner claims. For one thing, it would simply take too long. Consider the example of language where the child masters thousands of words and complex syntax and grammar by the time she enters school. The rapidity and seeming ease with which children acquire language does not fit well with the tedious process of shaping. Bandura points out that cognitive and social development would be greatly retarded if we learned only through the effects of our own actions. Fortunately, he claims, most human behavior is learned by observing the behavior of others (Bandura, 1986). Because people can learn what to do through first observing the behavior of others, they save not only time but the pain associated with trial-and-error mistakes. Imagine learning skills such as driving by the trial-and-error process of shaping!

Other behavioral theorists have accepted the importance of imitation but feel that learning only occurs when the person is directly reinforced after reproducing an observed action (Miller & Dollard, 1941). However, Bandura has produced evidence that reinforcement is not necessary for learning through modeling. For example, Freddie observes his friend David raising his hand to get the teacher's attention. Freddie learns to raise his hand in similar circumstances. In this case, Freddie learned a new behavior without responding or receiving reinforcement. Although reinforcement does play an important role in Bandura's theory, his conception of how it influences behavior is quite different from that of behaviorists.

Comparison with Cognitive Theory

Bandura's theory is similar to cognitive theories of learning in that he postulates mental processes or thoughts that intervene between stimulus events and people's reactions to these events. However, unlike cognitive theorists, who are primarily concerned with describing the properties of mental processes, Bandura's theory also specifies the mechanisms by which knowledge is translated into behavior. Cognitive theorists primarily study the acquisition of knowledge by individuals, while Bandura bases many of his principles on studies of social interactions, that is, on the interaction of two or more people.

Reciprocal Determinism

Many of the differences between Bandura's and other theoretical approaches to human learning are made apparent by contrasting their views of where the causes of human behavior are located. Behaviorists, especially radical behaviorists such as Skinner, espouse *environmental determinism.* In this view, behavior is controlled by environmental influences. This control by the environment is unidirectional in that "A person does not act upon the world, the world acts upon him," (Skinner, 1971, p. 211). Other theorists have located the causes of human behavior inside the person. *Personal determinism* claims that behavior is a function of instincts, traits, drives, beliefs, or motivational forces within the individual. For example, Freud believed that behavior stems from the dynamic interplay of inner psychic forces, most of which are below the level of consciousness. Trait theorists (e.g., Allport, 1961; Cattell, 1966) believe that human actions are governed by personality traits (e.g., aggression, dependence), which are broad, enduring dispositions to behave in certain ways.

Most cognitive theorists take the *interactional* view that behavior is determined by the interaction of internal forces and environmental influences. However, once again, the control is unidirectional. That is, cognitive theorists believe that people's thoughts and beliefs interact with information from the environment to produce behavior. However, this model does not take into account how a person's behavior may lead to environmental changes that, in turn, may influence how he thinks about the situation (see the example of John below).

Bandura views the relationship of behavior, person, and environment as a three-way reciprocal process which he calls *triadic reciprocality*. In this model, summarized in Figure 8.1, behavior, cognition, and other personal factors, as well as environmental influences, all operate as interlocking determinants of each other.

Consider the case of John, who puts forth little effort in math class because he believes he is not very bright. His self-conception (personal factor) influences his behavior. However, John observes that he does put a lot of effort into literature assignments. Perhaps, he reasons, he is basically intelligent but just not good in math. His self-examination brings his self-concept into line with his overall behavior and he begins to try harder. John's math teacher perceives John's new efforts and begins reinforcing them (environmental consequence). John begins to succeed in math which, in turn, further enhances his self-concept. And so the interactive process between cognition, behavior, and environmental consequences goes on and on.

It should also be noted that people can passively activate environmental reactions. That is, people may elicit reactions because of physical characteristics (gender, race, physical appearance) and social roles and status. What if John had been Joan? A biased math teacher might have concluded that, being a girl, she was unlikely to do well in math and, consequently, might not have reinforced her new efforts. This lack of teacher response might eventually have discouraged Joan from continuing her new efforts.

Bandura (1986) points out that the relative influence exerted by personal, behavioral, and environmental factors will vary across individuals and circumstances. In some cases, environmental conditions are all-powerful. For example, if people are dropped into deep water, they will all engage in swimming behavior

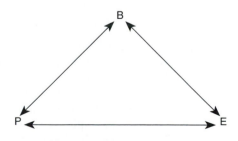

FIGURE 8.1   Bandura's view of the relationship of behavior (B), person (P), and environment (E) as a three-way reciprocal process.

regardless of differences in their cognitive processes and behavioral repertoires. Sometimes behavior and its intrinsic feedback are the central factors in the interacting system. An example would be a person's playing the piano for his own enjoyment. Such behavior is sustained over a long time by its sensory effects, with cognitive activities and situational influences involved to a lesser extent.

In some circumstances, such as deciding what book to check out of a large library, personal factors (i.e., one's interests and preferences) predominate. Defensive reactions are another instance of the predominance of personal factors. For example, a person with a false belief, say, a racial prejudice, will act on that belief and avoid contacts with persons from that race. This avoidance behavior keeps him out of touch with environmental conditions that might counteract his belief. Consequently, the belief-action pattern is protected from corrective environmental influence.

In most instances, the development and activation of the three sets of factors are highly interdependent. Bandura (1986) uses the example of television viewing to illustrate this interdependence. Personal preferences influence when and which programs, from among the available alternatives, individuals choose to watch. Through their viewing behavior they partly shape the kinds of programs that will be offered in the future (TV shows live and die by the ratings). Because production costs and commercial requirements also determine what people are shown, the options provided in the televised environment also shape the viewers' preferences. Hence, all three factors (viewer preferences, viewing behavior, and televised offerings) reciprocally affect each other.

Thus, Bandura proposes a process of causation that gives attention to the internal states of people (their thoughts and emotions), their observable behaviors, and the perceptions and actions of others. As we shall see, all of these factors play a role in observational learning.

OBSERVATIONAL LEARNING

According to Bandura, people acquire cognitive representations of behavior by observing models. These cognitive representations are in the form of memory codes stored in long-term memory. They may be either visual imagery codes or verbal propositional codes. Bandura uses the terms "observational learning" and "modeling" interchangeably to refer to learning that takes place in a social context. He prefers the term "modeling" (or "observational learning") over the term "imitation" because he believes that imitation is only one way in which we learn from models.

Question 8.2: What do you suppose is the difference between observational learning and imitation? Consider the following episode before answering. Suppose you watch someone at a party eat a mint from a tray of candies. The person turns blue, falls to the floor, and thrashes about, moaning loudly. You then eat a mint from the same tray. Even though you imitated the model's behavior, we could conclude that you learned very little from observing the model. So what's the difference between observational learning and imitation?_____

_____

_____
_____

CLASSIFICATION OF MODELING EFFECTS

The primary function of modeled behavior is to transmit information to the observer. Bandura has classified this information in terms of four different kinds of effects it produces in the observer: observational learning, inhibition, disinhibition, and response facilitation.

Observational Learning Effect

Observers can acquire new cognitive skills and new patterns of behavior by observing the performance of others. For example, after watching the physical education teacher demonstrate the proper way to hold a tennis racket, the student then holds the racket appropriately. In math class, after watching the teacher model how to find the reciprocal of a number, the students then work through several practice problems in which they find the reciprocal. In each instance, the model exhibited novel patterns of thought or behavior which the students did not already possess but which, following observation, they could reproduce. The modeling effect is also present when observers learn to organize already learned component skills into new structures. For example, students observing their teacher pronounce a new vocabulary word such as "onomatopoeia" already know how to produce the constituent phonemes. They are simply learning to place them into a new organization.

Inhibitory and Disinhibitory Effects

A second function of modeling is to strengthen or weaken inhibitions over behaviors that have been previously learned. An **inhibitory effect** occurs when an observer reduces his performance of some behavior as a result of watching a model experience negative consequences for producing that behavior. For example, Alice watches while Marcia is ridiculed by the teacher for volunteering an incorrect answer to the teacher's question. Subsequently, Alice volunteers less frequently in that teacher's class. You are driving on the freeway and see a car ahead of you get pulled over for speeding. You immediately reduce your speed to the legal limit. **Disinhibitory effects** occur when observers increase their performance of formerly inhibited behavior after seeing others engage in the behavior without adverse effects. For example, Axel begins to act out in class after observing that his friend's misbehavior is not punished by the teacher.

Response Facilitation Effects

In this case, the behavior of a model is a cue for observers to perform the same or similar behavior. For example, one member of the audience begins to clap and the rest of the audience follows suit. People's looking up upon seeing others gaze skyward is another common example of response facilitation by modeling. Response facilitation effects are distinguished from observational learning because no new responses have been acquired. Disinhibition is not involved because the facilitated behavior is socially acceptable and has not been restrained or inhibited by the observer. The various modeling effects are summarized in Table 8.1.

Exercise 8.1: Identify the following outcomes of modeling as observational learning, inhibition, disinhibition, or response facilitation.

1. Jan, a teenager from a very strict, conservative family, begins to smoke marijuana after seeing her friends who smoke dope gain acceptance among their peers.

2. Many of the kids in Jeff's class have volunteered to bring items for the school's annual food drive. Jeff volunteers also.

3. Six-year-old Kyle assembles a water bomb and drops it on pedestrians on the street below his apartment after viewing a similar episode on the *Little Rascals* TV show.

4. Gavin "cools it" after his friend gets busted for shoplifting.

TABLE 8.1   SUMMARY OF MODELING EFFECTS

Modeling effect	Description
Observational learning	Observers acquire cognitive skills and new patterns of behavior by observing the behavior of others
Inhibition	Observers reduce their performance of the modeled behavior as a result of seeing models experience negative consequences
Disinhibition	Observers increase their performance of formerly inhibited behavior after seeing others engage in the prohibited behavior without adverse consequences
Response facilitation	Observer performs some behavior that has been cued or activated by seeing a model engage in it; the behavior is neither new nor has it been previously inhibited

PROCESSES IN MODELING

According to Bandura (1986), learning is largely an information-processing activity in which information about behavior and about environmental events is transformed into symbolic representations that serve as guides for action. In his social-cognitive analysis of observational learning, which is schematically depicted in Figure 8.2, four constituent processes govern learning. **Attentional processes** govern exploration and perception of modeled activities. **Retention processes** transform perceptions into long-term memory codes that serve as internal models for response production and standards for response correction. **Production processes** regulate the organization of constituent subskills into new response patterns. Finally, **motivational processes** determine whether or not competencies acquired through observation will be put to use. The attention and retention processes are critical for learning a new behavior, while production and motivational processes are involved in performance of the behavior. Let's examine each of these components in more detail.

Attentional Processes

In order to learn from observing another's behavior, the observer must be paying attention to and correctly perceiving the modeled activity. That is obvious. What is not obvious is why students attend to some models and not others, and why they attend to only some parts of a model's behavior and not other parts. Attention seems to be influenced both by the nature of the modeled activity and the internal state of the observer. Factors related to the model include distinctiveness and complexity of the model's behavior. The more distinctive a model's behavior, the easier it is for the observer to attend to it. Moreover, when the modeled activity is an ongoing event (e.g., a dance performance), the more distinctive behaviors are the ones that will normally be attended to (e.g., a dramatic solo). The more complex the modeled activity, the more difficult it is for the observer to maintain his attention. Thus, simple, conspicuous acts are the ones most readily learned through observation.

Internal factors influencing attention and perception include observers' prior knowledge and expectations, which dispose them to look for some things but not others. An observer's level of cognitive development also influences the amount of observational learning. If the rate or complexity of the modeled activity overtaxes the observer's attentional capacity, observational learning will be fragmentary. The arousal level of the observer is another factor which influences the attention given to modeled events. Arousal level refers to a person's overall activity level. At the low end of the arousal continuum, a person is drowsy; at very high levels, a person is hyperactive. Observational learning is best when the learner is moderately to highly aroused. An important point is that high arousal can be experienced as an unpleasant state, what we call anxiety. Anxiety is often experienced when we are in new, unfamiliar situations where we are unsure of what to do. Under such circumstances, we are most likely to attend to the behavior of

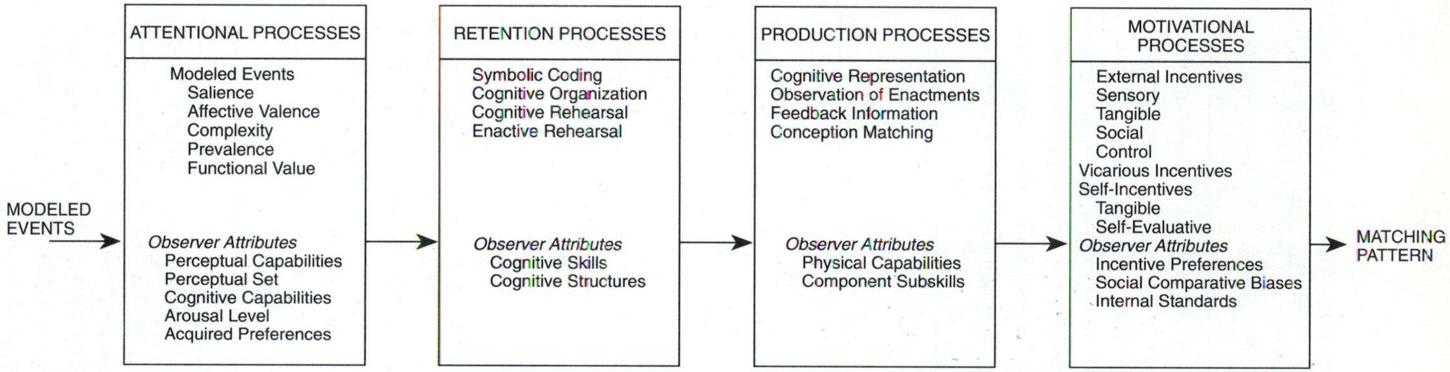
MODELED EVENTS
ATTENTIONAL PROCESSES
Modeled Events
Salience
Affective Valence
Complexity
Prevalence
Functional Value
Observer Attributes
Perceptual Capabilities
Perceptual Set
Cognitive Capabilities
Arousal Level
Acquired Preferences
RETENTION PROCESSES
Symbolic Coding
Cognitive Organization
Cognitive Rehearsal
Enactive Rehearsal
Observer Attributes
Cognitive Skills
Cognitive Structures
PRODUCTION PROCESSES
Cognitive Representation
Observation of Enactments
Feedback Information
Conception Matching
Observer Attributes
Physical Capabilities
Component Subskills
MOTIVATIONAL PROCESSES
External Incentives
Sensory
Tangible
Social
Control
Vicarious Incentives
Self-Incentives
Tangible
Self-Evaluative
Observer Attributes
Incentive Preferences
Social Comparative Biases
Internal Standards
MATCHING PATTERN

FIGURE 8.2 Subprocesses governing observational learning. (From Albert Bandura, *Social Foundations of Thought & Action: A Social Cognitive Theory.* Copyright 1986. Reprinted by permission of Prentice Hall, Englewood Cliffs, NJ.)

someone who appears to know the ropes. For example, if you are attending a formal dinner party for the first time, you might be inclined to learn such niceties as which fork to use for which course by observing the behavior of someone who seems to be experienced.

Question 8.3: The factors of distinctiveness and arousal can help us to understand some puzzling modeling behavior that can be observed in the classroom. Consider Johnny, a third grader who is popular with his classmates. He is very bright and when so inclined can be industrious and cooperative. At other times, however, he can be loud, disruptive, and downright devilish. It is these latter behaviors that his classmates attend to and subsequently reproduce. Can you explain to Johnny's despairing teacher why the children selectively attend to

Johnny's "bad" behavior?_____

_____

_____

_____

Retention Processes

The second major component in observational learning is retention of knowledge about the modeled activities. Retention involves active transformation and restructuring of information about modeled events. Learners convert modeled activities into images and/or verbal propositions that capture the essential features of the modeled performance.

Bandura's view of the retention process is similar to the constructive view of memory held by schema theorists (see Chapter 3). Thus, according to Bandura, the observer does not enter into memory an exact copy of the model's behavior. Rather, the observer abstracts out of the model's behavior a general rule or code which he then uses to generate or construct behaviors of his own. For example, consider a small child playing with her dolls. It may be possible to identify small bits of behavior that she has learned from watching her mother care for siblings or from watching TV ads showing children playing with similar dolls. But she does not go through an entire sequence of her mother's behavior of that of the TV models. Instead, her behavior indicates that she has abstracted small chunks of those behaviors and strung them together to form a unique pattern.

The child has developed a blueprint or schema of childcare behavior. The schema includes general categories of behavior such as singing to the baby, changing the baby's clothes, and putting the baby to bed. From these general categories the child can construct novel patterns. In other words, the observer does not learn an inflexible set of behaviors by observing a model. Rather, the observer learns general patterns or rules which can be used to generate behavior appropriate to a variety of settings. The memory codes formed during observation not only preserve pertinent information about the modeled activity but also include operations for translating this coded information into actions. Thus, both declarative and procedural knowledge about modeled events is stored in memory.

Rehearsal aids retention of modeled activities. People who cognitively rehearse or actually perform modeled patterns of behavior are less likely to forget them than those who do not rehearse. As in the learning of verbal information, elaborative rehearsal which serves to reorganize and make the modeled activity more meaningful to the learner results in better retention than maintenance rehearsal which simply repeats the modeled event.

Cognitive rehearsal, in which individuals visualize themselves executing the correct sequence of actions, plays an important role in observational learning since, often, what is observed cannot be easily practiced. Time, space, and resource limitations often make physical practice difficult. Studies have shown that cognitive rehearsal benefits subsequent performance of athletic skills, vocational activities, and conceptual tasks (Corbin, 1972). Such activities are mastered more rapidly by combining cognitive and physical rehearsal than by physical rehearsal alone. Moreover, daily cognitive rehearsal of an already learned psychomotor skill has been shown to aid its retention (Sackett, 1935). Cognitive rehearsal can also prepare people to perform well-learned skills. That is, individuals who visualize themselves performing what they are about to do usually perform better than if they do not visualize their performance (Richardson, 1967).

Cognitive rehearsal benefits skill acquisition because it helps learners to conceptualize the skill and to organize the psychological, neural, and muscular systems underlying the action pattern. Initial learning proceeds best by gaining a clear conception of the skilled performance and then alternating cognitive and physical rehearsal (Richardson, 1967). For example, following teacher demonstration, students might first study a list of the steps involved in setting up a piece of delicate scientific apparatus. They could then visualize themselves doing the procedure before actually doing it. Finally, cognitive and physical enactments could be alternated until the skill is mastered. It is important to give students clear feedback during physical rehearsals so that their cognitive rehearsals do not contain faulty procedures.

Production Processes

The third component of modeling involves converting the symbolic codes in memory into appropriate actions. This is done by sequencing and timing one's behavior according to one's cognitive representation of the activity. Thus, the conceptual representation stored in long-term memory represents learning of the modeled activity, while the behavioral enactment based on the conceptual representation represents performance.

Question 8.4: Suppose students have just observed their teacher model a complex new behavior, say, focusing a microscope. How could the teacher find out if students have learned the modeled activity before letting them get their hands on the school's limited equipment?

_____

_____

_____

_____

The conceptual representation provides the internal model for response production and its subsequent correction. According to Bandura (1986), behavioral production primarily involves a *conception-matching* process in which sensory feedback from motor performance is compared to the conception. Thus, the accuracy of the conceptual representation is essential for this matching process to result in good performance. That is why it's a good idea to evaluate students' conceptions independently from their motor performance.

Even when students have acquired an accurate conception of the modeled activity, their behavioral production can be faulty if performance requires component motor skills that have not been mastered. For example, students may fail to produce modeled utterances in French until they master the speech sounds needed to pronounce French words. Individual and developmental differences in physical strength and dexterity profoundly affect this observational learning process. Young children, for example, may be able to attend to and accurately encode a modeled activity such as driving a car. However, they will not be able to produce it because of physical limitations.

Conceptions are rarely transformed into corresponding actions without errors on the first few attempts. Initially, people try to correct themselves by monitoring the feedback from their actions and comparing it with their conceptual representations. Thus, people improve their performance by seeing, hearing, and feeling what they are doing. This intrinsic feedback can be augmented by extrinsic feedback from others who have observed and evaluated their actions. For example, a student attempting to perform the tennis stroke modeled by the PE teacher attends to the visual placement of his arm and wrist, the sound of the ball as it hits the racket, and the kinesthetic feedback from his movements. He also benefits from seeing what happens to the ball after he strokes it. Finally, his instructor can give him evaluative verbal feedback.

A common problem in learning new skills is that people cannot fully observe their own behavior. For example, in coordinated skills like tennis and swimming, students cannot see much of what they are doing. Similarly, speech and drama students are hampered by not being able to see themselves while performing. Self-observation through videotape replays is increasingly being used to overcome this problem. However, care should be taken when using self-observation. Simply letting students view replays of their performance will not be effective if students do not notice what they are doing wrong or know how to correct errors if they do spot them. Moreover, self-observation of flawed performance can reduce students' perceptions of their capabilities (Brown, 1980). Thus, the teacher needs to provide corrective feedback during self-observation to direct students' attention to relevant aspects of performance. Such teacher feedback should focus on successes, not just errors, and should inform students how to correct mistakes.

Motivational Processes

A person might attend to a modeled activity, store a cognitive representation of it in long-term memory, and be able to produce the behavior accurately but might still not enact the behavior. This, once again, is the distinction between learning and performance. The final process in the model deals with motivational factors that enhance or suppress the performance of behaviors learned through observation. Three types of consequences influence performance of modeled behavior—vicarious, direct, and self-produced.

Vicarious Consequences   This term refers to rewards or punishments given to the model after some behavior. Research indicates that an observer is more likely to reproduce behavior for which a model has received rewards than behavior that has been punished or ignored (Bandura, Ross, & Ross, 1963b). There is one important exception to this rule, however, that teachers and parents need to know about. When a model exhibits socially disapproved or prohibited behavior without receiving any adverse consequences, it may disinhibit the behavior in observers in much the same way as if the model were rewarded for the behavior. For example, a teacher may be trying to extinguish a disruptive behavior in one student by ignoring it. But this may provide a modeling situation in which other children not only learn that disruptive behavior through observation but also learn that it is safe to engage in it.

Question 8.5: Suppose you are out walking with your 12-year-old son and you pass by a homosexual couple. You, being proud of your liberal views, take no notice. Then along comes a group of teenagers who begin harassing the couple. They shout epithets like "queer," "fag," and "homo" and make lewd gestures. You and your son watch all this but neither of you say anything. Now the question

is, what have you taught your son?_____

Direct Consequences   Rewards or punishments for engaging in modeled behavior can also come directly to the observer. People are more likely to exhibit modeled behavior if it results in valued outcomes than if it is unrewarded or punished. In general, direct consequences are more powerful in motivating reproduction of modeled behavior than are vicarious consequences. Although seeing others rewarded may temporarily increase one's motivation, direct reinforcement is necessary to sustain behavior.

Self-produced Consequences   How people evaluate their own behavior also determines which observationally learned behaviors they are likely to exhibit.

They tend to reproduce observed behaviors they find self-satisfying and reject those they personally disapprove of. The processes by which self-reinforcement operates will be examined further in a later section.

Functions of Consequences   As you can see, consequences play a quite different role in Bandura's theory from that in behavioral theories like Skinner's. For one thing, Skinner viewed reinforcement as necessary for learning, while Bandura maintains that reinforcement is not necessary for learning (i.e., for forming cognitive representations). According to Bandura, reinforcement facilitates performance of learned behaviors, but it is only one among several determinants of performance. Direct reinforcement is necessary in Skinner's view, while in Bandura's theory vicarious and self-reinforcement play as important a role as direct reinforcement.

Finally, the mechanism by which reinforcement influences behavior is quite different for the two theorists. In Skinner's view, the strengthening of response tendencies through reinforcement is automatic. That is, when a person's actions are reinforced, it is not necessary for him to consciously think, "That worked, so I'll try that again in the future." Rather, the reinforcement unconsciously strengthens the response. Moreover, Skinner believed that for this automatic strengthening to be most effective, consequences must immediately follow the behavior.

Bandura disagrees with this view of reinforcement as an automatic response strengthener. He believes instead that reinforcement has an **informative** and **motivational** function. By informative, Bandura means that consequences tell a person under what circumstances it would be wise to try a particular action in the future. By motivational, he means that people will more likely perform a behavior if they value the consequences it seems to produce. This view of consequences allows Bandura to account for people's vicarious learning. That is, watching others receive valued consequences for certain behaviors gives an observer the same information that he gets from his own direct behavioral consequences. For example, if a student desires recognition and observes that the teacher gives recognition and approval to students who do well in arithmetic, she is motivated to work hard on arithmetic assignments. Notice that in both their informative and motivational roles, the effect of consequences is not to strengthen the responses that immediately preceded them. Rather, consequences are regulators of *future* behavior. They regulate by giving the individual information about likely future consequences and by motivating actions that lead to such consequences (Thomas, 1992).

In addition to providing information and motivating behavior, vicarious consequences serve an **emotive function** and a **valuation function.** Both of these functions come about as observers witness models' reactions to receiving consequences. People commonly display emotional reactions while experiencing rewarding or painful consequences. Observers of such reactions experience vicarious emotional arousal which enables them to learn what might be pleasurable or painful without having to go through the same experiences themselves. Through such vicarious emotional reactions observers can come to like, dislike, or fear persons, places, and things that they have had little direct contact with (Bandura, 1965). For example, a child who observes another child's emotional reaction to being bitten by a dog will not only become frightened, but she will also come to fear dogs. Once acquired, such fears become self-perpetuating through the avoidance reactions they promote. More positively, children can develop new values or preferences by observing others receiving rewards. For example, children come to value money after seeing adults' reactions to receiving money. Thus, modeling is a powerful technique for establishing new secondary reinforcers.

Internal standards are another example of values that can be acquired vicariously. That is, as people engage in behaviors, they frequently express approval or disapproval of their own behavior in accordance with their personal standards. They react approvingly when their behavior matches some internal standard, but self-critically when their behavior falls short or violates their standard. Through repeated exposure to the modeled self-evaluations of others, observers can acquire the same underlying standards and use them as guides for their own future behavior (Bandura, 1976). For example, the nonviolent resistance that Martin Luther King, Jr., modeled for millions of Americans became the internal standard by which many people subsequently judged their own reaction to injustice and oppression. We shall discuss the acquisition of internal standards for behavior in more detail later when we examine self-regulatory mechanisms. Table 8.2 summarizes the functions of vicarious consequences.

Self-efficacy   According to Bandura, another factor that influences people's motivation to perform modeled activities is their perceived efficacy. "Self-efficacy" is an academic term that refers to how capable someone judges herself to be in a given situation. It is a person's sense of "I can do it" or "I can't do it." In addition to its informative and motivational role, reinforcement, both direct and vicarious, influences performance by its effects on self-efficacy. That is, seeing other people succeed or fail (or succeeding or failing oneself) affects a person's judgment of her own capabilities (Brown & Inouye, 1978).

Perceptions of self-efficacy can have diverse effects on behavior, thought patterns, and emotional reactions. One's choice of activities and environments is

TABLE 8.2   FUNCTIONS OF VICARIOUS CONSEQUENCES

Informative	Vicarious consequences inform the observer what outcomes to expect if he were to reproduce the modeled behavior.
Motivational	Vicarious consequences motivate reproduction of modeled activities when they represent outcomes valued by the observer.
Emotive	Models' reaction to consequences produce vicarious emotional experiences in observers. These attractions and aversions are created in the absence of direct contact with consequences.
Valuational	Models' reactions to consequences can produce new values and preferences in observers. Self-evaluative reactions can produce new internal standards for observers.

influenced by one's perceived efficacy. Individuals tend to avoid tasks and situations which they believe exceed their capabilities, but they undertake tasks they feel capable of handling (Bandura, 1977). For example, students who do not view themselves as capable in math might attempt to avoid taking math classes, while students with high self-efficacy for math will choose more math electives. Perceived efficacy influences how much effort people will expend and how long they will persist at a task in the face of difficulty. When facing difficult learning tasks, students who perceive themselves as capable learners will expend more effort and persist longer than students who doubt their learning capabilities (Schunk, 1984).

Perceived efficacy also affects thought patterns and emotional reactions. Those who judge themselves to be inefficacious in coping with environmental demands dwell upon their inadequacy and envision potential difficulties as more formidable than they really are (Meichenbaum, 1977; Sarason, 1975). For example, a person who doubts his ability to drive on the freeway in heavy traffic may entertain thoughts of wreckage and mishap and consequently experience a high degree of stress. These thoughts and emotions can, in turn, interfere with his efforts to cope with the situation.

In general, outcome expectations and self-efficacy are distinct motivational processes that combine to influence performance. **Outcome expectations** are personal beliefs that certain behaviors will lead to certain outcomes or consequences. Such expectations are formed through direct and vicarious consequences. For example, a student believes that he can obtain the teacher's approval by doing well in spelling because he has observed the teacher praise others who made good grades on a spelling test. However, the student may not choose to study the spelling list or persist in studying it if he doubts his ability as a speller. On the other hand, a student who believes that he has high aptitude in spelling may also avoid studying if he perceives that this activity will not lead to valued outcomes such as teacher approval. Both positive outcome expectations and high self-efficacy appear to be necessary for students to choose and persist in academic tasks.

Sources of Self-efficacy Information   Knowledge about one's efficacy, whether accurate or faulty, comes from four principal sources: performance attainments, vicarious experiences, verbal persuasion, and physiological states. One of the best ways of knowing whether one is capable of some performance is to actually attempt it. Repeated success at an activity results in high self-efficacy, while failures will lower self-efficacy, unless lack of effort or adverse circumstances are involved (Bandura, Adams, & Beyer, 1977). Once a strong sense of efficacy (or inefficacy) is established, it will generalize to similar tasks and situations.

Often, we do not need to directly perform a task to gain efficacy information. Watching others succeed on a task can raise our own sense of efficacy, especially if we perceive ourselves to be similar to those observed. We reason that "If he can do it, so can I." By the same token, observing others who are similar to ourselves fail despite high effort lowers our own efficacy (Brown & Inouye, 1978). However, such vicarious experience can be overridden by direct experience. In general, efficacy information obtained from models is more potent when people have little prior experience on which to base evaluations of their personal competence. So Frank, who has never bowled before, might believe that he can perform adequately when he sees his friend, also a novice, roll a strike. However, this vicarious sense of efficacy will soon vanish if Frank rolls a long series of gutter balls.

Verbal persuasion is widely used to convince people that they possess the capabilities to achieve what they seek. As teachers, we have all attempted to bolster students' confidence in their own abilities. Such persuasion can be beneficial if it boosts students' self-efficacy to the point that they begin trying to succeed. However, raising unrealistic beliefs of competence invites failure that not only discredits the persuader but further undermines the student's self-efficacy.

Question 8.6: Persuading students of their inefficacy can have long-term effects. For example, Cathy's mother often lamented her own inefficacy in math and expressed the belief that "because of genes," Cathy was unlikely to be a good math student. Subsequently, throughout school, Cathy failed miserably in math. Can you explain why it is harder to boost students' self-efficacy than to undermine it? (Hint: Review the effects of self-efficacy on one's choice of activities.)

_____

_____

_____

A fourth source of self-efficacy information is one's physiological state. People judge their capabilities partly on information gained from monitoring their physiological state. Since anxiety or stress reactions usually debilitate performance, people are more likely to feel efficacious when they are not feeling aversive levels of arousal. For example, a student who is highly anxious over an upcoming exam is likely to have lower self-efficacy than one who has no test anxiety, even though both students are equally well-prepared for the exam. Fear reactions generate further fear by conjuring up fear-provoking thoughts related to one's ineptitude. Such elevated levels of stress can then produce the feared dysfunction. Treatments that eliminate emotional arousal to perceived threats heighten self-efficacy with corresponding improvements in performance (Bandura & Adams, 1977).

We shall leave the topic of self-efficacy for now and pick it up again in Chapter 9, where we examine various approaches to motivation. Self-efficacy is best understood in the context of attributional theories of motivation (Weiner, 1980) which examine how people explain their successes and failures. As Weiner points out, there are a number of factors to which success or failure can be attributed. Only some of these, such as ability and effort, reflect directly on the efficacy of the individual. Others, such as luck and task difficulty, are not under personal control and do not have direct implications for judgments of self-efficacy. In Chapter 9, we shall also examine the relationship of self-efficacy to school achievement and discuss ways of enhancing students' self-efficacy.

Modeling Processes and the Medium of Information

The term "model" can refer to an actual, physically present person whose behavior serves as a guide for someone else. A model might also be symbolic. **Symbolic models** include such things as books, verbal or written instructions, pictures, cartoon or film characters, TV programs, and so forth. According to social cognitive theory, the basic conception-matching process underlying observational learning is the same regardless of the type of model involved. That is not to say that different forms of modeling are equally effective. They may differ in the amount of information they convey and their power to command attention.

Comparing Types of Modeling   The effectiveness of different types of modeling depends upon the developmental level of the observer and the complexity and codability of the modeled activities. Young children at the preverbal level of development must acquire new behavior from observing physical models, either live or pictorial. When live and pictorial models (e.g., TV and film characters) command attention and convey the same amount of information, they produce comparable amounts of observational learning in very young children (Bandura, Ross, & Ross, 1963a). Older children who have a good grasp of language can learn new behaviors from verbal descriptions without the physical presence of a model (Bandura & Mischel, 1965). However, most people learn best from some combination of verbal instruction and behavioral demonstration. For example, children learn rule-governed behaviors (e.g., classifying objects according to size or shape) better when the rules are imparted both verbally and through demonstrations than when only verbal instruction or behavioral demonstration is used alone (Rosenthal & Zimmerman, 1978).

Verbal Modeling of Thought Processes   Modeling is an effective procedure for teaching students cognitive strategies for learning and thinking. However, that requires the model to adequately reflect covert mental processes while modeling the strategy. For example, teachers can verbalize their thought strategies aloud as they engage in problem-solving activities. They can verbally describe the mental processes they are using to remember new vocabulary words or the processes they use to comprehend a difficult text. Modeling of both thoughts and actions is a critical ingredient of good strategy instruction and is central to both the reciprocal teaching (see Chapter 7) and direct explanation approaches (Chapter 4) to strategy instruction.

IMPLICATIONS OF MODELING PROCESSES FOR TEACHING

Now let's put everything we have learned about the processes involved in modeling together and draw out some guidelines for using modeling in the classroom. Read carefully because some exercises are included.

Attentional Processes

When modeling cognitive skills and behaviors for students, teachers can use various procedures to heighten attention and insure accurate perception. The teacher can *physically accentuate* the essential aspects of the performance by using expressive gestures and body movements or by incorporating conspicuous objects into the behavior. For example, to model impulse control, a first-grade teacher might actually put on a brightly colored "thinking cap" to convey that she is thinking about a situation before acting on it. *Attention-directing narration* such as "pay close attention now" can be used to point out what is important. Teachers can also use *contrast modeling* of good and poor performance to make clear the features that are necessary for superior performance. For example, a foreign language teacher may model both correct and incorrect pronunciation or grammatical structure. *Subdividing complex activities* into segments and *highlighting the constituent skills* (e.g., the toss part of a tennis serve) will result in better observational learning than exposing students to an entire performance. Mass exposure to a lengthy performance can overwhelm students' attentional capacity and result in errors and misconceptions. *Repeating* the modeled performance is usually a good idea. However, *learners need opportunities to practice what they have seen between observations.* Students' errors during practice can show them what to look for in subsequent observation of modeled performance.

Retention Processes

Meaningfulness plays a large role in the comprehension and retention of novel behavior, just as it does in the learning of verbal knowledge. New response patterns are learned more easily if they are related to what is already known. When introducing new behaviors, teachers can point out how they are similar to familiar activities. Teachers can also help students code modeled activities into images or verbal symbols. For example, simplified line drawings of essential parts of a performance can be presented following their demonstration. Or, verbal descriptions that capture essential actions can be provided. Don't forget the mnemonic techniques such as the peg word method and method of loci (see Chapter 4) which can be used to help students remember sequences of actions. Instruct students to use both physical and cognitive rehearsal while learning new skills.

Production Processes

Providing students with opportunities to practice new skills is important. However, the timing and type of feedback given by the teacher is critical if such practice is to be beneficial. Especially during initial learning, feedback should be immediate. Positive feedback that highlights successes and gains while correcting deficiencies builds both confidence and skill (Dowrick, 1983). One of the best ways to provide feedback is through *corrective modeling* (Vasta, 1976). In this approach, problematic segments of a student's performance are identified, and correct ways of performing them are modeled by the instructor. Learners then rehearse those subskills until they master them.

Motivational Processes

In the social cognitive view, observational learning takes place as a result of cognitive processing that occurs during exposure to modeled events. The learning occurs before any responses have been performed by the learner and does not require any external reward. However, knowing that a given model's behavior is effective in producing valued outcomes or in averting punishing ones can improve observational learning by directing and increasing attentiveness to the model's actions. Anticipated rewards can also improve retention by motivating people to encode and rehearse modeled activities. Therefore, teachers can improve observational learning of their students by informing them in advance about the benefits of adopting modeled behavior. Then, of course, students should be directly reinforced for performing modeled activities. All the information in Chapter 2 concerning effective ways of delivering direct reinforcement applies in the observational learning situation just as in the operant conditioning situation. That is true even though the underlying explanations of the effects of reinforcement on performance are quite different in Bandura's and Skinner's theories.

Direct reinforcement of students for performing modeled activities can be given in a way that provides vicarious reinforcement to other students. For example, publicly praising a student for correctly enacting a modeled activity informs other students that they can expect your approval for similar behavior. Of course, the use of public praise can backfire for students who do not value it. Therefore, it is important to assess the incentive value of particular reinforcers for individual students when using both direct and vicarious reinforcement. It is important to remember that when it comes to motivating performance, direct reinforcement is more powerful than vicarious reinforcement. Just compare the motivational value of receiving your own paycheck versus seeing others being paid for doing their jobs. Finally, be aware that how students perceive their capability to perform the modeled activity influences their motivation as much as their expectation of receiving valued outcomes. We shall discuss ways of influencing students' self-efficacy in Chapter 9. These guidelines for teaching through modeling are summarized in Table 8.3.

Exercise 8.2: Most physical activities are learned through observation and practice. The object of this exercise is for you to create a plan for teaching someone a behavior sequence through modeling. Some examples of behaviors you could model are:

The toss and serve in tennis
Tying a square knot
Operating a ditto, photocopy, or other office machine

TABLE 8.3   GUIDELINES FOR MODELING

Process	Guidelines
Gaining learners' attention	1. Use expressive gestures and body movements and attention-directing narrative 2. Employ contrast modeling 3. Subdivide complex actions into segments and highlight constituent skills 4. Repeat the modeled performance with opportunities to practice between observations
Aiding retention	1. Relate new activity to familiar activities 2. Provide drawings and/or verbal descriptions that code essential actions 3. Instruct students to use physical and cognitive rehearsal
Facilitating production	1. Provide immediate feedback that corrects deficiencies while highlighting successes 2. Use corrective modeling
Motivating performance	1. Inform students in advance of the value of adopting the modeled behavior 2. Provide direct and vicarious reinforcement for performing modeled activity

The behavior sequence you choose should be complex enough so that some learning is necessary but simple enough to be completed in four to six steps. First identify your behavior sequence and then identify the level of student who would benefit from learning it. Then identify the steps of the sequence so that each part can be demonstrated. Next, determine what will focus the learner's attention at each step and what you need to say (if anything) at each step. After planning the sequence of steps, describe how you would help the student to remember the sequence, what type of practice and feedback you would give, and any motivational techniques you would use. You can check the end of the chapter for a sample plan before using the form given below for your planning.

Behavior to be taught _____

Student (brief description) _____

Step in modeling	**Draw learner's attention to**	**Verbal comments**
1. _____	_____	_____
	_____	_____
	_____	_____

2. _____   _____   _____
                      _____   _____
                      _____   _____

3. _____   _____   _____
                      _____   _____
                      _____   _____

4. _____   _____   _____
                      _____   _____
                      _____   _____

5. _____   _____   _____
                      _____   _____
                      _____   _____

6. _____   _____   _____
                      _____   _____
                      _____   _____

Describe retention aids _____

_____

Describe practice/feedback _____

_____

Describe motivational techniques _____

_____

Exercise 8.3: Modeling can also be used to teach cognitive skills and strategies. The object of this exercise is for you to create a plan for teaching someone a strategy, using modeling. Some examples of strategies are:

Key-word strategy for learning vocabulary words
Peg-word mnemonic technique
Outlining a section of text

First identify the strategy and the level and type of student who would benefit from learning it. Then fill in the instructional plan below. See an example at the end of the chapter before beginning.

Strategy to be taught _____

Student (brief description) _____

Step in modeling	Draw learner's attention to	Verbal comments
1. _____	_____	_____
	_____	_____
	_____	_____
2. _____	_____	_____
	_____	_____
	_____	_____
3. _____	_____	_____
	_____	_____
	_____	_____
4. _____	_____	_____
	_____	_____
	_____	_____
5. _____	_____	_____
	_____	_____
	_____	_____
6. _____	_____	_____
	_____	_____
	_____	_____

Describe retention aids _____

_____

Describe practice/feedback _____

_____

Describe motivational techniques _____

_____

SELF-REGULATION

According to Bandura (1986), theories that explain behavior solely in terms of external rewards and punishments do not accurately represent human nature because people have self-directive capabilities. This capacity for self-direction allows people to have some control over their behavior by the consequences they produce for themselves. Thus, *both external and self-generated consequences combine to regulate human behavior.*

Many activities are performed in order to achieve positive outcomes or to avoid trouble in the future. While these distant outcomes provide general direction for choosing present activities, they are too far off to provide specific guides for behavior. People have to create for themselves proximal (close in) behavioral guides and self-motivators to achieve distant outcomes. For example, a student may begin writing a term paper at midterm in order to achieve a good grade at the end of the course. Because the grade is too far in the future to regulate the student's writing behavior, the work on the paper may depend upon her standards of what constitutes good writing. Her standards may include the time needed to generate ideas and mentally rephrase them several times before putting anything on paper. She will then successively revise the written product until she is satisfied with what she has written. The more exacting the student's standards, the more revisions she will make. Self-editing sometimes exceeds the external standards of what would be acceptable to the teacher. Indeed, some students paralyze their own writing efforts by being overly critical of themselves.

SUBPROCESSES IN SELF-REGULATION

Self-regulation operates through a set of subprocesses that when developed and mobilized allow individuals to control their own behavior. People often have the intent or desire to change their behavior but lack the strategies for doing so. The subprocesses involved in self-regulation are shown in Figure 8.3.

FIGURE 8.3   Subprocesses in self-regulation of behavior. (From Albert Bandura, *Social Foundations of Thought & Action: A Social Cognitive Theory.* Copyright 1986. Reprinted by permission of Prentice Hall, Englewood Cliffs, NJ.)

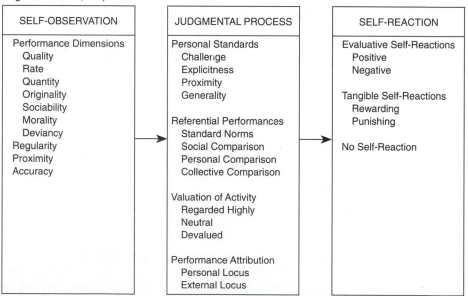

Self-observation

In order to influence their own actions people need to monitor relevant aspects of their behavior, some of which are listed in Figure 8.3. Naturally, the behaviors that are monitored must be appropriate to the situation. For example, people monitor physical dexterity in sports, comprehension and test performance in academic settings, and the sociability of their behavior in social settings. The consistency, accuracy, and timeliness of self-monitoring partially determines success in self-regulation. That is because self-observation provides the information needed for the other subprocesses in self-regulation: setting realistic performance standards and evaluating ongoing behavior. Several factors influence whether self-monitoring will produce effective goal or standard setting and self-evaluation that will, in turn, lead to changes in behavior.

One such factor is how close in time the self-monitoring is to the target behavior. Focusing on immediate behavior is more effective than monitoring the future effects of behavior. For example, when trying to lose weight, it is more effective to monitor one's daily caloric intake than to periodically weigh oneself (Romanczyk, 1974). Immediate self-observation provides continuing information and permits the kind of ongoing self-evaluation that most effectively influences behavior. Once the pounds have been put on, even severe self-criticism cannot alter the effects of past behavior. Intermittent self-monitoring, because it provides less information, is less effective in producing behavioral change than continuous monitoring (Mahoney, Moore, Wade, & Moura, 1973).

Another factor is whether an individual focuses on his successes or failures. Self-monitoring one's successes increases desired behavior, whereas observing one's failures causes little change or lowers performance (Kirschenbaum & Karoli, 1977). For example, the student who consistently focuses on her mistakes in math will become discouraged and lower her self-efficacy. Helping that student to pay more attention to her successes in math will increase her self-efficacy and decrease her anxiety, both of which will improve her performance.

Self-observation is most effective (1) when the person is motivated to change the monitored behavior, (2) when she perceives the behavior as being important, (3) when the information gained from monitoring can be clearly interpreted, and (4) when the motivated behavior can be voluntarily controlled (Bandura, 1986). For example, John's self-observation of his interactions with girls is likely to improve those interactions if he is highly motivated to change his present awkwardness, if he perceives dating and being popular with girls as important, and if he receives clear cues from those girls as to his progress. However, John may have more success in changing how he talks to girls than in changing his tendency to blush upon meeting one, because such involuntary responses are difficult to control.

Judgmental Process

Observing one's own behavior is only the first step in doing something about it. In order for the information gained through self-monitoring to influence behavior, it must elicit either positive or negative self-evaluations. However, whether a performance will be regarded favorably or negatively by an individual depends upon the personal standards against which it is judged. Thus, self-regulation requires internal standards for judging and guiding one's actions. Such standards are developed by direct instruction, by evaluative feedback from others, and by exposure to standards modeled by others.

Development of Internal Standards   How significant others (parents, peers, et al.) react to our behavior influences the behavioral standards we set. For example, parents are generally pleased when their child meets or exceeds their own standard for academic achievement and disappointed when the child's performance falls short of those standards. Quite often, the child internalizes his parents' standards and subsequently uses them to criticize his own achievement behavior depending upon whether it meets the standards of his parents.

Standards can also be acquired through direct instruction. Parents and teachers often use this approach when attempting to influence children's standards. Such tutelage is most effective when it is backed up by behavioral consequences. That is, parents may advocate honesty, but if they do not respond positively for behaving in accordance with this standard or negatively for violating it, then their words are unlikely to retain much impact. In many instances, instruction in performance standards is not effective because it is accompanied by inconsistent or inadequate follow-through (Bandura, 1986).

Evaluative standards can also be transmitted through modeling. That is shown through studies in which children observe models performing a task for purposes of self reward. The results of such studies show that children tend to adopt evaluative standards modeled by others and then judge and reward their own performance according to those standards. That is, children exposed to models who set high standards reward themselves only when they achieve superior performance, whereas children exposed to models favoring low self-standards reward themselves for minimal performance (Bandura & Kupers, 1964). Adult standards are influenced by modeling in the same way as those of children (Marston, 1965), especially in domains of activity in which they have little experience.

In the course of life, people are exposed to a variety of models having different standards. Bandura (1986) points out that theoretically it is more challenging to explain why people often adopt high performance standards than low ones that require less effort and result in greater self-generated reinforcement.

Question 8.7: In the context of education, there is often a conflict between the academic and conduct standards modeled by adults and those modeled by peers. Given what you know about motivational processes in modeling, how could children be encouraged to adopt the higher standards of adults?_____

In addition to providing social support, adults must be consistent if children are to adopt modeled standards. Adults sometimes preach one standard for children while adopting a different one for themselves. In some cases, adults hypocritically advocate high standards for children but require less of themselves. In other cases, adults set high standards for themselves but are more lenient with children. Although both forms of inconsistency will reduce the likelihood that high standards will be adopted, hypocrisy has stronger negative effects. Leniency simply encourages lesser standards. However, hypocrisy engenders resentment and encourages children to abandon performance standards and to reward themselves on the basis of expediency (Bandura, 1986). Finally, the chances of children's adopting high standards modeled by adults are increased if the standard is explicitly expressed in words as well as action (Liebert, Hanratty, & Hill, 1969). And when models possess status and social power, the chances of adoption are even better (Mischel & Liebert, 1967).

Social Referential Comparisons   Sometimes judging the adequacy of one's performance against internal standards requires comparisons with the performance of others. For example, a student who scores 123 on an examination and who aspires to be in the top of his class will have no basis for self-appraisal without knowing how others have performed. Comparisons with others may take different forms. For some activities, norms based upon representative groups are used to determine one's relative standing. This type of normative comparison is involved when percentile scores on a standardized achievement test are used to judge students' academic performance.

More often, people compare themselves with particular peers in similar situations. For example, a student may compare his performance with that of one or more classmates. Usually, students will choose to compare themselves with those whom they regard as similar or slightly higher in ability because such comparisons provide realistic challenges while ensuring some degree of success. However, some students may attempt to boost their self-appraisals by selecting for comparison classmates lower in ability, whom they can easily surpass. In other cases, students may pit themselves unfavorably against classmates much higher in ability. We shall come back to these problems when we consider dysfunctional self-evaluation systems.

A third type of referential judgment involves comparing present and past levels of performance. Such self-comparison can lead to changes in standards. That is, after a level of performance has been consistently attained, it is no longer challenging. Thus, people tend to raise their performance standards after experiencing success and to lower their standards after experiencing repeated failure on a task. Self-comparison can provide the personal challenges and success experiences necessary for self-development without the animosity and conflict often aroused by social comparison. Teachers can structure classroom activities to encourage students to judge themselves in terms of their own capabilities and standards rather than by comparing themselves with others. However, as Bandura (1986) points out, social comparison is inevitable in competitive, individualistic societies such as ours.

Valuation of Activities   In order for self-appraisals to influence behavior, they must involve valued activities. The more valued the activity, the greater the likelihood that the resulting self-appraisal will elicit either self-approval or criticism. For example, when people believe that a task taps their intellectual creativity, they are likely to be self-approving for appraisals of high performance and self-criticizing for appraisals of low performance. However, when people believe that a task taps nonintellectual skills, they are less likely to react evaluatively to either high or low performance (Simon, 1979).

Performance Attribution   Another factor influencing the effectiveness of self-appraisals is how people perceive the causes of their behavior. People are more likely to react positively (or negatively) to self-appraisals if they ascribe their successes (or failures) to their own abilities and efforts. They do not derive much self-satisfaction (or self-blame) when they view their performance as due to external factors. For example, Bryon is likely to take pride in and reward himself for his high score on the weekly math test if he perceives that his performance was due to his ability in math and to the time he put in studying. On the other hand, Cindy, who made the same grade as Bryon, doesn't feel much satisfaction because she believes her performance is due to the extra help the teacher gave her that week. Incidentally, it is not accidental that it was the girl in the example who attributed her success to a situational factor. Research indicates that in stereotypically male activities, girls are more prone than boys to attribute success to external factors and failure to internal factors (Parsons, Ruble, Hodges, & Small, 1976). We shall discuss the topic of performance attribution (including gender differences) in more detail in Chapter 9.

Self-reaction

The final process involved in self-regulation is self-reaction, which is possible after a person has observed his behavior and appraised it against some internal standard of performance. Self-reaction involves creating consequences (rewards and punishments) for one's own behavior depending upon how it measures up to an internal standard. Thus, a person pursues actions that produce positive self-reactions (rewards) and avoids behaving in ways that produce negative self-reactions (punishments). Bandura (1986) suggests that self-generated consequences affect behavior through their incentive or motivational function and can take the form of tangible outcomes or self-evaluative reactions.

Tangible Self-incentives   People often get themselves to do things they would otherwise put off or avoid by making tangible incentives dependent upon task completion. For example, while writing this book, one of the authors made going to movies and other desired leisure activities dependent upon writing so many pages a week. Research indicates that people who reward their own attainments accomplish more than people who perform the same activities but without rewarding themselves (e.g., Bandura & Perloff, 1967). Moreover, self-incentives are at least as effective as externally arranged incentives (Bandura & Perloff, 1967).

Self-evaluative Incentives   Most people value their self-approval for a job well done more highly than they value tangible rewards.

Question 8.8: How do you suppose that evaluative self-reactions come to have motivational force? (Hint: Consider self-approval and self-criticism as secondary reinforcers.)_____

_____

_____

In many instances, people exert influences over their behavior by using both evaluative and tangible self-incentives. For example, the author who got to go to the movies after writing so many pages a week also felt a sense of self-satisfaction at having achieved a self-set goal. Moreover, most authors make revisions and improvements based on self-evaluative reactions to what they have written.

DYSFUNCTIONAL SELF-REGULATIVE SYSTEMS

When working well, the self-regulative system not only serves to guide behavior but is a major source of personal satisfaction, interest, and self-esteem. However, self-regulation can also be a source of misery. We all know individuals who drive themselves to achieve impossibly high goals or who are excessively self-critical. In extreme cases, dysfunction in one or more of the subprocesses of self-regulation can operate to produce depression.

People who are depressed do not monitor their performance attainments accurately. They are prone to distort their perceptions (or recollections) of their performance in self-diminishing directions. Nondepressed people, by comparison, tend to distort observed performance in self-enhancing directions. Thus, despite achieving the same pattern of outcomes, depressed individuals underestimate their successes and overestimate their failures, whereas nondepressed people remember their successes well but underestimate their failures (Bandura, 1986).

Compared with nondepressed individuals, depressed people tend to set higher standards for themselves and evaluate their performances as poorer for similar accomplishments (e.g., Golin & Terrell, 1977). Depression is most likely to result when internal standards of accomplishment are set well above one's perceived efficacy to attain them (Kanfer & Zeiss, 1983).

Depressed people are also not very kind to themselves when judging their accomplishments. For example, while nondepressed people tend to attribute failure to situational factors, depressed persons tend to see themselves as responsible for failure (Kuiper, 1978). Finally, after comparable levels of performance, depressed people generally evaluate themselves less favorably and reward themselves less than do nondepressed people. The depressed also punish themselves more severely for poor performance (e.g., Rehm, 1982).

The correlations observed between dysfunctional processes of self-regulation and depression need to be interpreted with caution. That is, as Bandura (1986) implies, it may be that distorted self-observation, overly high standard setting, and excessively critical self-reaction produce depression. On the other hand, it may be that people who are depressed (for whatever reason) also tend to be more negative and harsh when it comes to observing and regulating their own behavior. Nevertheless, it seems apparent that effective self-regulation is crucial for students' success in almost all types of endeavor. Therefore, helping students acquire the skills involved in self-regulation is an important task for teachers.

IMPLICATIONS OF SELF-REGULATION FOR TEACHING

Teachers can do much to help students develop the capacity for self-regulation by teaching them goal setting, performance appraisal, and self-reinforcement.

Goal Setting

Teachers can help students identify and use appropriate internal evaluative standards by teaching them to set goals that are *specific, proximal,* and *challenging.* Specific goals (e.g., complete a page of math problems with no more than one error) clearly designate the type and amount of effort needed and provide unambiguous standards for judging performance. Specific goals are much more effective in directing behavior than global or general goals (e.g., do a good job on the math assignment) (Locke, Shaw, Saari, & Latham, 1981). Proximal goals refer to immediate performance on tasks (e.g., completing the page of math problems in the next 20 minutes) rather than to some distant future goal (e.g., receiving an "A" in math). Focusing on proximal goals mobilizes effort in the here and now, whereas focusing on distant goals can lull students into putting off immediate effort. Finally, goals that are effective in directing behavior are challenging (difficult but reachable) rather than too easy or too difficult.

Research indicates that getting students to set the kind of goals described above and making a commitment to reach those goals increases their performance (Bandura & Schunk, 1981). However, if goals are to be specific and challenging for all students, different students will need different goals. In the context of *individual goal-setting conferences,* students can be given guidance in setting challenging but realistic goals that require reasonable effort. Additionally, teachers can help students to set specific subgoals that will enable them to reach a desired long-range goal. In the process of doing that, teachers can point out the connection between achieving intermediate and ultimate goals (Bandura & Schunk, 1981).

Teachers can model goal setting. In modeling goal setting, a teacher can point out how she selects attainable yet challenging goals, describing how goals that are too easy and those that are unattainable can be impractical and frustrating. She can emphasize self-knowledge when setting goals and focus on setting self-improvement goals. After showing them how to set realistic goals, the teacher can provide students with many opportunities to practice goal setting.

Performance Appraisal

Teachers can help students in assessing their progress toward goals by *teaching them to use appropriate standards for judging their level of success.* In the case of specific performance goals (e.g., obtaining at least 80 percent correct on comprehension questions following a reading assignment), students can be taught to compare their performance with the absolute standard in order to appraise their success. In the case of self-improvement goals (e.g., raising one's previous score on comprehension questions), students can be directed to use comparisons with past performance to determine success. Both of these standards (absolute performance and self-improvement) can be encouraged, instead of comparisons with peers which can foster unrealistic goal setting. In general, it is a good idea to promote self-improvement goals because research indicates that students work harder and enjoy their classes more when they are striving for self-improvement goals (Ames & Archer, 1988).

It is essential to *provide students with accurate but encouraging feedback* to help them appraise their progress toward goals. Errors need to be pointed out so that they can be corrected. However, general evaluative comments should stress students' progress and encourage them to note improvements over past performance. Providing detailed, specific feedback is especially important in the case of complex tasks (e.g., compositions, research projects, laboratory experiments) that are graded on a qualitative rather than objective basis. For example, merely assigning a letter grade to a composition will not help a student appraise and improve his performance. But a student can benefit immensely from feedback concerning the relevance of the content, organization of the composition, structuring of paragraphs, variety and appropriateness of sentence structures and vocabulary, grammar, spelling, and punctuation (Good & Brophy, 1990).

Self-reinforcement

Many students will habitually reinforce themselves for making progress toward goals. However, some students need to be encouraged to take credit for their successes (that is, to attribute their accomplishments to their ability and hard work). Modeling self-reinforcement for accomplishing self-set goals is a valuable technique. The teacher can demonstrate the practice of making both tangible incentives and positive self-reactions dependent upon one's goal achievement and, in the process, point out the connection between effort and success in achieving realistic goals. Table 8.4 summarizes techniques for fostering self-regulation.

BANDURA'S POSITION ON THE CORE ISSUES

1. *What is learned according to the theory?* Bandura is concerned with the acquisition of cognitive representations of behavior through observation. His theory specifies four processes involved in learning through observation—attention,

TABLE 8.4   FOSTERING SELF-REGULATION

Teach	Function	Activity
Goal setting	Helps students to set specific, proximal, challenging goals	Modeling; individual goal-setting conferences
Performance appraisal	Enables students to use absolute and self-improvement standards for judging performance	Provide specific feedback that is accurate and detailed and general feedback that is encouraging
Self-reinforcement	Helps students to attribute success to ability and effort and to reinforce themselves for progress toward their goals	Model ability/effort attributions; model self-reinforcement

retention, production, and motivation. While Bandura stresses the cognitive aspects of learning, he is also very much concerned with factors governing the translation of cognition into behavior. Thus, his theory integrates cognitive and behavioral approaches to learning.

In this chapter, we have emphasized the acquisition of cognitive representations of behaviors important for performing academic tasks. However, Bandura has also investigated the darker side of observational learning which works to our detriment. For example, studies of child abusers consistently show that these parents were themselves abused when they were children. Moreover, studies of juvenile delinquents and criminals show that they acquire much of their antisocial habits from observing their parents (Bandura & Walters, 1959). Bandura also points out that "both children and adults have unlimited opportunities to learn from televised modeling aggressive coping styles and the whole gamut of felonious behavior within the comfort of their homes" (Bandura, 1973, p. 101). Finally, many phobias are acquired not through direct conditioning but through observational learning (Bandura & Menlove, 1968; Jones, 1924). For example, the child who observes his sibling's panic at going to school may vicariously acquire a school phobia. Thus, it is safe to say that any complete view of learning must take into account humans' tremendous capacity to learn through observation.

2. *What is the relative emphasis on environmental versus organismic factors in learning?* Bandura's notion of reciprocal determinism indicates that factors inside the organism (person variables) and environmental factors interact in influencing behavior and are, in turn, shaped by behavior. Compared with behavioral theorists, Bandura places much more emphasis on cognitive and affective factors, while compared with cognitive theorists, he emphasizes environmental influences more strongly. He would argue, no doubt, that it makes no sense to consider either the person, his behavior, or the environment in isolation because these factors are so tightly linked.

3. *What is the source of motivation for learning?* People are motivated to perform modeled activities when they expect desirable outcomes for doing so and when they believe that they are capable of performing the behavior. Thus, outcome expectations and self-efficacy are the major sources of motivation. The outcomes that motivate performance can be arranged by other people or can be controlled by the learner through self-reinforcement. It should be remembered, however, that Bandura believes that learning (i.e., formation of a cognitive representation) can occur in the absence of either internal or external incentives. Motivational processes are primarily important in facilitating the performance of behaviors learned through observation.

4. *How does transfer occur?* Bandura's notion of transfer is similar to that of information processing theory. That is . . . no wait, let's ask you.

Question 8.9: If you can recall how transfer occurs in information processing theory, you know how it occurs in social cognitive theory.

---

5. *What are important variables in instruction?* The important variables in instruction are those that enhance the processes of observational learning. These are the modeling practices that optimize attention, retention, and reproduction. Motivational techniques, such as providing direct and vicarious reinforcement and boosting students' self-efficacy, are important for enhancing students' performance of activities learned through modeling.

REVIEW OF MAJOR POINTS

1 Social learning theory is a framework that has encompassed the work of many theorists. The major proponent of this approach to learning is Albert Bandura, whose social cognitive theory incorporates features of both behavioral and cognitive explanations of human behavior.

2 Like behavioral theorists, Bandura is concerned with behavioral change. However, he differs from behavioral theorists in his claim that learning can occur through observation as well as through direct experience, and in his claim that reinforcement is not necessary for learning. Like cognitive theorists, Bandura postulates mental events that intervene between stimuli and responses. However, unlike cognitive theorists he is interested in the mechanisms that translate cognition into behavior.

3 Bandura sees behavior as being determined by factors in both the environment and in the person. In turn, behavior partially shapes personal and environmental factors. He called this three-way interaction between person, environment, and behavior triadic reciprocality.

4 People acquire cognitive representations of behavior by observing models.

Modeled behavior transmits information that can result in (1) a new skill in the observer (observational learning effect), (2) inhibition or disinhibition of some previously learned behavior, or (3) facilitation of some already acquired behavior (elicitation effect).

5 Bandura distinguishes between learning from observation, which entails attention, retention, and reproduction processes, and performance of modeled activities, which is governed by motivational processes. Reinforcers, which can be direct, vicarious, or self-generated, have both an informative and a motivational function rather than automatically strengthening the behaviors that they follow.

6 Self-efficacy refers to a person's sense that he can or cannot perform in a given situation. Such perceptions influence one's choice of activities, one's persistence on difficult tasks, and one's thoughts and emotions while attempting tasks. Knowledge about one's efficacy comes from performance attainments, vicarious experiences, verbal persuasion, and physiological states.

7 People can learn from physically present models or from symbolic models including books, instructions, pictures, and film or TV characters. The developmental level of the learner influences the relative effectiveness of live and symbolic models. Generally, young children tend to learn better from live models, while older children and adults can learn either that way or from verbal descriptions without the physical presence of a model. Modeling is a good technique for teaching cognitive strategies if the model adequately portrays the covert mental processes involved in the strategy.

8 Bandura posits a capacity for self-direction that allows people to have control over their own behavior through self-generated consequences. Self-regulation involves observing one's own behavior, judging that behavior against internal performance standards, and then reacting either positively or negatively to one's performance. Teachers can help students develop the capacity for self-regulation by teaching them to set specific, proximal, and challenging goals, to use appropriate standards for judging their performance, and to attribute their successes to ability and effort.

9 With regard to the core issues, Bandura asserts that: (1) We learn cognitive representations of behavior through observing models. (2) Learning is equally determined by the interaction of personal, environmental, and behavioral factors. (3) Learning can occur in the absence of incentives or even the intent to learn. However, people are motivated to perform modeled activities when they expect desirable outcomes and when they believe they are capable of performing the behavior. (4) Transfer occurs when cues in a new situation enable retrieval of a symbolic representation of a behavior stored in long-term memory. (5) The important variables in instruction are those that enhance the observational-learning processes of attention, retention, and reproduction, as well as motivational variables such as reinforcement and self-efficacy.

ANSWERS TO QUESTIONS AND EXERCISES

Question 8.1: Shaping is the concept behaviorists use to describe the acquisition of complex new behaviors. It is a process in which the organism is initially reinforced for responses that faintly resemble some target behavior. Then, over time, reinforcement is gradually reserved for behaviors that become increasingly similar to the target behavior until, at last, the target behavior is achieved. This is a very slow, laborious process.

Question 8.2: The difference between observational learning and imitation is the difference between learning and rote performance. Imitation is a process by which one individual simply matches the actions of another, usually close in time. Bandura asserts that modeling is not simply thoughtless repetition of observed behavior. Rather, modeling involves cognitive processes that intervene between one's observations and one's subsequent behavior. Those cognitions help us to fit the observed behavior to the present circumstances. In the case described, observational learning would result in *not* imitating the model. Moreover, in observational learning performance often occurs well after learning. For example, today you might watch the evaluation of a colleague's teaching. You notice that the evaluator praises your colleague's vigorous gestures but criticizes her for smiling constantly. The next time your teaching is evaluated, you will probably try to benefit from your fellow teacher's experience by using a lot of gestures but smiling only occasionally. You learned these things today, but you will demonstrate them much later. Observational learning and imitation are two different things.

Exercise 8.1: 1. Smoking marijuana is deviant by Jan's own standards, but seeing peers do it and thereby gain social prestige and acceptance within the group may well *disinhibit* this behavior. There is really no new learning involved since Jan has seen the act of smoking modeled many times by adults in the society. 2. Seeing others volunteer *facilitates* that response in Jeff. Similarly, if you see someone else put money into the sidewalk Santa's pot, you may be more inclined to give than if that response had not just been modeled. 3. Assembling a water bomb is a new behavior that Kyle *learned through observation.* Dropping it on passersby is a behavior that has been *disinhibited* by seeing the Little Rascals get away with it. Thus, a single modeling episode can produce several effects. 4. Gavin's deviant stealing behavior has been *inhibited,* at least temporarily, by observing his friend receive negative consequences for that behavior.

Question 8.3: Disruptive behaviors tend to occur during high arousal times. Or, if the arousal level of his classmates isn't already high, Johnny's disruptive behavior certainly raises it. Thus, arousal conditions are optimal for modeling during Johnny's "bad" behavior. Also, disruptive acts are clearly more distinctive than cooperative behavior that tends to blend into normal classroom routine. Johnny's teacher probably contributes to the problem by ignoring Johnny's good behavior and reprimanding or commenting upon his disruptive behavior.

Question 8.4: Although learning is inferred from performance, as we indicated in Chapter 1, there are indices of learning that are independent of *motor* performance. Degree of observational learning can be measured in several ways. One way is to simply have the students verbally describe what they have learned through observation (Bandura, Jeffery, & Bachicha, 1974). Another way is to give students a recognition test in which they have to pick out the modeled prototype from incorrect alternatives. Students could also be asked to construct the modeled pattern by rearranging scrambled photographs of the component acts. Research using multiple measures of acquisition show that people can learn by observing before they actually perform (Bandura & Jeffery, 1973; Rosenthal & Zimmerman, 1978).

Question 8.5: You may have taught your son that such behavior toward homosexuals is acceptable. You might protest this conclusion. After all, *you* did not engage in the behavior; you didn't even express approval of the teenagers' behavior. So how did you teach your son that such behavior is acceptable? By *saying nothing.* Not commenting negatively on the model's behavior may amount to implicit approval of that behavior (Donnerstein & Donnerstein, 1978). You may have inadvertently increased the likelihood that your son will behave in a similar manner. Think about that the next time you and your child see aggressive or discriminatory behavior live or "at the movies."

Question 8.6: Illusory boosts in self-efficacy can be quickly dispelled by one's actual performance. But those who have been persuaded of their inefficacy tend to avoid engaging in challenging activities and give up quickly in the face of difficulties. So Cathy might tend to avoid math assignments whenever she could and give up quickly when she couldn't avoid them. By restricting choices and undermining effort, self-disbeliefs can create their own validation (Bandura, 1986).

Exercise 8.2: The following is an abbreviated plan for modeling the toss and serve in tennis to a junior high school student of average athletic ability (adapted from Glover & Bruning, 1990).

Step in modeling	Draw attention to	Verbal comments
1. Holding ball correctly	How hand grips ball	"Hold the ball like this, between the thumb and first two fingers."
2. Racket back, preparing for the serve	How elbow is lifted; position of racket head	"Lift your elbow like this. Scratch your back with your racket."
3. Toss (further steps as needed)	Lifting of the ball	"Imagine you're pushing the ball up a pipe."

Retention Retention would be aided by the images conveyed in the verbal comments. Also the student would be instructed to visualize himself performing the sequence before actually performing.

Practice/feedback Following observation of the model and cognitive rehearsal, student would practice the toss and serve. The instructor would point out errors and provide corrective modeling. Feedback would also point out the student's progress and gains. Student would be encouraged to watch the ball after serving to see the outcome.

Motivational techniques Before beginning the demonstration, the instructor would point out that a good serve will allow the student to win more games. Praise would be used throughout practice and feedback to reinforce correct behavior. Verbal persuasion would be used to increase student's self-efficacy.

Exercise 8.3: Below is an abbreviated sample-modeling plan for teaching the key-word strategy to a ninth-grade student taking Spanish. The strategy will be modeled using the Spanish-English pair, "Pato-Duck."

Step in modeling	Draw attention to	Verbal comments
1. Forming the key word	How key word is a familiar word that sounds like part of the Spanish word	"The Spanish word 'Pato' sounds like the English word 'Pot.'"
2. Rehearsing the Spanish word/key-word connection	How to subvocalize the word/key-word connection	"'Pato-Pot,' 'Pato-Pot,' 'Pato-Pot.' It is necessary to rehearse so that the Spanish word elicits the key word strongly and rapidly."
3. Making up an image or sentence linking the key word/English translation	A drawing of a duck wearing a pot on its head	"In your mind's eye, see a duck wearing a pot on its head. So when you see 'Pato,' think of 'pot' and see the pot on the duck's head."

Retention The student cognitive rehearses the steps in the key-word strategy, using a code such as *first key word, second rehearse, third image.*

Practice/feedback The student is given a list of Spanish-English pairs to learn and is asked to write down his key word and image or sentence for each pair. Instructor suggests key words when student can't generate one or suggests a better key word if student's key word is not adequate. The list should contain pairs for which the method is not appropriate. For example, pairs that are naturally very easy to remember and pairs for which it is not possible to generate a familiar key word. These should be pointed out to the student so that he learns when to use the method and when not to use it. The student is tested over the list. The instructor points out how high performance is when using the key-word technique. The student could also be given a list of Spanish vocabulary to learn without using the key word, so that he can experience by comparison how much the key word helps his retention.

Motivational techniques Point out to students how the key-word technique will help them remember the translations of Spanish words. Also, indicate that using the key-word method requires some mental effort but that it is more fun than rote memorization and more effective. Praise students whenever they use the key-word method to learn new vocabulary words.

Question 8.7: Students are more likely to choose adult standards over lower ones modeled by peers if they are praised, admired, and honored for seeking excellence. Vicarious influences also support standard setting. Thus, observing others being recognized and publicly rewarded for pursuing high standards encourages similar behavior. It is no accident that effective schools are ones in which standards of excellence are modeled and socially supported.

Question 8.8: Self-evaluative reactions such as self-praise and self-criticism become reinforcers by being paired with primary reinforcers. People usually treat themselves well and think pleasant thoughts when they feel a sense of self-approval. They usually treat themselves badly and think unpleasant thoughts when they feel a sense of self-disapproval. Thus, through classical conditioning, positive self-reactions come to signal rewarding experiences while negative self-reactions become aversive. If people did not treat themselves differently following self-approving and self-censuring evaluations, such reactions would not acquire motivating power.

Question 8.9: A concept or skill learned in one situation will transfer to another situation provided there are cues within the new situation that will lead to retrieval of the learned material. Thus, good transfer requires (1) that students engage in elaborative rehearsal of modeled activities during acquisition and (2) that they practice modeled activities in a variety of situations. Varied practice situations ensure that a wide range of retrieval cues become associated with the cognitive representation of the new skill.

REFERENCES

Allport, G. W. (1961). *Pattern and growth in personality.* New York: Holt, Rinehart and Winston.

Ames, C., & Archer, J. (1988). Achievement goals in the classroom: Students' learning strategies and motivation processes. *Journal of Educational Psychology, 80,* 260–267.

Bandura, A. (1965). Vicarious processes: A case of no-trial learning. In L. Berkowitz (Ed.), *Advances in experimental social psychology* (Vol. 2). New York: Academic Press.

Bandura, A. (1973). *Aggression: A social learning analysis.* Englewood Cliffs, NJ: Prentice-Hall.

Bandura, A. (1976). Self-reinforcement: Theoretical and methodological considerations. *Behaviorism, 4,* 135–155.

Bandura, A. (1977). Self-efficacy: Toward a unifying theory of behavioral change. *Psychological Review, 84,* 191–215.

Bandura, A. (1986). *Social foundations of thought and action: A social cognitive theory.* Englewood Cliffs, NJ: Prentice-Hall.

Bandura, A., & Adams, N. E. (1977). Analysis of self-efficacy theory of behavioral change. *Cognitive Therapy and Research, 1,* 287–308.

Bandura, A., Adams, N. E., & Beyer, J. (1977). Cognitive processes mediating behavioral change. *Journal of Personality and Social Psychology, 35,* 125–129.

Bandura, A., & Jeffery, R. W. (1973). Role of symbolic coding and rehearsal processes in observational learning. *Journal of Personality and Social Psychology, 26,* 122–130.

Bandura, A., Jeffery, R. W., & Bachicha, D. L. (1974). Analysis of memory codes and cumulative rehearsal in observational learning. *Journal of Research in Personality, 7,* 295–305.

Bandura, A., & Kupers, C. J. (1964). Transmission of patterns of self-reinforcement through modeling. *Journal of Abnormal and Social Psychology, 69,* 1–9.

Bandura, A., & Menlove, F. L. (1968). Factors determining vicarious extinction of avoidance behavior through symbolic modeling. *Journal of Personality and Social Psychology, 8,* 99–108.

Bandura, A., & Mischel, W. (1965). The influence of models in modifying delay of gratification patterns. *Journal of Personality and Social Psychology, 2,* 698–705.

Bandura, A., & Perloff, B. (1967). Relative efficacy of self-monitored and externally imposed reinforcement systems. *Journal of Personality and Social Psychology, 7,* 111–116.

Bandura, A., Ross, D., & Ross, S. A. (1963a). Imitation of film-mediated aggressive models. *Journal of Abnormal and Social Psychology, 66,* 3–11.

Bandura, A., Ross, D., & Ross, S. A. (1963b). Vicarious reinforcement and imitative learning. *Journal of Abnormal and Social Psychology, 67,* 601–607.

Bandura, A., & Schunk, D. (1981). Cultivating competence, self-efficacy, and intrinsic interest through proximal self-motivation. *Journal of Personality and Social Psychology, 41,* 586–598.

Bandura, A., & Walters, R. H. (1959). *Adolescent aggression.* New York: Ronald Press.

Bandura, A., & Walters, R. H. (1963). *Social learning and personality development.* New York: Holt, Rinehart and Winston.

Brown, S. D. (1980). Videotape feedback: Effects on assertive performance and subjects' perceived competence and satisfaction. *Psychological Reports, 47,* 455–461.

Brown, I., Jr., & Inouye, D. K. (1978). Learned helplessness through modeling: The role of perceived similarity in competence. *Journal of Personality and Social Psychology, 36,* 900–908.

Cattell, R. B. (1966). *The scientific analysis of personality.* Chicago: Aldine.

Corbin, C. (1972). Mental practice. In W. Morgan (Ed.), *Erogenic aids and muscular performance.* New York: Academic Press.

Dollard, J., Doob, L. W., Miller, N., Mowrer, O.H., & Sears, R. R. (1939). *Frustration and aggression.* New Haven, CT: Yale University Press.

Donnerstein, M., & Donnerstein, E. (1978). Direct and vicarious censure in the control of interracial aggression. *Journal of Personality, 46,* 162–175.

Dowrick, P. W. (1983). Self modeling. In P. W. Dowrick & S. J. Biggs (Eds.), *Using video: Psychological and social applications.* London: Wiley.

Glover, J. A., & Bruning, R. H. (1990). *Educational psychology: Principles and applications.* Glenview, IL: Scott Foresman.

Golin, S., & Terrell, F. (1977). Motivational and associative aspects of mild depression in skill and chance tasks. *Journal of Abnormal Psychology, 86,* 389–401.

Good, T. L., & Brophy, J. E. (1990). *Educational psychology: A realistic approach.* New York: Longman.

Jones, M. C. (1924). The elimination of children's fears. *Journal of Experimental Psychology, 7,* 382–390.

Kanfer, R., & Zeiss, A. M. (1983). Depression, interpersonal standard-setting and judgments of self-efficacy. *Journal of Abnormal Psychology, 92,* 319–329.

Kirschenbaum, D. S., & Karoli, P. (1977). When self-regulation fails: Tests of some preliminary hypotheses. *Journal of Consulting and Clinical Psychology, 45,* 1116–1125.

Kuiper, N. A. (1978). Depression and causal attributions for success and failure. *Journal of Personality and Social Psychology, 36,* 236–246.

Liebert, R. M., Hanratty, M., & Hill, J. H. (1969). Effects of rule structure and training method on the adoption of a self-imposed standard. *Child Development, 40,* 93–101.

Locke, E. A., Shaw, K. N., Saari, L. M., & Latham, G. P. (1981). Goal setting and task performance: 1969–1980. *Psychological Bulletin, 90,* 125–152.

Mahoney, M. J., Moore, B. S., Wade, T. C., & Moura, N. G. M. (1973). The effects of continuous and intermittent self-monitoring on academic behavior. *Journal of Consulting and Clinical Psychology, 41,* 65–69.

Marston, A. R. (1965). Imitation, self-reinforcement, and reinforcement of another person. *Journal of Personality and Social Psychology, 2,* 255–261.

Meichenbaum, D. H. (1977). *Cognitive-behavior modification: An integrative approach.* New York: Plenum.

Miller, N. E., & Dollard, J. (1941). *Social learning and imitation.* New Haven, CT: Yale University Press.

Mischel, W., & Liebert, R. M. (1967). The role of power in the adoption of self-reward patterns. *Child Development, 38,* 673–683.

Parsons, J. E., Ruble, D. N., Hodges, K. L., & Small, A. W. (1976). Cognitive-developmental factors in emerging sex differences in achievement-related expectancies. *The Journal of Social Issues, 32,* 47–62.

Rehm, L. P. (1982). Self-management in depression. In P. Karoli & F. H. Kanfer (Eds.), *Self-management and behavior change: From theory to practice.* New York: Pergamon.

Richardson, A. (1967). Mental practice: A review and discussion. Part I. *Research Quarterly, 38,* 95–107.

Romanczyk, R. G. (1974). Self-monitoring in the treatment of obesity: Parameters of reactivity. *Behavior Therapy, 5,* 531–540.

Rosenthal, T. L., & Zimmerman, B. J. (1978). *Social learning and cognition.* New York: Academic Press.

Sackett, R. S. (1935). The relationship between amount of symbolic rehearsal and retention of a maze habit. *Journal of General Psychology, 13,* 113–130.

Sarason, I. G. (1975). Anxiety and self-preoccupation. In I. G. Sarason & D. C. Spielberger (Eds.), *Stress and anxiety* (Vol. 2). Washington, DC: Hemisphere.

Schunk, D. H. (1981). Modeling and attributional effects on children's achievement: A self-efficacy analysis. *Journal of Educational Psychology, 73,* 93–105.

Schunk, D. H. (1984). Self-efficacy perspective on achievement behavior. *Educational Psychologist, 19,* 48–58.

Simon, K. M. (1979). Self-evaluative reactions: The role of personal valuation of the activity. *Cognitive Therapy and Research, 3,* 111–116.

Skinner, B. F. (1971). *Beyond freedom and dignity.* New York: Knopf.

Thomas, R. M. (1992). *Comparing theories of child development.* Belmont, CA: Wadsworth.

Vasta, R. (1976). Feedback and fidelity: Effects of contingent consequences on accuracy of imitation. *Journal of Experimental Child Psychology, 21,* 98–108.

9

TRADITIONAL AND CURRENT VIEWS OF MOTIVATION

OBJECTIVES

1. Distinguish between extrinsic and intrinsic motivation.
2. Distinguish between the assumed sources of motivation for classical conditioning, operant conditioning, and social learning theory.
3. Describe strategies for motivating students from the perspective of classical conditioning, operant conditioning, and social learning theory.
4. Distinguish between the assumed sources of motivation for Piagetian theory, Case's neo-Piagetian theory, and Vygotsky's theory.
5. Describe strategies for motivating students from the perspective of Piagetian theory, Case's neo-Piagetian theory, and Vygotsky's theory.
6. Define "achievement motivation" and describe how it may influence achievement behaviors.
7. Describe the three dimensions of causal attributes and their potential effects on students' self-esteem, affect, and future expectations.
8. Define learned helplessness and its potential effects on student achievement behaviors.
9. Describe how instruction can influence the types of attributions that students employ within achievement settings.
10. Identify two contrasting types of goal orientation, their relation to achievement motivation, and their potential effects on related cognitive processes and achievement behaviors.
11. Describe how instruction can influence the type of goal orientation adopted by students within achievement settings.

Thus far, the chapters in this book have focused our attention on the learning and development process. As a teacher it is not only important to understand *how* your students learn, but also *why* they desire to learn certain things. For example, a football coach might spend months carefully teaching his players how to execute various plays. While this knowledge is essential, an equally important aspect of coaching is to motivate players to give their maximum effort. That is also true of education, where even the most thoughtfully designed curricula and the most modern teaching methods will not by themselves insure that learning occurs. If students lack the incentive to learn, little learning will occur.

In our previous discussion of the different learning and development theories, we identified the assumed source of motivation for each theory. For example, Piagetian theory assumes that we all have a built-in motivational system—equilibration—which motivates us to reduce cognitive conflict between our existing knowledge of the world and our current experiences. This, in turn, is responsible for changes in our cognitive development. In contrast, operant conditioning assumes that the consequences of our past behaviors provide our present source of motivation. We will choose to become actively involved in a task if related behavior was rewarded in the past.

For all theories of learning and development, motivation has a directive, sustaining quality that energizes and maintains our learning activities. It influences the tasks we choose to get involved in, the nature of our involvement in those tasks, and how much energy and persistence we put into them. For example, a motivated student will not only attend to instruction but will engage in activities such as repeated practice and elaboration that facilitate learning. Also, a motivated student will, when faced with roadblocks, be persistent and expend the effort to complete the learning task.

This chapter will follow a slightly different format from most of the previous ones. The first half of this chapter will review the role of motivation in each previously described theory, its assumed source, and instructional strategies that will foster its development. Then, in the second half of the chapter, we will review current views of motivation and their implications for teaching. This review will focus on specific motivational variables that influence the process of learning. For example, how will attributing our failures to a lack of ability influence our performance within the classroom? Given the somewhat different structure of this chapter, there will be no attempt to categorize the motivational theories and views presented here in terms of the five core issues reviewed in Chapter 1.

SOURCES OF MOTIVATION

To help compare and contrast the way motivation is explained by our various learning and development theories, we have chosen to categorize the theories according to those concerned primarily with extrinsic motivation and those concerned primarily with intrinsic motivation.

Extrinsic and Intrinsic Motivation

Heider (1958) was the first to propose a distinction between intrinsic and extrinsic motivation, which he described as personal and impersonal, respectively. According to Heider, behaviors that occur due to **intrinsic (personal) motives** are intentional and under the individual's control, while behaviors that occur due to **extrinsic (impersonal) motives** are not intentional and are under the control of some external source. An example of an intrinsic motive would be to voluntarily engage in an activity such as piano practice in order to become more competent at it. Alternatively, an example of an extrinsic motive would be to engage in piano practice in order to receive a reward from someone.

In recent years, Deci (1975) and Deci and Ryan (1985) have further elaborated on these two types of motives. According to these theorists, an *extrinsically motivated* individual is driven to obtain certain rewards that originate outside him. For example, the desire for extra recess may drive a student to do his homework on time, since his teacher has arbitrarily decided to tie homework performance to extra recess. However, the outcome (extra recess time) originates externally (from the teacher) and it has no natural relation to the student behavior (homework performance).

In contrast, an *intrinsically motivated* individual is driven by a need to display competency or exercise some control over the environment (Deci, 1975; Deci & Ryan, 1985). For example, a student who longs to know more about a particular subject would be intrinsically motivated to seek books and other resources in order to increase her knowledge of the subject. Notice that the outcome is internal (increased knowledge) and is very much related to the behavior of reading and seeking out sources of information.

The extrinsically motivated student is a passive player in the learning situation and will exhibit appropriate behavior only when attractive incentives are present or when compliance will allow her to avoid something aversive. For example, as long as an extrinsically motivated student is given extra privileges when she aces her exams, she is likely to continue studying for them; however, as soon as the privileges are withdrawn, she will cease doing so. In contrast, an intrinsically motivated student is an active player in the learning situation, one who feels some control over that situation, and exercises her right to choose. An intrinsically motivated student will study for and attempt to ace exams because she wants to master the material or feels a need to control her environment. Finally, an intrinsically motivated student will perceive that she has total or partial control of the learning situation while an extrinsically motivated student will not.

Exercise 9.1: After each of the following descriptions, please identify whether the individual is intrinsically or extrinsically motivated and why.

1. Timothy decides not to throw a snowball at a passing car because he knows that he will be punished for doing so.

_____

_____

2. June decides to work overtime to become more proficient at her current task.

_____

_____

3. Billy studies hard for his exam over the weekend because if he does well on the exam, he will receive extra allowance from his parents.

_____

_____

4. To be better prepared to deal with the outdoors, Jan enrolls in a Sierra Club class on orienteering and camping.

_____

_____

Exercise 9.2: Before we review and discuss the sources of motivation for the learning and development theories presented in previous chapters, please take a moment to speculate on those sources. You may want to go back to the previous chapters to briefly review each theory. Please justify your answers.

1. Classical and operant conditioning: _____

_____

2. Information processing theory: _____

_____

3. Piagetian theory: _____

_____

4. Social learning theory: _____

_____

5. Vygotskian theory: _____

_____

6. Case's neo-Piagetian theory: _____

_____

LEARNING AND DEVELOPMENT THEORIES AND SOURCES OF MOTIVATION

In addition to discussing the source of motivation within each of the previously presented theories, the following section will identify important instructional implications for motivating students.

Classical and Operant Conditioning

As indicated in Chapter 2, classical conditioning is responsible for many of our physical and emotional responses to particular situations. According to classical conditioning, the repeated pairing of an unconditioned stimulus (UCS) and a conditioned stimulus (CS) will elicit a specific response in the presence of the CS. For example, losing your balance or falling (UCS) typically produces anxiety and fear (unconditioned response—UCR). Consequently, if you are repeatedly pushed into water, you will eventually associate water (CS) with falling and anxiety (CR), and will avoid water. The association of the water and anxiety occurs somewhat automatically. Basically, if an organism is awake and somewhat alert, learning occurs whether or not the organism wants it to. So motivation plays little role in initial learning. However, once conditioned, it may take considerable motivation for people to become free of their conditioned responses.

According to operant conditioning, whether or not an individual is motivated and exhibits a particular behavior is a function of his reinforcement history. For example, a student will behave properly in class if the teacher has followed previous occurrences of appropriate behavior with reinforcement (e.g., increased recess time). According to operant conditioning, reinforcement strengthens responses automatically. That is, internal processes or cognitive factors do not influence the effects of reinforcement. *The environment is in control of the individual's level of motivation; in other words, the emphasis of this theory is on extrinsic motivation.* A student, then, does not have much control over his level of motivation and is a passive player within the learning sequence.

Instructional Implications   Motivating a student from the classical and operant conditioning perspective requires analyzing and manipulating the student's environment. As a first step, teachers should analyze their classroom situation and identify those activities and events which students voluntarily choose to do with some frequency. These activities can then be used as reinforcers. For example, students may choose to use the computer, read a new book, or just rest during their free time. These voluntary activities can be used as reinforcers that are tied to some desired behavior. Second, teachers should clearly state and make available the rules and regulations of their classroom. Without this, students may behave inappropriately simply because they are unsure of what constitutes proper behavior. For example, by using handouts or posting signs around the room, a teacher can list the classroom rules and regulations (what happens when someone breaks or follows the rules). Third, teachers should use frequent, consistent, specific, and immediate reinforcement whenever the desired behavior is exhibited. For example, to keep students engaged teachers should immediately follow the completion of each part of the task with verbal praise. Finally, to create a positive classroom atmosphere, teachers should associate positive and pleasant events with classroom learning activities. For example, teachers could embed classroom assignments in gamelike activities. The pleasure associated with the activities may eventually transfer to the subject matter itself (e.g., mathematics).

Social Learning Theory

As indicated in Chapter 8, according to social learning theory there are primarily two factors which influence motivation: (1) expectations and (2) personal goals (Bandura, 1986). There are two types of expectations: outcome expectations and efficacy expectations. **Outcome expectations** are what an individual expects to occur as a consequence of his behavior. For example, someone who has carefully reviewed both her class notes and the assigned textbook might expect to do well on a unit exam. Conversely, someone who has spent little time reviewing might expect to do poorly. Specific outcome expectations such as these result not only from the consequences of our own experiences (often self-imposed), but from our vicarious experiences (watching others being reinforced and punished) and from descriptions of possible consequences. From these different sources, we pick up informational and motivational cues that result in specific outcome expectations. When we are reinforced or see someone else reinforced for a specific behavior, we are thereby not only given some information about what constitutes appropriate behavior in that situation but also provided with incentives to behave in that way again. In contrast to this view, operant conditioning states that consequences *automatically* strengthen or weaken behavior. Also according to operant conditioning, only direct consequences will increase our motivation to exhibit particular behaviors.

"Efficacy expectations" (also known as self-efficacy) refers to an individual's judgments regarding his ability to execute specific behaviors. If a person believes he has the ability to be successful at some activity, then he will engage in that behavior, cope with any difficulties that may arise, and be more likely to persist in the face of obstacles or frustrations. Take for example the case of an individual who feels incapable of bargaining within a tense situation such as buying a new car or house. In this situation, even though the outcome expectations (saving money by bargaining) are very attractive, the individual may not choose to bargain because he feels incapable of doing so. Conversely, another individual may have a high level of efficacy concerning his bargaining behavior but may choose not to bargain because there are inadequate incentives (outcome expectations). For example, an individual may feel very capable of bargaining within a tense house-buying situation, but, if he is very wealthy and not particularly concerned about the price, he may have little incentive to do so. According to social learning theory, outcome and efficacy expectations constantly interact to influence an individual's level of motivation for performing a specific behavior.

Question 9.1: Briefly summarize the four factors (described in Chapter 8) which may influence an individual's efficacy expectations.

The second factor that influences our level of motivation is *goal setting.* Setting personal goals will focus an individual's activities and increase the degree to which she persists in reaching the goal. Not all goals, however, are equally effective at maintaining high levels of performance and persistence. Specific, moderately difficult, attainable goals are most effective. For example, if a student wants to maintain a high level of motivation for completing a term paper, she would be better off breaking that paper down into manageable subsections (introduction, topic one, topic two, etc., and conclusions) and then completing each section separately. The nature of each section should be specified clearly, as well as the standards for acceptability. *Given the importance of both external factors (consequences) and internal factors (expectancies and goal setting) on motivation, this theory embraces both extrinsic and intrinsic motives.*

Instructional Implications   According to social learning theory, the best way to enhance a student's motivation is to involve her in as many "mastery" experiences as possible. For example, if a student has a history of "failure" experiences, it is very likely that both her efficacy and outcome expectations are low and, consequently, she may avoid classroom activities. In order to motivate this student, the teacher may want to arrange for her a series of easy-to-difficult tasks which, when combined with extensive teacher support, ensures that student a set of mastery experiences. An alternative approach would be for the teacher or peers to model mastery and coping skills. A teacher could ask students who are similar to the unmotivated student to demonstrate mastery skills as well as ways of dealing with difficulties (i.e., coping skills) when trying to master new content. Finally, students should be taught how to set specific, attainable, and moderately difficult goals. For example, if a student wants to complete an extensive and complicated science project, the teacher should help her break the project into manageable subgoals which will lead to completion.

Exercise 9.3: Read the following scenario and describe how you would motivate this student from the perspective of both operant conditioning *and* social learning theory.

Scenario: In math class, John sits behind Annette. John has difficulty with math. Unfortunately, every time he is unable to answer a math question, Annette turns and smirks at him. Even though he has difficulty with math, John enjoys putting problems on the board. Like most students, John dislikes doing homework and presenting to the whole class. His favorite class is geography, primarily because he is smarter in geography than Annette. The day before the class picnic, John intermittently pulls Annette's hair. How might we motivate John to behave in class and not pull Annette's hair?

Operant conditioning:_____

_____

Social learning theory:_____

_____

In summary, classical conditioning, operant conditioning, and social learning theory all emphasize the influence of consequences on an individual's level of motivation. Whereas the two former theories focus exclusively on external factors, the last theory sees the influence of these external factors on motivation and behavior as being mediated by an individual's outcome and efficacy expectations and by his personal goals. All three theories take a reactive approach to the source of motivation in learning. That is, all three are useful for dealing with motivational problems that already exist within the classroom. Although these theories do make suggestions that may help avoid potential motivational problems (e.g., providing clear and precise rules and regulations, helping students set appropriate goals), the techniques derived from them would be most useful for eliminating existing problems.

In contrast to these behavioral theories, the theories of Piaget, Case, and Vygotsky all assume a motivated learner and, consequently, they are most useful for *maintaining* high levels of motivation. In this way, they take a proactive approach to motivation, learning, and development.

Piagetian Theory

Piagetian theory believes that individuals have built-in tendencies that motivate them to interact with the environment and, consequently, to learn and develop. Individuals are inherently active and are constantly attempting to accumulate and organize information about the nature of the world through the processes of assimilation and accommodation. In essence, they actively gather information and seek experiences that will help in their development. When new experiences fail to fit into their existing schemes, there occurs a need to resolve this conflict (i.e., equilibration). This need motivates individuals to further interact with the environment and reorganize their world view as a means of resolving the conflict. *For Piaget, then, individuals are intrinsically motivated to develop.*

Instructional Implications   In order to motivate learning, teachers need to set up learning situations which conflict with students' prior experience and knowledge. In order to reduce their cognitive tension, students will be motivated to seek new information which they can use to restore their lost sense of mental equilibrium. Consequently, instruction should always be at or slightly higher than students' existing developmental level. For example, given a student whose cognitive level is beginning to move from preoperational to concrete operations, it would be appropriate to begin supplementing hands-on counting activities with the rules of addition and subtraction. Having already mastered the process of counting physical objects, the student can now be challenged to count using symbolic representations of physical objects.

Case's Neo-Piagetian Theory

In Case's neo-Piagetian theory, the individual is viewed as a natural problem solver. Motivated by the inherent need to solve problems, we automatically organize our world into problem situations, identify objectives, and then devise appropriate problem-solving strategies. As the problems that we deal with become more and more complicated, the strategies we require to solve them become increasingly sophisticated. *As in Piagetian theory, the individual is intrinsically motivated to develop.*

Instructional Implications   In order to motivate learning, teachers are encouraged to structure learning activities within problem situations. Rather than forcing students into passive listening followed by a strict drill and practice routine, teachers should present new information within the context of a problem situation. For example, when teaching vocabulary, one could indicate that in order to decipher a secret message, certain vocabulary words need to be defined. One could have tight constraints on the process, that is, no access to dictionaries or other sources of definitions. Students would then have to draw on their problem-solving abilities to find alternative ways (contextual cues, word structure, etc.) to identify the mystery words.

As with Piagetian theory, there are important developmental constraints that need to be identified prior to the implementation of motivational strategies. According to Case's theory, both the capacity of short-term storage space (STSS; see Chapter 6) and the stage of cognitive development will constrain the level of tasks presented to learners. For example, with younger children it is important to use problems that are concrete and that do not have multiple dimensions. Otherwise, the student's STSS capacity may be overwhelmed to the point that he loses his problem-solving motivation. No matter how powerful your motivational strategy is, unless these constraints are taken into account, you will not be successful at motivating the student.

Question 9.2: After reading each of the following scenarios, indicate whether it is most consistent with Piagetian or neo-Piagetian views of motivation or both. Also, please justify your answer.

1. When teaching addition and subtraction to first graders, the teacher gives students an array of wooden blocks and asks them to find solutions by reorganizing that array._____

---

2. During a science class, a middle school teacher uses the following demonstration to introduce the idea of gravity: The teacher asks the students to predict which of the following two objects will hit the floor first when dropped from a 10-foot ladder, a balloon filled with air, or a soccer ball (both objects are the same size). Most students will predict that the soccer ball will hit first. However, in reality, the two objects should hit the floor about the same time. The students are asked to explain why._____

_____

3. A physical education teacher is trying to teach middle school students the value of passing the ball while playing soccer. She puts together a game board that consists of a field with movable players. She presents a series of scenarios that represent specific gamelike situations and asks the students to identify the most effective route (via passing) to get the ball up field toward the goal. Students receive points for identifying the most effective passing route. She gradually increases the difficulty of each problem scenario, giving students corrective comments when they do not choose the most effective passing route._____

_____

_____

Vygotsky's Theory

According to this theory, the source of motivation for learning and development resides both in the child and in the child's sociocultural environment. As in Piagetian theory, the child's inherent activity and curiosity impels exploration of his environment, including attention to other humans. The child's adult interactions include observing and imitating the adult's use of cultural tools such as language. Although Vygotsky rarely discusses the idea of motivation directly, one senses that a primary goal of interactions between children and adults is to gradually free the child from dependence on the adult. Both partners work toward this end, the child by internalizing tools for self-regulation and the adult by transferring more and more responsibility for task completion to the child. *The primary motivation, then, appears to be an increase in control over one's environment and an increase in feelings of competence. Thus, this is an intrinsic motivational theory.*

Instructional Implications According to this theory, teachers can build motivation through interactions between a student and a knowledgeable member of the culture (e.g., teacher, another student). As with Piagetian theory, the student brings to the situation an inherent need to explore and be active.

The role of the teacher in channeling and maintaining a student's level of motivation begins by having a clear understanding of the student's zone of proximal development (see Chapter 7), and then providing the student with appropriate support and guidance in moving through this zone. If tasks are below or above the student's zone of proximal development, low levels of motivation may result.

That is, a task that is below the zone will not be challenging and may lead to boredom, while a task above the zone may be frustrating and lead to task avoidance. *As with Piaget and Case, Vygotsky suggests the need to clearly evaluate the student's current level of functioning prior to developing and presenting instruction.* Again, a critical component to maintaining a high level of motivation is to have a clear idea of the developmental level of students within your classroom.

Question 9.3: Please identify the similarities among the motivational views of Piagetian, neo-Piagetian, and Vygotskian theory (i.e., the nature of motivation and how it influences learning and development)._____

_____

_____

Although there are important similarities among these three theories, they differ as to role of instruction in maintaining high levels of motivation. Piagetian theorists are the least prescriptive and suggest that appropriate environments be made available, while Case and Vygotsky suggest using direct instruction to help students acquire required information and skills. In this way, the latter theories put more emphasis on instruction while the former view puts a greater emphasis on exploratory experience. For example, to maintain high levels of motivation within the classroom, Piagetian theory would suggest that a variety of challenging experiences, activities, and materials be made available to students for their active exploration. In contrast, Case would suggest that specific problem-oriented instruction and practice be used to maintain high levels of motivation, while Vygotsky would suggest the use of specific dialogue and interactions between the student and the teacher to maintain high levels of motivation.

Information Processing Theory

We have chosen to review this theory last primarily because it devotes little attention to the source of motivation in learning. If one were to identify a potential source of motivation for these theorists, it would be a *need to make sense of the world.* Accordingly, humans are meaning-seeking creatures who derive satisfaction from constructing representations that allow them to understand the universe and their role in it. There have been some recent attempts to identify specific motivational factors that influence an individual's ability to process and remember information (cf. Borkowski, Carr, Rellinger, & Pressley, 1990; Graham & Golan, 1991). This research suggests that an individual who is motivated to learn because he wants to master the material will be better able to encode and retrieve that information than someone who is motivated in order to outscore other students or save face (Graham & Golan, 1991). *The information processing theorists' focus on the need to make sense of the world makes this an intrinsic motivational learning theory.* Given the lack of attention to motivational sources, no instructional implications are described for information processing theories.

In summary, various sources of motivation are identified within current learning and development theories (see Table 9.1). As you can see, depending upon a theory's assumptions about the source of motivation, different instructional strategies are used to produce highly motivated students. The behavioral theories tend to assume extrinsic sources of motivation, while the cognitive theories tend to assume intrinsic sources of motivation.

In the next section we will discuss current cognitive views of motivation. These current views adopt the perspective that an individual's goals, expectations, beliefs, and attitudes significantly influence the nature and direction of motivation. Rather than subscribing to a one-dimensional view of motivation (i.e., extrinsic versus intrinsic) these views adopt a multidimensional view of motivation.

CURRENT VIEWS OF MOTIVATION

Within the last 20 years, a number of cognitive frameworks have been developed to describe how motivation influences the process of learning (Weiner, 1992). Each of these frameworks has identified one or more cognitive factors which critically influence motivation and learning within classroom settings. Specifically, these frameworks describe how a student's beliefs, attitudes, and knowledge influence his achievement motivation and, consequently, his performance within the classroom.

ACHIEVEMENT MOTIVATION

Murray (1938) was one of the first theorists to focus on achievement motivation and he defined it as the need to

> accomplish something difficult. To master, manipulate, or organize physical objects, human beings, or ideas. To do this as rapidly and as independently as possible. To overcome obstacles and attain a high standard. To excel oneself. To rival oneself and surpass others. To increase self regard by the successful exercise of talent. (p. 164)

Embedded in this definition are issues of mastery, competency, control, standards, and competition. As you will see in the following sections, all these issues have found their way into current views of motivation and learning.

Murray (1938) went on to develop the Thematic Apperception Test (TAT) in order to measure the different need states. This instrument was later refined by McClelland, Atkinson, Clark, and Lowell (1953) and again by Atkinson (1958), and used as a research tool to assess the strength of achievement need and its influence on achievement motivation. This instrument presents an individual with pictures and asks him to describe a story related to the picture. For example, individuals would be presented with a picture of two men in a machine shop or two women who appear to be chemists. Responses such as "The men are trying to build a more efficient bicycle" or "The women are trying to be the best in their field" would be rated as indicating a high need for achievement. As you can well

TABLE 9.1   SUMMARY OF SOURCE AND NATURE OF MOTIVATION FOR LEARNING AND DEVELOPMENT THEORIES

Theory	Source of motivation	Nature of motivation	Instructional implications
Classical conditioning	Association with habitual or reflexive behavior	Extrinsic	Pair pleasant and attractive stimuli with classroom learning activities.
Operant conditioning	History of consequences of previous behaviors	Extrinsic	Identify a variety of meaningful reinforcers and apply them in a consistent, immediate, and precise fashion.
Social learning	Outcome and efficacy expectations; cognitive goals	Extrinsic and intrinsic	Identify a variety of meaningful direct and vicarious reinforcers and use them in a consistent, immediate, and precise way. Ensure that students are involved in primarily successful classroom experiences. Also, teach students to set proximal, specific, and meaningful goals and how to monitor their progress toward those goals.
Piagetian	Equilibration; need to reduce conflict	Intrinsic	Construct developmentally appropriate tasks which induce a manageable degree of conflict between reality and prior knowledge and experience.
Neo-Piagetian	Need to find solutions to problems	Intrinsic	Construct developmentally appropriate tasks which are structured to induce students to access and use their problem-solving skills.
Vygotskian	Curiosity, control over one's environment, and increasing one's level of competence	Intrinsic	Offer adequate support (through dialogue and social interaction) for students to apply their skills and knowledge to situations which are just beyond independent problem-solving capabilities.
Information processing	Need to make the world meaningful	Intrinsic	Identify students' prior knowledge and experiences and integrate them with current classroom activities.

imagine, the scoring of responses is complex. In the end, however, a final score for need for achievement is derived for each individual (Atkinson, 1958).

Atkinson (1957, 1964) went on to identify two conflicting factors as being responsible for an individual's need for achievement: a hope for success and a fear of failure. This conflict is fueled by an individual's anxiety about the future, the expectancy of success and failure, and the incentive value of success and failure. For example, a student who wishes to succeed may not engage in achievement-related behaviors (e.g., class participation, extra study) because he expects to fail. Atkinson's examination of multiple factors on motivation significantly influenced current cognitive views of motivation and learning.

Current views of achievement motivation have attempted to isolate specific sets of cognitive factors (e.g., attitudes and beliefs) which influence an individual's motivation and performance. The following sections will discuss two sets of factors which seem to influence achievement behaviors: causal attributions and goal orientation. The focus on causal attributions and motivation has primarily been concerned with how our perceived causes of our failures and successes influence our achievement behaviors. For example, attributing past successes to luck will have very different effects on our self-esteem and future expectations from attributing our past successes to ability or a high level of effort. These differential levels of self-esteem and expectations can produce different patterns of achievement behaviors. In contrast, the focus on goal orientation and motivation is concerned with how the types of goals we identify within achievement situations influence our approach to tasks, the types of tasks we engage in, and our persistence in the chosen task. For example, goals which focus on doing better than others will influence our achievement behaviors differently from goals that focus on increasing our personal competence.

Up to now, the discussion of learning and development has focused primarily on "cold cognition," that is, intellect devoid of emotion. However, within the following sections, there will be much discussion of emotional influences and reactions to the learning process.

CAUSAL ATTRIBUTIONS

According to Weiner (1985, 1992), individuals within achievement situations will try to identify why a certain outcome (success or failure) occurred. The reasons for the outcome are called causal attributions. The typical attributions for success and failure within achievement situations are ability, effort, task difficulty, and luck (Weiner, 1985, 1992). A student's prior experiences and beliefs, the behavior of others, and reasoning skills can all influence which of these attributes are selected. For example, if a student repeatedly fails (prior experiences), no matter how much effort she employs, she will begin to attribute her failures to a lack of ability.

Individuals have particular beliefs about the nature of ability, effort, task difficulty, and luck. For example, effort is viewed as a controllable cause as well as one that is unstable and that may fluctuate over time. Once an individual thinks she has identified the causes of her success or failure, these perceptions turn into beliefs that influence her future expectations of success or failure as well as her self-esteem and confidence. This, in turn, may influence her future achievement behaviors. Consequently, according to Weiner, a perception of why you failed or succeeded is the primary motivator in achievement settings. Figure 9.1 depicts Weiner's causal attribution model of motivation, which will be discussed in the following pages.

What are the factors that influence an individual's choice of attributions? For example, why will some individuals be more likely to attribute failure to a lack of ability rather than effort, or to view ability as unstable and controllable versus stable and uncontrollable? In short, what are the antecedents to causal attributions and beliefs?

Antecedents to Causal Attributions and Beliefs   According to Weiner (1992), the antecedents to causal attributions and beliefs include an individual's personal history and beliefs, the performance of others in her environment, and her causal schemas (see Figure 9.1).

Exercise 9.4: Please identify which one of the following pairs of statements reflects your views on your life. After completing this exercise, read the next section.

1. (a) If people are unhappy it is the result of the mistakes they have made.
   (b) Many of the unhappy things in people's lives are partly due to fate.
2. (a) There is no truth to the idea that teachers are biased and unfair to students.
   (b) Most students don't realize the extent to which accidental factors influence grades within a class.
3. (a) If I do well on a task it is because of the time and effort I have invested in preparing and performing the task.
   (b) If I do well on a task it is because it was an easy task which anyone would have easily completed without any difficulties.

(Adapted from Weiner, 1992.)

FIGURE 9.1   Weiner's causal attribution model of motivation. (Adapted from Bernard Weiner, *Human Motivation*. Copyright © 1992. Used by permission of Sage Publications, Inc., and the author.)

Antecedent Conditions	Perceived Causes	Causal Dimensions	Primary Effects	Consequences
Personal history and beliefs	Ability	Stability ⟶	Expectancy change (hope and helplessness)	Performance intensity
Causal schemata	Effort (typical and immediate)			Persistence
Performance of others	Others (students, family, teacher)	Locus ⟶	Esteem-related effects (pride)	Choice
	Luck	Control ⟶	Social-related effects (guilt and shame)	Others

Personal History and Beliefs   Rotter (1966) identified general beliefs that influence an individual's behaviors within a variety of situations. He indicated that individuals hold specific beliefs, referred to as locus of control, about whether their response to some situation will influence the outcome. Alternative ''a'' in all three questions in Exercise 9.4 represents an internal locus of control: that is, the belief that outcomes are caused by your own responses. In contrast, alternative ''b'' in all three questions represents an external locus: that is, the belief that outcomes are due to something other than your own responses (e.g., luck, task difficulty, or fate). An individual who has an external locus of control has less confidence in her ability and, consequently, will be less apt to initiate activities independently and will be less persistent in the face of failure. In contrast, an individual who has an internal locus of control will have high confidence and, consequently, will act independently and will persist in the face of failure. *The main distinction between internal and external locus of control is the degree to which one feels in control.*

Gilmor and Morton (1979) conducted a series of experiments which investigated the explanations that students give for success or failure. They found that students with an external locus of control will attribute both success and failure to luck, while students with an internal locus of control will attribute success and failure to both ability and effort. Thus, an individual's locus of control influences her judgments of why she succeeded or failed. How an individual develops her general beliefs about locus of control may partially be a function of past experiences. For example, someone who has experienced repeated success as a result of intense effort will develop an internal locus of control while repeated failure usually leads to an external locus of control.

Performance of Others   How closely one's own performance matches the performance of others also influences the choice of causal attributes (Weiner, 1992). The closer the match between the performance of self and others, the more likely it is that the outcome is attributed to the task (Weiner & Kukla, 1970). For example, if a student fails a test that everyone failed, then he is likely to attribute his failure to a difficult test. Conversely, the more one's own performance differs from the performance of others, the more likely it is that the outcome will be attributed to the person rather than the task (Weiner & Kukla, 1970). For example, if a student fails a test that everyone else has passed, then he is more likely to attribute his failure to a personal factor such as lack of effort or ability.

Causal Schemas   In most situations, there is too little information to make well-founded causal attributions. Consequently, we make a best guess as to the potential cause for an outcome. In these cases, we access causal schemas, which are heuristics that help us identify relations between specific causes and effects (Take a moment and see if you can remember the definition of ''heuristic''; if not, see Chapter 5). These rules are built up from prior experiences and are activated by cues within the achievement situation. One of the primary rules employed in these situations is covariation. That is, if an outcome (successful test grades) repeatedly follows a specific factor (intensive test reviews) but does not occur when the reviews are absent, the outcome covaries with the presence of the reviews and may be attributed to the reviews.

Another example of a general rule which may influence the attribution process concerns the number of causes which may be related to the outcome. According to this rule, if performance outcomes are uncommon, then attributions tend to include multiple causes: For example, success on an exam that most individuals failed is due to both ability and great effort. Conversely, when performance outcomes are common, then attributions tend to include only one cause: For example, failure on an exam that almost everyone failed is due to either low ability or a lack of effort. In other words, for common outcomes, we are willing to accept one cause, whereas for uncommon outcomes, we assume multiple causes (Kun & Weiner, 1973).

In summary, Figure 9.1 shows that there are multiple factors which may interact and influence the specific causes that we relate to our achievement outcomes. Some (e.g., causal schemas) influence the process of selection, whereas others (e.g., personal beliefs and experiences) influence the specific cause that is related to an outcome.

Causal Dimensions

As indicated earlier, individuals have particular beliefs about the nature of causal attributes (Weiner, 1992). Weiner identifies three dimensions or sets of beliefs that describe the nature of causal attributes: (1) **controllability,** (2) **locus of control,** (3) **stability** (see Figure 9.1). Specific causes for our successes and failures are categorized along all three dimensions. For example, ability, in most instances, is perceived as an internal, stable, and uncontrollable cause, while effort is an internal, unstable, and controllable cause. Luck and task difficulty are seen as uncontrollable, external, and unstable causes. Table 9.2 shows how Weiner's three-dimensional system can be used to analyze the causes of success and failure.

It is important to note that there is much variation in how individuals classify specific causes. For example, some individuals may believe that luck is stable (they are always running into bad luck) while others will view it as unstable (their luck varies). Even ability, which is generally perceived as innate and unchange-

TABLE 9.2   EXAMPLES OF WEINER'S THREE-DIMENSIONAL ATTRIBUTION SYSTEM APPLIED TO ACHIEVEMENT FAILURE

	Stable		Unstable	
	Internal	External	Internal	External
Controllable	student never studies	instructor is biased	did not study for this exam	friend failed to help
Uncontrollable	low aptitude	difficulty of exam	sick the day of the exam	bad luck

able, is viewed by some individuals as being open to development through individual effort.

As indicated above, both the actual attributions and the general beliefs supporting these attributions will influence an individual's attitudes, feelings, and expectations for future achievement. For example, Johnny, who often fails, attributes his failure to a lack of ability and views ability as internal, stable, and uncontrollable. Consequently, Johnny will very likely expect to fail in the future, have low self-confidence, and feel shame and depression. Alternatively, Mort, who also fails with some regularity and also attributes this failure to a lack of ability, views ability as internal, unstable, and controllable. Mort, therefore, is less likely to predict failure in the future and may feel guilty rather than ashamed and depressed. Also, Mort's failure is less likely to influence his level of self-confidence than is the case with Johnny. Consequently, the future academic behavior of the two boys is likely to be very different.

Within the following sections, we will review the potential effects of specific attributions and the dimensions of these attributions on an individual's attitudes, feelings, and future expectations (see Figure 9.1).

Causal Attributions   The specific causes to which we attribute our successes and failures will primarily influence our feelings and attitudes. Table 9.3 summarizes the affective outcomes of specific attributions. Affective responses may influence the intensity and direction of achievement behaviors. For example, pride will more likely lead to active involvement whereas resignation will more likely lead to a lack of involvement.

Controllability   Controllable causes such as help from others and personal effort are modifiable, while uncontrollable causes such as luck or mood are those that we cannot modify or influence. A controlled variable in school achievement could involve seeking help from a classmate. You are controlling the situation by making the contact for assistance. An uncontrolled variable could be the bias of the teacher. You could attribute your success or failure to the teacher's bias either

TABLE 9.3   AFFECTIVE OUTCOMES OF CAUSAL ATTRIBUTIONS

Causal attribution	Locus of control	Affective outcomes	
		Success	Failure
Ability	internal; controllable	competence; pride	incompetence; shame; apathy; resignation
Extended effort	internal; controllable	relaxation; pride	guilt
Others	external; uncontrollable	gratitude	anger
Luck	external; uncontrollable	surprise	surprise
Task difficulty	external; uncontrollable	gratitude	depression; frustration

against you or in support of you. In either case, this bias is out of the student's control.

The controllability dimension will primarily influence our socially related affect (Covington & Omelich, 1981), that is, how we feel we will be viewed by others. For example, guilt and shame are affective reactions that reflect our feelings of not living up to some external standards. According to Weiner (1985, 1992), attributing our success to a controllable factor (e.g., effort) will produce feelings of pride, while attributing success to an uncontrollable factor (e.g., luck) will produce feelings of gratefulness. Alternatively, attributing our failure to a controllable factor will produce feelings of guilt, while attributing failure to an uncontrollable factor will produce feelings of shame, anger, or depression.

Locus of Control   Internal causes such as ability, effort, and mood exist within the individual, while external causes such as task difficulty, luck, and help from others reside outside the individual. For example, if a student fails an English test, she could attribute her failure to being in a bad mood, which is internal. Alternatively, she could attribute the failure to the fact that the English teacher gives difficult tests, an external factor.

The internal/external dimension is said to influence our feelings of self-esteem and our confidence in ourselves. For example, if we have been successful and we attribute our success to an internal cause (e.g., effort or ability), then we will feel pride, and this will increase our confidence, while failing may produce feelings of shame. Alternatively, if we have been successful and we attribute our success to an external cause (e.g., luck or test difficulty), then we will feel gratitude, while if we fail we will feel anger. These affective reactions may modify our confidence in ourselves and may influence how motivated we are in future learning situations.

Question 9.4: Will attributing an outcome to an external or internal cause influence an individual's level of self-efficacy? For example, if an individual attributes success to an internal cause, would this be more likely to raise or lower her level of self-efficacy? Alternatively, if an individual attributes failure to an internal cause, would this be more likely to raise or lower her level of self-efficacy? Justify your answer._____

_____

_____

Exercise 9.5: You have just failed a math exam, and you think the failure was due to one of the causes indicated below. You expect to take another math exam in the same class very soon. Indicate your expectation for succeeding at the next exam. After answering the questions within this exercise, please continue reading for a discussion of your answers.

1. The prior failure occurred because of your *lack of math ability*. Likelihood of future success:

1	2	3	4	5
very low		intermediate		very high

2. The prior failure occurred because you *did not put enough effort* into studying for the exam. Likelihood of future success:

1	2	3	4	5
very low		intermediate		very high

3. The prior failure occurred because this *exam was particularly difficult*. Likelihood of future success:

1	2	3	4	5
very low		intermediate		very high

4. The prior failure occurred because *you were sick* when you took the exam. Likelihood of future success:

1	2	3	4	5
very low		intermediate		very high

(Adapted from Weiner, 1992.)

Stability Stable causes such as ability are constant and should not fluctuate over time, while unstable causes such as effort, mood, luck, and difficulty of task will fluctuate over time. For example, completing a task successfully could be attributed to the fact that you have a natural aptitude for that task (a stable cause) or that you put in enough effort (an unstable cause).

The stable/unstable dimensions will influence our success expectations. For example, in Exercise 9.5, if you identified a stable cause (ability) for your failure on a math exam, you probably indicated that it was very unlikely that you would succeed on future tests. That is, because ability is stable and will not change in the future, neither will your test performance. Alternatively, in the items that attributed your failure to an unstable cause (lack of effort, difficulty of exam, and sickness), it is more likely that you would expect things to be different in the future. That is, because these causes can fluctuate over time, the likelihood of success is greater than if the prior failure was attributed to a stable cause.

Fyans and Maehr (1979) found that students in a fifth- through twelfth-grade sample who attributed their success on achievement tasks to their own effort were likely to prefer tasks in which competence could determine the outcome. However, those students who attributed their success to luck were likely to avoid ability tasks and prefer games of chance. That suggests the importance of developing stable, controllable variables in students.

Consequences of Causal Attributes and Dimensions

According to Weiner (1992), changes in an individual's expectations and feelings directly influence both his choice of activity and the intensity and persistence with which he performs the activity. For example, if a student does not expect to succeed in the future, he will put little effort into performing a task (lack of intensity), may easily give up when faced with roadblocks, may choose not to perform the task, or, given the choice, may perform an easy and trivial task versus a difficult and significant one.

Certain repeated combinations of causal attributes, beliefs, and outcomes can have severe consequences. One in particular which has received much attention is the student who has developed feelings of **learned helplessness,** that is, a student who ascribes her repeated failures to a lack of ability which she believes to be an internal, uncontrollable, and stable cause. Seligman (1975), and Abrahamson, Seligman, and Teasdale (1978) indicate that when organisms (animal or human) are exposed to uncontrollable and stable events, they eventually give up trying to do anything about them. As an illustration, Hiroto (1974) exposed two groups of students to noxious noise during problem-solving activities. For one group, if the students solved the problems, the noxious noise was stopped. In the second group, there was no relationship between their performance and the noise. That is, the noxious noise was randomly turned off and on. Eventually, this second group stopped attempting to perform the tasks they were given.

These results and the idea of learned helplessness can be explained through attribution theory in the following way: Initially the helpless individual concludes that certain outcomes and responses are independent (uncontrollable) and then attributes the outcomes to an uncontrollable cause (ability, luck, fate, etc.). The individual at this point will continue to believe that his environment is uncontrollable, that that will not change, and that it will generalize to related outcomes. As an example, if a student repeatedly fails in science, he will develop the view that he has little control within this situation. He will then attribute the cause of his failure to something uncontrollable, such as ability, fate, or luck. Given this view, he may expect to continue failing in science in the future and may even generalize this expectation to other content areas. Eventually, this feeling of uncontrollable failure may result in a general low level of academic motivation, and he may cease preparing for exams.

Causal Attributions: Instructional Implications

Two sets of instructional implications can be derived from the literature on causal attributions: one reactive and one proactive. The reactive set focuses on how to change maladaptive attribution patterns, whereas the proactive set focuses on the development of adaptive attribution patterns.

Maladaptive Patterns of Attribution   Maladaptive attribution patterns generally consist of attributing one's failures to a lack of ability. This pattern usually develops following a history of failures that occur even after a student has devoted much effort to the failed tasks. Also, seeing other students who are similar to him succeed at tasks when he continues to fail may cause the student to attribute his failure to lack of ability. Social interactions can also have a rather direct influence on a student's future attributions, as for example when peers ridicule a student who constantly fails as being stupid or slow. As we will see in the next section, a teacher's reactions to students' failures may also predispose them to attribute their failures to a lack of ability.

Much research has focused on using **attribution retraining** to eliminate maladaptive attribution patterns. When students believe that past failures were due to insufficient effort rather than insufficient ability, they will persist longer and increase achievement (Weiner, 1979). Attribution retraining programs typically involve students in series of successful experiences (going from easy to more difficult tasks), getting them to attribute their success to effort, and then, given this link between success and effort, inducing them to attribute past failures to insufficient effort rather than insufficient ability (Dweck, 1975; Andrews & Debus, 1978; Anderson & Jennings, 1980; Fosterling, 1985; Schunk, 1989, 1991). In a review of this research, Graham (1991) concluded that these attribution retraining programs have been quite successful at changing students' attributions from ability to effort and have led to overall increases in achievement motivation.

Teacher-student Interactions One of the most powerful influences on students' attribution patterns is their interaction with teachers. For example, a teacher can subtly cue students to their expectations of success and failure by the way they distribute questions. They tend to ask students they perceive as having high ability more questions, give them longer to respond, and interrupt them less frequently than students they perceive as having low ability (Allington, 1980; Good & Brophy, 1984). Students who are perceived as having low ability are asked easier questions, allowed less time for answering, and are given fewer prompts (Woolfolk & Brooks, 1985). These differential treatments are easily picked up by students and may be translated into personal views of low or high ability.

Graham (1991) indicates that how teachers respond to students' success and failure can also act as a subtle cue to their views of students' abilities. For example, if a teacher seems angered at a student's failure, this sends the message that the teacher has high expectations of that student and feels the student has some control over succeeding and failing. Conversely, if a teacher reacts to failure with sympathy or pity, it sends the message that the student did the best he could and probably hasn't the ability to exert much control over succeeding or failing.

Excessive teacher help and teacher praise can also contribute to the development of inappropriate student attributions. Weiner, Graham, Taylor, and Meyer (1983) found that praise for a student's success and lack of criticism for a student's failure when a task is very easy suggests to students that they possess low ability. In addition, these researchers found that providing excessive help to students who do not request help will also foster views of low ability. Consequently, teachers must carefully monitor their reactions (e.g., sympathy, anger, praise, help) to students' successes and failures within the classroom.

GOAL ORIENTATION

As discussed in Chapter 8, social learning theorists believe that personal goals play an important part in motivating individuals within achievement settings. That is, social learning theory believes that an important characteristic of a successful learner is the ability to set appropriate goals and then monitor progress toward those goals. The focus is on identifying those factors (student self-efficacy, teacher feedback, etc.) which influence goal setting. Also, the characteristics of useful goals (specific, attainable, and moderately difficult) were studied in relation to maintaining high levels of motivation.

Current views of motivation, however, are concerned with identifying *why* the specific goals are chosen. For example, two students may set for themselves the goal of completing a reading assignment by the end of the school week. One student may pursue this goal in order to become a better reader or to learn more, while the other student may seek to become more competent than his classmates. Current views are more focused on broad—internal versus external—goal orientations than on specific goals.

According to current views of motivation, these two goal orientations can have a very different impact on a student's level of motivation and, consequently, on his cognitive processes, affective states, and academic performance (Dweck, 1989). That is, if a student's achievement goal is to acquire new information and skills, he is internally motivated and, consequently, would be less influenced by external factors such as other students' performance or negative feedback. Alternatively, if a student's goal is to do better than others, he is extrinsically motivated and may be significantly influenced by external factors such as teacher feedback, peer performance, or unexpected difficulties.

These two broad categories of achievement goal orientation have been variously labeled as learning and performance orientation (Dweck, 1989), task-involvement and ego-involvement orientation (Nicholls, 1984), and mastery and performance orientation (Ames & Archer, 1988), respectively. Learning, task-involvement, and mastery orientations are associated with the internal goal of increasing knowledge and competency, whereas ego-involvement and performance orientations are associated with the external goal of doing better than others. These two broad goal orientations are associated with qualitatively different student behaviors within the classroom and are elicited by different environmental or instructional demands (Ames, 1992). Consequently, as you will see in a later section, there are important reasons for guiding students toward one orientation and away from the other.

Rather than trying to superficially review all three pairs of orientation, we have chosen instead to present an in-depth summary of how learning goals and performance goals influence achievement motivation and behavior. Wherever appropriate, we will integrate conclusions derived from research on mastery and performance goals, and task-involved and ego-involved goals. Finally, we will discuss how student-teacher interactions and participation in specific academic tasks and classrooms can influence which orientation students choose.

Learning and Performance Goals

Dweck (1975, 1989, 1992) indicates that setting achievement goals is the single most critical influence on achievement motivation and behaviors. She defines achievement goals as those related to one's competence. For example, some achievement goals may focus on the enhancement of personal skills and competence, while others may focus on using one's skills and competence to outperform others.

According to Dweck (1989), the types of goals that an individual develops within achievement settings are primarily influenced by his "motivational sets." Recall from Chapter 5 that "sets" are a collection of beliefs and knowledge which focus our attention on specific aspects of our environment. For example, within a problem-solving situation we may believe that a two-dimensional answer is called for; consequently, we are "set" to search for only two-dimensional solutions.

Within the present context, we will examine a variety of motivational sets that are related to achievement behavior: individual's beliefs about competence, rules for identifying causes of outcomes (i.e., causal schemas), and values and preferences regarding approaches to achievement situations. For example, some individuals are set or predisposed to identify only external causes of success and failure and that, as seen earlier, may induce different patterns of achievement-related behaviors such as a lack of persistence and effort in attaining goals.

One motivational set that particularly influences achievement behaviors and the development of achievement goals is an individual's beliefs about competence (Dweck, 1992). According to Dweck (1989), there are two different views on the nature of competence: an entity view and an incremental view. An **entity view of competence** suggests that it is stable and uncontrollable and that we begin with a certain level of ability and competence that cannot be changed. In contrast, the **incremental view of competence** suggests that it is unstable and controllable and that we can increase our level of competence through our experiences. This latter view of competence is typically seen in young children because they do not judge their ability in comparison with norms or peers and because they typically believe that greater effort means greater competence (Nicholls, 1984, 1989).

Dweck (1989) indicates that these two divergent views on the nature of competence are related to the two types of goal orientation (learning and performance). An individual with an incremental view of competence will most likely adopt a **learning goal orientation.** That will lead to attempts to increase competence or master new material and is the more adaptive and desirable type of goal. With a learning goal orientation, an individual seeks to understand her work, develop new skills that will improve her level of competence, and achieve a sense of mastery based on self-referenced standards (Ames, 1992; Nicholls, 1989). For example, a student with internal learning goals may look at a new study skill as an important tool for increasing her ability to engage in self-paced and self-regulated learning.

On the other hand, an individual with an entity view of competence will most likely adopt a **performance goal orientation.** This choice will focus the individual on demonstrating higher levels of ability or competence than others rather than focusing on self-development, which is a more adaptive attitude. Performance goals tend to focus on strengthening one's sense of self-worth by doing better than others, by surpassing normative standards, or by achieving success with little effort (Ames, 1984; Covington, 1984). However, when faced with an achievement situation that is beyond their current ability level and, consequently, that threatens such favorable comparisons, performance-oriented students become insecure and often tend to withdraw from the situation. Dweck and Leggett (1988) suggest that this orientation tends to interfere with establishing attainable goals and often increases the probability that a student will give up in the face of difficult or frustrating events because they threaten his sense of competence and self-worth.

Question 9.5: Individuals who focus on learning goals view the nature of competence and ability differently from those who focus on performance goals. Earlier, we indicated that different beliefs about causal attributions will produce different expectations regarding future success. Given this previous discussion, distinguish between learning goals and performance goals in terms of (1) how they view ability (is it stable, controllable, etc.) and (2) how they view success expectancy.

(a) learning goal:_____

_____

(b) performance goal:_____

Research has found that both orientations can be associated with the selection of challenging tasks and persistence (Dweck, 1989). *However, a learning goal orientation should always produce these achievement behaviors, whereas a performance goal orientation will do so only if they are accompanied by a high level of confidence in one's ability* (see Figure 9.2). Consequently, the probability of choosing an appropriately challenging task and persisting in it is much higher if

FIGURE 9.2   Achievement goals and achievement behaviors. (Adapted from Carol Dweck, "Motivation," in Alan Lesgold and Robert Glaser, eds., *Foundations for a Psychology of Education.* Copyright © 1989. Used by permission of Lawrence Erlbaum Associates, Inc. Publishers and Carol Dweck.

Goal Orientation	Confidence in Present Ability	Task Difficulty Choice	Persistence
Performance	Lo →	Avoid challenge	Lo
	Hi →	Seek challenge	Hi
Learning	Lo ↘ Hi ↗	Seek challenge (that fosters learning)	Hi

one adopts a learning goal orientation and is not influenced by one's perception of ability. Also, individuals who adopt a learning goal orientation are more adaptive in dealing with difficulties. That is, they assume that the difficulty is due to inappropriate strategy selection or too little effort and, consequently, they adapt their strategy or expend more effort. In contrast, if an individual with a low level of confidence adopts a performance goal orientation, he is most likely to choose excessively easy tasks (to ensure success) or an excessively difficult one (to ensure that failure does not indicate a lack of ability) (Covington & Omelich, 1979; Raynor & Smith, 1966). In addition, when faced with roadblocks or difficulties, performance-oriented individuals tend to attribute the difficulty to a lack of ability and give up.

Perceived Control   A learning goal orientation will enhance an individual's sense of control in comparison with a performance goal orientation (Dweck, 1989, 1992). The perceived lack of control associated with a performance goal orientation stems from a variety of uncontrollable factors which intervene between one's performance and the sought after outcome. For example, an individual who is attempting to do better than others cannot control how well others do or how performances are judged by others. In contrast, individuals with a learning goal orientation are more likely to perceive themselves as having control over factors, such as individual effort, that they consider essential to goal attainment. This sense of perceived control motivates them to set attainable goals and to persist in their pursuit of these goals.

Outcome Attributions   As suggested by the earlier discussion of success expectations and perceived locus of control, a student with a learning goal orientation will attribute success to effort (Dweck, 1989; Ames & Archer, 1988; Ames, Ames, & Felker, 1977). Bandura and Dweck (1981) found that students with learning goals felt smarter after a high-effort mastery experience than after a low-effort one. In short, students with learning goal orientation have adopted the view that effort is critical to success, a belief that is central to maintaining high levels of achievement motivation.

For students with a learning goal orientation, effort is also at the center of their affective responses. For example, children with learning goals associated boredom and disappointment with low-effort mastery experiences and pride or relief with high-effort success experiences (Bandura & Dweck, 1981). Also, research has found that individuals who have adopted learning goals will associate pride and satisfaction with successful effort, and guilt with inadequate effort (Jagacinski & Nicholls, 1984, 1987; Wentzel, 1991).

Engagement in Learning Activities   Besides increasing time on learning tasks, the learning goal orientation is associated with the use of high-effort, elaborative learning strategies such as imagery and mnemonics (Ames & Archer, 1988; Deiner & Dweck, 1978; Nicholls, 1984). Students who indicate that they have adopted learning goals report using effective learning strategies related to attention, processing, self-monitoring, and elaborative processing of verbal materials (Nolen, 1988; Nolen & Haadyna, 1990). In contrast, the adoption of performance goals is associated with the use of superficial learning strategies (Nolen, 1988; Ryan & Grolnick, 1986). An example of a superficial learning strategy is using verbal rehearsal to remember new information.

Question 9.6: Why is it important to employ high-effort learning strategies? Hint: In addition to a focus on meaning, what other characteristic of encoding strategies is important to successful learning and remembering (see Chapter 4)?

As can be seen in Table 9.4, adopting a learning goal orientation is associated with beliefs, attitudes, and behavior which are conducive to being successful within achievement settings. Conversely, adopting a performance goal orientation has been associated with beliefs, attitudes, and behavior which may interfere with being successful within achievement settings. The final section will focus on how teachers can facilitate the adoption of a learning goal orientation.

Learning and Performance Goals: Instructional Implications

There has been much research evaluating the effects of task characteristics and classroom structure on students' achievement behaviors (cf. Epstein, 1988; Stipek & Daniels, 1988). In particular, tasks and classroom structures that focus students on effort versus ability, on intrinsic interest in learning, and on using effective learning strategies lead to behaviors consistent with the learning goal orientation (Ames, 1992). There are three types of learning modes that foster a learning goal orientation within achievement settings: **meaningful learning, self-directed learning** and **self-referenced learning.**

TABLE 9.4   BELIEFS, ATTITUDES, AND BEHAVIORS ASSOCIATED WITH LEARNING AND PERFORMANCE GOAL ORIENTATION

Learning goals	Performance goals
personal standards	normative standards
effort/outcome attributions	ability/outcome attributions
chooses challenging tasks	chooses challenging tasks only when confident
perceives high level of internal control	perceives high level of external control
persistent	not persistent
effective learning strategies	superficial learning strategies
appropriate affective reactions to success and failure	negative reactions to failure

Meaningful Learning   Meaningful tasks are more likely to get students to put forth effort and to become actively engaged in learning than are tasks that seem unconnected to their lives. That is, personally relevant, varied, and challenging tasks produce behaviors which are consistent with a learning goal orientation—for example, willingness to employ high-effort strategies and exhibit appropriate feelings and attitudes after successes and failures (Nicholls, 1989; Corno & Rohrkemper, 1985; Lepper & Hodell, 1989).

As a first step to creating meaningful tasks, the teacher needs to gather information about the experiences, knowledge, developmental level, and preferences of the children in his classroom. With this information the teacher can then identify tasks that are personally relevant and challenging to students. For example, if the majority of students are from an inner city environment, then tasks that reflect that environment would be most relevant. That could entail a world history lesson which compares the inner city ruins to those left by the Greeks and Romans. Alternatively, the teacher could develop an American history lesson which uses cultural diversity within the community to underscore the contribution of various groups to the founding and development of the United States. Finally, students could be presented with a contemporary issues lesson which uses ethical dilemmas related to surviving within the inner city as a basis for discussing values and moral development.

Question 9.7: How might knowing the developmental level of a student contribute to the development of meaningful tasks?_____

_____

_____

Self-directed Learning   Individuals who are guided by learning goals take more responsibility for their learning. Consequently, any attempt to increase the degree to which individuals are in control of their learning will support the development of a learning goal orientation. One way to foster the development of student self-direction and autonomy is for teachers to give students choices and allow them to participate in classroom decisions. That is, students could be given choices as to the tasks that they engage in, how these tasks are to be completed, the difficulty level of tasks, and how they will be evaluated (Stipek, 1992). For example, to develop mathematical problem-solving skills, the teacher could present a set of problems organized by difficulty level, and the students could choose which problems to complete first. Once they have completed their chosen problems, they could be allowed to check their work against an answer sheet. Alternatively, in order to give students even more control, the teacher could ask them to generate their own everyday problems requiring the use of mathematical skills. As an example, if a student is studying proportional reasoning, she might create a problem that focuses on the calculation of the ''best deals'' when shopping for groceries: ''Given an 11-ounce candy bar that costs 50 cents, and a 15-ounce candy bar that costs 60 cents, which is the best deal?''

The more choices a student is given, the more opportunities she has to develop personal responsibility for her learning. This will foster an atmosphere which supports developing higher levels of perceived control within the classroom. This, in turn, should help students see the relationship of personal effort to learning.

As suggested in the chapter on social learning theory, helping students to acquire self-regulatory skills (planning, organizing, and monitoring their learning) will foster higher levels of perceived control and focus students on the importance of effort for successful learning. A critical component of self-regulatory skills is the ability to set personal goals. According to Schunk (1989), when tasks are defined by specific and short-term personal goals, students are more likely to believe that they can accomplish a task with reasonable effort and more willing to apply the effort to complete the task. For example, students who can identify the number of spelling words that they should get correct each day or the number of pages that they will read in the history text each day will be more motivated toward these short, attainable goals than will students whose goals have not been so sharply defined.

Question 9.8: In the chapter on information processing theory (Chapter 4), we describe a direct strategy approach for acquiring metacognitive and cognitive skills. What aspects of this approach are specifically aimed at developing self-

direction and higher levels of perceived control?_____

_____

_____

Self-referenced Learning A self-referenced learner compares his current performance with personal standards when evaluating progress within achievement situations. The two most powerful influences on the development of self-referenced learning are the nature of the evaluation employed within the classroom and the nature and use of external rewards as incentives for achievement.

Nature of Evaluation Any method of evaluation that imposes social comparisons on students will increase the likelihood that they will focus on ability attributions and react negatively to failure. These, of course, are the classic characteristics of a performance orientation. For example, classrooms that publicly present highest and lowest grade scores, display student papers, and use ability groupings are imposing social comparison on students (Ames, 1992). Research indicates that these types of evaluative practices reduce the likelihood that students will pursue challenging tasks (Dweck, 1989) and use effective learning strategies (Ames, 1984). In essence, these practices make it less likely that students will adopt a learning goal orientation.

In order to help students develop a learning goal orientation, a teacher should individualize his grading policy. *That is, individual students should be evaluated on the progress they have made in acquiring appropriate skills and knowledge.* For example, a student would receive an "A" if she doubled the amount of information and skills acquired in the previous grading period. Alternatively, students could be graded on the acquisition of a prescribed set of skills and knowledge which could be identified by the teacher and/or student. For example, a student would receive an "A" if she acquired 80 percent of the prescribed set of skills and knowledge. Finally, teachers should employ frequent feedback which highlights each student's personal progress. For example, rather than indicating to students that they did better than many others in the classroom, the teacher should indicate that they are doing a great job of acquiring new and diverse skills.

Nature of Incentives Although rewards have a useful purpose within classrooms, they work against the development of a learning goal orientation when they are distributed publicly and given on a differential ability basis. Publicly distributed rewards motivate students to compete with each other and, consequently, support the development of a performance goal orientation. If rewards are related to comparative ability rather than exerted effort, then students will be more likely to attribute their successes and failures to ability rather than effort. For example, if students are rewarded for receiving the highest grade rather than for putting forth the most effort, they will be more apt to attribute differential performance to differential ability. Focusing on ability attributions rather than on effort attributions makes it less likely that students will adopt a learning goal orientation within the classroom.

Rewards can have positive effects if they are given for exhibiting high levels of effort and for making progress toward short-term goals (Brophy, 1987; Schunk, 1989). For example, if teachers monitor the amount of effort that students employ in attempting to complete a task and reward those who exhibit high levels of effort, they will be supporting a learning goal orientation within the classroom. In addition, teachers need to help students set specific, attainable short-term goals and then reward them for making progress toward those goals. Rewards should be given for individual progress and effort and not be based on comparisons with peers or the class as a whole.

Thus, teachers can significantly increase the probability that students will adopt learning goals by involving students in meaningful tasks, using self-referenced evaluation and rewards, and developing the self-directive skills of students. A summary of specific recommendations is presented in Table 9.5.

REVIEW OF MAJOR POINTS

1 Motivation has a directive, sustaining quality that energizes and maintains our learning activities. It influences the tasks we choose to involve ourselves in, the nature and intensity of our involvement in those tasks, and how long we persist at them. Also, a motivated student will, when faced with roadblocks, expend more effort at completing the learning task and be more persistent in completing it.

2 An extrinsically motivated individual is driven to obtain certain incentives that originate externally. When extrinsically motivated, the individual is a passive player in the learning situation and will exhibit appropriate behavior only when

TABLE 9.5   TEACHING STRATEGIES WHICH PROMOTE A LEARNING GOAL ORIENTATION

A. Engage students in meaningful learning by using . . .

a variety of tasks

diverse, challenging tasks

personally relevant tasks

B. Develop students' ability to engage in self-directed learning by . . .

allowing students to select the type, difficulty, and pace of tasks

allowing students to evaluate their own task performance

allowing students to create their own tasks

helping students acquire the self-regulatory skills of goal setting, self-monitoring, and self-evaluation

C. Develop students' ability to engage in self-referenced learning by . . .

comparing their performance with personal standards rather than to normative standards (that of other students)

rewarding effort expended, not ability exhibited

using feedback which highlights students' personal progress

---

attractive incentives are present or when compliance will allow him to avoid something aversive.

In contrast, an intrinsically motivated individual is driven by a need for competency and control over the environment, is an active player in the learning situation, is internally driven to exhibit appropriate behaviors, and exercises his right to choose. An intrinsically motivated student will perceive that he has total or partial control of the learning situation, while an extrinsically motivated student will not.

3 Classical conditioning, operant conditioning, and social learning theory all emphasize the influence of consequences on an individual's level of motivation. Whereas the former two theories focus exclusively on external factors, the last theory suggests that the influence of these external factors on motivation and behavior is mediated by an individual's outcome expectations, efficacy expectations, and personal goals.

These three theories take primarily a reactive view; that is, they are useful for dealing with motivational problems that already exist within the classroom. Although these theories do make suggestions that may help avoid potential motivational problems (present clear and precise rules and regulations, help students set appropriate goals, etc.) the techniques derived from these theories will be most useful for eliminating existing problems.

4 Piagetian, Vygotskian, and Case's neo-Piagetian theories all subscribe to an intrinsic view of motivation that sees individuals as having built-in tendencies to actively seek out learning opportunities. They also agree that an individual's current developmental level limits what she can learn and, consequently, limits the motivational strategies that can be effectively used on her.

5 According to Piagetian theory, motivation will be high if a student is presented with learning situations which conflict in some way with his prior experiences and knowledge. These types of situations threaten his mental equilibrium and challenge him to resolve the existing conflict. Consequently, instruction should always be at or slightly higher than students' developmental level. Also, given the active nature of individuals, students will be more motivated to learn within situations which allow active manipulation of objects and ideas.

6 According to neo-Piagetian theory, the primary instructional strategy for maintaining high levels of motivation involves tahe use of problem situations. Rather than forcing students into a strict drill and practice mode, students are presented with new information within the context of a problem situation. In addition, it is important to structure activities at or slightly higher than the student's existing cognitive level.

7 According to Vygotskian theory, the teacher needs to have a clear understanding of the student's zone of proximal development and must offer the student appropriate support and guidance in moving through this zone. If tasks are geared below or above this zone, low levels of motivation may result. Tasks that are below the zone will not be challenging and may lead to boredom, while those above the zone may be frustrating and cause the student to disengage. As with Piaget and Case, Vygotsky suggests the need to clearly evaluate the student's current level of functioning prior to designing and developing instructional lessons.

8 Causal attributions are the perceptions that individuals develop in order to explain their successes and failures in achievement situations. The four most common causes that people attribute their successes and failures to are ability, effort, task difficulty, and luck.

9 Weiner identifies three dimensions or sets of beliefs that describe the nature of causal attributes: (1) controllability, (2) locus of control, and (3) stability. Individuals categorize specific causes for their success and failure along all three dimensions. Controllable causes such as effort and help from others are modifiable, while uncontrollable causes such as luck and task difficulty cannot be modified. Those who customarily attribute achievement to controllable causes such as effort tend to operate from stable, internal standards. Those who attribute achievement to uncontrollable causes such as ability tend to operate from unstable, socially vulnerable standards.

10 Internal causes exist within the individual (e.g., ability, effort, mood) while external causes reside outside the individual (e.g., difficulty of task, luck, help from others). The internal/external dimension is believed to influence our self-esteem and our confidence in ourselves. Stable causes such as ability are constant and should not fluctuate over time, while unstable causes such as effort, mood, and task difficulty will fluctuate over time. This stable/unstable dimension influences our future expectations.

11 Students who attribute their repeated failures to a lack of ability that they believe to be internal, uncontrollable, and stable will often develop "learned helplessness." They begin to expect failure, that is, to view failure as stable and uncontrollable, and begin to generalize it to other achievement settings.

12 Teachers can modify their students' motivation in two ways: (1) by changing maladaptive attribution patterns and (2) by interacting with students in ways that develop adaptive attribution patterns. Maladaptive patterns generally consist of attributing one's failures to a lack of ability and can be eliminated by attribution retraining. Attribution retraining programs typically involve students in a series of successful experiences (going from easy to more difficult tasks), with the intent being to get them to attribute their success to effort rather than ability.

Adaptive attribution patterns involve student-teacher interaction patterns that are the same for all students. For example, teachers can subtly cue students to their expectations for success and failure and their level of ability by the way they question students and by the way they respond to student successes and failures. By asking low-ability students fewer and easier questions, and by giving them fewer cues and less time to answer, teachers communicate their low expectations. Also, when teachers respond to students' successes with surprise and to students' failures with pity or indifference, that too signals low expectations. In short, teachers must strive to give all students the benefit of high expectations in their interactions with them.

13 Researchers have identified two broad categories of achievement goal orientation: learning goals and performance goals. The learning goal orientation is associated with goals for increasing knowledge and competency, whereas the performance goal orientation is associated with goals aimed at doing better than others. These two broad categories of achievement goal orientation not only lead to qualitatively different student behaviors within the classroom but also respond to different instructional strategies.

14 Tasks and classroom structures that focus students on effort versus ability, on intrinsic interest in learning rather than public rewards, and on effective learning strategies all lead to behaviors consistent with the learning goal orientation.

15 There are three types of learning modes that foster a learning goal orientation: meaningful learning, self-directed learning, and self-referenced learning. Tasks that seem meaningful are more likely to induce students to put forth effort and to become actively engaged in learning than tasks that seem removed from their lives. That is, personally relevant, varied, and challenging tasks produce behaviors which are consistent with a learning goal orientation (e.g., willingness to employ effort-based strategies and to exhibit appropriate attitudes concerning successes and failure).

16 Individuals who are guided by self-directed learning goals take more responsibility for their learning. Consequently, any attempt to increase the degree to which students control their learning will support the development of a learning goal orientation. One way to foster the development of student self-direction and autonomy is for teachers to give students choices and allow them to participate in classroom decisions. Another way is to help students acquire self-regulatory skills (planning, organizing, and monitoring their learning). A critical component of self-regulatory skills is the ability to set personal goals. When tasks are defined by specific and short-term personal goals, students are more likely to believe that they can accomplish them with reasonable effort and are more willing to apply effort to completing the tasks.

17 Self-referenced learning involves the use of evaluation and reward systems which get students to compare their current and prior performances. Personal standards and the amount of effort expended on these standards are consistent with the adoption of a learning goal orientation. Conversely, grading procedures which compare students to others in the classroom and distribute rewards based on ability and competition will support the adoption of a performance goal orientation.

ANSWERS TO QUESTIONS AND EXERCISES

Exercise 9.1: 1. *Extrinsic*. Timothy refrains from throwing a snowball at the passing car in order to avoid an external consequence—being punished.

2. *Intrinsic*. June's decision to stay after work is motivated by a need to master her environment and to be more competent. These are internal personal factors that are tied to her current context.

3. *Extrinsic*. Billy's motivation to study depends upon the external reward of extra allowance. This extra incentive is arbitrarily (not naturally) related to his study behavior.

4. *Intrinsic*. Jan's need to be a competent outdoorsperson motivates her to enroll in the Sierra Club classes. Increased competence is intimately related to the task at hand.

Exercise 9.2: Classical conditioning and operant conditioning assume that behaviors are extrinsically motivated, while social learning theory assumes that behavior is both extrinsically and intrinsically motivated. Piagetian theory, Vygotskian theory, neo-Piagetian theory, and information processing theory assume that behavior is intrinsically motivated. The justification for these assumed sources is contained in the text.

Question 9.1: The four factors that influence an individual's level of self-efficacy are performance attainments, vicarious experiences, verbal persuasion, and physiological states. One of the best ways of knowing whether one is capable of some performance is to attempt it. Repeated success at an activity results in high self-efficacy, while failures will lower self-efficacy unless the poor performance can be attributed to lack of effort or adverse circumstances.

Often we do not need to directly perform a task to gain efficacy information. Watching others succeed at a task can raise our own sense of efficacy, especially if we perceive ourselves to be similar to those observed. We reason that "If he can do it, so can I." By the same token, observing others who are similar to ourselves fail despite high effort lowers our own sense of efficacy. In general, efficacy information obtained from models is more potent when people have little prior experience with which to compare themselves to the models.

Verbal persuasion is widely used to convince people that they possess the capabilities needed to achieve some goal. As teachers we have all attempted to bolster students' confidence in their own abilities. Such persuasion can be beneficial if it boosts students' self-efficacy to the point that they begin trying to succeed.

However, creating an unrealistic sense of competence invites failure that not only discredits the persuader but further undermines the student's self-efficacy.

Finally, self-efficacy information is tied to one's physiological state. People judge their capabilities partly on information gained from monitoring their physiological state. Since anxiety or stress reactions usually debilitate performance, people are more likely to feel most efficacious when they are not feeling aversive levels of arousal.

Exercise 9.3: An operant conditioning analysis of this problem would begin by identifying events or activities that could be used to reinforce John for not pulling Annette's hair or to punish him for doing so. Since John's most preferred activities are putting things on the board and going to geography class, while his least preferred activities are presenting to the whole class, doing homework, and going to math class, the teacher should plan her strategy around these events. The teacher might indicate to John that he has to abide by the following rules during math class: (1) each time he pulls Annette's hair, he will have to present a math homework problem to the whole class, and (2) for each math class in which he does not pull Annette's hair, he will be permitted to put a geography problem on the board during geography class. The teacher needs to deliver these consequences frequently, consistently, and immediately.

A social learning approach to motivating John would attempt to modify his expectations within the classroom situation. In addition to rewarding appropriate behavior and punishing inappropriate behavior, the teacher could recruit classmates who share similar characteristics with John to act as models. These models could be asked to interact with Annette in a courteous and polite manner and the teacher could reward them with consequences that are attractive to John (putting things on the board, not having to do homework, etc.).

Question 9.2: 1. The teacher is taking a hands-on approach to teaching subtraction and addition. Using manipulatives to maintain high levels of motivation is most consistent with Piagetian theory.

2. This demonstration is consistent with both Piagetian and Case's neo-Piagetian views. The demonstration is setting up a conflict between students' experimental observations and their prior knowledge and expectations (heavy objects fall faster). That is consistent with Piagetian theory. However, the teacher has also set up a problem situation: Here's the goal; explain these results. The problem is how to get students from their initial state of misconceptions (which produced an incorrect prediction) to the goal state: a correct understanding of the laws of gravity. This problem-solving demonstration approach is also consistent with Case's neo-Piagetian theory.

3. The physical education teacher has set up this learning activity within a problem format. She has set up a particular situation with a specific goal and has asked students to try to find the best way to arrive at the goal. Setting up classroom activities within problem formats is most consistent with Case's neo-Piagetian theory.

Question 9.3: These three theories have similar views on motivation because they assume that individuals have built-in tendencies that propel them to actively seek out learning opportunities. They also agree that an individual's current developmental level determines her ability to learn, which, in turn, determines what motivational strategies will be effective with her. For example, a student at the preoperational stage is incapable of classifying blocks of various sizes, shapes, and colors according to more than one of these characteristics at a time, and no cleverly contrived problem situation can motivate such learning.

Question 9.4: Belief in internal causation implies a higher level of self-efficacy because personal events are seen as a consequence of one's own actions and thereby potentially under one's own control. External locus of control, on the other hand, implies a lower level of self-efficacy because personal events are seen as beyond one's personal control.

Locus of control and self-efficacy are different, however. Perceptions regarding locus of control concern the outcomes of behaviors, that is, whether individuals have control over personal outcomes or whether they are controlled by external factors. In contrast, perceptions of self-efficacy concern an individual's ability to perform certain desired actions (e.g., be amusing or analyze a problem) regardless of the outcomes of those actions. That is an important difference between self-efficacy and locus of control: The former focuses on the action while the latter focuses on the outcome.

Question 9.5: Dweck and Leggett (1988) point out that students who employ performance goals typically view ability as stable and uncontrollable. That triggers motivational sets which lead students to minimize the amount of effort and energy devoted to pursuing and completing tasks and, when they fail, to expect to continue to do so in the future. In comparison, students who employ learning goals view ability as incremental and controllable. That, in turn, triggers motivational sets that seek challenges and persist in the face of difficulty. Also, these students will expect to succeed in the future.

Question 9.6: According to information processing theory, the more effort and energy you devote to encoding new information meaningfully, the better it will be remembered and learned. Consequently, it is critical that students be willing to employ high-effort learning strategies such as elaborative rehearsal (organization, imagery, mnemonics, etc.); otherwise, they will not be very effective learners.

Question 9.7: Tasks which challenge but stretch a student are considered meaningful. Therefore, if a teacher knows the developmental level of her students (stage of cognitive development or zone of proximal development), she can generate tasks which require skills and knowledge which are slightly more complicated and extensive than students at that developmental level typically possess. By engaging students in tasks that stretch them but are still attainable, the teacher will be providing challenging and meaningful tasks.

Question 9.8: The direct strategy approach emphasizes the important connection between high effort and success. Students are not only told that high effort and success go together but are also involved in experiences that demonstrate the connection. That should increase students' perceived control of their learning and remembering. Also, students who possess effective learning strategies and who have high levels of perceived control are more likely to engage in self-directed learning. Using a direct strategy approach is well-suited, then, to support students' adoption of learning goal orientation.

REFERENCES

Abrahamson, L., Seligman, M., & Teasdale, J. (1978). Learned helplessness in humans: Critique and reformulation. *Journal of Abnormal Psychology, 87,* 49–74.

Allington, R. (1980). Teacher interruption behaviors during primary-grade oral reading. *Journal of Educational Psychology, 71,* 371–377.

Ames, C. (1984). Achievement attributions and self-instructions under competitive and individualistic goal structures. *Journal of Educational Psychology, 76,* 478–487.

Ames, C. (1992). Classrooms: Goals, structures, and student motivation. *Journal of Educational Psychology, 84,* 261–271.

Ames, C., Ames, R., & Felker, D. (1977). Effects of competitive reward structure and valence of outcome on children's attributions. *Journal of Educational Psychology, 69,* 1–8.

Ames, C., & Archer, R. (1984). Systems of student and teacher motivation: Toward a qualitative definition. *Journal of Educational Psychology, 76,* 535–556.

Ames, C., & Archer, R. (1988). Achievement goals in the classroom: Students' learning strategies and motivation processes. *Journal of Educational Psychology, 80,* 260–267.

Anderson, C., & Jennings, D. (1980). When experiences of failure promote expectations of success: The impact of attributing failure to ineffective strategies. *Journal of Personality and Social Psychology, 45,* 393–407.

Andrews, G., & Debus, R. (1978). Persistence and the causal perception of failure: Modifying cognitive attributions. *Journal of Educational Psychology, 70,* 154–166.

Bandura, A. (1986). *Social foundations of thought and action: A social-cognitive theory.* Englewood Cliffs, NJ: Prentice-Hall.

Bandura, M., & Dweck, C. (1981). Children's theories of intelligence as predictors of achievement goals. Unpublished manuscript, Harvard University, Cambridge, MA.

Borkowski, J., Carr, M., Rellinger, E., & Pressley, M. (1990). Self-regulated cognition: Interdependence of metacognition, attributions, and self-esteem. In B. F. Jones and L. Idol (Eds.), *Dimensions of thinking and cognitive instruction.* Hillsdale, NJ: Lawrence Erlbaum.

Brophy, J. (1987). Synthesis of research on strategies for motivating students to learn. *Educational Leadership, 44,* 40–48.

Corno, L., & Rohrkemper, M. (1985). The intrinsic motivation to learn in classroom learning and motivation. In C. Ames & R. Ames (Eds.), *Research on motivation in education* (Vol. 2). San Diego, CA: Academic Press.

Covington, M. (1984). The motive for self-worth. In R. Ames & C. Ames (Eds.), *Research on motivation in education: Student motivation* (Vol. 1). San Diego, CA: Academic Press.

Covington, M., & Omelich, C. (1979). Effort: The double-edged sword in school achievement. *Journal of Educational Psychology, 71,* 169–182.

Covington, M., & Omelich, C. (1981). As failures mount: Affective and cognitive consequences of ability demotion in the classroom. *Journal of Educational Psychology, 73,* 796–808.

Covington, M., & Omelich, C. (1984). An empirical examination of Weiner's critique of attribution research. *Journal of Educational Psychology, 76,* 1199–1213.

Deci, E. (1975). *Intrinsic motivation.* New York: Plenum.

Deci, E., & Ryan, R. M. (1985). *Intrinsic motivation and self-determination in human behavior.* New York: Plenum.

Deiner, C., & Dweck, C. (1978). An analysis of learned helplessness: Continuous changes in performance, strategy, and achievement cognitions after failure. *Journal of Personality and Social Psychology, 36,* 451–462.

Dweck, C. (1975). The role of expectations and attributions in the alleviation of learned helplessness. *Journal of Personality and Social Psychology, 32,* 674–685.

Dweck, C. (1989). Motivation. In A. Lesgold & R. Glaser (Eds.), *Foundations for a Psychology of Education.* Hillsdale, NJ: Lawrence Erlbaum.

Dweck, C. (1992). The study of goals in psychology. *Psychological Science, 3,* 165–167.

Dweck, C., & Leggett, E. (1988). A social-cognitive approach to motivation and personality. *Psychological Review, 95,* 256–273.

Epstein, J. (1988). Effective schools and effective students: Dealing with diversity. In R. Haskins & D. MacRae (Eds.), *Policies for America's public schools: Teacher equity indicators.* Norwood, NJ: Ablex.

Fyans, L., & Maehr, M. (1979). Attributional style, task selection, and achievement. *Journal of Educational Psychology, 71,* 499–507.

Fosterling, F. (1985). Attributional retraining: A review. *Psychological Bulletin, 48,* 495–512.

Garner, R. (1990). When children and adults do not use learning strategies. *Review of Educational Research, 60,* 517–530.

Gilmor, T., & Morton, H. (1979). Locus of control and causal attributions for positive and negative outcomes on university examinations. *Journal of Research in Personality, 13,* 154–160.

Good, T., & Brophy, J. (1984). *Looking in the classrooms* (3rd Edition). New York: Harper & Row.

Graham, S. (1991). Attribution theory in achievement contexts. *Educational Psychology Review, 3,* 5–40.

Graham, S., & Golan, S. (1991). From motivation to cognition: The effects of ego- versus task-focused feedback on depth of processing. *Journal of Educational Psychology, 83,* 187–194.

Hiroto, D. S. (1974). Locus of control and learned helplessness. *Journal of Experimental Psychology, 102,* 187–193.

Jagacinski, C., & Nicholls, J. G. (1984). Conceptions of ability and related affects in task involvement and ego involvement. *Journal of Educational Psychology, 76,* 909–919.

Jagacinski, C., & Nicholls, J. G. (1987). Competence and affect in task involvement and ego involvement: The impact of social comparison information. *Journal of Educational Psychology, 79,* 107–114.

Kun, A., & Weiner, B. (1973). Necessary versus sufficient causal schemata for success and failure. *Journal of Research in Personality, 7,* 197–207.

Lepper, M., & Hodell, M. (1989). Intrinsic motivation in the classroom. In C. Ames & R. Ames (Eds.), *Research on motivation in education* (Vol. 3). New York: Academic Press.

McClelland, D., Atkinson, J., Clark, J., and Lowell, E. (1953). *The achievement motive.* New York: Appleton-Century Crofts.

Murray, H. A. (1938). *Explorations in personality.* New York: Oxford University Press.

Nicholls, J. (1984). Achievement motivation: Conceptions of ability, subjective experience, task choice and performance. *Psychological Review, 91,* 328–346.

Nicholls, J. (1989). *The competitive ethos and democratic education.* Cambridge, MA: Harvard University Press.

Nolen, S. (1988). Reasons for studying: Motivational orientations and study strategies. *Cognition and Instruction, 5,* 269–287.

Nolen, S., & Haldyna, T. (1990). Motivation and studying in high school science. *Journal of Research on Science Teaching, 27,* 115–126.

Raynor, J., & Smith, C. (1966). Achievement related motives and risk taking in games of skill and chance. *Journal of Personality, 34,* 176–198.

Rotter, J. (1966). Generalized expectancies for internal versus external control of reinforcement. *Psychological Monographs, 180,* 1–28.

Ryan, R., & Grolnick, W. (1986). Origins and pawns in the classroom: Self-report and projective assessments of individual differences in children's perceptions. *Journal of Personality and Social Psychology, 50,* 550–558.

Schunk, D. (1989). Self-efficacy and cognitive skill learning. In Ames, C. Ames, & R. Ames (Eds.), *Research on motivation in education.* (Vol. 3). New York: Academic Press.

Seligman, M. (1975). *Helplessness: On depression, development, and death.* San Francisco: W. H. Freeman.

Stipek, D. (1992). *Motivation to learn: From theory to practice.* Boston: Allyn & Bacon.

Stipek, D., & Daniels, D. (1988). Declining perceptions of competence: A consequence of changes in the child or in the educational environment? *Journal of Educational Psychology, 80,* 352–356.

Weiner, B. (1985). *An attributional theory of motivation and emotion.* New York: Springer-Verlag.

Weiner, B. (1992). *Human motivation: Metaphors, theories and research.* London: Sage Publications.

Weiner, B., & Graham, S. (1984). An attributional approach to emotional development. In C. Izard, J. Kagan, & R. Zacone (Eds.), *Emotions, cognition, and behavior* (pp. 167–191). Cambridge: Cambridge University.

Weiner, B., Graham, S., Taylor, S., & Meyer, W. (1983). Social cognition in the classroom, *Educational Psychologists.* 18, 109–124.

Weiner, B., & Kukla, A. (1970). An attributional analysis of achievement motivation. *Journal of Personality and Social Psychology, 15,* 1–20.

Wentzel, K. (1991). Social competence at school: Relationship of social responsibility and academic achievement. *Review of Educational Research, 81,* 131–142.

Woolfolk, A., & Brooks, D. (1985). The influence of teachers' nonverbal behaviors on students' perceptions and performance. *Elementary School Journal, 85,* 514–528.

ADDENDUM TO PART ONE

COMPARISON OF THEORIES ON THE CORE ISSUES

It occurred to us that a good way to end Part One of this book is by giving a reprise of the core issues. In the summary of the issues given below and in Table A.1 we have endeavored to compare and contrast the various theories that we have discussed in Part One.

What Is Learned?

In Chapter 1 we defined learning as a relatively permanent change in knowledge or behavior as a result of experience. The theories we have discussed focus on either changes in behavior (i.e., classical and operant conditioning theory) or changes in knowledge (i.e., information processing theory, Piaget, Case, Vygotsky, and Bandura). Each theory attempts to explain how a particular aspect of either behavior or knowledge is learned or developed (see Table A.1).

What Is the Relative Emphasis on Environmental versus Organismic Factors in Learning?

The behavioral theories (classical and operant conditioning) both place relatively greater weight on the role of the environment in bringing about changes in behavior, with the organism playing a passive role. In contrast to behavioral theory, all of the cognitive theories view the organism as playing a more active role in the learning process. The cognitive theories differ from one another in terms of the relative weight given to the two factors. For example, information processing theory attributes learning almost entirely to factors inside the organism. Piaget and

Case view learning/development as involving an interaction of the organism with the environment, so they place nearly equal weight on the two factors. Although Vygotsky clearly viewed the learner as an active participant in learning, he gave relatively more emphasis to the influence of sociocultural factors in learning. Bandura is unique in his insistence on reciprocal determination of organismic, environmental, and behavioral variables in learning. Compared with behavioral theorists, he places more emphasis on cognitive and affective factors, while compared with other cognitive theorists, he emphasizes environmental influences more strongly.

What Is the Source of Motivation for Learning?

Motivation plays a role in all of the theories except for classical conditioning theory which asserts that conditioning occurs whether the organism is motivated or not. Each theory views motivation in a different way. In operant theory, biological drives such as hunger must be present in primary conditioning. Additionally, reinforcers can become incentives which motivate behavior. Although information processing theory has little to say about motivation, most theorists within this framework consider the need to make sense of the world as the major source of motivation. Piaget's and Case's views are somewhat similar in that they view individuals as being intrinsically motivated to interact with the environment and, consequently, to develop and learn. In Vygotsky's view, the source of motivation resides both in the child and in the child's sociocultural environment. The child's inherent activity and curiosity, combined with the adult's motivation to pass on cultural knowledge, impel learning and development. According to Bandura, people are motivated to perform modeled activities when they expect desirable outcomes for doing so and when they believe that they are capable of performing the behavior. Motivation influences performance rather than learning. That is, the acquisition of a cognitive representation through observation of a model can occur without incentives.

How Does Transfer Occur?

In both behavioral theories, generalization is synonymous with transfer. In classical conditioning, the tendency for stimuli that are physically or semantically similar to the conditioned stimulus to elicit the conditioned response accounts for transfer. In operant conditioning, when a response is reinforced in a particular situation, other situations that are similar to the first, either physically or semantically, will serve to cue that response.

Information processing theory and Bandura's theory have similar views of transfer. Knowledge learned in one setting will transfer to a new setting to the extent that cues in the new setting activate appropriate representations in long-term memory.

Piaget viewed transfer of skills to new situations as occurring automatically as a function of global changes in the child's knowledge structures. For example,

TABLE A.1   COMPARISON OF THEORIES ON CORE ISSUES

Core issue	Classical conditioning	Operant conditioning	Information processing
What is learned or developed?	A reflexive response to a neutral stimulus	A particular response in a particular situation	New knowledge added to memory
Emphasis on environment versus organismic factors?	Learner is passively acted on by stimuli in the environment	Shaping of learner by reinforcement contingencies	Internal factors such as working memory capacity and knowledge base
What is the source of motivation?	Plays little role. Conditioning occurs whether person is motivated or not	Biological drives in primary conditioning; reinforcers become incentives	Humans seek meaning and derive satisfaction from gaining knowledge that enables them to understand the world
How does transfer occur?	Stimulus generalization	Stimulus generalization	Retrieval cues in the new setting must activate representations in memory
What are some important variables in instruction?	Timing and repetition of unconditioned and conditioned stimuli	Nature and timing of reinforcement; behavioral objectives, task analysis, supportive environment	Attention, schema activation, capacity of working memory, encoding strategies, retrieval cues

once a child develops the ability to reason concretely in one content area, that ability should transfer automatically to new content areas. Case, in contrast, does not believe that developments in one content domain necessarily transfer to other domains. However, practice of cognitive skills within a variety of content domains will help transfer.

According to Vygotsky, transfer depends upon the child's having first internalized skills and knowledge from external sources. Thereafter, the child can search for similarities between new and old problems. The child first learns to transfer knowledge and skills from more to less familiar situations under the guidance of a more capable adult who helps the child make connections.

What Are Important Variables in Instruction?

Both behavioral theories stress the importance of environmental stimuli in instruction. Classical conditioning theory focuses on the timing and repetition of the unconditioned and conditioned stimuli. Operant theory focuses on the nature and timing of reinforcement. Additional instructional elements important to operant theory include behavioral objectives, task analysis, entering behavior, instruction, assessment, and supportive environment.

Information processing theory emphasizes variables that influence perception,

TABLE A.1 *(continued)*

Bandura	Piaget	Case	Vygotsky
Cognitive representations of behavior	Ability to reason logically	Ability to reason logically	Ability to use culture's psychological tools
Internal factors, environmental factors, and behavior reciprocally determine each other	Equal weight to environmental and organismic factors in development	Equal weight to environmental and organismic factors in development	Greater emphasis on social-cultural than organismic factors
Outcome expectations and self-efficacy motivate people to perform	Child is intrinsically motivated to interact with the environment and to resolve conflict	Child is intrisically motivated to solve problems and to develop ever more sophisticated strategies	Curiosity and activity of child plus motivation of adults to pass on cultural tools
Retrieval cues in the new setting must activate representations in memory	Child automatically applies new level of reasoning across domains	Practice of skills across a variety of domains and increase in efficiency of STSS	Child learns to relate knowledge and skills to new problems under adult guidance
Variables that optimize attention, retention, and reproduction	Stage of reasoning; cognitive conflict; sequence of instruction	Capacity of child's STSS; practice on operations and strategies	The quality of interactions with adults and peers within the child's zone of proximal development

comprehension, and remembering. They include attention, activation of relevant schemas in long-term memory, encoding activities that elaborate upon and organize the material, and a variety of effective retrieval cues.

According to both Piaget and Case, one of the most important variables influencing instruction is the child's current developmental level. According to Piaget, instruction is a matter of exposing the child to situations that don't quite fit her existing system of schemes so that she will be challenged to develop. In addition to this, Case specifies that the mental processes and strategies involved in problem solving must be practiced and automatized.

According to Vygotsky, the most important instructional variables are the nature and quality of interactions between the teacher and child, and between the child and peers. The teacher must determine the child's region of sensitivity to instruction (zone of proximal development) and adjust instruction to support the child's emerging capabilities.

The important variables in instruction according to Bandura are those that enhance the processes of observational learning. These include modeling practices that optimize attention, retention, and reproduction. Additionally, motivational techniques such as providing direct and vicarious reinforcement and boosting students' self-efficacy are important for enhancing students' performance of activities learned through modeling.

APPLICATION OF THE THEORIES

10

INTRODUCTION TO THE APPLICATION CHAPTERS

OBJECTIVES

1. Describe the four steps to solving instructional problems.
2. Distinguish between learning and nonlearning problems and be able to classify novel examples of each type of problem.
3. Describe the four categories of learning problems, give examples of each category, and be able to classify novel examples of each category.
4. Describe key concepts and methods for solving each of the four categories of learning problems.
5. Describe the process of evaluating plans for solving learning problems.
6. Distinguish between evaluation tools which match the instructional intervention and those that do not match the instructional intervention.

In chapters 2 through 9, we described central ideas and instructional implications of major learning theories within educational psychology. You should now have a large battery of techniques and methods with which to tackle any instructional problem that you may encounter. For example, if your students are having difficulty remembering new vocabulary words, you can use elaborative and organizational techniques to help them remember (see Chapter 4). Also, if a student in your class constantly disturbs other students by cracking her knuckles, you might positively reinforce her for not cracking her knuckles (see Chapter 2).

Within this chapter we will discuss ways to approach instructional problems and how to use the techniques and methods previously discussed in solving these problems. Our discussion will be informed by current theory on problem solving (see Chapter 5) and by an instructional theory proposed by Robert Gagné (1985).

In addition, we will present an extended description of a fictitious school system (Howard City Independent School System) which serves as the context for the problem solving cases that follow. This description will include information about school services, personnel, students, and the community as well as a little history about current crises and conditions within the school system. Each of the following chapters (11–14) then focuses on a different type of instructional problem and techniques for solving these problems.

SOLVING PROBLEMS WITHIN THE CLASSROOM

As we described in Chapter 5, problem solving is a four-step process: analyzing problem information (coming up with a problem representation), searching for relevant knowledge and experience which may help solve the problem (creating a problem space), developing a plan to solve the problem, and, finally, verifying or evaluating whether the plan will solve the problem. The following sections will discuss each of these steps in detail.

Analysis of a Classroom Problem

The first step to solving a classroom problem is to gather vital information about the student or students involved (e.g., academic skills and prior classroom experiences) and the context of the problem (math class, during quiet activities, etc.), including nonclassroom factors such as student health and community and home environment. Analyzing this information allows us to identify potential causes for the problem behaviors. As an illustration, if a student is not paying attention in class (which is the problem), you would want to identify and investigate potential causes such as her reading and study skills, her history of failure and success, whether she has trouble paying attention during both simple and complex classroom activities, whether there are any preexisting physiological conditions, and the nature of her community and home environment. Once you have a detailed idea of the givens of a particular problem, then you can decide whether you have a learning or a nonlearning problem.

"Learning" Problems   A learning problem is due to a student's lack of appropriate knowledge, skill, attitude, or prior experience. Consequently, solving a learning problem requires the development and implementation of an instructional intervention which focuses on these factors. For example, in the situation described earlier, if the student's lack of attention occurs when she is faced with complex problems but not with simpler problems, then it may be due to inefficient attentional strategies and, consequently, would be classified as a "learning problem." In this case, an instructional intervention focusing on the teaching of attentional strategies to more efficiently process complex information may alleviate the problem.

If a classroom problem is due to community factors, school system factors, a student's family environment, or a student's health, then it is not a learning problem, and the techniques discussed in this book may not be helpful. For example, if the attentional problem just described is due to a preexisting health condition (e.g., hyperactivity), then the appropriate response is to ask the school and parents to consult a physician. Alternatively, if the student's lack of attention seems to be related to a community or home environment that bombards her with distracting, fast-paced, or upsetting stimuli, then the appropriate response is to discuss the situation with her parents and get their help in modifying the home or community environment.

In summary, learning and nonlearning problems differ in terms of both their perceived causes and the nature of their solution. Learning problems are due to a lack of appropriate knowledge, skills, attitudes, and/or experiences. Conversely, nonlearning problems are due to deficiencies in the student's health and/or family, community, and societal environment. Given these different perceived causes, learning and nonlearning problems require very different solutions. That is, learning problems can be solved with an instructional intervention, whereas nonlearning problems generally cannot be solved with one. The focus of the rest of this chapter and the chapters that follow is on analyzing and finding solutions for learning problems.

Exercise 10.1: Please classify each of the following problems as "learning" or "nonlearning" and justify your classification. Please note: This exercise contains both teacher and student problems.

Problem A: Mr. Apple needs to develop some lessons to help one of his students become a more proficient reader. Unfortunately, given his course load, he is unable to find the time to develop these lessons. How can Mr. Apple get more time to devote to this project?

Problem B: Brittany is always late to class in the morning because she has to take care of her younger brother (bathe and feed him) before she can come to school. How can we get Brittany to come to school on time?

Problem C: Mr. Lemon, an inexperienced teacher, has difficulty managing, particularly when the students first come into the classroom. Students complain that Mr. Lemon has not explicitly stated classroom rules and regulations. How can Mr. Lemon get his students to be better behaved?

Problem D: In a history class, although most students can clearly state the definition of "statement of fact" and "statement of opinion," many students are unable to discriminate between examples of statements of fact and of statements of opinion. How can we get these students to discriminate between fact and opinion?

_____

_____

Problem E: Richard has difficulty paying attention in class because he works evenings until 1:00 A.M. How can we get Richard to pay attention?

_____

_____

Analysis of the Learning Problem

After your preliminary analysis of the givens of a situation indicates that you are faced with a learning problem, the next step is to further analyze the learning problem and identify and describe the goal or outcome of instruction. Given a learning problem, the general goal of the instructional intervention is to modify or add to a student's existing knowledge, attitudes, and experiences. However, in order to begin developing an adequate intervention, one needs to identify the specific changes in the student's knowledge, attitudes, and experiences that are required to solve the problem. These specific changes are the learning outcome of your instructional intervention. For example, if you decide that the reason one student constantly pulls the hair of another is her disinterest in classroom activities, then the learning outcome of your instructional intervention would be to modify her level of motivation.

Taxonomies of Learning Outcomes   There is a variety of ways to categorize learning outcomes. Many of you may already be familiar with Bloom's Taxonomies (Bloom, Englehart, Frost, Hill, & Krathwohl, 1956; Harrow, 1972; Krathwohl, Bloom, & Masia, 1956). Bloom and his colleagues created taxonomies of learning outcomes within the cognitive, psychomotor, and affective domain. Each domain consists of multiple levels of outcomes which are arranged in hierarchical order from least to most complex. In contrast, Gagné (1985) generated a simple, usable taxonomy of learning outcomes which consists of the following five categories: attitude, verbal information, intellectual skills, motor skills, and cognitive strategies. The taxonomy employed within this and the next four chapters is a slightly modified version of Gagné's (1985) taxonomy.

Categories of Learning Problems   Our taxonomy consists of four learning outcomes or categories which involve the acquisition or modification of (1) positive attitude and motivation, (2) verbal information, (3) intellectual skills, and (4) cognitive strategies and metacognition.

Positive attitude and motivation problems concern a student's beliefs, attitudes, attributions, goals, and/or affect (emotion) related to learning and learning environments. This type of problem may require the modification of a student's declarative and procedural knowledge. Changes in declarative knowledge may involve modifying a student's internal statements describing her beliefs, attitudes, attributions, goals, and/or affect related to learning and learning environments. Changes in procedural knowledge may involve developing student goal-setting skills and coping skills. Typical indicators of positive attitude and motivation problems are a student's exhibiting inappropriate behaviors (e.g., acting out), consistently failing, choosing not to get involved in activities, and giving up easily on difficult tasks. For example, a student may have maladaptive attributions about the causes of her academic failures and successes. That is, she might wrongly attribute failure to a lack of ability, and that misapprehension interferes with her classroom performance. In this case, a useful instructional intervention might focus on changing the student's maladaptive attribution while teaching the student effective learning strategies.

Verbal information problems focus on a student's ability to verbalize previously presented information. This type of problem requires the modification of a student's factual declarative knowledge. Typical indicators of this problem are a student's inability to restate words or a sequence of words or to reconstruct an organized presentation of a verbal passage. A student's inability to remember and repeat important dates within a history class would be classified as a verbal information problem. A useful intervention in this case might involve presenting images that connect the dates with the event to help the student remember these dates.

Intellectual skills problems focus on a student's ability to apply a specific skill or concept or to discriminate between objects, events, or people. This type of problem focuses primarily on the modification of a student's procedural knowledge. Typical indicators of this problem are a student's inability to apply a specific skill or concept or to discriminate between characteristics, events, objects, or people. A student's inability to identify the main idea in a reading passage would be classified as an intellectual skills problem, that is, lack of a specific skill. An effective intervention in this instance might involve identifying the critical attributes of main ideas, creating examples and nonexamples of main ideas, and asking the student to separate the examples from the nonexamples.

As you have probably noticed, we have chosen not to focus on motor skills problems. This decision was based upon the following: (1) the discussion of skills within the previous chapters has been mainly focused on cognitive rather than motor skills, and (2) the extensive literature on motor skills and motor learning suggests that there are important differences between the acquisition and use of motor skills and intellectual skills (see Salmoni, 1989). Consequently, we felt that any attempt to include motor skills at this point would be inappropriate.

Finally, **cognitive strategy and metacognition problems** focus on diagnosing, planning, selecting, and monitoring the basic cognitive processes: perception, attention, memory, thinking, and problem solving. This type of problem requires the modification of a student's declarative, procedural, and metacognitive knowledge. Typical indicators of this problem are a student's inability to identify, use, and/or monitor appropriate strategies. If a student is having difficulty understanding a reading assignment, it may be due to a lack of appropriate cognitive strategies and metacognitive knowledge. The solution to this problem may be to explicitly teach the student specific strategies for monitoring his reading and for dealing with difficulties in comprehension.

Exercise 10.2: Classify each of the following learning problems, using these four categories: positive attitude and motivation, verbal information, intellectual skills, and cognitive strategies and metacognition. Please justify your classification.

Problem A: Within a Spanish course, John is having difficulty remembering definitions of new vocabulary words. John does not, however, have a problem remembering themes of stories or other verbal material when it is presented in a

meaningful context._____

Problem B: Timothy is unable to solve algebraic equations which have more

than one unknown._____

Problem C: Mary consistently fails to put much effort into solving science problems and gives up the minute one becomes difficult. However, when the teacher helps and guides her through the problem, it is clear that she has appropriate

content knowledge and problem-solving skills._____

_____

Problem D: Marcus is a class clown and constantly disrupts classroom activities

and lessons. Apparently, he has a high need for attention._____

_____

Problem E: Megan is able to correctly state the definition of the concept "de-

ciduous" but is unable to identify novel examples of this concept._____

_____

Problem F: Marcelle always has trouble doing well on essay exams. She uses the same study techniques for all other types of exams and she does well on them.

She wonders why the techniques don't work for essay exams._____

_____

We have presented four categories of learning outcomes and the typical behavioral indicators associated with each of them. However, it is important to note that in the "real world" of the classroom, learning problems are seldom as uni-dimensional as our descriptions, indicators, and examples suggest. For instance, when a student does not invoke strategies (a cognitive strategy and metacognition problem), it may well be because she does not think that strategies or anything else will improve performance (a positive attitude and motivation problem). In most cases, there are multiple causes for classroom learning problems.

Determine Relevant Theoretical Knowledge

The primary purpose of categorizing a learning problem is to accurately represent it, which then allows you to identify an appropriate problem space. These problem spaces will include schemas representing techniques and information that will help solve these types of problems. For example, a problem space for verbal information problems should include both a description of (declarative knowl-edge) and guidelines for using (procedural knowledge) techniques such as im-agery, networking, and outlining which help students remember new information. Such techniques should be applicable to a wide variety of settings and content areas (e.g., mathematics, social science, history, art, music). Tables 10.1 through 10.4 consist of representative problem spaces for each category of learning prob-lem.

Notice that techniques within each problem space are drawn from multiple theories. For example, in the cognitive strategy and metacognition category, there are techniques from information processing theory (repeated practice, metacog-nitive information), social cognitive theory (modeling), and Vygotsky's theory (re-ciprocal dialogue). When approaching problems in the classroom, it is often appropriate to draw from multiple theories. But organizing your knowledge of learning and instruction by theory rather than by learning outcome may actually interfere with the solution of classroom learning problems. That is why we have chosen to organize the application of these theories by learning problem rather than by theory.

Up to this point, we have used the following terms to describe the organization of knowledge related to solving problems: problem categories, problem spaces, and schemas. Let's take a moment to clearly differentiate these terms. "Problem categories" refers to the four broad learning outcomes: positive attitude and mo-tivation, verbal information, intellectual skills, and cognitive strategies and meta-cognition. Each category includes a description of the typical student behaviors associated with it. For example, a student's lack of persistence at completing a task is an indication of a positive attitude and motivation problem.

Once an instructional problem has been categorized, we gain access to the related problem space. As we indicated earlier, "problem space" consists of all relevant declarative and procedural knowledge which will allow us to analyze, develop, implement, and evaluate a solution to the problem at hand. It is organized into "schemas" to represent the different types of subproblems which fit into each problem space. For example, for intellectual skills, we have separated the problem space into a schema that focuses on concept learning problems and one that

TABLE 10.1 REPRESENTATIVE PROBLEM SPACE FOR POSITIVE ATTITUDE AND MOTIVATION PROBLEMS

Key concept: Importance of clear, specific, immediate, and positive feedback for maintaining high levels of motivation and a positive attitude.

Key concept: Importance of engaging students in meaningful, self-directed, and self-referenced learning activities for facilitating the development of a learning goal orientation.

Key concept: Student characteristics such as attentional and memory limitations, developmental level, and lack of prior knowledge and experience can interfere with the effectiveness of motivational interventions.

Method for modifying inappropriate behavior (e.g., acting out, disrupting class, not following stated rules)

---

1 Clearly specify problem behavior; then

2 identify antecedents and consequences to problem behavior; then

3 identify potential reinforcers for specific student; then

4 organize environment so that appropriate behaviors are followed by reinforcers but inappropriate behaviors have no reinforcers.

Methods for modifying inappropriate attitudes, attributions, and beliefs (e.g., consistently gives up or fails, chooses not to get involved in challenging tasks)

---

1 Establish a pattern of success on the target tasks and provide extensive feedback and reinforcement which focuses on the importance of effort.

AND/OR

1 Provide teacher or peer modeling of skills needed to successfully perform the target task. Also provide extensive feedback and reinforcement which focuses on the importance of effort.

AND/OR

1 Get student to identify a set of attainable, moderately difficult and specific goals related to the target task. Then monitor progress toward these goals with extensive feedback and reinforcement which focuses on the importance of effort.

Methods for modifying inappropriate affect (e.g., anxiety related to learning, learning environments, or teachers)

---

1 Identify stimulus which elicits inappropriate affect; then eliminate that stimulus.

OR

1 Identify stimulus which elicits inappropriate affect and, if you cannot eliminate it, pair stimulus with incompatible stimuli (e.g., relaxation, comfort, pleasure).

---

focuses on problem-solving problems. In summary, problem category information facilitates the identification and classification of an instructional problem. Once categorized, information within the related problem space and schema allows one to develop, implement, and evaluate a solution plan. We hope that, given the above discussion, you have a better understanding of these similar terms.

This book and related classroom experiences should help you organize your knowledge of learning and instructional techniques into usable problem spaces and schema such as those shown in tables 10.1 to 10.4. Such schemas, when organized into problem spaces, allow you to access relevant information more

TABLE 10.2   REPRESENTATIVE PROBLEM SPACE FOR VERBAL INFORMATION PROBLEMS

Key concept: The more effort required to meaningfully process the to-be-remembered information, the higher the probability of remembering and being able to access that information.

Key concept: There are important attentional limits on the amount of effort that can be devoted to the processing of information.

Key concept: There are important limits on the amount of information that can be stored in STM/ working memory.

Key concept: These limits (attentional and STM) are influenced by maturation (e.g., developmental level) and experience (e.g., schooling, practice).

Key concept: Match the context of instruction to the context within which the to-be-remembered information will be retrieved.

Methods for making information meaningful

1 Identify relevant and meaningful student schemas (e.g., prior experiences, familiar events and people) and relate these to the to-be-remembered information you present.

OR

1 Use elaboration techniques such as imagery, key-word method, verbal enhancement, and analogies (see pages 121–128). Imagery is well-suited for concrete words; key-word method is well-suited for vocabulary learning; and analogies are well-suited for abstract words. Verbal enhancements can be used with most types of words.

OR

1 Use organizational techniques such as outlining and networking (see pages 119–120). Outlining is well-suited for hierarchically organized materials.

efficiently. The intent of chapters 11 through 14 is to help you organize your knowledge of learning and instruction into the following learning problem categories: cognitive strategies and metacognition, positive attitude and motivation, verbal information, and intellectual skills.

Development of Proposed Instructional Solution

After you have categorized a learning problem and gained access to the relevant problem space in your long-term memory, the next step is to develop a plan for moving from the givens to the goal. That requires further analysis and questioning. For example, you might decide to use the difference-reduction heuristic (see Chapter 5) which helps find important differences between the current situation and the goal. Once you have identified these differences, then you can develop an appropriate plan for solving the problem. As illustrations, we will describe the process of solving certain problems from Exercise 10.2.

Positive Attitude and Motivation Problems

Problem C: Mary consistently fails to put much effort in solving science problems and gives up the minute they become difficult. However, when the teacher helps and guides her through the problem, it is clear that she has appropriate content knowledge and problem solving skills.

TABLE 10.3   REPRESENTATIVE PROBLEM SPACE FOR INTELLECTUAL SKILLS PROBLEMS

Key concept: Repeated practice is critical to the acquisition of intellectual skills. The nature of practice will differ depending upon the nature of the specific intellectual skill.

Key concept: There are important attentional limits on the amount of effort that can be devoted to the processing of information.

Key concept: There are important limits on the amount of information that can be stored in STM/working memory.

Key concept: These limits (attentional and STM) are influenced by maturation (e.g., developmental level) and experience (e.g., schooling, practice)

Key concept: The level of cognitive development plus limits on the intellectual skills that can be acquired.

Key concept: To the extent that it is possible, the context of instruction and practice should match the context within which the concepts and skills will be used.

Methods for teaching specific concepts

A) Concept definitions:

1 Identify critical attributes, prototypes, and distinctive exemplars of target concept; then use verbal information techniques (see Table 10.2) for encoding into memory.

THEN

B) Concept classification:

1 Create a concept taxonomy (see Chapter 5) and identify superordinate, coordinate, and subordinate categories.

2 Select and present nonexamples from the coordinate categories with matched examples, and ask students to practice identifying examples. Follow each student response with extensive feedback (e.g., "no, that is not an example because . . . .").

3 Present a wide variety of examples and nonexamples and ask students to practice identifying examples. Follow each student response with extensive feedback.

Method for teaching specific skills

1 Break the skill into its basic components.

2 Verbally describe and/or demonstrate (model) the first component; then ask student to practice first component until automatic.

3 Verbally describe and/or demonstrate (model) first and second component; then ask student to practice first and second component until automatic.

4 Add each component following the above procedure until student can perform all components of skill in smooth and automatic fashion.

Within this situation, the current state is Mary's lack of persistence in solving difficult science problems, and the goal is for Mary to develop a high level of persistence. Using the problem space depicted in Table 10.1 for positive attitude and motivation problems, the following internal dialogue illustrates a series of questions and answers that could be asked in order to move from the current state to the goal.

TABLE 10.4 REPRESENTATIVE PROBLEM SPACE FOR COGNITIVE STRATEGY AND METACOGNITION PROBLEMS

Key concept: Repeated practice is critical to the acquisition of cognitive strategies. The nature of practice will differ depending upon the nature of the specific strategy.

Key concept: It is important to establish metacognitive scaffolding for the appropriate selection, use, and monitoring of cognitive strategies.

Key concept: There are important attentional limits on the amount of effort that can be devoted to the processing of information.

Key concept: There are important limits on the amount of information that can be stored in STM/working memory.

Key concept: These limits (attentional and STM) are influenced by maturation (e.g., developmental level) and experience (e.g., schooling, practice).

Key concept: The level of cognitive development puts limits on the cognitive strategies that can be acquired.

Key concept: To the extent that it is possible, the context of instruction and practice should match the context within which the cognitive strategies will be used.

Methods for teaching cognitive strategies

A) Direct explanation approach (can be used with large groups):

1 Alert students that they are to learn a strategy.

2 Explicitly point out the connection between use of strategy and performance—strategy use requires effort but will pay off.

3 Model the strategy through verbal description and actual demonstration.

4 Provide students with metacognitive scaffolding by indicating why the strategy works and when to use it.

5 Ask students to practice the strategy, giving them extensive feedback.

6 Watch for independent use of strategy, rewarding its appropriate use and reminding students that good performance is linked to both effort and use of the strategy.

7 When testing over content learned via the strategy, give feedback on the strategy-performance link.

8 Monitor students for spontaneous use. If lacking, prompt students to use the strategy.

OR

B) Reciprocal teaching approach (best used with small groups):

1 Select a task (e.g., understanding narrative prose, solving mathematical problem) with which students are having difficulty. Identify critical strategies related to successfully completing the task. For example, for understanding narrative prose, the discussion should be centered around the use of four strategies—predicting, questioning, summarizing, and clarifying.

2 Select a discussion leader; then instruct each student in the group to read task material, and ask the leader to summarize the content of the material and pose a question about important information contained in the material.

3 Have the leader ask members of the group to discuss possible answer(s), with the teacher providing clarifications, modeling her strategies by "thinking aloud," identifying when and why the strategies work, and providing guidance and support to students.

4 After extensive discussion, have the leader predict future directions of the story or pose answers to problems raised in the story.

5 Repeat this process, with other students in the group taking on the role of leader.

Question: How can we get Mary to be persistent, able to overcome roadblocks, and motivated when solving science problems?

Answer: We can increase her level of self-efficacy.

Question: How can we increase her self-efficacy?

Answer: One way would be to increase the probability of success at solving science problems and to establish a history of success at solving science problems.

Question: How can we do that?

Answer: By giving her easier problems and working up to more difficult problems.

Given such a dialogue, an appropriate plan for solving the above problem might consist of the following steps:

1 Identify science problems that Mary is having difficulty completing.

2 Given these problems, identify progressively simpler ones and arrange them in a learning hierarchy from simplest to most complex.

3 Engage Mary in solving the easiest problems, giving her immediate and positive feedback after she successfully completes each one.

4 After she has established a history of success on these easier problems, move her to next level of problem, and so on.

It is important to note that the above plan will not solve all positive attitude and motivation problems. For example, classroom behavior problems (e.g., acting out) are best solved through the manipulation of consequences (e.g., positive reinforcement) without any reference to self-efficacy. The purpose of manipulating consequences would be to motivate the student who is acting out not to do so and to exhibit alternative appropriate behaviors. So, even after categorizing a problem and identifying an appropriate problem space, there is still a variety of possible solutions depending upon the exact nature and context of the learning problem.

Verbal Information Outcome

Problem A: Within a Spanish course, John is having difficulty remembering definitions of new vocabulary words. John does not, however, have a problem remembering themes of stories or other verbal material when it is presented in a meaningful context.

As indicated earlier, this situation can be categorized as a verbal information problem. Given the problem space presented in Table 10.2, let's employ a difference-reduction heuristic to find an appropriate solution.

Question: How can we get John to remember the new vocabulary words?

Answer: One way would be to make the words more meaningful for him.

Question: How can we make the words more meaningful?

Answer: We could use an elaboration method.

Question: Is there any particular elaboration method which is well suited for learning new words?

Answer: Yes: the key-word method (see Chapter 4).

Given the above, an appropriate plan for attacking this problem would consist of the following steps:

1 Identify new vocabulary words that are to be learned.

2 Identify John's prior abilities, experiences, and interests (as described in initial analysis of problem).

3 Employ the key-word method to create meaningful images for each vocabulary word.

4 Given John's abilities (e.g., processing limitations) create a lesson which includes meaningful images for each vocabulary word.

Depending upon the goals of the classroom teacher, the above situation could also be categorized as a cognitive strategy and metacognition problem. Using this problem-solving space, the teacher might elect to teach the student specific strategies (e.g., create meaningful images) that he could use on his own to help him remember new vocabulary. As is the case with nonlearning problems, there are often multiple ways to solve the same learning problem.

Intellectual Skills Problem

Problem E: Megan is able to correctly state the definition of "deciduous" but is unable to classify novel examples of this concept.

Given the problem space depicted in Table 10.3 for intellectual skills problems, the following is a series of questions that may help identify and plan a specific solution:

Question: How can I get Megan to correctly classify novel examples of the concept "deciduous"?

Answer: She needs to practice classifying novel examples and nonexamples.

Question: How do I identify appropriate teaching examples and nonexamples?

Answer: Create a taxonomy which includes superordinate, coordinate, and subordinate concepts (see pages 163–164 in Chapter 5 for examples) and use instances from these concepts as nonexamples. To generate appropriate teaching examples, consult existing reference works (e.g., biology books).

The plan for teaching Megan classification skills for the concept "deciduous" would be:

1 Create a taxonomy of the concept "trees."

2 Select close-in nonexamples (which possess one less critical attribute than examples) from coordinate concepts ("coniferous") and identify appropriate matching teaching examples (e.g., prototypical, distinctive).

3 Give practice classifying a wide variety of examples and matched example-nonexample pairs.

4 Give student explicit feedback on her performance.

Notice that in developing a plan, you need to draw from bodies of related knowledge to devise specific instructional techniques. For example, this classification problem used knowledge related to the nature of examples and nonexamples, while the previous problem, which dealt with retention of verbal information, used knowledge of the key-word method. It is important to emphasize that the plans presented here are merely examples of how such problems might be addressed. They should not be viewed as the only or necessarily the best intervention possible. More detailed knowledge of the situation would be needed in order to develop a detailed intervention plan. In the chapters which follow, more detailed intervention plans keyed to specific cases and vignettes will be presented.

Cognitive Strategy and Metacognition Problems

Problem F: Marcelle always has trouble doing well on essay exams. She uses the same study techniques for all other types of exams and she does well on them. She wonders why the techniques don't work for essay exams.

Given the problem space depicted in Table 10.4 for cognitive strategy and metacognition problems, the following is a series of questions and answers that may help identify and plan a specific solution:

Question: How can we help Marcelle study more effectively for essay exams?
Answer: Teach her study strategies specifically suited to essay exams.
Question: What are some effective ways to teach such strategies?
Answer: Use the direct explanation approach or the reciprocal teaching approach to teaching strategies.

The plan for teaching Marcelle an appropriate study strategy for essay exams might be:

1 Identify effective strategy (or strategies) for studying for essay exams.
2 Identify subject matter of exam (history, science, etc.) and student's prior study strategies for such subject matter.
3 Employ a direct explanation approach to teaching correct essay exam study strategies and contrast against her previous (e.g., objective test) study method.

As with the previous plans for solving learning problems, the above is a barebones outline of how to create an appropriate instructional intervention to solve the particular problem.

Evaluation of Instructional Solution

Evaluating your solution plan consists of two steps. The first occurs prior to the implementation of your plan and includes identifying and developing an evaluation tool. We are using the term "tool" very loosely. It may involve watching a student demonstrate a skill, fill out answers to a test, do an independent project, and so on. It is crucial to match the type of evaluation with the nature of the learning problem and its intended outcome. For example, in the positive attitude and motivation problem described earlier, it would be inappropriate to evaluate changes in this student's level of self-efficacy by asking her if she feels more confident and if she will be more persistent in solving science problems. In order to evaluate the success of the instructional plan, the student has to be given difficult, novel science problems and asked to solve them. Only when she demonstrates greater effort and persistence at solving such problems can you say that your intervention has succeeded.

Let's take another example. In developing an evaluation tool for the cognitive strategy and metacognition problem described earlier, asking the student to list the steps involved in effective use of strategies, or to describe when, how, and why to use a particular strategy (declarative knowledge) would be an inappropriate evaluation. The student has to be given a wide variety of tasks, some of which fit the strategy being taught and others which do not. Only then is it possible to evaluate the application and use (procedural knowledge) of the newly learned strategy.

Exercise 10.3: Each of the following paragraphs describes a learning problem, intervention, and related evaluation tool. After each paragraph indicate whether the evaluation tool is appropriate for the described intervention and justify your answer. If the tool does not match the intervention, suggest one that does match.

1. A student has difficulty identifying novel examples of the concept "hypocrite." The teacher gives her matched examples and nonexample pairs and a wide variety of practice with extensive feedback. In order to evaluate the effects of the intervention, the teacher asks the student to state the definition of "hypocrite."

    _____

    _____

    _____

2. A student is always misbehaving in class. The teacher identifies activities that the student likes and makes them contingent on good behavior within the classroom. In order to evaluate the effects of the intervention, the teacher asks the student to identify the value of abiding by classroom rules and the negative effects of disruptions caused by misbehaving.

    _____

    _____

    _____

3. A "shy" student is socially inept and has difficulty introducing himself to others. The teacher describes to the student the appropriate way to introduce oneself to others and, with the help of the student's friends, gets him to practice such introductions and provides extensive feedback and praise. The teacher evaluates the effect of this intervention by asking the shy student to introduce himself to other students in the classroom.

_____

_____

_____

4. A student has difficulty remembering historical facts and dates. The teacher uses the direct explanation approach to teach her the method of loci (see page 124) as a way to remember this type of information. In order to evaluate this intervention, the teacher gives the student a variety of tasks that may or may not lend itself to using the method of loci and asks her to (1) identify appropriate and inappropriate applications and (2) use the method of loci to remember the information within appropriate tasks.

_____

_____

_____

The second step in evaluating your solution plan occurs after its implementation and consists of verifying whether or not your intervention actually solved the problem. That means using your evaluation tool to assess any targeted changes in the student's knowledge, attitudes, and experiences. That tells you if you have solved your learning problem.

In this chapter, we have tried to prepare you for those that follow by bridging the gap between theory and application. As described earlier, each of the following chapters will focus on one of four common types of learning problems: cognitive strategies and metacognition, positive attitude and motivation, verbal information, and intellectual skills. Each chapter will begin with a case study, which will be followed by a detailed description of the solution to the problem in the case study. The four steps to solving learning problems described in the present chapter will serve to guide you through the analysis. They consist of identifying the problem, developing an intervention plan, developing an evaluation tool, and applying that evaluation tool to the intervention plan. Two cases will then be presented as practice exercises, with answers provided at the end of the chapter. Finally, at the end of Chapter 14, a new set of cases will be presented and you will be asked to identify the problem, develop a plan, and evaluate that plan for each cases. For this final set, we will not give you any detailed feedback, so you will be on your own!

The case studies which appear in the application chapters are taken from a fictitious school system. A description of school services, personnel, students, and the community as well as a little history about current crises and conditions within this fictitious school system are presented in the next section. After this extended description, you will be presented with six brief cases and asked to identify what type of learning problem exists within each one.

HOWARD CITY INDEPENDENT SCHOOL SYSTEM

Overview

Howard City Independent School System (HCISS) has a student population of approximately 1,950 students. There are three schools in the system: Sammy Pre- and Elementary School (preschool through grade 5), Eugenia Middle School (grades 6 through 8), and Norwood High School (grades 9 through 12). Each school is housed in a separate building and each has similar facilities: a gymnasium, a computer lab, an art lab, an extensive library, an intercom system to each classroom, and an auditorium. In addition to these facilities, Eugenia Middle School and Norwood High School have a baseball/football playing field with track and field facilities, while Sammy Pre- and Elementary School has an extensive playground area. Finally, Norwood High School has a weight room and a variety of classroom shops devoted to vocational training.

There are some unique features of the schools in this district. Teacher aides are available in the buildings (at all levels) to work with teachers and small groups of children. There is a variety of services for children classified as eligible for special education, for ESL students, and for "at-risk" students. In addition, the middle school and high school track students into three levels: honors, average, and remedial. Students typically enter one of the three tracks in sixth grade and are reevaluated before entering high school. Gifted students are served in a pullout program of accelerated activities for three half-days a week. Enrichment activities are offered to students in the regular classroom on a first-come, first-served basis. At all levels of instruction, teachers are encouraged to include students within classroom decisions in order to establish a democratic atmosphere. In order to get them involved in their children's education, parents are encouraged to spend one day a month as classroom volunteers.

The grading policy of all three schools is to automatically promote all students to the next level, irrespective of their accomplishments. However, those students who are not progressing at an expected and reasonable level (as identified via initial testing and case-study materials) will be given extensive support via one-on-one instruction and tutoring. Each student is expected to keep a portfolio of products developed within each subject area, and these portfolios are periodically evaluated. Students are given satisfactory or unsatisfactory ratings rather than a traditional "A" through "F" rating. An unsatisfactory rating automatically sets a procedure in motion which includes meetings of the student, teachers, and parents in an effort to identify ways to support the student within the particular subject area.

Approximately 75 percent of the students go on to further education after graduation from high school. The average daily attendance is approximately 95 percent of the student body, and the percentage of "at-risk" students is one of the lowest in the state of Bliss. The socioeconomic status of students ranges from upper-lower class to upper-middle class. The ethnically diverse student population (25 percent African-American, 20 percent Asian, 30 percent Hispanic, and 25 percent Caucasian) has been declining for several years. As a result, few new teachers have been hired, and the average length of service of the 250 teachers is now over 12 years.

Sammy Pre- and Elementary School

The preschool has four classrooms that serve children from 3 to 5 years of age. Average class size is 15, with two teachers in each classroom. The classrooms have extensive supplies (books, toys, etc.) and room for exploration and play. The preschool curriculum encourages children to take an active role in their learning and attempts to provide a supportive environment. The curriculum is organized around activities (e.g., creating products) rather than around subject areas. Much of the instruction that occurs within the preschool is individual and self-paced.

Grades 1 through 5 are taught in self-contained subject-oriented classrooms. Separate subjects are scheduled at specific and regular times during the day. Class sizes range from 10 to 20 students. There is no attempt to integrate the diverse areas (physical education, arithmetic, writing, reading, etc.). However, all subject areas are primarily concerned with developing the basic skills of students. Students are given standardized tests (arithmetic and reading) at the end of their second and fourth years in order to identify those who may be falling behind and, consequently, may need remedial activities.

Eugenia Middle School

The middle school is also subject-centered, and students are taught within self-contained, subject-oriented classrooms. The goals of the middle school are to continue developing students' basic skills, provide a solid cognitive program, offer exploratory experiences, prepare students for high school, help boys and girls successfully adapt to social and biological changes, and serve as a guidance center. Core subject areas in which all children are involved are science, reading, mathematics, foreign languages, arts, social studies, and physical education. Elective subject areas in which students have a choice are industrial arts, home economics, music, and typing.

Norwood High School

The goals of the high school are to provide a general education, to help students acquire employable skills which they can apply immediately upon graduation, and to prepare those who plan to go to college for further schooling. The curriculum of the school is a mix of college preparatory and vocationally based courses and reflects the city's white collar business and blue collar industrial population. The combined vocational curriculum (business education, home economics, industrial arts, distributive education, agriculture education, apprenticeship training, and trade and industry training) supports nearly as many teachers as the college preparatory curriculum (six different languages, mathematics, biology, chemistry, physics, ecology, history, philosophy, psychology, sociology, music, art, and geography). The high school has developed cooperative programs with local businesses, industries, and a nearby college, which offer students apprenticeship experiences with experts in their field of interest. These programs run year-round so that many students end up working full-time at their apprenticeship sites during the summer.

Historical Context of the School System

During the middle 1980s, HCISS was devastated by a revenue shortfall, a teachers' strike, and snow. Many parents placed their children in private or parochial schools rather than face the uncertainties of a fiscally and politically unsettled public school system. In 1986, many teachers were laid off as the result of declining enrollments and dwindling resources.

Now, however, the district shows signs of resurgence. In the fall of 1992 a large bond issue was passed by 70 percent of the voters, the largest margin of support in the school district's history. Many parents who had left the system began returning, and staff confidence and morale shot up. The superintendent of schools conducted a large-scale needs assessment and community goals survey and is using the information collected in these surveys to reconstruct the district one piece at a time. The superintendent maintains a constructive engagement approach with the teachers' union, community officials, and teachers. In general, all parties are cooperative and support the school system, which contributes greatly to the high quality of the schools.

Exercise 10.4: Classify each of the following case studies as describing either a positive attitudes and motivation, verbal information, intellectual skills, or cognitive strategies and metacognition problem. Please justify your classification of each case study.

Case Study #1   Mr. Globe is a sixth-grade history teacher in the Eugenia Middle School. He is having difficulty getting his students to remember important historical dates and events. Mr. Globe thought he might be able to get some new ideas by talking with Mr. Atlas, who was a history teacher at Norwood High School.

After listening to his dilemma, Mr. Atlas asked him to describe how he tried to get his students to remember historical facts and events. Mr. Globe indicated that he uses a chronological approach because it gives students an appreciation of the changes that have occurred in world economies over time. That was preferable, he felt, to studying the specific relationships between countries that had been isolated from the larger flow of world events. Using a chronological approach, according to Mr. Globe, should increase students' understanding of the evolving nature of history.

In addition to presenting history in a chronological manner, Mr. Globe indicated that he frequently gave students handouts containing a chronological list of important dates and asked them to fill in the important historical events next to each date. After the students had filled in the appropriate events, he would then ask them to repeatedly rehearse each pair of dates and events. The only thing that Mr. Atlas could suggest to Mr. Globe about changing his approach was to try not to treat historical events and dates as isolated facts. Mr. Atlas agreed that it was important to get students to understand the evolving nature of history, but not at the expense of remembering important historical information. However, his students did not seem to be learning the nature of history or to be remembering important dates and events.

Problem Category:_____

_____

_____

Case Study #2   Marsha's third grade class at Sammy Pre- & Elementary School was a difficult group of children. A few students liked school and really tried to learn, but overall the class just wasn't focused on learning. It was impossible to relax with them. If Marsha let down her guard and tried to engage them in a friendly, less formal manner, the class would disintegrate. This vigilant formality ran counter to Marsha's natural teaching style which was to maintain a friendly, relaxed manner. She usually enjoyed her students and her enjoyment showed. But in this particular case, she constantly had to be firm and vigilant ("witchlike", she thought) in order to keep the students under control.

The majority of her problems stemmed from a group of students who were in the "below grade level" reading group. This group provided the spark that set off fireworks for the entire class, day after day. Since they tended to be at their worst as a group, Marsha tried separating them, but that brought little improvement. Three weeks ago, in early October, she tried reorganizing her reading groups, distributing the slower readers among all three groups. The net result of this experiment, however, was to make all three groups disruptive. Moreover, mixing her slow and average readers dramatically reduced the pace of both groups. The slow readers put little effort into the group activities and, even when engaged, gave up easily when faced with obstacles. Finding this arrangement unfair to her other students, she finally went back to her original groupings.

Marsha did not think she ran her classroom in too lax a manner. She had procedures for incomplete work; she had rules for appropriate behavior; and she never hesitated to involve parents. Moreover, she was not afraid to use punishment. She sent individual troublemakers to the office, held detention during lunch, isolated misbehaving children for misbehavior by separating their desks from the rest of the class, and used denial of privileges. Marsha also tried talking honestly with the children, giving them pep talks about the value of education and their need to read and write and think in order to participate fully in life. But nothing seems to alter the poor behavior of her class. (Adapted from Silverman, Welty, & Lyon, 1992).

Problem Category:_____

_____

_____

Case Study #3   Mr. Kohlberg, who has 3 years of teaching experience, accepts a teaching position at Eugenia Middle School in Howard City. He is not very familiar with Howard City, but he does know that it is a more heterogeneous community (in terms of ethnicity and social class) than the one he just left.

During the first few weeks of class, he gets students involved in a unit on values clarification, which he developed. This unit makes students aware of value dilemmas and helps them to critically think through the issues related to those dilemmas. The students are very excited about the material and the activities, and he can see real growth in their critical thinking skills.

Unfortunately, the parents of his students do not share this enthusiasm for the new curriculum. He soon hears that groups of parents have begun discussing ways of counteracting the effects of his critical thinking curriculum. Apparently, the parents are upset that the students are being taught to deal openly and in a relativistic manner with traditional values and resent the fact that their children are beginning to challenge them on value-laden issues.

The principal of the middle school wants to talk to Mr. Kohlberg about this particular issue because he has been receiving phone calls from certain parents. Mr. Kohlberg is unsure of how to prepare for his meeting with the principal or how to deal with the current crisis.

Problem Category:_____

_____

_____

Case Study #4   Therese looked out over her class of 17 first graders and smiled as she watched them prepare for the science lesson. The children, while fidgety and noisy, were responsive to Therese's attention, and their immature behavior and dependence did not bother her.

Once all the desks were clear, Therese began her introduction to the lesson. She perched on the edge of her desk and held up several circles of different colors and sizes. "What are these?" she asked.

Some children responded, "Balls, dots . . . ."

"Yes, these look like balls and dots. What shape are they?" Therese emphasized the word "shape" and pointed to the bulletin board that showed circles, squares, and triangles.

"Circles." Most of the children called out.

"Good. These are circles. Are all the circles the same?"

The children were quiet. Some were no longer watching Therese. William called out, "Some are different."

"How are they different, William?"

"Some are red."

"Yes, some are red. Let's put the red ones here." Therese put the red circles on the flannel board and looked out at her students. Three or four had opened their desks and were looking inside. Others were bouncing in their seats or talking to the children next to them. Fewer than half the students were watching Therese.

"It's this damn science curriculum," Therese thought as she observed her students. It was written by a new science coordinator who had been appointed 2 years earlier. The elementary level of the new science curriculum evolved from her work with a committee of elementary school teachers. It took them 1 year and 2 summers to produce the curriculum that Therese was now trying, unsuccessfully, to use.

"OK, everybody. Eyes front. Look at Miss Carmen. Rosa, Anthony, Jacob." As she called the names of several students, all the children turned toward her.

"William told us that some circles are different because they are red. Kelly, how are some other circles different?"

Kelly shook her head but didn't answer.

"Tiffany, do you know?"

"Some are round."

"Yes, all circles are round. How are they different?"

When none of the students responded, Therese answered her own question. "Some of the circles are yellow," she said as she placed the yellow circles underneath the red ones on the flannel board.

"What colors do I have left?"

"Blue," several students responded.

"Good," Therese said enthusiastically as she put the blue circles on the flannel board. "We have circles that are different colors. What colors are they, class?"

A few children answered, but most were no longer looking at the teacher or the flannel board. Again, Therese thought about what a poor idea it was to teach classification this way to first graders. (Taken from Silverman, Welty, & Lyon, 1992.)

Problem category:_____

_____

_____

Case Study #5 Mr. Paul, the principal of Norwood High School, is concerned that his high school students are not "conscientious about school." He would like his students to be actively involved in the learning process and interested in expanding their horizons. He cites the high tardiness rate (on average, 40 percent of the students are late each day) as evidence that students are not really serious about school. In addition, approximately 20 percent of the students turn assignments in late.

Mr. Paul decides to gather some information from teachers and students by talking to them informally during lunch and recess. Unfortunately, teachers were not able to give Mr. Paul much information about why students were consistently tardy and also late with their assignments. They did, however, complain about the lack of planning time (no free period) and overcrowded classrooms. They also complained about lack of parent participation in parent-teacher conferences. Many parents either did not show or were very late. Also, those parents who did show spent the majority of their conference time complaining about the recent changes in class scheduling—which allows high school students to come one period later than middle school students—and about overcrowding in the classrooms.

In talking to students, Mr. Paul was again greeted with complaints. Their major complaint was that they often did not receive feedback on assignments for weeks after they turned them in. And when they finally did receive feedback, it was typically superficial and not very helpful.

Mr. Paul was discouraged by the information that he received from both the teachers and students. He decided that the next logical step was to contact parents and to talk with them about his concerns.

Problem category:_____

_____

_____

Case Study #6   Mr. Triton was in the teachers' lounge talking to another teacher, Ms. Nuclear, about how difficult it was to get students to take control of their own learning. Mr. Triton teaches seventh-grade social studies, and Ms. Nuclear teaches seventh-grade English at Eugenia Middle School.

Mr. Triton shook his head and said, "It seems as if we spend most of the school year reviewing old material and organizing new information to make it easier to learn. If I ask my students to learn new information without first outlining, organizing, and elaborating it for them, they just fall apart!"

"I know what you mean," replied Ms. Nuclear. "I don't understand it either! I spend too much class time getting students to remember new information by presenting it in distinctive and memorable ways. I also explain what I have done to make the material more distinctive and memorable. You would think that after doing this for the first third of the school year, they would be able to do these things for themselves!"

Ms. Nuclear paused for a moment, then continued. "For example, when we learn new vocabulary words, I present pictures that get students to connect the meaning with the sound and the pronunciation of the word. I think my educational psychology teacher called it the key-word method. The students seem to remember these words well, but when I give them an independent assignment to learn a new set of words, they seem unable to use this technique on their own."

"My students also have trouble taking control of their learning when I give them independent work," replied Mr. Triton. "For example, when I teach a new set of historical events and show how they have influenced the modern world, I present a graphic overview that gives them the big picture. It helps them organize the material. But when I give them a new history reading and ask them to create their own summary or overview, most students just copy bits and pieces of the reading.''

A bell rang in the background, indicating the start of a new class period. Mr. Triton and Ms. Nuclear said their good-byes, picked up their lesson materials, and went to their next class.

Problem category:_____

_____

_____

REVIEW OF MAJOR POINTS

1 The first step in solving an instructional problem is performing a detailed analysis of the givens within the classroom situation. That requires gathering vital information about the academic skills and prior classroom experiences of the student(s), the context of the problem, the health of the student(s), and the nature of the community and home environment.

2 Once you have a detailed idea of the givens in a particular instructional problem, you can then decide whether you have a ''learning'' or a ''nonlearning'' problem. Learning problems involve a student's lack of appropriate knowledge, attitude, or prior experience. Consequently, solving a learning problem requires planning and implementing an instructional intervention which focuses on the modification or acquisition of these factors. Nonlearning problems are due to factors outside the learner, such as family, health, school, and community influences, which cannot be solved with an instructional intervention.

3 The goal of a learning problem is to modify or add to a student's existing knowledge, attitudes, and experiences. The targeted knowledge, experience, and attitude will be identified as the ''learning outcome'' of your instructional intervention.

4 The four categories of learning problems that we have adapted from Gagné's (1985) taxonomy include the following: (1) positive attitude and motivation, (2) verbal information, (3) intellectual skills, and (4) cognitive strategies and metacognition. Positive attitude and motivation problems concern a student's beliefs, attitudes, attributions, goals, and/or affect related to learning and learning environments. Problems which fit into the verbal information category focus on a student's ability to verbalize previously presented information. Problems which fit into the intellectual skills category focus on a student's ability to apply a specific skill or concept or to discriminate between objects, events, or people. Finally, cognitive strategy and metacognition problems focus on the diagnosis, planning, selection, and/or monitoring of perceptual, attention, memory, thinking, and problem-solving processes.

5 The primary purpose of categorizing a learning problem is to accurately represent the problem, which then allows you to create a problem space in long-term memory. The problem space includes related techniques and information (schemas) that will help solve that learning problem. Techniques within each problem space are drawn from multiple theories.

6 After you have categorized a learning problem and created a problem space, the next step is to develop a plan for moving from the givens to the goal. The selection of appropriate techniques to include in this plan requires further analysis and questioning within the problem situation. A useful approach for selecting an appropriate technique is the difference-reduction heuristic which helps find the important differences between the current situation and the goal. Once you have identified these differences, you can develop an appropriate plan for solving the problem.

7 Evaluation of your solution plan involves two steps. The first step, which occurs prior to the implementation of your plan, involves identifying and developing an evaluation tool. An evaluation tool consists of watching a student demonstrate a skill, answer test questions, do an independent project, and so on. It is crucial at this point that you match your evaluation with the nature of the learning problem and desired outcome. For example, your evaluation should not be limited to declarative knowledge if the problem is a procedural one that involves applying a concept, skill, or strategy. The second step in evaluating your solution plan occurs after its implementation and consists of verifying whether your intervention solved the problem. That entails using your evaluation tool to assess any changes in the student's knowledge, attitudes, and experiences.

ANSWERS TO QUESTIONS AND EXERCISES

Exercise 10.1: Problem A: *Nonlearning problem.* The reason for Mr. Apple's lack of time is a large course load. Modifying his students' knowledge, attitudes, or experiences will not alleviate this problem. Possible solutions would include discussions with the principal to lessen his course load, paying someone else to write the lessons, or buying prepared lesson plans aimed at helping students become more proficient readers.

Problem B: *Nonlearning problem.* Britanny's tardiness is a function of family conditions. Modifying Britanny's knowledge, attitude, or experiences will not alleviate this problem. Possible solutions would require discussing with the family ways to lessen her household duties prior to the school day.

Problem C: *Learning problem.* Setting up clear rules about classroom behavior and enforcing them (with appropriate consequences) should help solve this problem. This solution involves changing the students' attitudes and experiences.

Problem D: *Learning problem.* This problem requires changing students' knowledge so that they can discriminate between statements of opinion and fact. Since the students have already acquired the definitions of statement of fact and of opinion, the teacher can solve this problem by giving them extensive practice (with feedback) identifying examples and nonexamples.

Problem E: *Nonlearning problem.* This problem is due to a lack of sleep. Trying to arrange for Richard not to have to work until 1:00 A.M. would help solve this problem (e.g., helping him find a job at school or restructuring his morning classes to allow him more rest). This problem cannot be solved with an instructional intervention.

Exercise 10.2: Problem A: *Verbal information problem.* John's difficulty centers on his inability to restate a sequence of words.

Problem B: *Intellectual skills problem.* Timothy's difficulty centers on his inability to apply a specific skill, that is, solving algebraic equations.

Problem C: *Positive attitude and motivation problem.* Mary's problem is not a lack of problem-solving skill but appears to be related to low motivation (e.g., low self-efficacy), which makes her give up easily.

Problem D: *Positive attitude and motivation problem.* Marcus's need for attention motivates him to be a class clown and disrupt the class. The problem is motivational, and the solution would require motivating him to exhibit appropriate behavior.

Problem E: *Intellectual skills problem.* Megan possesses appropriate declarative knowledge related to the concept "deciduous"; however, she lacks appropriate procedural knowledge which supports classification skills.

Problem F: *Cognitive strategy and metacognition problem.* Marcelle does not possess appropriate declarative, procedural, and metacognitive knowledge. She needs to identify appropriate strategies and to know when and how to use them to improve her performance on essay-type exams.

Exercise 10.3: 1. The evaluation tool does not match the intervention. The teacher needs to evaluate how well the student classifies novel examples. Being able to give the correct definition of a concept (declarative knowledge) does not indicate that she can correctly classify novel examples (procedural knowledge).

2. The evaluation tool does not match the intervention. The teacher needs to observe the student within the classroom over an extended period and monitor his behavior. Being able to describe the value of appropriate behavior is not a good indicator of how the student will behave in the classroom.

3. The evaluation tool matches the intervention. The intervention involves practice in introducing oneself to friends, and the evaluation tool involves evaluating the student introducing himself to others who are not friends.

4. The evaluation tool matches the intervention. The intervention is aimed at getting the student to acquire the method of loci as a strategy to remembering verbal information. The evaluation tool involves evaluating the student's declarative knowledge of when to use this memory technique and then evaluating her application of the strategy (procedural knowledge).

Exercise 10.4: *Case Study #1.* This is a verbal information problem. The students lack appropriate declarative knowledge and, consequently, are unable to correctly state historical facts and events. Please see Chapter 13 for an extended discussion of this type of problem its analysis, intervention plan, and proposed evaluation.

Case Study #2. This is a positive attitude and motivation problem. The problem students lack relevant experiences and incentives to behave appropriately. Please see Chapter 12 for an extended discussion of this type of problem and for the development and evaluation of an instructional intervention to solve the problem.

Case Study #3. This is not a learning problem. Solving this problem may require extended discussion with parents and, possibly, involving parents in the curriculum.

Case Study #4. This is an intellectual skills problem. The students lack appropriate declarative knowledge and, consequently, are having difficulty demonstrating classification skills. Please see Chapter 14 for an extended discussion of this type of problem and the development and evaluation of an instructional intervention to solve it.

Case Study #5. This is not a learning problem. Within this problem description, there is a variety of possible reasons for the high rate of student tardiness (e.g., change of schedule, lack of parental involvement, teacher apathy).

Case Study #6. This is a cognitive strategy and metacognition problem. The students lack appropriate declarative, procedural, and metacognitive knowledge and, consequently, cannot take control of their own learning. Please see Chapter 11 for an extended discussion of this type of problem and the development and evaluation of an instructional intervention to solve this problem.

REFERENCES

Bloom, B., Englehart, M., Frost, E., Hill, W., & Krathwohl, D. (1956). *Taxonomy of educational objectives. Handbook I: Cognitive domain.* New York: David McKay.

Gagné, R. (1985). *The conditions of learning and theory of instruction.* New York: Holt, Rinehart & Winston.

Harrow, A. (1972). *A taxonomy of the psychomotor domain: A guide for developing behavioral objectives.* New York: David McKay.

Krathwohl, D., Bloom, B., & Masia, B. (1956). *Taxonomy of educational objectives. Handbook II: Affective domain.* New York: David McKay.

Salmoni, A. (1989). Motor skill learning. In D. Holding (Ed.), *Human skills.* New York: John Wiley & Sons.

Silverman, R., Welty, W., & Lyon, S. (1992). *Case studies for teacher problem solving.* New York: McGraw-Hill.

11

TEACHING COGNITIVE
STRATEGIES AND
METACOGNITION

OBJECTIVES

Given case studies involving teaching strategies and metacognition:

1. Analyze the learning problem.
2. Determine relevant theoretical knowledge.
3. Develop a proposed instructional solution.
4. Evaluate the instructional solution.

Cognitive strategies are mental processes for controlling learning and thinking. Using strategies appropriately enables students to efficiently manage their own learning, remembering, and thinking. Cognitive strategies can be likened to intellectual devices or machines that magnify or extend the power of the mind, just as physical machines extend the power of the human arm and hand. Moreover, just as people have knowledge that enables them to select the best physical machine for a job (e.g., to use a hammer rather than a shovel when hanging a picture), they also have knowledge that enables them to select the best cognitive strategy for an intellectual task. Metacognition includes peoples' knowledge about strategies and the skills of diagnosing, selecting, and monitoring strategies.

BACKGROUND KNOWLEDGE FROM PART ONE

In Chapter 4, we described various categories of strategies for encoding and remembering information including rehearsal, elaboration, organization, and mnemonics. In Chapter 5, we discussed various strategies (i.e., heuristics) for solving problems. In Chapter 7, we discussed strategies for monitoring reading and dealing with difficulties in comprehension (i.e., summarizing, clarifying, questioning, and predicting). Altogether these cognitive strategies represent a formidable repertoire of ways in which people learn, remember, and solve problems.

Cognitive strategies are also techniques that teachers can design into their instruction. For example, a teacher can present students with analogies and images (forms of elaboration) to help them understand and remember verbal information (see Chapter 13). In this case, the teacher has designed instruction so that students are induced to use one or more cognitive strategies to learn the material. The students' learning performance is improved even though they may not be aware that they are using a strategy. However, one important goal of education is to provide students with the skills that will enable them to be independent learners.

To be independent learners requires that students be able to deliberately and consciously employ strategies on their own. To achieve this goal teachers must broaden the goals (outcomes) of their instruction. That is, rather than focusing entirely on the verbal information and intellectual skills that constitute the content of the various subject areas, they must also focus on the cognitive strategies which enable students to learn, remember, and think about that content.

In Chapters 4 and 7, we presented two well researched approaches to teaching cognitive strategies and metacognition: the direct explanation approach and the reciprocal teaching approach. In both approaches the teacher's role is to help students internalize cognitive strategies and thereby transfer control over the learning process to them. Each of these approaches to strategy instruction involves motivating students to use strategies independently. Chapter 9 also deals with motivating students to become independent learners.

Now that we have activated some schemas in your long-term memory, let's proceed to the case study. (If, per chance, none of your schemas were activated by this introduction, you might wish to go back and review relevant portions of Chapters 4, 5, 7, and 9 before proceeding).

CASE STUDY

Mr. Triton was in the teachers' lounge talking to another teacher, Ms. Nuclear, about how difficult it was to get students to take control of their own learning. Mr. Triton teaches seventh-grade social studies and Ms. Nuclear teaches seventh-grade English at Eugenia Middle School.

Mr. Triton shook his head and said, "It seems as if we spend most of the school year reviewing old material and organizing new information to make it easier to learn. If I ask my students to try to learn new information without first outlining, organizing, and elaborating it for them, they just fall apart!"

"I know what you mean," replied Ms. Nuclear. "I don't understand it either! I spend too much class time getting students to remember new information by presenting it in distinctive and memorable ways. I also explain what I have done to make the material more distinctive and memorable. You would think that after doing this for the first third of the school year, they would be able to do these things for themselves."

Ms. Nuclear paused for a moment, then continued. "For example, when we learn new vocabulary words, I present pictures that get students to connect the meaning with the sound and the pronunciation of the word. I think my educational psychology teacher called it the key-word method. The students seem to remember these words well, but when I give them an independent assignment to learn a new set of words, they seem unable to use this technique on their own."

"My students also have trouble taking control of their learning when I give them independent work," replied Mr. Triton. "For example, when I teach a new set of historical events and show how they have influenced the world, I present a graphic overview that gives them the big picture. It helps them to organize the material. But when I give them a new history reading and ask them to create their own summary or overview, most students just copy bits and pieces of the reading."

A bell rang in the background, indicating the start of a new class period. Mr. Triton and Ms. Nuclear said their good-byes, picked up their lesson materials, and went to their next class.

Analysis of the Learning Problem

It is clear from their conversation that these teachers are faced with a learning problem rather than a nonlearning problem. That is, the problem is not due to community, system, or family factors but concerns students' lack of knowledge and experience. The knowledge and experience that are lacking are cognitive strategies and metacognitive knowledge (surprise!). To understand why the teachers are faced with this learning problem, we have to look more deeply into the case information.

Both teachers appear to have an appreciation of the value of elaboration, organization, and mnemonic strategies for enhancing students' learning of lesson content. Moreover, both are exposing their students to such strategies. The problem is that students are not then using the strategies on their own. A likely reason for this is that the teachers, in their desire for students to learn lesson content, incorporate all of the organizing and elaborating into their instruction instead of explicitly teaching students how to do it for themselves. For example, instead of teaching students to generate their own key words and images for learning new vocabulary, Ms. Nuclear provides them with these learning aids. Instead of teaching students how to summarize and organize the material, Mr. Triton presents them with a ready-made graphic organizer. Thus, the students are not learning to execute such strategic procedures or to transfer them to new material. In summary, both teachers have been totally focused on learning outcomes involving verbal information. If they desire their students to take more responsibility for their own learning, they need to shift part of their focus to teaching cognitive strategies and metacognition.

Determination of Relevant Theoretical Knowledge

Now that we have identified our learning problem as one involving cognitive strategies and metacognition, we can search for relevant knowledge and experience. You might wish to refer to Table 10.4 for some key concepts related to cognitive strategy and metacognition problems. Additionally, a careful reading of the case might result in the activation of the following types of knowledge.

The students are seventh graders, so they are certainly capable of concrete operational reasoning, with many well into the formal stage. The types of strategies that Mr. Triton and Ms. Nuclear are trying to convey (e.g., key word, summarizing) are clearly developmentally appropriate for these students. However, given limits on students' processing capacity and short-term memory (STM), it would probably be wise to teach only one or two strategies during a semester.

Merely pointing out a strategy to students (as Ms. Nuclear has done) is clearly not effective. However, modeling the steps involved in a strategy (e.g., the steps in the key-word method; the steps in summarizing) is an appropriate approach for teaching strategies. The instructional techniques for enhancing the components of the modeling process (attention, retention, production, and motivation) are clearly relevant to this case (see especially Exercise 8.3 in Chapter 8). When modeling strategies, it is important that the covert mental processes involved in the strategy be made overt so that students can form an adequate cognitive representation of the strategic procedure.

Although students may learn how to execute a strategy through observing a model, it is doubtful that they will then transfer the strategy to new learning material for which it is appropriate. The teachers will need to devise ways to promote transfer of the strategies once students have learned them. For instance, having students practice a new strategy on a variety of tasks and in a variety of contexts will enhance transfer because elements of these tasks and situations then become cues for retrieving the strategy.

Students also need metacognitive knowledge if they are to use strategies appropriately and independently. It is important that strategy instruction impart knowledge concerning (1) the value of a particular strategy for enhancing learning and (2) when and where to use a strategy. The instruction also needs to equip students with ways of monitoring their performance while using a strategy so that they can assess its impact.

Finally, there are several approaches to teaching strategies, such as the direct explanation approach (see Chapter 4) and reciprocal teaching (see Chapter 7). Both of these approaches incorporate the above theoretical principles.

Development of Proposed Instructional Solution

Both teachers could devote part of their classtime early in the school year to explicitly teaching strategies. Because both teachers want students to remember new information, appropriate strategies to teach might include the following: (1) text elaboration strategies (e.g., summarizing, inferencing, generating images, asking questions), (2) organizational strategies (e.g., outlining, networking), and (3) mnemonic strategies (e.g., key-word method, peg method). The direct explanation approach would probably be the most useful method in this situation because the strategies need to be taught to a classroom-size group. Reciprocal teaching is best suited to small groups where everyone can interact. We will now illustrate how Mr. Triton might implement the direct explanation approach to teach his students to summarize material in their history text.

Teaching Students to Summarize Using Direct Explanation

1. The first step is to alert students that they are about to learn a new strategy. That focuses their attention on the strategy rather than the lesson content.

Mr. Triton might say, "Today, students, you are going to learn how to summarize what you are reading in your history text."

2. Explicitly point out the positive connection between use of the strategy and academic performance. Inform students that using strategies requires effort but will pay off.

Mr. Triton: "Creating good summaries will help you remember the material in your text. At first, it may take more time and effort than just reading the book, but it will pay off in higher test scores. After you practice summarizing for a while, it will become much easier to do."

3. Model the strategy. Analyze the steps in the summarizing strategy and demonstrate each one. Use verbal comments to direct students' attention to the important steps in the strategy.

Mr. Triton: "I will summarize the first paragraph in Chapter 1 of the text. The first thing I am going to do is *pick out the most important or main idea* of the paragraph." (reads paragraph aloud) "Let's see, the author is talking about how important it is to understand history. His main idea seems to be that if you don't study history, you are doomed to repeat it.

"The second step in creating a summary is to restate the main idea in your own words. So, my restatement is that studying history can help you avoid repeating the same old mistakes.

"Now I will summarize the second paragraph." (reads aloud) "Now I noticed that the author has underlined the third sentence in this paragraph. That means he thinks it's the most important thing to remember, so I will select that sentence and restate it."

Mr. Triton might model the process with several more paragraphs, each time pointing out how he selected the most important idea. He could describe various ways that authors indicate important material (e.g., by use of inserted questions, objectives, italics, boldface type, underlining, or positioning the idea [first, last] within a paragraph).

Mr. Triton: "I write down my summary for each paragraph here in my notebook. After I have done this for the entire chapter, I have summarized the chapter. Then, I can study for the chapter test by reviewing my summary instead of rereading the whole chapter."

4. The next step in teaching the strategy is to provide students with metacognitive scaffolding by telling them why the strategy works and when to use it.

Mr. Triton: "The summarizing strategy helps you remember what you read, because you select the most important ideas and then put them into your own words. To put an idea into your own words, you really have to understand it. You will remember an idea better if you understand it than if you don't understand it.

"You can use the summarizing strategy whenever you want to remember the gist or main points of what you are reading. It won't help you to remember specific facts like the dates of historical events or the names of the presidents. We will learn other memory strategies that will help with those. You can also use the summarizing strategy in your other classes. For example, you can use it when reading your science text."

5. Next the teacher should have the students practice the strategy. It is a good idea to have students initially practice with less complex material before tackling the actual text. Of course, the students will need feedback on the quality of their summaries. The teacher can provide this initially and then have students work together in small groups and critique each other's summaries.

Mr. Triton: "Now you practice writing summaries for the paragraphs on this sheet." (gives handout) "Jason, please read your summary for the first paragraph." "Good! You selected the most important idea, but you forgot to put it in your own words. Can you restate it in your own words?" "Great." "Barb, what was your summary for the second paragraph?" "That's a good restatement of that idea. But I wonder if that is the most important idea. It seems to me that the very first sentence contains the most important idea. What do the rest of you think?"

It is important that students get lots of practice in using the strategy with different types of material: newspaper articles, articles in magazines, and finally the history text itself. Extensive and varied practice with a strategy will lead to its being automatized and generalized to a variety of learning tasks. In fact, Mr. Triton and Ms. Nuclear could team up in their strategy teaching efforts. For example, after Mr. Triton has taught students how to use the summarizing strategy, Ms. Nuclear could prompt them to use it in her language arts class. And, after Ms. Nuclear has taught students how to use the key-word strategy for learning definitions of new vocabulary words, Mr. Triton could prompt its use in memorizing dates of historical events and other factual information. Once again, varied practice in different contexts increases the number of cues which will activate the strategy.

6. The teacher can inform students that he expects them to use the strategy and then reward them for doing so. The teacher also needs to repeatedly attribute good performance to effort and to the use of good strategies.

Mr. Triton: "Jeff, I noticed that you were using the summarizing strategy while you were reading your assignment. Good work! Your test scores are improving because of your hard work and use of summarizing."

7. When testing the content learned via the strategy, give feedback on the strategy-performance link. That could be done by writing comments on students' test papers.

Mr. Triton's comment on Angela's test: "Dear Angela, this is a very good test grade. You really understand the material much better since you have been using the summarizing strategy. Keep up the good work!"

It is also important to teach students ways to monitor their performance while using the strategy. In this case, it turns out that summarizing is a good monitoring strategy as well as a good memory strategy.

Mr. Triton: "The summarizing strategy helps you to know how well you are learning the material. If you are having difficulty creating a summary for a paragraph, chances are you don't understand it very well and need to seek assistance."

8. The final step in teaching a strategy is to follow up to see if students continue to use the strategy on their own. If students fail to use the strategy spontaneously when appropriate, prompt them to do so.

Mr. Triton (several weeks later): "Cary, did you use the summarizing strategy when you read Chapter 4?" "No?" "I didn't think so because your score was not as good as before. You need to keep using the strategy."

The steps involved in the direct explanation approach to teaching cognitive strategies and metacognition are listed in Table 11.1.

Evaluation of the Instructional Solution

The goal is for students to eventually use the strategies on their own without teacher prompting. Thus, the intervention must be evaluated by monitoring the students' independent use of instructed strategies. It would be wise to limit the number of strategies taught in any one semester so that appropriate follow-up and evaluation can be done.

Now it's time to let you apply your knowledge about cognitive strategies to two brief cases. Please answer the questions before turning to the back of the chapter.

TABLE 11.1   TEACHING STRATEGIES USING DIRECT EXPLANATION

1. Alert students that they are about to learn a new strategy.

2. Point out the positive connection between use of the strategy and academic performance. Inform students that using strategies requires effort but will pay off.

3. Model the strategy using verbal comments to direct students' attention to important steps.

4. Provide students with metacognitive knowledge by telling them why the strategy works and when and where to use it.

5. Provide practice in using the strategy on a variety of tasks in various contexts. Give feedback.

6. Reward students for using the strategy. Attribute good performance to effort and to the use of the strategy.

7. Give feedback on the strategy-performance link when testing the content learned via the strategy.

8. Follow up to see that students are using the strategy independently.

CASE #1

Mr. Lincoln is unhappy with his ninth-grade mathematics students' performance on word problems. They solve equations quickly and accurately, and most can complete a page containing 30 problems without errors. Yet, as soon as he gives them a few word problems, it's as if they had never heard of algebra. Some can't even begin, others guess the answer without showing any work, and still others represent the problems incorrectly and thus end up solving the wrong equation. Even students who do manage to get the right answer seem unsure of themselves when questioned. He has also noticed that many students give up quickly, and others become nervous when the lesson involves word problems.

The students can usually respond correctly when he guides them through these problems by asking a series of questions. For example: "Is this the first time that this kind of problem has come up, or have you done similar problems before? Are there parts of the problem that you understand and know how to handle and other parts that are causing difficulty?" Overall, Mr. Lincoln thinks that his students do not lack appropriate knowledge. Rather, it's as if, in his words, "they just don't get the point or are unable to pull it all together when I ask them to apply their knowledge to new word problems."

1 What is your **analysis of the learning problem?**

_____

_____

_____

_____

_____

_____

2 Please identify **relevant theoretical knowledge.**

_____

_____

_____

_____

_____

3 What is your **proposed instructional solution?**

_____

_____

_____

_____

_____

_____

_____

4 How will you **evaluate your proposed solution?**

_____

_____

_____

_____

_____

_____

_____

CASE #2

Ms. Bambi, a third-grade reading teacher, was reflecting on her day at school today. She was somewhat perplexed about some of her students' reading performance. There were about six students who seemed to have good decoding skills but didn't seem to comprehend what they were reading. Ms. Bambi thought about Jill, who was typical of the group. "She was reading the words from _Charlotte's Web_ just fine when I called on her to read, but she couldn't answer any of my questions about the passage she had just finished!"

Ms. Bambi thought back to her education courses on reading. "I know that there were certain activities designed to help poor readers to understand what they were reading. Wasn't one of them predicting what would happen next in the story? What were the other ones?" She remembered that activities like clarifying, summarizing, and asking questions would not only help students comprehend what they read but, in addition, help them to monitor their understanding of what they were reading. Then she thought, "How am I going to get my problem students to do these things? I can't just tell them to predict, clarify, summarize, and so on while reading. They will never be able to do these things on their own even if I show them how. What can I do to help them develop these reading strategies?"

1 What is your **analysis of the learning problem?**

_____

_____

_____

_____

_____

_____

2 Identify **relevant theoretical knowledge.**

_____

_____

_____

_____

_____

3 What is your **proposed instructional solution?**

_____

_____

_____

_____

_____

_____

_____

_____

_____

_____

_____

_____

4 How will you **evaluate your proposed solution?**

_____

_____

_____

_____

_____

_____

_____

_____

REVIEW OF MAJOR POINTS

The intent of this chapter is to help you to organize your knowledge related to cognitive strategies and metacognition so that you can use it to solve instructional problems. You are concerned with teaching cognitive strategies and metacognition whenever you want your students to be responsible for managing their own learning.

The cases presented in this chapter required applying theoretical knowledge to develop instructional solutions for learning-problems involving students' lack of cognitive strategies and metacognition. Developing these instructional solutions required decisions as to which strategies were most appropriate for the task and for the developmental level of the students and which instructional method was most appropriate for the setting and students. Evaluating the instructional solutions required long-term follow-up to determine whether students were using appropriate strategies on their own.

ANSWERS TO CASE EXERCISES

Case #1

1. Analysis of the learning problem. Mr. Lincoln's students appear to have the appropriate knowledge for solving algebra problems. That is, they appear to know mathematical algorithms and can apply them when given equations to solve. However, when given word problems they fail to represent the problems so that they can apply those algorithms. If Mr. Lincoln guides them through the problems by asking questions, they can eventually make such representations and then solve the problems. However, he needs to shift responsibility to the students by explicitly teaching them strategies for representing and solving algebra word problems and making sure that they learn to use these strategies independently.

2. Relevant theoretical knowledge. The two types of heuristics for solving problems, the analogical approach and the difference-reduction approach that we discussed in Chapter 5, are clearly relevant in this case. The analogical approach when used as a strategy involves comparing a novel problem to similar problems that students already know how to solve. Knowledge and methods can be transferred between problems depending upon the extent of their similarity. However, students need to have explicit training in finding analogous problems. One difference-reduction approach, called means-end analysis, involves finding the most important difference between the current state and the goal state and creating a subgoal which is directed toward eliminating this difference. This method proceeds as successive subgoals are identified and means are applied to attain each one until the final goal state is reached. Experts often solve problems using a difference-reduction strategy such as means-end analysis, and novices can also be taught to use this approach.

Research on problem solving indicates that when teaching heuristic strategies, it is important to teach students *when* to use them. This knowledge, as well as other metacognitive knowledge such as information concerning the effectiveness and value of the strategy, supports students' transfer and independent use of the strategies.

The students in this case are ninth graders who are either at the formal level of reasoning or are transitional between concrete and formal reasoning. Thus, the above strategies are appropriate for their developmental level. However, one would not attempt to teach the means-end strategy to students at the concrete level because it requires keeping systematic track of multiple aspects of a situation.

Any complex strategy for solving math word problems is likely to exceed students' attentional and STM capacity. Therefore, it will probably be necessary to break the strategy into small steps that can be practiced and automatized. Effectively teaching each step requires modeling in which the teacher explains his covert thinking process.

Finally, it appears that students' continual failure on word problems is producing learned helplessness and that the problems are becoming a conditioned stimulus for anxiety. Mr. Lincoln needs to address these motivational problems as he attempts to teach his students problem-solving strategies and metacognition.

3. Proposed instructional solution. Mr. Lincoln needs to teach his students a systematic heuristic strategy for solving algebra word problems. The first step is to identify the specific steps in the strategy. Here is one possible analysis. If you devised a slightly different strategic approach, that is OK, as long as the strategy works.

Strategy for Solving Algebra Word Problems

1. Read the problem carefully.

2. Ask yourself, "Have I done a similar problem before (analogical approach)?" If the answer is "yes," then recall how this previous problem was solved and solve this one as you did the old problem. If the answer is "no," or if the old method doesn't work, ask yourself:

3. "Are there parts of the problem that I understand?" If so, "What are the parts that I am having difficulty with?" For each difficult part, ask yourself:

4. "What is the difference between my current state and my goal of understanding this part? What do I need to know or do in order to understand or solve this part of the problem (means-end analysis)?"

5. Do whatever is called for in step 4. If you now understand that part of the problem, then repeat step 4 for each part of the problem that you are having difficulty with until you have solved the problem.

Mr. Lincoln could teach his students the above strategy using either the direct explanation approach or the reciprocal teaching approach. We would recommend the direct explanation approach because of the large number of students and the fact that they are older students. The reciprocal teaching approach works better with small groups, and with young or at-risk students.

Because we have already illustrated the direct explanation approach in the first case, we will not go through each of the instructional steps involved. However, *you* could benefit from actually scripting a lesson for directly teaching a problem-solving strategy (either the one above or one of your own devising). Your lesson script should address each of the steps in the direct explanation approach (see Table 11.1). Your script must not only teach the strategy but also enable students to transfer the strategy to new problems. That is, students must be provided metacognitive knowledge concerning when and why to use the strategy and be prompted to use the strategy on a variety of problems.

It is very important for Mr. Lincoln to emphasize *that part* of the direct explanation approach that deals with motivation because his students need this type of support. Students can be prompted to attribute success to effort and to good problem-solving strategies and to attribute failure to lack of effort or use of a poor strategy. That will make them more persistent in the problem-solving situation. While teaching the strategy, Mr. Lincoln can start with relatively easy problems and very gradually increase the difficulty level as students become more practiced in applying the strategy. This tactic ensures that students will consistently experience success in solving algebra word problems, which should counter their previously conditioned anxiety response to this type of problem.

4. Evaluation of the proposed solution. Mr. Lincoln must follow up on his students to determine if they are using the strategy spontaneously on new word problems. Achieving this goal of independent strategy usage will probably require practice and gradual fading of cues and prompts to use the strategy over at least a semester.

Case #2

1. Analysis of the learning problem. Ms. Bambi is faced with a situation in which she needs to teach her students comprehension and monitoring strategies. However, it is clear that she will have to provide her young students with much support in order for them to learn to use the strategies independently.

2. Relevant theoretical knowledge. Transmitting strategies to young students (or older at-risk students) requires the teacher to provide much support or scaffolding. In Chapter 7 we discussed how teachers might work with children on tasks that are within their zone of proximal development. Such tasks are ones which a child cannot accomplish alone but can do with help from an adult or more capable peer. Reciprocal teaching is an instructional technique that has been developed to help teachers implement collaborative learning of strategies. This approach to strategy instruction is particularly useful in the case of developmentally immature students, because it provides a structure in which the teacher can initially take most of the responsibility for task completion while supporting students' participation. As students begin to internalize the strategies, the teacher turns more and more responsibility for the task over to the students.

3. Proposed instructional solution. Ms. Bambi or an instructional aide can implement reciprocal teaching of reading comprehension strategies with the six students diagnosed as having difficulties. During the regular reading instruction period, these students would meet in a small group away from the rest of the class. During the session the students and the teacher discuss small sections of text. The discussions are focused on the use of four comprehension strategies: predicting, questioning, summarizing, and clarifying. These strategies both improve comprehension and provide the reader with means for monitoring his comprehension.

Plan for Implementing Reciprocal Teaching

1. Introduce students to reciprocal teaching

Ms. Bambi can discuss the purpose of reciprocal teaching with her students by telling them that they will be working together to help each other understand the meaning of stories and other selections from their readers. She can explain that each member of the group will take turns being the teacher. After everyone has read a section of the text, the "teacher" will first summarize the content and then pose a question about the text that might occur on a test. The rest of the group discusses the question and adds any needed clarification. Finally, the teacher makes a prediction about what will happen next.

Ms. Bambi can then provide the students with a structured overview of the four strategies and lead them in activities that involve the strategies. For example, she can introduce questioning by discussing the role that questions play in our lives. She can then have students generate information-seeking questions about everyday events. Following that she can give students simple informational sentences and ask them to generate a question. Next, she could have students evaluate questions that were written about short segments of text. Finally, she could have them generate their own questions from segments of text. She can conduct similar activities for the predicting, summarizing, and clarifying strategies. These activities will ensure that students learn to perform the strategies before being asked to employ them in the dialogue. Based on their performance, the teacher can infer how much support the individual children in the group might need in the dialogue.

2. Model the strategies

After several days of introduction, Ms. Bambi and the students begin the dialogue. Ms. Bambi should be the first teacher so that she can model the strategies in the context of the dialogue. Here is a sample dialogue based upon an expository piece about a relative of spiders, "Daddy Longlegs." Ms. Bambi models how she uses text to *clarify* the meaning of a word (all sample dialogues are taken from Palincsar, 1988).

Ms. Bambi reads:

"Daddy longlegs spend much of their time cleaning or preening their long legs."

Ms. Bambi inquires of the children:

"Now then, the question is, what does preening mean?"

The children offer a number of possible explanations:

"taking care of it"
"not doing bad things to it"
"giving it special air and food"
Ms. Bambi comments:
"These are all good things that you would do for the whole body."
She then calls their attention to the text again . . .
"Let's read again and listen for a word that is used in the sentence that might give you a clue." (rereading) "Daddy longlegs spend much of their time cleaning or preening their long legs."
Susan interjects:
"Cleaning?"
Ms. Bambi responds by modeling how she uses the text to assist her in figuring out the meaning of the word, preening:
"Yes. Did you hear the little word that they used after cleaning? Cleaning *or* preening. When I hear that little word, 'or,' I know that it is saying, another word for this is, and so, cleaning or preening. You are exactly right. Preening does mean cleaning."
In this example, Ms. Bambi has made her covert comprehension processes overt so that the children can apprehend them. An important key in using dialogue for the purpose of modeling comprehension processes is for teachers to put themselves in the place of their novice students and ask themselves how they would try to infer meaning if they didn't know the meaning.

3. Support students' acquisition and use of strategies

The following dialogue illustrates how Ms. Bambi supports and guides Sara, a child who is having difficulty leading the discussion and applying the strategies. For example, Ms. Bambi supports Sara by modifying the requests she makes of her and providing additional modeling.
Ms. Bambi reads:
"One thing you need is an air tank. The air tank gives you air to breathe underwater. You wear the tank on your back. A short hose from the tank brings the air to your mouth. Before you dive, a lot of air is pumped into your tank. The tank can hold enough air for you to breathe underwater for about an hour. Your hour is almost over. It's time to go up. As you swim slowly to the top, the pressure gets lighter. The water is warmer too. The top of the water looks like a wavy mirror. At last your head comes out. Now you can take off your mask. You can breathe the air around you."
Ms. Bambi then asks:
"Now when it says 'you' who are they talking about?"
Students:
"The aquanauts."
Ms. Bambi:
"Yes. Now, Sara, think about what the section was about and a question you might ask us." (pause)
When Sara is unable to generate a question, Ms. Bambi modifies the task:
"Well, maybe you could think of a summary. What did this paragraph tell us about?"

Sara responds:

"About whenever that tank is not filled up, he has to come up."

Ms. Bambi:

"Yes! Now we could make up a question about that, couldn't we?"

This is still not enough assistance to Sara and so the teacher models such a question, using the information that Sara has suggested:

"We could say, 'Why does the aquanaut have to come up?' Would you like to ask that question?"

Sara repeats the teacher's question:

"Why does the aquanaut come up?" and calls another child, "Candy?"

Candy:

"Because it didn't have enough air."

Sara:

"That's right."

Rather than proceed with the discussion, Ms. Bambi asks Sara to try for another question, providing more opportunity for scaffolded instruction:

"Let's try for another question. Let me read a part of this again."

Ms. Bambi then rereads the second paragraph and asks:

"Can you think of a question?"

Sara, while not generating a question, is able to identify a topic:

"I know. They can see themselves."

Ms. Bambi:

"Aha! You could ask a question about that couldn't you?" (pause) "Start the question with the word, 'how.'"

Sara, with Ms. Bambi's help, then generates a question:

"How can the . . ."

Ms. Bambi:

"aquanauts . . ."

Sara:

"see themselves in the mirror?"

Ms. Bambi:

"OK! That was close! You answered your own question. What is the mirror, Sara?"

Sara:

"The water."

Ms. Bambi:

"So you might ask, 'How could the aquanauts see themselves?' or 'what was the water like?' Let's go on now. What do you suppose, Sara, we will learn about next?"

Sara:

"More about breathing in the water."

4. Turn over control to students

As students begin to internalize the strategies, Ms. Bambi allows them to take more responsibility for the task of constructing the text's meaning. In the following discussion, Dan functions very independently of the teacher.

Ms. Bambi (reading):

"Some aquanauts have already lived and worked under water for many days. Wearing their gear, they went out of the underwater houses. They took pictures of coral. They gathered rocks from the ocean floor. They looked for signs of oil and minerals. They watched fish feed and lay their eggs. They learned a lot about life in the sea."

Dan:

"How does the aquanaut get air in his house?"

Bobby:

"By the hose."

Dan:

"Yes. And what did the aquanauts do under the water?"

Devon:

"Gather rocks."

Dan:

"And take pictures of the coral."

Ms. Bambi:

"Well, you've covered that section very well."

Dan:

"Also, what did the aquanauts build under the water?"

Candy:

"Houses."

Dan:

"Yes. And my summary: This was about that they build houses under the water."

Ms. Bambi elaborates upon Dan's summary:

"Excellent. And they told us what they used them for, to observe the life underwater. Dan did an excellent job of being our teacher. Let's go ahead."

Ms. Bambi and her students would continue the dialogue sessions for four or five weeks or until the teacher is assured that students are using the strategies independently.

4. Evaluation of the instructional solution. Ms. Bambi could look at several indicators to evaluate the success of the reciprocal teaching. First, students should improve in their use of the four strategies over the course of the intervention. Second, their comprehension of texts should improve. She can assess comprehension by periodically giving students questions to answer about short passages they have read independently. Finally, she should observe that the students are using the strategies independently in settings other than the dialogue sessions.

REFERENCE

Palincsar, A. M. (1988, April). *Dialogue, private speech, and the development of self-regulatory behavior.* Paper presented at the American Educational Research Association, New Orleans, LA.

12

FACILITATING POSITIVE ATTITUDES AND MOTIVATION

OBJECTIVES

Given case studies describing student behavior, attitudes, and motivation:

1. Analyze the learning problem.
2. Determine relevant theoretical knowledge.
3. Develop a proposed instructional solution.
4. Evaluate the instructional solution.

A student's attitudes and motivational orientation influence the degree to which she follows classroom rules and regulations, the academic tasks she chooses, the nature of her involvement in those tasks, and how much energy and persistence she puts into them. For example, a student with positive attitudes will be motivated not only to attend to instruction but also to engage in activities such as repeated practice and elaboration that facilitate learning. Also, when faced with roadblocks, this student will be persistent and expend the effort needed to complete the learning task. Conversely, a student with negative attitudes toward learning will likely exhibit disruptive behaviors which may interfere with learning and classroom activities. For example, she may fail to follow classroom rules and regulations and may give up easily after putting little effort into learning.

It is important to note, however, that these same disruptive behaviors and halfhearted learning efforts sometimes result from not knowing how to behave appropriately or how to learn rather than from a negative attitude. For example, if a teacher does not make her classroom rules explicit, a student may behave inappropriately because she is unsure or unaware of these rules. Consequently, when dealing with student attitude and motivation to learn, it is important to gather as much information as possible about the classroom environment and a student's internal states before identifying potential solutions for undesirable behavior.

A student's attitudes and motivational orientations are significantly influenced by declarative and procedural knowledge related to learning and achievement. His declarative knowledge consists of his internalized beliefs, attitudes, goals, and affect related to learning and achievement. For example, a student who believes that he has control over whether he succeeds or fails will most likely possess a positive attitude and motivation to learn. Likewise, a student's ability to set appropriate goals and to cope with potential difficulties (procedural knowledge) will also significantly influence his attitudes and motivational orientations. For example, a student who can set appropriate goals and overcome most learning difficulties is likely to have a positive attitude toward learning and be highly motivated to learn. In most instances, instructional interventions aimed at modifying a student's attitudes and motivational orientation will involve changes in either his declarative or his procedural knowledge.

BACKGROUND KNOWLEDGE FROM PART ONE

In contrast to the other three learning outcomes dealt with in chapters 11, 13, and 14, attempts to improve students' attitudes and motivation toward learning integrate techniques *from both behavioral and cognitive approaches to learning.* Depending upon the problem, one may focus on the modification of a student's behavior and environment, on the modification of a student's declarative and procedural knowledge, or on both. Part One contained a variety of techniques for modifying students' attitudes and level of motivation and, consequently, their classroom behavior. For example, our discussion of behavioral learning theory in Chapter 2 described techniques for identifying and manipulating the antecedents and consequences of student behaviors in order to help develop positive and motivated learners. Similarly, Chapter 8 explained how the use of teacher and peer modeling of positive and motivated behaviors can significantly influence student classroom behaviors.

Also within Chapter 8, we saw how explicit instruction in setting and monitoring goals can help students maintain positive attitudes and develop high levels of self-efficacy. This will influence the tasks a student chooses, the amount of effort she puts into completing the task, and the degree to which she persists at academic tasks. Also, helping a student to consistently attribute successes and failures to controllable factors such as effort will facilitate appropriate behaviors and attitudes within the classroom (see Chapter 9). Likewise, the use of instructional and evaluative techniques that focus students on learning that is meaningful, self-directed, and self-referenced helps cultivate positive and effective classroom behavior (see Table 9.5).

In Chapter 9, we also discussed the importance of knowing the developmental level of students. Developmentally appropriate tasks (see chapters 6 and 7) are needed to sustain positive student attitudes and high levels of motivation. Also, engaging students in challenging conflict resolution and problem-solving tasks generally motivates them to actively participate in classroom activities and learning. Let us now proceed to analyze our first case study. If further cues are needed to activate your problem-solving schema, see Table 10.1.

CASE STUDY

Marsha's third-grade class at Sammy Pre- and Elementary School was a difficult group of children. A few students liked school and really tried to learn, but overall the class just wasn't focused on learning. It was impossible to relax with them. If Marsha let down her guard and tried to engage them in a friendly, less formal manner, the class would disintegrate. This vigilant formality ran counter to Marsha's natural teaching style which was to maintain a friendly, relaxed manner. She usually enjoyed her students, and her enjoyment showed. But in this particular class, she constantly had to be firm and vigilant ("witchlike," she thought) in order to keep the students under control.

The majority of her problems stemmed from a group of students who were in the "below grade level" reading group. This group provided the spark that set off fireworks for the entire class, day after day. Since they tended to be at their worst as a group, Marsha tried separating them, but that brought little improvement. Three weeks ago, in early October, she tried reorganizing her reading groups, distributing the slow readers among all three groups. The net result of this experiment, however, was to make all three groups disruptive. Moveover, mixing her slow and average readers dramatically reduced the pace of both groups. The slow readers put little effort into the group activities and, even when engaged, gave up easily when faced with obstacles. Finding this arrangement unfair to her other students, she finally went back to her original groupings.

Marsha did not think she ran her classroom in too lax a manner. She had procedures for incomplete work; she had rules for appropriate behavior; and she never hesitated to involve parents. Moreover, she was not afraid to use punishment. She sent individual troublemakers to the office, held detention during lunch, isolated misbehaving children by separating their desks from the rest of the class, and used denial of privileges. Marsha also tried talking honestly with the children, giving them pep talks about the value of education and their need to read and write and think in order to participate fully in life. But nothing seem to alter the poor behavior of her class.

Analysis of the Learning Problem

The primary problem in this case is the disruptive behavior of the students who are performing below grade level in reading. Marsha has attempted to deal with their problem behavior in a number of ways. First, she separated these problem students into different groups. Presumably, that was to expose them to the more positive behavior models of the higher achieving students. She also actively taught rules and regulations for appropriate classroom behavior and employed both positive and negative punishment techniques when these rules were violated. Finally, she tried to motivate positive behavior by discussing the importance of reading and writing to success outside the classroom.

Given the limited information provided in this case, a variety of causes could be contributing to the students' poor attitude and misbehavior. Consequently, a multifaceted approach may be best in this situation. First, Marsha might check out the possibility that these "disruptive" students may be receiving reinforcement for their disruptive behavior. If being in class is uncomfortable for them, then any behavior which gets them out of the classroom becomes a negative reinforcer. For example, disruptions which send them to the office during reading activities may save them from painful feelings of incompetence and, consequently, negatively reinforce that behavior.

Second, it appears that Marsha is not reinforcing appropriate behavior. Although she has clear rules for appropriate behavior, she tends to use punishment rather than positive reinforcement to support those rules. Third, the "disruptive" students probably have a history of school failure due to their below grade level reading ability. This history, together with their conspicuous placement into a "low ability" reading group, has likely produced feelings of low innate ability, lack of control, and a performance goal orientation. Their tendency to put little effort or persistence into classroom activities supports this suggestion. It is important, however, that this assessment be verified by observing these students over time and in a variety of situations to see if they exhibit other attitudes, beliefs, and behaviors which are consistent with these patterns and orientation. For example, does their motivation seem to consistently revolve around the need to maintain feelings of self-worth?

Finally, Marsha seems to be aware of the need to take a student's developmental level into consideration when planning instructional activities (e.g., ability groupings). However, as indicated earlier, ability groupings can have detrimental effects on students' motivational orientation. Consequently, Marsha may need to use a more private and individualized approach when designing instruction for those low-achieving students.

Determination of Relevant Theoretical Knowledge

As indicated earlier, both behavioral and cognitive learning theories can be used to remedy attitude and motivation problems. From a behavioral perspective, inappropriate student behaviors such as the low achievers' disruptions can be modified or eliminated by manipulating the antecedents and consequences that have historically surrounded them. In Chapter 2, we listed the types of direct consequences: positive and negative reinforcement and positive and negative punishment. In Chapter 8, we indicated that seeing someone else reinforced or punished (vicarious reinforcement and punishment) can also be used to modify or eliminate behaviors. However, as we discussed in Chapter 2, it is preferable to primarily use reinforcement to modify or eliminate behavior because punishment can lead to some undesirable side effects. Finally, in Chapter 2, discriminative stimuli were identified as important antecedents that can influence student behaviors by indicating which will be reinforced and which will be punished (e.g., classroom rules and regulations).

It is important to note that the use of reinforcement theory requires a sensitive and observant teacher, one who is truly "tuned in" to the likes and dislikes of her students. Many well-intentioned teachers have actually embarrassed or turned off their students by indiscriminant use of unwanted or undeserved praise or some other form of attention. However, once appropriate reinforcers have been identified, it is important that the teacher administer them frequently, consistently, and immediately.

In Chapter 9, we saw that when students devote little effort and persistence to completing a task, it is often an indication that they attribute academic outcomes to uncontrollable causes such as ability or luck, have low self-efficacy, and possess a performance goal orientation. Disruptive behaviors are often symptomatic of these motivational beliefs and orientations. That is, these students may be too depressed and frustrated to put any effort into learning. Instead, they prefer to be disruptive because they are more successful at that. In order to help these students believe they have some control over their learning, a teacher would need to (1) develop their learning skills and strategies (see chapters 11 and 14) and (2) prepare developmentally appropriate learning activities that allow each problem student to begin building a history of success in academic tasks (see chapters 6 and 7). Finally, the teacher needs to adopt instructional and evaluation practices that will encourage her problem students to adopt a learning goal motivational orientation (see Table 9.5).

Development of Proposed Instructional Solution

Marsha needs to deal both with the external behavioral "disruptions" and with the internal maladaptive motivational patterns. However, before any work on the students' motivational patterns and orientations can occur, she will need to reduce the problem students' penchant for disrupting the class.

At the behavioral level, Marsha should develop specific guidelines for appropriate classroom behaviors and ensure that all students understand and remember these rules. She can use elaborative techniques to help students remember these guidelines (see Chapter 13 for ways to help students remember verbal information). Examples of typical classroom guidelines appear in Table 12.1. Weinstein and Mignano (1993) indicate that classroom rules and guidelines need to be appropriate to the particular grade level. For example, it would be unreasonable to expect fourth-grade students to employ sophisticated conflict resolution techniques such as mutual negotiation. However, it would not be unreasonable to expect this behavior of high school students. The guidelines also need to be understandable and meaningful to students. The more students are involved in the development and enforcement of the guidelines, the more meaningful they become. The guidelines also need to be specific and stated in behavioral terms. Finally, the guidelines need to be consistent with the goals of the classroom and

TABLE 12.1 EXAMPLES OF CLASSROOM GUIDELINES

Guidelines

1. Stay in your seats.
2. Raise your hand to talk.
3. No eating or drinking in the classrooms.
4. Listen when someone is talking.
5. Don't fight; settle your disagreements peacefully.

with the rules of school. For example, it is important not to create guidelines which will hinder student learning within the classroom.

Marsha should create guidelines for the whole class and should not single out the low-achieving students. If the disruptive behaviors are being maintained by high levels of attention, singling them out via the guidelines will only reinforce them. As indicated earlier, Marsha needs to consistently and immediately administer the consequences of following and not following classroom rules. In addition, it is important to tailor reinforcers to each student within the classroom. That is, the reinforcer needs to be meaningful to the student to have any reinforcing effect. For example, one student may prefer to read fiction or play games on a computer, while another may prefer to socialize with other students or lead group discussions. These preferred activities should be noted and used to reinforce each student, respectively. Within the present context, Marsha can set up a token system to reward students who follow classroom guidelines. At the end of the day or week, she can allow students to redeem their tokens for a personalized reward such as participating in one of their preferred activities.

Giving students choices among meaningful reinforcers should also help them adopt a learning goal orientation within the classroom. As indicated in Chapter 9, engaging students in relevant activities and allowing them some self-direction will facilitate the adoption of a learning goal orientation. Another way to encourage self-direction is to solicit the students' help in identifying and enforcing the classroom guidelines.

With respect to the low-achieving reading students, Marsha should create a set of graded activities which gradually moves them from relatively easy tasks to more difficult ones. She also needs to ensure that these students develop a history of success within these tasks. Moreover, she should continually point out the connection between their efforts and their successes. Marsha also needs to ensure that these students possess the learning and study strategies that will allow them to be successful. Although it is unclear from the case description whether these students have the requisite strategies, it is likely that they do not. In that case, Marsha should design instruction that will develop the cognitive strategies of these students (see Chapter 11 for ways to teach cognitive strategies).

Finally, Marsha needs to stop using ability groups in her classroom. Such groups tend to highlight differential ability and foster social comparisons. Focusing on ability and social comparisons encourages students to adopt a performance goal orientation. Marsha needs to get rid of the ability groups and individualize instruction and evaluation for each student. In addition, she should provide each student with private feedback concerning his academic progress within the class. Also, positive reinforcement should be made contingent upon a student's devoting higher levels of effort to completing tasks and making consistent progress toward attaining important academic goals. Finally, she should help students acquire the intellectual skill of creating important personal goals and monitoring the attainment of these goals. See Chapter 14 for ways to help students acquire such skills.

Evaluation of the Instructional Solution

Marsha can evaluate her instructional interventions by monitoring the behavioral changes of her students, particularly her low-achieving students. She should create a checklist which includes both appropriate and inappropriate behaviors (see Table 12.2 for an example of an abbreviated behavioral checklist). This checklist should include behaviors which relate directly to the classroom guidelines as well as other behaviors such as amount of effort devoted to academic tasks, amount of persistence in the face of difficulty, and use of effective learning strategies. Including these other behaviors will allow Marsha to evaluate whether the students have developed an appropriate motivational orientation. That is, these items will assess whether students are attributing successes and failures to differential effort, have developed a higher level of self-efficacy, and have developed a learning goal orientation to achievement situations.

This checklist should be filled out daily for each student within the classroom. Once students begin consistently exhibiting appropriate behaviors, Marsha can cut back the checklist to twice a week and then to once a week. However, it is

---

TABLE 12.2   BEHAVIORAL CHECKLIST

Instruction: For each student in the class, put "yes" next to those behaviors which were consistently exhibited today, and "no" next to those which were not consistently exhibited. For those behaviors which are not applicable to today's class, please put "NA." For example, there may not be assigned homework every day or students may not volunteer to ask questions every day.

1. _____ Given a task, student remains on task without interruption.

2. _____ Completes and returns assigned homework.

3. _____ Responds to teacher's cues to line up and become quiet.

4. _____ Stays in seat except when given permission to get up.

5. _____ Raises hand and waits to be acknowledged by teacher before talking.

6. _____ Given the opportunity, chooses to engage in challenging tasks.

7. _____ Devotes considerable effort to completing tasks.

8. _____ Persists at completing a task even when having difficulty.

9. _____ Exhibits appropriate emotional reactions to successes and failures within the classroom.

10. _____ Cooperates with others to complete classroom tasks.

---

important not to discontinue the checklist entirely since it alerts students to the fact that their behavior is being monitored. Thus, the checklist acts as a cue or discriminative stimulus (see Chapter 2) that encourages students to behave appropriately within the classroom. Gradually, the teacher can withdraw and fade the monitoring when it is clear that students are no longer dependent upon the teacher for cues.

Now it is time for you to apply your knowledge of learning theory to two brief cases involving attitude and motivation problems.

CASE #1

Sally, a tenth grader, frequently shouts out answers in her social studies class without being recognized by the teacher. Most often her answers are correct. Sally's behavior is annoying to other students, but their comments to her have had no effect. Mr. Tribble has attempted to deal with this inappropriate behavior by taking Sally aside and discussing with her how the behavior disrupts the class and upsets the other students. Unfortunately, this has only produced an increase in the shouting behavior.

Social studies is Sally's favorite class, one in which she has produced many high-quality portfolios. She particularly enjoys leading social studies group activities as that gives her the opportunity to speak without being recognized. In other subjects, Sally is quiet and rarely gets involved in class discussions. Although she enjoys interacting with others, she dreads getting up in front of the class to present her homework. Also, even though she does everything that is required in her other subjects, she maintains barely passing grades.

Interestingly enough, her ability to think quickly has helped her to become the most effective member of the student council, where she has successfully obtained a variety of student privileges from the school administration. She is currently president of council.

1 What is your **analysis of the learning problem?**

_____

_____

_____

_____

2 Please determine **relevant theoretical knowledge.**

_____

_____

_____

_____

_____

3 What is your **proposed instructional solution?**

_____

_____

_____

_____

4 How will you **evaluate your proposed solution?**

_____

_____

_____

_____

_____

CASE #2

Bruce, a seventh grader, is a star football player who enjoys the game very much. Because he spends so much time on sports, his academic progress has suffered. Some students have begun to give him demeaning nicknames like "blockhead" and "dunce."

On the few occasions when Bruce has put extra effort into his studies, he has attained satisfactory progress reports. In most instances, however, Bruce offers up only minimal effort on academic tasks. In addition, he has a limited repertoire of study strategies and relies primarily on repetition when trying to remember verbal materials. This may contribute to his mediocre performance in school. His history of academic failure has led him to attribute his difficulty with academic subjects to a lack of inherent ability. In contrast, Bruce often attributes his success in football to the fact that he was born with natural athletic ability.

As with most other boys in his grade, his favorite activity in school is physical education class, and he dreads going to arts and crafts. Bruce has recently begun to be very physical with other students in the hall and in the classroom. He has been seen using his notebook to swat others, both males and females. He pinches girls. He often bumps into other students or shoulders them aside. Because of this physical behavior, almost all students try to ignore him. Unfortunately, this has merely exacerbated the situation and led Bruce to escalate his physically inappropriate behaviors.

1 What is your **analysis of the learning problem?**

_____

_____

_____

_____

_____

2 Please determine **relevant theoretical knowledge.**

_____

_____

_____

_____

3 What is your **proposed instructional solution?**

_____

_____

_____

_____

_____

4 How will you **evaluate your proposed solution?**

_____

_____

_____

_____

_____

REVIEW OF MAJOR POINTS

The intent of this chapter is to help you to organize your knowledge related to facilitating positive attitudes and motivation to learn so that you can use it to solve instructional problems. Positive attitude and motivation problems concern a student's beliefs, attitudes, attributions, goals, and/or affect (emotion) related to learning and learning environments. Typical indicators of this type of problem are a student's exhibiting inappropriate behaviors (e.g., acting out), consistently failing, choosing not to get involved in activities, and giving up easily on difficult tasks.

The three cases presented in this chapter required applying your knowledge of cognitive and behavioral learning theories to develop instructional solutions for learning problems involving the modification of a student's behaviors and/or his declarative and procedural knowledge. Changes in behaviors require the manipulation of the antecedents to and consequences of these behaviors. Changes in declarative knowledge involve modifying a student's internal statements describing his beliefs, attitudes, attributions, goals, and/or affect related to learning and learning environments. Finally, changes in procedural knowledge involve developing student goal-setting skills and coping skills.

ANSWERS TO CASE EXERCISES

Case #1

1. Analysis of the learning problem. There are two learning problems described in this case: Sally's shouting behavior and her anxiety about getting up in front of the class. There is not enough information to establish any maladaptive motivational patterns or orientations. Although Sally is not doing well in most classes, there is no indication that it is due to a lack of effort or persistence on her part. Given the lack of information about internal states, the best approach to solving these problems is to focus on Sally's overt behavior, that is, to teach her to wait for recognition prior to answering questions and, through controlled practice, to overcome her fear of presenting homework to the whole class.

2. Relevant theoretical knowledge. In chapters 2 and 8, we saw how inappropriate student behaviors such as Sally's shouting-out can be modified or eliminated by consistently applying the principles of both direct and vicarious reinforcement. Negative and positive punishments can also be used but must be applied judiciously as they can easily lead to student's withdrawing altogether from the problem situation. As indicated earlier, the use of reinforcement theory requires a sensitive and observant teacher, one who is truly "tuned in" to the likes and dislikes of his students. Once appropriate reinforcers have been identified, it is important that the teacher administer them frequently, consistently, and immediately.

A technique that may be helpful in dealing with Sally's anxiety about presenting to the class is counterconditioning (see Chapter 2). That involves pairing positive emotional stimuli with situations which normally produce negative emotions such as anxiety. The key to using counterconditioning is to *gradually* immerse the student into the anxiety-producing situation. After the student has become comfortable with a miniature version of the situation, she can then be confronted with a series of slightly expanded versions until she is finally able to deal effectively with the full-blown situation.

3. Proposed instructional solution. Let's deal first with Sally's shouting-out behavior which, as indicated, occurs primarily in social studies, a class in which she is quite successful. Despite negative feedback from both her classmates and Mr. Tribble, the frequency of Sally's shouting-out has not been reduced. As a first step in reducing her disruptive behavior, Mr. Tribble should carefully observe her behavior patterns both inside and outside his classroom. That will enable him to identify those activities that she most enjoys and that can be used to positively reinforce desired behavior or to negatively punish undesired behavior. For example, he should note that Sally likes to lead small group discussions and that she enjoys her membership on the student council, which allows her to negotiate with school faculty. Armed with these reinforcement tools, Mr. Tribble is now ready to help Sally learn appropriate question-asking behavior.

First, however, Mr. Tribble must be sure that Sally understands that she must wait for recognition before answering questions. Once he is sure she understands that, he is ready to manipulate the consequences of her behavior. For Sally, the consequences of raising her hand and waiting to be acknowledged might be allowing her to lead a small group discussion within his social science class (positive reinforcement).

Mr. Tribble should also tell Sally that unless she consistently raises her hand and waits to be acknowledged before answering questions, she could be removed as president of the student council (negative punishmnent). Initially, "consistently" can be defined as behaving appropriately during two out of five social studies classes. Once this level of performance has been attained for three consecutive weeks, the level of consistency can be increased to three out five classes, and eventually five out of five classes. After attaining a certain level of consistent performance (e.g., three out of five classes), any sliding back to a previous level (e.g., one or two out of five classes) will result in Sally's removal as president of the student council. If it occurs a second time, she could be removed from student council altogether.

Finally, Mr. Tribble can also consistently and immediately reinforce other students within the class for exhibiting appropriate question-answering behavior. Observing other students receive positive consequences for modeling appropriate behavior will, it is hoped, motivate Sally to do the same.

In order to deal with Sally's anxiety regarding whole-group presentations, Mr. Tribble can create a series of tasks which will gradually move Sally from small-group presentations of familiar topics to large group presentations of unfamiliar topics. As indicated earlier, an example of a topic familiar to Sally might be useful negotiation techniques. By starting with a small-group and working toward a large-group presentation, the teacher is allowing Sally to gradually overcome her anxiety associated with large group presentation. Finally, as with question-asking behavior, the teacher should reinforce other students for volunteering to present to the class.

4. Evaluation of the instructional solution. As indicated earlier, the most appropriate way to evaluate changes in behavior is to systematically observe students within the classroom. In the current context, that would involve keeping a record of Sally's question-answering behavior. It is important to continue monitoring her behavior even after she consistently behaves appropriately. It is very likely that as long as Sally knows that the teacher is monitoring her behavior, the monitoring may act as cue or discriminative stimulus (see Chapter 2) to continue behaving appropriately. Gradually, the teacher can withdraw and fade the monitoring when it becomes clear that Sally is no longer dependent on the teacher for cues.

The best way to evaluate Sally's anxiety about presenting to groups is to monitor the number of times she volunteers to present to the class. As it becomes more comfortable for her, she will be more likely to volunteer. That would signal a reduction in her anxiety.

Case #2

1. Analysis of the learning problem. There are two learning problems described in this case: Bruce's poor academic performance and his physical behavior with fellow students. With respect to his poor academic performance, there is evidence that Bruce attributes his failures to a lack of ability. Feeling that he has no control over his academic outcomes, he rarely puts any effort into his studies. Consequently, there is a need to help Bruce to consistently attribute his academic outcomes to controllable causes. One way to accomplish that is to ensure that Bruce accumulates a history of successful academic experiences.

The physical behavior may have multiple causes: (1) a reaction to student's calling him demeaning nicknames, (2) the fact that in football, extreme physical interaction is reinforced because it is critical to success, and (3) need for attention from his peers. The name calling may cue Bruce to retaliate, and given Bruce's athletic and football experience, becoming more physical may be his way of reestablishing himself. Also, the fact that Bruce's physical abuse escalated when other students began to ignore him suggests that physical behavior is either highly reinforced for Bruce or it is his way of getting attention from peers.

2. Relevant theoretical knowledge. In Chapter 9, we saw how poor academic performance is often due, in part, to inappropriate attributions on the part of students. Attributing failure to factors outside the student's control (e.g., luck or lack of ability) leads to a lack of effort and low persistence when faced with obstacles to successful task completion. While attribution retraining will undoubtedly contribute to improved academic performance, it cannot do the job alone. In most instances, students with a history of academic failure also lack the study strategies needed to convert increased effort and persistence into maximum academic performance (see chapters 4, 5, 7, and 11).

Turning to inappropriate social behavior, chapters 2 and 8 presented reinforcement and punishment techniques that can be used to eliminate undesirable behavior. However, before rewards and punishments can be applied, it is necessary to determine the likes and dislikes of the student in question. That entails getting to know the student. At that point, the teacher can be a sensitive and informed (rather than an arbitrary) dispenser of rewards and punishments.

3. Proposed instructional solution. In order to deal with Bruce's maladaptive attributional pattern, the teacher needs to engage him in attributional retraining. That means getting Bruce involved in tasks that require small but noticeable amounts of effort and that are likely to lead to success. Then, as Bruce shows more willingness to exert effort, the teacher could involve him in tasks that require more effort and that, once again, are likely to produce success. The teacher should avoid tasks that can be done successfully without any effort, because she may then lose credibility.

As indicated in an earlier case study, it is also important to develop Bruce's academic skills, that is, his cognitive and metacognitive strategies, in order to give him the tools with which to successfully complete tasks. In short, increased effort alone cannot guarantee success. Chapter 4 describes a variety of strategies for remembering information, such as rehearsal, elaboration, organization, and mnemonics. Chapter 5 then discusses various strategies (i.e., heuristics) for solving problems. Chapter 7 discusses strategies such as summarizing, clarifying, questioning, and predicting, which are useful in reading comprehension. Finally, Chapter 11 illustrates how a teacher can actively teach these strategies. As indicated in that chapter, an integral part of teaching students strategies is to focus them on the importance of effort to success within the classroom.

In order to eliminate Bruce's inappropriate physical behaviors, a variety of interventions can be used. First, the help of the other students should be enlisted by asking them to refrain from calling Bruce names. That will eliminate a potential cue for his physical behavior. Second, indicate to Bruce that if he refrains from being physical with others, he will be given extra time in physical education class. However, if there is no reduction in this behavior after one week, Bruce will be given less physical education time and will not be allowed to play on the football team. If that occurs, he will be allowed to return to the football team only when he refrains from being physical for two consecutive weeks.

4. Evaluation of the instructional solution. The teacher can evaluate the effects of attributional retraining by monitoring Bruce's performance on academic tasks. She should look at the amount of effort he devotes to academic tasks and note any improvement in his grades, the amount of persistence he exhibits in the face of difficulty, and his use of effective learning strategies. The teacher may eventually want to set up more challenging tasks that will slow Bruce's progress in order to evaluate his effort, persistence, and ability to use effective strategies.

As indicated earlier, the most appropriate way to evaluate changes in student behavior is to systematically observe students within the classroom. In the current context, that would involve keeping a record of the number of times Bruce exhibits inappropriate physical behavior toward others. Such observations can be recorded during the changing of classes and by asking students to report any inappropriate physical behavior.

REFERENCE

Weinstein, C., & Mignano, A., Jr. (1993). *Elementary classroom management.* New York: McGraw-Hill, Inc.

13

TEACHING VERBAL INFORMATION

OBJECTIVES

Given case descriptions involving teaching verbal information:

1. Analyze the learning problem.
2. Determine relevant theoretical knowledge.
3. Develop a proposed instructional solution.
4. Evaluate the instructional solution.

The outcome of verbal information refers to students' ability to retrieve and verbalize previously presented information. Thus, this outcome deals with the acquisition of declarative knowledge which is verbalizable knowledge about the world. Verbal information can vary in complexity. The simplest kind of verbal information is a label or name. Students are expected to learn the labels or names for many objects and concepts. Note that learning the name of a concept is quite distinct from learning the concept. *Forming* concepts is an intellectual skill and is examined in Chapter 14. Another form of verbal information is the *fact,* which is expressed as a simple proposition. Students are expected to learn many facts, such as "Columbus discovered America in 1492," or "There are limits on how much information can be stored in working memory." Finally, verbal information may also be learned as sets of interrelated facts or bodies of knowledge. For example, students are expected to learn American history or theories of learning.

It appears to be fashionable today to disparage the learning of facts and "mere verbal knowledge." The major reason for that seems to be a desire to emphasize loftier goals such as teaching students to think creatively. It is important to remember, however, that *verbal information is a vehicle for thought.* In Chapter 5 we pointed out that expert problem solvers have more factual knowledge within their areas of expertise than novices do. Problem solving is facilitated by the acquisition of a large store of relevant declarative knowledge. However, we also noted that in order for factual knowledge to facilitate problem solving it must be organized around important concepts and principles.

BACKGROUND KNOWLEDGE FROM PART ONE

In chapters 3 and 4 we discussed processes involved in comprehending and remembering information. We emphasized that comprehending new information entails relating it to existing schemas in long-term memory. Remembering the comprehended information depends upon elaborating the meaning of the material and organizing it into meaningful patterns. Additionally, we discussed specific techniques that teachers can use to activate schemas (e.g., use advance organizers), stimulate elaboration (e.g., use imagery and analogies, ask students questions that require elaboration), and enhance organization (e.g., provide students with an organizational scheme using concept maps and/or outlines). Finally, we discussed specific mnemonic strategies (e.g., peg-word, key-word, and method of loci) that are useful for remembering verbal information.

In attempting to enhance learning of verbal information, teachers can either supply students with appropriate elaborations and organization for the material or they can teach students to construct their own elaborations and organization. In this chapter we will deal with the former approach. The other approach involves teaching students cognitive strategies and metacognition, and was dealt with in Chapter 11. Now that we have stimulated some of your schemas, let us proceed to the case study.

CASE STUDY

Mr. Globe is a sixth-grade history teacher in the Eugenia Middle School. He is having difficulty getting his students to remember important historical dates and events. Mr. Globe thought he might be able to get some new ideas by talking with Mr. Atlas, who was a history teacher at Norwood High School.

After listening to his dilemma. Mr. Atlas asked him to describe how he tried to get his students to remember historical facts and events. Mr. Globe indicated that he uses a chronological approach because it gives students an appreciation of the changes that have occurred over time. The historical evolution of current conditions is, to Mr. Globe, the most important lesson to be learned from history. For example, it is best to discuss the changes that have occurred in world economies over time rather than isolating and discussing specific current relationships such as those between the United States and Japan. Using a chronological approach, according to Mr. Globe, emphasizes the evolving nature of history, something students need to understand. However, his students did not seem to be grasping either the evolutionary nature of history or the important dates and events within that evolutionary process.

In addition to presenting history in a chronological manner, Mr. Globe indicated that he gives students handouts with a chronological list of important dates and asks them to fill in the important historical events next to each date. After they have filled in the appropriate events, he then asks them to repeatedly rehearse each pair of dates and events.

The only change that Mr. Atlas could suggest was to avoid treating historical events and dates as isolated facts. Mr. Atlas agreed that it was important to get students to understand the evolving character of history, but not at the expense of remembering important historical information.

Analysis of the Learning Problem

Mr. Globe is aware that students need an organizational structure in order to assimilate large bodies of verbal information. Thus, he has chosen a chronological organization for his history course. Time, or narration, does appear to be a natural chunking strategy for history; however, it is not the only possible organizational scheme. In fact, organizing historical content in terms of time provides a relatively weak structure in the sense that it tends to be fairly abstract and remote from students' personal experience and, consequently, tends not to be very memorable. Also, this structure often contains so much information that students may become overloaded with facts that they see as having little relevance to their own world. Presumably Mr. Globe does not intend for students to acquire an inert set of facts unrelated to anything else in their knowledge base.

In summary, Mr. Globe's sole reliance on temporal organization plus his emphasis upon maintenance rehearsal to acquire isolated facts inhibits meaningful learning and good retention of verbal information.

Determination of Relevant Theoretical Knowledge

According to Gestalt and information processing theory, learning of verbal information best begins with a big picture, a schema, a holistic structure. Providing students with such a big picture at the beginning of a lesson or before a selection of text helps them to organize the details of the lesson and, at the same time, to identify the most important concepts and principles. In Mr. Globe's case, the temporal organization fails to provide a structure that pulls together the important concepts. On the other hand, a narrative organization is concrete and familiar and can be very interesting to students. If well written, it is like reading an exciting novel. This ''story-like'' organization is particularly suitable for many of Mr. Globe's sixth-grade students who are still at the concrete operational stage of reasoning.

For students to be able to use verbal information in solving problems, their knowledge must be organized into manageable chunks that do not overload their working memories and that are organized around fundamental themes. Requiring students to perform problem-solving exercises with recently acquired verbal information can enhance this type of organization. This principle should be quite familiar to you by now after working through the many exercises in this text. A chronological approach does not lend itself to this sort of phrasing or segmenting of content into coherent chunks.

Retention of verbal information is also enhanced if students are instructed to study lesson material using encoding strategies that elaborate the meaning of the material. Students' retention of specific facts can be enhanced by instructing them to use an appropriate elaboration or mnemonic device. For example, imagery is a good method for memorizing dates of historical events. The peg method or the method of loci is appropriate for memorizing historical sequences of events (e.g., the presidents in order of term, the sequence of major civil war battles).

Finally, providing students with several ways to organize the material can enhance retention because it provides several retrieval routes. For example, studying the information about the Civil War organized chronologically provides temporal cues for recalling important events. Subsequently viewing the same information organized around the goals and plans of the Union and Confederacy provides alternative retrieval cues. The exercise of rechunking or reorganizing the material facilitates recall.

Development of Proposed Instructional Solution

Mr. Globe might continue to use a chronological organization but supplement it with other organizational schemes. Other ways of organizing the material include the following: *cause-effect* (e.g., the causes and effects of the revolutionary war), *similarities and differences* (e.g., the similarities and differences between capitalist and socialist economic systems), *advantages and disadvantages* (e.g., the pros and cons of democracy), *goal frames* (e.g., what was the goal of the English government with respect to the colonies? What plan, action, and outcome followed from this goal?).

Mr. Globe could continue to use a textbook that has a chronological organization. Or, to capture student interest even more, he might have them read historically accurate novels related to particular historical periods (e.g., *Johnny Tremain*). His lessons, however, could use one of the above alternative organizational schemes to highlight major themes and concepts. For example, after students have read the story of the revolutionary war, Mr. Globe could present a lesson on the causes and effects of the war. Before beginning his lesson, Mr. Globe could present students with the big picture in an overview or concept map. He could point out that the lesson is organized in terms of the causes and effects of the war. Then, during the actual lesson, he could fill in the details. As a follow-up, problem-solving exercise, Mr. Globe could present information about a current-day revolution and have students hypothesize its causes and effects based upon their knowledge of the causes and effects of the American revolution. The use of exercises in which students must apply their knowledge not only helps students to retain the material but also to transfer their knowledge to relevant problems in today's world.

If Mr. Globe wishes his students to remember dates of specific events of the revolutionary war, he could provide them with elaborations that will enhance their retention. For example, he could ask his students to imagine the founding fathers signing the Declaration of Independence on the basketball court of the Philadelphia (17) 76ers. Or, if that is not familiar to his students, he could have them imagine the signing's taking place at a Union (17) 76 gas station. Any image that meaningfully connects the event with the date is appropriate. Students enjoy coming up with such images and can be challenged to think up and share images with classmates.

Mr. Globe could help students remember the sequence of revolutionary war battles by teaching them the rhyme that goes with the peg method (one is a bun, two is a shoe, etc.; see Chapter 4). After they have learned the rhyme, he can help them construct images linking each battle with its appropriate peg word (e.g., an image of a bun with a cord draped over it for the Battle of Concord, a shoe on top of a hill for the Battle of Bunker Hill). The peg rhyme can then be used ever after to remember sequences of events from various historical epochs.

In other lessons on American history, Mr. Globe can continue to use alternative organizational schemes to supplement the chronological organization of the text. The first step in developing these lessons is to inspect the material in the text to discover the major ideas, concepts, and principles. The second step is to decide which type of organization (e.g., comparison/contrast, cause and effect, advantages/disadvantages) the material lends itself to. The third step is to construct an overview of the lesson which highlights the organizational scheme. The fourth step is to teach the lesson, filling in the details of the organizational scheme. Following the lesson students can be given short exercises in which they are asked to apply the knowledge they have acquired to some contemporary problem. Finally, Mr. Globe could provide students with elaborations and mnemonic devices to help them retain specific facts.

Evaluation of the Instructional Solution

Mr. Globe can evaluate his instructional approach by constructing tests that require students to retrieve and verbalize their knowledge of American history. Appropriate items are ones that ask students to state, discuss, compare/contrast, list, describe, and so on. In constructing his tests, Mr. Globe should reinstate the retrieval cues that were present during the lesson. This will allow a better estimate of what knowledge students have stored in their long-term memories. For example, the test following the lessons on the revolutionary war might ask students to state four causes and three effects of the war. An examination of students' responses enables him to ascertain whether students are retaining the material or not. If a majority of students fail to answer certain questions correctly, he can reteach that material. Using his sense of students' level of performance in prior semesters, he can evaluate whether his attempts to reorganize the material and introduce elaborative study methods are improving students' learning of verbal information.

Now you can apply your knowledge of teaching verbal information to several small cases.

CASE #1

Ms. Smith and Ms. Jones are using the same second-grade science curriculum that deals with animals. They are teaching a unit on cows, and today's lesson focuses on the milking process. Ms. Smith teaches in a small cow-farming community in Vermont, so many of the students have firsthand experience with cows and the milking process. Others have either attended public milking demonstrations or have friends who have shown them the process.

Ms. Jones teaches in inner city Chicago. Few of her students have ever been outside the city, let alone traveled to the country, so most have never seen a live cow. Since most of their exposure to cows and milk is either on TV or in grocery stores, many of them assume that milk is man-made. They don't have a clue as to the connection between milk and cows.

1 What is your **analysis of the learning problem** facing Ms. Smith? Ms. Jones?

_____

_____

_____

_____

_____

_____

_____

_____

_____

2 Please determine **relevant theoretical knowledge.**

_____

_____

_____

_____

3 What is your **proposed instructional solution?**

4 How will you **evaluate your proposed solution?**

CASE #2

Mr. Bolivar, who teaches ninth-grade science, is currently covering a unit on engines. He cannot understand why his students are having so much trouble understanding today's lesson on turbine engines. "They seemed to have grasped the previous lesson on piston engines," he mused. "So why can't they see that the operation of the two kinds of engines is really quite similar? Why don't they just apply what they already know about piston engines to turbines?" he wondered.

As he reflected more on today's lesson, he realized that it often surprised him that his students rarely carried over what they learned from one lesson to another, even when there were obvious connections between them. "Why don't they see the similarities?" he asked himself.

1 What is your **analysis of the learning problem?**

_____

_____

_____

_____

_____

_____

_____

_____

2 Please determine **relevant theoretical knowledge.**

_____

_____

_____

_____

_____

_____

_____

_____

3 What is your **proposed instructional solution?**

_____

_____

_____

_____

_____

_____

_____

_____

_____

_____

_____

4 How will you **evaluate your proposed solution?**

_____

_____

_____

_____

_____

_____

_____

REVIEW OF MAJOR POINTS

The outcome of verbal information refers to students' ability to retrieve and verbalize previously presented information. This important educational outcome includes learning the names of objects, facts, and organized bodies of knowledge. Such factual information is a necessary prerequisite for expert problem solving.

Learning new verbal information entails relating it to existing schemas in long-term memory. Remembering verbal information depends upon elaborating the meaning of material and organizing it into meaningful patterns. Teachers can use specific techniques to activate schemas, stimulate elaboration, and enhance organization. The case studies required application of these principles from information processing theory to problems involving learning verbal information.

ANSWERS TO CASE EXERCISES

Case #1

1. Analysis of the learning problem. The problem centers around students' background knowledge related to the topic of the lesson. Ms. Smith's students appear to have schemas related to cows and the milking process that will enable them to readily comprehend and remember the lesson material. However, Ms. Jones's students have not had the opportunity to acquire this requisite background knowledge. Thus, they will have difficulty in understanding the material. The tables are likely to be turned in a later lesson on urban transportation systems. When teaching verbal information, teachers must take students' background knowledge into account.

2. Relevant theoretical knowledge. As discussed in Chapter 3, students' background knowledge in the form of schemas plays a critical role in the comprehension process. Comprehension fails when students either lack the necessary background schemas for assimilating new material (as is the case for Ms. Jones's students) or when students possess requisite schemas but fail to activate them (something Ms. Smith wants to avoid). If either of these circumstances prevails, students may acquire material by rote without understanding it. Such rote-acquired information is quickly forgotten.

3. Proposed instructional solution. Because her students have a wealth of knowledge related to farms, cows, and the milking process, Ms. Smith simply needs to activate that knowledge in her students immediately prior to teaching the lesson. There are a number of ways to accomplish that. One method might be to present a short, oral advance organizer that provides an overview of major concepts with which students are already familiar. The teacher could then indicate how the new material will relate to the old material. Another form that schema activation could take is to have students discuss their cow-milking experiences in small groups. According to Piaget, with students of this developmental level, concrete materials and interactions are preferred over abstract material and teacher verbalization.

Because her students have no knowledge of farms, cows, and the milking process, Ms. Jones will have to expose them to this background material before she can attempt the lesson. Given the developmental level of her students and the fact that some have misconceptions (e.g., that milk is man-made), it would be ideal if Ms. Jones could arrange a trip to a dairy-farm. Direct contact with the farm environment, cows, and the milking process would provide perceptual experiences on which new schemas are based. If a field trip is not possible, perhaps a film of life on a dairy farm could be shown. These forms of direct perceptual experience would be preferable to more abstract verbal presentation of information about dairy farms. Ms. Jones must be sure to direct students' attention to relevant objects and events during the field trip or film. Such attention directing is particularly necessary when students lack relevant schemas that enable them to distinguish important from unimportant information. Once she is confident that students have acquired some familiarity with the *dairy-farm* schema, Ms. Jones can proceed with the lesson material, being careful to link the new material with students' prior experiences.

4. Evaluation of the proposed solution. As always, evaluation of verbal information acquisition involves requiring students to retrieve and state the target information. Ms. Smith and Ms. Jones could ask students questions about the milking process. It is important that teachers ask questions that require students to state information in their own words rather than parrot back a verbal statement contained in the lesson. A student can state verbatim information from the lesson without having comprehended it, that is, without having assimilated it to a schema in long-term memory.

Case #2

1. Analysis of the learning problem. The problem appears to be that students are treating each lesson as entirely new and unconnected to prior lessons. That may be occurring because the instruction is proceeding from lesson to lesson with little or no attempt at connecting or bridging. To an expert in the area, the connections between the material on piston and turbine engines are obvious. However, to novices these connections may be totally lacking. By failing to point out connections from unit to unit and from lesson to lesson, Mr. Bolivar may be unconsciously conditioning students not to seek meaningful connections when learning or manipulating information. Without such connections, learning may be rote and quickly forgotten.

2. Relevant theoretical knowledge. Formulating connections between new material and previously learned material enables students to interact meaningfully with new information. One approach to helping students form such connections is to use advance organizers. As we pointed out in Chapter 3, the term "advance organizer" refers to any kind of overview material presented at the start of a lesson which serves to activate relevant schemas so that the new material can be assimilated to them.

In the context of this case, the advance organizer would serve to link new lesson material with material from prior lessons. The foundation is *similarities* between the old and new material. The advance organizer would outline the new information *and* restate prior knowledge. Such an advance organizer provides students with a structure for the new information and encourages them to transfer or apply what they know.

3. Proposed instructional solution. Mr. Bolivar needs to focus on building bridges or connections between lessons by constructing advance organizers that are presented to students at the beginning of lessons. We will illustrate this solution with an advance organizer for a lesson on turbine engines.

Advance Organizer for a science lesson on engines

In our last lesson we learned about *piston engines.* For our next lesson we will study *turbine engines.* Piston engines and turbine engines have one important feature in common: Combustion of fuel produces hot gases at high pressures. In our last lesson we learned that for piston engines to operate, *first,* a fuel must be burned at high pressure. *Second,* this burning or combustion creates hot gases under high pressure. This high pressure occurs in a restricted chamber. *Third,* under this pressure the hot gases expand and push against pistons. In this next lesson on turbine engines we will see that turbine engines work in very similar ways, but with one major difference. In this next lesson we will examine the operation of turbine engines by tracing these three similar operations, then investigate the major difference between the piston engine and the turbine engine. (Taken from West, Farmer, & Wolff, 1991.)

The major steps in creating advance organizers are as follows (West, Farmer, & Wolff, 1991):

1. Examine the new lesson for necessary prerequisite knowledge.

2. Find out if students know the prerequisite material. If they don't, reteach material from previous lessons.

3. List or summarize the major principles or ideas in the new lesson.

4. Write the advance organizer, emphasizing the similarities between major principles across old and new lessons.

5. Then teach the new material, covering the main ideas in the same sequence as they are presented in the advance organizer.

If Mr. Bolivar consistently uses advance organizers as a means for helping students recognize connections between topics, he should find that their learning and retention of the material improves.

4. Evaluation of the proposed instructional solution. Tests requiring students to retrieve and state verbal information (e.g., What important feature do piston and turbine engines have in common?) contained in the lessons are an appropriate way for assessing the instructional effectiveness of advance organizers. Once again, the outcome of verbal information does not ensure that students will be able to *use* the information to solve problems or draw inferences. These latter outcomes involve intellectual skills which are the subject of the next chapter.

REFERENCE

West, C. K., Farmer, J. A., & Wolff, P. M. (1991). *Instructional design: implications from cognitive science.* Englewood Cliffs, NJ: Prentice-Hall.

14

TEACHING INTELLECTUAL SKILLS

OBJECTIVES

Given case studies involving teaching strategies and intellectual skills:

1. Analyze the learning problem.
2. Determine relevant theoretical knowledge.
3. Develop a proposed instructional solution.
4. Evaluate the instructional solution.

Intellectual skills involve the application of a mental procedure. Thus, this outcome deals with the acquisition of procedural knowledge which involves learning *how* to do something. There are three types of intellectual skills which are typically taught within classrooms. These include the ability to discriminate between events, objects, or people; the ability to categorize a novel example of a specific concept; and the ability to apply a specific rule or principle. The first skill—the ability to discriminate between events, objects, or people—involves such things as differentiating between different colored objects. It is important to note that this skill concerns the ability to differentiate between similar but different objects without categorizing them. For example, in order to learn letters of the alphabet, a student should be able to differentiate between figures such as "b" and "p." This can be done without being able to categorize the figures as alphabet letters. The second skill, categorizing a novel example of a specific concept, involves putting things into a category and responding to instances of that category. For example, a student who has acquired the concept of "ball"—when faced with tennis balls, footballs, medicine balls, and bowling balls—will be able to categorize all these different instances into the single category of ball. As indicated earlier, categorizing novel instances of a concept and differentiating between instances are not synonymous. However, in order to acquire specific concepts, a student must first be able to differentiate examples from each other based on their characteristics. To illustrate, a student who can categorize a novel instance of ''ball'' has to be able to differentiate balls from other similar objects such as globes and balloons.

The third type of intellectual skill involves the application of a specific rule or principle. Mathematics, for example, consists of many rules for operating on numbers, such as how to multiply fractions and add whole numbers. Similarly, language arts consists of many grammatical rules such as maintaining agreement between subject and verb and capitalizing proper names. Typically, rules consist of the relationship between several concepts. For example, in order to multiply fractions, it is helpful to know the concepts ''numerator,'' ''denominator,'' ''cross-multiply,'' and ''quotient'' as well as how they relate to each other. Also, ensuring subject-verb agreement requires knowledge of the concepts ''verb'' and ''subject'' and the relational concept ''agreement.''

As we indicated in Chapter 13, learning an intellectual skill or *how* to do something is very different from being able to verbally describe it. For example, describing how to multiply fractions is not a good measure of whether or not a student can actually solve a problem which requires the use of this skill. On the other hand, being able to verbally describe a concept, rule, or characteristic is often an important prerequisite to its application. In summary, it is important to clearly differentiate between learning problems which focus on intellectual skill outcomes and those which focus on verbal information outcomes.

BACKGROUND KNOWLEDGE FROM PART ONE

In Chapter 3, when we discussed the nature and development of procedural knowledge, we emphasized its reactive and dynamic nature. Procedural knowledge is reactive because specific procedures will be triggered by specific environmental cues. For example, for a student who has acquired the concept ''tree,'' either a picture or a verbal description of a tree will automatically trigger the procedure for categorizing trees. Procedural knowledge is dynamic because it involves coordinating a series of activities: identifying defining characteristics, matching them to a specific procedure, and—if they match—engaging in a specific mental activity such as categorizing the instance or applying a rule. A well-practiced intellectual skill will quickly flow through the above sequence of steps. Given the reactive and dynamic quality of procedural knowledge, methods for helping students acquire these skills involve developing an understanding of when to use them and then providing repeated practice in performing them.

In Chapter 5, we looked specifically at the nature of concepts and the implications for teaching them. We indicated that before we can help students acquire concept classification skills (procedural knowledge), they must learn the concept definition (declarative knowledge) attributes, which serve as cues that trigger the categorization procedure. A variety of techniques for acquiring declarative knowledge were discussed in Chapter 13.

In order to help students acquire an understanding of the attributes associated with particular concepts, we indicated that the teacher needs to present a variety of meaningful examples and nonexamples of the target concept. By focusing students on the defining characteristic of a concept (e.g., balls are roundish, they are used in a game, they are somewhat rigid), students will be learning a series of cues that trigger the use of that concept. Once the defining characteristics or cues are acquired, students should be given extensive practice in classifying novel examples and nonexamples and should be provided with specific feedback to their responses (e.g., yes, that is correct because it possesses . . . or no, that is not correct because it does not possess. . . .).

In Part One, we identified a variety of factors that may influence the kinds of skills that students can acquire. In Chapter 4, we discussed how individuals have distinct limits on their attentional processes and on the amount of information they can store in working memory, and how these limitations may constrain the skills that can be acquired. In Chapter 6, we discussed the importance of recognizing that children have a qualitatively different view of the world from that of adults. That is, children go through a series of cognitive developmental stages, each with its own unique set of characteristics and capabilities which may significantly influence what skills they can learn within the classroom. For example, a child operating at the preoperational level of thinking has schemas which are centered, unidimensional, and irreversible. Consequently, a preoperational child would have difficulty learning a skill which required the manipulation of multiple dimensions.

In Chapter 6, we also indicated that practice not only improves one's ability to apply specific skills but also increases the amount of attention and space that one can devote to the acquisition of other important skills. In Chapter 7, we specifically identified the importance of cultural influences on cognitive development, including the ability to regulate acquisition and use of skills. Also, we discussed the importance of differentiating between skills whose performance still requires outside support and those which can be demonstrated without support. This "zone of proximal development" can be used to identify how much support is required for the acquisition of specific skills. Finally, as described in chapters 4 and 5, the context of instruction and practice should match the context within which the intellectual skills will be used. Otherwise, an individual may learn a skill but not know when to employ it.

We hope that this discussion has activated relevant schemas in your long-term memory. However, if it did not, please take a moment to review relevant portions of chapters 3, 4, 5, 6, 7, and Table 10.3 before reading the case study.

CASE STUDY

Therese looked out over her class of 17 first graders and smiled as she watched them prepare for the science lesson. The children, while fidgety and noisy, were responsive to Therese's attention, and their immature behavior and dependence did not bother her.

Once all the desks were clear, Therese began her introduction to the lesson.

She perched on the edge of her desk and held up several circles of different colors and sizes. "What are these?" she asked.

Some children responded, "Balls, dots. . . ."

"Yes, these look like balls and dots. What shape are they?" Therese emphasized the word "shape" and pointed to the bulletin board that showed circles, squares, and triangles.

"Circles." Most of the children called out the answer.

"Good. These are circles. Are all the circles the same?"

The children were quiet. Some were no longer watching Therese. William called out, "Some are different."

"How are they different, William?"

"Some are red."

"Yes, some are red. Let's put the red ones here." Therese put the red circles on the flannel board and looked out at her students. Three or four had opened their desks and were looking inside. Others were bouncing in their seats or talking to the children next to them. Fewer than half the students were watching Therese.

"It's this damn science curriculum," Therese thought as she observed her students. It was written by a new science coordinator who had been appointed two years earlier. The new elementary science curriculum evolved from the co-ordinator's work with a committee of elementary school teachers. It took them one year and two summers to produce the curriculum that Therese was now trying, unsuccessfully, to use.

"OK, everybody. Eyes front. Look at Miss Carmen. Rosa, Anthony, Jacob." As she called the names of several students, all the children turned toward her.

"William told us that some circles are different because they are red. Kelly, how are some other circles different?"

Kelly shook her head but didn't answer.

"Tiffany, do you know?"

"Some are round."

"Yes, all circles are round. How are they different?"

When none of the students responded, Therese answered her own question. "Some of the circles are yellow," she said as she placed the yellow circles underneath the red ones on the flannel board.

"What colors do I have left?"

"Blue," several students responded.

"Good," Therese said enthusiastically as she put the blue circles on the flannel board. "We have circles that are different colors. What colors are they, class?"

A few children answered, but most were no longer looking at the teacher or the flannel board. Again, Therese thought about what a poor idea it was to teach classification this way to first graders.

Analysis of the Learning Problem

Clearly, the learning problem described here concerns the inability of the first graders to acquire classification skills, that is, the grouping of objects on the basis of some set of defining characteristics. Therese is not satisfied with the science curriculum and blames it for her students' inability to acquire the targeted classification skills. Although not explicitly stated in the case study, she probably believes that the types of stimuli and examples used in the lesson are not very meaningful to the students. Early in the lesson, you can see that students are attempting to make the stimuli meaningful by relating them to objects that they are familiar with, such as balls and dots.

Although there is nothing in the case study which describes the first graders' prior knowledge or level of cognitive development, it is clear that Therese feels they are not ready to acquire classification skills. That is, no matter how instructionally sound the lesson is, Therese feels that her students may be incapable of grasping the intellectual skill of classification.

Finally, it is important to note that her students were easily distracted and often drifted from the task. That could be due to their limited cognitive skills and prior experiences, the complexity of the task, or the nature of the teaching stimuli and examples used in the lesson. For example, in order to be able to compare multiple dimensions (size and color), students must be able to attend to both dimensions simultaneously. Asking them to process a variety of different-sized and different-colored circles may have overloaded their attentional and working memory capacity. When that occurs, students become easily distracted, which is what we saw happen in the case study.

Determination of Relevant Theoretical Knowledge

Now that we have identified the intended learning outcome and the factors that may be influencing its attainment, let's identify those learning principles and ideas from Part One that may help us produce an instructional solution for this problem (also see Table 10.3).

As described in Chapter 6, Piagetian theory suggests that first graders are preoperational thinkers and are likely to be incapable of acquring classification skills. Preoperational thinkers typically lack flexibility and reversibility and have difficulty focusing on more than one dimension at a time. In essence, students at this stage have not developed the ability to reason about events in a way that would allow them to classify objects along multiple dimensions.

In contrast to Piagetian theory, Case's neo-Piagetian theory would identify first-grade students as relational thinkers and would indicate that they are capable of acquiring classification skills. Within this theory, the primary limitation on a student's ability to develop more and more complicated thinking skills is a lack of practice of the to-be-acquired skill. As indicated in chapters 3 and 6, children of this age have specific limitations on their ability to store and manipulate information within working memory or short-term sensory store. Practicing the skill until it is automatized is the primary way to overcome memory capacity limitations.

Finally, as described in chapters 3 and 4, in order to help students acquire new information, whether it is declarative or procedural knowledge, the information has to be meaningful to the students. The more meaningful it is, the more likely students will pay attention and remember it. Also, our discussion in Chapter 9 suggested that making to-be-learned material meaningful will also help maintain high levels of student motivation.

Development of Proposed Instructional Solution

This problem requires a multifaceted instructional solution. It involves (1) increasing the variety of manipulative experiences which challenge students to classify objects within the classroom, (2) directly training students to classify objects on one and two dimensions, (3) setting up a cooperative support system to help students acquire classification skills, and (4) identifying meaningful objects to be classified within the classroom.

Therese should make available a variety of games and activities that involve the classification of objects such as blocks, pictures, and toys. For example, students can be given a ball and asked to identify other spherelike objects in the class such as globes, light bulbs, and so on. Since it is clear that the students in this class are having difficulty with objects that vary along more than one dimension, the teacher should include a variety of tasks requiring classification along one dimension only. For example, the teacher can use a set of black and white balls that differ only by color. However, in order to challenge them, the teacher should also include tasks which require classifying objects along two dimensions. For example, she could make available another set of black and white balls which are all slightly larger than those described earlier. The students would then be manipulating objects which vary along two dimensions. It is important to note that this part of the proposed solution does not involve any direct instruction but rather focuses on changing the classroom environment and encouraging students to actively investigate and manipulate objects.

In order to directly teach classification skills, a series of tasks should be developed which will induce students to practice classifying according to one dimension, then two dimensions, and so on. In all cases, the students should be asked to classify objects based on concrete and visible characteristics such as shape, color, size, or texture, in contrast to abstract characteristics such as function. Once students have acquired the ability to classify specific objects, then, in order to help generalize that skill, they should be asked to classify other objects such as cubes, boxes, containers, and the like along the same dimension. After mastering classification of a variety of objects along this single dimension, the students should be given other objects to classify which vary along a different dimension, such as sweet and sour (as in candy), tall and short (as in ice cream bar sticks), and so on.

After students can successfully classify a variety of objects (e.g., blocks, sticks, containers, balls) along a variety of single dimensions (color, size, height, taste), they should practice classifying objects along two dimensions (large and black versus short and white, and so on). Further classification lessons could include expanding from bipolar characteristics such as black versus white to multiple categories such as black, white, yellow, and the like. While moving students through this set of graded classification exercises, the teacher should not give them more complicated classification exercises until they have mastered the prerequisite skills. Also, the difficulty of the classification should be increased by small increments. For example, it would be inappropriate to jump from classifying an object along one dimension to classifying objects along three or four dimensions.

Before using direct instruction to help students acquire classification skills, the teacher should identify their existing cognitive skills. Some students may require extensive support and direction in working through the classification tasks, while others may not. Therese must be ready to individualize this support and to monitor when the student is ready to exhibit these skills independently. In addition, she should pair students who have already acquired independent classification skills with those who have not, in order to help the slower students.

Finally, the objects that are used in these classification exercises need to be meaningful to students. For example, they can be shown short clips of recent movies such as *Aladdin* or *Beauty and the Beast* and asked to identify objects which are examples of spheres or cubes. Also, students could be asked to organize pieces of an erector set into those which are yellow and those which are blue. The notion here is to see what kinds of objects the students seem to use frequently and the kinds of experiences they tend to get excited about and then use them to construct the classification exercises.

Evaluation of the Instructional Solution

In evaluating the acquisition of an intellectual skill, there are two things to keep in mind. First, acquiring an intellectual skill involves learning *how* to do something, that is, acquiring procedural knowledge. Consequently, students must be asked to demonstrate their knowledge by actually using the skill. Describing the nature of the skill or how one might use it and under what conditions does not indicate whether the student has actually acquired a target skill.

Second, skills can be used in a variety of contexts. Consequently, it is important to identify those contexts within which the targeted skills will be applied, to develop instruction to fit those contexts, and then to match the evaluation tool to that context. In some instances, skill training may take place within a narrow set of contexts, while at other times it takes place within a wide variety of settings. Finally, students may be given practice using a skill for a specific purpose such as solving particular problems. In each case, it is important to evaluate a student's acquisition of the target skills in these specific contexts.

Within the present case, the way to evaluate whether or not the targeted classification skills have been acquired is to ask students to classify a new set of concrete objects in the same manner as in their instruction. Students should never be asked to make classification judgments that go beyond those contained in instruction. That is, if Therese decides to use instructional exercises which require classification along two bipolar dimensions only (e.g., black and white, large and small), then her evaluation exercises should also be limited to these kinds of classifications.

CASE #1

Timmy, age 15, was having a difficult time preparing for his high school psychology test. "Is negative reinforcement the addition of an aversive event or the subtraction of an aversive event?" he asked himself. "Or is it the subtraction of an attractive event?" He had to look in his class notes again. He just didn't seem to be able to keep this attractive/aversive and add/subtract business straight.

Timmy wished that Mr. Hammy had given them an easy way to differentiate between the different labels so that he could correctly state the definition of each concept. He kept mixing up negative reinforcement with the two types of punishment. Also, Mr. Hammy focused primarily on important characteristics of each concept but did not indicate how they differed from similar concepts. In addition, the few teaching examples that Mr. Hammy presented in class involved only animals. As a matter of fact, they all had to do with modifying the behavior of a rat in a Skinner Box.

The next day, when Timmy received the test in Mr. Hammy's psychology class, his heart skipped a beat. Not only were there questions asking for definitions of the four different types of consequences, but the test also included application questions which went well beyond the Skinner Box and included novel examples and nonexamples from a variety of settings.

1. What is your **analysis of the learning problem?**

_____

_____

_____

_____

2. Please determine **relevant theoretical knowledge.**

_____

_____

_____

_____

3. What is your **proposed instructional solution?**

_____

_____

_____

_____

_____

4. How will you **evaluate your proposed solution?**

_____

_____

_____

_____

_____

CASE #2

Tim Einstein is a sixth-grade science teacher who wants his students to learn how to use the scientific method. According to Mr. Einstein, the method consists of the following six steps: (1) recognizing a problem or discrepancy, (2) guessing at an explanation, (3) designing an experiment to test the guess, (4) collecting data from the experiment, (5) analyzing the data, and (6) arriving at a tentative conclusion. In the first part of his instruction, he clearly defined all the terms and concepts related to each step and made sure all the students understood them. Next, he described how famous scientists used the scientific method, going into great detail about each step. He also liked to talk about great discoveries and how they were a product of the scientific method. Finally, Tim Einstein presented science problems to the class and modeled each step of the scientific method in solving the problems. However, when he gave students problems which required the application of the scientific method, they failed miserably. Mr. Einstein was frustrated because he felt he had done a good job.

1. What is your **analysis of the learning problem?**

_____

_____

_____

_____

_____

2. Please determine **relevant theoretical knowledge.**

_____

_____

_____

_____

3. What is your **proposed instructional solution?**

_____

_____

_____

_____

_____

4. How will you **evaluate your proposed solution?**

_____

_____

_____

_____

_____

REVIEW OF MAJOR POINTS

Intellectual skill outcomes refer to students' ability to apply their procedural knowledge. There are three types of intellectual skills which are typically taught within classrooms: the ability to discriminate between events, objects, or people; the ability to categorize a novel example of a specific concept; and the ability to apply a specific rule or principle.

Learning an intellectual skill entails developing procedures by repeatedly practicing their application within a variety of meaningful contexts. Oftentimes, in order to acquire intellectual skills, students will need to possess appropriate declarative knowledge such as concept definitions or a description of the conditions under which to apply a skill. Consequently, the techniques described in Chapter 13 will often be relevant to the development of intellectual skills.

ANSWERS TO CASE EXERCISES

Case #1

1. Analysis of the learning problem. Timmy's problems are due to inappropriate concept instruction. Given the nature of the test, Mr. Hammy must have wanted his students to be able to state the definition of the concepts *and* categorize a wide variety of novel instances of the concepts. His instruction, however, seems to have focused on the formal definition of the concepts and on a narrow set of examples involving rats in Skinner Boxes. This problem is clearly an intellectual skills learning one and requires that Mr. Hammy modify his instruction.

2. Relevant theoretical knowledge. As we discussed in Chapter 5, acquiring the ability to classify novel examples of a concept is a two-step process that requires students to (1) encode the definition of the concepts (see chapters 4 and 13) and (2) practice classifying and comparing a variety of meaningful examples and nonexamples of the target concept. Encoding may be accomplished through the teaching of critical or prototypical attributes or with the use of visual imagery. Important superordinate and subordinate examples and nonexamples of the target concepts can be identified through a taxonomy. Finally, when asking students to classify novel examples and nonexamples, the teacher should give them specific feedback to their responses. Chapters 3 and 4 suggest that a student's prior cognitive skills and experiences need to be monitored because these may influence their ability to acquire target intellectual skills. That is, students may fail to acquire a skill not because they cannot master it but because they do not have the processing capabilities to engage in appropriate practice. Also, the types of examples and nonexamples used to teach concepts need to be drawn from the students' experiences in order to make them meaningful and permit elaborative processing of target information.

3. Proposed instructional solution. From the case study information, it is clear that Mr. Hammy has already done a preliminary concept analysis and has identified the critical attributes of the four target concepts. Table 14.1 includes a 2 × 2 matrix which describes the dimensions of the two critical attributes. As shown in this table, the two critical attributes are the nature of an event (attractive versus aversive) and direction of change (added versus subtracted). In addition, however, Mr. Hammy should also identify the variable attributes of the target concepts (see Chapter 5 and Table 14.1). With a complete concept analysis, Mr. Hammy can create both matched example and nonexample pairs and a wide variety of illustrations to be used during instruction. For instance, a matched example and nonexample pair for the concept "positive reinforcement" is a teacher's giving a student verbal praise for a correct answer (example) and a teacher's insulting a student for giving an incorrect answer (nonexample). They are matched because the only difference between the two instances is that in the former case there is the addition of something attractive whereas in the latter case there is the addition of something aversive.

A wide variety of examples would involve interactions between husband and wife, parent and child, and teacher and student as well as both tangible and social rewards. In addition, the teacher would want to create prototypical and distinctive examples which may also be used during instruction. As an illustration, using M&M's to reward appropriate behavior is a prototypical example, while winning a $5 million lottery is a distinctive example.

Once the concept analysis has been completed, Mr. Hammy is ready to begin helping students acquire the coordinate concepts. He should present the 2 × 2 matrix depicted in Table 14.1 to the students and should clearly define and illustrate the dimensions of the two critical attributes. The intent of this step is to get the students to acquire the definitions of the concepts (declarative knowledge). Students often have difficulty (as Timmy does) understanding what the words mean when used in such an abstract manner. For example, it is hard for most students

TABLE 14.1   CRITICAL AND VARIABLE ATTRIBUTES FOR POSITIVE AND NEGATIVE REINFORCEMENT
AND PUNISHMENT

How the stimulus is perceived	Critical attributes	
	Direction of change of stimulus	
	Onset (turned on)	Offset (turned off)
Attractive	Positive reinforcement	Negative punishment
Aversive	Positive punishment	Negative reinforcement

Variable attributes

1. Age relationship between agent and recipient:
   a) Both adult
   b) Both child
   c) Adult-child
   d) Not applicable

2. Role relationship between agent and recipient:
   a) One a socially defined authority figure
   b) Family
   c) None

3. Status relationship between agent and recipient:
   a) Agent and recipient equal
   b) Agent and recipient unequal
   c) Indeterminate

4. Nature of the event:
   a) Physical-tangible
   b) Verbal-social

Source: Taken from Tiemann and Markle, 1983.

to think of "negative reinforcement" as a favorable consequence. One method for getting around this problem and helping students remember the definitions is to assign a plus or a minus sign to each dimension of the two critical attributes. "Attractive" and "added" can be represented with a plus sign, while "aversive" and "subtracted" can be represented with a minus sign. Students would then be asked to multiply the signs. Those quotients which end up being positive are favorable and are reinforcers, and those that end up being negative are unfavorable and are punishers.

After students have demonstrated their verbal knowledge of the critical attributes of each coordinate concept, Mr. Hammy needs to present a series of matched example and nonexample pairs (see Table 14.2) in order to help them isolate the critical attributes of each concept. Mr. Hammy should describe the similarities and differences between each example and nonexample. That should be followed by another set of matched pairs in which students are asked to identify how the example and nonexample are similar and different. The next step would involve asking students to compare a wide variety of novel examples and nonexamples with a prototypical example of each concept and to categorize each novel

TABLE 14.2   MATCHED EXAMPLE AND NONEXAMPLE PAIRS FOR POSITIVE AND NEGATIVE REINFORCEMENT AND PUNISHMENT

Matched example and nonexample pairs	
Positive reinforcement:	
Example:	Teacher gives student a pat on the back for giving a correct answer.
Nonexample:	Teacher gives student a slap on the hand for giving an incorrect answer.
Negative reinforcement:	
Example:	Teacher takes away a homework assignment for a student who gives a correct answer.
Nonexample:	Teacher takes away a student's privileges for giving an incorrect answer.
Positive punishment:	
Example:	Teacher gives student a slap on the hand for giving an incorrect answer.
Nonexample:	Teacher gives student a pat on the back for giving a correct answer.
Negative punishment:	
Example:	Teacher takes away a student's privileges for giving an incorrect answer.
Nonexample:	Teacher takes away a homework assignment for a student who gives a correct answer.

instance (see Table 14.3 for prototypical examples). Finally, students should be given a new set of novel examples and nonexamples and then asked to categorize them. At every step in the lesson, students should receive extensive feedback to their categorization responses (e.g., yes, that is correct because it possesses . . . or no, that is not correct because it does not possess. . . .).

4. Evaluation of instructional solution. The original test that Timmy was given would now be an appropriate evaluation tool for checking his knowledge of the concepts of positive and negative reinforcement and punishment. That is, Timmy should be asked to classify a wide variety of novel examples and nonexamples of these target concepts.

TABLE 14.3   PROTOTYPICAL EXAMPLES FOR POSITIVE AND NEGATIVE REINFORCEMENT AND PUNISHMENT

Positive reinforcement:	A teacher gives a student candy for behaving appropriately.
Negative reinforcement:	A mother stops nagging her son to pick up his clothes after he cleans up.
Positive punishment:	A father spanks his child for misbehaving.
Negative punishment:	A son is grounded for staying out past curfew.

Case #2

1. Analysis of the learning problem. It is clear that the problem presented in this case study is an intellectual skills problem. The objective of the lesson is to know how to use the scientific method, which involves the development of procedural knowledge. Nevertheless, the students are never given the opportunity to actually use the scientific method in dealing with problems. The techniques used by Mr. Einstein are sound instructional devices for teaching declarative knowledge concerning the scientific method, but the students are never shown *how* to use that knowledge.

2. Important theoretical knowledge. As described in Chapter 3, in order to encourage students to acquire procedural knowledge (how to do something), the teacher needs to engage them in extensive practice of the target skill. In addition, complicated skills may have to be broken down into subcomponents, acquired individually, and then combined into the more complex skill. Also, in chapters 4 and 9, we underlined the importance of using meaningful stimuli and activities in order to facilitate learning new knowledge and skills.

Chapter 5 described the importance of matching the retrieval context to the encoding context. In order to maximize the retrieval of knowledge, instruction should include the future contexts within which students will be asked to apply this knowledge. This was reiterated within Chapter 6 when we discussed the importance of integrating problem-solving activities into the initial instruction when the objective of the lesson is for students to use newly learned information to solve problems. For example, if you want students to be able to apply the concept of mass and gravity to help solve a physics problem, then your initial instruction of these two concepts should include their application to various physics problems.

3. Proposed instructional solution. As indicated earlier, Mr. Einstein is already using instructional techniques which should produce a good declarative knowledge base from which to begin the development of appropriate procedural knowledge. Let's briefly review these techniques.

Mr. Einstein is clearly defining all the terms and concepts related to each step. In addition, he is presenting a wide variety of examples of the scientific method in action. That not only demonstrates the application of the scientific method but also makes it more interesting to students by tying it to real-life situations and illustrations. Finally, he personally demonstrated how the scientific method can be used by modeling each step in solving a science problem. In summary, Mr. Einstein is using interesting activities, a wide variety of examples, and detailed descriptions of the steps involved in applying the scientific method. How might he improve his instruction?

First of all, although Tim Einstein is using real-life illustrations of the scientific method to maintain student interest, it is unclear whether these are meaningful to the students. If he used illustrations that were relevant to the students' lives, such as applying the scientific method to the development of sugarless gum, their attention and motivation might increase.

Second, Mr. Einstein needs to include illustrations of scientific problem solving in which the scientific method *has not* been applied appropriately and the consequences of this inappropriate application. There are a multitude of real-life examples in which scientists have made up data, modified the analysis, and stolen ideas from other scientists—interesting and distinctive illustrations of how not to apply the scientific method! It would be important to emphasize the consequences of misapplication in terms of cost and public trust.

Finally, Mr. Einstein needs to create activities which allow the students to actually apply the scientific method to solve a problem. The steps should be practiced individually prior to being applied in a coordinated fashion. For example, students can be given problem scenarios in which they are asked only to identify problems or discrepancies that need to be explained. Then, after they can do that reliably, they can be asked to identify problems and discrepancies and then guess at an explanation. After students have mastered this second step, additional steps can gradually be added to the practice activities until the students can reliably employ all six steps of the scientific method in a coordinated fashion. Just as it was important to give a variety of meaningful illustrations of the scientific method in action, it is equally important to ask students to practice using the scientific method within a variety of meaningful problem scenarios.

4. Evaluation of instructional solution. Mr. Einstein should evaluate the students' ability to use the scientific method by giving them a series of novel science problems and asking them to apply the method to solve these problems. He should require the students to clearly identify each step in their answer so that he can evaluate their ability to use each of the six steps.

REFERENCE

Tiemann, P., and Markle, S. (1983). *Analyzing instructional content: A guide to instruction and evaluation.* Champaign, IL: Stipes.

ADDENDUM TO PART TWO

This addendum to Part Two contains six additional cases on which to practice your problem-solving skills. No feedback is provided, and not all the cases contain a "learning" problem. Our hope is that they will be used both for class discussion and as a means of personal review. So good luck and good problem solving!

CASE #1

Teachers have started complaining to school administrators about Joel's inability to do his work. During writing assignments and reading group, Joel often becomes tearful, causing his classmates to label him a "crybaby." During recess, Joel is unable to keep up with his fellow third graders' structured games, and the physical education teacher reports that Joel cannot remember the rules for games. These problems are causing Joel to become a social outcast. His peers have been ridiculing him, calling him "stupid" and a "wimp."

During classes, Joel frequently asks to go to the bathroom, and when refused, he wets his pants. That elicits further ridicule from the other children. Joel rarely attempts his assignments, and when his teachers insist that he can do the work, Joel turns in almost illegible papers that are full of errors and contain vivid drawings in the margins of boys in spaceships and on horses. At the end of the first semester, Joel received all "F's" on his report card.

1. What is your **analysis of the problem?** Is it a learning problem?

_____

_____

2. Please determine **relevant theoretical knowledge.**

_____

_____

_____

_____

3. What is your **proposed instructional solution?**

_____

_____

_____

_____

4. How will you **evaluate your proposed solution?**

_____

_____

_____

_____

_____

CASE #2

Madeline has difficulty paying attention in science class. The only time she seems interested is when the class discusses topics concerned with the application of scientific theory of modern technology. She seems very interested and attentive in other classes and has earned the privilege of doing an independent study in social sciences. In the science class, however, she is often intimidated by the breadth of scientific theory and facts. She compensates by getting class notes from a girlfriend who is a good student. Madeline frequently asks the teacher not only to look over her work but also to make suggestions and to supply her with the correct answers. She makes some attempt to do homework problems but eventually resorts to copying the work from her friend during her first class period.

1. What is your **analysis of the problem?** Is it a learning problem?

_____

_____

_____

_____

2. Please determine **relevant theoretical knowledge.**

_____

_____

_____

_____

3. What is your **proposed instructional solution?**

_____

_____

_____

_____

4. How will you **evaluate your proposed solution?**

_____

_____

_____

_____

CASE 3#

Tommy is always behind in his assignments and in class. While other students are finishing their work, Tommy daydreams and slowly proceeds with his work. Tommy's completed work is usually above average. It is clear that Tommy has the ability but not the motivation to finish his work on time. He wastes time and is often engaged in off-task activitites. Tommy's inability to complete assignments on time is beginning to disrupt the flow of the class. For group and class projects, he holds everyone up. Consequently, while others are waiting for him to finish, they often exhibit disruptive behavior because of their boredom. Unfortunately, individualizing instruction puts a strain on the teacher's time and resources because Tommy seems to fall so far behind.

1. What is your **analysis of the problem?** Is it a learning problem?

_____

_____

_____

_____

_____

2. Please determine **relevant theoretical knowledge.**

_____

_____

_____

_____

_____

3. What is your **proposed instructional solution?**

_____

_____

_____

_____

_____

4. How will you **evaluate your proposed solution?**

_____

_____

_____

_____

_____

_____

CASE #4

Megan was discussing her performance on the recent exam in world geography with her teacher, Mrs. Juniper. The exam covered one chapter of their text on the history and colonization of Australia. Although the chapter was a relatively long one, it was not particularly difficult. "I read the chapter four times before the test, and I took extensive notes," Megan said, showing Mrs. Juniper some well-written notes. When Mrs. Juniper looked them over, she noticed that the notes were organized in exactly the same way as the chapter and were written in almost the exact words as the book. She also noticed that there was no attempt to connect the chapter notes to information presented in class (which was related to the chapter information).

Given the nature of Megan's notes, it was not surprising that she had trouble with Mrs. Juniper's exams, which included essay questions asking students to summarize information related to a particular issue and to integrate information from multiple sources (text, class discussion, and lecture).

---

1. What is your **analysis of the problem?** Is it a learning problem?

_____

_____

_____

_____

_____

2. Please determine **relevant theoretical knowledge.**

_____

_____

_____

_____

_____

3. What is your **proposed instructional solution?**

_____

_____

_____

_____

_____

4. How will you **evaluate your proposed solution?**

_____

_____

_____

_____

_____

_____

CASE #5

Mr. Glick's tenth-grade science class did poorly on the midterm exam, which focused on some basic biological concepts. The majority of the students claimed that they had studied hard and knew the concepts. In order to gain more information about the discrepancy between the students' anecdotal comments and their performance, Mr. Glick asked them to define five of the concepts presented on the exam. To his surprise, almost everyone in the class is able to correctly define each concept. Mr. Glick is now at a loss to try and figure out why the students did so poorly on the exam.

As he continues to discuss the situation with his students, one of them tells him that the test asked for a lot more than just the definitions of concepts. Mr. Glick goes back and looks over the test; he notices that in addition to definitions, the exam consists of classification exercises which included novel examples of the biological concepts. Now he is even more confused and doesn't understand why there is a problem, since his students should be able to successfully complete the classification exercises if they already know the definitions.

1. What is your **analysis of the problem?** Is it a learning problem?

_____

_____

_____

_____

2. Please determine **relevant theoretical knowledge.**

_____

_____

_____

_____

3. What is your **proposed instructional solution?**

_____

_____

_____

_____

_____

4. How will you **evaluate your proposed solution?**

_____

_____

_____

_____

_____

CASE #6

John looked over his spelling test and found that he recognized many of the words but could not recall most of the definitions. Mrs. Mabel has spent considerable time in class listing the words on the blackboard, pairing them with their definitions, and asking students to read each word and definition with her every day. Each night she sent home work sheets, which consisted of one column of words and a second column of definitions, and instructed the students to match the words with the definitions.

Mrs. Mabel also uses a word game to get students interested in learning the new vocabulary. The game consists of putting students into groups of five and seeing which group is able to integrate the greatest number of new vocabulary words into one sentence. Students are encouraged to use reference sources such as a thesaurus and dictionary to help them during this game. The group that is able to integrate the most words in one sentence does not have to do homework over the weekend.

1. What is your **analysis of the problem?** Is it a learning problem?

_____

_____

_____

_____

2. Please determine **relevant theoretical knowledge.**

_____

_____

_____

_____

3. What is your **proposed instructional solution?**

_____

_____

_____

_____

4. How will you **evaluate your proposed solution?**

_____

_____

_____

_____

_____

NAME INDEX

SUBJECT INDEX